The Baker Encyclopedia *of* Bible People

The Baker Encyclopedia *of* Bible People

A Comprehensive Who's Who From Aaron to Zurishaddai

Edited by Mark Water

Published by Baker Books
a division of Baker Publishing Group
P.O. Box 6287, Grand Rapids, MI 49516-6287

Published in 2006 under license from John Hunt Publishing Ltd., UK

Printed in the United States of America

Library of Congress Cataloging-in-Publication Data is on file at the Library of Congress, Washington, D.C.

ISBN 10: 0-8010-6604-2 (pbk.)
ISBN 978-0-8010-6604-7 (pbk.)

Contents

List of Abbreviations

BC	Alexander Whyte, *Bible Characters*
BH	Albert Edersheim, *Bible History*, Book 1
CBC	Ashley S. Johnson, *Condensed Biblical Cyclopedia*
CCEB	Robert Jamieson, A. R. Fausset, and David Brown, *A Commentary, Critical and Explanatory on the Whole Bible*
EDNTW	W. E. Vine, Merrill F. Ungar, and William White Jr., *An Expository Dictionary of New Testament Words*
FBD	Andrew Robert Fausset, *Bible Dictionary*
HCC	Philip Schaff, *History of the Christian Church*, Volume 1, *Apostolic Christianity, A.D. 1–100*
IBD	Matthew George Easton, *Illustrated Bible Dictionary*, Third edition
ISBE	James Orr, *The International Standard Bible Encyclopaedia*
NTB	*Nave's Topical Bible*
NTT	R. A. Torrey, *New Topical Textbook*
SBD	William Smith, *Smith's Bible Dictionary*
SERK	*The New Schaff-Herzog Encyclopedia of Religious Knowledge*
TCB	*The Companion Bible*
TT	A. B. Bruce, *The Training of the Twelve*

Introduction

The Baker Encyclopedia of Bible People, a comprehensive "Who's Who in the Bible," has collated material on over two thousand people mentioned in the Bible, from Aaron to Zurishaddai.

Significant Summary

Each entry starts with a *significant summary* of the person. This gives a short overall view of the person and his or her significance in the Bible.

Family Connections

The entries from Adam up to and including the patriarchal period of biblical history will include the names of other family members. For example, in the entry for Abraham, the following people are listed as family:

father: Terah; *siblings:* Nahor, Haran, Sarai; *married to:* Sarai, Hagar, Keturah; *children:* Ishmael, Isaac, Zimran, Jokshan, Medan, Midian, Ishbak, Shuah

Meaning of Name

In Bible times, a person was often given a name that had a special meaning. Such names predicted a characteristic of the person or recorded something about the circumstances of a birth.

Isaiah's children are a case in point. Shear-Jashub, Isaiah's first son, was given his symbolic name to foreshadow the restoration of the Jews after their exile, as it means "a remnant shall return." Isaiah's second son was given the name "Maher-Shalal-Hash-Baz," which is, incidentally, the longest word in the Bible. The meaning of Maher-Shalal-Hash-Baz's name is "speed-spoil-hasten-plunder" and refers to a specific incident in biblical history when Damascus and Israel would be attacked by the Assyrians.

A more well-known example of the important meaning attached to a name is spelled out in the opening chapter of the New Testament: "She will give birth to a son, and you are to give him the name Jesus, because he will save his people from their sins" (Matt. 1:21 NIV). To make sure no one misses the significance of the name given to Jesus and the link it has to salvation, the NIV footnote spells it out: "Jesus is the Greek form of Joshua, which means the LORD saves."

Whenever we know the meaning of a person's name, it is given toward the beginning of his or her entry. In part 3, I've included Rev. Roswell D. Hitchcock's famous list of Bible names with their meanings.

Bible Dictionary/Encyclopedia Entry

All major entries include a "life" of the person. Most of these come under the heading of "Bible dictionary/encyclopedia entry." There are over 230 such entries. The following people, as authors and editors of Bible dictionaries and Bible encyclopedias, have contributed to these features:

- Matthew George Easton, M.A., D.D., from his *Illustrated Bible Dictionary*, third edition, has nearly seventy such entries. Easton (1823–1894) was a Scottish Presbyterian preacher and writer. His best-known work is the *Easton's Bible Dictionary* (1897), published three years after his death. Easton also translated into English two of Franz Delitzsch's commentaries.
- Dr. William Smith, from his *Smith's Bible Dictionary*, also has about seventy of these entries. Smith, noted English theologian and scholar, completed his original three-volume dictionary in 1863, and it has been a classic reference and comprehensive Bible dictionary ever since.
- Andrew Robert Fausset (1821–1910), from his *Bible Dictionary*, has nine entries under the heading of "Bible dictionary/encyclopedia entry." Fausset was one of the contributors to *A Commentary,*

Critical and Explanatory on the Whole Bible along with Robert Jamieson and David Brown.
- James Orr, M.A., D.D., general editor, has twenty-two entries from a galaxy of international Bible scholars in the articles included from *The International Standard Bible Encyclopaedia*, 1915.
- Ashley S. Johnson has twelve entries from the *Condensed Biblical Cyclopedia*. This encyclopedia, written in 1896 by Johnson, the founder of Johnson Bible College, was meant for busy people who "wish to increase their knowledge of the oracles of God."

A Bible Commentator's Portrait

Under this heading there are some entries from Robert Jamieson, A. R. Fausset, and David Brown, *A Commentary, Critical and Explanatory on the Whole Bible* (1871).

The Companion Bible

From a number of the appendixes of *The Companion Bible* the following entries have been included: Noah being referred to as "perfect," Nimrod, Pharaoh, the man of God, Jeremiah as a type of the Messiah, the six Marys, and the Sadducees.

All the entries from the classic Bible dictionaries and encyclopedias. have been updated, but the individual styles of each writer have been left unchanged.

Bible Study

In the Old Testament section of this book introductions to each of the subsections have been included.

Entries in *The Baker Encyclopedia of Bible People* roughly follow the order in which they occur in the Bible. They are also placed together in their different groups, so Judah's prophets come together in one section, as do, for example, the people associated with the apostle John. Such entries do not follow the exact Bible order.

The Baker Encyclopedia of Bible People enables the reader to engage in a Bible study on all of the Bible people who have entries in this volume. There are nearly four hundred of these under the heading of *Bible study on the life of*. These range from Adam in the Old Testament to Drusilla in the New Testament and have been provided by Orville J. Nave's classic work, *Nave's Topical Bible*. This best known of all topical Bibles has been a valuable Bible study reference and a bestseller for decades. Orville J. Nave, A.M., D.D., LL.D., compiled this magnificent reference work while serving as a chaplain in the United States Army. He referred to his work as "the result of fourteen years of delighted and untiring study of the Word of God."

All the People of the Bible

Part 3 includes an alphabetical list of the people who are mentioned in the Bible, from Aaron and Abagtha to Zuriel and Zurishaddai. Just the briefest sentence about them, the meaning of the name, and a relevant Bible reference or two, is given for each person.

Studying Bible People

There are countless benefits to be derived from studying Bible characters, as they give us an overall picture of the Bible, help us to appreciate Bible history, and tie together the Old Testament and New Testament. Jesus himself often referred to people in the Old Testament in his teaching. And every person in both the Old Testament and New Testament teaches us some helpful spiritual lesson. As Paul put it when referring to the sinful deeds of the Israelites in their wanderings in the desert, "These things happened to them as examples and were written down as warnings for us, on whom the fulfillment of the ages has come" (1 Cor. 10:11 NIV). Paul was convinced that the Old Testament was crammed full of lessons that Christians should learn: "For everything that was written in the past was written to teach us, so that through endurance and the encouragement of the Scriptures we might have hope" (Rom. 15:4 NIV).

The writer to the Hebrews was a great fan of the Old Testament people who lived their lives based on faith in God. He wrote about them to encourage his readers to emulate such faith (see Hebrews 11).

Part One

People in the Old Testament

The First Humans

Adam • Eve • Cain • Abel • Seth • Enoch, Cain's son • Lamech, Cain's descendant • Enoch, Methuselah's father • Methuselah • Lamech, Methuselah's son • Noah • Shem • Japheth • Ham • Cush • Canaan • Nimrod

Job and His Comforters

Job • Eliphaz • Bildad • Zophar • Elihu

The Patriarchs

Nahor, Abraham's grandfather • Terah • Abraham • Melchizedek • Sarah • Hagar • Ishmael • Keturah • Nahor, Abraham's brother • Chedorlaomer • Eliezer • Lot • Moab • Isaac • Rebekah • Esau • Jacob • Rachel • Dinah • Shechem • Naphtali • Gad • Issachar • Leah • Zilpah • Zebulun • Laban • Bilhah

Egypt: Arrival, Living, and Exodus

Joseph • Benjamin • Judah • Tamar, Judah's daugher-in-law • Levi • Gershon • Merari • Reuben • Simeon • Ephraim • Manasseh • Potiphar • Kohath • Moses • Jethro (Reuel) • Zipporah • Miriam • Aaron • Nadab • Eleazar • Phinehas, Eleazar's son • Bezalel • Abiram • Korah • Dathan • Og • Sihon • Balaam • Balak • Joshua • Rahab • Jabin I • Caleb • Achan

Israel's Judges

Othniel • Ehud • Eglon • Jael • Cushan-Rishathaim • Shamgar • Sisera • Barak • Jabin II • Deborah • Gideon (Jerubbaal) • Tola • Jair • Ibzan • Elon • Abdon • Samson • Manoah • Delilah • Jephthah • Abimelech

Ruth and Her Circle

Naomi • Elimelech • Mahlon • Orpah • Kilion • Ruth • Boaz

Samuel and the First King

Samuel • Hannah • Elkanah • Eli • Hophni • Phinehas, Eli's son • Saul • Kish • Ziba • Merab • Rizpah

King David and His Circle

Jesse • Jonathan • Goliath • David • Doeg • Ahimaaz • Ahimelech • Nathan • Obed-edom • Hushai • Achish • Mephibosheth • Uzzah • Shimei • Jeduthun • Araunah (Ornan) • Asahel • Asaph • Eliab • Ittai • Hadadezer (Hadarezer) • Barzillai • Absalom • Tamar, Absalom's daughter • Michal • Bathsheba • Abishag • Abishai • Nabal • Joab • Tamar, David's daughter • Solomon • Uriah • Hiram, King of Tyre • Abigail • Adonijah • Rezon • Hiram, the craftsman • Ish-bosheth • Amnon • Abner • Ahithophel • Abiathar • Zadok

Judah's Kings

Rehoboam • Abijam • Asa • Zerah • Jehoshaphat • Jehoram • Ahaziah • Athaliah • Joash/Jehoash • Jehoiada • Amaziah • Azariah • Jotham • Ahaz • Hezekiah • Sennacherib • Manasseh • Esarhaddon • Rabsaris • Rab-shakeh • Tartan • Shebna(h) • Merodach-Baladan • Amon • Josiah • Hilkiah • Shaphan • Jehoahaz • Jehoiakim • Jehoiachin • Evil-merodach • Zedekiah • Tiglath-Pileser

Judah's Prophets

Joel • Shemaiah • Oded • Jahaziel • Zechariah • Isaiah • Shear-Jashub • Maher-Shalal-Hash-Baz • Nahum • Jeremiah • Baruch • Uriah • Jehudi • Ebed-melech • Pashur • Johanan • Hanamel • Hananiah • Micah • Zephaniah • Habakkuk • Obadiah • Huldah

Israel's Kings

Jeroboam I • Abijah • Nadab • Baasha • Elah • Ben-hadad I • Ben-hadad II • Hazael • Zimri • Ethbaal • Rezin • Omri • Ahab • Jezebel • Naboth • Obadiah • Ahaziah • Jehoram (Joram) • Jehu • Jehoahaz • Jehoash • Jeroboam II • Zedekiah • Zachariah • Shallum • Menahem • Pekahiah • Pekah • Nebuzaradan • Hoshea • Shalmaneser

Israel's Prophets

Ahijah • Iddo • Jehu • Elijah • Gehazi • Micaiah • Naaman • Elisha • Amos • Hosea • Gomer • Jonah

In Exile

Nebuchadnezzar • Gedaliah • Ezekiel • Gog • Abednego • Shadrach • Meshach • Belshazzar • Cyrus • Daniel • Michael • Darius I • Darius II

Return from Exile

Nehemiah • Sanballat • Tobiah • Darius III • Geshem • Ezra • Zerubbabel (Sheshbazzar) • Esther • Xerxes (Ahasuerus) • Haman • Mordecai • Haggai • Zechariah • Malachi • Joshua

The First Humans

Adam • Eve • Cain • Abel • Seth • Enoch, Cain's son • Lamech, Cain's descendant • Enoch, Methuselah's father • Methuselah • Lamech, Methuselah's son • Noah • Shem • Japheth • Ham • Cush • Canaan • Nimrod

ADAM

Significance in summary

The first man

Meaning of name

red, earth

Family connections

Married to: Eve
Children: Cain, Abel, Seth

Bible dictionary/encyclopedia entry (IBD)

Red, a Babylonian word, the generic name for man, has the same meaning in Hebrew and Assyrian. It was the name given to the first man, whose creation, fall, and subsequent history and that of his descendants are detailed in the book of Genesis. "God created man [Heb., *Adam*] in his own image, in the image of God created he him; male and female created he them."

Adam was formed out of the dust of the earth (and hence his name); God breathed into his nostrils the breath of life and gave him dominion over all the lower creatures (Gen. 1:26; 2:7). After his creation he was put in the Garden of Eden, to cultivate it, and to enjoy its fruits under this one prohibition: "Of the tree of the knowledge of good and evil thou shalt not eat of it; for in the day that thou eatest thereof thou shalt surely die."

In his first recorded act Adam gave names to the animals and birds. Then the Lord made Adam fall into a deep sleep, and while unconscious took one of his ribs, and closed up his flesh again; and from this rib he made a woman, whom he presented to him when he awoke. Adam received her as his wife and said, "This is now bone of my bones, and flesh of my flesh: she shall be called Woman, because she was taken out of Man." He called her Eve, because she was the mother of all living.

Beguiled by the tempter in the form of a serpent to eat the forbidden fruit, Eve persuaded Adam, and he also did eat. Thus man fell, and brought on himself and his posterity all the sad consequences of his transgression. The narrative of the Fall includes the great promise of a Deliverer (Gen. 3:15), the "first gospel" message to man. They were expelled from Eden, and at the east of the garden God placed a flame, which turned every way, to prevent access to the tree of life (Genesis 3). How long they were in Paradise is a matter of mere conjecture.

Shortly after their expulsion Eve gave birth to her firstborn and called him Cain. Although we have the names of only three of Adam's sons, Cain, Abel, and Seth, yet it is obvious that he had several sons and daughters (Gen. 5:4). He died at the age of 930 years.

Adam and Eve were the progenitors of the whole human race. The investigations of science, independent of historical evidence, lead to the conclusion that God "hath made of one blood all nations of men for to dwell on all the face of the earth" (Acts 17:26; compare Rom. 5:12–21; 1 Cor. 15:22–49).

Bible study on the life of Adam (NTB)

Creation of: Genesis 1:26–28; 2:7; 1 Corinthians 15:45; 1 Timothy 2:13
History of, before he sinned: Genesis 1:26–30; 2:16–25
Temptation and sin of: Genesis 3; Job 31:33; Isaiah 43:27; Hosea 6:7
Subsequent history of: Genesis 3:20–24; 4:1–2, 25; 5:1–5
His death: Genesis 5:5
Progenitor of the human race: Deuteronomy 32:8; Malachi 2:10

Brought sin into the world: 1 Corinthians 15:22, 45
Type of Christ: Romans 5:14

Did Adam exist as a person?

Adam really lived according to Jesus (Matt. 19:4–5); Paul (Rom. 5:14); Jude (Jude 14).

EVE

Significance in summary

The first woman, Adam's wife, mother of all living

Meaning of name

life, living

Family connections

Married to: Adam
Children: Cain, Abel, Seth

Bible dictionary/encyclopedia entry (IBD)

Life; living, the name given by Adam to his wife (Gen. 3:20; 4:1). The account of her creation is given in Genesis 2:21–22. The Creator, by declaring that it was not good for man to be alone, and by creating for him a suitable companion, sanctions monogamy.

The commentator Matthew Henry says: "This companion was taken from his side to signify that she was to be dear unto him as his own flesh. Not from his head, lest she should rule over him; nor from his feet, lest he should tyrannize over her; but from his side, to denote that species of equality which is to subsist in the marriage state." And again, "That wife that is of God's making by special grace, and of God's bringing by special providence, is likely to prove a helpmeet to her husband."

Through the subtle temptation of the serpent she violated God's commandment by taking the forbidden fruit, which she then gave to her husband (2 Cor. 11:3; 1 Tim. 2:13–15).

Bible study on the life of Eve (NTB)

Creation of: Genesis 1:26–28; 2:21–24; 1 Timothy 2:13
Named by Adam: Genesis 2:23; 3:20
Beguiled by Satan: Genesis 3; 2 Corinthians 11:3; 1 Timothy 2:14
Clothed with fig leaves: Genesis 3:7

Clothed with animal skins: Genesis 3:21
Curse denounced against: Genesis 3:16
Messiah promised to: Genesis 3:15
Children of: Genesis 4:1–2, 25; 5:3–4

CAIN

Significance in summary

Adam and Eve's eldest son; killed Abel

Family connections

Parents: Adam and Eve
Siblings: Abel, Seth
Son: Enoch

Meaning of name

acquire

Bible dictionary/encyclopedia entry (IBD)

The firstborn son of Adam and Eve (Genesis 4). He became a farmer, tilling the ground, while his brother Abel became a shepherd.

He was "a sullen, self-willed, haughty, vindictive man; lacking any religious side to his character, and defiant even in his attitude towards God."

It came to pass "in process of time" (marg. "at the end of days"), i.e., probably on the Sabbath, when the two brothers presented their offerings to the Lord. Abel's offering was from the "firstlings of his flock and of the fat," while Cain's was "of the fruit of the ground."

Abel's sacrifice was "more excellent" (Heb. 11:4) than Cain's, and was accepted by God. On this account Cain was "very angry," and cherished murderous feelings towards his brother, and was guilty of killing him (1 John 3:12). For this crime he was expelled from Eden, and led the life of an exile, bearing some mark which God had set on him in reply to his own cry for mercy, so he might be protected from the anger of his fellow-men; or it may be that God only gave him some sign to assure him that he would not be killed (Gen. 4:15).

Doomed to be a wanderer and a fugitive on the earth, he went out to the "land of Nod," i.e., the land of "exile," which is said to have been in the "east of Eden." There he built the first city we read about, and called it after his son's name, Enoch. His descendants are listed to the sixth generation. They gradually degenerated in their moral and spiritual condition until they became wholly corrupt before God. This corruption prevailed, and the flood was sent by God to prevent the final triumph of evil.

Bible study on the life of Cain (NTB)

Son of Adam: Genesis 4:1
Jealousy and crime of: Genesis 4:3–15; Hebrews 11:4; 1 John 3:12; Jude 11
Lives in the land of Nod: Genesis 4:16
Children and descendants of: Genesis 4:17–18

ABEL

Significance in summary

Adam and Eve's second son, killed by his brother Cain

Family connections

Parents: Adam and Eve
Siblings: Cain, Seth

Meaning of name

mankind

Bible dictionary/encyclopedia entry (ISBE)

The second son of Adam and Eve.

A shepherd. "Abel was a keeper of sheep, but Cain was a tiller of the ground," thus representing the two fundamental pursuits of civilized life, the two earliest subdivisions of the human race.

A worshipper. "In process of time," the two brothers came to sacrifice to Yahweh, in order to express their gratitude to Him for all His gifts (Gen. 4:3–4).

A righteous man. The reason for the divine preference is found in the disposition of the brothers. The correct actions did not consist in the outward offering (Gen. 4:7) but in the right state of mind and feeling. Whether the offering is accepted or not depends on the inner motives and moral characters of the offerers. "By faith Abel offered unto God a more excellent [abundant, *pleiona*] sacrifice than Cain" (Heb. 11:4). The "more abundant sacrifice," Westcott thinks, "suggests the deeper gratitude of Abel, and shows a fuller sense of the claims of God." Cain's deeds (the collective expression of his inner life) "were evil, and his brother's righteous" (1 John 3:12). Cain's heart was no longer pure; it had a criminal propensity, springing from envy and jealousy, which made both his offering and person unacceptable. His evil deeds and hatred of his brother culminated in the act of murder, specifically evoked by the opposite character of Abel's deeds and the acceptance of his offering. The evil man cannot endure the sight of goodness in another.

A martyr. Abel ranks as the first martyr (Matt. 23:35), whose blood cried for vengeance (Gen. 4:10; compare Rev. 6:9–10) and brought despair (Gen. 4:13), whereas that of Jesus appeals to God for forgiveness and speaks peace (Heb. 12:24) and is preferred to Abel's.

A type. The first two brothers in history stand as the types and representatives of the two main and enduring divisions of humankind, and bear witness to the absolute antithesis and eternal enmity between good and evil.

Bible study on the life of Abel (NTB)

Son of Adam, history of: Genesis 4:1–15, 25
References to the death of: Matthew 23:35; Luke 11:51; Hebrews 11:4; 12:24; 1 John 3:12

SETH

Significance in summary

Replaced Abel as ancestor of the promised seed

Family connections

Parents: Adam and Eve
Siblings: Cain, Abel
Son: Enosh

Meaning of name

compensation

Bible dictionary/encyclopedia entry (IBD)

Seth was a substitute, the third son of Adam and Eve (Gen. 4:25; 5:3). His mother gave him this name, "for God," said she, "hath appointed me [i.e., compensated me with] another seed instead of Abel, whom Cain slew."

Bible study on the life of Seth (NTB)

The third son of Adam and Eve: Genesis 4:25–26; 5:3, 8; 1 Chronicles 1:1; Luke 3:38

ENOCH, Cain's son

Significance in summary

Cain's eldest son

Family connections

Father: Cain
Son: Irad

Meaning of name

consecrated, dedicated

Bible dictionary/encyclopedia entry (SBD)

The eldest son of Cain (Gen. 4:17), who called the city which he built after him (Gen. 4:18).

Bible study on the life of Enoch (NTB)

Oldest son of Cain: Genesis 4:17–18
A city built by Cain, named after Enoch: Genesis 4:17

LAMECH, Cain's descendant

Significance in summary

A descendant of Cain

Family connections

Married to: Adah, Zillah
Children: Jabal, Jubal, Tubal-Cain, Naamah

Meaning of name

powerful

Bible dictionary/encyclopedia entry (IBD)

The fifth in descent from Cain. He was the first to violate the ordinance of marriage (Gen. 4:18–24) and practice polygamy.

His address to his two wives, Adah and Zillah (4:23–24), is the only extant example of antediluvian poetry.

"Lamech said to his wives, 'Adah and Zillah, listen to me; wives of Lamech, hear my words. I have killed a man for wounding me, a young man for injuring me. If Cain is avenged seven times, then Lamech seventy-seven times'" (Gen. 4:23–24).

It has been called "Lamech's sword-song." He was a "rude ruffian," fearing neither God nor man. With him the curtain falls on the race of Cain. We know nothing of his descendants.

ENOCH, Methuselah's father

Significance in summary

Father of Methuselah

Family connections

Father: Jared
Son: Methuselah

Meaning of name

consecrated, dedicated

Bible dictionary/encyclopedia entry (SBD)

The son of Jared and father of Methuselah (Gen. 5:21; Luke 3:37). In the Epistle of Jude (Jude 14) he is described as "the seventh from Adam"; and the number is probably noticed as conveying the idea of divine completion and rest, while Enoch was himself a type of perfected humanity. After the birth of Methuselah it is said (Gen. 5:22–24) that Enoch "walked with God . . . three hundred years . . . and he was not; for God took him."

The phrase "walked with God" is elsewhere only used of Noah (Gen. 6:9; cf. Gen.17:1, etc.), and is explained by a prophetic life being spent in immediate presence of God.

Like Elijah, he was translated without seeing death. In the Epistle to the Hebrews the spring of Enoch's life is clearly pinpointed. Both the Latin and Greek fathers often linked Enoch and Elijah as historic witnesses of the possibility of a resurrection of the body and of a true human existence in glory (Rev. 11:3).

Bible study on the life of Enoch (NTB)

Father of Methuselah: Genesis 5:18–24; Luke 3:37
Called Henoch: 1 Chronicles 1:3

METHUSELAH

Significance in summary

Noah's grandfather, ancestor of Jesus Christ, the longest living human recorded in the Bible

Family connections

Father: Enoch
Son: Lamech

Meaning of name

man of the javelin

Bible dictionary/encyclopedia entry (IBD)

Man of the dart, the son of Enoch, and grandfather of Noah. He was the oldest man we have any record of. He died at the age of nine hundred and sixty-nine years, in the year of the flood.

Bible study on the life of Methuselah (NTB)

Son of Enoch and grandfather of Noah: Genesis 5:21–27; 1 Chronicles 1:3

LAMECH, Methuselah's son

Significance in summary

Father of Noah and ancestor of Jesus Christ

Family connections

Father: Methuselah
Son: Noah

Meaning of name

powerful

Bible study on the life of Lamech (NTB)

Son of Methuselah, and father of Noah; Lamech lived for 777 years: Genesis 5:25–31; 1 Chronicles 1:3
Ancestor of Jesus: Luke 3:36

NOAH

Significance in summary

Son of Lamech, grandson of Methuselah, builder of the ark

Family connections

Father: Lamech
Children: Japheth, Shem, Ham

Meaning of name

rest

Bible dictionary/encyclopedia entry (CBC, TCB)

CBC

His sons. Noah had three sons—Shem, Ham, and Japheth (Gen. 5:32).

God's revelation to him. God revealed to Noah His reason for destroying the human race (Gen. 6:3, 11–13).

The ark. Noah was commanded to make an ark of gopher wood. The dimensions, allowing eighteen inches to the cubit, were four hundred fifty feet long, seventy-five feet wide, and forty-five feet high (Gen. 6:15). During the building of the ark Noah preached righteousness to his contemporaries (2 Peter 2:5).

People in the ark. The ark contained eight people—Noah, his wife, three sons and their wives—and two of every kind of unclean animals, seven pair of animals that were clean, and seven pair of all kinds of birds (Gen. 6:17–22; 7:1–16).

The flood. The water fell in ceaseless torrents for forty days and forty nights until the highest mountains were covered by twenty-two and a half feet of water (Gen. 7:12, 20). This brought about the destruction of everything on the dry land (Gen. 7:21–24).

Noah's salvation. Noah's salvation is ascribed to faith, fear, the ark, obedience, and water (Gen. 6:22; 7:5; Heb. 11:7; 1 Peter 3:19–21).

God's covenant with Noah. After the flood God established a covenant with Noah that He would never again destroy all living flesh by water (Gen. 8:18–22; 9:1–17).

TCB

Noah is referred to as "perfect" in Genesis 6:9 in the KJV.

The Hebrew word *tamim* means without blemish, and is the technical word for bodily and physical perfection, and not for moral perfection. Hence it is used of animals and their sacrificial purity. It is translated:

- "without blemish" in Exodus 12:5; 29:1; Leviticus 1:3,10; 3:1, 6; 4:3, 23, 28, 32; 5:15, 18; 6:6; 9:2, 3; 14:10; 22:19; 23:12, 18; Numbers 6:14; 28:19, 31; 29:2, 8, 13, 20, 23, 29, 32, 36; Ezekiel 43:22, 23, 25; 45:18, 23; 46:4, 6, 13
- "without spot" in Numbers 19:2; 28:3, 9, 11; 29:17, 26
- "undefiled" in Psalm 119:1

This shows that Genesis 6:9 does not speak of Noah's moral perfection, but tells us that he and his family alone had kept themselves pure, in spite of the prevailing corruption brought about by the fallen angels.

Bible study on the life of Noah (NTB)

Son of Lamech: Genesis 5:28–29
Builds an ark (ship) and saves his family from the great flood: Genesis 6:14–22; 7; 8; Matthew 24:38; Luke 17:27; Hebrews 11:7; 1 Peter 3:20
Builds an altar and offers sacrifices: Genesis 8:20–21
Receives the covenant from God that no flood would ever again come to the earth; the rainbow instituted as a token of the covenant: Genesis 8:20–22; 9:9–17
Intoxication of, and his curse on Canaan: Genesis 9:20–27
His blessing on Shem and Japheth: Genesis 9:26–27
Dies at the age of nine-hundred and fifty: Genesis 9:28–29

SHEM

Significance in summary

Noah's eldest son

Family connections

Father: Noah
Siblings: Japheth, Ham
Children: Elam, Asshur, Arphaxad, Lud, Aram

Meaning of name

name, renown

Bible dictionary/encyclopedia entry (IBD)

The first mentioned of the sons of Noah (Gen. 5:32; 6:10). He was probably the eldest of Noah's sons. The words "brother of Japheth the elder" in Genesis 10:21 are more correctly translated "the elder brother of Japheth," as in the Revised Version. Shem's name is generally mentioned first in the list of Noah's sons. He and his wife were saved in the ark (7:13). Noah foretold his preeminence over Canaan (9:23–27). He died when he was six hundred years old, having been for many years contemporary with Abraham, according to the usual chronology. The Israelite nation sprang from him (Gen. 11:10–26; 1 Chron. 1:24–27).

Bible study on the life of Shem (NTB)

Preserved in the ark (ship): Genesis 7:13; 9:18
His filial conduct: Genesis 9:23–27
Descendants of: Genesis 10:1, 21–31; 11:10–29; 1 Chronicles 1:17–54
Called Sem (KJV): Luke 3:36

JAPHETH

Significance in summary

Noah's second son

Family connections

Father: Noah
Siblings: Shem, Ham
Children: Gomer, Magog, Madai, Javan, Tubal, Meshech, Tiras

Meaning of name

may God enlarge

Bible study on the life of Japheth (NTB)

Son of Noah: Genesis 5:32; 6:10; 9:18; 10:21
His life preserved at the time of the great flood: Genesis 7:13; 9:18
Prudence of, on the occasion of Noah's drunkenness: Genesis 9:23, 27
Descendants of: Genesis 10:2–5; 1 Chronicles 1:5–7

HAM

Significance in summary

Noah's youngest son

Family connections

Father: Noah
Siblings: Japheth, Shem
Children: Cush, Mizraim, Put, Canaan

Meaning of name

hot

Bible dictionary/encyclopedia entry (IBD)

The youngest son of Noah (Gen. 5:32; compare 9:22, 24). The curse pronounced by Noah against Ham, appropriately against Canaan his fourth son, was accomplished when the Jews subsequently exterminated the Canaanites.

One of the most important facts recorded in Genesis 10 is the foundation of the earliest monarchy in Babylonia by Nimrod the grandson of Ham (vv. 6, 8, 10). The early Babylonian empire was thus Hamitic, and has a similar race to the early inhabitants of Arabia and of Ethiopia.

The race of Ham was the most energetic of all the descendants of Noah in the early days of the post-diluvian world.

Bible study on the life of Ham (NTB)

Son of Noah: Genesis 5:32; 9:18, 24; 1 Chronicles 1:4
Provokes his father's anger and is cursed by him: Genesis 9:18–27
His children: Genesis 10:6–20; 1 Chronicles 1:8–16

CUSH

Significance in summary

Ham's eldest son

Family connections

Father: Ham
Siblings: Mizraim, Put, Canaan
Children: Seba, Havilah, Sabtah, Raamah, Sabteca, Nimrod

Meaning of name

black

CANAAN

Significance in summary

A son of Ham, grandson of Noah

Family connections

Father: Ham
Siblings: Cush, Mizraim, Put
Children: Sidon, Hittites, Jebusites, Amorites, Girgashites, Hivites, Arkites, Sinites, Arvadites, Zemarites, Hamathites

Meaning of name

merchant, or lowly

NIMROD

Significance in summary

Cush's son, Ham's grandson

Family connections

Father: Cush
Siblings: Seba, Havilah, Sabtah, Raamah, Sabteca

Meaning of name

let us rebel, rebellion

Bible dictionary/encyclopedia entry (FBD, TCB)

FBD

Cush's son or descendant, Ham's grandson (Gen. 10:8). "[Nimrod] began to be a mighty one in the earth," i.e., he was the first of Noah's descendants who became renowned for bold and daring deeds.

"He was a mighty hunter before Jehovah," so that it became a proverb or the refrain of ballads in describing hunters and warriors, "even as Nimrod the mighty hunter before Jehovah."

The Hebrew name Nimrod means "let us rebel," given by his contemporaries to Nimrod as one who always had in his mouth words to stir up a rebellion. Nimrod subverted the existing patriarchal order of society by setting up leadership based on personal valor and maintained by aggression.

TCB

Josephus says: "Nimrod persuaded mankind not to ascribe their happiness to God, but to think that his own excellency was its source. And he soon changed things into a tyranny, thinking there was no other way to wean men from the fear of God, than by making them rely on his own power."

The Targum of Jonathan says: "From the foundation of the world no one was like Nimrod, powerful in hunting, and in rebellions against the Lord."

The Jerusalem Targum says: "He was powerful in hunting and in wickedness before the Lord, for he was a hunter of the sons of men, and he said to them, 'Depart from the judgment of the Lord, and adhere to the judgment of Nimrod!' Therefore is it said: 'As Nimrod [is] the strong one, strong in hunting, and in wickedness before the Lord.'"

The Chaldee paraphrase of 1 Chronicles 1:10 says: "Cush begat Nimrod, who began to prevail in wickedness, for he shed innocent blood, and rebelled against Jehovah."

Nimrod founded Babylon, which adopted his character and became the great antagonist of God's truth and God's people.

We cannot fail to see, in Nimrod, Satan's first attempt to raise up a human universal ruler of men. There have been many subsequent attempts, such as Nebuchadnezzar, Alexander, Napoleon, and others. He will finally succeed in the person of the Antichrist.

Bible study on the life of Nimrod (NTB)

"A mighty hunter before the Lord": Genesis 10:8–9; 1 Chronicles 1:10

Job and His Comforters

Job • Eliphaz • Bildad
• Zophar • Elihu

Introduction (BH)

Two things may be regarded as quite settled about the book of Job. Its scene and actors are set in patriarchal times and are outside the family or immediate ancestry of Abraham. It is an account of Gentile life in the time of the earliest patriarchs. And yet anything more noble, grand, devout, or spiritual than what the book of Job contains is not found, "no, not in Israel."

This is not the place to give either the history of Job, or to point out the depth of thought, the vividness of imagery, and the beauty and grandeur of language with which it is written. Job had evidently perfect knowledge of the true God; and he was a humble, earnest worshipper of Jehovah. Without any acquaintance with "Moses and the prophets," he knew that of which Moses and the prophets spoke. Reverent, believing acknowledgment of God, submission, and spiritual repentance formed part of his experience, which had the approval of

God Himself. Then Job offered sacrifices; he speaks about the great tempter; he looks for the resurrection of the body; and he expects the coming of Messiah.

JOB

Significance in summary

A godly man from Uz whose endurance of calamities resulted in God's blessings

Meaning of name

persecuted

Bible dictionary/encyclopedia entry (IBD)

An Arabian patriarch who lived in the land of Uz. While living in the middle of great prosperity, he was suddenly overwhelmed by a series of calamities. In all his sufferings he maintained his integrity. Once more God visited him with the rich tokens of his goodness and even greater prosperity than he had enjoyed before. He survived the period of trial for one hundred and forty years, and died in a good old age, an example to succeeding generations of integrity (Ezek. 14:14, 20) and of submissive patience under the sorest calamities (James 5:11). His history, so far as it is known, is recorded in his book.

A Bible commentator's portrait (CCEB)

Job: a real person. It has been supposed by some that the book of Job is an allegory, not a real narrative, on account of the artificial character of many of its statements. Thus the sacred numbers, three and seven, often occur. He had seven thousand sheep, seven sons, both before and after his trials; his three friends sit down with him seven days and seven nights; both before and after his trials he had three daughters. So also the number and form of the speeches of the several speakers seem to be artificial. The name of Job too is derived from an Arabic word signifying repentance.

But Ezekiel 14:14 (compare Ezek. 14:16, 20) speaks of "Job" in connection with "Noah and Daniel," real people. James (James 5:11) also refers to Job as an example of "patience," which he would not have been likely to do had Job been only a fictitious person. Also the names of people and places are specified with a particularity not to be looked for in an allegory. As to the exact doubling of his possessions after his restoration, no doubt the round number is given for the exact number;

this is often done in undoubtedly historical books. As to the studied number and form of the speeches, it seems likely that the arguments were substantially those that appear in the book, but that the studied and poetic form was given by Job himself, guided by the Holy Spirit. He lived one hundred and forty years after his trials, and nothing would be more natural than that he should, at his leisure, mold into a perfect form the arguments used in the momentous debate, for the instruction of the Church in all ages. Probably too the debate itself occupied several sittings; and the number of speeches assigned to each was arranged in advance, and each was allowed the interval of a day or more to prepare carefully his speech and replies; this will account for the speakers bringing forward their arguments in regular series, no one speaking out of his turn. As to the name Job—repentance (supposing the derivation correct)—it was common in old times to give a name from circumstances which occurred at an advanced period of life, and this is no argument against the reality of the person.

Did Job write the book of Job? Its style, thought patterns, and imagery are those we would look for in the work of an Arabian emir. There is precisely that degree of knowledge of early tradition (see Job 31:33, as to Adam) which had become well known in the days of Noah and Abraham, and which was subsequently embodied in the early chapters of Genesis. Job, in his speeches, shows that he was much more competent to compose the work than Elihu. The style prevents it from being attributed to Moses, to whom its composition is by some attributed. But the fact that it, though not a Jewish book, appears among the Hebrew sacred writings, makes it likely that it came to the knowledge of Moses during the forty years which he passed through parts of Arabia, mainly near Horeb; and that he, by divine guidance, introduced it as a sacred writing to the Israelites, to whom, in their affliction, the patience and restoration of Job were calculated to be a lesson of special usefulness.

That it is inspired appears from the fact that Paul (1 Cor. 3:19) quotes it (Job 5:13) with the formula, "It is written." Compare also James 4:10 and 1 Peter 5:6 with Job 22:29; Romans 11:34–35 with Job 15:8. It is probably the oldest book in the world. It stands among the Hagiographa in the threefold division of Scripture into the Law, the Prophets, and the Hagiographa ("Psalms," Luke 24:44).

Bible study on the life of Job (NTB)

A man who lived in Uz: Job 1:1
Righteousness of: Job 1:1, 5, 8; 2:3; Ezekiel 14:14, 20
Riches of: Job 1:3
Trial of, by affliction of Satan: Job 1:13–19; 2:7–10

Fortitude of: Job 1:20–22; 2:10; James 5:11
Visited by Eliphaz, Bildad, and Zophar as comforters: Job 2:11–13
Complaints of, and replies by his three friends to: Job 3–37
Replied to by God: Job 38–41
Submission of, to God: Job 40:3–5; 42:1–6
Later blessings and riches of: Job 42:10–16
Death of: Job 42:16–17

ELIPHAZ

Significance in summary

First of Job's three friends

Meaning of name

God his strength

Bible dictionary/encyclopedia entry (ISBE)

The first and most prominent of the three friends of Job (Job 2:11), who came from distant places to comfort him, when they heard of his affliction.

That he is to be regarded as their leader and spokesman is shown by the greater weight and originality of his speeches (contained in Job 4; 5; 15; 22), the speeches of the other friends being mainly echoes and emotional enforcements of his thoughts, and by the fact that he is taken as their representative (Job 42:7) when, after the address from the whirlwind, Yahweh points to their expiation for the wrong done to Job and to the truth.

He is represented as a venerable sage from Teman in Idumaea, a place noted for its wisdom (compare Jer. 49:7), as was also the whole land of Edom (compare Obad. 1:8). This wisdom is the result of ages of thought and experience (compare Job 15:17–19), of long study (compare Job 5:27), and claims the authority of revelation.

In his first speech he deduces Job's affliction from the natural sequence of effect from cause (Job 4:7–11), which cause he makes broad enough to include innate impurity and depravity (Job 4:17–19); evinces a quietism which deprecates Job's self-destroying outbursts of anger (Job 5:2–3; compare Job's answer, Job 6:2–3; 30:24); and promises restoration as the result of penitence and submission.

In his second speech he is irritated because Job's blasphemous words are calculated to hinder devotion (Job 15:4); he attributes them to iniquity (Job 15:5–6), reiterates his depravity doctrine (Job 15:14–16), and initiates the lurid descriptions of the wicked man's fate, in which the friends go on to overstate their case (Job 15:20–35).

In the third speech he is moved by the exigencies of his theory to impute actual crimes to Job, iniquities indulged in because God was too far away to see (22:5–15); but as a close friend holds open to him still the way of penitence and restoration to health and wealth (22:21–30). His utterances are well composed and judicial (too coldly academic, Job thinks, 16:4–5), full of good religious counsel abstractly considered.

Their error is in their inveterate presupposition of Job's wickedness, their unsympathetic clinging to theory in the face of fact, and his lack of friendship.

BILDAD

Significance in summary

Second of Job's three friends

Meaning of name

son of contention

Bible dictionary/encyclopedia entry (ISBE)

The second of the three friends of Job who, coming from distant regions, set about trying to comfort him in his affliction (Job 2:11). He is from Shuah, an unknown place somewhere in the countries east and southeast of Palestine (or the designation Shuhite may refer to his ancestor Shuah, one of Abraham's sons by Keturah, Gen. 25:2), and from his name (compounded with Bel, the name of a Babylonian deity) would seem to represent the wisdom of the distant East. His three speeches are contained in Job 8; 18; they are mainly an echo of what Eliphaz has maintained, but made with greater vehemence (compare Job 8:2; 18:3–4) because he deems Job's words so impious. He is the first to attribute Job's calamity to actual wickedness; but he gets at it indirectly by accusing his children (who were destroyed, Job 1:19) of sin which brings about their punishment (Job 8:4). For his contribution to the discussion he appeals to tradition (Job 8:8–10), and taking Eliphaz's cue of cause and effect (Job 8:11) he gives, evidently from the literary stores of wisdom, a description of the precarious state of the wicked, to which he contrasts, with whatever implication it involves, the felicitous state of the righteous (Job 8:11–22).

His second speech is an intensified description of the wicked man's woes, made as if to match Job's description of his own desperate case (compare Job 18:5–21 with Job 16:6–22), thus tacitly identifying Job with the reprobate wicked.

His third speech (Job 25), which is the last utterance of the friends, is brief, subdued in tone, and is a kind of Parthian shot, reiterating Eliphaz's depravity idea, the doctrine that dies hardest. This speech marks the final silencing of the friends.

ZOPHAR

Significance in summary

Third of Job's three friends

Bible dictionary/encyclopedia entry (ISBE)

One of the three friends of Job who, hearing of his affliction, visits and comforts him. He is from the tribe of Naamah, a tribe and place otherwise unknown, for as all the other friends and Job himself are from lands outside of Palestine, it is not likely that this place was identical with Naamah in the West of Judah (Josh. 15:41). He speaks only twice (Job 11; 20); by his silence the third time the writer seems to intimate that with Bildad's third speech (Job 25), the friends' arguments are exhausted. He is the most impetuous and dogmatic of the three (compare Job 11:2–3; 20:2–3); stung in to a passionate response by Job's presumption in maintaining that he is wronged and is seeking light from God. His words are intense amounting to reckless exaggeration. He is the first to accuse Job directly of wickedness, averring indeed that his punishment is too good for him (11:6); he rebukes Job's impious presumption in trying to find out the unsearchable secrets of God (11:7–12); and yet, like the rest of the friends, promises peace and restoration on the basis of penitence and rejecting iniquity (11:13–19). Even from this promise, however, he reverts to the fearful peril of the wicked (11:20); and in his second speech, outdoing the others, he presses their lurid description of the wicked man's woes to the extreme (20:5–29), and asks for a denial from Job, who, not in anger, but in dismay, is constrained by loyalty to truth to acknowledge things as they are. Zophar seems to represent the wrong-headedness of the odium theologicum.

ELIHU

Significance in summary

The fourth and youngest of Job's advisors

Meaning of name

he is my God

Bible dictionary/encyclopedia entry (ISBE)

One of the disputants in the book of Job; a young man who, having listened in silence to the arguments of Job and his friends, is moved to prolong the discussion and from his more just views of truth set both parties right. He is from the tribe of Buz (compare Gen. 22:21), a brother-tribe to Uz, and from the family of Ram, or Aram, that is, an Aramean. He is not mentioned as one of the characters of the story until chapter 32; and then, as the friends are silenced and Job's words are ended, Elihu has the whole field to himself, until the theophany of the whirlwind proves too overwhelming for him to bear. His four speeches take up chapters 32–37.

Consider the situation at the end of Job's words (Job 31:40). Job has vindicated his integrity and stands ready to present his cause to God (Job 31:35–37). The friends, however, have exhausted their resources, and through three discourses have been silent, as it were, snuffed out of existence. It is at this point, then, that Elihu is introduced, to renew their contention with young constructive blood, and represent their cause (as he sees it) better than they can themselves. He is essentially at one with them in condemning Job (Job 34:34–37); his only quarrel with them is on the score of the inconclusiveness of their arguments (32:2–3). His self-portrayal is conceived in a decided spirit of satire on the part of the writer, not unmingled with a sardonic humor. He is very egotistic, very sure of the value of his ideas. This, whether inferior composition or not, admirably adapts his words to his character. He adds materially to what the friends have said, but in a more rationalistic vein; speaks edifyingly, as the friends have not done, of the disciplinary value of affliction, and of God's means of revelation by dreams and visions and the interpreting of an intercessory friend (Job 33:13–28).

Very evidently, however, his ego is the center of his words; it is he who sets up as Job's mediator (Job 33:5–7; compare Job 9:32–35), and his sage remarks on God's power and wisdom in nature are full of self-importance. All this seems designed to accentuate the almost ludicrous humiliation of his collapse when from a natural phenomenon the storm shows unusual and supernatural signs. His words become disjointed and incoherent, and cease with an attempt to recant his pretensions. And the verdict from the whirlwind is: "darkeneth counsel by words without knowledge." Elihu thus has a real function in the story, as honorable as overweening self-confidence is apt to be.

The Patriarchs

Nahor, Abraham's grandfather • Terah • Abraham • Melchizedek • Sarah • Hagar • Ishmael • Keturah • Nahor, Abraham's brother •Chedorlaomer • Eliezer • Lot • Moab • Isaac • Rebekah • Esau • Jacob • Rachel • Dinah • Shechem • Naphtali • Gad • Issachar • Leah • Zilpah • Zebulun • Laban • Bilhah

Introduction

A patriarch is a "father" of a tribe, or the chief ancestor of a race.

David is referred to as a patriarch in Acts 2:29. The twelve sons of Jacob are referred to as patriarchs in Acts 7:8–9, while in Hebrews 7:4 Abraham is called a patriarch.

To the Jews, the patriarchs of the Old Testament refer to Abraham, Isaac, and Jacob, and Judaism thinks of the patriarchal age as the period from the birth of Abraham to the death of Jacob.

NAHOR, Abraham's grandfather

Significance in summary

Abraham's grandfather

Family connections

Father: Serug
Son: Terah

TERAH

Significance in summary

Abraham's father and ancestor of Jesus Christ

Family connections

Father: Nahor
Children: Abram, Nahor, Haran, Sarai

Bible dictionary/encyclopedia entry (IBD)

Tenth from Noah through Shem; father of Abram, Nahor, Haran, and Sarai (Gen. 11:27). Accompanied Abram from Ur on the way to Canaan (an act of faith on the part of one so very old; persuaded by his godly son), but died at Haran when 205 years old. He was 70 when Haran his oldest son was born, 130 when Abram was born (Gen. 11:26; 11:32; 12:4; Acts 7:2–4).

Bible study on the life of Terah (NTB)

The father of Abraham: Genesis 11:24–32
Was an idolater: Joshua 24:2
Called Thara: Luke 3:34

ABRAHAM

Significance in summary

The founder of the Jewish nation and ancestor of Jesus Christ

Family connections

Father: Terah
Siblings: Nahor, Haran, Sarai
Married to: Sarai, Hagar, Keturah
Children: Ishmael, Isaac, Zimran, Jokshan, Medan, Midian, Ishbak, Shuah

Meaning of name

father of a multitude

Bible dictionary/encyclopedia entry (CBC, SBD)

CBC

Birth. He was born in Ur of the Chaldees, and was a direct descendant of Shem (Gen. 11:10–32).

His call. The Lord first spoke to him in Ur of the Chaldees (Gen. 12:1; Acts 7:1–5).

The promises. God gave him two great promises,

- that he would make of him a great nation, bless him, make his name great, make him a blessing, bless those who blessed him, and curse those who cursed him;
- that in him all families of the earth would be blessed (Gen. 12:1–3).

These promises were renewed on Mount Moriah (Gen. 22:1–18) and subsequently fulfilled in

- the covenant dedicated at Mount Sinai (Exod. 24:1–8);
- the new covenant (Gal. 4:22–31).

Last days of Abraham. The closing years of Abraham's life were notable for:

- his marriage to Keturah (Gen. 25:1–2);
- the birth of Esau and Jacob (Gen. 21:5; 25:1–26);
- giving his property to Isaac and sending the sons of his concubines away with gifts (Gen. 25:5–6).

SBD

Abraham (father of a multitude) was the son of Terah, and founder of the great Hebrew nation. His family, a branch of the descendants of Shem, was settled in Ur of the Chaldees, beyond the Euphrates, where Abraham was born. Terah had two other sons, Nahor and Haran. Haran died while his father was in Ur of the Chaldees, leaving a son, Lot. Terah, taking with him Abram, with Sarai his wife and his grandson Lot, emigrated to Haran in Mesopotamia, where he died. On the death of his father, Abram, then seventy-five years old, with Sarai and Lot, moved to the land of Canaan, where he was directed by divine command (Gen. 12:5). There he received the general promise that he would become the founder of a great nation, and that all the families of the earth would be blessed in him. He passed through the heart of the country over the great highway to Shechem, and pitched his tent beneath the terebinth of Moreh (Gen. 12:6). Here he received a vision from Jehovah that this was the land that his descendants would inherit (Gen. 12:7). The next stopping place of the wanderer was on a mountain between Bethel and Ai (Gen. 12:8), but the country was suffering from famine, and Abram journeyed farther south to the rich corn lands of Egypt. There, fearing that the great beauty of Sarai might tempt the powerful monarch of Egypt and endanger his own life, he passed off Sarai as his sister. But the king was told about her beauty, and she was taken into the royal harem. The deception was uncovered, and Pharaoh with some indignation sent Abram out of the country (Gen. 12:10–20). He left Egypt with great possessions, and, accompanied by Lot, returned by the south of Palestine to his former encampment between Bethel and Ai. The increased wealth of the two relatives caused their separation. Lot chose the fertile plain of the Jordan near Sodom, while Abram pitched his tent among the groves of Mamre, near Hebron (Gen. 13:1).

Lot with his family and possessions was captured by Chedorlaomer, king of Elam, who had invaded Sodom. Abram pursued the conquerors and defeated them not far from Damascus. The captives and plunder were all recovered, and Abram was greeted on his return by the king of Sodom, and by Melchizedek, king of Salem, priest of the most high God, who mysteriously appears on the scene to bless the patriarch and receive from him a tenth of the spoil (Gen. 14:1–18).

After this the promise, repeated for a third time, that his descendants would become a mighty nation and possess the land in which he was a stranger was confirmed with all the solemnity of a religious ceremony (Genesis 15).

Ten years had passed since he had left his father's house, and the fulfillment of the promise was apparently more distant than ever. At the suggestion of Sarai, who despaired of having children of her own, he took as his concubine Hagar, her Egyptian maid, who bore him Ishmael (Genesis 16).

But this was not the fulfillment of the promise. Thirteen years elapsed, during which Abram still lived in Hebron, when the covenant was renewed, and the rite of circumcision was established as its sign. This most important crisis in Abram's life, when he was 99 years old, is marked by the significant change of his name to Abraham, "father of a multitude," while his wife's from Sarai became Sarah.

The promise that Sarah would have a son was repeated in the remarkable scene described in Genesis 18. Three men stood before Abraham as he sat at the entrance of his tent in the heat of the day. The patriarch, with true Eastern hospitality, welcomed the strangers, and invited them to rest and refresh themselves. After the meal, they foretold the birth of Isaac, and went on their way to Sodom. Abraham accompanied them, and is represented as an interlocutor in a dialogue with Jehovah, in which he pleaded in vain to avert the vengeance threatened on the cities of the plain (Gen. 18:17–33).

Isaac, the long-looked-for child, was born. Sarah, her jealousy of Hagar aroused by the mockery of Ishmael at the "great banquet" which Abram made to celebrate the weaning of her son (Gen. 21:9), demanded that, with his mother Hagar, Ishmael be thrown out of their home (Gen. 21:10). But the severest trial of Abraham's faith was yet to come. For a long time nothing is recorded about Abraham. Then he receives the strange command to take Isaac, his only son, and offer him as a burnt offering. Abraham obeyed. His faith, up to now unshaken, supported him in this final trial, "accounting that God was able to raise up his son, even from the dead, from where also he received him in a figure" (Heb. 11:19). The sacrifice was prevented by the Lord's angel, the promise of spiritual blessing made for the first time, and Abraham with his son returned to Beersheba, and for a time lived there (Genesis 22).

But we find him, after a few years, in his original residence at Hebron, for there Sarah died (Gen. 23:2) and was buried in the cave of Machpelah. The remaining years of Abraham's life are marked by just a few incidents. After Isaac's marriage with Rebekah and his move to Lahai-roi, Abraham took Keturah as his wife, by whom he had six children, Zimran, Jokshan, Medan, Midian, Ishbok, and Shuah, who became the ancestors of nomadic tribes inhabiting the countries south and southeast of Palestine. Abraham lived to see the gradual accomplishment of the promise in the birth of his grandchildren Jacob and Esau, and witnessed their growth to manhood (Gen. 25:26). At the goodly age of 175 he was "gathered to his people," and laid beside Sarah in the tomb of Machpelah by his sons Isaac and Ishmael (Gen. 25:7–10).

Bible study on the life of Abraham (NTB)

Son of Terah: Genesis 11:26–27
Marries Sarah: Genesis 11:29
Lives in Ur, but moves to Haran: Genesis 11:31; Nehemiah 9:7; Acts 7:4
Lives in Canaan: Genesis 12:4–6
Divine call of: Genesis 12:1–3; Joshua 24:3; Nehemiah 9:7; Isaiah 51:2; Acts 7:2–3; Hebrews 11:8
Canaan given to: Genesis 12:1, 7; 15:7–21; Ezekiel 33:24
Lives in Bethel: Genesis 12:8
Lives in Egypt: Genesis 12:10–20
Deferring to Lot, chooses Hebron: Genesis 13; 14:13; 35:27
Lives in Gerar: Genesis 20; 21:22–34

Defeats Chedorlaomer: Genesis 14:5–24
Is blessed by Melchizedek: Genesis 14:18–20; Hebrews 7:1–10
God's covenant with: Genesis 15; 17:1–22; Micah 7:20; Luke 1:73; Romans 4:13; 15:8; Galatians 3:6–18, 29; 4:22–31; Hebrews 6:13–14
Called Abraham: Genesis 17:5; Nehemiah 9:7
Circumcision of: Genesis 17:10–14, 23–27
Angels appear to: Genesis 18:1–16; 22:11, 15; 24:7
His questions about the destruction of the righteous and wicked in Sodom: Genesis 18:23–32
Witnesses the destruction of Sodom: Genesis 19:27–28
Ishmael born to: Genesis 16:3, 15
Deceives Abimelech concerning Sarah, his wife: Genesis 20
Isaac born to: Genesis 21:2–3; Galatians 4:22–30
Sends Hagar and Ishmael away: Genesis 21:10–14; Galatians 4:22–30
Trial of his faith in the offering of Isaac: Genesis 22:1–19; Hebrews 11:17; James 2:21
Sarah, his wife, dies: Genesis 23:1–2
He purchases a place for her burial and buries her in a cave: Genesis 23:3–20
Marries Keturah: Genesis 25:1
Provides a wife for Isaac: Genesis 24
Children of: Genesis 16:15; 21:2–3; 25:1–4; 1 Chronicles 1:32–34
Testament of: Genesis 25:5–6
Wealth of: Genesis 13:2; 24:35; Isaiah 51:2
Age of, at different periods: Genesis 12:4; 16:16; 21:5; 25:7
Death: Genesis 25:8–10
In Paradise: Matthew 8:11; Luke 13:28; 16:22–31
Friend of God: 2 Chronicles 20:7; Isaiah 41:8; James 2:23
Piety of: Genesis 12:7–8; 13:4, 18; 20:7; 21:33; 22:3–13; 26:5; Nehemiah 9:7–8; Romans 4:16–18
A prophet: Genesis 20:7
Faith of: Genesis 15:6; Romans 4:1–22; Galatians 3:6–9; Hebrews 11:8–10, 17–19; James 2:21–24
Unselfishness of: Genesis 13:9; 21:25–30
Independence of, in character: Genesis 14:23; 23:6–16
Ancestors of, idolatrous: Joshua 24:2
How regarded by his descendants: Matthew 3:9; Luke 13:16, 28; 19:9; John 8:33–40

MELCHIZEDEK

Significance in summary

King and high priest of Salem

Meaning of name

king of righteousness

Bible dictionary/encyclopedia entry (CBC)

During Abram's stay in Canaan this priest and king met him and was hospitable to him (Gen. 14:18–20). Much mystery surrounds this distinguished person. Various theories have been advanced concerning him. Some assert that he was God Almighty. This is not a fact, for he was "the priest of the most high God" (Gen. 14:18). Others assert that he was Jesus Christ. This is not a fact, for he was "made like the Son of God" (Heb. 7:3). It is asserted in the Scriptures that he was a man (Heb. 7:1–4). If you will reflect that the Scriptures deal with him in his official capacity, the difficulties and mysteries surrounding him will immediately vanish. Let us take a closer view. The history of the world, from the biblical standpoint, naturally divides itself into three different periods, which for lack of better terms I will designate, the Patriarchal dispensation, the Jewish dispensation, the Christian dispensation.

They are each characterized by a priesthood peculiarly its own. There was no regular priestly line from the transgression to the giving of the law of Moses. In a general way, it may be asserted that every man was his own priest (Gen. 4:1–4; 12:7–8; 15:8–18; 26:19–25; 31:43–55; 35:1–15; 46:1). During this age Melchizedek appeared. He was king of Salem and priest of the most high God. We know nothing of his duties or prerogatives as priest or king. We know that he did not belong to any special priestly order. His priestly office was independent of all other men. In the priestly office he was without father, and without mother, and without descent. No record was kept of his installation as priest, his official acts, or his death, hence, so far as the record is concerned, he was without beginning of days or end of life.

At the inauguration of the second dispensation an entire family was set apart to the priestly office, and the priestly office remained in that family, and was transmitted from father to son and from generation to generation to the death of Christ (Exod. 29:1, 29; Num. 17; 18:1–7; Heb. 7:11, 23–28). David predicted that a priest would appear who was similar to the order of Melchizedek (Ps. 110:4). This is repeatedly affirmed by the author of Hebrews. The priesthood of the Christian dispensation is similar to the order of Melchizedek, and does not follow the order of Aaron. Jesus became a priest when he entered heaven by his own blood (Heb. 8:1–4; 10:11–12). His priesthood is independent. He had no predecessor, and he will have no successor. He will remain in heaven and officiate as priest until the work of redemption is done.

Bible study on the life of Melchizedek (NTB)

King of Salem: Genesis 14:18–20
A priest and type of Christ: Hebrews 5:6, 10; 6:20; 7:1–21

SARAH

Significance in summary

Abraham's wife and mother of Isaac

Family connections

Father: Terah
Siblings: Abram, Nahor, Haran
Married to: Abram
Son: Isaac

Meaning of name

princess

Bible dictionary/encyclopedia entry (ISBE)

In Genesis 17:15 the woman who up to that time has been known as Sarai receives by divine command the name Sarah.

The former name appears to be derived from the same root as Israel, if, indeed, Genesis 32:28 is intended as an etymology of Israel. "She that strives," a contentious person, is a name that might be given to a child at birth (compare Hos. 12:3–4, of Jacob), or later when the child's character developed; in Genesis 16:6 and 21:10 a contentious character appears. Yet comparison with the history of her husband's name warns us not to operate solely on the basis of the Hebrew language. Sarai was the name this woman brought with her from Mesopotamia. On the other hand there can be little doubt that the name Sarah, which she received when her son was promised, means "princess," for it is the feminine form of the extremely common title *sar*, used by the Semites to designate a ruler of greater or lesser rank. In the verse following the one where this name is conferred, it is declared of Sarah that "kings of people shall be of her" (Gen. 17:16).

We are introduced to Sarai in Genesis 11:29. She is here mentioned as the wife that Abraham "took," while still in Ur of the Chaldees, that is, while among his family. It is immediately added that "Sarai was barren; she had no child" (v. 30). By this simple remark the writer sounds the motif that is to be developed later on. When the migration to Haran occurs, Sarai is named along with Abram and Lot as accompanying Terah.

Sarai's career as described in Genesis 11 was not dependent on her being the daughter of Terah. Terah had other descendants who did not accompany him. Her movements were determined by her being Abram's wife. It appears, however, that she was a daughter of Terah by a different mother from the mother of Abram. The language of 20:12 could mean that she was Abram's niece, but the fact that there was only ten years difference between their ages (Gen. 17:17) makes this hypothesis less probable. Marriage with half-sisters seems to have been not uncommon in antiquity (even in the Old Testament; compare 2 Sam. 13:13).

This double relationship was used by Abraham twice when he lacked faith in God to protect his life. In a cowardly way he thought about his own safety at the price of his wife's honor.

Although the births of Ishmael and Isaac are separated by fourteen years, they are closely linked in the Bible record. Sarah's barrenness persisted. She was now far past middle life, even on a patriarchal scale of longevity, and there appeared no hope of her ever bearing that child who would inherit the promise of God. She therefore adopts the expedient of being "builded by" her personal slave, Hagar the Egyptian (see Gen. 16:2 margin). That is, according to contemporary law and custom as witnessed by the Code of Hammurabi, a son born of this woman would be the freeborn son and heir of Abraham and Sarah.

Such was in fact the position of Ishmael later. But the insolence of the maid aroused the jealousy of the mistress and led to an unjustified expulsion. Hagar, however, returned at God's instruction, humbled herself before Sarah, and bore Ishmael in his own father's house. Here he remained the sole and rightful heir, until the miracle of Isaac's birth disappointed all human expectations and resulted in the ultimate expulsion of Hagar and her son.

The change of name from Sarai to Sarah when Isaac was promised has already been noted. Sarah's laughter of incredulity when she hears the promise is associated with the origin of the name of Isaac, but it serves also to emphasize the miraculous character of his birth, coming as it does after his parents are both so "well stricken in age" as to make parenthood seem an absurdity.

Before the birth of this child of promise, however, Sarah is again exposed, through the cowardice of her husband, to dishonor and ruin. Abimelech, king of Gerar, desiring to be allied by marriage with a man of Abraham's power, sends for Sarah, whom he knows only as Abraham's sister, and for the second time she takes her place in the harem of a prince. But the divine promise is not to be thwarted, even by persistent human weakness and sin. In a dream God reveals to Abimelech Sarah's true position, and Sarah is restored to her husband. Then the long-delayed son is born, the jealous mother expels Hagar and Ishmael, and her career comes to a close at the age of 127, at Hebroni. The grief and devotion of Abraham are displayed in Genesis 23, in which he seeks and obtains a burying place for his wife. She is the first to be interred in that cave of the field of Machpelah, which was to be the common resting place of the fathers and mothers of the future Israel.

The character of Sarah is a mixture of light and shade. On the one hand we have seen that lapse from faith which resulted in the birth of Ishmael, and that lack of self-control and charity which resulted in a quarrel with Abraham, an act of injustice to Hagar, and the disinheriting of Ishmael. Yet on the other hand we see in Sarah, as the New Testament writers point out (Heb. 11:11; 1 Peter 3:6), one who through a long life of companionship with Abraham shared his hope in God, his faith in the promises, and his power to become God's agent for achieving what was humanly impossible. In fact, to Sarah is ascribed a sort of spiritual maternity, correlative with Abraham's position as "father of the faithful"; for all women are declared to be the (spiritual) daughters of Sarah, who like her are adorned in "the hidden man of the heart," and who are "doers of good" and "fearers of no terror" (1 Peter loc. cit., literally translated). That in spite of her dealings with Hagar and Ishmael she was in general "in subjection to her husband" and of "a meek and quiet spirit," appears from her husband's genuine grief when she died, and still more clearly from her son's prolonged mourning for her (Gen. 24:67). And He who makes even the anger of man to praise Him used even Sarah's jealous anger to accomplish His purpose that "the son of the freewoman," Isaac, "born through promise," should alone inherit that promise (Gal. 4:22–31).

Apart from the three New Testament passages already cited, Sarah is alluded to only in Isaiah 51:2 ("Sarah that bare you," as the mother of the nation), in Romans 4:19 ("the deadness of Sarah's womb"), and in Romans 9:9, where God's promise in Genesis 18:10 is quoted. Yet her existence and her history are of course presupposed wherever allusion is made to the stories of Abraham and of Isaac.

Bible study on the life of Sarah (NTB)

Wife of Abraham: Genesis 11:29–31; 12:5
Close relative of Abraham: Genesis 12:10–20; 20:12
Abraham passes her off as his sister, and Abimelech, king of Gerar, takes her; she is restored to Abraham by means of a dream: Genesis 20:1–14
Is sterile; gives her handmaiden, Hagar, to Abraham as a concubine: Genesis 16:1–3
Her jealousy of Hagar: Genesis 16:4–6; 21:9–14
Her miraculous conception of Isaac: Genesis 17:15–21; 18:9–15
Name changed from Sarai to Sarah: Genesis 17:15
Gives birth to Isaac: Genesis 21:3, 6–8
Death and burial of: Genesis 23; 25:10
Character of: Hebrews 11:11; 1 Peter 3:5–6

HAGAR

Significance in summary

Sarah's servant, and mother of Ishmael by Abraham

Family connections

Married to: Abram
Son: Ishmael

Meaning of name

flight

Bible dictionary/encyclopedia entry (IBD)

According to some, a stranger; an Egyptian, Sarah's handmaid (Gen. 16:1; 21:9–10), whom she gave to Abraham as a secondary wife (16:2). When she was about to become a mother she fled from the cruelty of her mistress, intending apparently to return to her relatives in Egypt, by way of the desert of Shur. Exhausted she had reached the place she called Beer-lahai-roi ("the well of the visible God"), where the angel of the Lord appeared to her. In obedience to the heavenly visitor she returned to Abraham, where her son Ishmael was born, and where she remained until after the birth of Isaac, that is, for fourteen years. Sarah showed her disapproval of both Hagar and her child. Ishmael insulted Sarah, and Sarah insisted that he and his mother should be dismissed. This was then carried out, but reluctantly by Abraham (Gen. 21:14). They wandered out into the wilderness, where Ishmael, exhausted by his journey and from lack of water seemed about to die. Hagar "lifted up her voice and wept," and the angel of the Lord, as before, appeared to her, and she was comforted and delivered (Gen. 21:18–19).

Ishmael later lived in the wilderness of Paran, where he married an Egyptian (Gen. 21:20–21).

"Hagar" allegorically represents the Jewish church (Gal. 4:24), in bondage to the ceremonial law; while "Sarah" represents the Christian church, which is free.

Bible study on the life of Hagar (NTB)

Given by Sarah to Abraham to be his wife: Genesis 16
Descendants of: Genesis 25:12–15; 1 Chronicles 5:10, 19–22; Psalm 83:6
Called Agar: Galatians 4:24–25

ISHMAEL

Significance in summary

Son of Abraham and Hagar

Family connections

Parents: Abram and Hagar
Siblings: Isaac, Zimran, Jokshan, Medan, Midian, Ishbak, Shuah
Married to: a wife from Egypt
Children: Nebaioth, Kedar, Adbeel, Mibsam, Mishma, Dumah, Massa, Hadad, Tema, Jetur, Naphish, Kedemah, Mahalath

Meaning of name

God heard

Bible dictionary/encyclopedia entry (CBC)

Sarai, Abram's wife, was barren (Gen. 11:30). Impatient at the long delay of the promise, she agreed for Abram to cohabit with her maid Hagar, and as a result Ishmael was born eleven years after Abram and Sarai entered Canaan (Gen. 16:1–16). He was finally thrown out of Abraham's house at Sarah's request and the Lord's approval, for Abraham's descendants were to come from Isaac (Gen. 21:1–21).

KETURAH

Significance in summary

Abraham's second wife

Family connections

Married to: Abraham
Children: Zimran, Jokshan, Medan, Midian, Ishbak, Shuah

Meaning of name

incense

Bible study on the life of Keturah (NTB)

Wife (concubine) of Abraham: Genesis 25:1–4; 1 Chronicles 1:32

NAHOR, Abraham's brother

Significance in summary

Abraham's brother

Family connections

Father: Terah
Siblings: Abram, Haran, Sarai
Married to: Milcah, Tebah (concubine)
Children: Uz, Buz, Kemuel, Kesed, Hazo, Pildash, Jidlaph, Bethuel, Tebah, Gaham, Tahash, Maacah
Granddaughter: Rebekah

Bible dictionary/encyclopedia entry (IBD)

A son of Terah, and elder brother of Abraham (Gen. 11:26–27; Josh. 24:2 RSV). He married Milcah, the daughter of his brother Haran, and remained in the land of his birth on the east of the river Euphrates at Haran (Gen. 11:27–32). The family of Abraham in Canaan kept in touch with the relatives in the old ancestral home at Haran until the time of Jacob. When Jacob fled from Haran all links between the two branches of the family came to an end (Gen. 31:55). His granddaughter Rebekah became Isaac's wife (24:67).

CHEDORLAOMER

Significance in summary

King of Elam who fought against Sodom and Gomorrah

Bible dictionary/encyclopedia entry (FBD)

King of Elam, who for twelve years subjected the kings of Sodom, Gomorrah, Admah, Zeboiim, and Bela, or Zoar. In Genesis 13 they revolted, whereupon Chedorlaomer, with his subordinate allies, the kings of Shinar (Babylonia), and Ellasar, and Tidal, "king of nations" (Median Scyths, belonging to the old population) defeated the Rephaims in Ashteroth Karnaim, the Zuzims in Ham, the Emims in Shaveh Kiriathaim, the Horites in Mount Seir, the Amalekites, and the Amorites in Hazezon Tamar; and finally encountered and defeated the five allied kings in the vale of Siddim. Among the captives whom he took was Lot. Abraham with three hundred and eighteen armed servants defeated him in turn, and rescued Lot, and made him flee to Hobah, near Damascus.

ELIEZER

Significance in summary

The steward of Abram's house

Meaning of name

God is help

Bible dictionary/encyclopedia entry (FBD)

Genesis 15:2, "the steward of Abram's house, Eliezer of Damascus," literally, "the son of the business," or possession (i.e., heir) of my house. Arriving at Canaan, Abram took with him his chief retainer, and adopted him in the absence of a son and heir. He was not "born in Abram's house" but, as Hebrew expresses, was "son of his house," i.e., adopted as such, as was customary between patriarchs and their servants.

Thus, he faithfully carried out the delicate commission of choosing a wife from his master's relatives for his master's son Isaac. Eliezer's prayer, "O Lord God of my master Abraham, I pray thee, send me good speed this day, and show kindness unto my master"; his looking for a providential token to guide him; God's gracious answer; and his thanksgiving, "Blessed be the Lord God . . . who hath not left destitute my master of his mercy and his truth: I being in the way, the Lord led me" are examples of God's special care for His people's earthly concerns (Genesis 24).

LOT

Significance in summary

Haran's son, Abraham's nephew

Family connections

Father: Haran
Siblings: Milcah, Iscah
Married to: one wife who died when running from Sodom
Children: two daughters (names unknown), Moab, Ben-Ammi

Meaning of name

covering

Bible dictionary/encyclopedia entry (IBD)

The son of Haran, and nephew of Abraham (Gen. 11:27). On the death of his father, he was left in the care of his grandfather Terah (11:31), after whose death he accompanied his uncle Abraham into Canaan (12:5), from there into Egypt (12:10), and back again to Canaan (13:1). After this he separated from him and settled in Sodom (13:5–13). There his righteous soul was "vexed" from day to day (2 Peter 2:7), and he had good reason to regret living there. A few years after his separation from Abraham he was taken captive by Chedorlaomer, and then rescued by Abraham (Genesis 14). When God's judgment descended on the guilty cities of the plain (Gen. 19:1–20), Lot was miraculously delivered. While fleeing from the doomed city his wife "looked back from behind him, and became a pillar of salt." There is to this day a peculiar crag at the south end of the Dead Sea, near Kumran, which the Arabs call Bint Sheik Lot, i.e., Lot's wife. It is "a tall, isolated needle of rock, which really does bear a curious resemblance to an Arab woman with a child on her shoulder." From the words of warning in Luke 17:32, "Remember Lot's wife," it would seem as if she had gone back, or delayed trying to save some of her possessions, that she became involved in the destruction which fell on the city, and became a stiffened corpse, fixed in the saline incrustations. She became "a pillar of salt," i.e., as some think, of asphalt.

Lot and his daughters sought refuge first in Zoar, and then, fearing to stay there any longer, went to a cave in the neighboring mountains (Gen. 19:30).

Bible study on the life of Lot (NTB)

Accompanies Terah from Ur of the Chaldees to Haran: Genesis 11:31
Migrates with Abraham to the land of Canaan: Genesis 12:4

Accompanies Abraham to Egypt; returns with him to Beth-el: Genesis 13:1–3
Rich in flocks, and herds, and servants; separates from Abraham, and lives in Sodom: Genesis 13:5–14
Taken captive by Chedorlaomer; rescued by Abraham: Genesis 14:1–16
Providentially saved from destruction in Sodom: Genesis 19; Luke 17:28–29
Disobediently protests against going to the mountains, and chooses Zoar: Genesis 19:17–22
His wife disobediently yearns after Sodom, and becomes a pillar of salt: Genesis 19:26; Luke 17:32
Commits incest with his daughters: Genesis 19:30–38

MOAB

Significance in summary

The incestuous son of Lot's older daughter, and an ancestor of the Moabites

Family connections

Parents: Lot and Lot's first daughter
Sibling: Ben-Ammi

Meaning of name

from my father

ISAAC

Significance in summary

Son of Abraham and Sarah, the second patriarch

Family connections

Parents: Abraham and Sarah
Siblings: Ishmael, Zimran, Jokshan, Medan, Midian, Ishbak, Shuah
Married to: Rebekah
Children: Esau, Jacob

Meaning of name

laughter

Bible dictionary/encyclopedia entry (CBC, FBD)

CBC

After Abram's arrival in Canaan the Lord promised him an heir by Sarai his wife (Gen. 17:15–17). Isaac was preeminently the child of promise (Gen. 17:19; 18:9–15; 21:1–5). He was married to Rebekah, his cousin (Gen. 24:1–67). He was Abraham's heir (Gen. 25:5). God renewed the two great promises (Gen. 12:1–3; 26:1–5). Isaac was a farmer and herdsman (Gen. 26:12–25).

FBD

Named "laughter," because Abraham laughed in joy at the promise of his birth, a type of the annunciation of Messiah's birth (Gen. 17:17); and Sarah too, with some incredulity because of the improbability at her age (Gen. 18:12), but at his birth with thankful joy toward God, saying "God hath made me to laugh, so that all that hear will laugh with me" (Gen. 21:6; compare Isa. 54:1). His miraculous conception and naming before birth typify Messiah (Luke 1; Matthew 1). Born at Gerar when Abraham was 100 years old. "Mocked" by Ishmael (who was "born after the flesh") at the weaning feast; the mocking, as Paul implies, containing the germ and spirit of persecution, profanely sneering at the object of the promise. The child of the slave-woman must therefore give place to the child of the freewoman born "by promise."

While the believing parents "laughed," Ishmael "mocked," with the laugh of derision and spite. Isaac is type of the believing "children of the promise," "born after the Spirit," therefore, "children of the free" church, "heirs according to the promise," persecuted by the children of legal and godless slavery, but ultimately about to "inherit all things" (Gal. 4:22–31; 3:29; 5:1; Rev. 21:7). Isaac's submission to his father's will, when carrying the wood for his own sacrifice and being tied up, make him a type of Him who bore His own cross to Calvary (John 19:17), and who said, "Lo, I come to do Thy will, O God" (Heb. 10:7). Being still alive after the three days (Gen. 22:4) prefigures the Messiah's resurrection on the third day.

The scene of the sacrifice, Mount Moriah, was probably that of Christ's suffering. What Isaac's sacrifice lacked was actual death and vicarious substitution; the offering of the ram's life, instead of the human life, provided the defect; the ram and Isaac jointly complete the type. Isaac typifies Christ's Godhead, the ram typifies His manhood (Theodoret) "caught in a thicket by his horns" as Jesus was crowned with thorns. Isaac should not have been killed, for God's law gives no sanction to human sacrifices.

His contemplative character appears in his "going out to meditate" or pray "in the field at the eventide." The death of his mother Sarah just before (Genesis 23) naturally pressed on his spirit, and his resource in affliction was prayerful meditation, a type of Him who "went up into a mountain apart to pray" (Matt. 14:23), his calm and submissive temper also prefiguring the meek and lowly Lamb of God (Isa. 53:7). Solitude and prayer suit best the wounded spirit. That Sarah's death was uppermost in his meditation is implied in what follows: Isaac "brought Rebekah into his mother Sarah's tent, and he loved her, and was comforted after his mother's death." Rebekah supplied the void in his heart and home. Weakness and partiality for Esau, probably owing to the contrast which Esau's bold spirit presented to his own gentle character, were his failings; his partaking of his favorite dish, venison, the produce of his son's hunting, confirmed his selfish partiality. The mother loved the steady, quiet Jacob.

The gift from God of the twin sons was the answer to Isaac's prayer, after twenty years of childless marriage; for God in giving the greatest blessings delays fulfilling His promise in order to call forth His people's persevering, waiting, prayerful faith (Gen. 25:21). When Isaac was 137, the age at which Ishmael died fourteen years before, the thought of his brother's death at that age suggested thoughts of his own, and the desire to bless his favorite before dying. As he lived forty-three years afterward, to see Jacob return from Mesopotamia, he probably was now dangerously sick; hence, loathing ordinary food, he longed to have "savory meat such as he loved." Esau invited him to "arise and sit" to eat of his venison, implying that he was laid in his bed. Moreover "he trembled exceedingly" when Esau came in. Esau's words imply his thinking Isaac near death: "the days of mourning for my father are at hand." Isaac's unexpected prolongation of life probably deterred Esau from his murderous purpose against Jacob for having stolen his blessing.

He reverenced his father in the middle of all his wildness, and finally joined Jacob in paying respect at his father's grave, even as Isaac and Ishmael had met at Abraham's burial. Isaac's carnal partiality and Rebekah's tortuous policy resulted in their being left in their old age by both children—Esau disappointed and disinherited, Jacob banished to a long and distant servitude, the idols of God's children becoming their scourges, in order to bring them back to Himself (1 Cor. 11:32; Jer. 2:19). His equivocation as to his wife, as if she were his sister, through fear of Abimelech's people at Gerar, was another blemish in Isaac (Genesis 26). So Abram had erred in Egypt and in this same Philistine kingdom. Isaac had obeyed God's vision in not going down to Egypt, a place of spiritual danger though abundant in food, but sojourning in Gerar during the famine. Lack of godly and manly firmness betrayed him into the untruth.

His wife was not taken into Abimelech's house, as Sarah had been. Abimelech, discovering the real state of the case, reproved him and warned his people not to touch him or Rebekah. His meek character appears in his successively yielding to the grasping herdsmen of Gerar the wells Esek ("strife") and Sitnah ("hatred"). So, the Lord who had given him a hundredfold increase in his harvests made room for him at last; and he retained the well Rehoboth ("room") without further contention, and made a covenant with Abimelech (compare Rom. 12:18–21; Matt. 5:5, 25; Prov. 16:7). Isaac lived to see Jacob, whom he had sent with his blessing (for faith at last prevailed over his partiality, and he gave Jacob the blessing of Abraham, Gen. 28:1; 28:4) to seek a wife in Padan-aram, return with a large family to him at Hebron (Gen. 35:27).

He died at 180, the longest living of the three patriarchs, the least migratory, the least prolific, and the least favored with revelations. He was buried in the cave of Machpelah. His blessing Jacob and Esau "even (Greek) concerning things to come," as if they were actually present, and not merely concerning things present, is quoted (Heb. 11:20) as evidencing his faith; similar dying charges evidenced Jacob's and Joseph's faith. A faithful husband of one wife (compare Eph. 5:23, etc.), unlike Abraham and Jacob, of tender affections, he was a man of suffering rather than action; having the divine favor so markedly that Abimelech and his officers said, "we saw certainly that the LORD was with thee" (Gen. 26:28).

As Abraham foreshadows the unsettled early history of the nation, and Jacob their commercial unwarlike later course, so Isaac their intermediate days of peace and separation from the nations in their fertile land of promise. As Abraham is associated with morning prayer, and Jacob associated with night prayer, so Isaac with evening prayer (Gen. 19:27; 28:11; 24:63). God is still "the God of Isaac," who is one of the triad with whom the children of the kingdom shall sit down at the resurrection of the just (Luke 20:37–38, etc.; Matt. 8:11, etc.).

Bible study on the life of Isaac (NTB)

The miraculous son of Abraham: Genesis 17:15–19; 18:1–15; 21:1–8; Joshua 24:3; 1 Chronicles 1:28; Galatians 4:28; Hebrews 11:11
Ancestor of Jesus: Matthew 1:2
Offered in sacrifice by his father: Genesis 22:1–19; Hebrews 11:17; James 2:21
Is provided a wife from among his relatives: Genesis 24; 25:20
Abrahamic covenant confirmed in: Genesis 26:2–5; 1 Chronicles 16:15–19

Lives in the south country at the well called Lahai-roi: Genesis 24:62; 25:11
With Ishmael, buries his father in the cave of Machpelah: Genesis 25:9
Esau and Jacob born to: Genesis 25:19–26; Joshua 24:4; 1 Chronicles 1:34
Lives in Gerar: Genesis 26:6–11
Prospers: Genesis 26:12–14
Possesses large flocks and herds: Genesis 26:14
Digs wells, and is defrauded of them by the herdsmen of Abimelech: Genesis 26:15, 21
Moves away to the valley of Gerar, afterward called Beer-sheba: Genesis 26:22–33
His old age, last blessing on his sons: Genesis 27:18–40
Death and burial of: Genesis 35:27–29; 49:31
His filial obedience: Genesis 22:9
Was a prophet: Genesis 27:28–29, 38–40; Hebrews 11:20
His devoutness: Genesis 24:63; 25:21; 26:25; Matthew 8:11; Luke 13:28
Prophecies concerning: Genesis 17:16–21; 18:10–14; 21:12; 26:2–5, 24; Exodus 32:13; 1 Chronicles 16:16; Romans 9:7

REBEKAH

Significance in summary

Isaac's wife, and mother of Jacob and Esau

Family connections

Grandfather: Nahor (Abraham's brother)
Father: Bethuel
Sibling: Laban
Married to: Isaac
Children: Esau, Jacob

Meaning of name

flattering

Bible dictionary/encyclopedia entry (SBD)

Daughter of Bethuel (Gen. 22:23) and sister of Laban, married to Isaac. She is first presented to us in Genesis 24:1 where the beautiful story of her marriage is related. For nineteen years she was childless; then Esau and Jacob were born, the younger being the mother's companion and favorite (Gen. 25:19–28). Rebekah suggested the deceit that was engaged in by Jacob on his blind father. She directed and aided him in carrying it out, foresaw the probable consequence of Esau's anger, and prevented it by making Isaac send Jacob away to Padan-aram (Gen. 27:1), to her own family (Gen. 29:12). Rebekah's beauty once became a source of danger to her husband (Gen. 26:7).

Bible study on the life of Rebekah (NTB)

The daughter of Bethuel, the grandniece of Abraham: Genesis 22:20–23
Becomes Isaac's wife: Genesis 24:15–67; 25:20
Mother of Esau and Jacob: Genesis 25:21–28
Passes as Isaac's sister: Genesis 26:6–11
Displeased with Esau's wives: Genesis 26:34, 35
Prompts Jacob to deceive Isaac: Genesis 27:5–29
Sends Jacob to Laban, her brother: Genesis 27:42–46
Burial place of: Genesis 49:31
Called Rebecca: Romans 9:10

ESAU

Significance in summary

Isaac and Rebecca's elder son, and twin of brother Jacob

Family connections

Parents: Isaac and Rebekah
Sibling: Jacob
Married to: Judith, Bashemath, Oholibamah, Mahalath
Children: Eliphaz, Reuel, Jeush, Jalam, Korah

Meaning of name

hairy

Bible dictionary/encyclopedia entry (IBD)

Rebekah's firstborn twin son (Gen. 25:25). The name of Edom, "red," was also given to him because of his conduct in connection with the red lentil "pottage" for which he sold his birthright (vv. 30–31). The circumstances connected with his birth foreshadowed the enmity which afterwards existed between the twin brothers and the nations they founded (25:22–23, 26). Jacob, following his natural bent, became a shepherd, while Esau, a "son of the desert," devoted himself to hunting. On one occasion, on returning from a hunt, famished with hunger, Esau sold his birthright to his brother, Jacob, who thereby obtained the covenant blessing (Gen. 27:28–29, 36; Heb. 12:16–17). He later tried to regain what he had so recklessly parted with, but was outwitted by his brother (Gen. 27:4, 34, 38).

At the age of forty, to the great sadness of his parents, he married (Gen. 26:34–35) two Canaanite women, Judith, the daughter of Beeri, and Bashemath, the daughter of Elon. When Jacob was sent away to Padan-aram, Esau tried to conciliate his parents (Gen. 28:8–9) by marrying his cousin Mahalath, the daughter of Ishmael. This led him to throw in his lot with the Ishmaelite tribes; driving the Horites out of Mount Seir, he settled in that region. After some thirty years' stay in Padan-aram Jacob returned to Canaan and was reconciled to Esau, who went out to meet him (33:4). Twenty years later, their father Isaac died; the two brothers met, probably for the last time, beside his grave (35:29). Esau now permanently left Canaan, and established himself as a powerful and wealthy chief in the land of Edom.

Long after this, when the descendants of Jacob came out of Egypt, the Edomites remembered the old quarrel between the brothers and opposed Israel.

Bible study on the life of Esau (NTB)

Birth of: Genesis 25:19–26; 1 Chronicles 1:34
Called Edom: Genesis 36:1, 8
A hunter: Genesis 25:27–28
Beloved by Isaac: Genesis 25:27–28
Sells his birthright for a single meal: Genesis 25:29–34; Malachi 1:2; Romans 9:13; Hebrews 12:16
Marries Hittite women: Genesis 26:34
Polygamy of: Genesis 26:34; 28:9; 36:2, 3
Is defrauded of his father's blessing by Jacob: Genesis 27; Hebrews 11:20
Meets Jacob on the return of the latter from Haran: Genesis 33:1
With Jacob, buries his father: Genesis 35:29
Descendants of: Genesis 36
Hostility of descendants of, toward the descendants of Jacob: Obadiah 1:10–14
Ancestor of Edomites: Jeremiah 49:8
Mount of Edom, called Mount of Esau: Obadiah 1:8, 9, 18–21
His name used to denote his descendants and their country: Deuteronomy 2:5; Jeremiah 49:8, 10; Obadiah 1:6
Prophecies concerning: Obadiah 1:18

JACOB

Significance in summary

Isaac and Rebekah's younger son, twin of Esau, and an ancestor of Jesus Christ

Family connections

Parents: Isaac and Rebekah
Sibling: Esau
Married to: Leah, Rachel, Bilhah, Zilpah
Children: Reuben, Simeon, Levi, Judah, Dan, Naphtali, Gad, Asher, Issachar, Zebulun, Dinah, Joseph, Benjamin

Meaning of name

supplanter

Bible dictionary/encyclopedia entry (FBD)

"Supplanter," or "holding the heel." Esau's twin brother, but second in priority. Son of Isaac, then 60 years old, and Rebekah. As Jacob "took his brother by the heel [the action of a wrestler] in the womb" (Hos. 12:3), so the spiritual Israel, every believer, having no right in himself to the inheritance, by faith when being born again of the Spirit takes hold of the bruised heel, the humanity, of Christ crucified, "the Firstborn of many brethren." He by becoming a curse for us became a blessing to the true Israel; contrast Hebrews 12:16–17. Jacob was a "plain," i.e., an upright man, steady and affectionate, and so became his mother's favorite (Gen. 25:24). He preferred staying at home, minding the flocks and performing household duties; he was not, like Esau, wandering around in search for game, "a man of the field," wild, restless, self indulgent, and seldom at home in the tent.

Having bought the birthright from Esau, he later, at Rebekah's instigation, stole the blessing which his father intended for Esau, but which God had given him when the two sons were yet unborn; "the elder shall serve the younger" (Gen. 25:23; 27:29; Mal. 1:3; Rom. 9:12). His seeking a right end by wrong means (Genesis 27) entailed a lifelong retribution in kind. Instead of occupying the first place of honor in the family he had to flee for his life; instead of a double portion, he fled with only the staff in his hand.

Jacob's grand superiority lay in his abiding trust in the living God. Faith made him "covet earnestly the best gift," though his mode of getting it (first by taking advantage of his brother's hunger; next by deceit) was most unworthy.

When sent by his parents to escape Esau and to find a wife in Padan-aram, he for the first time is presented as enjoying God's manifestations at Bethel in his vision of the ladder set up on earth, and the top reaching heaven, with "Jehovah standing above, and the angels of God ascending and descending on it," typifying God's providence and grace arranging all things for His people's good through the ministry of "angels" (Genesis 28; Heb. 1:14). When his conscience made him feel his flight was the just penalty of his deceit God comforts him by promises of His grace.

He typifies the Messiah again, through whom heaven is opened and also linked to earth, and angels minister to Him first, then to His people (John 14:6; Acts 7:56; Heb. 9:8; 10:19–20; Rev. 4:1). The process was then beginning which shall eventuate in the restoration of the union between heaven and earth, with greater glory than before (Rev. 5:8; 21:1–22:21). Then followed God's promise of (1) the land and (2) of universal blessing to all families of the earth "in his seed," i.e., Christ; meanwhile he would have (1) God's presence, (2) protection in all places, (3) restoration to home, (4) unfailing faithfulness (Gen. 28:15; compare Gen. 28:20–21).

Recognizing God's manifestation as sanctifying the spot, he made his stony pillow into a pillar, consecrated with oil and taking up God's word he vowed that as God would fulfill His promises Jehovah would be his God, and of all God gave he would give a tenth to Him (compare Gen. 32:10). Next follows his seven years' service under greedy Laban, in lieu of presents to the parents (the usual way of securing a wife in the East [Gen. 24:53], which Jacob was unable to give), and the imposition of Leah on him instead of Rachel—the first installment of his chastisement for his own deceit.

Jacob's polygamy was contrary to the original law of paradise (Gen. 2:23–24; Matt. 19:5). Leah was imposed on him when he had planned to marry Rachel only, and the maids were given him by his wives to obtain offspring. The times of ignorance, when the gospel had not yet restored the original standard, tolerated evils which would be inexcusable now.

The most characteristic scene of Jacob's life was his wrestling until break of day (compare Luke 6:12) with the Angel of Jehovah, in human form, for a blessing. "By his strength he had power with God, yea he had power over the Angel and prevailed, he wept and made supplication unto Him" (Hos. 12:3–4). So he received the name Israel, "contender with God," a pattern to us (Matt. 11:12; 15:22; Rev. 3:21; Luke 13:24). His "strength" was conscious weakness constraining him, when his thigh was put out of joint and he could no longer rely on his own efforts he had to hang on Him; teaching us the irresistible might of conscious weakness hanging on Almighty strength (Job 23:6; Isa. 27:5; 40:29–31; 2 Cor. 12:9–10).

"I will not let Thee go except Thou bless me" is a model prayer (Gen. 32:26). Tears and supplications were his weapons; type of Messiah (Heb. 5:7). The vision of the two encampments of angels on either side of him prepared him for the vision of the Lord of angels. Thus he saw "they that be with us (believers) are more than they that be with" our enemies (2 Kings 6:16–17). Wrestling first with God, we can victoriously wrestle with Satan (Eph. 6:12). Jacob like David felt "what time I am afraid, I will trust in Thee" (Ps. 56:3–4, 11; 1 Sam. 30:6). His is one of the earliest prayers on record (Gen. 32:7, 9–12).

Having left Canaan in guilt, now on his return Jacob must reenter it with deep searchings of heart and wrestlings with God for the recovery of that sinless faith which he had forfeited by deceit and which lays hold of the covenant. Jacob is made to know he has more to fear from God's displeasure than from Esau's enmity. Once he stands right with God he need not fear Esau. There followed therefore the wrestling "alone" with Jehovah (compare Matt. 14:23; Mark 1:35); his being named "Israel"; and his asking God's name, to which the only reply was, God "blessed him there." Blessing is God's name, i.e., the character wherein He reveals Himself to His people (Exod. 34:5–7). Jacob called the place Peniel, "the face of God." Next Jacob came to Succoth, then crossed the Jordan, and near Shechem bought his only possession in Canaan, the field on which he tented.

He erected an altar, *El Elohe Israel*, claiming God as his own ("the God of Israel"). Still God saw need for calling him to a personal and domestic revival. Jacob called his household to put away their strange gods, their earrings (used as idolatrous phylacteries), and uncleanness; he then proceeded to perform what he had vowed so long ago, namely, to make the stone pillar God's house (Gen. 28:22). Reaching Bethel once more after forty years, where he had seen the heavenly ladder, he has a vision of God confirming his name "Israel" and the promise of nations springing from him, and of his seed inheriting the land; he rears again the stone pillar to *El Shaddai*, "God Almighty," the name God used when He changed Abram's name to Abraham.

Then followed the birth of Benjamin, which completed the tribal twelve (Genesis 35). The loss of his favorite son Joseph was his heaviest trial, his deceit to Isaac now being repaid by his sons' cruel deceit to himself. Tender affection for wife and children was his characteristic (Gen. 37:33–35; 42:36; 45:28). By special revelation at Beersheba (Genesis 46) allaying his fears of going to Egypt, which Isaac had been expressly forbidden to do (Gen. 26:2), he went down. This marks the close of the first stage in the covenant and the beginning of the second stage. Leaving Canaan as a family, Israel returned as a nation.

In Egypt the transformation took place; the civilization, arts, and sciences of Egypt adapted it well for the divine purpose of training Israel in this second stage of their history; Jacob and his family numbered approximately seventy. In the genealogy those named are the heads of tribes and of families. At 130 Jacob blessed Pharaoh and termed his life a "pilgrimage" of days "few and evil" (Gen. 47; Heb. 11:9, 13). The list of ills includes his sufferings: from Esau; from Laban; maiming by the Angel; Dinah's violation and Simeon and Levi's cruelty; loss of Joseph; Simeon's imprisonment; Benjamin's departure; Rachel's death; Reuben's incest.

The general promise of "the seed" sprung from Abraham, Isaac, and Jacob he now limits to Judah. His faith in "bowing on his bed" after Joseph promised to bury him in Canaan (Gen. 47:29–30) consisted in his confidence of God's giving Canaan to his seed, and he therefore earnestly desired to be buried there. His life is epitomized in "I have waited for Thy salvation, O Lord" (Gen. 49:18). At 147 he died, and his body was embalmed and after a grand state funeral procession buried with his fathers in the cave of Machpelah before Mamre (Gen. 50:13).

Bible study on the life of Jacob (NTB)

Son of Isaac, and the twin brother of Esau: Genesis 25:24–26; Joshua 24:4; 1 Chronicles 1:34; Acts 7:8
Ancestor of Jesus: Matthew 1:2
Given in answer to prayer: Genesis 25:21
Obtains Esau's birthright for just one bowl of stew: Genesis 25:29–34; Hebrews 12:16
Fraudulently obtains his father's blessing: Genesis 27:1–29; Hebrews 11:20
Esau seeks to kill, escapes to Padan-aram: Genesis 27:41–46; 28:1–5; Hosea 12:12
His vision of the ladder: Genesis 28:10–22
God confirms the covenant of Abraham to: Genesis 28:13–22; 35:9–15; 1 Chronicles 16:13–18
Lives in Haran with his uncle, Laban: Genesis 29:30; Hosea 12:12
Serves fourteen years for Leah and Rachel: Genesis 29:15–30; Hosea 12:12
Sharp practice of, with the flocks and herds of Laban: Genesis 30:32–43
Dissatisfied with Laban's treatment and returns to the land of Canaan: Genesis 31

Meets angels of God on the journey, and calls the place "Mahanaim": Genesis 32:1–2
Dreads to meet Esau; sends him presents; wrestles with an angel: Genesis 32
Name of, changed to "Israel": Genesis 32:28; 35:10
Reconciliation of, with Esau: Genesis 33:4
Journeys to Succoth: Genesis 33:17
Journeys to Shalem, where he purchases a parcel of ground from Hamor and erects an altar: Genesis 33:18–20
His daughter, Dinah, is raped: Genesis 34
Returns to Beth-el, where he builds an altar, and erects and dedicates a pillar: Genesis 35:1–7
Journeys to Ephrath; Benjamin is born to; Rachel dies; and is "buried on the way to Ephrath, which is Bethlehem": Genesis 35:16–19; 48:7
Erects a monument at Rachel's grave: Genesis 35:20
The incest of his son, Reuben, with his concubine, Bilhah: Genesis 35:22
List of the names of his twelve sons: Genesis 35:23–26
Returns to Arbah, the city of his father: Genesis 35:27
Lives in the land of Canaan: Genesis 37:1
His partiality for his son, Joseph, and the consequent jealousy of his other sons: Genesis 37:3–4
Joseph's prophetic dream concerning: Genesis 37:9–11
His grief over the loss of Joseph: Genesis 37:34–35
Sends to Egypt to buy corn (grain): Genesis 42:1–2; 43:1–14
His grief over the detention of Simeon and the demand for Benjamin to be taken into Egypt: Genesis 42:36
His love for Benjamin: Genesis 43:14; 44:29
Hears that Joseph is still alive: Genesis 45:26–28
Moves to Egypt: Genesis 46:1–7; 1 Samuel 12:8; Psalm 105:23; Acts 7:14–15
The list of his children and grandchildren who went down into Egypt: Genesis 46:8–27
Meets Joseph: Genesis 46:28–34
Pharaoh receives him, and is blessed by Jacob: Genesis 47:1–10
The land of Goshen assigned to: Genesis 47:11–12, 27
Lives in Egypt for seventeen years: Genesis 47:28
Exacts a promise from Joseph to bury him with his forefathers: Genesis 47:29–31
His benediction on Joseph and his two sons: Genesis 48:15–22
Gives the land of the Amorites to Joseph: Genesis 48:22; John 4:5
His final prophetic benedictions on his sons: Genesis 49:3–27

Charges his sons to bury him in the field of Machpelah: Genesis 49:29–30
Death of: Genesis 49:33
Body of, embalmed: Genesis 50:2
Forty Days mourning for: Genesis 50:3
Burial of: Genesis 50:4–13
Descendants of: Genesis 29:31–35; 30:1–24; 35:18, 22–26; 46:8–27; Exodus 1:1–5; 1 Chronicles 2:9
Prophecies concerning himself and his descendants: Genesis 25:23; 27:28–29; 28:10–15; 31:3; 35:9–13; 46:3; Deuteronomy 1:8; Psalm 105:10–11
His wealth: Genesis 36:6–7
The well of: John 4:5–30

RACHEL

Significance in summary

Laban's daughter, Jacob's wife, and mother of Joseph and Benjamin

Family connections

Father: Laban
Sibling: Leah
Married to: Jacob
Children: Joseph, Benjamin

Meaning of name

ewe

Bible dictionary/encyclopedia entry (IBD)

Ewe, "the daughter," "the somewhat petulant, peevish, and self-willed though beautiful younger daughter" of Laban, and one of Jacob's wives (Gen. 29:6, 28). Jacob served Laban fourteen years for her, so deep was his affection for her. She was the mother of Joseph (Gen. 30:22–24). Afterwards, on Jacob's departure from Mesopotamia, she took with her her father's teraphim (31:34, 35). As they journeyed on from Bethel, Rachel died in giving birth to Benjamin (35:18–19), and was buried "in the way to Ephrath, which is Bethlehem. And Jacob set a pillar upon her grave." Her sepulcher is still regarded with great veneration by the Jews. Its traditional site is about half a mile from Jerusalem.

This name is used poetically by Jeremiah (Jer. 31:15–17) to denote God's people mourning under their calamities. This passage is also quoted by Matthew as fulfilled in the lamentation at Bethlehem on account of the slaughter of the infants there at Herod's command (Matt. 2:17–18).

Bible study on the life of Rachel (NTB)

Meets Jacob at a well: Genesis 29:9–12
Jacob serves Laban an additional seven years to obtain her as his wife: Genesis 29:15–30
Sterility of: Genesis 29:31
Her grief in consequence of her sterility; gives her maid to Jacob in order to obtain children in her own name: Genesis 30:1–8, 15, 22–34
Later productiveness of; becomes the mother of Joseph, Benjamin: Genesis 30:22–25; 35:16–18, 24
Steals the household images (teraphim, legal deed) of her father: Genesis 31:4, 14–19, 33–35
Her death and burial: Genesis 35:18–20; 48:7; 1 Samuel 10:2

DINAH

Significance in summary

Jacob and Leah's daughter who was raped by Shechem

Family connections

Parents: Jacob and Leah
Siblings: Reuben, Simeon, Levi, Judah, Dan, Naphtali, Gad, Asher, Issachar, Zebulun, Joseph, Benjamin

Meaning of name

justice

Bible dictionary/encyclopedia entry (SBD)

Dinah accompanied her father from Mesopotamia to Canaan, and, having ventured among the inhabitants, was raped by Shechem the son of Hamor, the chieftain of the territory in which her father had settled (Genesis 34). Shechem proposed to make the usual reparation by paying a sum to the father and marrying her (Gen. 34:12). This proposal was accepted, the sons of Jacob demanding as a condition of the proposed union the circumcision of the Shechemites. They assented; and on the third day, when the pain and fever resulting from the operation were at the highest, Simeon and Levi, the brothers of Dinah, attacked them unexpectedly, killed all the males, and plundered their city.

SHECHEM

Significance in summary

Hamor's son who raped Dinah

Family connections

Father: Hamor

Meaning of name

shoulder

Bible study on the life of Shechem (NTB)

Son of Hamor; seduces Jacob's daughter; killed by Jacob's sons: Genesis 33:19; 34; Joshua 24:32; Judges 9:28

NAPHTALI

Significance in summary

Jacob's sixth son, whose descendants became one of the twelve tribes

Family connections

Parents: Jacob and Bilhah
Siblings: Reuben, Simeon, Levi, Judah, Dan, Gad, Asher, Issachar, Zebulun, Dinah, Joseph, Benjamin
Children: Jahziel, Guni, Jezer, Shillem

Meaning of name

wrestle

GAD

Significance in summary

Jacob's seventh son, whose descendants became one of the twelve tribes

Family connections

Parents: Jacob and Zilpah

Siblings: Reuben, Simeon, Levi, Judah, Dan, Naphtali, Asher, Issachar, Zebulun, Dinah, Joseph, Benjamin
Children: Zephon, Haggi, Shuni, Ezbon, Eri, Arodi, Areli

Meaning of name

fortune

ISSACHAR

Significance in summary

Jacob's ninth son, whose descendants became one of the twelve tribes

Family connections

Parents: Jacob and Leah
Siblings: Reuben, Simeon, Levi, Judah, Dan, Naphtali, Gad, Asher, Zebulun, Dinah, Joseph, Benjamin
Children: Tola, Puah, Jashub, Shimron

LEAH

Significance in summary

Jacob's wife, on account of her father's (Laban) deception

Family connections

Father: Laban
Sibling: Rachel
Married to: Jacob
Children: Reuben, Simeon, Levi, Judah, Issachar, Zebulun, Dinah

Meaning of name

wild cow

Bible dictionary/encyclopedia entry (IBD)

The eldest daughter of Laban, and sister of Rachel (Gen. 29:16). Jacob took her to wife through a deceit of her father (Gen. 29:23). She was "tender-eyed" (17). She bore to Jacob six sons (32–35), and one daughter, Dinah (30:21). She accompanied Jacob into Canaan, died there before the time of the going down into Egypt (Genesis 31), and was buried in the cave of Machpelah (49:31).

ZILPAH

Significance in summary

Leah's servant, given by Laban and by Leah to Jacob, who bore Jacob Gad and Asher

Family connections

Married to: Jacob
Children: Gad, Asher

Bible study on the life of Zilpah (NTB)

Leah's handmaiden: Genesis 29:24
Mother of Gad and Asher by Jacob: Genesis 30:9–13; 35:26; 37:2; 46:18

ZEBULUN

Significance in summary

Tenth of Jacob's sons, sixth and last of Leah's sons

Family connections

Parents: Jacob and Leah
Siblings: Reuben, Simeon, Levi, Judah, Dan, Naphtali, Gad, Asher, Issachar, Dinah, Joseph, Benjamin
Children: Sered, Elon, Jahleel

Meaning of name

dwelling, or honor

Bible dictionary/encyclopedia entry (FBD)

Named from Leah's anticipation, "now will my husband dwell with me, for I have borne him six sons." Jacob's blessing (Gen. 49:13) was "Zebulun shall dwell at the haven of the sea, and he shall be for an haven of ships, and his border shall be unto Sidon."

Bible study on the life of Zebulun (NTB)

Son of Jacob and Leah: Genesis 30:20; 35:23; 46:14; 49:13; Exodus 1:3; 1 Chronicles 2:1
Descendants of: Genesis 46:14; Numbers 26:26, 27

LABAN

Significance in summary

Bethuel's son, grandson of Nahor, Rebekah's brother, father of Rachel and Leah

Family connections

Father: Bethuel
Sibling: Rebekah
Children: Leah, Rachel

Meaning of name

white

Bible dictionary/encyclopedia entry (SBD)

Son of Bethuel, brother of Rebekah and father of Leah and Rachel. The elder branch of the family remained at Haran, Mesopotamia, when Abraham removed to the land of Canaan, and it is there that we first meet with Laban, as taking the leading part in the betrothal of his sister Rebekah to her cousin Isaac (Gen. 24:10, 29–60; 27:43; 29:5). The next time Laban appears in the sacred narrative it is as the host of his nephew Jacob at Haran (Gen. 29:13–14). Jacob married Rachel and Leah, daughters of Laban, and remained with him twenty years. But Laban's dishonest and overreaching practice toward his nephew shows from what source Jacob inherited his tendency to sharp dealing. Nothing is said of Laban after Jacob left him.

Bible study on the life of Laban (NTB)

Brother of Rebekah: Genesis 22:23; 24:15, 29
Receives the servant of Abraham: Genesis 24:29–33
Receives Jacob, and gives him his daughters in marriage: Genesis 29:12–30
Jacob becomes his servant: Genesis 29:15–20, 27; 30:27–43
Outwitted by Jacob: Genesis 30:37–43; 31:1–21
Pursues Jacob, overtakes him at Mount Gilead, and covenants with him: Genesis 31:22–55

BILHAH

Significance in summary

Rachel's servant, mother of Dan and Naphtali

Family connections

Married to: Jacob
Children: Dan, Naphtali

Bible study on the life of Bilhah (NTB)

Bears children by Jacob: Genesis 29:29; 30:3–4; 37:2
Mother of Dan and Naphtali: Genesis 30:1–8; 35:25; 46:23–25
Reuben's incest with: Genesis 35:22; 49:4

Egypt: Arrival, Living, and Exodus

Joseph • Benjamin • Judah • Tamar, Judah's daughter-in-law • Levi • Gershon • Merari • Reuben • Simeon • Ephraim • Manasseh • Potiphar • Kohath • Moses • Jethro (Reuel) • Zipporah • Miriam • Aaron • Nadab • Eleazar • Phinehas, Eleazar's son • Bezalel • Abiram • Korah • Dathan • Og • Sihon • Balaam • Balak • Joshua • Rahab • Jabin I • Caleb • Achan

Introduction (IBD)

The great deliverance God undertook for the children of Israel, known as the Exodus, occurred when God brought them out of the land of Egypt with "a mighty hand and with an outstretched arm" (Exod. 12:51; Deut. 26:8; Ps. 114; 136).

They had lived in Egypt, according to Exodus 12:40, for four hundred and thirty years. In Genesis 15:13–16, the period is prophetically given (in round numbers) as four hundred years. This passage is quoted by Stephen in his defense before the council (Acts 7:6).

The Israelites never forgot how God had miraculously rescued them and gave them the Passover as an annual reminder of the Lord their God and his mighty act of salvation.

JOSEPH

Significance in summary

Son of Jacob and Rachel; sold as a slave into Egypt; became second in command in Egypt

Family connections

Parents: Jacob and Rachel
Siblings: Reuben, Simeon, Levi, Judah, Dan, Naphtali, Gad, Asher, Issachar, Zebulun, Dinah, Benjamin
Married to: Asenath
Children: Manasseh, Ephraim

Meaning of name

may God add, increaser

Bible dictionary/encyclopedia entry (CBC)

Early life. Joseph was the son of Rachel, born to Jacob in his old age (Gen. 30:1–24), and was therefore the favorite (Gen. 37:3); Joseph had two remarkable dreams, resulting in the estrangement of his brothers and the suspicion of his father (Gen. 37:5–11). His brothers sold him into slavery, and deceived their father by dipping the coat of many colors into the blood of a goat, assuring him that they had found it (Gen. 37:15–35).

Early life in Egypt. Joseph was sold to Potiphar, an officer of Pharaoh (Gen. 39:1; Acts 7:9). On a false charge he was thrown into prison. In prison he enjoyed the confidence of the keeper, and interpreted the dreams of the butler and baker (Gen. 39:21–23; 40:1–23).

Pharaoh's dreams. The king had two dreams:

He stood by the river and saw seven well-favored and fat-fleshed cows come up out of the river and feed in a meadow; seven other cows that were ill-favored and lean-fleshed followed and devoured them.

He saw seven ears of corn on one stalk, rank and good, and they were followed by seven scorched ears by which they were devoured (Gen. 41:1–7).

Joseph's interpretation. The wise men failed to give the king's mind any relief, and Pharaoh, on the suggestion of the chief butler, called for Joseph, who declared that the dreams were one, and predicted that there would immediately follow seven years of plenty, succeeded by seven years of famine (Gen. 41:8–32).

His elevation. Pharaoh immediately clothed Joseph in royal robes, made him ride in the second chariot, and required the people to bow down before him (Gen. 41:33–45).

His marriage. Pharaoh gave him the name Zaphnath-paaneah (preserver of the age, or revealer of secrets), and also gave him Asenath, the daughter of Potipherah, priest of On, to wife. By this union were two sons (Gen. 41:44–52).

Preparation for the famine. Joseph immediately began to make preparations for the famine. He gathered corn "as the sands of the sea" and stored it in the cities (Gen. 41:47–52).

Famine in Egypt. The famine began as Joseph had predicted and covered the entire land of Egypt (Gen. 41:53–57).

Famine in Canaan. The famine extended to Canaan (Gen. 42:1–2; Acts 7:11). Jacob sent his sons to Egypt to buy corn. Joseph recognized them, but they did not know him. He supplied their wants, and they returned to their home (Gen. 42:3–38). On their return to Egypt, Joseph made himself known to them and sent for his father to come to Egypt (Gen. 43:1–34; 44:1–34; 45:1–24; Acts 7:12, 14). Jacob received the news of Joseph's glory with incredulity (Gen. 45:25–28).

Lessons from Joseph's brothers. We may learn from this to investigate thoroughly before coming to a conclusion and that, after a man is once settled in error, it takes a tremendous influence to deliver him from it.

Last days of Joseph. Joseph's last days were characterized by:

- forgiving his brothers;
- enjoying the pleasures of family relation;
- predicting the restoration of his brothers to the land of Abraham, Isaac, and Jacob;
- and taking a pledge of his brethren to carry his bones with them on their departure (Gen. 50:15–26).

Bible study on the life of Joseph (NTB)

Personal appearance of: Genesis 39:6
His father's favorite child: Genesis 33:2; 37:3–4, 35; 48:22; 1 Chronicles 5:2; John 4:5
His father's partiality for, excites the jealousy of his brethren: Genesis 37:4, 11, 18–28; Psalm 105:17; Acts 7:9
His prophetic dreams of his fortunes in Egypt: Genesis 37:5–11
Sold as a slave into Egypt: Genesis 37:27–28
Is falsely reported to his father as killed by wild beasts: Genesis 37:29–35
Is bought by Potiphar, an officer of Pharaoh: Genesis 37:36
Is prospered of God: Genesis 39:2–5, 21, 23
Is falsely accused, and thrown into prison; is delivered by the friendship of another prisoner: Genesis 39; 40; Psalm 105:18

Is an interpreter of dreams, of the two prisoners: Genesis 40:5–23; *of Pharaoh:* Genesis 41:1–37
Name changed to Zaphnath-paaneah: Genesis 41:11
Is promoted to authority next to Pharaoh at thirty years old: Genesis 41:37–46; Psalm 105:19–22
Marries the daughter of the priest of On: Genesis 41:45
Provides against the seven years of famine: Genesis 41:46–57
Exports the produce of Egypt to other countries: Genesis 41:57
Sells the stores of food to the people of Egypt, exacting from them all their money, flocks and herds, lands and lives: Genesis 47:13–26
Exempts the priests from the exactions: Genesis 47:22, 26
His father sends down into Egypt to buy corn (grain): Genesis 42–44
Reveals himself to his brothers; sends for his father; provides the land of Goshen for his people; and sustains them during the famine: Genesis 45; 46; 47:1–12
His two sons: Genesis 41:50, 52
Mourns the death of his father: Genesis 50:1–14
Exacts a pledge from his brothers to convey his remains to Canaan: Genesis 50:2, 4, 25; Hebrews 11:22; Exodus 13:19; Joshua 24:32; Acts 7:16
Death of: Genesis 50:22–26
Kindness of heart: Genesis 40:7–8
Joseph's integrity: Genesis 39:7–12
His humility: Genesis 41:16; 45:7–9
His wisdom: Genesis 41:33–57
His piety: Genesis 41:51
His faith: Genesis 45:5–8
Was a prophet: Genesis 41:38, 39; 50:25; Exodus 13:19
God's providence with: Genesis 39:2–5; Psalm 105:17–22
Descendants of: Genesis 46:20; Numbers 26:28–37

BENJAMIN

Significance in summary

Jacob's youngest son

Family connections

Parents: Jacob and Rachel
Siblings: Reuben, Simeon, Levi, Judah, Dan, Naphtali, Gad, Asher, Issachar, Zebulun, Dinah, Joseph
Children: Bela, Beker, Ashbel, Gera, Naaman, Ehi, Rosh, Muppim, Huppim, Ard

Meaning of name

son of my right hand

Bible dictionary/encyclopedia entry (IBD)

The younger son of Jacob by Rachel (Gen. 35:18). His birth took place at Ephrath, on the road between Bethel and Bethlehem, at a short distance from the latter place. His mother died in giving him birth, and with her last breath named him Ben-oni, son of my pain, a name which was changed by his father into Benjamin. His posterity are called Benjamites (Gen. 49:27; Deut. 33:12; Josh. 18:21).

The tribe of Benjamin at the Exodus was the smallest but one (Num. 1:36–37; Ps. 68:27). During the march its place was along with Manasseh and Ephraim on the west of the tabernacle. At the entrance into Canaan it counted 45,600 warriors. It has been inferred by some from the words of Jacob (Gen. 49:27) that the figure of a wolf was on the tribal standard. This tribe is mentioned in Romans 11:1; Philippians 3:5.

The inheritance of this tribe lay immediately to the south of that of Ephraim, and was about twenty-six miles in length and twelve in breadth. Its eastern boundary was the Jordan. Dan intervened between it and the Philistines. Its chief towns are named in Joshua 18:21–28.

The history of the tribe contains a sad record of a desolating civil war in which they were engaged with the other eleven tribes. By it they were almost exterminated (Judges 20:20–21; 21:10).

The first king of the Jews was Saul, a Benjamite. A close alliance was formed between this tribe and that of Judah in the time of David (2 Sam. 19:16–17), which continued after his death (1 Kings 11:13; 12:20). After the Exile these two tribes formed the great body of the Jewish nation (Ezra 1:5; 10:9).

The tribe of Benjamin was famous for its archers (1 Sam. 20:20, 36; 2 Sam. 1:22; 1 Chron. 8:40; 12:2) and slingers (Judg. 20:6).

The gate of Benjamin, on the north side of Jerusalem (Jer. 37:13; 38:7; Zech. 14:10), was so called because it led in the direction of the territory of the tribe of Benjamin. It is called (Jer. 20:2) "the high gate of Benjamin" and also "the gate of the children of the people" (17:19). (Compare 2 Kings 14:13.)

Bible study on the life of Benjamin (NTB)

Son of Jacob by Rachel: Genesis 35:18, 24; 46:19
Taken into Egypt: Genesis 42–45
Prophecy concerning: Genesis 49:27
Descendants of: Genesis 46:21; Numbers 26:38–41

JUDAH

Significance in summary

The fourth son of Jacob and Leah

Family connections

Parents: Jacob and Leah
Siblings: Reuben, Simeon, Levi, Dan, Naphtali, Gad, Asher, Issachar, Zebulun, Dinah, Joseph, Benjamin
Married to: daughter of Shua, Tamar
Children: Er, Onan, Shelah, Perez, Zerah

Meaning of name

praise

Bible dictionary/encyclopedia entry (SBD)

The fourth son of Jacob and Leah. Of Judah's personal character more traits are preserved than of any other of the patriarchs, with the exception of Joseph, whose life he saved in conjunction with Reuben (Gen. 37:26–28). During the second visit to Egypt for corn it was Judah who was understood to be responsible for the safety of Benjamin (Gen. 43:3–10), and when, through Joseph's artifice, the brothers were brought back to the palace, he is again the leader and spokesman of the band. So too it is Judah who is sent before Jacob to smooth the way for him in the land of Goshen (Gen. 46:28). This ascendancy over his brothers is reflected in the last words addressed to him by his father. The families of Judah occupy a position among the tribes similar to that which their progenitor had taken among the patriarchs.

Bible study on the life of Judah (NTB)

Intercedes for Joseph's life when his brothers were about to kill him, and proposes that they sell him to the Ishmaelites: Genesis 37:26–27
Takes two wives: Genesis 38:1–6
Lives at Chezib: Genesis 38:5
His incest with his daughter-in-law: Genesis 38:12–26
Goes down into Egypt for corn (grain): Genesis 43:1–10; 44:14–34; 46:28
Prophetic benediction of his father: Genesis 49:8–12
The ancestor of Jesus: Matthew 1:2–3; Revelation 5:5

TAMAR, Judah's daughter-in-law

Significance in summary

Widow of Er, Judah's son; bore Judah twin sons, Perez and Zerah; an ancestor of Jesus Christ

Family connections

Married to: Er and Onan
Children with Judah: Perez and Zerah

Meaning of name

palm tree

Bible dictionary/encyclopedia entry (SBD)

The wife successively of the two sons of Judah, Er and Onan (Gen. 38:8–30). Her importance in the sacred narrative depends on the great anxiety to keep up the lineage of Judah. It seemed as if the family was about to become extinct. Er and Onan had perished suddenly. Judah's wife, Bathshuah, died, and there only remained a child, Shelah, whom Judah was unwilling to trust to the dangerous union as it appeared, with Tamar, in case he met with the same fate as his brothers. Accordingly she resorted entrapping the father himself into the union which he feared for his son. The fruits of this intercourse were twins, Perez and Zerah, and through Perez the sacred line was continued.

Bible study on the life of Tamar (NTB)

Wife of the sons of Judah: Genesis 38:6–24; Ruth 4:12; 1 Chronicles 2:4
Called Thamar: Matthew 1:3

LEVI

Significance in summary

Third son of Jacob and Leah, whose descendants became one of the twelve tribes of Israel

Family connections

Parents: Jacob and Leah
Siblings: Reuben, Simeon, Judah, Dan, Naphtali, Gad, Asher, Issachar, Zebulun, Dinah, Joseph, Benjamin
Children: Gershon, Kohath, Merari, Jochebed

Meaning of name

joined

Bible dictionary/encyclopedia entry (SBD)

The name of the third son of Jacob by his wife Leah. The name, derived from *lavah*, "to adhere," gave utterance to the hope of the mother that the affections of her husband, which had previously rested on the favored Rachel, would at last be drawn to her: "This time will my husband be joined unto me, because I have borne him three sons" (Gen. 29:34).

Levi, with his brother Simeon, avenged with a cruel slaughter the outrage of their sister Dinah.

Levi, with his three sons, Gershon, Kohath, and Merari, went down to Egypt with his father Jacob (Gen. 47:11). When Jacob's death draws near, and the sons are gathered around him, Levi and Simeon hear the old crime brought up again to receive its sentence. They, no less than Reuben, the incestuous firstborn, had forfeited the privileges of their birthright (Gen. 49:5–7).

Bible study on the life of Levi (NTB)

Son of Jacob: Genesis 29:34; 35:23; 1 Chronicles 2:1
Avenges the seduction of Dinah: Genesis 34; 49:5–7
Jacob's prophecy regarding: Genesis 49:5–7
His age at death: Exodus 6:16

GERSHON

Significance in summary

Levi's eldest son and an important priest

Family connections

Siblings: Kohath, Merari, Jochebed
Children: Libni, Shimei

Bible dictionary/encyclopedia entry (FBD)

Oldest of Levi's three sons, born apparently before Jacob's going down to Egypt (Gen. 46:11). Kohath and his descendants Moses and Aaron's priestly line eclipsed Gershon's line. Gershon's sons were Libni and Shimei (1 Chron. 6:17, 20–21, 39–43). Some of his descendants took part in the service of the sanctuary (1 Chron. 23:7–11). Asaph, the famous sacred singer and seer, was one of them. Compare also under Hezekiah

(2 Chron. 29:12). At the Sinai census the males of the sons of Gershon were 7500 (Num. 3:21–22). The serving men were 2,630 (Num. 4:38–41). They had charge of the tabernacle, tent, covering, hangings, curtain of the door, and cords (Num. 3:25–26; Num. 4:25–26). They had two covered wagons and four oxen for the service (Num. 7:3, 7–8).

They were stationed "behind the tabernacle westward" (Num. 3:23). When they traveled they were in the rear of the first three tribes. Thirteen of the Levitical cities were allotted to them, all in the northern tribes, two of them cities of refuge (Josh. 21:27–33; 1 Chron. 6:62, 71–76).

Bible study on the life of Gershon (NTB)

Son of Levi: Genesis 46:11; Exodus 6:16–17; Numbers 3:17–26; 4:22–28, 38; 7:7; 10:17; 26:57; Joshua 21:6; 1 Chronicles 6:1, 16–17, 20, 43, 62, 71; 15:7; 23:6

MERARI

Significance in summary

Levi's third son, whose descendants formed one of the three groups of Levites

Family connections

Father: Levi
Siblings: Gershon, Kohath, Jochebed
Children: Mahli, Mushi

Meaning of name

bitter

Bible study on the life of Merari (NTB)

Son of Levi: Genesis 46:11
Headed the Merarite Levites: Numbers 3:17, 33–35

REUBEN

Significance in summary

Jacob and Leah's oldest son, whose descendants became one of the twelve tribes of Israel

Family connections

Parents: Jacob and Leah
Siblings: Simeon, Levi, Judah, Dan, Naphtali, Gad, Asher, Issachar, Zebulun, Dinah, Joseph, Benjamin
Married to: Bilhah
Children: Hanoch, Pallu, Hezron, Carmi

Meaning of name

see, a son

Bible dictionary/encyclopedia entry (ISBE)

The eldest son of Jacob, born to him by Leah in Paddan-aram (Gen. 29:32).

Of his boyhood we are only told about the story of the mandrakes (Gen. 30:14). As the firstborn he should really have been leader among his father's sons. His birthright was forfeited by a deed of peculiar infamy (Gen. 35:22). Of this repulsive crime which mars his history, and which turned the blessing of his dying father into a curse—his adulterous connection with Bilhah—we only know from the Scriptures. As far as we know, his tribe never took the lead in Israel. It is named first, indeed, in Numbers 1:5, 20, but thereafter it falls to the fourth place, Judah taking the first (Num. 2:10, etc.). To Reuben's intervention Joseph owed his escape from the fate proposed by his other brothers (Gen. 37:29). Some have thought Reuben designed to set him free, from a desire to rehabilitate himself with his father. But there is no need to deny to Reuben certain noble and chivalrous qualities. Jacob seems to have appreciated these, and, perhaps, therefore all the more deeply lamented the lapse that spoiled his life (Gen. 49:3). It was Reuben who felt that their perils and anxieties in Egypt were a fit recompense for the unbrotherly conduct (Gen. 42:22). To assure his father of Benjamin's safe return from Egypt, where Joseph required him to be taken, Reuben was ready to pledge his own two sons (Gen. 42:37). Four sons born to him in Canaan went with Reuben when Israel went down to Egypt (Gen. 46:8).

Bible study on the life of Reuben (NTB)

Son of Jacob: Genesis 29:32; 1 Chronicles 2:1
Brings mandrakes (an aphrodisiac) to his mother: Genesis 30:14
Commits incest with one of his father's concubines, and, in consequence, forfeits his birthright: Genesis 35:22; 49:4; 1 Chronicles 5:1
Seeks to save Joseph from the conspiracy of his brothers: Genesis 37:21–30; 42:22

Jacob's prophetic benediction: Genesis 49:3–4
His children: Genesis 46:9; Exodus 6:14; 1 Chronicles 5:3–6; Numbers 16:1

SIMEON

Significance in summary

Jacob and Leah's second son, whose descendants became one of the twelve tribes of Israel

Family connections

Parents: Jacob and Leah
Siblings: Reuben, Levi, Judah, Dan, Naphtali, Gad, Asher, Issachar, Zebulun, Dinah, Joseph, Benjamin
Married to: a Canaanite woman
Children: Jemuel, Jamin, Ohad, Jakin, Zohar, Shaul

Meaning of name

he hears, or hearing

Bible dictionary/encyclopedia entry (IBD)

The second son of Jacob by Leah (Gen. 29:33). He was associated with Levi in the terrible act of vengeance against Hamor and the Shechemites (34:25–26). He was detained by Joseph in Egypt as a hostage (42:24). His father, when dying, pronounced a malediction against him (49:5–7).

Bible study on the life of Simeon (NTB)

Son of Jacob: Genesis 29:33; 35:23; Exodus 1:1–2; 1 Chronicles 2:1
With Levi avenges on the Shechemites the seduction of Dinah: Genesis 34; 49:5–7
Jacob's denunciation of: Genesis 34:30; 49:5–7
Goes down into Egypt to buy corn; is imprisoned by Joseph, and is detained: Genesis 42:24, 36; 43:23
His sons: Genesis 46:10; Exodus 6:15; 1 Chronicles 4:24–37
Descendants of: Numbers 26:12–14

EPHRAIM

Significance in summary

Joseph's second son

Family connections

Parents: Joseph and Asenath
Sibling: Manasseh

Meaning of name

fruitful

Bible dictionary/encyclopedia entry (IBD)

Double fruitfulness ("for God had made him fruitful in the land of his affliction"). The second son of Joseph, born in Egypt (Gen. 41:52; 46:20). The first incident recorded about him is his being placed, along with his brother Manasseh, before their grandfather, Jacob, that he might bless them (48:10; compare 27:1). The intention of Joseph was that the right hand of the aged patriarch should be placed on the head of the elder of the two; but Jacob set Ephraim the younger before his brother, "guiding his hands wittingly." Before Joseph's death, Ephraim's family had reached the third generation (Gen. 50:23).

Bible study on the life of Ephraim (NTB)

Second son of Joseph: Genesis 41:52
Adopted by Jacob: Genesis 48:5
Blessed before Manasseh; prophecies concerning: Genesis 48:14–20
Descendants of: Numbers 26:35–37; 1 Chronicles 7:20–27
Mourned for his sons: 1 Chronicles 7:21–22

MANASSEH

Significance in summary

Joseph's first son, whose descendants became one of the twelve tribes of Israel

Family connections

Parents: Joseph and Asenath
Sibling: Ephraim
Son: Makir

Meaning of name

one who causes forgetfulness

Bible dictionary/encyclopedia entry (SBD)

The eldest son of Joseph (Gen. 41:51; 46:20). Both he and Ephraim were born before the commencement of the famine. He was placed after his younger brother, Ephraim, by his grandfather Jacob, when he adopted them into his own family and made them heads of tribes. Whether the elder of the two sons was inferior in form or promise to the younger, or whether there was any external reason to justify the preference of Jacob, we are not told. In the division of the promised land half of the tribe of Manasseh settled east of the Jordan in the district embracing the hills of Gilead with their inaccessible heights, impassable ravines, and the almost impregnable tract of Argob (Josh. 13:29–33). From here they pushed their way northward over the rich plains of Jaulan and Jedur to the foot of Mount Hermon (1 Chron. 5:23). But they gradually assimilated themselves with the old inhabitants of the country and were punished for their misdoing. They, first of all Israel, were carried away by Pul and Tilgath-pilneser, and settled in the Assyrian territories (1 Chron. 5:25–26). The other half of the tribe settled to the west of the Jordan, north of Ephraim (Josh. 17:1).

Bible study on the life of Manasseh (NTB)

Son of Joseph and Asenath: Genesis 41:50, 51; 46:20
Adopted by Jacob on his deathbed: Genesis 48:1, 5–20
Called Manasses: Revelation 7:6

POTIPHAR

Significance in summary

The Egyptian officer who bought Joseph, made him overseer, then later threw him in prison on false charges.

Meaning of name

whom Re (the sun god) has given

Bible dictionary/encyclopedia entry (IBD)

He was "captain of the guard," i.e., chief, probably, of the state police, who, while they formed part of the Egyptian army, were also mainly employed in civil duties (37:36; marg., "chief of the executioners"). Joseph, though a foreigner, gradually gained his confidence, and became overseer over all his possessions. Believing the false accusation his wife brought against Joseph, Potiphar cast him into prison, where he remained for some years.

KOHATH

Significance in summary

Levi's second son and grandfather of Moses

Family connections

Father: Levi
Siblings: Gershon, Merari, Jochebed
Children: Amram, Izhar, Hebron, Uzziel

Bible study on the life of Kohath (NTB)

Son of Levi: Genesis 46:11; Exodus 6:16
Grandfather of Moses, Aaron, and Miriam: Numbers 26:58–59
Father of the Kohathites, one of the divisions (shifts) of the Levites: Exodus 6:18; Numbers 3:19, 27

MOSES

Significance in summary

Israel's deliverer, prophet, and lawgiver

Family connections

Parents: Amram and Jochebed
Siblings: Miriam, Aaron
Married to: Zipporah, a Cushite
Children: Gershom, Eliezer

Meaning of name

drawn-out

Bible dictionary/encyclopedia entry (IBD)

On the invitation of Pharaoh (Gen. 45:17–25), Jacob and his sons went down into Egypt. This immigration took place probably about 350 years before the birth of Moses.

The Israelites began to "multiply exceedingly" (Gen. 47:27), and extended to the west and south. The descendants of Jacob were allowed to retain their possession of Goshen undisturbed, but after the death of Joseph their position was not so favorable. The Egyptians began to despise them, and the period of their "affliction" (Gen. 15:13) began. They continued, however, to increase in numbers, and "the land was filled with them" (Exod. 1:7). The native Egyptians regarded them with suspicion.

In process of time "a king arose who knew not Joseph" (Exod. 1:8). This king thought it necessary to weaken his Israelite subjects by oppressing them, and by degrees reducing their number. They were made public slaves, and were employed in connection with his numerous buildings, especially in the erection of store-cities, temples, and palaces. But this cruel oppression did not reduce their number. On the contrary, "the more the Egyptians afflicted them, the more they multiplied and grew" (Exod. 1:12).

The king next tried, through a compact secretly made with the guild of midwives, to bring about the destruction of all the Hebrew male children that might be born. But the male children were spared by the midwives, so that "the people multiplied" more than ever. Baffled, the king issued a public proclamation calling on the people to put to death all the Hebrew male children by casting them into the river (Exod. 1:22).

One of the Hebrew households into which this cruel edict brought great alarm was that of Amram, of the family of the Kohathites (Exod. 6:16–20), who with his wife Jochebed and two children, Miriam, a girl of perhaps fifteen years old, and Aaron, a boy of three years, lived in or near Memphis, the capital city of that time. In this quiet home a male child was born. His mother concealed him in the house for three months, but when that became difficult, she contrived to bring her child under the notice of the daughter of the king by constructing for him an ark of bulrushes, which she laid at the edge of the river, near the spot where the princess would come down to bathe. Her plan was successful. The king's daughter "saw the child; and behold the child wept." The princess sent Miriam, who was standing by, to fetch a nurse. She went and brought the mother of the child, to whom the princess said, "Take this child away, and nurse it for me, and I will give thee thy wages." Thus Jochebed's child, whom the princess called "Moses," i.e., "Saved from the water" (Exod. 2:10), was ultimately restored to her.

As soon as the natural time for weaning the child had come, he was transferred to the royal palace, where he was brought up as the adopted son of the princess, his mother probably accompanying him and still caring for him. He grew up amid all the grandeur and excitement of the Egyptian court, maintaining, however, probably a constant fellowship with his mother. He at length became "learned in all the wisdom of the Egyptians" (Acts 7:22). Egypt had then two chief seats of learning, or universities, at one of which, probably that of Heliopolis, his education was completed. Moses, being now about twenty years old, spent over twenty more before he came into prominence in Bible history. These twenty years were probably spent in military service. There is a tradition recorded by Josephus that he took a lead in the war which was then waged between Egypt and Ethiopia, in which he gained renown as a skillful general, and became "mighty in deeds" (Acts 7:22).

After the war in Ethiopia, Moses returned to the Egyptian court, where he might reasonably have expected to be loaded with honors and enriched with wealth. But Moses, amid all his Egyptian surroundings, had never forgotten that he was a Hebrew. He now resolved to make himself acquainted with the condition of his countrymen, and "went out unto his brethren, and looked upon their burdens" (Exod. 2:11). Assured that God would bless his resolution for the welfare of his people, he left the palace of the king and took up his abode, probably in his father's house, as one of the Hebrew people who had for forty years been suffering cruel wrong at the hands of the Egyptians.

He could not remain indifferent to the state of things around him, and one day his indignation was roused against an Egyptian who was maltreating a Hebrew. He rashly lifted up his hand and slew the Egyptian, and hid his body in the sand. The next day he found that the deed of the previous day was known. It reached the ears of Pharaoh (the "great Rameses," Rameses II), who "sought to slay Moses" (Exod. 2:15). Moved by fear, Moses fled from Egypt to Midian, the southern part of the peninsula of Sinai, probably by much the same route as that by which, forty years afterwards, he led the Israelites to Sinai. He was providentially led to find a new home with the family of Reuel, where he remained for forty years (Acts 7:30), under training unconsciously for his great life's work.

An angel of the Lord appeared to him in the burning bush (Exodus 3), and commissioned him to go down to Egypt and "bring forth the children of Israel" out of bondage. He was at first unwilling to go, but at length he was obedient and left the land of Midian (4:18–26). On the way he was met by Aaron and the elders of Israel (vv. 27–31). He and Aaron had a hard task before them; but the Lord was with them (ch. 7–12). After an eventful journey to and fro in the wilderness, we see them at length encamped in the plains of Moab, ready to cross over the Jordan into the Promised Land. There Moses addresses the assembled elders (Deut. 1:1–4; 5:1–26:19; 27:11–30:20); he gives the people his last counsels, and then rehearses the great song (Deuteronomy 32) reviewing the marvelous history in which he had so conspicuous a part. Then, after blessing the tribes (33), he ascends to "the mountain of Nebo, to the top of Pisgah, that is over against Jericho" (34:1) and surveys the land. "Jehovah shewed him all the land of Gilead, unto Dan, and all Naphtali, and the land of Ephraim, and Manasseh, and all the land of Judah, unto the utmost sea, and the south, and the plain of the valley of Jericho, the city of palm trees, unto Zoar" (Deut. 34:2–3), the magnificent inheritance of the tribes of whom he had been so long the leader; and there he died, being one hundred and twenty years old, and was buried by the Lord "in a valley in the land of Moab, over against Beth-peor" (34:6). The people mourned for him for thirty days.

Thus died "Moses the man of God" (Deut. 33:1; Josh. 14:6). He was characterized by his meekness and patience and firmness, and "he endured as seeing him who is invisible." "There arose not a prophet since in Israel like unto Moses, whom the Lord knew face to face, in all the signs and the wonders, which the Lord sent him to do in the land of Egypt to Pharaoh, and to all his servants, and to all his land, and in all that mighty hand, and in all the great terror which Moses shewed in the sight of all Israel" (Deut. 34:10–12).

The name of Moses occurs frequently in the Psalms and Prophets as the chief of the prophets.

In the New Testament he is referred to as the representative of the law and as a type of Christ (John 1:17; 2 Cor. 3:13–18; Heb. 3:5–6). Moses is the only character in the Old Testament to whom Christ likens himself (John 5:46; compare Deut. 18:15, 18–19; Acts 7:37). In Hebrews 3 this likeness to Moses is set forth in various particulars.

In Jude 9 mention is made of a contention between Michael and the devil about the body of Moses. This dispute is supposed to have had reference to the concealment of the body of Moses so as to prevent idolatry.

Bible study on the life of Moses (NTB)

A Levite and son of Amram: Exodus 2:1–4; 6:20; Acts 7:20; Hebrews 11:23

Hidden in a small basket: Exodus 2:3

Discovered and adopted by the daughter of Pharaoh: Exodus 2:5–10

Learned in all the wisdom of Egypt: Acts 7:22

His loyalty to his race: Hebrews 11:24–26

Takes the life of an Egyptian taskmaster; flees from Egypt; finds refuge among the Midianites: Exodus 2:11–22; Acts 7:24–29

Joins himself to Jethro, priest of Midian; marries his daughter Zipporah; has one son, Gershom: Exodus 2:15–22

Is a herdsman for Jethro in the desert of Horeb: Exodus 3:1

Has the vision of the burning bush: Exodus 3:2–6

God reveals to him his purpose to deliver the Israelites and bring them into the land of Canaan: Exodus 3:7–10

Commissioned as leader of the Israelites: Exodus 3:10–22; 6:13

His rod miraculously turned into a serpent, and his hand was made leprous and then restored: Exodus 4:1–9, 28

With his wife and sons, he leaves Jethro to perform his mission in Egypt: Exodus 4:18–20
His controversy with his wife on account of circumcision: Exodus 4:20–26
Meets Aaron in the wilderness: Exodus 4:27–28
With Aaron assembles the leaders of Israel: Exodus 4:29–31
Along with Aaron, goes before Pharaoh and demands the liberties of his people in the name of Jehovah: Exodus 5:1
Rejected by Pharaoh; hardships of the Israelites increased: Exodus 5
People complain against Moses and Aaron: Exodus 5:20–21; 15:24; 16:2–3; 17:2–3; Numbers 14:2–4; 16:41; 20:2–5; 21:4–6; Deuteronomy 1:12, 26–28
Receives comfort and assurance from the Lord: Exodus 6:1–8
Unbelief of the people: Exodus 6:9
Renews his appeal to Pharaoh: Exodus 6:11
Under divine direction brings plagues on the land of Egypt: Exodus 7–12
Secures the deliverance of the people and leads them out of Egypt: Exodus 13
Crosses the Red Sea; Pharaoh and his army are destroyed: Exodus 14
Composes a song for the people of Israel on their deliverance from Pharaoh: Exodus 15
Joined by his family in the wilderness: Exodus 18:1–12
Institutes a system of government: Exodus 18:13–26; Numbers 11:16–30; Deuteronomy 1:9–18
Receives the law and ordains various statutes: Exodus 19:10–23:33
Transfigured face: Exodus 34:29–35; 2 Corinthians 3:13
Sets up the tabernacle; reproves Aaron for making the golden calf: Exodus 32:2–23
Irregularity in the offerings: Leviticus 10:16–20
Jealousy of Aaron and Miriam toward: Numbers 12
Rebellion of Korah, Dathan, and Abiram against: Numbers 16
Appoints Joshua as his successor: Numbers 27:22–23; Deuteronomy 31:7–8, 14, 23; 34:9
Not permitted to enter Canaan, but views the land from atop Mount Pisgah: Numbers 27:12–14; Deuteronomy 1:37; 3:23–29; 32:48–52; 34:1–8
Death and burial of: Numbers 31:2; Deuteronomy 32:50; 34:1–6
Body of, disputed over: Jude 9
120 years old at death: Deuteronomy 31:2
Mourning for, thirty days in the plains of Moab: Deuteronomy 34:8
His virility: Deuteronomy 31:2; 34:7

Present with Jesus on the Mount of Transfiguration: Matthew 17:3–4; Mark 9:4; Luke 9:30
A type of the Messiah: Deuteronomy 18:15–18; Acts 3:22; 7:37

JETHRO (REUEL)

Significance in summary

Moses' father-in-law

Meaning of name

excellence

Bible dictionary/encyclopedia entry (SBD)

Jethro was priest or prince of Midian. Moses married his daughter Zipporah. On account of his local knowledge he was asked to stay with the Israelites throughout their journey to Canaan (Num. 10:31, 33). Reuel is probably his proper name, and Jethro his official title.

Bible study on the life of Jethro (NTB)

Also called Raguel and Reuel, a priest of Midian
Moses spent forty years of exile with Jethro, and married his daughter: Exodus 2:15–22; 3:1; 4:18; Numbers 10:29

ZIPPORAH

Significance in summary

Jethro's daughter, wife of Moses

Family connections

Father: Jethro/Reuel
Siblings: six sisters
Married to: Moses
Son: Gershom

Meaning of name

bird

Bible study on the life of Zipporah (NTB)

Wife of Moses: Exodus 2:16–22
Reproaches Moses: Exodus 4:25–26

Separates from Moses, is brought again to him by her father: Exodus 18:2–6
Miriam and Aaron reprimand Moses concerning his marriage to Zipporah: Numbers 12:1

MIRIAM

Significance in summary

Moses and Aaron's sister

Family connections

Parents: Amram and Jochebed
Siblings: Aaron, Moses

Meaning of name

loved by God

Bible dictionary/encyclopedia entry (SBD)

The sister of Moses, she was the eldest of that sacred family; she first appears, probably as a young girl, watching her infant brother's cradle in the Nile (Exod. 2:4) and suggesting her mother as a nurse (v. 7). After the crossing of the Red Sea, "Miriam the prophetess" was her acknowledged title (Exod. 15:20). The prophetic power showed itself in her the same way it did in the days of Samuel and David—poetry, accompanied with music and processions (Exod. 15:1–19). She took the lead, with Aaron, in the complaint against Moses for his marriage with a Cushite (Num. 12:1–2) and for this became leprous. This affliction and its removal, which took place at Hazeroth, form the last public event of Miriam's life (Num. 12:1–15). She died toward the close of the wanderings at Kadesh and was buried there (Num. 20:1).

Bible study on the life of Miriam (NTB)

Watched over Moses when he was in the little basket: Exodus 2:4–8
Song of, after the destruction of Pharaoh and his army: Exodus 15:20–21; Micah 6:4
Jealous of Moses, stricken with leprosy, healed on account of the intercession of Moses: Numbers 12; Deuteronomy 24:9
Died and is buried at Kadesh: Numbers 20:1

AARON

Significance in summary

Brother of Moses and Miriam

Family connections

Parents: Amram and Jochebed
Siblings: Miriam, Moses
Married to: Elisheba
Children: Nadab, Abihu, Eleazar, Ithamar

Meaning of name

enlightened

Bible dictionary/encyclopedia entry (SBD)

Aaron was a Levite, and is first mentioned in Exodus 4:14. He was appointed by Jehovah to be the interpreter (Exod. 4:16) of his brother Moses, who was "slow of speech"; accordingly he was not only the organ of communication with the Israelites and with Pharaoh (Exod. 4:30; 7:2) but also the actual instrument of working most of the miracles of the Exodus (Exod. 7:19, etc). On the way to Mount Sinai, during the battle with Amalek, Aaron and Hur stayed up the weary hands of Moses when they were lifted up for the victory of Israel (Exod. 17:12). He is mentioned as dependent on his brother and deriving all his authority from him. Left, on Moses's departure into Sinai, to guide the people, Aaron is tried for a moment on his own responsibility, and he fails to withstand the demand of the people for visible "gods to go before them," by making an image of Jehovah, in the well-known form of Egyptian idolatry (Apis or Mnevis). He repented of his sin, and Moses sought and was given forgiveness for him (9:20). Aaron was not consecrated by Moses to the new office of the high priesthood (Exod. 29:9). From this time the history of Aaron is almost entirely that of the priesthood, and its chief feature is the great rebellion of Korah and the Levites. Leaning, as he seems to have done, wholly on Moses, it is not strange that he should have shared his sin at Meribah and its punishment (Num. 20:10–12). Aaron's death seems to have followed very speedily. It took place on Mount Hor, after the transference of his robes and office to Eleazar (Num. 20:28). This mount is still called the "Mountain of Aaron." Aaron's wife was Elisheba (Exod. 6:23) and the two sons who survived him, Eleazar and Ithamar. The high priesthood descended to the former, and to his descendants until the time of Eli, who, although of the house of Ithamar, received the high priesthood and transmitted it to his children; with them it continued till the accession of Solomon, who took it from Abiathar and restored it to Zadok (of the house of Eleazar).

Bible study on the life of Aaron (NTB)

Lineage of: Exodus 6:16–20; Joshua 21:4, 10; 1 Chronicles 6:2–3; 23:13
Marriage of: Exodus 6:23
Children of: Exodus 6:23, 25; 1 Chronicles 6:3; 24:1–2
Descendants of: Exodus 6:23, 25; 1 Chronicles 6:3–15, 50–53; 24
Meets Moses in the wilderness and is made spokesman for him: Exodus 4:14–16, 27–31; 7:1 2
Inspiration of: Exodus 12:1; Leviticus 10:8; 11:1; 13:1; 15:1; Numbers 2:1; 4:1, 17; 18:1; 19:1; 20:12
Commissioned as a deliverer of Israel: Exodus 6:13, 26–27; Joshua 24:5; 1 Samuel 12:8; Psalm 77:20; 105:26; Micah 6:4
Summoned to Sinai with Nadab, Abihu, and seventy elders: Exodus 19:24; 24:1, 9–10
Priesthood of: Exodus 28:1; 29:9; Numbers 17; 18:1; Psalm 99:6; Hebrews 5:4
Consecration of, to the priesthood: Exodus 28–29; Leviticus 8
Begins the priestly office: Leviticus 9
Descendants of, ordained priests forever: Exodus 28:40–43; 29:9; Numbers 3:3; 18:1; 1 Chronicles 23:13; 2 Chronicles 26:18
Judges Israel in the absence of Moses: Exodus 24:14
Makes the golden calf: Exodus 32; Deuteronomy 9:20–21; Acts 7:40
Rod of, buds: Numbers 17; Hebrews 9:4
Murmured against, by the people: Exodus 5:20–21; 16:2–10; Numbers 14:2–5, 10; 16:3–11, 41; 20:2; Psalm 106:16
Places pot of manna in the ark: Exodus 16:34
With Hur supports the hands of Moses during battle: Exodus 17:12
His benedictions on the people: Leviticus 9:22; Numbers 6:23
Forbidden to mourn the death of his sons, Nadab and Abihu: Leviticus 10:6–7
Intercedes for Miriam: Numbers 12:11–12
Stays the plague by priestly intercession: Numbers 16:46–48
Jealous of Moses: Numbers 12:1
His presumption, when the rock is smitten: Numbers 20:10–12
Not permitted to enter Canaan: Numbers 20:12, 23–29
Age of, at death: Exodus 7:7; Numbers 33:38–39
Death and burial of: Numbers 20:27–28; Deuteronomy 10:6; 32:50
Character of: Psalm 106:16

NADAB

Significance in summary

Aaron's first son

Family connections

Parents: Aaron and Elisheba
Siblings: Abihu, Eleazar, Ithamar

Meaning of name

liberal

Bible study on the life of Nadab (NTB)

Called to Mount Sinai with Moses and Aaron to worship: Exodus 24:1, 9–10
Set apart to priesthood: Exodus 28:1, 4, 40–43
Offers "strange" (unauthorized) fire to God, and is destroyed: Leviticus 10:1–2; Numbers 3:4; 26:61
Is buried: Leviticus 10:4–5
His father and brothers forbidden to mourn: Leviticus 10:6–7

ELEAZAR

Significance in summary

Aaron's third son, who became high priest

Family connections

Parents: Aaron and Elisheba
Siblings: Nadab, Abihu, Ithamar
Married to: a daughter of Putiel
Son: Phinehas

Meaning of name

God has helped

Bible study on the life of Eleazar (NTB)

Son of Aaron: Exodus 6:23; 28:1
Married a daughter of Putiel, who bore him Phinehas: Exodus 6:25
After the death of Nadab and Abihu is made chief of the tribe of Levi: Numbers 3:32
Duties of: Numbers 4:16

Succeeds Aaron as high priest: Numbers 20:26, 28; Deuteronomy 10:6
Assists Moses in the census: Numbers 26:63
With Joshua, divides Palestine: Numbers 34:17
Death and burial of: Joshua 24:33
Descendants of: 1 Chronicles 24:1–19

PHINEHAS, Eleazar's son

Significance in summary

Aaron's grandson, who became high priest

Family connections

Parents: Eleazar and a daughter of Putiel

Meaning of name

mouth of brass

Bible study on the life of Phinehas (NTB)

High priest: Exodus 6:25; 1 Chronicles 6:4, 50
Religious zeal of, in killing the Israelite woman who had committed abomination: Numbers 25:7–15; Psalm 106:30
Chief of the Korahite Levites: 1 Chronicles 9:19–20
Sent to sound the trumpets in the battle with the Midianites: Numbers 31:6
Sent to inquire of the Israelites what the monument they had erected signified: Joshua 22:13–32
Inheritance allotted to: Joshua 24:33
Mediator in behalf of the people: Judges 20:28

BEZALEL

Significance in summary

A chief craftsman of the tabernacle

Meaning of name

protected by God

Bible study on the life of Bezalel (NTB)

A divinely-inspired master craftsman who built the tabernacle: Exodus 31:2; 35:30–35; 36:1; 37:1; 38:1–7, 22

ABIRAM

Significance in summary

Leader of a rebellion against Moses, with Dathan and Korah, for which he was killed

Meaning of name

father is exulted

Bible study on the life of Abiram (NTB)

An Israelite who conspired with Dathan against Moses and Aaron: Numbers 16; 26:9–10; Deuteronomy 11:6; Psalm 106:17

KORAH

Significance in summary

Leader of a rebellion against Moses, with Dathan and Abiram, for which he was killed

Meaning of name

bald

Bible study on the life of Korah (NTB)

A Korhite Levite: Exodus 6:18, 21, 24

Jealous of Moses, leads two-hundred and fifty people in an insurrection, and is swallowed up in the earth: Numbers 16; 26:9–10; Deuteronomy 11:6; Psalm 106:17; Jude 11

DATHAN

Significance in summary

Chief of Reuben's tribe who, with Korah and Abiram, led an unsuccessful rebellion against Moses

Bible study on the life of Dathan (NTB)

A conspirator against Moses: Numbers 16:1–35; 26:9; Deuteronomy 11:6; Psalm 106:17

OG

Significance in summary

A giant king of Bashan

Bible study on the life of Og (NTB)

A man of gigantic stature: Numbers 21:33; Deuteronomy 3:11; Joshua 12:4; 13:12
Defeated and killed by Moses: Numbers 21:33–35; Deuteronomy 1:4; 3:1–7; 29:7; 31:4; Joshua 2:10; 9:10; Psalms 135:10, 11; 136:18–20
Land of, given to the tribes of Gad, Reuben, and Manasseh: Numbers 32:33, Deuteronomy 3:8–17; 4:47–49; 29:7–8; Joshua 12:4–6; 13:12, 30–31; 1 Kings 4:19; Nehemiah 9:22; Psalm 136:20–21

SIHON

Significance in summary

Amorite king defeated by Israel

Bible study on the life of Sihon (NTB)

Governed from Heshbon: Numbers 21:26
The proverbial chant celebrating the victory of Sihon over the Moabites: Numbers 21:26–30
Conquest of his kingdom by the Israelites: Numbers 21:21–25; Deuteronomy 2:24–37; 3:2, 6, 8

BALAAM

Significance in summary

A prophet whom the king of Moab asked to curse Israel

Meaning of name

devourer

Bible dictionary/encyclopedia entry (IBD)

The son of Beor, he was a man of some standing among the Midianites (Num. 31:8; compare 16). He lived at Pethor (Deut. 23:4) in Mesopotamia (Num. 23:7). Though living among idolaters he had some knowledge of the true God; it was supposed that he whom he blessed was blessed, and he whom he cursed was cursed. When the

Israelites were camping on the plains of Moab, on the east of Jordan, near Jericho, Balak sent for Balaam "from Aram, out of the mountains of the east," to curse them; but by God's remarkable intervention he was unable to fulfill Balak's wish, no matter how hard Balak pressed him. The apostle Peter (2 Peter 2:15–16) refers to this as a historical event. In Micah 6:5 reference also is made to the relationship between Balaam and Balak. Though Balaam could not curse Israel, he suggested a way in which divine displeasure might come on them (Numbers 25). In a battle between Israel and the Midianites Balaam was killed while fighting on the side of Balak (Num. 31:8).

The "doctrine of Balaam" is spoken of in Revelation 2:14, and is an allusion to the fact that through the teaching of Balaam Balak learned the way the Israelites might be led into sin. Balaam uttered beautiful prophecies regarding the future of Israel (Num. 24:5–9, 17).

Bible study on the life of Balaam (NTB)

From Mesopotamia: Deuteronomy 23:4
Practiced divination: Joshua 13:22
A prophet: Numbers 24:2–9; 2 Peter 2:15–16
Balak sends for, to curse Israel: Numbers 22:5–7; Joshua 24:9; Nehemiah 13:2; Micah 6:5
Anger of, rebuked by his donkey: Numbers 22:22–35; 2 Peter 2:16
Counsel of, an occasion of Israel's corruption with the Midianites: Numbers 31:16; Revelation 2:14–15
Covetousness of: 2 Peter 2:15; Jude 11
Death of: Numbers 31:8; Joshua 13:22

BALAK

Significance in summary

The king of Moab who asked Balaam to curse Israel

Meaning of name

devastator

Bible dictionary/encyclopedia entry (IBD)

A son of Zippor, and king of the Moabites (Num. 22:2, 4). From fear of the Israelites, who were camped near his territory, he tried to force Balaam to curse them; but in vain (Josh. 24:9).

Bible study on the life of Balak (NTB)

King of Moab: Numbers 22:4; Joshua 24:9; Judges 11:25; Micah 6:5
Tries to bribe Balaam to curse Israel: Numbers 22:5–7, 15–17

JOSHUA

Significance in summary

Moses's successor who led the Israelites into the Promised Land

Meaning of name

God is salvation

Bible dictionary/encyclopedia entry (IBD)

The son of Nun, from the tribe of Ephraim, the successor of Moses as the leader of Israel. He is called Jehoshua in Numbers 13:16 (KJV), and Jesus in Acts 7:45 and Hebrews 4:8 (RSV, Joshua).

He was born in Egypt, and was probably the same age as Caleb, with whom he is linked. He shared in all the events of the exodus, and commanded the Israelites at the great battle against the Amalekites in Rephidim (Exod. 17:8–16). He became Moses's minister or servant, and accompanied him part of the way when he ascended Mount Sinai to receive the two stone tablets (Exod. 32:17). He was also one of the twelve sent by Moses to explore the land of Canaan (Num. 13:16–17); only he and Caleb gave an encouraging report. Under the direction of God, Moses, before his death, made Joshua his successor (Deut. 31:23). Joshua was visited by the captain of the Lord's host, who spoke to him encouraging words (1:1–9). The people were encamped at Shittim when Joshua assumed the command; crossing the Jordan, they encamped at Gilgal, where, having circumcised the people, he kept the Passover.

Then followed the wars of conquest which Joshua engaged in for many years, and which are recorded in the book bearing his name. Six nations and thirty-one kings were conquered by him (Josh. 11:18–23; 12:24). After he had subdued the Canaanites, Joshua divided the land among the tribes; Timnath-serah in Mount Ephraim became his own inheritance.

His work being done, he died, at the age of one hundred and ten years, twenty-five years after crossing the Jordan. He was buried in his own city of Timnath-serah (Joshua 24); and "the light of Israel for the time faded away."

Joshua has been regarded as a type of Christ (Heb. 4:8) for the following reasons: (1) in the name they shared; (2) Joshua brings the people into the possession of the Promised Land, as Jesus brings his people to the heavenly Canaan; and (3) as Joshua succeeded Moses, so the gospel succeeds the Law.

Bible study on the life of Joshua (NTB)

Also called Jehoshua, and Jehoshuah, and Oshea; son of Nun: Numbers 13:8; 1 Chronicles 7:27
Intimately associated with Moses: Exodus 24:13; 32:17; 33:11
A religious zealot: Numbers 11:28
Sent with others to view the Promised Land: Numbers 13:8
Makes a favorable report: Numbers 14:6–10
Rewarded for his courage and fidelity: Numbers 14:30, 38; 32:12
Commissioned, ordained, and charged with the responsibilities of Moses's office: Numbers 27:18–23; Deuteronomy 1:38; 3:28; 31:3, 7, 23; 34:9
Divinely inspired: Numbers 27:18; Deuteronomy 34:9; Joshua 1:5, 9; 3:7; 8:8
His life miraculously preserved when he made a favorable report about the land: Numbers 14:10
Promises to: Joshua 1:5–9
Leads the people into the land of Canaan: Joshua 1–4; Acts 7:45; Hebrews 4:8
Renews circumcision of the children of Israel; reestablishes the Passover; has a vision of the angel of God: Joshua 5
Besieges and captures Jericho: Joshua 6
Captures Ai: Joshua 7–8
Makes a treaty with the Gibeonites: Joshua 9:3–27
The kings of the six nations of the Canaanites band together against him: Joshua 9:1–2
The six kings make war on the Gibeonites; are defeated and killed: Joshua 10
Defeats seven other kings: Joshua 10:28–43
Conquers Hazor: Joshua 11
Completes the conquest of the whole land: Joshua 11:23
List of the kings whom Joshua struck down: Joshua 12
Allots the land: Joshua 13–19
Sets up the tabernacle at Shiloh: Joshua 18:1
Sets apart several cities of refuge: Joshua 20
Cities for the Levites: Joshua 21
Exhortation of, before his death: Joshua 23–24
Survives the Israelites who refused to enter the Promised Land: Numbers 26:63–65
His part of the land: Joshua 19:49–50

Death and burial of: Joshua 24:29–30
Esteem with which he was held: Joshua 1:16–18
Faith of: Joshua 6:16
Military genius of, as exhibited
  at the defeat of the Amalekites: Exodus 17:13
  at Ai: Joshua 8
  at Gibeon: Joshua 10
  at Hazor: Joshua 11
Age of, at death: Judges 2:8

RAHAB

Significance in summary

A prostitute who lived in Jericho and helped Israel's spies; an ancestor of Jesus Christ

Meaning of name

insolence, pride, violence

Bible dictionary/encyclopedia entry (IBD)

A poetical name applied to Egypt in Psalms 87:4; 89:10; Isaiah 51:9, as "the proud one." Rahab (Heb. *Rahab*; i.e., "broad," "large").

When the Hebrews were camped at Shittim, in the "Arabah" or Jordan valley opposite Jericho, ready to cross the river, Joshua, as a final preparation, sent out two spies to "spy the land." After five days they returned, having swum across the river, which at this season, the month Abib, overflowed its banks from the melting of the snow on Lebanon. The spies reported back (Josh. 2:1–7). They had been exposed to danger in Jericho, and had been saved by the faithfulness of Rahab the prostitute, to whose house they had gone for protection. When the city of Jericho fell (6:17–25), Rahab and her whole family were preserved in line with the promise of the spies, and joined the Jewish people. She afterwards became the wife of Salmon, a prince from the tribe of Judah (Ruth 4:21; 1 Chron. 2:11; Matt. 1:5).

"Rahab's being asked to bring out the spies to the soldiers (Josh. 2:3) sent for them, is in strict keeping with Eastern manners, which would not permit any man to enter a woman's house without her permission. The fact of her covering the spies with bundles of flax which lay on her house-roof (2:6) is an 'undesigned coincidence' which strictly corroborates the narrative. It was the time of the barley harvest, and flax and barley are ripe at the same time in the Jordan valley, so that the bundles of flax stalks might have been expected to be drying just then" (Geikie's *Hours*, ii., 390).

Bible study on the life of Rahab (NTB)

Assists the spies of the Israelites: Joshua 2
Is spared when the Israelites captured Jericho: Joshua 6:17–25
An ancestor of Joseph of Nazareth: Matthew 1:5
The faith of, commended: Hebrews 11:31; James 2:25

JABIN I

Significance in summary

A king of Hazor whom Joshua defeated

Meaning of name

intelligent, discerning

Bible study on the life of Jabin (NTB)

Name of two kings of Hazor: Joshua 11:1–14; Judges 4:2, 7, 17, 23–24; Psalm 83:9

CALEB

Significance in summary

One of the spies sent out by Moses to view the Promised Land

Meaning of name

dog

Bible dictionary/encyclopedia entry (ISBE)

The son of Jephunneh, occurs in the story of the spies (Numbers 13). He represents the tribe of Judah as its prince (Num. 13:6; compare Num. 13:2). While the majority of the men sent out by Moses bring back a very negative report, Caleb and Hoshea, or Joshua, the son of Nun, are the only people to support the idea to invade the Promised Land (Num. 13:30; 14:6). Accordingly, these two alone are allowed to survive (Num. 14:38; 32:12). After the conquest and distribution of the land by Joshua, Caleb reminds the leader of the promise made by God through Moses, and so he receives Hebron as an inheritance for himself and his descendants (Josh. 14:6–15) after driving out the Anakim (Josh.

15:14). In the parallel account in Judges 1:8, the dispossession of the Canaanite inhabitants of Hebron is ascribed to Judah (Judg. 1:10). Both accounts agree in mentioning Othniel, a younger brother of Caleb, as the conqueror of Kiriath-sepher or Debir; as his reward he receives the hand of Achsah, Caleb's daughter. Achsah is given by her father part of the south land; but, in response to her request, she is given a more fruitful site with flowing springs (Josh. 15:15–19; Judg. 1:12–15).

Nabal, with whom David had an encounter, is called a Calebite, i.e., one belonging to the house of Caleb (1 Sam. 25:3).

Bible study on the life of Caleb (NTB)

One of the two survivors of the Israelites permitted to enter the land of promise: Numbers 14:30, 38; 26:63–65; 32:11–13; Deuteronomy 1:34–36; Joshua 14:6–15
Sent to Canaan as a spy: Numbers 13:6
Brings favorable report: Numbers 13:26–30; 14:6–9
Assists in dividing Canaan: Numbers 34:19
Life of, miraculously saved: Numbers 14:10–12
Leader of the Israelites after Joshua's death: Judges 1:11–12
Age of: Joshua 14:7–10
Inheritance of: Joshua 14:6–15; 15:13–16
Descendants of: 1 Chronicles 4:15

ACHAN

Significance in summary

Stole part of the spoil from Jericho

Meaning of name

troubler

Bible dictionary/encyclopedia entry (SBD)

An Israelite from the tribe of Judah, who, when Jericho and all that it contained were accursed and devoted to destruction, secreted a part of the spoil in his tent. For this sin he was stoned to death with his whole family by the people, in a valley between Ai and Jericho, and their remains, together with his property, were burnt (Josh. 7:19–26). From this event the valley received the name of Achor (i.e., trouble).

Bible study on the life of Achan (NTB)

Sin and punishment of: Joshua 7; 22:20; 1 Chronicles 2:7

Israel's Judges

Othniel • Ehud • Eglon • Jael • Cushan-Rishathaim • Shamgar • Sisera • Barak • Jabin II • Deborah • Gideon (Jerubbaal) • Tola • Jair • Ibzan • Elon • Abdon • Samson • Manoah • Delilah • Jephthah • Abimelech

Introduction (SBD, CBC)

SBD

The judges were temporary and special deliverers, sent by God to deliver the Israelites from their oppressors. Their power usually only extended over a limited part of their country. They were, in the first place, leaders in war; secondly, they dispensed justice to their people. Even while Samuel's administration gave a more settled state of affairs in the south, that still left plenty of scope for the irregular exploits of judges like Samson to mount daring attacks on the armies of the hated and feared Philistines.

CBC

It is not possible to exactly determine the time when the reign of the judges began, or the precise length of all their reigns.

After the death of Joshua the children of Israel asked the Lord for a leader, and he gave them Judah (Judg. 1:1–2). Judah, subsequently, formed an alliance with Simeon, and a number of victories followed (Judg. 1:3–20). The other tribes, however, did not drive out the inhabitants of the land, but reduced them to tribute (Judg. 1:21–36).

The Lord destroyed the Canaanites because (a) the cup of their iniquity was full (Gen. 15:16), and (b) to fulfill His promise made to Abraham, Isaac, and Jacob (Deut. 7:1–5; 9:5).

After the people had failed to execute the Lord's vengeance on the inhabitants of Canaan, He sent an angel to them at Bochim, who reminded them of the commandments they had broken, and announced that their enemies would be thorns in their sides and that their gods would be a great hindrance to them. When the people heard this they lifted up their voices and wept (Judg. 2:1–5).

The people served the Lord all the days of Joshua and during the lives of his contemporaries who survived him; but after that generation died, they forsook the Lord and served Baal and Ashtaroth. The Lord delivered them into the hands of their enemies, but, when they cried to the Lord, He sent them judges to whom they paid only the tribute of temporary allegiance and obedience; and finally the Lord declared that He would not drive out their enemies before them (Judg. 2:6–23).

From this time on the children of Israel were surrounded by the Canaanites, Hittites, Amorites, Perizzites, Hivites, and Jebusites (Judg. 3:1–5). Subsequently they intermarried with these nations, contrary to the law of God (Deut. 7:1–6); they forgot the Lord their God, and served Baalim and the groves (Judg. 3:6–7).

OTHNIEL

Significance in summary

Israel's first judge

Meaning of name

God is might

Bible dictionary/encyclopedia (CBC)

The anger of the Lord was roused against Israel, and he sold them into the hands of Chushan-rishathaim, king of Mesopotamia, and they served him eight years. They cried to the Lord, and He raised up Othniel, the son of Kenaz, who delivered them from their oppressor, and the land had rest forty years (Judg. 3:8–11).

Bible study on the life of Othniel (NTB)

Son of Kenaz and nephew of Caleb; conquers Kirjath-sepher, and as reward receives Caleb's daughter as a wife: Joshua 15:16–20; Judges 1:12–13
Becomes the deliverer and leader of Israel: Judges 3:8–11
Death of: Judges 3:11
Descendants of: 1 Chronicles 4:13–14

EHUD

Significance in summary

Israel's second judge, who killed King Eglon of Moab

Bible dictionary/encyclopedia (CBC)

After the death of Othniel, the children of Israel fell into their evil ways, and the Lord allowed Eglon, king of Moab, to invade their territory, capture the city of palm trees, and rule Israel for eighteen years (Judg. 3:11–14). Feeling the iron heel of the despot, they cried to the Lord for help, and He raised up for them a deliverer in the person of Ehud, a Benjamite, who was well-known for being left-handed. By an extraordinary stratagem he took the life of the king, rallied his countrymen to Mount Ephraim, and led them in a triumphant march against their foes; and the land had rest for eighty years (Judg. 3:15–30).

Bible study on the life of Ehud (NTB)

A Benjamite, the assassin of Eglon: Judges 3:16

EGLON

Significance in summary

A king of Moab who harassed the Israelites for eighteen years; was assassinated by Ehud

Meaning of name

circle

Bible study on the life of Eglon (NTB)

King of Moab; assassinated by Ehud: Judges 3:12–30

JAEL

Significance in summary

Wife of Heber; assassinated Sisera, commander of the Canaanite army

Meaning of name

mountain goat

Bible dictionary/encyclopedia entry (IBD)

The wife of Heber the Kenite (Judg. 4:17–22). When the Canaanites were defeated by Barak, Sisera, the captain of Jabin's army, fled and sought refuge with the friendly tribe of Heber, beneath the oaks of Zaanaim. As he arrived, Jael invited him to enter her tent. He did so, and as he lay exhausted on the floor he fell into a deep sleep. She took a mallet and drove a tent peg through his temples (Judg. 5:26–27). She then led Barak, who was in pursuit, into her tent, and showed him what she had done.

Bible study on the life of Jael (NTB)

Wife of Heber, and the one who killed Sisera: Judges 4:17–22; 5:6, 24

CUSHAN-RISHATHAIM

Significance in summary

King of Mesopotamia who ruled over Israel for eight years during the time of the judges

Bible study on the life of Cushan-Rishathaim (NTB)

King of Mesopotamia: Judges 3:8–10

SHAMGAR

Significance in summary

Israel's third judge

Bible dictionary/encyclopedia entry (CBC)

Shamgar was well-known for killing six hundred Philistines with an ox goad, and delivering Israel (Judg. 3:31).

Bible study on the life of Shamgar (NTB)

A deliverer of Israel: Judges 3:31; 5:6

SISERA

Significance in summary

Commander of the Canaanite army who was assassinated by Jael

Bible dictionary/encyclopedia entry (IBD)

The captain of Jabin's army (Judg. 4:2), which was routed and destroyed by the army of Barak on the plain of Esdraelon. After all was lost he fled to the settlement of Heber the Kenite in the plain of Zaanaim. Jael, Heber's wife, received him into her tent with apparent hospitality, and "gave him butter" (i.e., *lebben*, or curdled milk) "in a lordly dish." Having drunk the refreshing beverage, he lay down, exhausted, and soon sank into a deep sleep. While he lay asleep Jael killed him with a tent peg. Part of Deborah's song (Judg. 5:24–27) refers to the death of Sisera.

Bible study on the life of Sisera (NTB)

Captain of a Canaanite army, defeated by Barak; killed by Jael: Judges 4; 5:20–31; 1 Samuel 12:9; Psalm 83:9

BARAK

Significance in summary

Deborah's military leader who defeated the Canaanites and their stranglehold on Israel

Meaning of name

lightning

Bible dictionary/encyclopedia entry (IBD)

The son of Abinoam (Judg. 4:6). At the summons of Deborah he fought against Jabin. She accompanied him into the battle, and gave the signal for the little army to make the attack in which the troops of Jabin were completely routed. The battle was fought (Judg. 4:16) in the plain of Jezreel. This deliverance of Israel is commemorated in Judges 5. Barak's faith is commended (Heb. 11:32). The character of Barak, though pious, does not seem to have been heroic. Like Gideon, and in a sense Samson, he is an illustration of the words in Hebrews 11:34, "Out of weakness were made strong."

Bible study on the life of Barak (NTB)

A judge in Israel: Judges 4–5; Hebrews 11:32

JABIN II

Significance in summary

King of Hazor whom Deborah defeated

Meaning of name

intelligent, discerning

Bible study on the life of Jabin (NTB)

Name of two kings of Hazor: Joshua 11:1–14; Judges 4:2, 7, 17, 23–24; Psalm 83:9

DEBORAH

Significance in summary

Israel's only woman judge

Meaning of name

honeybee

Bible dictionary/encyclopedia entry (SBD)

A prophetess who judged Israel (Judges 4–5). She lived under the palm tree of Deborah between Ramah and Bethel in Mount Ephraim (Judg. 4:5), which, as palm trees were rare in Palestine, "is mentioned as a well-known and solitary landmark." She was probably from Ephraim. Lapidoth was probably her husband, and not Barak as some say. She was not so much a judge as one gifted with prophetic command (Judg. 4:6, 14; 5:7) and by virtue of her inspiration "a mother in Israel." The tyranny of Jabin, a Canaanite king, was peculiarly felt in the northern tribes, who were near his capital and under her jurisdiction. Under her direction Barak encamped on the broad summit of Tabor. Deborah's prophecy was fulfilled (Judg. 4:9), and the enemy's general Sisera perished among the "oaks of the wanderers" (Zaanaim), in the tent of the Bedouin Kenite's wife (Judg. 4:21) in the northern mountains. Deborah's title of "prophetess" includes the notion of inspired poetry (as in Exod. 15:20), and in this sense the glorious triumphal ode, Judges 5, well vindicates her claim to the office.

Bible study on the life of Deborah (NTB)

The prophetess, a judge of Israel: Judges 4:4–5; 5:7
Inspires Barak to defeat Sisera: Judges 4:6–16
The triumphant song of: Judges 5

GIDEON (Jerubbaal)

Significance in summary

A fifth judge of Israel; defeated the Midianites

Meaning of name

great warrior

Bible dictionary/encyclopedia entry (IBD)

Gideon, also called Jerubbaal (Judg. 6:29, 32), was the first of the judges whose life is recorded at length, (Judges 6–8). His calling coincides with the beginning of the second dynasty of the history of the judges. After the victory won by Deborah and Barak over Jabin, Israel once more sank into idolatry, and the Midianites and Amalekites, with other "children of the east," crossed the Jordan each year for seven successive years to plunder the land. Gideon received a direct call from God to deliver the land from these warlike invaders.

He was from the family of Abiezer (Josh. 17:2; 1 Chron. 7:18), and from the little township of Ophrah (Judg. 6:11). First, with ten of his servants, he overthrew the altars of Baal and cut down the asherah there, and then he blew the trumpet to sound the alarm. Twenty-two thousand men flocked to his standard on the crest of Mount Gilboa. They were, however, reduced to only three hundred. These men, armed with torches and jars and trumpets, rushed in from three different points on the camp of Midian at midnight, in the valley to the north of Moreh, with the war cry, "For the Lord and for Gideon" (Judg. 7:18 RSV). Terror-stricken, the Midianites were in total confusion, and in the darkness killed one another, so that only fifteen thousand out of the great army of one hundred and twenty thousand escaped alive. The memory of this great deliverance impressed itself deeply on the mind of the nation (1 Sam. 12:11; Ps. 83:11; Isa. 9:4; 10:26; Heb. 11:32). The land now had rest for forty years. Gideon died at a good old age, and was buried in the sepulcher of his fathers.

Soon after his death a change came over the people. They again forgot Jehovah, and turned to the worship of Baalim, "neither shewed they kindness to the house of Jerubbaal" (Judg. 8:35). Gideon left behind him seventy sons, a feeble, sadly degenerated race, with one exception, that of Abimelech, who seems to have had much of the courage and energy of his father, yet of restless and unscrupulous ambition. He gathered around him a group of people who killed all Gideon's sons on one stone, except Jotham.

Bible study on the life of Gideon (NTB)

Call of, by an angel: Judges 6:11, 14
His excuses: Judges 6:15
Promises of the Lord to: Judges 6:16
Angel attests the call to, by miracle: Judges 6:21–24
He destroys the altar of Baal, and builds one to the Lord: Judges 6:25–27
His prayer tests: Judges 6:36–40
Leads an army against and defeats the Midianites: Judges 6:33–35; 7; 8:4–12
Reproaches the Ephraimites for not joining in the campaign against the Midianites: Judges 8:1–3
Avenges himself on the people of Succoth: Judges 8:14–17
Israel desires to make him king; he refuses: Judges 8:22–23
Makes an ephod which becomes a snare to the Israelites: Judges 8:24–27
Had seventy sons: Judges 8:30
Death of: Judges 8:32
Faith of: Hebrews 11:32

TOLA

Significance in summary

The sixth judge of Israel; served for twenty-three years

Meaning of name

worm; grub; scarlet

Bible study on the life of Tola (NTB)

Judge of Israel: Judges 10:1–2

JAIR

Significance in summary

The seventh judge of Israel; served for twenty-two years

Meaning of name

my light; who diffuses light

Bible study on the life of Jair (NTB)

Judge of Israel: Judges 10:3–5

IBZAN

Significance in summary

The ninth judge of Israel; served for seven years

Meaning of name

father of a target; father of coldness

Bible study on the life of Ibzan (NTB)

Judge of Israel: Judges 12:8–10

ELON

Significance in summary

The tenth judge of Israel; served for ten years

Meaning of name

oak; grove; strong

Bible study on the life of Elon (NTB)

Judge of Israel: Judges 12:11–12

ABDON

Significance in summary

The eleventh judge of Israel; served for eight years

Meaning of name

servant; cloud of judgment

Bible study on the life of Abdon (NTB)

Judge of Israel: Judges 12:13–15

SAMSON

Significance in summary

Israel's most famous judge

Meaning of name

distinguished

Bible dictionary/encyclopedia entry (ISBE)

Samson was a judge, perhaps the last before Samuel. His home was near Bethshemesh, which means "house of the sun." He was a Nazirite from the tribe of Dan (Judg. 13:5); a man of prodigious strength, a giant and a gymnast—the Hebrew Hercules, a strange champion for Yahweh! He hated the Philistines, who had oppressed Israel for some forty years (Judg. 13:1), and was willing to fight them alone. He seems to have been actuated by little less than personal vengeance, yet in the New Testament he is named among the heroes of faith (Heb.11:32), and was in no ordinary sense an Old Testament worthy. He was good-natured, sarcastic, full of humor, and fought with his wits as well as with his fists. Milton has graphically portrayed his character in his dramatic poem *Samson Agonistes* (1671), on which Handel built his oratorio *Samson* (1743).

The story of Samson's life is unique among the biographies of the Old Testament. It is related in Judges 13–16. Like Isaac, Samuel, and John the Baptist, he was a child of prayer (13:8, 12). To Manoah's wife the angel of Yahweh appeared twice (13:3, 9), directing that the child which would be born to them would be a Nazirite from the womb, and that he would "begin to save Israel out of the hand of the Philistines" (13:5, 7, 14). The spirit of Yahweh first began to move him in Mahaneh-dan, between Zorah and Eshtaol (13:25). On his arriving at manhood, five remarkable circumstances are recorded of him.

1. His marriage with a Philistine woman of Timnah (Judges 14). His parents objected to the alliance (Judg. 14:3), but Samson's motive in marrying her was that he "sought an occasion against the Philistines." At the wedding feast Samson propounded to his guests a riddle, stat-

ing that if they guessed its answer he would give them thirty changes of raiment.

The Philistines threatened the life of his bride, and she in turn wrung from Samson the answer.

In revenge, Samson went down to Ashkelon, killed thirty men, and paid his debt; he even went home without his wife, and her father, to save her from shame, gave her to Samson's "best man" (Judg. 14:20). Not knowing this, Samson went down to Timnah to visit her, with a kid; when he discovered that he had been taken advantage of, he caught three hundred jackals, and put firebrands between every two tails, and burned up the grain fields and olive yards of the Philistines. The Philistines, however, showed they could play with fire too and burned his wife and her father. Samson smote the Philistines in revenge, "hip and thigh" (Judg. 15:1–8).

2. When he escaped to Etam, an almost vertical rock cliff in Judah not far from Zorah, Samson's home, the Philistines invaded Judah, encamped at Lehi above Etam, and demanded the surrender of their archenemy. The men of Judah were willing to hand Samson over to the Philistines, and went down to Etam, bound Samson, and brought him up where the Philistines were camped (Judg. 15:9–13). When Samson came to Lehi the Philistines shouted as they met him; the spirit of Yahweh came mightily on him, so that he broke loose from the two new ropes with which the three thousand men of Judah had bound him. Seizing a fresh jawbone of an ass he killed one thousand of the Philistines. At the same time, Samson reverently gave Yahweh the glory of his victory (Judg. 15:18). Samson being thirsty, Yahweh provided water for him (Judg. 15:17–19).

3. Samson next went down to Gaza, to the very stronghold of the Philistines, their chief city. There he saw a prostitute, and, his passions not being under control, he went in to her. It soon became known that Samson, the Hebrew giant, was in the city. So, the Philistines laid in wait for him. But Samson got up at midnight and took hold of the doors of the gate and their two posts, and carried them a quarter of a mile up to the top of the mountain that overlooks Hebron (Judg. 16:1–3).

4. From Gaza Samson went to the valley of Sorek where he fell in love with another Philistine woman, named Delilah, through whose machinations he lost his spiritual power. The Philistine lords bribed her with a very large sum of money to deliver him into their hands. Three times Samson deceived her about the secret of his strength, but eventually he explains that he is a Nazirite, and that his hair, which has never been cut, is the secret of his extraordinary power. Thus, Samson fell. By disclosing to Delilah this secret, he broke his covenant vow, and the Spirit of God departed from him (Judg. 16:4–20). The Philistines

took hold of him, put out his eyes, brought him down to Gaza, bound him in chains, and forced him to grind in the prison house.

5. The final incident recorded of Samson is in connection with a great sacrificial feast the Philistine lords gave in honor of Dagon, their god. They called for Samson to play the buffoon, and by his pranks to entertain the assembled multitude. The house of Dagon was full of people; about three thousand were on the roof looking down as Samson was paraded around. With the new growth of his hair his strength had returned to him. The disabled giant longed to be avenged on his adversaries for his blindness (Judg. 16:28). He prayed, and Yahweh heard his prayer. Guided by his attendant, he took hold of the wooden posts of the two middle pillars on which the portico of the house rested, and slipping them off their pedestals, caused the house to fall on all the people there. "So the dead which he slew at his death were more than they which he slew in his life" (Judg. 16:30). His family came and carried him up and buried him near his boyhood home, between Zorah and Eshtaol, in the burial place of his father. "And he judged Israel twenty years" (Judg. 16:31).

The story of Samson is a faithful mirror of his times: "Every man did that which was right in his own eyes" (Judg. 17:6; 21:25). There was no king in those days, i.e., no central government. Each tribe was separately occupied, driving out their individual enemies. For forty years the Philistines had oppressed Samson's tribal compatriots. Their authority was also recognized by Judah (Judg. 14:4; 15:11). Samson was the hero of his tribe, and he received the local popularity which a man of extraordinary prowess would naturally be given.

There are many important lessons to learn from the hero's life: Samson was the object of parental solicitude from even before his birth; Manoah prayed for guidance in the training of his yet unborn child (Judg. 13:8). Whatever our estimate of his personality is, Samson was closely linked to the covenant.

He was endowed with the Spirit of Yahweh (Judg. 13:25; 14:6, 19; 15:14).

He also prayed, and Yahweh answered him, though in judgment (Judg. 16:30). Samson had spiritual power and performed feats an ordinary man would hardly perform. But he was unconscious of his high vocation. In a moment of weakness he yielded to Delilah and divulged the secret of his strength. He was careless about his personal endowment. He did not realize that physical endowments no less than spiritual are gifts from God, and that to retain them we must be obedient.

He was passionate and therefore weak. The animal part of his nature was never curbed, but rather ran unchained and free. Samson was a wild, self-willed man. Passion ruled. He could not resist the blandishments of women.

He brought about no permanent deliverance for Israel; he lacked the spirit of cooperation. He undertook a task far too great for even a giant single-handed. Yet, Samson paved the way for Saul and David. He began the deliverance of Israel from the Philistines. He must, therefore, be judged according to his times. In his days there was unrestrained, individual, independence on every side, each one doing as he pleased. Samson differed from his contemporaries in that he was a hero of faith (Heb. 11:32). He was a Nazirite, and therefore dedicated to God. He was given to revenge, yet he was ready to sacrifice himself in order that his own and his people's enemies might be overthrown. He was willing to lay down his own life for the sake of his fellow-tribesmen—not to save his enemies, however, but to kill them. (Compare Matt. 5:43; Rom. 5:10.)

Bible study on the life of Samson (NTB)

A judge (leader, hero) of Israel: Judges 16:31
A Danite, son of Manoah; miraculous birth of; a Nazirite from his mother's womb; the mother forbidden to drink wine or strong drink, or to eat any ceremonially unclean thing during pregnancy: Judges 13:2–7, 24–25
Desires a Philistine woman for his wife; kills a lion: Judges 14:1–7
His marriage feast and the riddle propounded: Judges 14:8–19
Kills thirty Philistines: Judges 14:19
Wife of, estranged: Judges 14:20; 15:1–2
Is avenged for the estrangement of his wife: Judges 15:3–8
His great strength: Judges 15:7–14; Hebrews 11:32
Kills one-thousand Philistines with the jawbone of a donkey: Judges 15:13–17
Miraculously supplied with water: Judges 15:18–19
Cohabits with Delilah, a prostitute; her machinations with the Philistines to overcome him: Judges 16:1–20
Is blinded by the Philistines and confined to hard labor in prison; pulls down the pillars of the temple, meets his death, and kills a multitude of his enemies: Judges 16:21–31; Hebrews 11:32

MANOAH

Significance in summary

Father of Samson

Meaning of name

rest

Bible study on the life of Manoah (NTB)

A Danite of Zorah and the father of Samson: Judges 13:2–24

DELILAH

Significance in summary

A Philistine woman who betrayed Samson

Meaning of name

small, dainty

Bible dictionary/encyclopedia entry (IBD)

A Philistine woman who lived in the valley of Sorek (Judg. 16:4–20). She was bribed by the "lords of the Philistines" to obtain from Samson the secret of his strength and the means of overcoming it (Judg. 16:4–18). She tried in vain on three occasions. On the fourth occasion she wrung it from him. She made him sleep on "her knees," and then called the man who was waiting to help her; he "cut off the seven locks of [Samson's] head," and so his "strength went from him."

Bible study on the life of Delilah (NTB)

Samson's mistress: Judges 16:4–18

JEPHTHAH

Significance in summary

An Israelite judge who sacrificed his daughter in order to keep a rashly made vow

Bible study on the life of Jephthah (NTB)

Illegitimate, and therefore not entitled to inherit his father's property: Judges 11:1–2
Escapes the violence of his half-brothers; lives in the land of Tob: Judges 11:3
Recalled from the land of Tob by the elders of Gilead: Judges 11:5
Made captain of the army: Judges 11:5–11
Made head of the land of Gilead: Judges 11:7–11

His message to the king of the Ammonites: Judges 11:12–28
Leads the army of Israel against the Ammonites: Judges 11:29–33
His rash vow concerning his daughter: Judges 11:31, 34–40
Falsely accused by the Ephraimites: Judges 12:1
Leads the army of the Gileadites against the Ephraimites: Judges 12:4
Leads Israel for six years, dies, and is buried in Gilead: Judges 12:7
Faith of: Hebrews 11:32

ABIMELECH

Significance in summary

One of Gideon's sons who murdered his two brothers in order to become king himself

Meaning of name

my father is king

Bible dictionary/encyclopedia entry (IBD)

A son of Gideon (Judg. 9:1), who was proclaimed king after the death of his father (Judg. 8:33–9:6). One of his first acts was to murder his brothers, seventy in all "on one stone," at Ophrah. Only one, named Jotham, escaped. Abimelech was an unprincipled, ambitious ruler, often engaged in war with his own subjects. When attacking the town of Thebez, which had revolted, he was wounded by a millstone, thrown by the hand of a woman from the wall above. Seeing that the wound was mortal, he asked his armor-bearer to run him through with his sword, so that it could not be said he had been killed by the hand of a woman (Judg. 9:50–57).

Bible study on the life of Abimelech (NTB)

Son of Gideon: Judges 8:31; 9; 2 Samuel 11:21

Ruth and Her Circle

Naomi • Elimelech • Mahlon •
Orpah • Kilion • Ruth • Boaz

Introduction (Adapted from Matthew Henry's Commentary)

This short history of the domestic affairs of one particular family follows the book of Judges, and the events related here happened at the time of the judges. It is placed before the books of Samuel, because it ends by introducing David. It does not record miracles, or laws, or wars or victories, but the affliction, and later, the comfort of Naomi, and the conversion of Ruth.

The book of Ruth has recorded how God cared for Ruth, which should lead us to acknowledge His providence in everything that happens to us (see 1 Samuel 2:7–8; Psalm 113:7–9). It also shows the ancestry of Christ, who descended from Ruth, and part of whose genealogy concludes the book, which is quoted in Matthew 1. We should remember that the book is set in Bethlehem, the city where our Redeemer was born.

NAOMI

Significance in summary
Ruth's mother-in-law

Meaning of name
my joy, pleasantness

Bible dictionary/encyclopedia entry (IBD)
The wife of Elimelech and mother-in-law of Ruth (Ruth 1:2, etc.; Ruth 2:1, etc.; Ruth 3:1; 4:3, etc.). The name is derived from a root signifying sweetness or pleasantness. Naomi left Judea with her husband and two sons in time of famine and went to the land of Moab. There her husband and sons died; on her return to Bethlehem she asked to be known as Mara, bitterness, instead of Naomi, sweetness.

ELIMELECH

Significance in summary
Naomi's husband

Meaning of name
God is king

MAHLON

Significance in summary
Ruth's first husband

ORPAH

Significance in summary
Naomi's daughter-in-law

KILION

Significance in summary
Orpah's husband

Meaning of name

pining

RUTH

Significance in summary

Widow of Mahlon, who later married Boaz; an ancestor of Jesus Christ

Meaning of name

companion

Bible dictionary/encyclopedia entry (SBD)

A Moabite woman, the wife, first of Mahlon, second of Boaz, the ancestress of David and Christ, and one of the four women named by Matthew in the genealogy of Christ. A severe famine in the land of Judah induced Elimelech, a native of Bethlehem, to emigrate into the land of Moab, with his wife, Naomi, and his two sons, Mahlon and Chilion. This was probably about the time of Gideon. At the end of ten years Naomi, now a widow and childless, having heard that there was plenty again in Judah, decided to return to Bethlehem, and her daughter-in-law Ruth returned with her. They arrived at Bethlehem just at the beginning of barley harvest, and Ruth, going out to glean, happened to go into the field of wheat owned by a wealthy man and a close relative of her father-in-law, Elimelech. When he learned who the stranger was, Boaz treated her with the utmost kindness and respect, and sent her home laden with corn which she had gleaned. Encouraged by this incident, Naomi instructed Ruth to ask Boaz to carry out the duty of her husband's close relative by purchasing the inheritance of Elimelech and having Ruth as his wife. Boaz took Ruth to be his wife, in the middle of the blessings and congratulations of their neighbors. Their son, Obed, was "the father of Jesse, who was the father of David."

Bible study on the life of Ruth (NTB)

The daughter-in-law of Naomi: Ruth 1:4
Her devotion to Naomi: Ruth 1:16–17; 1:6–18
Goes to Bethlehem: Ruth 1:19, 22
Gleans in the field of Boaz: Ruth 2:3
Receives kindness from Boaz: Ruth 2:4–17; 3:15

Under Naomi's instructions claims from Boaz the duty of a kinsman: Ruth 3:1–9
Marries Boaz: Ruth 4:9–13
Becomes an ancestor of Jesus: Ruth 4:13, 21–22

BOAZ

Significance in summary

Ruth's husband, King David's great-grandfather

Meaning of name

strength or quickness

Bible dictionary/encyclopedia entry (SBD)

A wealthy Bethlehemite relative of Elimelech, the husband of Naomi. He married Ruth and redeemed the estate of her deceased husband Mahlon (Ruth 4:1). Boaz is mentioned in the genealogy of Christ (Matt. 1:5).

Samuel and the First King

Samuel • Hannah • Elkanah • Eli • Hophni • Phinehas, Eli's son • Saul • Kish • Ziba • Merab • Rizpah

Introduction (IBD)

Samuel was a great statesman as well as a reformer, and people looked up to him as the "seer," the prophet of the Lord. When he was an old man, the elders of Israel came to him at Ramah (1 Sam. 8:4–5, 19–22). They felt that their nation was exposed to great danger by the misbehavior of Samuel's sons, whom Samuel had appointed as his assistants, and by a threatened invasion from the Ammonites. So they demanded that they should have their own king to rule over them, just as the other nations had. This request displeased Samuel. He argued with them, and warned them of the consequences of such a step. Eventually, however, referring the matter to God, he acceded to their desires, and anointed Saul to be their king (11:15). Before retiring from public life Samuel convened an assembly of the people at Gilgal (chapter 12), and there spoke to them about him being their judge and prophet.

SAMUEL

Significance in summary

Israel's last judge and first prophet

Meaning of name

asked of God

Bible dictionary/encyclopedia entry (CBC)

Samuel was the thirteenth judge of Israel (1 Sam. 1:15–17). At the time of his birth the condition of Israel was deplorable; there was no recognized leader, and every man did that which was right in his own eyes (Judg. 21:25; 1 Sam. 4:1–28).

Samuel was the son of Elkanah and Hannah, who lived at Ramathaim-zophim, near Mount Ephraim. Shiloh was still the center of the national worship. Elkanah and his family were devout servants and worshippers of God, and they attended the annual feasts required by the law of Moses (Exod. 22:15–17; 1 Sam. 1:1–3). Hannah was very upset by Elkanah's other wife, Peninnah, who was continually reminding her of her barrenness. Hannah was so troubled that she refused to participate in the festivities, and in the bitterness of her soul she wept and prayed to God. She vowed that if the Lord would look on her affliction and grant her a male child, she would devote him to the Lord all the days of her life, and no razor should come on his head (Num. 6:1–21; 1 Sam. 1:4–11).

Eli, the priest, observed her as she was praying to the Lord and accused her of drunkenness; after she explained her condition to him, he told her to go in peace and asked the Lord to grant her the blessing she had asked. She returned with her husband to her home. The Lord remembered her, and she bore a son; she named him Samuel because she had asked and received him of the Lord. When the child was weaned, she took him, with an appropriate sacrifice, and presented him to the Lord according to her vow (1 Sam. 1:12–28). After this she poured out her soul in thanksgiving to the Lord (1 Sam. 2:1–10).

His early life was spent at Shiloh in the service of the Lord (1 Sam. 2:11). At this time the worship of God had been neglected and dishonored to such an extent that the people neglected the sacrifices required by the law (1 Sam. 2:12–17). Eli's sons, Hophni and Phinehas, were profligate and worthless, and towards the end of their father's life disgraced themselves by sleeping with the women who served at the entrance to the tent of meeting. Eli heard of this and only rebuked his sons mildly for it, and therefore the sons continued in their old ways

(1 Sam. 2:23–25). In the meantime Samuel grew in favor with God and men (1 Sam. 2:26). During these troubled times a man of God came to Eli and predicted the destruction and disgrace of Eli's house (1 Sam. 2:27–36).

Samuel's tribal relation is not very clearly established, but his life's work indicates that he was a Levite (Num. 1:51; 16:40; 1 Sam. 3:1–10).

Samuel continued to minister to the Lord before Eli the priest, but the word of the Lord was rare in those days, there being no open vision. Then, one night the Lord called him, and at the command of Eli, he replied reverently, submitting to the will of the Lord (1 Sam. 3:1–10). The Lord revealed to Samuel the destiny of Eli and his house, and the next morning he told everything to the priest, who expressed his submission to the will of the Lord (1 Sam. 3:11–18).

The young man grew in public esteem, the Lord was true to His word, and all Israel from Dan to Beersheba recognized him as a prophet of the Lord, and the Lord continued to reveal Himself to him in Shiloh (1 Sam. 3:19–21).

The Philistines invaded the land and camped in Aphek, and the children of Israel were camped at Ebenezer. In the battle that followed, Israel suffered an inglorious defeat (1 Sam. 4:1–2). When the people returned to the camp, they decided to send to Shiloh for the ark of the covenant and carry it on the field of battle. When the ark was brought into camp, a great shout went up from the people which sent terror to the hearts of the enemy, but they rallied their warriors by an appeal to their manhood, and by assuring them that in the event of defeat, they would be enslaved by the Hebrews (1 Sam. 4:3–9). The battle was engaged, Israel was defeated, the ark of God was taken by the Philistines, and the two wicked sons of Eli were killed (1 Sam. 4:10–11). When Eli heard of the disastrous result of the battle, he fell over and died; the wife of Phinehas gave birth to a son and with her last breath named him Ichabod, signifying that the glory had departed from Israel (1 Sam. 4:12–22). The victorious Philistines carried the ark in triumph to Ashdod and placed it next to their god Dagon. Disaster and death followed, until, after seven months, they returned it to Israel (1 Sam. 5:1–7:2).

Soon after the return of the ark, Samuel again appeared and inaugurated a reformation that amounted to a revolution in its far-reaching effects. All Israel assembled at Mize, and they drew water and poured it out before the Lord, fasted, acknowledged their sins, and Samuel judged the people (1 Sam. 7:3–6). When the Philistines heard that they were gathered at Mize, they went up to attack them, and the people, in great fear, asked Samuel to pray constantly for them (1 Sam. 7:7, 8). Samuel presented a burnt offering to the Lord and cried to Him for Israel; He answered by sending a terrific thunderstorm, which frightened the Philistines. The men of Israel pursued the fleeing soldiers, and great destruction followed (1 Sam. 7:9–11). Samuel set up a monument of this victory between Mize and Shen and called it Ebenezer, declaring that up to that point the Lord had been their helper (1 Sam. 7:12). After the subjection of the Philistines, Samuel judged Israel and went on tour from year to year to Bethel, Gilgal, Mize, and Ramah, his home, where he built an altar to the Lord (1 Sam. 7:13–17).

By the destruction of the Egyptians, the Lord designed to make His power known to all people of the earth (Exod. 9:16; 14:4). That this purpose was accomplished is evident from the fact that the people of Canaan had heard of this destruction at the time the Hebrews entered the land and were afraid (Josh. 2:8–11); also the Philistines, in the days of Samuel, were well acquainted with the fact of the destruction of the Egyptians (1 Sam. 4:7–8).

The people who possessed the prophetic gift before Samuel were: Enoch (Gen. 5:22–24; Jude 14), Noah (Gen. 9:24–27), Abram (Gen. 20:1–7), Jacob (Gen. 49:1–33), Joseph (Gen. 50:24–26), Aaron (Exod. 7:1), Miriam (Exod. 15:20), the seventy elders (Num. 11:25), Balaam (Num. 21:17), Moses (Deut. 34:10), and Deborah (Judg. 4:4).

Bible study on the life of Samuel (NTB)

Miraculous birth of: 1 Samuel 1:7–20
Consecrated to God before his birth: 1 Samuel 1:11, 22, 24–28
His mother's song of thanksgiving: 1 Samuel 2:1–10
Ministered in the house of God: 1 Samuel 2:11, 18–19
Blessed of God: 1 Samuel 2:21; 3:19
His vision concerning the house of Eli: 1 Samuel 3:1–18
A prophet of the Israelites: 1 Samuel 3:20–21; 4:1
A judge (leader) of Israel, his judgment seat at Bethel, Gilgal, Mize, and Ramah: 1 Samuel 7:15–17
Organizes the tabernacle service: 1 Chronicles 9:22; 26:28; 2 Chronicles 35:18
Israelites repent because of his reproofs and warnings: 1 Samuel 7:4–6
The Philistines defeated through his intercession and sacrifices: 1 Samuel 7:7–14
Makes his corrupt sons judges in Israel: 1 Samuel 8:1–3
People desire a king; he protests: 1 Samuel 8:4–22
Anoints Saul to be king of Israel: 1 Samuel 9:10
Renews the kingdom of Saul: 1 Samuel 11:12–15
Reproves Saul; foretells that his kingdom will not continue: 1 Samuel 13:11–15; 15

Anoints David to be king: 1 Samuel 16
Shelters David while escaping from Saul: 1 Samuel 19:18
Death of; the lament for him: 1 Samuel 25:1
Called up by the witch of Endor: 1 Samuel 28:3–20
His integrity as a judge and ruler: 1 Samuel 12:1–5; Psalm 99:6; Jeremiah 15:1; Hebrews 11:32
Chronicles of: 1 Chronicles 29:29
Sons of: 1 Chronicles 6:28, 33
Called Shemuel: 1 Chronicles 6:33

HANNAH

Significance in summary

Samuel's mother

Meaning of name

grace

Bible dictionary/encyclopedia entry (SBD)

One of the wives of Elkanah, and mother of Samuel (1 Sam. 1:2). A hymn of thanksgiving for the birth of her son is in the form of prophetic poetry; its similarity to that of the Virgin Mary (compare 1 Sam. 2:1–10 with Luke 1:46–55) has been noticed. See also Psalm 113:1.

ELKANAH

Significance in summary

Hannah's husband

Meaning of name

God has taken possession

Bible study on the life of Elkanah (NTB)

Father of Samuel: 1 Samuel 1:1, 4, 8, 19, 21, 23; 2:11, 20; 1 Chronicles 6:27, 34

ELI

Significance in summary

A judge and priest in Israel who raised Samuel

Meaning of name

God is exalted

Bible dictionary/encyclopedia entry (SBD)

A descendant of Aaron through Ithamar, the youngest of his two surviving sons (Lev. 10:1–2, 12; compare 1 Kings 2:27 with 2 Samuel 8:17 and 1 Chronicles 24:3). He was the first of the line of Ithamar who held the office of high priest. The office remained in his family until Abiathar was thrown out by Solomon (1 Kings 1:7; 2:26–27) when it reverted to the family of Eleazar in the person of Zadok (1 Kings 2:35). Its return to the elder branch was one part of the punishment to Eli during his lifetime for his negligence (1 Sam. 2:22–25), when his sons profaned the priesthood; compare 1 Samuel 2:27–36 with 1 Kings 2:27.

Despite this one great blemish, the character of Eli is marked by great piety, as is seen by his meek submission to divine judgment (1 Sam. 3:18) and his regard for the ark of God (1 Sam. 4:18). In addition to the office of high priest he was also a judge. He died at the age of 98 (1 Sam. 4:18), overcome by the disastrous news that the ark of God had been taken in battle by the Philistines, who had killed his sons Hophni and Phinehas.

Bible study on the life of Eli (NTB)

High priest: 1 Samuel 1:25; 2:11; 1 Kings 2:27
Judge of Israel: 1 Samuel 4:18
Misjudges and mistakenly rebukes Hannah: 1 Samuel 1:14
His benediction on Hannah: 1 Samuel 1:17–18; 2:20
Officiates when Samuel is presented at the tabernacle: 1 Samuel 1:24–28
Indulgent to his corrupt sons: 1 Samuel 2:22–25, 29; 3:11–14
His solicitude for the ark: 1 Samuel 4:11–18
Death of: 1 Samuel 4:18
Prophecies of judgments on his house: 1 Samuel 2:27–36; 3; 1 Kings 2:27

HOPHNI

Significance in summary

One of Eli's sons, and a priest at Shiloh

Bible study on the life of Hophni (NTB)

Son of Eli: 1 Samuel 1:3
Sin of: 1 Samuel 2:12–36; 3:11–14
Death of: 1 Samuel 4:4, 11, 17

PHINEHAS, Eli's son

Significance in summary

One of Eli's sons, and a priest at Shiloh

Meaning of name

mouth of brass

Bible dictionary/encyclopedia entry (IBD)

One of the sons of Eli, the high priest (1 Sam. 1:3; 2:12). He and his brother Hophni were guilty of great crimes, for which destruction came on the house of Eli (1 Sam. 2:31). He died in battle with the Philistines (1 Sam. 4:4, 11); his wife, on hearing of his death, gave birth to a son, whom she called Ichabod, and then she died (1 Sam. 4:19–22).

SAUL

Significance in summary

Israel's first king

Meaning of name

asked

Bible dictionary/encyclopedia entry (IBD)

The son of Kish (probably his only son, and a child of prayer, "asked for"), from the tribe of Benjamin, the first king of the Jewish nation. The singular providential circumstances linked with his election as king are recorded in 1 Samuel 8–10. His father's donkeys had strayed, and Saul was sent with a servant to find them. Leaving his home at Gibeah, Saul and his servant searched until they eventually came to the district of Zuph, near Samuel's home at Ramah (9:5–10). At this point Saul thought he would return after three days' fruitless search, but his servant suggested that they should first consult the "seer." Hearing that he was about to offer a sacrifice, the two went quickly into Ramah, and "behold, Samuel came out against them," on his way to the "bamah," i.e., the "height," where sacrifice was to be offered; and in reply to Saul's question, "Tell me, I pray thee, where the seer's house is," Samuel made himself known to him.

Samuel had been divinely prepared for Saul's coming (9:15–17), and received Saul as his guest. He took him with him to the sacrifice, and then after the feast "communed with Saul on the top of the house" of all that was in his heart. The next day Samuel "took a vial of oil and poured it on his head," and anointed Saul as king over Israel (9:25–10:8), giving him three signs in confirmation of his call to be king. When Saul reached his home in Gibeah the last of these signs was fulfilled; the Spirit of God came on him, and "he was turned into another man." The simple countryman was transformed into the king of Israel, and a remarkable change suddenly took place in his whole demeanor.

The link between Saul and Samuel was as then not known to the people. The "anointing" had been in secret. But now this had to be witnessed to so the nation became aware of it. So Samuel summoned the people to a solemn assembly "before the Lord" at Mize. Here the lot was drawn (10:17–27), and it fell on Saul; when he was presented before them, the stateliest man in all Israel, the cry for the first time in Israel went up: "God save the king!" He then returned to his home in Gibeah, in the company of a kind of bodyguard, "a band of men whose hearts God had touched." On reaching his home he dismissed them, and resumed the quiet work of his previous life.

Soon after this, on hearing of the conduct of Mahesh the Ammonite at Jabesh-gilead, an army from all the tribes of Israel rallied to him at Bezek, and he led them into battle, winning a decisive victory over the Ammonite invaders at Jabesh (11:1–11). He was now fully recognized as the king of Israel. Samuel officially anointed him as king at Gilgal (11:15). Although Samuel never ceased to be a judge in Israel, his work in that capacity practically came to an end.

Saul now undertook the great and difficult task of freeing the land from its hereditary enemies the Philistines, and so he collected an army of three thousand men (1 Sam. 13:1–2). The Philistines were camped at Geba. Saul, with two thousand men, occupied Michmash and Mount Bethel; his son Jonathan, with one thousand men, occupied Gibeah, to the south of Geba, and without any direction from his father "smote" the Philistines in Geba. Thus roused, the Philistines, who gathered an army of thirty thousand chariots and six thousand horsemen, camped in Michmash, which Saul had evacuated for Gilgal. Saul now waited for seven days in Gilgal before making any movement, as Samuel had advised (10:8), but becoming impatient, on the seventh day, made a burnt offering. Samuel appeared and warned him of the fatal consequences of his act of disobedience, for he had not waited long enough (13:13–14).

When Saul, after Samuel had left, left from Gilgal with his six hundred men, his followers having decreased to that number (13:15), against the Philistines at Michmash, he had his headquarters under a pomegranate tree at Migron, near Michmash. Here at Gibeah-Geba Saul and his army rested, uncertain what to do. Jonathan became impatient and with his armor-bearer planned an assault against the Philistines, unknown to Saul and the army (14:1–15). Jonathan and his armor-bearer climbed to the top of the narrow rocky ridge called Bozez, where was the outpost of the Philistine army. They surprised and killed twenty of the Philistines. Immediately the whole Philistine army was thrown into disorder and fled in great terror; a supernatural panic seized the people. Saul and his six hundred men, a band which speedily increased to ten thousand, seeing the confusion, pursued the army of the Philistines. While pursuing the Philistines, Saul rashly told the people, "Cursed be the man that eateth any food until evening." Though faint and weary, the Israelites "smote the Philistines that day from Michmash to Aijalon" (a distance of from fifteen to twenty miles).

Jonathan had, while passing through the wood in pursuit of the Philistines, tasted a little of the honeycomb which was abundant there (14:27). This was later discovered by Saul (v. 42), and he threatened to put his son to death. The people interposed, saying, "There shall not one hair of his head fall to the ground" (v. 45). He whom God had so signally owned, who had "wrought this great salvation in Israel," must not die. "Then Saul went up from following the Philistines: and the Philistines went to their own place" (1 Sam. 14:24–46); and thus the campaign against the Philistines came to an end. This was Saul's second great military success.

Saul's reign, however, continued to be one of almost constant war against his enemies (14:47–48), in all of which he proved victorious. The war against the Amalekites is the only one recorded at length (1 Samuel 15). These old (Exod. 17:8; Num. 14:43–45) enemies of Israel occupied the territory to the south and southwest of Palestine. Samuel summoned Saul to execute the "ban" which God had pronounced (Deut. 25:17–19) on this cruel and relentless foe of Israel. This command was "the test of his moral qualification for being king." Saul proceeded to execute the divine command; and gathering the people together, marched from Telaim (1 Sam. 15:4) against the Amalekites, destroying all that fell into his hands. He was, however, guilty of rebellion and disobedience in sparing Agag their king, and in conniving at his soldiers' sparing the best of the sheep and cattle; Samuel, following Saul to Gilgal, said to him, "Because thou hast rejected the word of the Lord, he hath also rejected thee from being king" (15:23). The kingdom was torn from Saul and was given to David, whom the Lord chose to be Saul's successor, and whom Samuel anointed (16:1–13). From that day "the Spirit of the Lord departed from Saul, and an evil spirit from the Lord troubled him" (v. 14).

David was now sent for as a "cunning player on an harp" (1 Sam. 16:16, 18) to play before Saul when the evil spirit troubled him, and thus was introduced to the court of Saul. He became a great favorite with the king. Then David returned to his father's house and to his vocation as a shepherd for perhaps three years. The Philistines once more invaded the land, and collected their army in Ephes-dammim, on the southern slope of the valley of Elah. Saul and the men of Israel went out to meet them, and camped on the northern slope of the same valley. It was here that David killed Goliath of Gath, the champion of the Philistines (17:4–54), an exploit which led to the flight and utter defeat of the Philistine army. Saul now took David permanently into his service (18:2); but he became jealous of him (v. 9), which showed itself in a number of attempts on David's life.

After some time the Philistines pitched their camp at Shunem, on the slope of Little Hermon; and Saul "gathered all Israel together," and "pitched in Gilboa" (1 Sam. 28:3–14). Being unable to discover the mind of the Lord, Saul, accompanied by two of his group, visited the "witch of Endor," some seven or eight miles away. Here he was overwhelmed by a communication from Samuel (vv. 16–19), who appeared to him. "He fell straightway all along on the earth, and was sore afraid, because of the words of Samuel" (v. 20). The Philistine host "fought against Israel: and the men of Israel fled from before the Philistines, and fell down slain in mount Gilboa" (31:1). In his despair at the disaster that had befallen his army, Saul "took a sword and fell on it." The next day the Philistines "found Saul and his three sons fallen in mount Gilboa." Having cut off his head, they sent it with his weapons to Philistia, and hung up the skull in the temple of Dagon at Ashdod. They suspended his headless body, with those of his sons, from the walls of Bethshan. The men of Jabesh-gilead afterwards removed the bodies from this position; and having burnt the flesh, they buried the bodies under a tree at Jabesh. The remains of Saul and Jonathan were, however, moved afterwards to the family sepulcher at Zelah (2 Sam. 21:13–14).

Bible study on the life of Saul (NTB)

A Benjamite, son of Kish: 1 Samuel 9:1–2
Sons of: 1 Chronicles 8:33
His personal appearance: 1 Samuel 9:2; 10:23
Made king of Israel: 1 Samuel 9; 10; 11:12–15; Hosea 13:11
Lives at Gibeah of Saul: 1 Samuel 14:2; 15:34; Isaiah 10:29
Defeats the Philistines: 1 Samuel 13; 14:46, 52
Strikes the Amalekites: 1 Samuel 15
Is reproved by Samuel for usurping the priestly functions: 1 Samuel 13:11–14
Samuel rebukes him for disobedience by not exterminating the Amalekites; the loss of his kingdom is foretold: 1 Samuel 15
Dedicates the spoils of war: 1 Samuel 15:21–25; 1 Chronicles 26:28
Sends messengers to Jesse, asking that David be sent to him as a musician and an armor-bearer: 1 Samuel 16:17–23
Defeats the Philistines after Goliath is killed by David: 1 Samuel 17
His jealousy of David; gives his daughter, Michal, to David to be his wife; becomes David's enemy: 1 Samuel 18
Tries to kill David; Jonathan intercedes and incurs his father's displeasure; David's loyalty to Jonathan; Saul's temporary remorse; prophesies: 1 Samuel 19
Hears Doeg against Ahimelech, and kills the priest and his family; pursues David to wilderness of Ziph; the Ziphites betray David to: 1 Samuel 23
Pursues David to En-gedi: 1 Samuel 24:1–6
His life spared by David: 1 Samuel 24:5–8
Saul's contrition for his bad faith: 1 Samuel 24:16–22
David is again betrayed to, by the Ziphites; Saul pursues him to the hill of Hachilah; his life spared again by David; his confession, and his blessing on David: 1 Samuel 26
Kills the Gibeonites; crime avenged by the death of seven of his sons: 2 Samuel 21:1–9
His kingdom invaded by Philistines; seeks counsel of the witch of Endor, who foretells his own death: 1 Samuel 28:3–25; 29:1
Is defeated, and is killed with some of his sons: 1 Samuel 31
Their bodies exposed in Beth-shan; rescued by the people of Jabesh and burned; bones of, buried under a tree at Jabesh: 1 Samuel 31; 2 Samuel 1–2; 1 Chronicles 10
His death is a judgment on account of his sins: 1 Chronicles 10:13

KISH

Significance in summary

Saul's father

Meaning of name

bow or power

Bible study on the life of Kish (NTB)

Father of Saul: 1 Samuel 9:1–3; 10:21; 2 Samuel 21:14
Called Cis (KJV): Acts 13:21

ZIBA

Significance in summary

King Saul's servant

Meaning of name

plant

Bible study on the life of Ziba (NTB)

His faithfulness to Mephibosheth: 2 Samuel 9
His faithfulness to David: 2 Samuel 16:1–4; 19:17, 26–29

MERAB

Significance in summary

King Saul's daughter, whom Saul promised in marriage to David, but was given in marriage to Adriel instead

Meaning of name

increase

Bible study on the life of Merab (NTB)

Daughter of King Saul: 1 Samuel 14:49
Betrothed to David by Saul: 1 Samuel 18:17–18
Given to Adriel for a wife: 1 Samuel 18:19

RIZPAH

Significance in summary

One of King Saul's concubines

Meaning of name

hot stone

Bible study on the life of Rizpah (NTB)

Concubine of Saul: 2 Samuel 3:7
Guards the bodies of her sons who were hanged on David's command: 2 Samuel 21:8–11

King David and His Circle

Jesse • Jonathan • Goliath • David • Doeg • Ahimaaz • Ahimelech • Nathan • Obed-edom • Hushai • Achish • Mephibosheth • Uzzah • Shimei • Jeduthun • Araunah (Ornan) • Asahel • Asaph • Eliab • Ittai • Hadadezer (Hadarezer) • Barzillai • Absalom • Tamar, Absalom's daughter • Michal • Bathsheba • Abishag • Abishai • Nabal • Joab • Tamar, David's daughter • Solomon • Uriah • Hiram, King of Tyre • Abigail • Adonijah • Rezon • Hiram, the craftsman • Ish-bosheth • Amnon • Abner • Ahithophel • Abiathar • Zadok

Introduction (IBD)

"The greatness of David was felt when he was gone. He had lived in harmony with both the priesthood and the prophets; a sure sign that the spirit of his rule had been throughly loyal to the higher aims of the theocracy. The nation had not been oppressed by him, but had enjoyed its ancient freedom. As far as his power went he had tried to act justly towards everyone (2 Sam. 8:15). His indulgence towards his sons, and his own great sin, had been bitterly atoned for, and were forgotten at his death when the great successes of his reign were recalled. He had reigned thirty-three years in Jerusalem and seven and a half at Hebron (2 Sam. 5:5). Israel at his accession had reached the lowest point of national depression; its new-born unity had been cut in two, and its territory had been attacked by the Philistines. But David bequeathed an imperial power to Solomon, which had imposing territories, like those of Egypt or Assyria. The throne was prepared for Solomon to succeed, before his father's death, and stretched from the Mediterranean to the Euphrates, and from the Orontes to the Red Sea" (Geikie's *Hours*).

JESSE

Significance in summary

Ruth and Boaz's grandson, and father of King David

Meaning of name

God exists

Bible dictionary/encyclopedia entry (SBD)

The wealthy father of David, he was the son of Obed, who was the fruit of the union of Boaz and the Moabitess Ruth. His great-grandmother was Rahab the Canaanite, of Jericho (Matt. 1:5). Jesse's genealogy is twice given in full in the Old Testament (see Ruth 4:18–22 and 1 Chronicles 2:5–12). He is often called "Jesse the Bethlehemite" (1 Sam. 16:1, 18; 17:58), but his full title is "the Ephrathite of Bethlehem Judah" (1 Sam. 17:12). He is an "old man" when we first meet him (1 Sam. 17:12), with eight sons (1 Sam. 16:10; 17:12), living in Bethlehem (1 Sam. 16:4–5). Jesse's wealth seems to have consisted of a flock of sheep and goats, which were under the care of David (1 Sam. 16:11; 17:34–35). After David's rupture with Saul David took his father and mother into the country of Moab and deposited them with the king, and there they disappear from our view in the records of Scripture.

Bible study on the life of Jesse (NTB)

Father of David: Ruth 4:17; 1 Samuel 17:12
Ancestor of Jesus: Matthew 1:5–6
Samuel visits, under divine command, to select a successor to Saul from his sons: 1 Samuel 16:1–13
Saul asks, to send David to become a member of his court: 1 Samuel 16:19–23
Sons in Saul's army: 1 Samuel 17:13–28
Lives with David in Moab: 1 Samuel 22:3–4
Descendants of: 1 Chronicles 2:13–17

JONATHAN

Significance in summary

King Saul's eldest son and David's best friend

Meaning of name

God is given

Bible dictionary/encyclopedia entry (CBC, IBD)

CBC

Jonathan, the son of Saul, was a valiant warrior (1 Sam. 13:4; 1 Sam. 14:1–16), but his name will forever live because of his love for David (1 Sam. 19:1–7; 1 Sam. 20:1–42).

IBD

The eldest son of king Saul, and the bosom friend of David. He is first mentioned when he was about thirty years old, some time after his father's accession to the throne (1 Sam. 13:2). Like his father, he was a man of great strength and activity (2 Sam. 1:23), and excelled in archery and slinging (1 Chron. 12:2; 2 Sam. 1:22). The affection that evidently existed between him and his father was interrupted by the growth of Saul's insanity. At length, "in fierce anger," he left his father's presence and threw in his lot with David's cause (1 Sam. 20:34). After an eventful career, interwoven to a great extent with David, he was killed, along with his father and his two brothers, at the battle of Gilboa (1 Sam. 31:2, 8). He was first buried at Jabesh-gilead, but his remains were later taken with those of his father to Zelah, in Benjamin (2 Sam. 21:12–14). His death was the occasion of David's famous elegy "the Song of the Bow" (2 Sam. 1:17–27). He left one son, five-year-old Merib-baal, or Mephibosheth (2 Sam. 4:4; compare 1 Chron. 8:34).

Bible study on the life of Jonathan (NTB)

Son of Saul: 1 Samuel 14:49
Victory of, over the Philistine garrison of Geba: 1 Samuel 13:3–4, 16
Victory of, over the Philistines at Michmash: 1 Samuel 14:1–18
Under Saul's curse pronounced against anyone who might eat before Saul finished his battle: 1 Samuel 14:24–30, 43
Rescued by the people: 1 Samuel 14:43–45
Love of, for David: 1 Samuel 18:1–4; 19:1–7; 20; 23:16–18
Killed in the battle with the Philistines: 1 Samuel 31:2, 6; 1 Chronicles 10:2; 2 Samuel 21:12–14
Buried by inhabitants of Jabesh-gilead: 1 Samuel 31:11–13

Mourned by David: 2 Samuel 1:12, 17–27
Son of, cared for by David: 2 Samuel 4:4; 9; 1 Chronicles 8:34

GOLIATH

Significance in summary

The giant killed by David

Meaning of name

soothsayer or an exile

Bible dictionary/encyclopedia entry (IBD)

A famous giant of Gath, who for forty days openly defied the armies of Israel, but was killed by David with a stone from a sling (1 Sam. 17:4). He was probably descended from the Rephaim who found refuge among the Philistines after they were dispersed by the Ammonites (Deut. 2:20–21). His height was "six cubits and a span," which, taking the cubit at twenty-one inches, is ten feet six inches. David cut off his head (1 Sam. 17:51) and brought it to Jerusalem, while he hung the armor he took from him in his tent. His sword was preserved at Nob as a religious trophy (21:9). David's victory over Goliath was the turning point in his life. He came into public notice now as the deliverer of Israel and the chief among Saul's men of war (18:5), and the devoted friend of Jonathan.

Bible study on the life of Goliath (NTB)

Defied armies of Israel and is killed by David: 1 Samuel 17; 21:9; 22:10
His sons: 2 Samuel 21:15–22; 1 Chronicles 20:4–8

DAVID

Significance in summary

Israel's second and greatest king

Meaning of name

beloved

Bible dictionary/encyclopedia entry (CBC)

After the death of Saul, David inquired of the Lord if he should go to any of the cities of Judah, and He told him to go to Hebron. He was accompanied by his two wives and the men who had been with him (2 Sam. 2:1–3). When he arrived the men of Judah anointed him king over Judah. They also informed him that the men of Jabesh-gilead had buried Saul, and he sent messengers to them, informing them that the house of Judah had made him king (2 Sam. 2:4–7).

Abner, the son of Ner, the captain of Saul's hosts, took Ish-bosheth, the son of Saul, brought him to Mahanaim and made him king over Israel, and he reigned two years. War followed, and the house of David became stronger while the house of Saul became weaker (2 Sam. 2:8–3:1). Finally Abner disagreed with Ish-bosheth and declared that he would transfer the kingdom to David. Abner, with twenty of his men, visited David at Hebron; the arrangement was ratified, and David sent Abner away in peace (2 Sam. 3:17–21). During the conference between David and Abner, Joab, the captain of David's men, was absent pursuing a troop. When Joab returned and discovered what had been done, he reproached the king, sent messengers after Abner, and on his return killed him (2 Sam. 3:22–27). David expressed great sorrow and indignation, declared that he and his kingdom were guiltless, and called Abner a great man and a prince in Israel (2 Sam. 3:28–39; 1 Chron. 2:16–17).

Ish-bosheth was murdered by two of his captains, Baanah and Rechab (2 Sam. 4:1–8). David had these men put to death (2 Sam. 4:9–12).

After the death of Ish-bosheth, all the tribes of Israel assembled at Hebron; David made an agreement with them before the Lord, and they anointed him king over Israel (2 Sam. 5:1–3).

Soon after this David, with his army, attacked Jerusalem and took the city (2 Sam. 5:4–7). David proclaimed throughout his army that the man who successfully attacked the Jebusites would be captain of his army (1 Chron. 11:6). The distinction was gained by Joab, and the king subsequently took up residence in the conquered city, improved it, and grew on in favor with God and man (2 Sam. 5:9–10; 1 Chron. 11:4–9).

Hiram, king of Tyre, sent messengers to David and building material, and built him a house, and David recognized the fact that the Lord was with him and that He had made him king for Israel's sake (2 Sam. 5:11–12).

David's prosperity was too great for his faith, consequently he flagrantly violated the law of God by having more concubines (Deut. 17:14–17; 2 Sam. 5:13–16).

When the Philistines heard of the anointing of David they invaded the land, but with the help of the Lord David won two great victories over them (2 Sam. 5:17–25).

David collected thirty thousand chosen men of Israel to take the ark of God from Kirjath-jearim to his own city. They placed the ark on a new cart, and the two sons of Abinadab, Uzzah and Ahio, drove the cart. The king and all the people expressed their joy by playing musical instruments (2 Sam. 6:1–9). When they came to Nachon's threshing floor, the oxen made the ark shake; Uzzah put out his hand to support it, and God struck him dead for his error (2 Sam. 6:7–8). David was displeased and frightened, and carried the ark into the house of Obed-edom, the Gittite, where it remained three months. David was informed that the Lord had blessed the house of Obed-edom (2 Sam. 6:12). He therefore prepared a place for the ark of God, and pitched a tent for it. He also followed the law of the Lord and had the ark of the covenant borne on the shoulders of the Levites (Num. 4:1–15; 7:9). The priests and Levites sanctified themselves, and the ark was transported according to the law of Moses (1 Chron. 15:14–15). The ark was placed where David had prepared. David celebrated the return of the ark by writing a psalm (1 Chron. 16:1–36).

After the arrival of the ark, David enjoyed a time of peace, and he was interested in building a house for the Lord. Nathan told David that God would not permit David to build Him a house, but assured him that when his days were fulfilled, He would raise up a son for him and establish his kingdom, and that he would build the house of the Lord.

David subsequently subdued the Philistines and Moabites, and won victories as far as the river Euphrates, thus fulfilling the Lord's promise to Abraham (Gen. 15:18; 2 Sam. 8:1–3). Numerous battles followed, in all of which David was victorious (2 Sam. 8:4–14).

In the days of David's prosperity, he asked if any were left from the house of Saul, as he wanted to show them kindness on account of Jonathan. Ziba told him of Mephibosheth, a crippled son of Jonathan. David called him, restored to him the land that belonged to his grandfather Saul, and invited him to be a permanent guest at the table of the king (2 Sam. 9:1–13).

At the beginning of another year, the king sent Joab and the army against the Ammonites. During the absence of the army, David committed adultery with Bathsheba, the wife of Uriah, the Hittite. Joab, on David's instructions, placed Uriah in a dangerous position, and he was killed (2 Sam. 11:1–17). As soon as Uriah's wife had ceased to mourn for her husband David brought her into his house; she became his wife and bore him a son.

David's actions displeased the Lord (2 Sam. 11:18–27), and He sent Nathan the prophet to him, who, with a clever parable, made him condemn and pass the death sentence on himself (2 Sam. 12:1–7). The prophet predicted that the sword would never depart from the house because he had taken the wife of Uriah to be his wife; he also predicted terrible calamities on his house (2 Sam. 12:7–12). The king acknowledged his sin, and the prophet assured him that he would not be put to death, but in view of the disgrace he had brought on his people, the child born to Bathsheba would die (2 Sam. 12:13–14). The child became dangerously sick, and his father fasted and prayed constantly until the baby died, after which David stopped fasting (2 Sam. 12:15–23). Subsequently Bathsheba bore David another son, and he named him Solomon, but Nathan the prophet called him Jedidiah (2 Sam. 12:24–25).

Joab fought until the royal city was overcome. He sent a message to the king requesting him to come and lead the final charge and receive the honor of the victory. He did this and took the king's crown; he enslaved the conquered people, and then returned to Jerusalem (2 Sam. 12:26–31).

In the fulfillment of the prediction of Nathan the prophet (2 Sam. 12:7–11), trouble began to arise in the king's family; Amnon defiled his sister Tamar and was killed for his crime by his brother Absalom, who was forced to flee from home and live in Geshur (2 Sam. 13:1–38). David longed to see Absalom (2 Sam. 13:39), and Joab, by a clever trick, procured the king's consent for his return to his native land, but the king refused to meet him face–to-face until after two years, when they met in love and peace (2 Samuel 14).

After this Absalom lived in royal splendor and inaugurated a rebellion against his father (2 Sam. 12:7–11), through which the young and brilliant leader attracted many of the people and also David's distinguished counselor, Ahithophel the Gilonite (2 Sam. 15:1–12). A messenger came to David and informed him that the hearts of the men of Israel had turned to Absalom. He and his servants, therefore, fled from the city. The priests stayed loyal to David, and followed him with the ark of God, but he commanded them to return with it to Jerusalem. As David ascended Mount Olivet in great distress he heard that Ahithophel was among the conspirators with Absalom; he asked the Lord to turn the counsels of Ahithophel into foolishness (2 Sam. 15:30–31). When David arrived at the top of the mountain, he was met by Hushai the Archite. The king sent him back to the city with instructions to defeat, if possible, the counsels of Ahithophel, and told him to communicate the results to him by the sons of the priests, Ahimaaz and Jonathan (2 Sam. 15:32–37).

Absalom and his followers rallied in Jerusalem. Hushai also arrived there and proclaimed his allegiance to the new king. Ahithophel, in reply to Absalom's request, counseled him to defile his father's concubines, which he did, thus making a reconciliation impossible (2 Sam. 16:15–23). Ahithophel also proposed to choose an army of twelve thousand men, pursue David and kill him, and bring the people back to Absalom. This suggestion met with Absalom's approval and with the approval of all Israel, but Absalom called Hushai the Archite in order to hear what he had to say. Hushai declared that the counsel of Ahithophel was not good at that time; he also said that a very large army should be collected and war made on David and his followers until they were all defeated. Absalom and all the men of Israel declared that the counsel of Hushai was better than that of Ahithophel. The Lord was helping Hushai bring evil on Absalom (2 Sam. 17:1–14). When Hushai sent messengers to David informing him of the situation, David went to Mahanaim. After Ahithophel saw that his counsel was not accepted, he returned to his home, put his business in order, and hanged himself (2 Sam. 17:15–24).

Absalom crossed over Jordan with his army and pitched in the land of Gilead. David and his army were comforted and refreshed by Shobi, Machir, and Barzillai (2 Sam. 17:24–29). David hastily organized his army and placed Joab, Abishai, and Ittai at the heads of the three grand divisions. He commanded the leaders of the army to deal gently with the young man Absalom for his sake. The battle was fought in the wood of Ephraim, and ended in the death of Absalom and a great victory for the forces of David. The news of the victory was carried to the king, and he went up into the chamber over the gate and wept bitterly for his lost son (2 Sam. 18:4–33).

Joab was informed that David was weeping for his son, and all Israel mourned that day out of sympathy for the king. Joab approached the king while he was pouring out his soul in sorrow and rebuked him with great severity (2 Sam. 19:1–7). The king got up and sat in the gate, and the restoration of peace began.

Sometime later Sheba, the son of Bichri, a Benjamite, inaugurated what appeared to be a formidable rebellion. David commanded Amasa to assemble the army and suppress it, but he was not prompt in meeting the demands of the situation, so Joab was given command. Subsequently Joab murdered Amasa, and succeeded in suppressing the rebellion, after which he occupied his old position as captain of the king's forces (2 Sam. 20:1–26).

After the suppression of the rebellion the country experienced famine, which lasted for three years. The Lord informed David that it was because Saul had broken the covenant with the Gibeonites (Josh.

9:1–21). David asked the Gibeonites what would satisfy them, and they replied by asking for seven of the sons of Saul. This request was granted, and the seven men were executed. David also buried the remains of Saul and Jonathan; after that the Lord answered prayer on behalf of the land (2 Sam. 21:1–14).

The Philistines again fought against Israel, and in one of the battles the king came close to losing his life, but he was rescued by Abishai; the war resulted in the death of four of the champions of the Philistines (2 Sam. 21:15–22). David celebrated his great deliverances and his victories over his enemies with a psalm of thanksgiving (2 Samuel 22).

The Lord again became angry with Israel, and Satan provoked David to number the people (2 Sam. 24:1; 1 Chron. 21:1). Joab was delegated by the king to number the people, and despite his strong opposition to David's request, he was eventually compelled to submit. Joab and the captains of the army left, and returning after nine months and twenty days reported that, although the counting was still not finished, Judah and Israel numbered one million three hundred thousand (2 Sam. 24:1–9; 1 Chron. 21:1–8). David saw his mistake and prayed for forgiveness (2 Sam. 24:10; 1 Chron. 21:7–8). The Lord sent Gad, the seer, to David, who gave him his choice between seven years of famine, three months of defeat in war, and three days of pestilence. David acknowledged that he was in great difficulty but expressed his willingness to abide by the will of the Lord. The Lord sent a pestilence on the people and seventy thousand died between Dan and Beersheba, but the angel of the Lord spared Jerusalem. When David saw the angel he expressed his willingness to take the punishment due his sin. The prophet Gad came to David and commanded him to set up an altar at the threshing floor of Araunah the Jebusite. After David built an altar he offered sacrifices, and the Lord stopped the plague (2 Sam. 24:11–25; 1 Chron. 21:9–27).

Toward the close of David's life the Lord gave him a plan for the future temple (1 Chron. 28:11–12); David made extensive preparations for it in stone, wood, gold, silver and brass. He also charged Solomon to build the house, assuring him that it was the will of the Lord (1 Chron. 22:1–19).

When David became old and feeble, Adonijah attempted to usurp the throne. He attracted to his cause Joab, Abiathar, and other distinguished men of the nation (1 Kings 1:1–10). The prophet Nathan told Bathsheba, who immediately laid the matter before King David. The king announced that Solomon would be inaugurated; David's chief men expressed their agreement with the king's desire and made Solomon king. The people received the young king with great shouts of joy, and when Adonijah's followers heard it they forsook him, and he fled.

After Solomon became king, David urged him to obey the law of Moses, assuring him that the perpetuity of his throne depended on it. He also commanded him to punish Joab and Shimei, and to show kindness to the sons of Barzillai the Gileadite (1 Kings 2:1–9). Solomon later had Adonijah, Joab, and Shimei killed.

David died and was buried in the city of David. He reigned seven years in Hebron and thirty-three years in Jerusalem (1 Kings 2:10–11). It is declared of him that he died in a good old age, full of riches and honor (1 Chron. 29:28).

Bible study on the life of David (NTB)

Genealogy of: Ruth 4:18–22; 1 Samuel 16:11; 17:12; 1 Chronicles 2:3–15; Matthew 1:1–6; Luke 3:31–38
A shepherd: 1 Samuel 16:11
Kills a lion and a bear: 1 Samuel 17:34–36
Anointed king, while a youth, by the prophet Samuel: 1 Samuel 16:1, 13; Psalm 89:19–37
Chosen of God: Psalm 78:70
Described to Saul: 1 Samuel 16:18
Detailed as armor-bearer and musician at Saul's court: 1 Samuel 16:21–23
Kills Goliath: 1 Samuel 17
The love of Jonathan for: 1 Samuel 18:1–4
Popularity and discreetness of: 1 Samuel 18
Saul's jealousy of: 1 Samuel 18:8–30
Is defrauded of Merab, and given Michal to marry: 1 Samuel 18:17–27
Jonathan intercedes for: 1 Samuel 19:1–7
Conducts a campaign against, and defeats the Philistines: 1 Samuel 19:8
Saul attempts to kill him; he escapes to Ramah, and lives at Naioth, where Saul pursues him: 1 Samuel 19:9–24
Returns, and Jonathan makes covenant with him: 1 Samuel 20
Escapes by way of Nob, where he obtains shewbread and Goliath's sword from Abimelech: 1 Samuel 21:1–6; Matthew 12:3, 4
Escapes to Gath: 1 Samuel 21:10–15
Recruits an army of insurgents, goes to Moab, returns to Hareth: 1 Samuel 22
Makes second covenant with Jonathan: 1 Samuel 23:16–18
Goes to the wilderness of Ziph, is betrayed to Saul: 1 Samuel 23:13–26
Writes a psalm on the betrayal: Psalm 54
Saul is diverted from pursuit of: 1 Samuel 23:27–28
Goes to En-gedi: 1 Samuel 23:29
Refrains from killing Saul: 1 Samuel 24

Covenants with Saul: 1 Samuel 26
Marries Nabal's widow, Abigail, and Ahinoam: 1 Samuel 25
Lives in the wilderness of Ziph, has opportunity to kill Saul, but only takes his spear; Saul is contrite: 1 Samuel 26
Flees to Achish and lives in Ziklag: 1 Samuel 27
The list of men who join him: 1 Chronicles 12:1–22
Conducts an expedition against Amalekites, misstates the facts to Achish: 1 Samuel 27:8–12
Is refused permission to accompany the Philistines to battle against the Israelites: 1 Samuel 28:1–2; 29
Rescues the people of Ziklag, who had been captured by the Amalekites: 1 Samuel 30
Death and burial of Saul and his sons: 1 Samuel 31; 2 Samuel 21:1–14
Kills the murderer of Saul: 2 Samuel 1:1–16
Lamentation over Saul: 2 Samuel 1:17–27
David goes to Hebron, and is anointed king by Judah: 2 Samuel 2:1–4, 11; 5:5; 1 Kings 2:11; 1 Chronicles 3:4; 11:1–3
The list of those who join him at Hebron: 1 Chronicles 12:23–40
Ish-bosheth, son of Saul, crowned: 2 Samuel 2:8–10
David wages war against and defeats Ish-bosheth: 2 Samuel 2:13–32; 3:4
Demands the restoration of Michal, his wife: 2 Samuel 3:14–16
Abner revolts from Ish-bosheth, and joins David, but is killed by Joab: 2 Samuel 3
Punishes Ish-bosheth's murderers: 2 Samuel 4
Anointed king over all Israel, after reigning over Judah at Hebron for seven years and six months, and reigns thirty-three years: 2 Samuel 2:11; 5:5; 1 Chronicles 3:4; 11:1–3; 12:23–40; 29:27
Makes conquest of Jerusalem: 2 Samuel 5:6; 1 Chronicles 11:4–8; Isaiah 29:1
Builds a palace: 2 Samuel 5:11; 2 Chronicles 2:3
Friendship of, with Hiram, king of Tyre: 2 Samuel 5:11; 1 Kings 5:1
Prospered of God: 2 Samuel 5:10; 1 Chronicles 11:9
Fame of: 1 Chronicles 14:17
Philistines make war against, and are defeated by him: 2 Samuel 5:17, 25
Assembles thirty-thousand men to escort the ark of the covenant to Jerusalem: 2 Samuel 6:1–5
Uzzah is struck down when he attempts to steady the ark of the covenant: 2 Samuel 6:6–11
David is terrified, and leaves the ark at the house of Obed-edom: 2 Samuel 6:9–11

After three months, David brings the ark of the covenant to Jerusalem: 2 Samuel 6:12–16; 1 Chronicles 13
Organizes the tabernacle service: 1 Chronicles 9:22; 15:16–24; 16:4–6, 37–43
Offers sacrifice, distributes gifts, and blesses the people: 2 Samuel 6:17–19
Desires to build a temple, is forbidden, but receives God's promise that his seed would reign forever: 2 Samuel 7:12–16; 23:5; 1 Chronicles 17:11–14; 2 Chronicles 6:16; Psalms 89:3–4; 132:11–12; Acts 15:16; Romans 15:12
Interpretation and fulfillment of this prophecy: Acts 13:22–23
Conquers the Philistines, Moabites, and Syria: 2 Samuel 8
Treats Mephibosheth, the lame son of Saul, with great kindness: 2 Samuel 9:6; 19:24–30
Defeats the combined armies of the Ammonites and Syrians: 2 Samuel 10; 1 Chronicles 19
Commits adultery with Bathsheba: 2 Samuel 11:2–5
Wickedly causes the death of Uriah: 2 Samuel 11:6–25
Takes Bathsheba to be his wife: 2 Samuel 11:26, 27
Is rebuked by the prophet Nathan: 2 Samuel 12:1–14
Repents of his crime and confesses his guilt: Psalms 6; 32; 38–40; 51
Is chastised with grievous affliction on account of his crime: Psalms 38; 41; 69
Death of his infant son (born from Bathsheba): 2 Samuel 12:15–23
Solomon is born to: 2 Samuel 12:24–25
Ammonites defeated and tortured: 2 Samuel 12:26–31
Amnon's crime, his murder by Absalom, and Absalom's flight: 2 Samuel 13
Absalom's return: 2 Samuel 14:1–24
Absalom's usurpation: 2 Samuel 14–15
David's flight from Jerusalem: 2 Samuel 15:13–37
Shimei curses him: 2 Samuel 16
Crosses the Jordan River: 2 Samuel 17:21–29
Absalom's defeat and death: 2 Samuel 18
Laments the death of Absalom: 2 Samuel 18:33; 19:1–4
Rebuked by Joab: 2 Samuel 19:5–7
David rebukes the priests for not showing loyalty amid the complaints of the people against him: 2 Samuel 19:9–15
Shimei begs for clemency: 2 Samuel 19:16–23
Mephibosheth begs for the king's favor: 2 Samuel 19:24–30
Barzillai rewarded: 2 Samuel 19:31–40
Judah accused by the ten tribes of stealing him away: 2 Samuel 19:41–43

Returns to Jerusalem: 2 Samuel 20:1–3
Sheba's conspiracy against David, and his death: 2 Samuel 20
Makes Amasa general: 2 Samuel 19:13
Amasa is killed: 2 Samuel 20:4–10
Consigns seven sons of Saul to the Gibeonites to be killed to atone for Saul's persecution of the Gibeonites: 2 Samuel 21:1–14
Buries Saul's bones and the bones of his sons: 2 Samuel 21:12–14
Defeats the Philistines: 2 Samuel 21:15–22; 1 Chronicles 20:4–8
Takes the military strength of Israel without divine authority and is reproved: 2 Samuel 24; 1 Chronicles 21; 27:24
Marries Abishag: 1 Kings 1:1–4
Adonijah usurps the sceptre; Solomon appointed to the throne: 1 Kings 1; 1 Chronicles 23:1
Delivers his charge to Solomon: 1 Kings 2:1–11; 1 Chronicles 22:6–19; 28; 29
Last words of: 2 Samuel 23:1–7
Death of: 1 Kings 2:10; 1 Chronicles 29:28; Acts 2:29–30
Sepulcher of: Acts 2:29
Length of reign, forty years: 1 Kings 2:11; 1 Chronicles 29:27–28
Wives of: 2 Samuel 3:2–5
Descendants of: 1 Chronicles 3
Civil and military officers of: 2 Samuel 8:16–18
Lists of his heroes, and of their exploits: 2 Samuel 23; 1 Chronicles 11; 12:23–40
Devoutness of: 1 Samuel 13:14; 2 Samuel 6:5, 14, 18; 7:18–29; 8:11; 24:25; 1 Kings 3:14; 1 Chronicles 17:16–27; 29:10; 2 Chronicles 7:17; Zechariah 12:8; Psalms 6; 7; 11; 13; 17; 22; 26; 27:7–14; 28; 31; 35; 37
Justice in the administration of: 2 Samuel 8:15; 1 Chronicles 18:14
Discreetness of: 1 Samuel 18:14, 30
Meekness of: 1 Samuel 24:7; 26:11; 2 Samuel 16:11; 19:22–23
Merciful: 2 Samuel 19:23
David as musician: 1 Samuel 16:21–23; 1 Chronicles 15:16; 23:5; 2 Chronicles 7:6; 29:26; Nehemiah 12:36; Amos 6:5
David as poet: 2 Samuel 22
David as prophet: 2 Samuel 23:2–7; 1 Chronicles 28:19; Matthew 22:41–46; Acts 2:25–38; 4:25
Type of Christ: Psalms 2; 16; 18:43; 69:7–9
Jesus called son of: Matthew 9:27; 12:23; 15:22; 20:30–31; 21:9; 22:42; Mark 10:47–48; Luke 18:37, 39
Prophecies concerning him and his kingdom: Numbers 24:17, 19; 2 Samuel 7:11–16; 1 Chronicles 17:9–14; 22; 2 Chronicles 6:5–17;

13:5; 21:7; Psalm 89:19–37; Isaiah 9:7; 16:5; 22:20–25; Jeremiah 23:5; 33:15–26; Luke 1:32–33

Chronicles of, written by Samuel, Nathan, and Gad: 1 Chronicles 29:29–30

A prophetic name for Christ: Jeremiah 30:9; Ezekiel 34:23–24; 37:24–25; Hosea 3:5

DOEG

Significance in summary

Saul's head shepherd who told Saul that Ahimelech had helped David and killed the priests at Nob

Meaning of name

anxious

Bible study on the life of Doeg (NTB)

An Edomite, present when Ahimelech helped David: 1 Samuel 21:7; Psalm 52

Murdered eighty-five priests: 1 Samuel 22:18–19

AHIMAAZ

Significance in summary

Spied on Absalom for King David

Meaning of name

brother is wrath

Bible study on the life of Ahimaaz (NTB)

Son of Zadok, the high priest; Loyal to David: 2 Samuel 15:36; 17:17–20; 18:19–33; 1 Chronicles 6:8–9, 53

AHIMELECH

Significance in summary

A priest at Nob who assisted King David

Meaning of name

my brother is king

Bible study on the life of Ahimelech (NTB)

Also called Ahia; a high priest, during the reign of David; gives shew-bread and the sword of Goliath to David: 1 Samuel 21; Mark 2:26
Killed by the command of Saul: 1 Samuel 22:9–22

NATHAN

Significance in summary

A prophet and faithful adviser to King David

Meaning of name

gift

Bible dictionary/encyclopedia entry (SBD)

An eminent Hebrew prophet in the reigns of David and Solomon. He first appears in the consultation with David about the building of the temple (2 Sam. 7:2–3, 17). He next comes forward as the reprover of David for the sin with Bathsheba; his famous apologue on the rich man and the ewe lamb is the only direct example of his prophetic power (2 Sam. 12:1–12).

Bible study on the life of Nathan (NTB)

His message to David concerning the building of a temple: 2 Samuel 7:1–17; 1 Chronicles 17:1–15
Reproves David for his adultery with Bathsheba and his murder of Uriah: 2 Samuel 12:1–15
Gives Solomon the name Jedidiah: 2 Samuel 12:25
Assists Bathsheba in securing for Solomon, her son, the succession to the throne: 1 Kings 1:10–14, 22–27
Assists in anointing Solomon to be king: 1 Kings 1:32–45
Kept the chronicles: 1 Chronicles 29:29; 2 Chronicles 9:29
Assists David in the organization of the tabernacle: 2 Chronicles 29:25

OBED-EDOM

Significance in summary

A Philistine who housed the covenant box for King David

Meaning of name

servant of Edom

Bible study on the life of Obed-edom (NTB)

A Korhite Levite; doorkeeper of the ark of the covenant: 1 Chronicles 15:18, 24; 26:4–8
David leaves the ark of the covenant with: 2 Samuel 6:10; 1 Chronicles 13:13–14
The ark of the covenant removed from: 2 Samuel 6:12; 1 Chronicles 15:25
Appointed to sound with harps: 1 Chronicles 15:21
Appointed to minister before the ark of the covenant: 1 Chronicles 16:4, 5, 37–38

HUSHAI

Significance in summary

A friend and counselor to King David

Bible study on the life of Hushai (NTB)

David's friend: 2 Samuel 15:32–37; 16:16–19; 17; 1 Chronicles 27:33

ACHISH

Significance in summary

A king of Gath who helped King David

Meaning of name

the king gives

Bible study on the life of Achish (NTB)

David escapes to: 1 Samuel 21:10–15; 27; 28:1–2; 29; 1 Kings 2:39–40

MEPHIBOSHETH

Significance in summary

Jonathan's son whom King David looked after

Meaning of name

he scatters shame

Bible dictionary/encyclopedia entry (SBD)

The name borne by two members of the family of Saul—his son and his grandson.

The son of Jonathan, grandson of Saul; also called Merib-baal (1 Chron. 8:34). His life seems to have been, from beginning to end, one of trial and discomfort. When his father and grandfather were killed on Gilboa he was five years old. At this age he met with an accident which deprived him for life the use of both feet (2 Sam. 4:4). After this he is found a home with Machir ben-Ammiel, a powerful Gadite, who raised him; while here he was married. Later on David invited him to Jerusalem, and there treated him and his son Michah with the greatest kindness. From this time forward he lived in Jerusalem. Of Mephibosheth's behavior during the rebellion of Absalom we possess two accounts—his own (2 Sam. 13:24–30) and that of Ziba (2 Sam. 16:1–4). They are naturally at variance with each other.

Bible study on the life of Mephibosheth (NTB)

Son of Jonathan: 2 Samuel 4:4
Called Merib-baal: 1 Chronicles 8:34; 9:40
Was lame: 2 Samuel 4:4
David entertains him at his table: 2 Samuel 9:1–7; 21:7
Property restored to: 2 Samuel 9:9–10
His ingratitude to David at the time of Absalom's usurpation: 2 Samuel 16:1–4; 19:24–30
Property of, confiscated: 2 Samuel 16:4; 19:29–30

UZZAH

Significance in summary

Died after touching the covenant box when it was moved to Jerusalem

Meaning of name

strength

Bible study on the life of Uzzah (NTB)

Driver of the cart when moving the ark of the covenant: 2 Samuel 6:3; 1 Chronicles 13:7

Struck dead for touching the ark of the covenant: 2 Samuel 6:6–8; 1 Chronicles 13:9–11

SHIMEI

Significance in summary

Spoke against King David during Absalom's rebellion

Meaning of name

God hear me

Bible study on the life of Shimei (NTB)

A Benjamite; curses David; David's magnanimity toward: 2 Samuel 16:5–13; 19:16; 23; 1 Kings 2:36–46

JEDUTHUN

Significance in summary

One of the three chief musicians during the reigns of David and Solomon

Bible study on the life of Jeduthun (NTB)

A musician of the temple: 1 Chronicles 16:41; 25:1

ARAUNAH (Ornan)

Significance in summary

Sold his threshing-floor to King David

Meaning of name

noble

Bible study on the life of Araunah/Ornan (NTB)

A Jebusite from whom David bought a site for an altar: 2 Samuel 24:16–24
Also called Ornan: 1 Chronicles 21:15–25

ASAHEL

Significance in summary

Commander in David's army

Meaning of name

God has made

Bible study on the life of Asahel (NTB)

Nephew of David, and one of his captains: 2 Samuel 2:18–24, 32; 3:27; 23:24; 1 Chronicles 2:16; 11:26; 27:7

ASAPH

Significance in summary

One of the chief musicians during David's reign

Meaning of name

collector

Bible study on the life of Asaph (NTB)

Son of Berachiah; one of three leaders of music in David's organization of the tabernacle service: 1 Chronicles 15:16–19; 16:5–7; 25:1–9; 2 Chronicles 5:12; 35:15; Nehemiah 12:46
Appointed to sound the cymbals in the temple choir: 1 Chronicles 15:17, 19; 16:5, 7
A composer of sacred lyrics: 2 Chronicles 29:13–30
See title of: Psalms 50; 73–83
Descendants of, in the temple choir: 1 Chronicles 25:1–9; 2 Chronicles 20:14; 29:13; Ezra 2:41; 3:10; Nehemiah 7:44; 11:22

ELIAB

Significance in summary

David's brother

Meaning of name

God is father

Bible study on the life of Eliab (NTB)

Son of Jesse and eldest brother of David: 1 Samuel 16:6; 17:13, 28; 1 Chronicles 2:13
A prince in the tribe of Judah: 1 Chronicles 27:18

ITTAI

Significance in summary

Commander in King David's army

Bible study on the life of Ittai (NTB)

A chief of David: 2 Samuel 18:2; 1 Chronicles 11:31

HADADEZER (HADAREZER)

Significance in summary

King of Zobah whom King David defeated

Meaning of name

Hadad is help

Bible study on the life of Hadadezer (NTB)

Also called Hadarezer; King of Zobah, vanquished by David: 2 Samuel 8:3–13; 10:15–19; 1 Kings 11:23; 1 Chronicles 18:3–10; 19:6–19

BARZILLAI

Significance in summary

Befriended David when David fled from Absalom

Meaning of name

of iron

Bible study on the life of Barzillai (NTB)

A friend of David: 2 Samuel 17:27–29; 19:31–39; 1 Kings 2:7; Ezra 2:61; Nehemiah 7:63

ABSALOM

Significance in summary

King David's son, who rebelled against his father

Meaning of name

father of peace

Bible dictionary/encyclopedia entry (IBD)

David's son by Maacah (2 Sam. 3:3; compare 1 Kings 1:6). He was noted for his personal beauty and for the extraordinary amount of hair on his head (2 Sam. 14:25–26). The first public act of his life was blood-revenge against Amnon, David's eldest son, who had wronged Absalom's sister Tamar. David's other sons fled and brought the tidings of the death of Amnon to Jerusalem. Alarmed for the consequences of the act, Absalom fled to his grandfather at Geshur, and stayed there for three years (2 Sam. 3:3; 13:23–38).

David mourned his absent son, now branded with the guilt of fratricide. Joab received David's sanction to invite Absalom back to Jerusalem. He returned, but two years elapsed before his father admitted him into his presence (2 Sam. 14:28). Absalom was now probably the oldest surviving son of David, and as he was of royal descent by his mother as well as by his father, he began to desire the throne. His pretensions were favored by the people. After his return from Geshur (2 Sam. 15:7; marg., RSV) he went up to Hebron, the old capital of Judah, along with many of the people, and proclaimed himself king. The revolt was so successful that David found it necessary to flee to Mahanaim, beyond Jordan; Absalom returned to Jerusalem and took possession of the throne without opposition. Ahithophel, who had been David's chief counselor, deserted him, joined Absalom, and became his chief counselor. Hushai also joined Absalom, but only for the purpose of trying to counteract the counsels of Ahithophel, and so to advantage David's cause. He was so successful that by his advice, which was preferred to that of Ahithophel, Absalom delayed to march an army against his father, who gained time to prepare for the defense.

Absalom at length marched out against his father, whose army, under the command of Joab, he encountered on the borders of the forest of Ephraim. Twenty thousand of Absalom's army were killed in that battle, and the rest fled. Absalom fled on a swift mule; but his long flowing hair, or more probably his head, was caught in the bough of an oak, and there he was left suspended until Joab came up and pierced him through with three darts. His body was then taken down and cast into a pit dug in the forest, and a heap of stones was raised over his grave. When David was told that Absalom had been killed, he gave way to the bitter lamentation: "O my son Absalom, my son, my son Absalom! would God I had died for thee, O Absalom, my son, my son!" (2 Sam. 18:33; compare Exod. 32:32; Rom. 9:3).

Absalom's three sons (2 Sam. 14:27; compare 18:18) had all died before him, so he left only a daughter, Tamar, who became the grandmother of Abijah.

Bible study on the life of Absalom (NTB)

Also called Abishalom; son of David by Maacah: 2 Samuel 3:3; 1 Chronicles 3:2
Beauty of: 2 Samuel 14:25
Kills Amnon: 2 Samuel 13:22–29
Flees to Geshur: 2 Samuel 13:37–38
Is permitted by David to return to Jerusalem: 2 Samuel 14:1–24
His demagogism: 2 Samuel 15:2–6, 13
Conspiracy: 2 Samuel 15:17
Death and burial: 2 Samuel 18:9–17
David's mourning for: 2 Samuel 18:33; 19:1–8
Children of: 2 Samuel 14:27; 18:18; 1 Kings 15:2; 2 Chronicles 11:20
Pillar of: 2 Samuel 18:18

TAMAR, Absalom's daughter

Significance in summary

Absalom's daughter

Meaning of name

palm tree

Bible study on the life of Tamar (NTB)

Daughter of Absalom: 2 Samuel 14:27

MICHAL

Significance in summary

Saul's youngest daughter and King David's wife.

Meaning of name

who is like God?

Bible dictionary/encyclopedia entry (IBD)

The younger of Saul's two daughters by his wife Ahinoam (1 Sam. 14:49–50). Attracted by the graces of his person and the gallantry of his conduct, she fell in love with David and became his wife (1 Sam. 18:20–28). She showed her affection for him by helping him to escape to Naioth when Saul sought his life (1 Sam. 19:12–17; compare Psalm 59). After this she did not see David for many years. Meanwhile she was given in marriage to another man, Phalti or Phaltiel of Gallim (1 Sam. 25:44), but David afterwards formally reclaimed her as his lawful wife (2 Sam. 3:13–16). The relationship between her and David soon after this was altered. They became alienated from each other. This happened on that memorable day when the ark was brought up in great triumph from its temporary resting place to the Holy City. In David's conduct on that occasion she saw nothing but a needless humiliation of the royal dignity (1 Chron. 15:29). She remained childless, and thus the races of David and Saul were not mixed. In 2 Samuel 21:8 her name again occurs, but the name Merab should probably be here substituted for Michal (compare 1 Sam. 18:19).

Bible study on the life of Michal (NTB)

Given to David as a reward for killing two hundred Philistines: 1 Samuel 18:22–28
Rescues David from death: 1 Samuel 19:9–17
Saul forcibly separates them and she is given in marriage to Phalti: 1 Samuel 25:44
David recovers, to himself: 2 Samuel 3:13–16
Ridicules David on account of his religious zeal: 2 Samuel 6:16, 20–23

BATHSHEBA

Significance in summary

Wife of Uriah whom David committed adultery with and married after Uriah was killed in battle

Meaning of name

the seventh daughter

Bible dictionary/encyclopedia entry (IBD)

Daughter of the oath, or of seven, called also Bath-shua (1 Chron. 3:5), was the daughter of Eliam (2 Sam. 11:3) or Ammiel (1 Chron. 3:5), and wife of Uriah the Hittite. David committed adultery with her (2 Sam. 11:4–5; Ps. 51:1). The child born from this union died (2 Sam. 12:15–19). After her husband was killed (2 Sam. 11:15–17) she married David (11:27) and became the mother of Solomon (12:24; 1 Kings 1:11; 2:13). She took a prominent part in securing the succession of Solomon to the throne (1 Kings 1:11, 16–21).

Bible study on the life of Bathsheba (NTB)

Wife of Uriah and later one of the wives of David; called Bath-shua: 1 Chronicles 3:5
Adultery of: 2 Samuel 11:2–5
Solomon's mother: 1 Kings 1:11–31; 2:13–21; 1 Chronicles 3:5

ABISHAG

Significance in summary

King David's wife who nursed him in his old age

Meaning of name

my father was a wanderer

Bible study on the life of Abishag (NTB)

Wife of David in his old age: 1 Kings 1:1–4; 2:13–25

ABISHAI

Significance in summary

King David's nephew and one of his commanders

Bible study on the life of Abishai (NTB)

Son of Zeruiah, David's sister: 1 Chronicles 2:16
One of David's chief men: 2 Samuel 23:18
Seeks Saul's life: 1 Samuel 26:6–8
Pursues and kills Abner: 2 Samuel 2:24; 3:30
Defeats the Edomites: 1 Chronicles 18:12
Defeats the Ammonites: 2 Samuel 10:10, 14
Seeks the life of Shimei: 2 Samuel 16:9; 19:21

Leads a division of David's army against Absalom: 2 Samuel 18:2, 5
Overthrows Sheba: 2 Samuel 20:1–22
Saves David from being killed by a Philistine: 2 Samuel 21:17
Obtains water from the well of Bethlehem for David: 1 Chronicles 11:15–20

NABAL

Significance in summary

A wealthy Carmelite who refused to give David food

Meaning of name

foolish

Bible study on the life of Nabal (NTB)

Husband of Abigail (Hebrew means "fool"); history of: 1 Samuel 25:2–38

JOAB

Significance in summary

King David's nephew and commander of his army

Meaning of name

God is father

Bible dictionary/encyclopedia entry (IBD)

One of the three sons of Zeruiah, David's sister, and "captain of the host" during the whole of David's reign (2 Sam. 2:13; 10:7; 11:1; 1 Kings 11:15). His father's name is nowhere mentioned, although his sepulcher at Bethlehem is mentioned (2 Sam. 2:32). His two brothers were Abishai and Asahel, the swift of foot, who was killed by Abner (2 Sam. 2:13–32), whom Joab afterwards treacherously murdered (3:22–27). He led the assault at the storming of the fortress on Mount Zion, and for this service was raised to the rank of "prince of the king's army" (2 Sam. 5:6–10; 1 Chron. 27:34). His chief military achievements were (1) against the allied forces of Syria and Ammon; (2) against Edom (1 Kings 11:15–16); and (3) against the Ammonites (2 Sam. 10:7–19; 11:1, 11). His character is deeply stained by the part he willingly took in the murder of Uriah (11:14–25). He acted apparently from a sense of duty in putting Absalom to death (18:1–14). David was unmindful of the many services Joab had given to him, and afterwards gave the command of the army to Amasa, Joab's cousin (2 Sam. 20:1–13; 19:13). When David was dying Joab espoused the cause of Adonijah in preference to that of Solomon. He was afterwards killed by Benaiah, by the command of Solomon, in accordance with his father's injunction (2 Sam. 3:29; 20:5–13), at the altar to which he had fled for refuge. Thus he died without anyone to lift up a voice in his favor. He was buried in his own property in the "wilderness," probably northeast of Jerusalem (1 Kings 2:5, 28–34). Benaiah succeeded him as commander-in-chief of the army.

Bible study on the life of Joab (NTB)

Son of David's sister: 1 Chronicles 2:16
Commander of David's army: 2 Samuel 8:16; 20:23; 1 Chronicles 11:6; 18:15; 27:34
Dedicated the plunder of his battles: 1 Chronicles 26:28
Defeated the Jebusites: 1 Chronicles 11:6
Defeats and kills Abner: 2 Samuel 2:13–32; 3:27; 1 Kings 2:5
Destroys all the males in Edom: 1 Kings 11:16
Defeats the Ammonites: 2 Samuel 10:7–14; 1 Chronicles 19:6–15
Captures Rabbah: 2 Samuel 11:1, 15–25; 12:26–29; 1 Chronicles 20:1–2
Procures the return of Absalom to Jerusalem: 2 Samuel 14:1–24
Barley field of, burned by Absalom: 2 Samuel 14:29–33
Pursues and kills Absalom: 2 Samuel 18
Censures David for lamenting the death of Absalom: 2 Samuel 19:1–8
Replaced by Amasa as commander of David's army: 2 Samuel 17:25; 19:13
Kills Amasa: 2 Samuel 20:8–13; 1 Kings 2:5
Causes Sheba to be put to death: 2 Samuel 20:16–22
Opposes the numbering of the people: 2 Samuel 24:3; 1 Chronicles 21:3
Numbers the people: 2 Samuel 24:4–9; 1 Chronicles 21:4–5; 27:23–24
Supports Adonijah as successor to David: 1 Kings 1:7; 2:28
Killed by Benaiah, under Solomon's order: 1 Kings 2:29–34

TAMAR, David's daughter

Significance in summary

King David's daughter, who was raped by her half-brother, Amnon

Meaning of name

palm tree

Bible study on the life of Tamar (NTB)

Daughter of David: 2 Samuel 13:1–32; 1 Chronicles 3:9

SOLOMON

Significance in summary

Son of Bathsheba and David and famous king of Israel

Meaning of name

peace

Bible dictionary/encyclopedia entry (IBD)

David's second son by Bathsheba, i.e., the first after their legal marriage (2 Samuel 12). He was probably born about 1035 BC (1 Chron. 22:5; 29:1). He succeeded his father on the throne at about sixteen or eighteen years of age. Nathan, to whom his education was entrusted, called him Jedidiah, i.e., "beloved of the Lord" (2 Sam. 12:24–25). He was the first king of Israel "born in the purple." His father chose him as his successor, passing over the claims of his elder sons: "Assuredly Solomon my son shall reign after me." His history is recorded in 1 Kings 1–11 and 2 Chronicles 1–9. His elevation to the throne took place before his father's death, and was hastened on mainly by Nathan and Bathsheba, in consequence of the rebellion of Adonijah (1 Kings 1:5–40). During his long reign of forty years the Hebrew monarchy gained its highest splendor. This period has well been called the "Augustan age" of the Jewish annals. The first half of his reign was by far the brighter and more prosperous; the latter half was clouded by the idolatries into which he fell, mainly from his heathen intermarriages (1 Kings 11:1–8; 14:21, 31).

Before his death David gave parting instructions to his son (1 Kings 2:1–9; 1 Chron. 22:7–16; 28). As soon as he had settled himself in his kingdom, and arranged the affairs of his extensive empire, he entered into an alliance with Egypt by the marriage of the daughter of Pharaoh (1 Kings 3:1), of whom nothing further is recorded. He surrounded himself with all the luxuries and the external grandeur of an Eastern monarch, and his government prospered. He also allied with Hiram, king of Tyre, who in many ways assisted him in his numerous undertakings.

For some years before his death David was engaged in the active work of collecting materials (1 Chron. 29:6–9; 2 Chron. 2:3–7) for building a temple in Jerusalem as a permanent abode for the ark of the covenant. He was not permitted to build the house of God (1 Chron. 22:8); that honor was reserved for his son Solomon.

After the completion of the temple, Solomon erected many other buildings of importance in Jerusalem and in other parts of his kingdom. For thirteen years he was engaged in the erection of a magnificent royal palace on Ophel (1 Kings 7:1–12). It was one hundred cubits long, fifty broad, and thirty high. Its lofty roof was supported by forty-five cedar pillars, so that the hall was like a forest of cedar wood, and hence probably it received the name of "The House of the Forest of Lebanon." In front of this "house" was another building—the Porch of Pillars—and in front of this was the "Hall of Judgment," or Throne-room (1 Kings 7:7; 10:18–20; 2 Chron. 9:17–19), "the King's Gate," where he administered justice and gave audience to his people. A part of the palace was set apart as the residence of the queen consort, the daughter of Pharaoh. From the palace there was a private staircase of red scented sandalwood which led up to the temple.

Solomon also constructed great works for the purpose of securing a plentiful supply of water for the city (Eccles. 2:4–6). He then built Millo (LXX., "Acra") for the defense of the city, completing a line of ramparts around it (1 Kings 9:15, 24; 11:27). He erected many other fortifications for the defense of his kingdom at various points where it was exposed to the assault of enemies (1 Kings 9:15–19; 2 Chron. 8:2–6). Among his great undertakings was the building of Tadmor in the wilderness as a commercial depot.

During his reign Palestine enjoyed great commercial prosperity. Extensive traffic was carried on by land with Tyre and Egypt and Arabia, and by sea with Spain and India and the coasts of Africa, by which Solomon accumulated vast stores of wealth and of the produce of all nations (1 Kings 9:26–28; 10:11–12; 2 Chron. 8:17–18; 9:21). This was the "golden age" of Israel. The royal magnificence and splendor of Solomon's court were unrivalled. He had seven hundred wives and three hundred concubines, evidence of his pride, his wealth, and his sensuality. The maintenance of his household involved immense expenditure. The provision required for one day was "thirty measures of fine flour, and threescore measures of meal, ten fat oxen, and twenty oxen out of the pastures, and an hundred sheep, beside harts, and roebucks, and fallowdeer, and fatted fowl" (1 Kings 4:22–23).

Solomon's reign was not only a period of great material prosperity, but was equally remarkable for its intellectual activity. He was the leader of his people in this new intellectual life. "He spake three thousand proverbs: and his songs were a thousand and five. And he spake of trees, from the cedar tree that is in Lebanon even unto the hyssop that springeth out of the wall: he spake also of beasts, and of fowl, and of creeping things, and of fishes" (1 Kings 4:32–33).

His fame had become well known through all lands, and people came from far and near "to hear the wisdom of Solomon." Among those attracted to Jerusalem was "the queen of the south" (Matt. 12:42), the queen of Sheba, a country in Arabia Felix. "When the queen of Sheba heard of the fame of Solomon . . . she came to prove him with hard questions. And she came to Jerusalem with a very great train, with camels that bare spices, and very much gold" (1 Kings 10:1–12; see also 2 Chron. 9:1–12). She was filled with amazement by all she saw and heard: "there was no more spirit in her." After an exchange of presents she returned to her native land.

But that golden age of Jewish history passed away. The bright day of Solomon's glory ended in clouds and darkness. His decline and fall from his high estate is a sad record. Chief among the causes of his decline were his polygamy and his great wealth. As he grew older he began to imitate the heathenish ways of his wives and concubines. He did not cease to believe in the God of Israel with his mind. He did not cease to offer the usual sacrifices in the temple at the great feasts. But his heart was not right with God; his worship became merely formal. Now for the first time a worship was publicly set up amongst the people of the Lord which was not simply irregular or forbidden, like that of Gideon (Judg. 8:27), or the Danites (Judg. 18:30, 31), but was downright idolatrous (1 Kings 11:7; 2 Kings 23:13).

This brought on him the divine displeasure. His enemies prevailed against him (1 Kings 11:14–40), and one judgment after another fell on the land. And now the end of all came, and he died, after a reign of forty years; he was buried in the city of David, and with him was buried the short-lived glory and unity of Israel.

Bible study on the life of Solomon (NTB)

Son of David by Bathsheba: 2 Samuel 12:24; 1 Kings 1:13, 17, 21
Named Jedidiah, by Nathan the prophet: 2 Samuel 12:24–25
An ancestor of Joseph: Matthew 1:6
Succeeds David to the throne of Israel: 1 Kings 1:11–48; 2:12; 1 Chronicles 23:1; 28; Ecclesiastes 1:12
Anointed king a second time: 1 Chronicles 29:22
His prayer for wisdom, and his vision: 1 Kings 3:5–14; 2 Chronicles 1:7–12
Covenant renewed in a vision after the dedication of the Temple: 1 Kings 9:1–9; 2 Chronicles 7:12–22

His rigorous reign: 1 Kings 2
Builds the temple: 1 Kings 5–6; 9:10; 1 Chronicles 6:10; 2 Chronicles 2–4; 7:11; Jeremiah 52:20; Acts 7
Dedicates the temple: 1 Kings 8; 2 Chronicles 6
Renews the courses of the priests and Levites, and the forms of service according to the commandment of Moses and the regulations of David: 2 Chronicles 8:12–16; 35:4; Nehemiah 12:45
Builds his palace: 1 Kings 3:1; 7:1, 8; 9:10; 2 Chronicles 7:11; 8:1; Ecclesiastes 2:4
Builds his house—the forest of Lebanon: 1 Kings 7:2–7
Builds a house for Pharaoh's daughter: 1 Kings 7:8–12; 9:24; 2 Chronicles 8:11; Ecclesiastes 2:4
Ivory throne of: 1 Kings 7:7; 10:18–20
Porches of judgment: 1 Kings 7:7
Builds Millo (a stronghold), the wall around Jerusalem, the cities of Hazor, Megiddo, Gezer, Beth-horon, Baalath, Tadmor, store cities, and cities for chariots, and for cavalry: 1 Kings 9:15–19; 2 Chronicles 9:25
Provides an armory: 1 Kings 10:16–17
Plants vineyards and orchards of all kinds of fruit trees; makes pools: Ecclesiastes 2:4–6
Imports apes and peacocks: 1 Kings 10:22
Drinking vessels of his houses: 1 Kings 10:21; 2 Chronicles 9:20
Musicians and musical instruments of his court: 1 Kings 10:12; 2 Chronicles 9:11; Ecclesiastes 2:8
The splendor of his court: 1 Kings 10:5–9, 12; 2 Chronicles 9:3–8; Ecclesiastes 2:9; Matthew 6:29; Luke 12:27
Commerce of: 1 Kings 9:28; 10:11–12, 22, 28–29; 2 Chronicles 1:16–17; 8:17–18; 9:13–22, 28
Presents received by: 1 Kings 10:10; 2 Chronicles 9:9, 23–24
Is visited by the Queen of Sheba: 1 Kings 10:1–13; 2 Chronicles 9:1–12
Wealth of: 1 Kings 9; 10:10, 14–15, 23, 27; 2 Chronicles 1:15; 9:1, 9, 13, 24, 27; Ecclesiastes 1:16
Has seven hundred wives and three hundred concubines: 1 Kings 11:3; Deuteronomy 17:17
Their influence over him: 1 Kings 11:4
Marries one of Pharaoh's daughters: 1 Kings 3:1
Builds idolatrous temples: 1 Kings 11:1–8; 2 Kings 23:13
His idolatry: 1 Kings 3:3–4; Nehemiah 13:26
Extent of his dominions: 1 Kings 4:21, 24; 8:65; 2 Chronicles 7:8; 9:26
Receives taxes: 1 Kings 4:21; 9:21; 2 Chronicles 8:8
Officers of: 1 Kings 2:35; 4:1–19; 2 Chronicles 8:9–10

His purveyors: 1 Kings 4:7–19
Military equipment of: 1 Kings 4:26, 28; 10:16–17, 26, 28; 2 Chronicles 1:14; 9:25; Deuteronomy 17:15–16
Cedes some inferior cities to Hiram: 1 Kings 9:10–13; 2 Chronicles 8:2
Wisdom and fame of: 1 Kings 4:29–34; 10:3–4, 8, 23–24; 1 Chronicles 29:24–25; 2 Chronicles 9:2–7, 22–23; Ecclesiastes 1:16; Matthew 12:42
Piety of: 1 Kings 3:5–15; 4:29; 8
Beloved of God: 2 Samuel 12:24
Justice of, illustrated in his judgment of the two prostitutes: 1 Kings 3:16–28
Oppressions of: 1 Kings 12:4; 2 Chronicles 10:4
Reigns for forty years: 2 Chronicles 9:30
Death of: 2 Chronicles 9:29–31
Prophecies concerning: 2 Samuel 7:12–16; 1 Kings 11:9–13; 1 Chronicles 17:11–14; 28:6–7; Psalm 132:11
A "type" of Christ: Psalm 45:2–17

URIAH

Significance in Summary

Husband of Bathsheba and Hittite soldier in King David's army

Meaning of name

God is light

Bible dictionary/encyclopedia entry (IBD)

A Hittite, the husband of Bathsheba, whom David first seduced and then married after Uriah's death. He was one of the band of David's "mighty men." The sad story of the cruel wrongs inflicted on him by David and of his mournful death are simply told in the sacred record (2 Sam. 11:2–12:26).

Bible study on the life of Uriah (NTB)

One of David's mighty men: 2 Samuel 23:39; 1 Chronicles 11:41
David's adultery with the wife of: 2 Samuel 11:2–5; 1 Kings 15:5
Summoned from seat of war by David: 2 Samuel 11:6–13
Noble spirit of: 2 Samuel 11:11
David compasses the death of: 2 Samuel 11:14–25
David marries the widow of: 2 Samuel 11:26–27
Called Urias (KJV): Matthew 1:6

HIRAM, King of Tyre

Significance in summary

King of Tyre who supplied King David with cedar and fir trees from Lebanon for the building of the temple

Meaning of name

my brother is exalted

Bible study on the life of Hiram (NTB)

Called Huram, king of Tyre; builds a house for David: 2 Samuel 5:11; 1 Chronicles 14:1; 2 Chronicles 2:3
Helps Solomon in building the temple: 1 Kings 5; 2 Chronicles 2:3–16
Dissatisfied with the cities given to him by Solomon: 1 Kings 9:11–13
Makes presents of gold and sailors to Solomon: 1 Kings 9:14, 26–28; 10:11

ABIGAIL

Significance in summary

Nabal's wife whom King David married after Nabal's death

Meaning of name

father rejoices

Bible dictionary/encyclopedia entry (IBD)

The wife of the churlish Nabal, who lived in the district of Carmel (1 Sam. 25:3). She showed great prudence at a critical period of her husband's life. She was "a woman of good understanding, and of a beautiful countenance." After Nabal's death she became the wife of David (1 Sam. 25:14–42), and was his companion in all his future fortunes (1 Sam. 27:3; 30:5; 2 Sam. 2:2). By her David had a son called Chileab (2 Sam. 3:3), elsewhere called Daniel (1 Chron. 3:1).

Bible study on the life of Abigail (NTB)

Her wisdom and tact, and marriage to David: 1 Samuel 25; 27:3; 2 Samuel 2:2
Mother of Chileab by David: 2 Samuel 3:3; 1 Chronicles 3:1
Taken captive and rescued by David: 1 Samuel 30:1–18

ADONIJAH

Significance in summary

David's fourth son

Meaning of name

God is Lord

Bible study on the life of Adonijah (NTB)

Son of David and Haggith: 2 Samuel 3:4; 1 Kings 1:5–6; 1 Chronicles 3:2
Usurpation of, and downfall: 1 Kings 1
Executed by Solomon: 1 Kings 2:13–25

REZON

Significance in summary

King of Syria who troubled King Solomon

Meaning of name

prince

Bible study on the life of Rezon (NTB)

An adversary of Solomon: 1 Kings 11:23–25

HIRAM, the craftsman

Significance in summary

A craftsman who helped build Solomon's palace and temple

Meaning of name

my brother is exalted

Bible study on the life of Hiram (NTB)

Also called Huram; a craftsman sent by King Hiram to execute the artistic work of the interior of the temple: 1 Kings 7:13–45; 2 Chronicles 2:13; 4:11–16

ISH-BOSHETH

Significance in summary

King Saul's son who reigned for two years before David defeated him

Meaning of name

man of shame

Bible study on the life of Ish-bosheth (NTB)

Called Esh-Baal in: 1 Chronicles 8:33; 9:39
Made king by Abner: 2 Samuel 2:8–10
Deserted by Abner: 2 Samuel 3:6–12
Restores Michal (David's first wife) to David: 2 Samuel 3:14–16
Assassinated: 2 Samuel 4:5–8
Avenged by David: 2 Samuel 4:9–12

AMNON

Significance in summary

King David's eldest son who raped his half-sister, Tamar

Meaning of name

faithful

Bible study on the life of Amnon (NTB)

Son of David: 2 Samuel 3:2; 1 Chronicles 3:1
Incest of, and death: 2 Samuel 13

ABNER

Significance in summary

First cousin and commander of King Saul's army

Meaning of name

father is a lamp

Bible dictionary/encyclopedia entry (IBD)

The son of Ner and uncle of Saul. He was commander-in-chief of Saul's army (1 Sam. 14:50; 17:55; 20:25). He first introduced David to the court of Saul after the victory over Goliath (1 Sam. 17:57). After the death of Saul, David was made king over Judah, and reigned in Hebron. Among the other tribes there was a feeling of hostility to Judah; Abner, at the head of Ephraim, fostered this hostility in the interest of the house of Saul, whose son Ish-bosheth he proclaimed king (2 Sam. 2:8). A state of war existed between these two kings. A battle fatal to Abner, who was the leader of Ish-bosheth's army, was fought with David's army under Joab at Gibeon (2 Sam. 2:12). Abner, escaping from the field, was overtaken by Asahel, who was "light of foot as a wild roe," the brother of Joab and Abishai, whom he thrust through with his spear (2 Sam. 2:18–32).

Being rebuked by Ish-bosheth for the impropriety of taking to wife Rizpah, who had been a concubine of King Saul, he found an excuse for going over to the side of David, whom he now regarded as anointed by the Lord to reign over all Israel. David received him favorably, and promised that he would have command of the armies. At this time Joab was absent from Hebron, but on his return he found what had happened. Abner had just left the city; Joab recalled him, and meeting him at the gate of the city on his return, killed him (2 Sam. 3:27, 31–39; 4:12; compare 1 Kings 2:5, 32). David lamented in pathetic words the death of Abner, "Know ye not that there is a prince and a great man fallen this day in Israel?" (2 Sam. 3:38).

Bible study on the life of Abner (NTB)

Cousin of Saul: 1 Samuel 14:50–51
Captain of the host: 1 Samuel 14:50; 17:55; 26:5, 14
Dedicated spoils of war to the tabernacle: 1 Chronicles 26:27–28
Loyalty of, to the house of Saul: 2 Samuel 2:8–32
Alienation of, from the house of Saul: 2 Samuel 3:6–21
Murdered by Joab; David's sorrow for: 2 Samuel 3:27–39

AHITHOPHEL

Significance in summary

Leader of Absolom's rebellion against King David

Meaning of name

brother of foolishness

Bible study on the life of Ahithophel (NTB)

One of David's counselors: 2 Samuel 15:12; 1 Chronicles 27:33

Joins Absalom: 2 Samuel 15:31, 34; 16:15, 20–23; 17:1–23
Suicide of: 2 Samuel 17:1–14, 23

ABIATHAR

Significance in summary

High priest who tried to put Adonijah on the throne instead of Solomon

Meaning of name

father of abundance

Bible study on the life of Abiathar (NTB)

Son of Ahimelech: 1 Samuel 22:20
Escapes to David from the vengeance of Saul, who slew the priests in the City of Nob: 1 Samuel 22:20–23; 22:6–19
Consults the ephod for David: 1 Samuel 22:9–12; 30:9–12
Associate high priest with Zadok in the reign of David: 2 Samuel 15:35; 20:25; 1 Kings 4:4; 1 Chronicles 15:11
Loyal to David when Absalom rebelled; leaves Jerusalem with the ark of the covenant, but is directed by David to return with the ark: 2 Samuel 15:24–29
Helps David by sending his son from Jerusalem to David with secret information concerning the counsel of Ahithophel: 2 Samuel 15:35–36; 17:15–22; 1 Kings 2:26
Supports Adonijah's pretensions to the throne: 1 Kings 1:7
Thrust out of office by Solomon: 1 Kings 2:26–27

ZADOK

Significance in summary

High priest in King David's reign

Meaning of name

righteous

Bible dictionary/encyclopedia entry (SBD)

Son of Ahitub and one of the two chief priests in the time of David, Abiathar being the other. Zadok was of the house of Eleazar the son of Aaron (1 Chron. 24:3) and eleventh in descent from Aaron. Zadok and Abiathar were of nearly equal dignity (2 Sam. 15:35–36; 19:11). The duties of the office were divided; Zadok ministered before the tabernacle at Gibeon (1 Chron. 16:39), and Abiathar had the care of the ark at Jerusalem. Zadok joined David at Hebron after Saul's death (1 Chron. 12:28), and from then on his fidelity to David was inviolable. When Absalom revolted and David fled from Jerusalem, Zadok and all the Levites bearing the ark accompanied him. When Absalom was dead, Zadok and Abiathar persuaded the elders of Judah to invite David to return (2 Sam. 19:11). When Adonijah, in David's old age, set up for king, and had persuaded Joab and Abiathar the priest to join his party, Zadok was unmoved, and was employed by David to anoint Solomon to be king (1 Kings 1:34). For this fidelity he was rewarded by Solomon, who dismissed Abiathar and put Zadok in his room (1 Kings 2:27, 35). From this time, however, we hear little of him.

Bible study on the life of Zadok (NTB)

The high priest during the time of David's reign: 2 Samuel 19:11; 20:25; 1 Chronicles 15:11; 16:39

Removes the ark of the covenant from Jerusalem at the time of Absalom's usurpation; returns with the ark of the covenant at David's command: 2 Samuel 15:24–36; 17:15, 17–21

Stands aloof from Adonijah at the time of his attempted usurpation: 1 Kings 1:8, 26

Summoned by David to anoint Solomon to be king: 1 Kings 1:32–40, 44–45

Performs the function of a high priest after Abiathar was deposed by Solomon: 1 Kings 2:35; 1 Chronicles 29:22

Judah's Kings

Rehoboam • Abijam • Asa • Zerah • Jehoshaphat • Jehoram • Ahaziah • Athaliah • Joash (Jehoash) • Jehoiada • Amaziah • Azariah • Jotham • Ahaz • Hezekiah • Sennacherib • Manasseh • Esarhaddon • Rabsaris • Rab-shakeh • Tartan • Shebna(h) • Merodach-Baladan • Amon • Josiah • Hilkiah • Shaphan • Jehoahaz • Jehoiakim • Jehoiachin • Evil-merodach • Zedekiah • Tiglath-pileser

REHOBOAM

Significance in summary

Solomon's son who set up the southern kingdom of Judah

Bible dictionary/encyclopedia entry (IBD)

The successor of Solomon on the throne, and apparently his only son. He was the son of Naamah, an Ammonite princess (1 Kings 14:21; 2 Chron. 12:13). He was forty-one years old when he ascended the throne, and he reigned seventeen years. Although he was acknowledged as the rightful heir to the throne, the people desired to modify the character of the government. The burden of taxation to which they had been subjected during Solomon's reign was very oppressive, so they assembled at Shechem and demanded from the king an alleviation of their burdens. He went to meet them at Shechem, and heard their demands for relief (1 Kings 12:1–4). After three days, having consulted with a younger generation of courtiers that had grown up around him, instead of following the advice of elders, he answered the people haughtily. "The king hearkened not unto the people; for the cause was from the LORD" (1 Kings 12:15; compare 11:31). This brought matters speedily to a crisis. The terrible cry was heard: "What portion have we in David? Neither have we inheritance in the son of Jesse: to your tents, O Israel: Now see to thine own house, David" (1 Kings 12:16; compare 2 Sam. 20:1).

And now at once the kingdom was rent in two. Rehoboam was appalled, and tried concessions, but it was too late (1 Kings 12:18). The tribe of Judah, Rehoboam's own tribe, alone remained faithful to him. Benjamin was reckoned along with Judah, and these two tribes formed the southern kingdom, with Jerusalem as its capital; while the northern ten tribes formed themselves into a separate kingdom, choosing Jeroboam as their king. Rehoboam tried to win back the revolted ten tribes by making war against them, but he was prevented by the prophet Shemaiah (1 Kings 12:21–24; 2 Chron. 11:1–4) from fulfilling his purpose.

In the fifth year of Rehoboam's reign, Shishak, one of the kings of Egypt of the Assyrian dynasty, stirred up, no doubt, by Jeroboam his son-in-law, made war against him. Jerusalem submitted to the invader, who plundered the temple and virtually reduced the kingdom to the position of a vassal of Egypt (1 Kings 14:25–26; 2 Chron. 12:5–9). A remarkable memorial of this invasion has been discovered at Karnac, in Upper Egypt, in certain sculptures on the walls of a small temple there. These sculptures represent the king, Shishak, holding in his hand a train of prisoners and other figures, with the names of the captured towns of Judah, the towns Rehoboam had fortified (2 Chron. 11:5–12).

The kingdom of Judah, under Rehoboam, sank more and more into moral and spiritual decay, and "there was war between Rehoboam and Jeroboam all their days" (1 Kings 14:30). At the age of fifty-eight, Rehoboam "slept with his fathers, and was buried with his fathers in the city of David" (1 Kings 14:31). He was succeeded by his son Abijah.

Bible study on the life of Rehoboam (NTB)

Successor to Solomon as king: 1 Kings 11:43; 2 Chronicles 9:31
Refuses to reform abuses: 1 Kings 12:1–15; 2 Chronicles 10:1–15
Ten tribes, under the leadership of Jeroboam, successfully revolt from: 1 Kings 12:16–24; 2 Chronicles 10:16–19; 11:1–4
Builds fortified cities; is temporarily prosperous: 2 Chronicles 11:5–23
Invaded by the king of Egypt and plundered: 1 Kings 14:25–28; 2 Chronicles 12:1–12
Death of: 1 Kings 14:31; 2 Chronicles 12:16
Genealogy and descendants of: 1 Chronicles 3; Matthew 1
Called Roboam: Matthew 1:7

ABIJAM

Significance in summary

Rehoboam's son who reigned as the second king of Judah for three years

Meaning of name

Jehovah is father

Bible dictionary/encyclopedia entry (CBC)

Abijam walked in the ways of his father and sinned against God (1 Kings 15:1–5). The war that had begun between the two kingdoms was continued during the reign of Abijam, and finally resulted in the defeat of Jeroboam (2 Chron. 13:1–20). During the latter part of Abijam's reign he became powerful and married fourteen wives (2 Chron. 13:21–22). He reigned three years contemporaneously with Jeroboam (1 Kings 14:20; 15:1–2).

Bible study on the life of Abijam (NTB)

Also called Abijah and Abia; king of Judah: 1 Kings 14:31; 15:1; 2 Chronicles 12:16
History of: 1 Kings 15:1–8; 2 Chronicles 11:22; 13
Succeeded by Asa: 1 Kings 15:8; 2 Chronicles 14:1

ASA

Significance in summary

Judah's third king, son of Abijam and ancestor of Jesus Christ

Meaning of name

healer

Bible dictionary/encyclopedia entry (CBC)

Immediately on his accession to the throne Asa inaugurated a reformation: he removed the sodomites from the land; removed all the idols his father had made; removed his mother from being queen and destroyed her idol. His heart was perfect toward the Lord; the things his father had dedicated, he brought into the house of the Lord (1 Kings 15:9–15). There was war between Asa and Baasha, and success seemed to attend Baasha for a time, but finally Asa induced Ben-hadad to make a league with him which resulted in favor of Asa (1 Kings 15:16–22).

Asa greatly improved his military equipment and increased the army (2 Chron. 14:1–8). He gained a victory over the mighty host of Zerah the Ethiopian (2 Chron. 14:9–15). After this victory he was met by Azariah, a servant of God, who strengthened and encouraged him (2 Chron. 15:1–7). He was also greatly encouraged by Oded, the prophet, and, as a result of his words, pushed his reforms and gathered his people together at Jerusalem, where they offered sacrifices and entered into a covenant to seek and serve the Lord (2 Chron. 15:8–19).

Later, Asa was severely rebuked by Hanani because he had relied on the Syrians to assist him in war. Asa was angry with the seer and imprisoned him, and he also oppressed some of the people (2 Chron. 16:7–10). Asa's closing years were clouded by disease and sorrow; he sought physicians and not the Lord. He slept with his fathers, and his countrymen buried him with distinguished honors in the city of David (2 Chron. 16:11–14). Asa reigned forty-one years (2 Kings 15:8–10), and was contemporary with seven of the kings of Israel: (1) Jeroboam, two years (1 Kings 14:20, 31; 15:1, 2; 2 Chron. 12:13); (2) Nadab, two years (1 Kings 14:20; 15:25); (3) Baasha, twenty-four years (1 Kings 15:33); (4) Elah, two years (1 Kings 16:8); (5) Zimri, seven days (1 Kings 16:8–10, 15); (6) Omri, six years (1 Kings 16:23, 28, 29); (7) Ahab, three years (1 Kings 16:29).

ZERAH

Significance in summary

Ethiopian commander who attacked King Asa of Judah

Meaning of name

shining, or, risen

JEHOSHAPHAT

Significance in summary

Son of King Asa who became the fourth king of Judah

Meaning of name

God is judge

Bible dictionary/encyclopedia entry (IBD)

After fortifying his kingdom against Israel (2 Chron. 17:1–2), Jehoshaphat set himself to cleanse the land of idolatry (1 Kings 22:43). In the third year of his reign he sent out priests and Levites over the land to instruct the people in the law (2 Chron. 17:7–9). He enjoyed a great measure of peace and prosperity, the blessing of God resting on the people "in their basket and their store."

The great mistake of his reign came when he made an alliance with Ahab, the king of Israel, which involved him in much disgrace, and brought disaster on his kingdom (1 Kings 22:1–33). Escaping from the bloody battle of Ramoth-gilead, the prophet Jehu (2 Chron. 19:1–3) reproached him for the course he had been pursuing; once more Jehoshaphat entered his former course of opposition to all idolatry, and of deepening interest in the worship of God and in the righteous government of the people (2 Chron. 19:4–11).

He subsequently joined Jehoram, king of Israel, in a war against the Moabites, who were under tribute to Israel. This war was successful. The Moabites were subdued, but the dreadful act of Mesha, king of Moab, in offering his own son as a sacrifice on the walls of Kir-haresheth in the sight of the armies of Israel filled him with horror, and he withdrew and returned to his own land (2 Kings 3:4–27).

The last most notable event of his reign was that recorded in 2 Chronicles 20. The Moabites formed a powerful confederacy with the surrounding nations, and came against Jehoshaphat. The allied forces were encamped at En-gedi. The king and his people were filled with alarm, and went to God in prayer. The king prayed in the court of the temple, "O our God, wilt thou not judge them? for we have no might against this great company that cometh against us" (2 Chron. 20:12). Amid the silence that followed, the voice of Jahaziel the Levite was heard announcing that on the next day all this great host would be overthrown. So it was, for they quarreled among themselves, and killed one another, leaving to the people of Judah only to gather the rich spoils of the dead. This was recognized as a great deliverance performed for them by God. Soon after this Jehoshaphat died, after a reign of twenty-five years, being sixty years old, and was succeeded by his son Jehoram (1 Kings 22:50). He had this testimony, that "he sought the Lord with all his heart" (2 Chron. 22:9). The kingdom of Judah was never more prosperous than under his reign.

Bible study on the life of Jehoshaphat (NTB)

Succeeds Asa: 1 Kings 15:24; 22:41; 1 Chronicles 3:10; 2 Chronicles 17:1; Matthew 1:8

Strengthens himself against Israel: 2 Chronicles 17:2

Inaugurates a system of public instruction in the law: 2 Chronicles 17:7–9
His wise reign: 1 Kings 22:43; 2 Chronicles 17:7–9; 19:3–11
His system of taxation: 2 Chronicles 17:11
His military forces and armaments: 2 Chronicles 17:12–19
Joins Ahab in an invasion of Ramoth-gilead: 1 Kings 22; 2 Chronicles 18
Rebuked by the prophet Jehu: 2 Chronicles 19:2
The allied forces of the Amorites, Moabites, and other tribes invade his territory, and are defeated by: 2 Chronicles 20
Builds ships for commerce with Tarshish, ships are destroyed: 1 Kings 22:48–49; 2 Chronicles 20:35–37
Joins Jehoram, king of Israel, in an invasion of the land of Moab, defeats the Moabites: 2 Kings 3
Makes valuable gifts to the temple: 2 Kings 12:18
Death of: 1 Kings 22:50; 2 Chronicles 21:1
Religious zeal of: 1 Kings 22:43, 46; 2 Chronicles 17:1–9; 19; 20:1–32; 22:9
Prosperity of: 1 Kings 22:45, 48
Bequests of, to his children: 1 Chronicles 21:2–3

JEHORAM

Significance in summary

Son of Jehoshaphat, the fifth king of Judah, and ancestor of Jesus Christ

Meaning of name

God is high

Bible dictionary/encyclopedia entry (CBC)

Jehoram's reign was characterized by murder, war, devastation, and great trouble. Elijah prophesied that a great plague would devastate his family and that Jehoram himself would suffer with sickness. He reigned eight years (2 Chron. 21:1, 5); contemporary of Jehoshaphat, king of Israel (1 Kings 22:42; 2 Kings 3:1). He died, a disgrace, but was buried in the city of David.

Bible study on the life of Jehoram (NTB)

King of Judah: 1 Kings 22:50; 2 Kings 8:16; 1 Chronicles 3:11; 2 Chronicles 21:5

Marries Athaliah, whose wicked counsels influence his reign for evil: 2 Kings 8:18–19; 2 Chronicles 21:6–13
Murders his brothers to strengthen himself in his sovereignty: 2 Chronicles 21:4, 13
Edom revolts from: 2 Kings 8:20–22; 2 Chronicles 21:8–10
The Philistines and Arabians invade his territory: 2 Chronicles 21:16–17
Death of: 2 Chronicles 21:18–20; 2 Kings 8:24
Prophecy concerning: 2 Chronicles 21:12–15
Ancestor of Jesus: Matthew 1:8

AHAZIAH

Significance in summary

Son of Jehoram, the sixth king of Judah who reigned for one year

Meaning of name

God sustains

Bible dictionary/ encyclopedia entry (CBC)

Ahaziah's reign was distinguished on account of his wickedness (2 Chron. 22:1–4). He went to Jezreel to visit Joram, king of Israel, who had been wounded in war with the Syrians, where he was killed by Jehu, the son of Nimshi (2 Chron. 22:5–9). Ahaziah reigned contemporaneously with Joram one year (2 Kings 8:24–26).

Bible study on the life of Ahaziah (NTB)

Called Azariah and Jehoahaz: 2 Chronicles 21:17; 25:23
History of: 2 Kings 8:25–29; 9:16–29
Gifts of, to the temple: 2 Kings 12:18
Brethren of, killed: 2 Kings 10:13–14
Succeeded by Athaliah: 2 Chronicles 22:10–12

ATHALIAH

Significance in summary

The only queen to rule over Judah

Meaning of name

God is strong

Bible dictionary/encyclopedia entry (IBD)

The daughter of Ahab and Jezebel, and the wife of Jehoram, king of Judah (2 Kings 8:18), who "walked in the ways of the house of Ahab" (2 Chron. 21:6), called "daughter" of Omri (2 Kings 8:26). On the death of her husband and of her son Ahaziah, she resolved to seat herself on the vacant throne. She slew all Ahaziah's children except Joash, the youngest (2 Kings 11:1, 2). After a reign of six years she was put to death in an insurrection (2 Kings 11:20; 2 Chron. 21:6; 22:10–12; 23:15), stirred up among the people in connection with Josiah's being crowned as king.

Bible study on the life of Athaliah (NTB)

Wife of Jehoram, king of Judah: 2 Kings 8:18, 26; 11:1–3, 12–16, 20; 2 Chronicles 22:10–12; 23:12–15, 21

JOASH/JEHOASH

Significance in summary

Son of King Ahaziah; became the seventh king of Judah when he was 7 years old

Meaning of name

God has given

Bible dictionary/encyclopedia entry (IBD)

While still an infant, he was saved from the general massacre of the family by his aunt Jehosheba, and was apparently the only surviving descendant of Solomon (2 Kings 11:1–3). His uncle, the high priest Jehoiada, brought him to public attention when he was seven years old, and crowned and anointed him king of Judah with the usual ceremonies. Athaliah was taken by surprise when she heard the shout of the people, "Long live the king"; and when she appeared in the temple, Jehoiada commanded her to be taken away and killed (2 Kings 11:13–20). While the high priest lived, Joash favored the worship of God and observed the law; but on the high priest's death he fell away into evil behavior, and the land was defiled with idolatry. Zechariah, the son and successor of the high priest, was put to death. These evil deeds brought down the judgment of God on the land.

He is one of the three kings omitted (Matt. 1:8) in the genealogy of Christ, the other two being Ahaziah and Amaziah. He was buried in the city of David (2 Kings 12:21) and was succeeded by his son.

Bible study on the life of Joash (NTB)

Saved from his grandmother by Jehosheba, his aunt, and hidden for six years: 2 Kings 11:1–3; 2 Chronicles 22:11–12
Anointed king by the priest Jehoiada: 2 Kings 11:12–21; 2 Chronicles 23
Righteousness of, under influence of Jehoiada: 2 Kings 12:2; 2 Chronicles 24:2
Repaired the temple: 2 Kings 12:4–16; 2 Chronicles 24:4–14, 27
Wickedness of, after Jehoiada's death: 2 Chronicles 24:17–22
Procured peace from Hazael, king of Syria, by gift of dedicated treasures from the temple: 2 Kings 12:17–18; 2 Chronicles 24:23–24
Prophecy against: 2 Chronicles 24:19–20
Put Jehoiada's son to death: 2 Chronicles 24:20–22; Matthew 23:35
Diseases of: 2 Chronicles 24:25
Conspired against and killed: 2 Kings 12:20–21; 2 Chronicles 24:25–26

JEHOIADA

Significance in summary

Chief priest in Jerusalem during the reigns of Ahaziah, Athaliah, and Joash

Meaning of name

The Lord knows

Bible study on the life of Jehoiada (NTB)

Overthrows Athaliah, the usurping queen of Judah, and establishes Joash on the throne: 2 Kings 11; 2 Chronicles 23
Salutary influence of, over Joash: 2 Kings 12:2; 2 Chronicles 24:2, 22
Directs the repairs of the temple: 2 Kings 12:4–16; 2 Chronicles 24:4–14
Death of: 2 Chronicles 24:4–16

AMAZIAH

Significance in summary

Succeeded his father Joash to the throne of Judah as the eighth king of Judah

Meaning of name

the Lord is mighty

Bible dictionary/encyclopedia entry (CBC)

Amaziah's reign was a mixture of good and evil, but the evil finally triumphed. He made great military preparations and defeated the Edomites in battle. Subsequently he challenged the king of Israel to war and was ingloriously defeated (2 Chron. 25:1–28). Amaziah reigned twenty-nine years (2 Kings 12:19–21; 14:1–2). He was contemporary with Jehoash fourteen years (2 Kings 13:10; 14:1–2) and Jeroboam fifteen years (2 Kings 14:23).

Bible study on the life of Amaziah (NTB)

History of: 2 Kings 14; 2 Chronicles 25

AZARIAH

Significance in summary

The ninth king of Judah, also known by the name Uzziah

Meaning of name

the Lord has helped

Bible dictionary/encyclopedia entry (CBC)

Azariah's reign was similar to his predecessors. He had a large army, and was successful in war because the Lord helped him (2 Chron. 26:1–15). Driven by his great success he became disobedient to the law of God; when he attempted to perform the duties of priest, the Lord sent on him the terrible disease of leprosy (2 Chron. 26:16–21). Uzziah reigned fifty-two years (2 Kings 15:1–2; 2 Chron. 26:1, 3). He was contemporary with Jeroboam fourteen years (2 Kings 15:1–2); Zachariah six months (2 Kings 15:8); Shallum one month (2 Kings 15:13); Menahem ten years (2 Kings 15:17); Pekahiah two years (2 Kings 15:23); and Pekah one year (2 Kings 15:27).

Bible study on the life of Azariah (NTB)

King of Judah, also called Uzziah: 2 Kings 14:21ff; 2 Chronicles 26

JOTHAM

Significance in summary

The tenth king of Judah

Meaning of name

God is perfect

Bible dictionary/encyclopedia entry (CBC)

The reign of Jotham was characterized by internal improvements and a successful contest with the Ammonites. His success is attributed to his fidelity to the Lord his God (2 Chron. 27:1–7). Jotham reigned sixteen years contemporaneously with Pekah (2 Kings 15:32–33).

Bible study on the life of Jotham (NTB)

Son of Azariah, king of Judah: 2 Kings 15:5–7, 32, 38; 1 Chronicles 3:12; 2 Chronicles 26:21–23; 27
Piety of: 2 Chronicles 27
The moral condition of Israel during his reign: Hosea 4
Ancestor of Jesus: Matthew 1:9

AHAZ

Significance in summary

The eleventh king of Judah and an ancestor of Jesus Christ

Meaning of name

he holds

Bible dictionary/encyclopedia entry (IBD)

The son and successor of Jotham, king of Judah (2 Kings 16; Isa. 7–9; 2 Chronicles 28). He gave himself over to a life of wickedness and idolatry. Despite the warnings of Isaiah, Hosea, and Micah, he appealed to Tiglath-pileser, the king of Assyria, for help against Rezin, king of Damascus, and Pekah, king of Israel, who threatened Jerusalem; great harm came to his kingdom (2 Kings 16:7, 9). He also introduced among his people many heathen and idolatrous customs (Isa. 8:19; 38:8; 2 Kings 23:12). He died at the age of thirty-five, after reigning sixteen years, and was succeeded by his son Hezekiah. Because of his wickedness he was "not brought into the sepulcher of the kings."

Bible study on the life of Ahaz (NTB)

King of Judah, son and successor of Jotham: 2 Kings 15:38; 16:1; 2 Chronicles 27:9; 28:1
Idolatrous abominations of: 2 Kings 16:3, 4; 2 Chronicles 28:2–4, 22–25
Kingdom of, invaded by the kings of Syria and Samaria: 2 Kings 16:5, 6; 2 Chronicles 28:5–8
Robs the temple to purchase aid from the king of Asia: 2 Kings 16:7–9, 17–18; 2 Chronicles 28:21
Visits Damascus, obtains a novel pattern of an altar, which he substitutes for the altar in the temple in Jerusalem, and otherwise perverts the forms of worship: 2 Kings 16:10–16
Sundial of: 2 Kings 20:11; Isaiah 38:8
Prophets in the reign of: Isaiah 1:1; Hosea 1:1; Micah 1:1
Prophecies concerning: Isaiah 7:13–25
Succeeded by Hezekiah: 2 Kings 16:20

HEZEKIAH

Significance in summary

The twelfth king of Judah; instituted godly religious reforms during his reign

Meaning of name

God is strength

Bible dictionary/encyclopedia entry (IBD)

Son of Ahaz (2 Kings 18:1; 2 Chron. 29:1), whom he succeeded on the throne of the kingdom of Judah. He reigned twenty-nine years. The history of this king is contained in 2 Kings 18–20, Isaiah 36–39, and 2 Chronicles 29–32. He is spoken of as a great and good king. In public life he followed the example of his great-grandfather Uzziah. He set himself to abolish idolatry from his kingdom, and so destroyed the "brazen serpent," which had been taken to Jerusalem, and had become an object of idolatrous worship (Num. 21:9). A great reformation took place in the kingdom of Judah in his day (2 Kings 18:4; 2 Chron. 29:3–36).

On the death of Sargon and the accession of his son Sennacherib to the throne of Assyria, Hezekiah refused to pay the tribute which his father had paid, and "rebelled against the king of Assyria, and served him not," but entered into an alliance with Egypt (Isa. 30–31; 36:6–9). This led to the invasion of Judah by Sennacherib (2 Kings 18:13–16), who took forty cities, and besieged Jerusalem with mounds. Hezekiah yielded to the demands of the Assyrian king, and agreed to pay him three hundred talents of silver and thirty of gold (18:14).

But Sennacherib dealt treacherously with Hezekiah (Isa. 33:1), and a second time within two years invaded his kingdom (2 Kings 18:17; 2 Chron. 32:9; Isaiah 36). This invasion resulted in the destruction of Sennacherib's army. Hezekiah prayed to God, and that night the angel of the Lord went out, and smote in the camp of the Assyrians 185,000 men. Sennacherib fled with the shattered remnant of his forces to Nineveh, where, seventeen years later, he was assassinated by his sons Adrammelech and Sharezer (2 Kings 19:37).

The narrative of Hezekiah's sickness and miraculous recovery is found in 2 Kings 20:1–11; 2 Chronicles 32:24; and Isaiah 38:1–8. Various ambassadors came to congratulate him on his recovery; among them was Berodach-baladan, the viceroy of Babylon (2 Kings 20:12). He closed his days in peace and prosperity, and was succeeded by his son Manasseh. He was buried in the "chiefest of the sepulchers of the sons of David" (2 Chron. 32:33). "After him was none like him among all the kings of Judah, nor any that were before him" (2 Kings 18:5).

Bible study on the life of Hezekiah (NTB)

King of Judah: 2 Kings 16:20; 18:1–2; 1 Chronicles 3:13; 2 Chronicles 29:1; Matthew 1:9
Religious zeal of: 2 Chronicles 29–31
Purges the nation of idolatry: 2 Kings 18:4; 2 Chronicles 31:1; 33:3
Restores the true forms of worship: 2 Chronicles 31:2–21
His piety: 2 Kings 18:3, 5, 6; 2 Chronicles 29:2; 31:20–21; 32:32; Jeremiah 26:19
Military operations of: 2 Kings 18:19; 1 Chronicles 4:39–43; 2 Chronicles 32; Isaiah 36–37
Sickness and restoration of: 2 Kings 20:1–11; 2 Chronicles 32:24; Isaiah 38:1–8
His psalm of thanksgiving: Isaiah 38:9–22
His lack of wisdom in showing his resources to commissioners of Babylon: 2 Kings 20:12–19; 2 Chronicles 32:25–26, 31; Isaiah 39
Prospered by God: 2 Kings 18:7; 2 Chronicles 32:27–30
Conducts the Gihon Brook into Jerusalem: 2 Kings 18:17; 20:20; 2 Chronicles 32:4, 30; 33:14; Nehemiah 2:13–15; 3:13, 16; Isaiah 7:3; 22:9–11; 36:2
Scribes of: Proverbs 25:1
Death and burial of: 2 Kings 20:21; 2 Chronicles 32:33
Prophecies concerning: 2 Kings 19:20–34; 20:5–6, 16–18; Isaiah 38:5–8; 39:5–7; Jeremiah 26:18–19

SENNACHERIB

Significance in summary

As king of Assyria he attacked Jerusalem but never succeeded in taking it

Meaning of name

Sin (the moon god) has increased the brothers

Bible dictionary/encyclopedia entry (IBD)

Son of Sargon, whom he succeeded on the throne of Assyria, in the twenty-third year of Hezekiah. He first set himself to break up the powerful combination of princes who were in league against him. Among these was Hezekiah, who had entered into an alliance with Egypt against Assyria. So he led a very powerful army of at least two hundred thousand men into Judea, and devastated the land on every side, taking and destroying many cities (2 Kings 18:13–16; 2 Chron. 32:1–8).

Hezekiah looked to Egypt for help (2 Kings 18:20–24). Sennacherib, hearing of this, marched a second time into Palestine (2 Kings 18:17, 37; 19; 2 Chron. 32:9–23; Isa. 36:2–22. Isaiah 37:25 should be translated "dried up all the Nile-arms of Matsor," i.e., of Egypt, so called from the "Matsor" or great fortification across the isthmus of Suez, which protected it from invasions from the east). Sennacherib sent envoys to try to persuade Hezekiah to surrender, but in vain. He next sent a threatening letter (2 Kings 19:10–14), which Hezekiah carried into the temple and spread before the Lord. Isaiah again brought an encouraging message to the pious king (2 Kings 19:20–34). That night the angel of the Lord smote the camp of the Assyrians. The Assyrian army was annihilated. This great disaster is not, as was to be expected, taken notice of in the Assyrian annals. Though Sennacherib survived this disaster some twenty years, he never again renewed his attempt against Jerusalem. He was murdered by two of his own sons (Adrammelech and Sharezer), and was succeeded by another son, Esarhaddon, after a reign of twenty-four years.

MANASSEH

Significance in summary

Reigned for fifty years as the thirteenth king of Judah

Meaning of name

One who causes forgetfulness

Bible dictionary/encyclopedia entry (IBD)

The only son and successor of Hezekiah on the throne of Judah. He was twelve years old when he began to reign (2 Kings 21:1), and he reigned fifty-five years. Though he reigned so long, comparatively little is known about this king. His reign was a continuation of that of Ahaz, both in religion and national polity. He quickly fell under the influence of the heathen court circle, and his reign was characterized by a sad relapse into idolatry with all its vices, showing that the reformation under his father had been, to a large extent, only superficial (Isa. 7:10; 2 Kings 21:10–15). A systematic and persistent attempt was made, and all too successfully, to banish the worship of Jehovah out of the land. Amid this widespread idolatry there were faithful prophets (Isaiah, Micah) who lifted up their voice in reproof and in warning. But their fidelity only aroused bitter hatred, and a period of cruel persecution against all the friends of the old religion began. There is an old Jewish tradition that Isaiah was put to death at this time (2 Kings 21:16; 24:3–4; Jer. 2:30), having been sawn asunder in the trunk of a tree. Manasseh has been called the "Nero of Palestine."

Esarhaddon, Sennacherib's successor on the Assyrian throne, who had his residence in Babylon for thirteen years (the only Assyrian monarch who ever reigned in Babylon), took Manasseh prisoner to Babylon. Such captive kings were usually treated with great cruelty. They were brought before the conqueror with a hook or ring passed through their lips or their jaws, having a cord attached to it, by which they were led. This is referred to in 2 Chronicles 33:11, where the Authorized Version reads that Esarhaddon "took Manasseh among the thorns"; while the Revised Version renders the words, "took Manasseh in chains"; or literally, as in the margin, "with hooks" (compare 2 Kings 19:28).

The severity of Manasseh's imprisonment brought him to repentance. God heard his cry, and he was restored to his kingdom (2 Chron. 33:11–13). He abandoned his idolatrous ways, and enjoined the people to worship Jehovah; but there was no thorough reformation. After a lengthened reign extending through fifty-five years, the longest in the history of Judah, he died, and was buried in the garden of Uzza, the "garden of his own house" (2 Kings 21:17–18; 2 Chron. 33:20), and not in the city of David, among his ancestors. He was succeeded by his son Amon.

Bible study on the life of Manasseh (NTB)

History of: 2 Kings 21:1–18; 2 Chronicles 33:1–20

ESARHADDON

Significance in summary

Made Manasseh, king of Judah, subject to him

Meaning of name

Assur has given a brother

Bible study on the life of Esarhaddon (NTB)

Succeeds Sennacherib: 2 Kings 19:37; Isaiah 37:38
Called Asnapper: Ezra 4:2, 10

RABSARIS

Significance in summary

Title given to Assyrian official visiting Jerusalem in King Hezekiah's reign

Bible study on the life of Rabsaris (NTB)

Sent by Sennacherib against Jerusalem: 2 Kings 18:17

RAB-SHAKEH

Significance in summary

Title given to Assyrian official visiting Jerusalem in King Hezekiah's reign

Bible study on the life of Rab-shakeh (NTB)

Sent by Sennacherib against Jerusalem; undertakes to cause disloyalty to Hezekiah and the surrender of Jerusalem by a speech in the Jews' native language: 2 Kings 18:17–36; 19:4, 8; Isaiah 36–37

TARTAN

Significance in summary

Title given to Assyrian official visiting Jerusalem in King Hezekiah's reign

Bible study on the life of Tartan (NTB)

An Assyrian general: 2 Kings 18:17; Isaiah 20:1

SHEBNA(H)

Significance in summary

One of King Hezekiah's most important officials

Meaning of name

youthfulness

Bible study on the life of Shebna(h) (NTB)

A scribe of Hezekiah: 2 Kings 18:18, 26, 37; 19:2; Isaiah 36:3, 11, 22; 37:2

MERODACH-BALADAN

Significance in summary

A king of Babylon who reigned during King Hezekiah's reign

Meaning of name

Marduk has given a son

Bible study on the life of Merodach-Baladan (NTB)

Sends congratulatory letters and a present to Hezekiah: 2 Kings 20:12; Isaiah 39:1

AMON

Significance in summary

Succeeded to the throne of Judah after his father Manasseh, and became its fourteenth king

Meaning of name

workman

Bible dictionary/encyclopedia entry (IBD)

Amon restored idolatry and set up the images his father had thrown down. Zephaniah (1:4; 3:4, 11) refers to the moral depravity prevailing in this king's reign.

He was assassinated (2 Kings 21:18–26; 2 Chron. 33:20–25) by his own servants, who conspired against him.

Bible study on the life of Amon (NTB)

King of Judah: 2 Kings 21:18–26; 2 Chronicles 33:21–25; Zephaniah 1:1; Matthew 1:10

JOSIAH

Significance in summary

Judah's fifteenth king and one of its most godly rulers; the book of the law was found in the Temple during his reign

Meaning of name

God supports

Bible dictionary/encyclopedia entry (IBD)

The son of Amon, and his successor on the throne of Judah (2 Kings 22:1; 2 Chron. 34:1). His history is contained in 2 Kings 22–23. He stands foremost among all the kings of the line of David for unswerving loyalty to Jehovah (23:25). He ascended the throne at the early age of eight years, and it appears that not till eight years afterwards did he begin "to seek after the God of David his father." At that age he devoted himself to God. He distinguished himself by beginning a war of extermination against the prevailing idolatry, which had practically been the state religion for some seventy years (2 Chron. 34:3; compare Jer. 25:3, 11, 29).

In the eighteenth year of his reign he repaired and beautified the temple, which had become very dilapidated (2 Kings 22:3, 5–6; 23:23; 2 Chron. 34:11). While this work was being carried on, Hilkiah, the high priest, discovered a roll, which was probably the original copy of the law, the entire Pentateuch, written by Moses.

When this book was read to him, the king was alarmed by the things it contained, and sent for Huldah the prophetess for her counsel. She spoke to him words of encouragement, telling him that he would be gathered to his fathers in peace before the threatened days of judgment came (2 Kings 22:3–20). Josiah immediately gathered the people together, and engaged them in a renewal of their ancient national covenant with God. The Passover was then celebrated, as in the days of his great predecessor, Hezekiah, with unusual magnificence (2 Chron. 35:1–19). Nevertheless, "the LORD turned not from the fierceness of his great wrath, wherewith his anger was kindled against Judah" (2 Kings 23:26). Jeremiah helped this great religious revolution on by his earnest exhortations.

Soon after this, Pharaoh-nechoh II, king of Egypt, in an expedition against the king of Assyria, with the view of gaining possession of Carchemish, sought a passage through the territory of Judah for his army. Josiah refused. He had probably entered into some new alliance with the king of Assyria, and faithful to his word he sought to oppose the progress of Nechoh.

The army of Judah went out and encountered the Egyptian army at Megiddo, on the verge of the plain of Esdraelon. Josiah went into the field in disguise, and was fatally wounded by a random arrow. His attendants took him toward Jerusalem but had only reached Hadadrimmon, a few miles south of Megiddo, when he died (2 Kings 23:28, 30; compare 2 Chron. 35:20–27), after a reign of thirty-one years. He was buried with the greatest honors in fulfillment of Huldah's prophecy (2 Kings 22:20; compare Jer. 34:5). Jeremiah composed a funeral elegy on this the best of the kings of Israel (2 Chron. 35:25; Lam. 4:20). The outburst of national grief on account of his death became proverbial (Zech. 12:11; compare Rev. 16:16).

Bible study on the life of Josiah (NTB)

King of Judah: 2 Kings 21:24–26; 22:1; 1 Chronicles 3:14; 2 Chronicles 33:25
Ancestor of Jesus: Matthew 1:10–11
Killed in battle with Pharaoh-nechoh: 2 Kings 23:29–30; 2 Chronicles 35:20–24
Lamentations for: 2 Chronicles 35:25
Piety of: exemplified in his repairing of the temple: 2 Kings 22:3–7; 2 Chronicles 34:1–4
Copy of the law was discovered and read to him: 2 Kings 22:8–20; 2 Chronicles 34:14–33
In keeping a solemn Passover: 2 Kings 23:21–23; 2 Chronicles 35:1–19
Called Josias: Matthew 1:10–11
Prophecies concerning: 1 Kings 13:1–3
Destroys the altar and high places of idolatry: 2 Kings 23:3–20, 24–25

HILKIAH

Significance in summary

High priest in Jerusalem during King Josiah's reign

Meaning of name

the Lord is my portion

Bible dictionary/encyclopedia entry (IBD)

To him and his deputy (2 Kings 23:5), along with the ordinary priests and the Levites who were in charge of the gates, was entrusted the purification of the temple in Jerusalem. While this was in progress, he discovered in some hidden corner of the building a book called the "book of the law" (2 Kings 22:8) and the "book of the covenant" (23:2). Some have supposed that this "book" was nothing else than the original copy of the Pentateuch written by Moses (Deut. 31:9–26). This remarkable discovery occurred in the eighteenth year of Josiah's reign, a discovery which permanently affected the whole subsequent history of Israel.

Bible study on the life of Hilkiah (NTB)

High priest: 2 Kings 22:4, 8, 10, 12, 14; 23:4, 24; 1 Chronicles 6:13; 9:11; 2 Chronicles 34:9, 14–15, 18, 20, 22; Ezra 7:1; Jeremiah 29:3

SHAPHAN

Significance in summary

The official who told King Josiah about the finding of the book of the law in the temple

Meaning of name

rock badger

Bible study on the life of Shaphan (NTB)

A scribe of King Josiah: 2 Kings 22:3–14; 2 Chronicles 34:8–20
Father of Gemariah: Jeremiah 36:10–12

JEHOAHAZ

Significance in summary

Judah's sixteenth king, who ruled for three months

Meaning of name

God has grasped

Bible dictionary/encyclopedia entry (IBD)

Josiah's third son, usually called Shallum (1 Chron. 3:15). He succeeded his father on the throne, and reigned over Judah for three months (2 Kings 23:31, 34). He fell into the idolatrous ways of his predecessors (23:32), was deposed by Pharaoh-nechoh from the throne, and carried away prisoner into Egypt, where he died in captivity (23:33–34; Jer. 22:10–12; 2 Chron. 36:1–4).

Bible study on the life of Jehoahaz (NTB)

Also called Shallum; king of Judah and successor of Josiah: 2 Kings 23:30–31; 1 Chronicles 3:15; 2 Chronicles 36:1; Jeremiah 22:11
Wicked reign of: 2 Kings 23:32
Pharaoh-nechoh, king of Egypt, invades his kingdom and takes him away captive to Egypt: 2 Kings 23:33–35; 2 Chronicles 36:3–4
Prophecies concerning: Jeremiah 22:10–12

JEHOIAKIM

Significance in summary

Judah's seventeenth king who was cruel and greedy

Meaning of name

God establishes

Bible study on the life of Jehoiakim (NTB)

King of Judah: 1 Chronicles 3:15
Ancestor of Jesus: Matthew 1:11
Wicked reign and final overthrow of: 2 Kings 23:34–37; 24:1–6; 2 Chronicles 36:4–8; Jeremiah 22:13–19; 26:22–23; 36; Daniel 1:1–2
Dies, and is succeeded by his son, Jehoiachin: 2 Kings 24:6

JEHOIACHIN

Significance in summary

The eighteenth king of Judah, who reigned for only three months before he was taken to Babylon by King Nebuchadnezzar

Meaning of name

God will establish

Bible study on the life of Jehoiachin (NTB)

King of Judah and successor to his father, Jehoiakim: 2 Kings 24:6–8; 2 Chronicles 36:8–9
Called Jeconiah: 1 Chronicles 3:16; Jeremiah 24:1
Called Coniah: Jeremiah 22:24; 37:1
Wicked reign of: 2 Kings 24:9; 2 Chronicles 36:9
Nebuchadnezzar invades his kingdom, takes him away captive to Babylon: 2 Kings 24:10–16; 2 Chronicles 36:10; Esther 2:6; Jeremiah 27:20; 29:1–2; Ezekiel 1:2
Confined in prison for thirty-seven years: 2 Kings 25:27
Released from prison by Evil-merodach, promoted above other kings, and honored until death: 2 Kings 25:27–30; Jeremiah 52:31–34
Prophecies concerning: Jeremiah 22:24–30; 28:4
Sons of: 1 Chronicles 3:17–18
Ancestor of Jesus: Matthew 1:12

EVIL-MERODACH

Significance in summary

The king of Babylon who released Jehoiachin of Judah from prison

Meaning of name

man of (the god) Marduk

Bible dictionary/encyclopedia entry (IBD)

The son and successor of Nebuchadnezzar, king of Babylon (2 Kings 25:27; Jer. 52:31, 34). He seems to have reigned for only two years. Influenced probably by Daniel, he showed kindness to Jehoiachin, who had been a prisoner in Babylon for thirty-seven years. He released him, and “spoke kindly to him.” He was murdered by Nergal-sharezer, that is, Neriglissar, his brother-in-law, who succeeded him (Jer. 39:3, 13).

Bible study on the life of Evil-merodach (NTB)

Released Jehoiachin from prison: 2 Kings 25:27–30; Jeremiah 52:31–34

ZEDEKIAH

Significance in summary

The nineteenth and last king of Judah; was blinded before being carted off to Babylon

Meaning of name

Jehovah is mighty

Bible dictionary/encyclopedia entry (IBD)

Zedekiah was the third son of Josiah; his mother's name was Hamutal, the daughter of Jeremiah of Libnah, and hence he was the brother of Jehoahaz (2 Kings 23:31; 24:17–18). His original name was Mattaniah, but when Nebuchadnezzar placed him on the throne as the successor to Jehoiachin he changed his name to Zedekiah. The prophet Jeremiah was his counselor, yet he did evil in the sight of the Lord (2 Kings 24:19–20; Jer. 52:2–3). He ascended the throne at the age of twenty-one. The kingdom was then under the control of Nebuchadnezzar; despite the strong remonstrances of Jeremiah and others, as well as the example of Jehoiachin, he threw off the yoke of Babylon, and entered into an alliance with Hophra, king of Egypt. This brought Nebuchadnezzar, "with all his host" (2 Kings 25:1), to launch an attack against Jerusalem. During this siege, which lasted about eighteen months, a severe famine plagued the city (2 Kings 25:3; Lam. 4:4–5, 10). The city was plundered and laid in ruins. Zedekiah and his followers, attempting to escape, were made captive and taken to Riblah. There, after seeing his own children put to death, his own eyes were put out, and, being loaded with chains, he was carried captive to Babylon (2 Kings 25:1–7; 2 Chron. 36:12; Jer. 32:4–5; 34:2–3; 39:1–7; 52:4–11; Ezek. 12:12), where he remained a prisoner, how long is unknown, to the day of his death.

After the fall of Jerusalem, Nebuzaraddan was sent to carry out its complete destruction. The city was razed to the ground. Only a few vinedressers and husbandmen were permitted to remain in the land (Jer. 52:16). Gedaliah, with a Chaldean guard stationed at Mizpah, ruled over Judah (2 Kings 25:22, 24; Jer. 40:1–2, 5–6).

Bible study on the life of Zedekiah (NTB)

Made king of Judah by Nebuchadnezzar: 2 Kings 24:17–18; 1 Chronicles 3:15; 2 Chronicles 36:10; Jeremiah 37:1
Throws off his allegiance to Nebuchadnezzar: 2 Kings 24:20; 2 Chronicles 36:13; Jeremiah 52:3; Ezekiel 17:12–21
Forms an alliance with the king of Egypt: Ezekiel 17:11–18
The allegiance denounced by Jeremiah and Ezekiel: 2 Chronicles 36:12; Jeremiah 21; 24:8–10; 27:12–22; 32:3–5; 34; 37:7–10, 17; 38:14–28; Ezekiel 12:10–16; 17:12–21
Imprisons Jeremiah on account of his denunciations: Jeremiah 32:2–3; 37:15–21; 38:5–28
Seeks the intercession of Jeremiah with God on his behalf: Jeremiah 21:1–3; 37:3; 38:14–27
The evil reign of: 2 Kings 24:19–20; 2 Chronicles 36:12–13; Jeremiah 37:2; 38:5, 19, 24–26; 52:2
Nebuchadnezzar destroys the city and temple, takes him captive to Babylon, kills his sons, blinds his eyes: 2 Kings 25:1–10; 2 Chronicles 36:17–20; Jeremiah 1:3; 32:1–2; 39:1–10; 51:59; 52:4–30

TIGLATH-PILESER

Significance in summary

The king of Assyria who was powerful enough to help both King Pekah of Israel and King Ahaz of Judah

Bible dictionary/encyclopedia entry (IBD)

Tiglath-Pileser III, or Tilgath-Pilneser, the Assyrian throne-name of Pul. He appears in the Assyrian records as gaining, in the fifth year of his reign, a victory over Azariah (that is, Uzziah in 2 Chron. 26:1), king of Judah, whose achievements are described in 2 Chronicles 26:6–15. He is first mentioned in Scripture, however, as gaining a victory over Pekah, king of Israel, and Rezin of Damascus, who were confederates. He put Rezin to death, and punished Pekah by taking a considerable part of his kingdom, and carrying off a vast number of its inhabitants into captivity (2 Kings 15:29; 16:5–9; 1 Chron. 5:6, 26), the Reubenites, the Gadites, and half the tribe of Manasseh, whom he settled in Gozan. In the Assyrian annals it is further related that, before he returned from Syria, he held a court at Damascus, and received submission and tribute from the neighboring kings, among whom were Pekah of Samaria and "Yahu-khazi [i.e., Ahaz], king of Judah" (compare 2 Kings 16:10–16).

He was the founder of what is called "the second Assyrian empire," an empire meant to embrace the whole world, the center of which would be Nineveh. He died in 728 BC, and was succeeded by a general of his army, Ulula, who assumed the name Shalmaneser IV.

Bible study on the life of Tiglath-Pileser (NTB)

Also called Tilgath-Pilneser, king of Assyria; invades Israel; carries part of the people captive to Assyria: 2 Kings 15:29; 1 Chronicles 5:6, 26

Forms an alliance with Ahaz; captures Damascus: 2 Kings 16:7–10; 2 Chronicles 28:19–21

Judah's Prophets

Joel • Shemaiah • Oded • Jahaziel • Zechariah • Isaiah • Shear-Jashub • Maher-Shalal-Hash-Baz • Nahum • Jeremiah • Baruch • Uriah • Jehudi • Ebed-melech • Pashur • Johanan • Hanamel • Hananiah • Micah • Zephaniah • Habakkuk • Obadiah • Huldah

Introduction (TCB, CCEB)

TCB

The first occurrence of the expression "the man of God" is in Deuteronomy 33:1, and is used of Moses.

He was so called, not because he foretold, but because he spoke for God. This is the meaning of the word "prophet" as taught by its first occurrence in Genesis 20:7. The prophet was God's "spokesman" (Exod. 4:16; compare Exod. 7:1).

God's spokesman could know what to speak for Him only (1) from His Spirit (Neh. 9:30; compare Hos. 9:7, margin, and see Num. 11:16, 17, 25–29); (2) from Jehovah making Himself known (Num. 12:6; Ezek. 3:17; Jer. 15:19; compare 2 Chron. 36:12); and (3) from God's written word. This is why Timothy is the only one called a "man of God" in the New Testament (1 Tim. 6:11), and why, today, one, and only one who knows "all scripture," which is so profitable, can be called a "man of God" (2 Tim. 3:17).

All such are God's spokesmen because they alone know what He wishes to be spoken. They are His witnesses (Acts 1:8; 22:15). Christ was the prophet because He spoke only those things which were given to him to speak, and He alone is "the faithful witness" (Rev. 1:5).

It was for the above reasons that the expression "the man of God" became the general name for a prophet among ordinary people.

CCEB

History, as written by the prophets, is retroverted prophecy. As the past and future alike proceed from the essence of God, an inspired insight into the past implies an insight into the future, and vice versa. Hence most of the Old Testament histories are written by prophets and are classed with their writings; the Chronicles being not so classed, cannot have been written by them, but are taken from historical monographs of theirs; for example, Isaiah's life of Uzziah, 2 Chronicles 26:22; also of Hezekiah, 2 Chronicles 32:32; of these latter all that was important for all ages has been preserved for us, while the rest, which was local and temporary, has been lost.

JOEL

Significance in summary

Remembered for his vision of a plague of locusts; his prophecies are recorded in an Old Testament book named after him

Meaning of name

the Lord is God

Bible dictionary/encyclopedia entry (SBD)

The second of the twelve minor prophets, the son of Pethuel, probably prophesied in Judah during the reign of Uzziah, about 800 BC. The book of Joel contains an outline of a terrible scene, which was to be depicted in more and more detail by subsequent prophets. The actual event to which the prophecy related was a public calamity then impending on Judah—a plague of locusts—and continuing for several years. The prophet exhorts the people to turn to God with penitence, fasting, and prayer; and then, he says, the plague will cease, and the rain will cause the land to yield her accustomed fruit. God, by the outpouring of His Spirit, will extend the blessings of true religion to heathen lands. The prophecy is referred to in Acts 2.

A Bible commentator's portrait (CCEB)

Joel (meaning "one to whom Jehovah is God," i.e., worshipper of Jehovah) seems to have belonged to Judah, as no reference occurs to Israel; whereas he speaks of Jerusalem, the temple, the priests, and the ceremonies, as if he were intimately familiar with them (compare Joel 1:14; 2:1, 15, 32; 3:1–2, 6, 16–17, 20–21). His predictions were probably delivered in the early days of Joash, for no reference is made in them to the Babylonian, Assyrian, or even the Syrian invasion, and the only enemies mentioned are the Philistines, Phoenicians, Edomites, and Egyptians (Joel 3:4, 19). Had he lived after Joash, he would doubtless have mentioned the Syrians among the enemies whom he enumerates since they took Jerusalem and carried off spoil to Damascus (2 Chron. 24:23, 24). No idolatry is mentioned; and the temple services, the priesthood, and other institutions of the theocracy, are represented as flourishing. This all answers to the state of things under the high priesthood of Jehoiada, through whom Joash had been placed on the throne and who lived in the early years of Joash (2 Kings 11:17, 18; 12:2–16; 2 Chron. 24:4–14).

Bible study on the life of Joel (NTB)

One of the twelve minor prophets, probably lived in the days of Uzziah: Joel 1:1; Acts 2:16
Declares the terribleness of God's judgments: Joel 1; 2:1–11
Denounces judgments against the enemies of God: Joel 3:1–17
Sets forth the blessings of the church: Joel 3:18–21

SHEMAIAH

Significance in summary

The prophet who warned King Rehoboam not to go to war

Meaning of name

the Lord hears

Bible dictionary/encyclopedia entry (CBC)

Shemaiah flourished during the reign of Rehoboam and communicated to him the command of the Lord not to go to war against the ten tribes when they rebelled against his authority (1 Kings 12:22–24).

Bible study on the life of Shemaiah (NTB)

Prevents Rehoboam from war with Jeroboam: 1 Kings 12:22–24; 2 Chronicles 11:2–4
Prophesies the punishment of Rehoboam by Shishak, king of Egypt: 2 Chronicles 12:5, 7
Writes chronicles: 2 Chronicles 12:15

ODED

Significance in summary

Prophet who managed to persuade King Pekah of Israel not to inflict great cruelty on the prisoners he took when he invaded Judah

Meaning of name

restorer

Bible dictionary/encyclopedia entry (ISBE)

According to 2 Chronicles 28, Oded protested against the enslavement of the captives Pekah had brought from Judah and Jerusalem on his return from the Syro-Ephraimitic attack on the Southern Kingdom (735 BC). He was joined in this protest by some of the leaders of Ephraim, and the captives were well treated. After those who were naked (i.e., those who had scanty clothing; compare the meaning of the word "naked" in Mark 14:51) had been supplied with clothing from the spoil, and the bruised anointed with oil, the prisoners were escorted to Jericho.

Bible study on the life of Oded (NTB)

Father of the prophet Azariah: 2 Chronicles 15:1
A prophet in Samaria, in the time of Ahaz and Pekah: 2 Chronicles 28:9–15

JAHAZIEL

Significance in summary

A prophet who encouraged King Jehoshaphat in his fight against the Moabites

Meaning of name

God sees

Bible dictionary/encyclopedia entry (CBC)

The prophets Jehu, the son of Hanani (2 Chron. 19:1–3), and Jahaziel flourished during the reign of Jehoshaphat (2 Chron. 20:14–17).

Bible study on the life of Jahaziel (NTB)

A disaffected Israelite who joined David at Ziklag: 1 Chronicles 12:4
A priest: 1 Chronicles 16:6
Son of Hebron: 1 Chronicles 23:19; 24:23
A Levite and a prophet: 2 Chronicles 20:14
A chief, or the father of a chief, among the exiles, who returned from Babylon: Ezra 8:5

ZECHARIAH

Significance in summary

Eleventh of the twelve minor prophets

Meaning of name

the Lord remembers

Bible dictionary/encyclopedia entry (FBD)

Son of Berechiah, grandson of Iddo. Zechariah was probably, like Ezekiel, priest as well as prophet. His priestly birth suits the sacerdotal character of his prophecies (Zech. 6:13).

He left Babylon, the city of his birth, when he was very young. Zechariah began prophesying in youth (Zech. 2:4). In the eighth month of Darius's second year, Zechariah first prophesied with Haggai (who began two months earlier) in support of Zerubbabel and Shealtiel in the rebuilding of the temple, which had been suspended.

Bible study on the life of Zechariah (NTB)

Son of Berechiah: Zechariah 2:4
Prophesied during the reign of Darius: Ezra 4:24; 5:1; 6:14; Zechariah 1:1, 7; 7:1
Probably the priest mentioned in: Nehemiah 12:16; Ezra 8:3, 11, 16

ISAIAH

Significance in summary

Known as "the prince of the prophets"; prophesied for over sixty years

Meaning of name

salvation of God

Bible dictionary/encyclopedia entry (CBC)

An Old Testament prophet who vividly predicted the coming of the Messiah. The chief events in the life of Isaiah were:

- He began his public ministry in the days of Uzziah, king of Judah, by denouncing the wickedness of Judah and Israel (Isa. 1:1–31).
- He predicted that the word of the Lord would go out from Jerusalem, and that finally the nations would beat their implements of war into implements of peace and learn war no more (Isa. 2:1–4).
- He had a vision of the glory of God (Isa. 6:1–12).
- He comforted Ahaz, the king of Judah, and assured him that a virgin would conceive and bring forth a son whose name would be Immanuel (Isa. 7:1–16).
- He predicted the birth of Jesus Christ and the triumphs of his kingdom (Isa. 9:1–7).
- He predicted the gathering again of Israel (Isa. 10:20–27; 11:11–16; 14:1–3).
- He predicted the downfall of Babylon (Isa. 13:1–22).
- He predicted the destruction of Moab (Isa. 15:1–9; 16:1–14).
- He predicted the downfall of Damascus (Isa. 17:1–3).
- He predicted the downfall of Egypt (Isa. 19:1–25).
- He comforted Hezekiah, and predicted the overthrow of the Assyrians (2 Kings 19:6–37; Isa. 37:6–38).
- He predicted the sickness and restoration of Hezekiah and the sign given him (2 Kings 20:1–11; Isa. 38:1–8).
- He condemned Hezekiah for showing his treasures to the ambassadors of the king of Babylon and predicted the captivity of the people of Judah (2 Kings 20:12–19; Isa. 39:1–8).
- He predicted the coming of the harbinger of the Lord (Isa. 40:1–8).

- He predicted the restoration of the captives and the rebuilding of the temple under Cyrus (Isa. 44:28; 45:1–13).
- He predicted the humiliation and sufferings of the Messiah (Isa. 53:1–12).
- He predicted the call of the Gentiles (Isa. 54:1–4; 60:1–11).
- He heard with prophetic ear the glorious invitation of the gospel (Isa. 55:1–5; Matt. 11:28–30).
- He predicted the giving of the new name (Isa. 62:1–4; Acts 11:1–26).
- He described the conquering march of the Messiah (Isa. 63:1–9).

A Bible commentator's portrait (CCEB)

Isaiah, son of Amoz (not Amos); contemporary of Jonah, Amos, Hosea, in Israel, but younger than they; and of Micah, in Judah. His call to a higher degree of the prophetic office (Isa. 6:1–13) is assigned to the last year of Uzziah, that is, 754 BC. The first through fifth chapters belong to the closing years of that reign; not, as some think, to Jotham's reign; in the reign of the latter he seems to have exercised his office only orally, and not to have left any record of his prophecies because they were not intended for all ages. The first through sixth chapters are all that was designed for the church universal of the prophecies of the first twenty years of his office. New historical epochs, such as occurred in the reigns of Ahaz and Hezekiah, when the affairs of Israel became interwoven with those of the Asiatic empires, are marked by prophetic writings. The prophets now had to interpret the judgments of the Lord, so as to make the people conscious of His punitive justice as well as His mercy. Isaiah 7:1–10:4 belong to the reign of Ahaz. The thirty-sixth through thirty-ninth chapters are historical, reaching to the fifteenth year of Hezekiah; probably the tenth through twelfth chapters and the thirteenth through twenty-sixth chapters, inclusive, belong to the same reign; thus we have Isaiah's office extending from about 760 to 713 BC, forty-seven years.

Tradition (Talmud) represents him as having been sawn in half by Manasseh with a wooden saw for having said that he had seen Jehovah (Exod. 33:20; 2 Kings 21:16; Heb. 11:37). The second part, the fortieth through sixty-sixth chapters, containing complaints of gross idolatry, is not restricted to Manasseh's reign, but is applicable to previous reigns. At the accession of Manasseh, Isaiah would be eighty-four, and if he prophesied for eight years afterwards, he must have endured martyrdom at ninety-two; so Isaiah prophesied for sixty years. And Eastern tradition reports that he lived to one hundred and twenty. The conclusive argument against the tradition is that, according to the inscription, all Isaiah's prophecies are included in the time from Uzziah to Hezekiah; the internal evidence accords with this.

His wife is called the prophetess (Isa. 8:3), that is, endowed, as Miriam, with a prophetic gift.

His children were considered by him as not belonging merely to himself; in their names, Shear-jashub, "the remnant shall return" (Isa. 7:3, margin), and Maher-shalal-hash-baz, "speeding to the spoil, he hasteth to the prey" (Isa. 8:1, marg.), the two chief points of his prophecies are intimated to the people—the judgments of the Lord on the people and the world and His mercy to the elect.

His wearing of sackcloth (Isa. 20:2) too was a silent sermon; he appears as the embodiment of that repentance which he taught.

Bible study on the life of Isaiah (NTB)

Also called Esaias; son of Amos: Isaiah 1:1
Prophesies in the days of Uzziah, Jotham, Ahaz, and Hezekiah, kings of Judah: Isaiah 1:1; 6:1; 7:1, 3; 14:27; 20:1; 36:1; 38:1; 39:1
Prophecy at the time of the invasion by Tartan of Assyria: Isaiah 20:1
Symbolically wears sackcloth, and walks barefoot as a sign to Israel: Isaiah 20:2–3
Comforts and encourages Hezekiah and the people during the siege of Jerusalem by Rab-shakeh: 2 Kings 18; 19; Isaiah 37:6–7
Comforts Hezekiah in his affliction: 2 Kings 20:1–11; Isaiah 38
Performs the miracle of the returning shadow to confirm Hezekiah's faith: 2 Kings 20:8–11
Reproves Hezekiah's folly in exhibiting his resources to the commissioners from Babylon: 2 Kings 20:12–19; Isaiah 39
Is the chronicler of the times of Uzziah and Hezekiah: 2 Chronicles 26:22; 32:32
Foretells punishment of the Jews for idolatry, and reproves self-confidence and distrust of God: Isaiah 2:6–20
Foretells the destruction of the Jews: Isaiah 3
Promises restoration of divine favor to the remnant: Isaiah 4:2–6; 6
Delineates the ingratitude of the Jews in the parable of the vineyard, and reproves it: Isaiah 5:1–10
Denounces existing corruptions: Isaiah 5:8–30
Foretells the failure of the plot of the Israelites and Syrians against Judah: Isaiah 7:1–16
Denounces calamities against Israel and Judah: Isaiah 7:16–25; 9:2–6
Foretells prosperity under Hezekiah, and the manifestation of the Messiah: Isaiah 9:1–7
Denounces vengeance on the enemies of Israel: Isaiah 9:8–12

Denounces the wickedness of Israel, and foretells the judgments of God: Isaiah 9:13–21
Denounces judgments against false prophets: Isaiah 10:1–4
Foretells the destruction of Sennacherib's armies: Isaiah 10:5–34
Foretells the restoration of Israel and the triumph of the Messiah's kingdom: Isaiah 11
Foretells the burden of Babylon: Isaiah 13; 14:1–28
Denounces the Philistines: Isaiah 14:9–32
Burden of Moab: Isaiah 15–16
Burden of Damascus: Isaiah 17
An obscure prophecy, supposed by some authorities to be directed against the Assyrians, by others against the Egyptians, and by others against the Ethiopians: Isaiah 18
Burden of Egypt: Isaiah 19–20
Denounces Babylon: Isaiah 21:1–10
Prophecy concerning Seir: Isaiah 21:11, 12
Burden of Arabia: Isaiah 21:13–17
Prophecy concerning the conquest of Jerusalem, the captivity of Shebna, and the promotion of Eliakim: Isaiah 22:1–22
Foretells the overthrow of Tyre: Isaiah 23
Prophesies the judgments on the land, but that a remnant of the Jews would be saved: Isaiah 25–27
Reproves Ephraim for his wickedness, and foretells the destruction by Shalmaneser: Isaiah 28:1–5
Declares the glory of God on the remnant who are saved: Isaiah 28:5–6
Exposes the corruptions in Jerusalem and exhorts to repentance: Isaiah 28:7–29
Foretells the invasion of Sennacherib, the distress of the Jews, and the destruction of the Assyrian army: Isaiah 29:1–8
Denounces the hypocrisy of the Jews: Isaiah 29:9–17
Promises a reformation: Isaiah 29:18–24
Reproves the people for their confidence in Egypt, and their contempt of God: Isaiah 30:1–17; 31:1–6
Declares the goodness and longsuffering of God toward them: Isaiah 30:18–26; 32–35
Reproves the Jews for their spiritual blindness and infidelity: Isaiah 42:18–25
Promises ultimate restoration of the Jews: Isaiah 43:1–13
Foretells the ultimate destruction of Babylon: Isaiah 43:14–17; 47
Exhorts the people to repent: Isaiah 43:22–28
Comforts the Jewish community with promises, exposes the folly of idolatry, and their future deliverance from captivity by Cyrus: Isaiah 44; 45:1–5; 48:20

Foretells the conversion of the Gentiles and the triumph of the gospel: Isaiah 45:5–25
Denounces the evils of idolatry: Isaiah 46
Reproves the Jews for their idolatries and other wickedness: Isaiah 48
Exhorts to sanctification: Isaiah 56:1–8
Foretells calamities to Judah: Isaiah 59:9–12; 57–59
Foreshadows the person and the kingdom of the Messiah: Isaiah 32

SHEAR-JASHUB

Significance in summary

Isaiah's first son, given this symbolic name to foreshadow the restoration of the Jews after their exile

Meaning of name

a remnant shall return

Bible study on the life of Shear-Jashub (NTB)

A son of Isaiah: Isaiah 7:3

MAHER-SHALAL-HASH-BAZ

Significance in summary

Symbolic name, meaning "quick to the plunder," given to Isaiah's second son

Meaning of name

the spoil speeds

Bible study on the life of Maher-shalal-hash-baz (NTB)

A symbolic name: Isaiah 8:1–4

NAHUM

Significance in summary

Prophecies against Nineveh are recorded in an Old Testament book named after him

Meaning of name

comforter

Bible dictionary/encyclopedia entry (SBD)

Nahum, called "the Elkoshite," is the seventh in the order of the minor prophets. His personal history is quite unknown. The site of Elkosh, his birthplace, is disputed, some placing it in Galilee, others in Assyria. Those who maintain the latter view assume that the prophet's parents were carried into captivity by Tiglath-pileser and that the prophet was born at the village of Alkush, on the east bank of the Tigris, two miles north of Mosul. On the other hand, the imagery of his prophecy is such that it would be natural to an inhabitant of Palestine (Nahum 1:4) to whom the rich pastures of Bashan, the vineyards of Carmel, and the blossoms of Lebanon were emblems of all that was luxuriant and fertile. The language used in 1:15 and 2:2 is appropriate to one who wrote for his countrymen in their native land.

The date of Nahum's prophecy can be determined with as little precision as his birthplace. It is, however, certain that the prophecy was written before the final downfall of Nineveh and its capture by the Medes and Chaldeans, about 625 BC. The allusions to the Assyrian power imply that it was still unbroken (Nahum 1:12; 2:8, 13; 3:16–17). It is most probable that Nahum flourished in the latter half of the return of Hezekiah, and wrote his prophecy either in Jerusalem or its neighborhood. The subject of the prophecy is, in accordance with the superscription, "the burden of Nineveh," the destruction of which he predicts. As a poet Nahum occupies a high place in the first rank of Hebrew literature. His style is clear and uninvolved, though pregnant and forcible; his diction sonorous and rhythmical, the words reechoing to the sense.

Bible study on the life of Nahum (NTB)

One of the minor prophets; prophesies against the Assyrians; declares the majesty of God and his care for his people: Nahum 1

Foretells the destruction of Nineveh: Nahum 2–3

JEREMIAH

Significance in summary

Prophesied during the last five reigns of the kings of Judah

Meaning of name

God is high

Bible dictionary/encyclopedia entry (CBC)

The chief events of the life of Jeremiah were:

- He was called to the prophetic office in the days of Josiah (Jer. 1:1–2).
- He denounced Jerusalem and Judah on account of their sins (Jer. 2:1–37; 3:1–10).
- He announced to the people the Lord's willingness to receive them if they would repent (Jer. 3:11–25).
- He was cast into prison by Pashur (Jer. 20:1–2).
- He announced to Zedekiah his impending doom (Jer. 21:1–10).
- He predicted the coming of a righteous king (Jer. 23:5–6).
- He foretold the seventy years' captivity (Jer. 25:11–12).
- He fled from Jehoiakim to Egypt (Jer. 26:12–21).
- He condemned the false prophet Hananiah (Jer. 28:1–16).
- He predicted the restoration of Judah and Israel (Jer. 30:1–3).
- He predicted the establishment of a new covenant (Jer. 31:31–34).
- He was imprisoned by Zedekiah (Jer. 32:1–12).
- He predicted the captivity of Zedekiah (Jer. 34:1–7).
- He was rescued from the dungeon by Ebed-melech (Jer. 38:1–13).
- He predicted the downfall of Jerusalem (2 Chron. 36:11–21; Jer. 39:1–10).
- He was kindly treated by Nebuzaradan (Jer. 39:11–14; 40:1–5).
- He departed into Egypt with a few of his countrymen (Jer. 43:5–7).
- He predicted the overthrow of Egypt by the king of Babylon, and the destruction of all the Jews who went into Egypt except a small remnant (Jer. 43:8–13; 44:1–28).
- He predicted the downfall of Babylon (Jer. 50:1–46; 51:1–64).

A Bible commentator's portrait (CCEB) (TCB)

CCEB

Jeremiah, son of Hilkiah, one of the ordinary priests, living in Anathoth of Benjamin (Jer. 1:1), not the Hilkiah the high priest who discovered the book of the law (2 Kings 22:8); had he been the same, the designation would have been "the priest," or "the high priest." Besides, his residence at Anathoth shows that he belonged to the line of Abiathar, who was deposed from the high priesthood by Solomon (1 Kings 2:26–35), after which the office remained in Zadok's line. Mention is made of Jeremiah in 2 Chronicles 35:25; 36:12, 21. In 629 BC, the thirteenth year of King Josiah, while still very young (Jer. 1:5), he received his prophetic call in Anathoth (Jer. 1:2); along with Hilkiah the high priest, the prophetess Huldah, and the prophet Zephaniah, he helped forward Josiah's reformation of religion (2 Kings 23:1–25). Among the first charges to him was one that he should go and proclaim God's message in Jerusalem (Jer. 2:2). He also took an official tour to announce to the cities of Judah the contents of the book of the law found in the temple (Jer. 11:6) five years after his call to prophesy. On his return to Anathoth, his countrymen, offended at his reproofs, conspired against his life. To escape their persecutions (Jer. 11:21), as well as those of his own family (Jer. 12:6), he left Anathoth and lived in Jerusalem. During the eighteen years of his ministry in Josiah's reign he was unharmed; also during the three months of Jehoahaz's or Shallum's reign (Jer. 22:10–12).

On Jehoiakim's accession it became evident that Josiah's reformation effected nothing more than a forcible repression of idolatry and the establishment of the worship of God outwardly. The priests, prophets, and people then brought Jeremiah before the authorities, urging that he should be put to death for his denunciations of evil against the city (Jer. 26:8–11). The princes, however, especially Ahikam, interposed on his behalf (Jer. 26:16, 24), but he was put under restraint, or at least thought it best not to appear in public. In the fourth year of Jehoiakim, he was commanded to write the predictions given orally through him, and to read them to the people. Being "shut up," he could not himself go into the house of the Lord (Jer. 36:5); he therefore asked Baruch, his scribe, to read them in public on the fast day. The princes then advised Baruch and Jeremiah to hide themselves from the king's displeasure. Meanwhile they read the roll to the king, who was so enraged that he cut it with a knife and threw it into the fire, at the same time giving orders for the apprehension of the prophet and Baruch. They escaped Jehoiakim's violence, which had already killed the prophet Urijah (Jer. 26:20–23). Baruch rewrote the words, with additional prophecies, on another roll (Jer. 36:27–32).

In the three months' reign of Jehoiachin or Jeconiah, he prophesied the carrying away of the king and the queen mother (Jer. 13:18; 22:24–30; compare 2 Kings 24:12). In this reign he was imprisoned for a short time by Pashur (Jer. 20:1–18), the chief governor of the Lord's house; but at Zedekiah's accession he was free (Jer. 37:4), for the king sent to him to "inquire of the Lord" when Nebuchadnezzar came up against Jerusalem (Jer. 21:1–3; Jer. 37:3). The Chaldeans withdrew on hearing of the approach of Pharaoh's army (Jer. 37:5), but Jeremiah warned the king that the Egyptians would forsake him, and the Chaldeans would return and burn up the city (Jer. 37:7–8). The princes, irritated at this, made the departure of Jeremiah from the city during the respite a pretext for imprisoning him, on the allegation of his deserting to the Chaldeans (Jer. 38:1–5). He would have been left to perish in the dungeon of Malchiah had it not been for the intercession of Ebed-melech, the Ethiopian (Jer. 38:6–13). Zedekiah, though he consulted Jeremiah in secret, was induced by his princes to leave Jeremiah in prison (Jer. 38:14–28) until Jerusalem was taken. Nebuchadnezzar directed his captain, Nebuzar-adan, to give him his freedom, so that he might either go to Babylon or stay with the remnant of his people as he chose. As a true patriot, despite the forty and a half years during which his country had repaid his services with neglect and persecution, he stayed with Gedaliah, the ruler appointed by Nebuchadnezzar over Judea (Jer. 40:6). After the murder of Gedaliah by Ishmael, Johanan, the recognized ruler of the people, in fear of the Chaldeans avenging the murder of Gedaliah, fled with the people to Egypt, and forced Jeremiah and Baruch to accompany him, in spite of the prophet's warning that the people would perish if they went to Egypt, but would be preserved by remaining in their land (Jer. 41:1–43:13). At Tahpanhes, a boundary city on the Tanitic or Pelustan branch of the Nile, he prophesied the overthrow of Egypt (Jer. 43:8–13). Tradition says he died in Egypt. The Jews so venerated him that they believed he would rise from the dead and be the forerunner of the Messiah (Matt. 16:14).

One writer observes that the combination of features in Jeremiah's character proves his divine mission: he was timid yet intrepid in the discharge of his prophetic functions, with the Spirit of prophecy controlling his natural temper and qualifying him for his hazardous undertaking. Zephaniah, Habakkuk, Daniel, and Ezekiel were his contemporaries. The last forms a good contrast to Jeremiah, the Spirit in his case acting on a temperament as strongly marked by firmness as Jeremiah's was by shrinking and delicate sensitiveness. Ezekiel views the nation's sins as opposed to righteousness—Jeremiah, as productive of misery; the former takes the objective, the latter the subjective view of the evils of the times. Jeremiah's style corresponds to his character: he is peculiarly marked by pathos and sympathy with the wretched. His Lamentations illustrate this; the whole series of elegies has but one object—to express sorrow for his fallen country—yet the lights and images in which he presents this are so many that the reader is charmed with the variety of the plaintive strains throughout. The language is marked by Aramaeisms, which probably was the ground of Jerome's charge that the style is "rustic."

TCB

In many ways Jeremiah was a type of Christ, sometimes by way of contrast (marked *). The following passages may be compared:

Book of Jeremiah

Jeremiah Type	Christ Antitype
11:18	Isaiah 11:2; John 2:25
11:19	Isaiah 53:7–8
11:19*	Isaiah 53:10
11:20*	Isaiah 53:11
13:17	Matthew 26:38; Luke 19:41; 22:41, 44–45
18:23	John 11:53
18:23*	Luke 23:34, 61
20:7	Mark 5:40
20:10	Luke 11:54 (compare Psalm 55:12–13)
26:11	Matthew 26:65–66
26:15	Matthew 27:4–25
26:15–16	Luke 23:13–15; John 10:21
29:26	John 7:20; 10:20, 39
29:27	Luke 7:39; John 8:53

Book of Lamentations

1:12	Isaiah 53:10; John 1:29
3:8	Matthew 27:46
3:14	Psalm 69:12
3:48	Luke 19:41

BARUCH

Significance in summary

Jeremiah's friend and scribe

Meaning of name

blessed

Bible study on the life of Baruch (NTB)

An amanuensis (copyist) of Jeremiah: Jeremiah 32:12–16; 36:4–32; 43:3–6; 45:1–2

URIAH

Significance in summary

Prophesied at the same time as Jeremiah and was killed by King Jehoiakim of Judah

Meaning of name

God is light

Bible study on the life of Uriah (NTB)

A prophet killed by Jehoiakim: Jeremiah 26:20–23

JEHUDI

Significance in summary

King Jehoiakim's official who read to him Jeremiah's scroll

Bible study on the life of Jehudi (NTB)

A Jew, an official at Jehoiakim's court who read Jeremiah's scroll to the king: Jeremiah 36:14, 21, 23

EBED-MELECH

Significance in summary

An Ethiopian eunuch who rescued Jeremiah from the bottom of a cistern

Meaning of name

king's servant

Bible study on the life of Ebed-melech (NTB)

Jeremiah rescued by: Jeremiah 38:7–13
Prophecy concerning: Jeremiah 39:16–18

PASHUR

Significance in summary

A priest who persecuted Jeremiah

Bible study on the life of Pashur (NTB)

Son of Immer and governor of the temple; beats and imprisons Jeremiah: Jeremiah 20:1–6

JOHANAN

Significance in summary

Linked up with Gedaliah after the fall of Jerusalem and led some people into Egypt

Meaning of name

the Lord is gracious

Bible study on the life of Johanan (NTB)

A Jewish captain: 2 Kings 25:22–24
Warns Gedaliah against Ishmael: Jeremiah 40:13–16
Ishmael defeated by: Jeremiah 41:11–15
Sought prayers of Jeremiah: Jeremiah 42:2–3
Disobeyed Jeremiah and took him to Egypt: Jeremiah 43:1–7

HANAMEL

Significance in summary

Jeremiah's cousin who sold him a field

Meaning of name

grace of God

Bible study on the life of Hanamel (NTB)

Cousin of Jeremiah, to whom he sold a field in Anathoth: Jeremiah 32:7–12

HANANIAH

Significance in summary

The prophet who falsely prophesied that the people of Judah would be freed of Babylonian rule after two years

Meaning of name

the Lord is gracious

Bible study on the life of Hananiah (NTB)

A prophet of Gibeon who uttered false prophecies in the temple during the reign of Zedekiah: Jeremiah 28

MICAH

Significance in summary

The Old Testament prophet who prophesied at the same time as Isaiah and Hosea

Meaning of name

who is like God?

Bible dictionary/encyclopedia entry (SBD)

The sixth in the order of the minor prophets. He is called the Morasthite, that is, a native of Moresheth, a small village near Eleutheropolis to the east, where formerly the prophet's tomb was shown, though in the days of Jerome it had been succeeded by a church. Micah exercised the prophetic office during the reigns of Jotham, Ahaz, and Hezekiah, kings of Judah, giving thus a maximum limit of fifty-nine years, from the accession of Jotham to the death of Hezekiah, and a minimum limit of sixteen years from the death of Jotham to the accession of Hezekiah. He was contemporary with Hosea and Amos during the part of their ministry in Israel, and with Isaiah in Judah.

A Bible commentator's portrait (CCEB)

His full name is Micaiah (not the Micaiah mentioned in 1 Kings 22:8, the son of Imlah), signifying, Who is like Jehovah? The time of his prophesying is said to be during the reigns of Jotham, Ahaz, and Hezekiah. Jeremiah (Jer. 26:18) quotes Micah 3:12 as delivered in the reign of Hezekiah. He was thus a contemporary of Isaiah and Hosea. The idolatries practiced in the reign of Ahaz accord with Micah's denunciations of such gross evils, and confirm the truth of the time assigned in Micah 1:1. His prophecies are partly against Israel (Samaria), partly against Judah. He prophesies the capture of both, the Jews' captivity and restoration, and the coming and reign of the Messiah.

Bible study on the life of Micah (NTB)

One of the minor prophets: Jeremiah 26:18–19; Micah 1:1, 14–15
Denounces the idolatry of his times: Micah 1
The oppressions of the covetous: Micah 2:1–11
Foretells the restoration of Israel: Micah 2:12–13
The injustice of judges and falsehoods of false prophets: Micah 3
Prophesies the coming of the Messiah: Micah 4–5

ZEPHANIAH

Significance in summary

Prophesied in King Josiah's reign; his prophesies are recorded in a Bible book named after him

Meaning of name

God has treasured

Bible dictionary/encyclopedia entry (SBD)

The ninth in order of the twelve minor prophets. His pedigree is traced to his fourth ancestor, Hezekiah (Zeph. 1:1), supposedly the celebrated king of that name. The chief characteristics of this book are the unity and harmony of the composition; the grace, energy, and dignity of its style; and the rapid and effective alternations of threats and promises. The general tone of the last portion is Messianic but without any specific reference to the person of our Lord. The date of the book is given in the inscription—the reign of Josiah.

Bible study on the life of Zephaniah (NTB)

A prophet in the days of Josiah: Zephaniah 1:1

HABAKKUK

Significance in summary

Prophesied during the reigns of Jehoiakim and Josiah; his prophesies are recorded in a Bible book named after him

Meaning of name

God is strength

Bible dictionary/encyclopedia entry (SBD)

The eighth in the order of the minor prophets. We have no certain information about the facts of the prophet's life. He probably lived about the twelfth or thirteenth year of Josiah.

Bible study on the life of Habakkuk (NTB)

A prophet and poet who probably prophesied after the destruction of Nineveh: Habakkuk 1:1; 3:1

His hymn of praise of the majesty of God: Habakkuk 3

OBADIAH

Significance in summary

Spoke against Edom; his prophesies are recorded in a Bible book named after him

Meaning of name

servant of God

Bible dictionary/encyclopedia entry (SBD)

The fourth of the twelve minor prophets. We know nothing about him except what we can gather from the short book which bears his name. The book of Obadiah is a sustained denunciation of the Edomites, melting into a vision of the future glories of Zion when the arm of the Lord will have delivered her and judged her enemies.

Bible study on the life of Obadiah (NTB)

A prophet who prophesied the destruction of Edom: Obadiah 1:1

HULDAH

Significance in summary

The prophetess who prophesied during the reign of King Josiah

Meaning of name

weasel

Bible study on the life of Huldah (NTB)

Foretells the destruction of Jerusalem: 2 Kings 22:14–20; 2 Chronicles 34:22–28

Israel's Kings

Jeroboam I • Abijah • Nadab • Baasha • Elah • Ben-hadad I • Ben-hadad II • Hazael • Zimri • Ethbaal • Rezin • Omri • Ahab • Jezebel • Naboth • Obadiah • Ahaziah • Jehoram (Joram) • Jehu • Jehoahaz • Jehoash • Jeroboam II • Zedekiah • Zachariah • Shallum • Menahem • Pekahiah • Pekah • Nebuzaradan • Hoshea • Shalmaneser

Introduction (CBC)

The accounts of the kings, in the Bible's books of Samuel, Kings, and Chronicles, reveal God's expectations for leaders.

The answer to the question, "Why study the kings of the Bible?" is that if we want to discover what God loves in a leader and what he hates in a leader, the stories of the kings give us the answers.

JEROBOAM I

Significance in summary

The first king of Israel after the division of the kingdom into Judah and Israel, who reigned for eleven years

Meaning of name

the people multiplied

Bible dictionary/encyclopedia entry (CBC)

During Solomon's building operations he discovered a young man by the name of Jeroboam, the son of Nebat an Ephrathite, who was industrious, and he put him over the charge of the house of Joseph (1 Kings 11:26–29). Subsequently Jeroboam was going out of Jerusalem, he was met by the prophet Ahijah who assured him that he would reign over ten of the tribes of Israel (1 Kings 11:29–39). Solomon on hearing of this attempted to kill Jeroboam, and for protection he fled to Egypt (1 Kings 11:40). On the accession of Rehoboam to the throne the people sent for Jeroboam, and he joined his countrymen in requesting the new king to lighten their burdens which he emphatically refused to do, and Jeroboam led the revolt (1 Kings 11:1–24; 1 Chron. 10:1–19).

Jeroboam established himself at Shechem in Mount Ephraim, and in order to prevent the people from going to Jerusalem to worship, set up two golden calves, one at Bethel and the other at Dan, assuring the people that these were the gods that had brought them out of the land of Egypt (1 Kings 12:25–30). He also disregarded the law of God and made priests of the lowest of the people, and changed the time of holding the annual feasts ordained by Moses (1 Kings 12:31–33). During these troubled times one of the Lord's prophets from Judah went to Bethel and found Jeroboam officiating at the altar. The prophet cried vehemently against the altar and predicted that a child would be born to the house of David, Josiah by name, who would destroy the priests of this altar on account of their sacrilegious work, and emphasized the authenticity of his commission by making the altar split apart so that its ashes poured out. Jeroboam was furious and attempted to arrest the man of God with disastrous results, but through the intercession of the prophet he was restored (1 Kings 13:1–32).

After this Jeroboam increased in wickedness (1 Kings 13:33–34). Jeroboam's son Abijah fell sick, and he sent his wife to Shiloh to talk with the prophet Ahijah in order to find out the destiny of the child. Ahijah told her that the child would die, and predicted the extinction of Jeroboam's house because of his unparalleled wickedness (1 Kings 14:1–18). Jeroboam reigned twenty-two years (1 Kings 14:19–20). He reigned contemporaneously with Rehoboam seventeen years (1 Kings 12:1–20; 14:20; 2 Chron. 14:20), Abijah three years (1 Kings 14:31–15:2), and with Asa two years (1 Kings 14:20, 31; 15:1–2, 8–10; 2 Chron. 12:13).

ABIJAH

Significance in summary

Son of King Jeroboam of Israel; died as a child

Meaning of name

the Lord is my father

Bible study on the life of Abijah (NTB)

Son of Jeroboam: 1 Kings 14:1–18

NADAB

Significance in summary

The second king of Israel, who ruled for two years

Meaning of name

liberal

Bible study on the life of Nadab (NTB)

Son and successor of Jeroboam: 1 Kings 14:20
His wicked reign; murdered by Baasha: 1 Kings 15:25–31

BAASHA

Significance in summary

The third king of Israel, who reigned for twenty-four years

Meaning of name

boldness

Bible dictionary/encyclopedia entry (CBC)

Nadab was overthrown and succeeded by Baasha, who, as soon as he reached the throne, exterminated the house of Jeroboam because of his extreme wickedness (1 Kings 15:2–30). Baasha walked in the footsteps of Jeroboam (1 Kings 15:34). He was visited by the prophet of the Lord who predicted the destruction of his house on account of his sins (1 Kings 16:1–7). Baasha reigned over all Israel twenty-four years (1 Kings 15:34). He reigned contemporaneously with Asa (1 Kings 15:9, 10, 33).

Bible study on the life of Baasha (NTB)

King of Israel: 1 Kings 15:16–22, 27–34; 16:1–7; 21:22; 2 Kings 9:9; 2 Chronicles 16:1–6; Jeremiah 41:9

ELAH

Significance in summary

The fourth king of Israel who reigned for two years

Meaning of name

oak

Bible study on the life of Elah (NTB)

Son and successor of Baasha, king of Israel: 1 Kings 16:6–14

BEN-HADAD I

Significance in summary

King of Syria who opposed King Ahab of Israel

Meaning of name

son of Hadad

Bible study on the life of Ben-hadad I (NTB)

King of Syria: 1 Kings 15:18–20; 2 Chronicles 16:2–4

BEN-HADAD II

Significance in summary

King of Syria who fought against Israel in Elijah's time

Meaning of name

son of Hadad

Bible study on the life of Ben-hadad II (NTB)

A king of Syria, who reigned during the time of Ahab, son of Ben-hadad I: 1 Kings 20; 2 Kings 5; 6; 7; 8:7–15

HAZAEL

Significance in summary

King of Syria who fought against both Israel and Judah

Meaning of name

God sees

Bible study on the life of Hazael (NTB)

Anointed king by Elijah: 1 Kings 19:15
Conquests by: 2 Kings 8:28–29; 9:14; 10:32–33; 12:17–18; 13:3, 22; 2 Chronicles 22:5–6
Conspires against, murders, and succeeds to the throne of Ben-hadad: 2 Kings 8:8–15
Death of: 2 Kings 13:24

ZIMRI

Significance in summary

The fifth king of Israel, who reigned for seven days

Bible dictionary/encyclopedia entry (CBC)

Elah was assassinated by his servant Zimri who, as soon as he ascended the throne, destroyed all the house of Baasha according to the word of the Lord. Zimri reigned contemporaneously with Asa, for just seven days (1 Kings 15:9, 10; 16:8–30).

Bible study on the life of Zimri (NTB)

King of Israel: 1 Kings 16:9–20; 2 Kings 9:31

ETHBAAL

Significance in summary

A king of Sidon, father of Jezebel, the wife of King Ahab

Meaning of name

man of Baal

Bible study on the life of Ethbaal (NTB)

King of Sidon: 1 Kings 16:31

REZIN

Significance in summary

The last king of Syria, who made an alliance with King Pekah of Israel to attack the kingdom of Judah

Bible study on the life of Rezin (NTB)

A king of Syria who harassed the southern kingdom (Judah): 2 Kings 15:37; 16:5–9
Prophecy against: Isaiah 7:1–9; 8:4–8; 9:11

OMRI

Significance in summary

The sixth king of Israel, who reigned for twelve years

Bible dictionaray/encyclopedia entry (CBC)

Omri reigned six years in undisputed authority. He was contemporary with Asa (1 Kings 15:9, 10; 16:21–23). The chief act of Omri's reign was the founding of the city of Samaria (1 Kings 16:23, 24). His reign was characterized by evil (1 Kings 16:25–27).

Bible study on the life of Omri (NTB)

Was commander of the army of Israel, and was proclaimed king by the army on news of the assassination of King Elah: 1 Kings 16:16
Defeats his rival, Tibni, and establishes himself: 1 Kings 16:17–22
Surrendered cities to king of Syria: 1 Kings 20:34
Wicked reign and death of: 1 Kings 16:23–28
Denounced by Micah: Micah 6:16

AHAB

Significance in summary

The seventh king of Israel, who reigned for twenty-two years

Meaning of name

father is brother

Bible dictionary/encyclopedia entry (IBD)

The son of Omri, whom he succeeded as the seventh king of Israel. His history is recorded in 1 Kings 16–22. His wife was Jezebel, who exercised a very evil influence over him. To the calf-worship introduced by Jeroboam he added the worship of Baal. He was severely admonished by Elijah for his wickedness. His anger was on this account kindled against the prophet, and he sought to kill him. He undertook three campaigns against Ben-hadad II, king of Damascus. In the first two, which were defensive, he gained a complete victory over Ben-hadad, who fell into his hands and was afterwards released on the condition of his restoring all the cities of Israel he then held, and granting certain other concessions to Ahab. After three years of peace, for some cause Ahab renewed war (1 Kings 22:3) with Ben-hadad by assaulting the city of Ramoth-gilead, although the prophet Micaiah warned him that he would not succeed, and that the four hundred false prophets who encouraged him were only leading him to his ruin. Micaiah was imprisoned for trying to dissuade Ahab from his purpose. Ahab went into the battle disguised, so he might escape his enemies, but an arrow from a bow "drawn at a venture" pierced him and he died towards evening; thus Elijah's prophecy (1 Kings 21:19) was fulfilled. Because of his idolatry, lust, and covetousness, Ahab is referred to as preeminently the type of a wicked king (2 Kings 8:18; 2 Chron. 22:3; Micah 6:16).

Bible study on the life of Ahab (NTB)

King of Israel: 1 Kings 16:29
Marries Jezebel: 1 Kings 16:31
Idolatry of: 1 Kings 16:30–33; 18:18–19; 21:25–26
Other wickedness of: 2 Kings 3:2; 2 Chronicles 21:6; 22:3–4; Micah 6:16
Reproved by Elijah; assembles the prophets of Baal: 1 Kings 18:17–46
Fraudulently confiscates Naboth's vineyard: 1 Kings 21
Defeats Ben-hadad: 1 Kings 20
Closing history and death of: 1 Kings 22; 2 Chronicles 18
Succeeded by his son, Ahaziah: 1 Kings 22:40
Prophecies against: 1 Kings 20:42; 21:19–24; 22:19–28; 2 Kings 9:8, 25–26
Sons of, murdered: 2 Kings 10:1–8

JEZEBEL

Significance in summary

Wife of King Ahab, and wicked, idolatrous queen of Israel

Meaning of name

unexalted

Bible dictionary/encyclopedia entry (SBD)

Jezebel was a Phoenician princess, the daughter of Ethbaal, king of the Zidonians. In her hands her husband became a mere puppet (1 Kings 21:25). The first effect of her influence was the immediate establishment of the Phoenician worship on a grand scale in the court of Ahab. At her table were supported no less than four hundred fifty prophets of Baal and four hundred of Asherah (1 Kings 16:31; 18:19). The prophets of Jehovah were attacked by her orders and put to the sword (1 Kings 18:13; 2 Kings 9:7). At last the people, at the instigation of Elijah, rose against her ministers and slaughtered them at the foot of Carmel.

When Ahab was disappointed that Naboth would not sell him his vineyard (1 Kings 21:7), she wrote a warrant in Ahab's name, and sealed it with his seal. To her, and not to Ahab, was sent the announcement that the royal wishes were accomplished and Naboth had been killed (1 Kings 21:14); on her accordingly fell the prophet's curse, as well as on her husband (1 Kings 21:23)—a curse fulfilled by Jehu, whose chariot-horses trampled out her life. The body was left in that open space called in modern eastern language "the mounds," where offal is thrown from the city walls (2 Kings 9:30–37).

Bible study on the life of Jezebel (NTB)

Daughter of Ethbaal, a Zidonian, and wife of Ahab: 1 Kings 16:31
Was an idolatress and persecuted the prophets of God: 1 Kings 18:4, 13, 19; 2 Kings 3:2, 13; 9:7, 22
Vowed to kill Elijah: 1 Kings 19:1–3
Wickedly accomplishes the death of Naboth: 1 Kings 21:5–16
Death of, foretold: 1 Kings 21:23; 2 Kings 9:10
Death of, at the hand of Jehu: 2 Kings 9:30–37
Used figuratively: Revelation 2:20

NABOTH

Significance in summary

Owned a vineyard next to King Ahab's palace and was stoned to death for not giving it over to Ahab

Meaning of name

a sprout

Bible study on the life of Naboth (NTB)

A Jezreelite; his vineyard forcibly taken by Ahab; was stoned at the instigation of Jezebel: 1 Kings 21:1–19
His murder avenged: 2 Kings 9:21–36

OBADIAH

Significance in summary

A steward in King Ahab's court, who hid one hundred prophets, despite being ordered by Jezebel to kill all the Lord's prophets

Meaning of name

servant of the Lord

Bible study on the life of Obadiah (NTB)

Conceals in a cave one hundred prophets persecuted by Jezebel: 1 Kings 18:3–4
Meets Elijah and receives a commission from him: 1 Kings 18:3–16

AHAZIAH

Significance in summary

The eighth king of Israel, who reigned for one year

Meaning of name

the Lord sustains

Bible dictionary/encyclopedia entry (CBC)

Ahab was succeeded by his son Ahaziah. He followed in the footsteps of his wicked ancestors (1 Kings 22:51–53). As he became dangerously ill he sent messengers to find out from Baalzebub, the god of Ekron, if he would recover. The angel of the Lord commanded Elijah to go and tell the messengers to declare to the king that he would certainly die. When the king recognized the prophet from their description, he sent a deputation of soldiers requesting him to come to him at once. Disaster followed disaster until the prophet appeared in the court of the king and predicted his speedy death (2 Kings 1:1–16). Ahaziah reigned contemporaneously with Jehoshaphat two years (1 Kings 22:42–51; 2 Kings 3:1).

Bible study on the life of Ahaziah (NTB)

History of: 1 Kings 22:40, 49, 51–53; 2 Chronicles 20:35–37; 2 Kings 1
Succeeded by Jehoram: 2 Kings 3:1

JEHORAM (JORAM)

Significance in summary

The ninth king of Israel, who reigned for eleven years

Meaning of name

God is exalted

Bible dictionary/encyclopedia entry (CBC)

Ahaziah was succeeded by his brother Jehoram (2 Kings 1:17; 3:1). His reign was characterized by evil (2 Kings 3:1–2). The peace of his kingdom was disturbed by the rebellion of the king of Moab. In order to suppress this rebellion he associated with the king of Judah and the king of Edom. Great destruction and sorrow followed (2 Kings 3:1–27). He reigned contemporaneously with Jehoshaphat (2 Kings 3:1) and Ahaziah (2 Kings 9:29).

Bible study on the life of Jehoram (NTB)

Also called Joram: 2 Kings 1:17; 3:1
King of Syria sends Naaman to, so that Naaman may be healed of his leprosy: 2 Kings 5:1–27
Fights against the king of Syria: 2 Kings 6:8–23; 7; 8:28–29; 2 Chronicles 22:5–6
Asks details about Elisha's miracles: 2 Kings 8:4–5
Killed by Jehu: 2 Kings 9:14–26

JEHU

Significance in summary

The tenth king of Israel, who reigned for twenty-eight years

Meaning of name

he is the Lord

Bible dictionary/encyclopedia entry (SBD)

The founder of the fifth dynasty of the kingdom of Israel, son of Jehoshaphat (2 Kings 9:2). His first appearance in history is when he heard the warning of Elijah against the murderer of Naboth (2 Kings 9:25). During the reigns of Ahaziah and Jehoram, Jehu rose to importance. He was, under Jehoram, captain of the host in the siege of Ramoth-gilead. During this siege he was anointed by Elisha's servant and told that he was appointed to be king of Israel and destroyer of the house of Ahab (2 Kings 9:12). The army at once ordained him king, and he set off full speed for Jezreel. Jehoram, who was lying ill in Jezreel, came out to meet him in the field of Naboth (2 Kings 9:21–24). Jehu seized his opportunity, and shot him through the heart (2 Kings 9:24). Jehu himself advanced to the gates of Jezreel and fulfilled the divine warning on Jezebel as already on Jehoram. He entered on a work of extermination until then unparalleled in the history of the Jewish monarchy. All the descendants of Ahab that remained in Jezreel were swept away. His next step was to secure Samaria. For the pretended purpose of inaugurating anew the worship of Baal, he called all the prophets of Baal together at Samaria. The vast temple raised by Ahab was crowded from end to end. The chief sacrifice was offered, as if in the excess of his zeal, by Jehu himself. As soon as it was ascertained that all, and none but, the idolaters were there, the signal was given to eighty trusted guards, and sweeping massacre removed at one blow the whole heathen population of the kingdom of Israel. This is the last public act recorded of Jehu. He was buried in state in Samaria, and was succeeded by his son Jehoahaz (2 Kings 10:35). His name is the first of the Israelite kings which appears in the Assyrian monuments.

Bible study on the life of Jehu (NTB)

Son of Nimshi, king of Israel: 1 Kings 19:16; 2 Kings 9:1–14
Religious zeal of, in killing idolaters: 2 Kings 9:14–37; 10:1–28; 2 Chronicles 22:8–9
His territory invaded by Hazael, king of Syria: 2 Kings 10:32–33
Prophecies concerning: 1 Kings 19:17; 2 Kings 10:30; 15:12; Hosea 1:4
Death of: 2 Kings 10:35

JEHOAHAZ

Significance in summary

The eleventh king of Israel, who reigned for seventeen years

Meaning of name

God has grasped

Bible dictionary/encyclopedia entry (CBC)

Jehu was succeeded by his son Jehoahaz, who reigned in Samaria seventeen years. His reign was characterized by a continuance of the idolatrous practice inaugurated by Jeroboam. The anger of the Lord was kindled against Israel, and He delivered them into the hands of the Syrians. The king seemed to be penitent but did not reform (2 Kings 12:2–8). He was contemporary with Jehoash for seventeen years (2 Kings 12:1; 13:1).

Bible study on the life of Jehoahaz (NTB)

Son of Jehu and king of Israel: 2 Kings 10:35; 13:1–9

JEHOASH

Significance in summary

The twelfth king of Israel, who reigned for sixteen years

Meaning of name

God has given

Bible dictionary/encyclopedia entry (CBC)

Jehoahaz was succeeded by his son Jehoash, who followed in the footsteps of his wicked progenitors. During Elisha's last illness he was visited by Jehoash to whom he communicated the information that he would fight against the Syrians three times (2 Kings 13:14–19). Jehoash reigned sixteen years, and was contemporary with Joash two years (2 Kings 13:9–10; 12:1; 14:1) and Amaziah fourteen years (2 Kings 14:1–2).

Bible study on the life of Jehoash (NTB)

Also called Joash; successor of Jehoahaz: 2 Kings 13:10–25
Defeats Amaziah: 2 Kings 13:12; 14:8–15; 2 Chronicles 25:17–24
Death of: 2 Kings 13:13; 14:16

JEROBOAM II

Significance in summary

The thirteenth king of Israel, who reigned for forty years

Meaning of name

the people multiplied

Bible dictionary/encyclopedia entry (CBC)

Jehoash was succeeded by his son Jeroboam. He followed the ways of his ancestors. He restored the coast of Israel from the "entering of Hamath unto the sea of the plain," according to the prediction of Jonah the son of Amittai (2 Kings 14:23–25). Israel was severely oppressed during these times, but the Lord granted them deliverance by the hand of the king (2 Kings 14:26, 27). Jeroboam reigned forty-one years, and was contemporary with Amaziah fifteen years (2 Kings 14:1–2, 23) and Uzziah fourteen years (2 Kings 15:1).

Bible study on the life of Jeroboam II (NTB)

Successor to Jehoash: 2 Kings 14:16, 23
Captures Hamath and Damascus: 2 Kings 14:25–28
Wicked reign of: 2 Kings 14:24
Prophecies concerning: Amos 7:7–13
Death of: 2 Kings 14:29
Genealogies written during his reign: 1 Chronicles 5:17

ZEDEKIAH

Significance in summary

A false prophet who spoke in King Ahab's reign

Meaning of name

Jehovah is mighty

Bible study on the life of Zedekiah (NTB)

Prophesies to Ahab that he will be victorious over the Syrians instead of being defeated: 1 Kings 22:11; 2 Chronicles 18:10
Strikes Micaiah, the true prophet: 1 Kings 22:24; 2 Chronicles 18:23

ZACHARIAH

Significance in summary

The fourteenth king of Israel, who reigned for six months

Meaning of name

the Lord remembers

Bible study on the life of Zachariah (NTB)

Son of Jeroboam, and the last of the household of Jehu: 2 Kings 14:29; 15:8–12

SHALLUM

Significance in summary

The fifteenth king of Israel, who reigned for one month

Meaning of name

recompense

Bible study on the life of Shallum (NTB)

King of Israel: 2 Kings 15:10, 13–15

MENAHEM

Significance in summary

The sixteenth king of Israel, who reigned for ten years

Meaning of name

comforter

Bible dictionary/encyclopedia entry (CBC)

Shallum was killed and succeeded by Menahem. His reign was characterized by very great wickedness, war, and excessive taxation (2 Kings 15:14–22). He reigned ten years contemporaneously with Uzziah (2 Kings 15:1, 2, 17).

Bible study on the life of Menahem (NTB)

King of Israel: 2 Kings 15:13–22

PEKAHIAH

Significance in summary

The seventeenth king of Israel, who reigned for two years

Meaning of name

the Lord opens

Bible dictionary/encyclopedia entry (CBC)

Menahem was succeeded by his son Pekahiah. His reign was characterized by wickedness. He reigned two years contemporaneously with Uzziah (2 Kings 15:1, 2, 22–24).

Bible study on the life of Pekahiah (NTB)

Son of Menahem; king of Israel: 2 Kings 15:22–26
Plotted against and killed by Pekah: 2 Kings 15:25

PEKAH

Significance in summary

The eighteenth king of Israel, who reigned for twenty years

Meaning of name

he sees, or, he opens

Bible dictionary/encyclopedia entry (SBD)

Son of Remaliah, originally a captain of Pekahiah, king of Israel, murdered his master, seized the throne, and became the eighteenth sovereign of the northern kingdom. Under his predecessors Israel had been much weakened through the payment of enormous tribute to the Assyrians (2 Kings 15:20) and by internal wars and conspiracies. Pekah seems to have steadily applied himself to the restoration of power. For this purpose he contracted a foreign alliance, and fixed his mind on the plunder of the sister kingdom of Judah. He must have made the treaty by which he proposed to share its spoil with Rezin, king of Damascus, when Jotham was still on the throne of Jerusalem (2 Kings 10:37), but its execution was long delayed, probably in consequence of that prince's righteous administration (2 Chron. 27:1). When his weak son Ahaz succeeded to the crown of David, the allies no longer hesitated but started the siege of Jerusalem. The history of the war is found in 2 Kings 13 and 2 Chronicles 28. It is famous as the occasion of the great prophecies in Isaiah 7–9. Its chief result was the Jewish port of Elath on the Red Sea, but the unnatural alliance of Damascus and Samaria was punished through the complete overthrow of the ferocious confederates by Tiglath-pileser. The kingdom of Damascus was finally suppressed and Rezin put to death while Pekah was deprived of at least half his kingdom, including all the northern part and the whole district to the east of Jordan. Pekah himself, now fallen into the position of an Assyrian vassal was of course compelled to abstain from further attacks on Judah. Whether his continued tyranny exhausted the patience of his subjects, or whether his weakness emboldened them to attack him, is not known; but, from one or the other cause, Hoshea the son of Elah conspired against him and put him to death.

Bible study on the life of Pekah (NTB)

Son of Remaliah; captain of the army of Israel: 2 Kings 15:25
Conspires against and assassinates King Pekahiah: 2 Kings 15:25
Is made king of Israel: 2 Kings 15:27
Victorious in war with Judah: 2 Chronicles 28:5–6
Is plotted against and killed by Hoshea: 2 Kings 15:30–31
Prophecies against: Isaiah 7:1–16; 8:4–10

NEBUZARADAN

Significance in summary

Captain of King's Nebuchadnezzar's guard, who treated Jeremiah kindly

Meaning of name

Nebo has given offspring

Bible study on the life of Nebuzaradan (NTB)

Captain of the guard of King Nebuchadnezzar; commands the Assyrian army which besieged Jerusalem and carried the inhabitants to Babylon: 2 Kings 25:8–21; Jeremiah 39:9–10; 43:6; 52:12–30
Protects Jeremiah: Jeremiah 39:11–14; 40:1–5

HOSHEA

Significance in summary

The nineteenth king of Israel, who reigned for nine years

Meaning of name

deliverer

Bible study on the life of Hoshea (NTB)

Assassinates Pekah and usurps the throne: 2 Kings 15:30
The evil reign of: 2 Kings 17:1–2
Becomes subject to Assyria: 2 Kings 17:3
Conspires against Assyria and is imprisoned: 2 Kings 17:4
Last king of Israel: 2 Kings 17:6; 18:9–12; Hosea 10:3, 7

SHALMANESER

Significance in summary

King of Assyria who defeated King Hoshea of Israel

Meaning of name

Sulman (the god) is chief

Bible dictionary/encyclopedia entry (SBD)

The Assyrian king who reigned probably between Tiglath-pileser and Sargon. He led the forces of Assyria into Palestine, where Hoshea, the last king of Israel, had revolted against his authority (2 Kings 17:3). Hoshea submitted and consented to pay tribute but soon after concluded all alliance with the king of Egypt, and withheld his tribute in consequence. In 723 BC Shalmaneser invaded Palestine for the second time, and, as Hoshea refused to submit, laid siege to Samaria. The siege lasted to 721 BC, when the Assyrian arms prevailed (2 Kings 17:4–6; 18:9–11). It is uncertain whether Shalmaneser conducted the siege to its close, or whether he did not lose his crown to Sargon before the city was taken.

Bible study on the life of Shalmaneser (NTB)

Overthrows the kingdom of Israel: 2 Kings 17:3–6; 18:9–11

Kings of the United Kingdom (c. 1025–925 BC)

King	Relationship to Previous King	God's Judgment
Saul	none	did evil
Ish-bosheth	son	unknown
David	none	did right
Solomon/ Jedidiah	son	did right in youth, evil in old age

Kings of Judah (c. 925–586 BC)

King	Relationship to Previous King	God's Judgment
Rehoboam	son	did evil
Abijam/ Abijah	son	did evil
Asa	son	did right
Jehoshaphat	son	did right
Jehoram	son	did evil
Ahaziah/ Azariah/ Jehoahaz	son	did evil
Athaliah	mother	did evil
Joash/ Jehoash	son of Ahaziah	did right in youth, evil in old age
Amaziah	son	did right in youth, evil in old age
Azariah/ Uzziah	son	did right
Jotham	son	did right
Ahaz	son	did evil
Hezekiah	son	did right
Manasseh	son	did evil
Amon	son	did evil
Josiah	son	did right
Jehoahaz/ Shallum	son	did evil
Jehoiakim/ Eliakim	son of Josiah	did evil
Jehoiachin/ Coniah/ Jeconiah	son	did evil
Zedekiah/ Mattaniah		did evil

Kings of Israel (c. 925–721 BC)

King	Relationship to Previous King	God's Judgment
Jeroboam I	servant	did evil
Nadab	son	did evil
Baasha	none	did evil
Elah	son	did evil
Zimri	captain	did evil
Omri	captain	did evil
Ahab	son	did evil
Ahaziah	son	did evil
Jehoram/ Joram	son of Ahab	did evil
Jehu	captain	mixed
Jehoahaz	son	did evil
Jehoash/ Joash	son	did evil
Jeroboam II	son	did evil
Zachariah	son	did evil
Shallum	none	did evil (assumed)
Menahem	none	did evil
Pekahiah	son	did evil
Pekah	captain	did evil
Hoshea	none	did evil

Israel's Prophets

Ahijah • Iddo • Jehu • Elijah • Gehazi • Micaiah • Naaman • Elisha • Amos • Hosea • Gomer • Jonah

Introduction (IBD)

Prophecies of sixteen Old Testament prophets form part of the Old Testament. They can be divided into four groups:

1. The prophets of Israel (the northern kingdom): Hosea, Amos, Joel, Jonah.
2. The prophets of Judah (the southern kingdom): Isaiah, Jeremiah, Obadiah, Micah, Nahum, Habakkuk, Zephaniah.
3. The prophets of the exile: Ezekiel and Daniel.
4. The prophets of the restoration: Haggai, Zechariah, and Malachi.

In addition to these prophets who left written records of their ministries there were the following prophets, sometimes referred to as the "oral" prophets who ministered to Israel: Ahijah, Iddo, Jehu, Elijah, Micaiah, Elisha.

AHIJAH

Significance in summary

Prophesied during the reign of Jeroboam I that Solomon's kingdom would be split into two

Meaning of name

the Lord is brother

Bible dictionary/encyclopedia entry (ISBE)

The distinguished prophet of Shiloh, who was active in Jeroboam I's reign. In Solomon's lifetime Ahijah clothed himself with a new robe, met Jeroboam outside Jerusalem, tore the robe into twelve pieces, and gave him ten, in token that he would become king of the ten tribes (1 Kings 11:29–39). Later, when Jeroboam had proved unfaithful to Yahweh, he sent his wife to Ahijah to ask in regard to their sick son. The prophet received her harshly, foretold the death of the son, and threatened the extermination of the house of Jeroboam (1 Kings 14).

Bible study on the life of Ahijah (NTB)

A prophet in Shiloh: 1 Kings 11:29–39

IDDO

Significance in summary

A prophet who wrote about the kings of Israel

Meaning of name

adorned

Bible study on the life of Iddo (NTB)

A prophet: 2 Chronicles 9:29; 12:15; 13:22

JEHU

Significance in summary

The prophet who brought bad news to King Baasha of Israel

Meaning of name

he is Yahweh

Bible study on the life of Jehu (NTB)

The prophet who announced the wrath of Jehovah against Baasha, king of Israel: 1 Kings 16:1, 7, 12; 2 Chronicles 19:2; 20:34

ELIJAH

Significance in summary

The great prophet who spoke fearlessly to King Ahab and Queen Jezebel

Meaning of name

the Lord is my God

Bible dictionary/encyclopedia entry (SBD)

Elijah (my God is Jehovah) has been well entitled "the grandest and the most romantic character that Israel ever produced." Elijah the Tishbite, of the inhabitants of Gilead, is literally all we know of his parentage and locality. His chief characteristic was his hair, long and thick, and hanging down his back. His ordinary clothing consisted of a girdle of skin round his loins (1 Kings 18:46). In addition to this he occasionally wore the "mantle" or cape of sheepskin which has supplied us with one of our most familiar figures of speech.

His introduction, in what we may call the first act of his life, is startling. He suddenly appears before Ahab, prophesies a three-year drought in Israel, and proclaims the vengeance of Jehovah for the apostasy of the king. Obliged to flee from the vengeance of the king, or more probably of the queen (compare 1 Kings 19:2) he was directed to the brook Cherith. There he remained, fed miraculously by ravens, until the brook dried up. His next refuge was at Zarephath. Here in the house of a widow Elijah performed the miracles of prolonging the oil and the meal, and restoring the son of the widow to life (1 Kings 17). In this or some other retreat an interval of more than two years must have elapsed. The drought continued, and at last the full horrors of famine descended on Samaria. Again Elijah suddenly appears before Ahab. There are few more sublime stories in history than the account of the succeeding events with the servant of Jehovah and his single attendant on the one hand, and the 850 prophets of Baal on the other—the altars, the descending fire of Jehovah consuming both sacrifice and altar, the rising storm, and the ride across the plain to Jezreel (1 Kings 18).

Jezebel vows vengeance, and again Elijah takes refuge in flight into the wilderness, where he is again miraculously fed, and goes forward, in the strength of that food, a journey of forty days to Mount Horeb, where he takes refuge in a cave, and witnesses a remarkable vision of Jehovah (1 Kings 19:9–18). He receives the divine communication, sets forth in search of Elisha, whom he finds plowing in the field, and anoints him prophet in his place (v. 19).

For a time little is heard of Elijah, and Ahab and Jezebel probably believed they had seen the last of him. But after the murder of Naboth, Elijah again suddenly appears before the king. Then follows Elijah's fearful denunciation of Ahab and Jezebel, which may possibly be recovered by putting together the words recalled by Jehu (2 Kings 9:26, 36–37) and those given in 1 Kings 21:19–25. A space of three or four years now elapses (compare 1 Kings 22:1, 51; 2 Kings 1:17) before we again catch a glimpse of Elijah. Ahaziah is on his deathbed (2 Kings 1:1–2) and sends messengers to an oracle or shrine of Baal to determine the severity of his illness; but Elijah suddenly appears on the path of the messengers, utters his message of death, and as rapidly disappears. The wrathful king sends two bands of soldiers to seize Elijah, and they are consumed with fire; but finally the prophet delivers to Ahaziah's face the message of death. Not long after, Elijah sends a message to Jehoram denouncing his evildoings, and predicting his death (2 Chron. 21:12–15).

It is at Gilgal—probably on the western edge of the hills of Ephraim—that the prophet receives word from the Lord that his departure is at hand. He is at the time with Elisha, who seems now to have become his constant companion, and who would not consent to leave him. "And it came to pass as they still went on, and talked, that, behold, there appeared a chariot of fire, and horses of fire, and parted them both asunder; and Elijah went up by a whirlwind into heaven" (2 Kings 2:11).

Fifty men of the sons of the prophets ascended the hills behind the town, and witnessed the scene. So deep was the impression Elijah made on the mind of the nation that many centuries later people believed he would again appear for the relief and restoration of his country, as Malachi prophesied (Mal. 4:5). He spoke, but left no written words, except for the letter to Jehoram king of Judah (2 Chron. 21:12–15).

Bible study on the life of Elijah (NTB)

The Tishbite, a Gileadite and prophet, called Elias in the King James Version of the New Testament; persecuted by Ahab: 1 Kings 17:2–7; 18:7–10
Escapes to the wilderness, where he is miraculously fed by ravens: 1 Kings 17:1–7
Goes to Zarephath; is sustained in the household of a widow, whose meal and oil are miraculouly increased: 1 Kings 17:8–16
Returns, and sends a message to Ahab: 1 Kings 18:1–16
Meets Ahab and directs him to assemble the prophets of Baal: 1 Kings 18:17–20
Derisively challenges the priests of Baal to offer sacrifices: 1 Kings 18:25–29
Kills the prophets of Baal: 1 Kings 18:40
Escapes to the wilderness from the fierceness of Jezebel: 1 Kings 19:1–18
Fasts for forty days: 1 Kings 19:8
Despondency and complaints of: 1 Kings 19:10, 14
Consolation given to: 1 Kings 9:11–18
Flees to the wilderness of Damascus; directed to anoint Hazael king over Syria, Jehu king over Israel, and Elisha to be a prophet in his own place: 1 Kings 19:9–21
Personal aspects of: 2 Kings 1:8
Piety of: 1 Kings 19:10, 14; Luke 1:17; Romans 11:2; James 5:17
His translation to heaven: 2 Kings 2:11
Appears to Jesus at his transfiguration: Matthew 17:3–4; Mark 9:4; Luke 9:30
Antitype of John the Baptist: Matthew 11:14; 16:14; 17:10–12; Mark 9:12–13; Luke 1:17; John 1:21–25
Miracles of:
- *Increases the oil of the widow of Zarephath:* 1 Kings 17:14–16
- *Raises the son of the woman of Zarephath from the dead:* 1 Kings 17:17–24
- *Causes rain after seven years of drought:* 1 Kings 18:41–45; James 5:17, 18
- *Causes fire to consume the sacrifice:* 1 Kings 18:24, 36–38
- *Calls fire down on the soldiers of Ahaziah:* 2 Kings 1:10–12; Luke 9:54

Prophecies of:
- *Foretells a drought:* 1 Kings 17:3
- *The destruction of Ahab and his house:* 1 Kings 21:17–29; 2 Kings 9:25–37
- *The death of Ahaziah:* 2 Kings 1:2–17

The plague sent as a judgment on the people in the time of Jehoram, king of Israel: 2 Chronicles 21:12–15

GEHAZI

Significance in summary

Elisha's servant

Meaning of name

valley of vision

Bible study on the life of Gehazi (NTB)

Servant of Elisha: 2 Kings 4:12, 29, 31
Covetousness of, and the judgment of leprosy on: 2 Kings 5:20–27
Mentions to King Jehoram the miracles of Elisha, his master: 2 Kings 8:4–5

MICAIAH

Significance in summary

Prophesied during the reign of King Ahab

Meaning of name

who is like the Lord?

Bible dictionary/encyclopedia entry (CBC)

During the reign of Ahab two distinguished prophets flourished, Elijah and Micaiah.

Micaiah's history is very brief. Ahab formed a military alliance with Jehoshaphat, and they went to war against the king of Syria. Before they went into the battle, Ahab's prophets were called, and they uttered their predictions concerning the result of the contest, after which Micaiah was called, and in a very impressive manner predicted the result of the engagement, and his predictions were fulfilled (2 Chron. 18:1–34).

Bible study on the life of Micaiah (NTB)

A prophet who reproved King Ahab: 1 Kings 22:8–28; 2 Chronicles 18:4–27

NAAMAN

Significance in summary

The Syrian commander whom Elisha cured of leprosy

Meaning of name

pleasantness

Bible dictionary/encyclopedia entry (SBD)

Naaman was commander-in-chief of the army of Syria and was nearest to the person of the king, Ben-hadad, whom he accompanied officially and supported when he went to worship in the temple of Rimmon (2 Kings 5:18) at Damascus, the capital (885 BC). A Jewish tradition at least as old as the time of Josephus, and which may very well be a genuine one, identifies him with the archer whose arrow, whether at random or not, struck Ahab with his mortal wound, and thus "gave deliverance to Syria." The expression in 2 Kings 5:1 is remarkable—"because that by him Jehovah had given deliverance to Syria." The most natural explanation perhaps is that Naaman in delivering his country had killed one who was the enemy of Jehovah not less than he was of Syria. Whatever the particular exploit referred to was, it had given Naaman a great position at the court of Ben-hadad. Naaman was afflicted with a leprosy of the white kind, which had defied cure. A little Israelite captive maiden tells him of the fame and skill of Elisha, and he is cured by following Elisha's simple directions to bathe in the Jordan seven times (see 1 Kings 5:14). His first business after his cure is to thank his benefactor and gratefully acknowledge the power of the God of Israel and promise "henceforth to offer neither burnt offering nor sacrifice unto other gods, but unto the Lord." How long Naaman lived to continue a worshipper of Jehovah while assisting officially at the worship of Rimmon we are not told.

Bible study on the life of Naaman (NTB)

A Syrian general, healed of leprosy by Elisha: 2 Kings 5:1–23; Luke 4:27

ELISHA

Significance in summary

The prophet who took over the prophetic role from Elijah

Meaning of name

God is Savior

Bible dictionary/encyclopedia entry (SBD)

Son of Shaphat of Abel-meholah; the attendant and disciple of Elijah, and subsequently his successor as prophet of the kingdom of Israel. The earliest mention of his name is in the cave at Horeb when the Lord commands Elijah to anoint Elisha as a prophet (1 Kings 19:16–17). Elijah sets forth to obey the command, and finds Elisha engaged in plowing. He throws over Elisha's shoulders his rough mantle—a token at once of investiture with the prophet's office and of adoption as a son. Elisha bids farewell to his father and mother, presides at a parting feast with his people, and then follows the great prophet on his northward road. We hear nothing more of Elisha for eight years, until Elijah's translation to heaven, when he reappears to become the most prominent figure in the history of his country during the rest of his long life.

In almost every respect Elisha presents the most complete contrast to Elijah. Elijah was a true Bedouin child of the desert. If he entered a city it was only to deliver his message of fire and be gone. Elisha, on the other hand, was a civilized man, an inhabitant of cities. His dress was the ordinary garment of an Israelite, the *beged*, probably similar in form to the long abbeyeh of the modern Syrians (2 Kings 2:12). His hair was trimmed, in contrast to the disordered locks of Elijah, and he used a walking staff (2 Kings 4:29) of the kind ordinarily carried by aged citizens (Zech. 8:4). After the departure of his master, Elisha returned to dwell at Jericho (2 Kings 2:18), where he miraculously purified the springs.

We next meet with Elisha at Bethel, in the heart of the country, on his way from Jericho to Mount Carmel (2 Kings 2:23). The mocking children, Elisha's curse, and the catastrophe which follow are familiar to all. Later he extricates Jehoram, king of Israel, and the kings of Judah and Edom from their difficulty in the campaign against Moab arising from want of water (2 Kings 3:4–27). Then he multiplies the widow's oil (2 Kings 4:5). At Shunem he is hospitably entertained by a woman whose son dies and whom he brings to life again (2 Kings 4:8–37). Then at Gilgal he purifies the deadly pottage (2 Kings 4:38–41) and multiplies the loaves (2 Kings 4:42–44). The simple records of these domestic incidents are now interrupted by the occurrence of a more important character (2 Kings 5:1–27). The chief captain of the army of Syria, Naaman, is attacked with leprosy, and is sent by an Israelite maid to the prophet Elisha, who directs him to dip seven times in the Jordan, which he does and is healed (2 Kings 5:1–14). Naaman's servant, Gehazi, is stricken with leprosy for his unfaithfulness (2 Kings 5:20–27).

Again the scene changes. It is probably at Jericho that Elisha causes the iron axe to swim (2 Kings 6:1–7). A band of Syrian marauders are sent to seize him, but are struck blind; he leads them to Samaria, where they find themselves in the presence of the Israelite king and his troops (2 Kings 6:8–23). During the famine in Samaria (2 Kings 6:24–33) he prophesies incredible plenty (2 Kings 7:1–2), which is soon fulfilled (2 Kings 7:3–20). We next find the prophet at Damascus. Ben-hadad the king is sick and sends Hazael to Elisha to find out the result. Elisha prophesies the king's death and announces that Hazael is to be king (2 Kings 8:7, 15). Finally this prophet of God, after having filled the position for sixty years, is found on his deathbed (2 Kings 13:14–19). The power of the prophet, however, does not end with his death. Even in the tomb he restores the dead to life (2 Kings 13:21).

Bible study on the life of Elisha (NTB)

Elijah instructed to anoint: 1 Kings 19:16
Called by Elijah: 1 Kings 19:19
Ministers to Elijah: 1 Kings 19:21
Witnesses Elijah's translation to heaven, receives a double portion of His spirit: 2 Kings 2:1–15; 3:11
Mocked by the young men of Beth-el: 2 Kings 2:23–24
Causes the king to restore the property of the hospitable Shunammite woman: 2 Kings 8:1–6
Instructs that Jehu be anointed as king of Israel: 2 Kings 9:1–3
Life of, sought by Jehoram: 2 Kings 6:31–33
Death of: 2 Kings 13:14–20
Bones of, restore a dead man to life: 2 Kings 13:21
Miracles of:
- *Divides the Jordan:* 2 Kings 2:14
- *Purifies the waters of Jericho by casting salt into the fountain:* 2 Kings 2:19–22
- *Increases the oil of the woman whose sons were to be sold for her debt:* 2 Kings 4:1–7
- *Raises the son of the Shunammite woman from the dead:* 2 Kings 4:18–37
- *Neutralizes the poison of the stew:* 2 Kings 4:38–41
- *Increases the bread to feed one hundred men:* 2 Kings 4:42–44
- *Heals Naaman the leper:* 2 Kings 5:1–19; Luke 4:27
- *Sends Naaman's leprosy on Gehazi as a judgment:* 2 Kings 5:26–27
- *Recovers the axe that had fallen into a stream by causing it to float:* 2 Kings 6:6

Reveals the counsel of the king of Syria: 2 Kings 6:12
Opens the eyes of his servant to see the hosts of the Lord: 2 Kings 6:17
Brings blindness on the army of Syria: 2 Kings 6:18
Prophecies of:
Foretells the birth of a son to the Shunammite woman: 2 Kings 4:16
Predicts bounty for the starving people in Samaria: 2 Kings 7:1
Foretells the death of the unbelieving prince: 2 Kings 7:2
Predicts seven years of famine in the land of Canaan: 2 Kings 8:1–3
Foretells the death of Ben-hadad, king of Syria: 2 Kings 8:7–10
Foretells the elevation of Hazael to the throne: 2 Kings 8:11–15
Predicts the victory of Jehoash over Syria: 2 Kings 13:14–19

AMOS

Significance in summary

Prophet from Judah, whose prophecies were directed against Israel

Meaning of name

burden-bearer

A Bible commentator's portrait (CCEB)

A shepherd of Tekoa, a small town of Judah, six miles southeast from Bethlehem and twelve from Jerusalem, on the borders of the great desert (2 Chron. 20:20; compare 2 Chron. 11:6). The region being sandy was more fit for pastoral than for agricultural purposes. Amos owned and tended flocks, and collected sycamore figs; he seems to have been of humble rank.

Though belonging to Judah, he was commissioned by God to exercise his prophetic work in Israel; since there were many impostors in Israel, the prophets of God generally fled to Judah through fear of the kings of Israel, and a true prophet from Judah was needed more there. His name is not to be confused with that of Isaiah's father, Amoz.

The time of his prophesying was during the reigns of Uzziah, king of Judea, and Jeroboam II, son of Joash, king of Israel (Amos 1:1), that is, during part of the time in which the two kings were contemporary, probably in Jeroboam's latter years, after he had recovered from Syria "the coast of Israel from the entering of Hamath to the sea of the plain" (2 Kings 14:25–27). Amos foretells that these same coasts, "from the entering in of Hamath unto the river of the wilderness," would be the scene of Israel's being afflicted (Amos 6:14); also his references to the state of luxurious security then existing (Amos 6:1, 4, 13), and to the speedy termination of it by the Assyrian foe (Amos 1:5; 3:12, 15; 5:27; 8:2), point to the latter part of Jeroboam's reign, which terminated in 784 BC, the twenty-seventh year of Uzziah's reign, which continued to 759 BC.

He was contemporary with Hosea, only in the fact that Hosea continued to prophesy in reigns subsequent to Uzziah (Hos. 1:1) while Amos ceased to prophesy during Uzziah's reign. The scene of his ministry was Beth-el, where the idol calves were set up (Amos 7:10–13). There his prophecies roused Amaziah, the idol priest, to accuse him of conspiracy and to try to drive him back to Judah.

Bible study on the life of Amos (NTB)

A prophet: Amos 1:1
Forbidden to prophesy in Israel: Amos 7:10–17
Vision of: Amos 8:2

HOSEA

Significance in summary

Prophesied against the idolatry of the people of Israel

Meaning of name

God has saved

Bible dictionary/encyclopedia entry (SBD)

Son of Beeri, and first of the minor prophets. Probably the life, or rather the prophetic career, of Hosea extended from 784 to 723 BC, a period of fifty-nine years. The prophecies of Hosea were delivered in the kingdom of Israel. Jeroboam II was on the throne, and Israel was at the height of its earthly splendor.

Bible study on the life of Hosea (NTB)

Called Osee: Romans 9:25

GOMER

Significance in summary

The prophet Hosea's unfaithful wife

Bible study on the life of Gomer (NTB)

Wife (concubine?) of Hosea: Hosea 1:3

JONAH

Significance in summary

The prophet who preached against Nineveh

Meaning of name

dove

Bible dictionary/encyclopedia entry (SBD)

The fifth of the minor prophets, the son of Amittai, and a native of Gath-hepher (2 Kings 14:25). Jonah flourished during or before the reign of Jeroboam II. Having already, as it seems, prophesied to Israel, he was sent to Nineveh. The time was one of political revival in Israel, but before long the Assyrians were to be a scourge on them. Jonah, shrinking from a commission which he felt sure would result (Jonah 4:2) in the sparing of a hostile city, attempted to escape to Tarshish. The providence of God, however, watched over him, first in a storm, and then in his being swallowed by a large fish, in whose belly he remained for three days and three nights. After his deliverance, Jonah went to Nineveh; the king, having heard of his miraculous deliverance, ordered a general fast, and averted the threatened judgment. But Jonah, not from personal but national feelings, grudged the mercy shown to a heathen nation. God then taught him by the significant lesson of the "gourd," whose growth and decay brought the truth at once home to him, that he was sent to testify by deed, as other prophets would afterward testify by word, the capacity of Gentiles for salvation and the purpose of God to make them partakers of it. This was "the sign of the prophet Jonas" (Luke 11:29–30). The resurrection of Christ itself was also shadowed forth in the history of the prophet (Matt. 12:39–41; 16:4). The mission of Jonah was highly symbolical. The facts contained a concealed prophecy.

Bible study on the life of Jonah (NTB)

Also called Jonas: 2 Kings 14:25
Sent by God to warn the city of Nineveh: Jonah 1:1–2
Disobedience and punishment of: Jonah 1:3–17
Repentance and deliverance of: Jonah 2; Matthew 12:40
Brought Ninevites to repentance: Jonah 3; Matthew 12:41
Displeased with God's mercy to Nineveh; reproved: Jonah 1:4
Is a sign: Matthew 16:4; Luke 11:29–30

In Exile

Nebuchadnezzar • Gedaliah • Ezekiel • Gog • Abednego • Shadrach • Meshach • Belshazzar • Cyrus • Daniel • Michael • Darius I • Darius II

Introduction (IBD)

The kingdom of Israel. In the time of Pekah, Tiglath-pileser II carried captive into Assyria (2 Kings 15:29; compare Isa. 10:5–6) some of the inhabitants of Galilee and of Gilead (741 BC).

After the destruction of Samaria (720 BC) by Shalmaneser and Sargon, there was a general deportation of the Israelites into Mesopotamia and Media (2 Kings 17:6; 18:9; 1 Chron. 5:26).

The kingdom of the two tribes, the kingdom of Judah. Nebuchadnezzar, in the fourth year of the reign of Jehoiakim (Jer. 25:1), invaded Judah, and carried away some royal youths, including Daniel and his companions (606 BC), together with the sacred vessels of the temple (2 Chron. 36:7; Dan. 1:2). In 598 BC (Jer. 52:28; 2 Kings 24:12), at the beginning of Jehoiachin's reign (2 Kings 24:8), Nebuchadnezzar carried away captive 3,023 eminent Jews, including the king (2 Chron. 36:10) with his family and officers (2 Kings 24:12), and a large number of warriors, as well as very many people of note, and workers, leaving behind only the poor. This was the first general deportation to Babylon.

In 588 BC, after Zedekiah's revolt, there was a second general deportation of Jews by Nebuchadnezzar (Jer. 52:29; 2 Kings 25:8), including 832 more leaders of the kingdom. He also took away the rest of the sacred vessels (2 Chron. 36:18). The period of time when the temple was destroyed (2 Kings 25:9) to its complete restoration in 517 BC (Ezra 6:15) is referred to as "seventy years."

In 582 BC the last and final deportation took place. Nebuchadnezzar took 4,600 heads of families with their wives and children and dependents (Jer. 52:30; 43:5–7; 2 Chron. 36:20, etc.). The exiles formed a large community in Babylon.

When Cyrus granted permission to the Jews to return to their own land (Ezra 1:5; 7:13), only a comparatively small number at first availed themselves of the privilege. But many joined the Jews who went back with Ezra, Zerubbabel, and Nehemiah, and later returned to them in Jerusalem (Jer. 50:4, 5, 17–20, 33–35).

NEBUCHADNEZZAR

Significance in summary

The powerful king of the Babylonian Empire who captured Jerusalem three times

Bible dictionary/encyclopedia entry (SBD)

The greatest and most powerful of the Babylonian kings. His name is explained to mean "Nebo is the protector against misfortune." He was the son and successor of Nabopolassar, the founder of the Babylonian empire. In the lifetime of his father Nebuchadnezzar led an army against Pharaoh-nechoh, king of Egypt, defeated him at Carchemish in a great battle (Jer. 46:2–12), recovered Coele-Syria, Phoenicia, and Palestine, took Jerusalem (Dan. 1:1–2), pressed forward to Egypt, and was engaged in that country when intelligence recalled him hastily to Babylon. Nabopolassar, after reigning twenty-one years, had died and the throne was vacant. In alarm about the succession, Nebuchadnezzar returned to the capital, accompanied only by his light troops; crossing the desert, probably by way of Tadmor or Palmyra, he reached Babylon before any disturbance had arisen and entered peaceably on his kingdom.

Within three years of Nebuchadnezzar's first expedition into Syria and Palestine, disaffection again showed itself in those countries. Jehoiakim, who, although threatened at first with captivity (2 Chron. 36:6) had been finally maintained on the throne as a Babylonian vassal, after three years of service "turned and rebelled" against his suzerain, probably trusting to be supported by Egypt for support (2 Kings 24:1). Not long afterward, Phoenicia seems to have broken into revolt, and the Chaldean monarch once more took the field in person, and marched first of all against Tyre. Having invested that city and left a part of his army there to continue the siege, he proceeded against Jerusalem, which submitted without a struggle. According to Josephus, Nebuchadnezzar punished Jehoiakim with death (Jer. 36:30) but placed his son Jehoiachin on the throne. Jehoiachin reigned only three months, because, on his showing symptoms of disaffection, Nebuchadnezzar came up against Jerusalem for the third time, deposed Jehoiachin, whom he carried to Babylon together with a large portion of the population of the city and the chief of the temple treasures, and made his uncle, Zedekiah, king. Tyre still held out; and it was not till the thirteenth year from the time of its first investment that the city of merchants fell. Before this, Jerusalem had been totally destroyed. Nebuchadnezzar had commenced the final siege of Jerusalem in the ninth year of Zedekiah—his own seventeenth year—and took it two years later. Zedekiah escaped from the city but was captured near Jericho (Jer. 39:5) and brought to Nebuchadnezzar at Riblah in the territory of Hamath, where his eyes were put out by the king's order and his sons and chief nobles were killed. Nebuchadnezzar then returned to Babylon with Zedekiah, whom he imprisoned for the remainder of his life. The military successes of Nebuchadnezzar cannot be traced minutely beyond this point. It may be gathered from the prophetic Scriptures and from Josephus that the conquest of Jerusalem was rapidly followed by the fall of Tyre and the complete submission of Phoenicia (Ezek. 26–28) after which the Babylonians carried their arms into Egypt, and inflicted severe injuries on it (Jer. 46:13–26; Ezek. 23:2–20).

On obtaining quiet possession of his kingdom after the first Syrian expedition, Nebuchadnezzar rebuilt the temple of Bel (Bel-Merodach) at Babylon out of the spoils of the Syrian war. He then proceeded to strengthen and beautify the city, which he renovated throughout and surrounded with several lines of fortifications, adding one entirely new quarter. Having finished the walls and adorned the gates magnificently, he constructed a new palace. On the grounds of this palace he formed the celebrated "hanging garden," which the Greeks placed among the seven wonders of the world. But he did not confine his efforts to the ornamentation and improvement of his capital. Throughout the empire he built or rebuilt cities, repaired temples, constructed quays, reservoirs, canals, and aqueducts, on a scale of grandeur surpassing nearly everything of its kind. We read of the wealth, greatness, and general prosperity of Nebuchadnezzar in the book of Daniel.

Toward the close of his reign the glory of Nebuchadnezzar suffered a temporary eclipse. As a punishment for his pride and vanity, a strange form of madness was sent on him which the Greeks called Lycanthropy, wherein the sufferer imagines himself a beast and insists on leading the life of a beast (Dan. 4:33). After four or perhaps seven years (Dan. 4:16) Nebuchadnezzar's malady left him. We are told that his reason returned, and he was established in his kingdom (Dan. 4:36). He died at an advanced age (eighty-three or eighty-four), having reigned forty-three years. A son, Evil-merodach, succeeded him.

Bible study on the life of Nebuchadnezzar (NTB)

Also called Nebuchadrezzar; king of Babylon: Jeremiah 21:2
His administration: Daniel 1–4
Conquests:
Of Jerusalem: 2 Kings 24–25; 1 Chronicles 6:15; 2 Chronicles 36:5–21; Ezra 1:7; Jeremiah 39
Of Egypt: 2 Kings 24:7; Jeremiah 46:2
Of Tyre: Ezekiel 29:18
An instrument of God's judgments: Jeremiah 27:8
Prophecies concerning: Jeremiah 21:7, 10; 22:25; 25:9; 27:6–9; 32:28; 43:10; 46:13; 49:30–33; Ezekiel 26:7–12

GEDALIAH

Significance in summary

The governor of Jerusalem after the exile

Meaning of name

the Lord is great

Bible study on the life of Gedaliah (NTB)

Governor appointed by Nebucbadnezzar after carrying the Jews into captivity: 2 Kings 25:22–24
Jeremiah committed to the care of: Jeremiah 39:14; 40:5–6
Warned of the conspiracy of Ishmael by Johanan and the captains of his army: Jeremiah 40:13–16
Killed by Ishmael: 2 Kings 25:25–26; Jeremiah 41:1–10

EZEKIEL

Significance in summary

Spoke to the exiles in Babylon

Meaning of name

God strengthens

Bible dictionary/encyclopedia entry (SBD)

One of the four greater prophets, was the son of a priest named Buzi, and was taken captive in the captivity of Jehoiachin, eleven years before the destruction of Jerusalem. He was a member of a community of Jewish exiles who settled on the banks of the Chebar, a "river" or stream of Babylonia. He began prophesying in 595 BC, and continued until 573 BC. We learn from an incidental allusion (Ezek. 24:18) that he was married, had a house (Ezek. 8:1) in his place of exile, and lost his wife by a sudden stroke. He lived in the highest consideration among his companions in exile, and their elders consulted him on all occasions. He is said to have been buried on the banks of the Euphrates. Ezekiel was characterized by his stern character and his devoted adherence to the rites and ceremonies of his national religion.

The book is divided into two great parts, of which the destruction of Jerusalem is the turning point. Chapters 1–24 contain predictions delivered before that event, and chapters 25–48 after it, as we see from Ezekiel 26:2. Again, chapters 1–32 are mainly occupied with correction, denunciation, and reproof, while the remainder deal chiefly in consolation and promise. A parenthetical section in the middle of the book, chapters 25–32, contains a group of prophecies against seven foreign nations. There are no direct quotations from Ezekiel in the New Testament, but in the Apocalypse there are many parallels and obvious allusions to the later chapters 40–48.

Bible study on the life of Ezekiel (NTB)

Time of his prophecy: Ezekiel 1:1–3
Persecution of: Ezekiel 3:25
Visions of:
- *God's glory:* Ezekiel 1; 8; 10; 11:22
- *Jews' abominations:* Ezekiel 8:5–6
- *The Jews' punishment:* Ezekiel 9:10
- *The valley of dry bones:* Ezekiel 37:1–14
- *A man with a measuring line:* Ezekiel 40–48
- *The river:* Ezekiel 47:1–14

Teaches by dramatic actions:
Feigns dumbness: Ezekiel 3:26; 24:27; 33:22
Symbolizes the siege of Jerusalem by drawings on a tile: Ezekiel 4
Shaves himself: Ezekiel 5:1–4
Removes his belongings to illustrate the approaching Jewish captivity: Ezekiel 12:3–7
Employs a boiling pot to symbolize the destruction of Jerusalem: Ezekiel 24:1–14
Does not show mourning on the death of his wife: Ezekiel 24:16–27
Prophesies by parable of an eagle: Ezekiel 17:2–10
Other parables: Ezekiel 15–16; 19; 23
His popularity: Ezekiel 33:31–32

GOG

Significance in summary

Featured in the books of Ezekiel and Revelation, as the ruler of Magog

Bible study on the life of Gog (NTB)

A Scythian prince; prophecy against: Ezekiel 38–39; Revelation 20:8

ABEDNEGO

Significance in summary

The name given to Azariah, one of Daniel's three friends

Meaning of name

servant of Nego

Bible study on the life of Abednego (NTB)

Also called Azariah; a Jewish captive in Babylon: Daniel 1:6–20; 2:17, 49; 3:12–30; Hebrews 11:34

SHADRACH

Significance in summary

The name given to Hananiah, one of Daniel's three friends

Bible dictionary/encyclopedia entry (SBD)

The Hebrew, or rather Chaldee name of Hananiah. The history of Shadrach or Hananiah, as told in Daniel 1–3, is well known. After their deliverance from the furnace, we hear no more of Shadrach, Meshach, and Abednego, except in Hebrews 11:33–34, but there are repeated allusions to them in the later apocryphal books, and the martyrs of the Maccabaean period seem to have been much encouraged by their example.

Bible study on the life of Shadrach (NTB)

Also called Hananiah; a Hebrew captive in Babylon: Daniel 1; 2:17, 49; 3

MESHACH

Significance in summary

The name given to Mishael, one of Daniel's three friends

Bible dictionary/encyclopedia entry (SBD)

One of the companions of Daniel, who with three others was taught (Dan. 1:4) and qualified to "stand before" King Nebuchadnezzar (Dan. 1:5) as his personal attendants and advisers (Dan. 1:20). Despite their Chaldean education, these three young Hebrews were strongly attached to the religion of their fathers, and their refusal to join in the worship of the image on the plain of Dura gave a handle of accusation to the Chaldeans. The rage of the king, the condemnation passed on the three offenders, their miraculous preservation from the fiery furnace heated seven times hotter than usual, the king's acknowledgement of the God of Shadrach, Meshach, and Abednego, and their restoration to office are written in the third chapter of Daniel; there the history leaves them.

Bible study on the life of Meshach (NTB)

A name given by the chief eunuch to Mishael, one of the three Hebrew young men: Daniel 1:7; 2:49; 3:12–30

BELSHAZZAR

Significance in summary

The co-regent in Babylon who witnessed the strange writing on the wall of his palace

Meaning of name

Bel protect the king

Bible dictionary/encyclopedia entry (SBD)

The last king of Babylon. In Daniel 5:2 Nebuchadnezzar is called the father of Belshazzar. This, of course, need only mean grandfather or ancestor. According to the well-known narrative Belshazzar gave a splendid feast in his palace during the siege of Babylon, using the sacred vessels of the temple, which Nebuchadnezzer had brought from Jerusalem. The miraculous appearance of the handwriting on the wall, the calling of Daniel to interpret its meaning (it being a prophecy about the overthrow of the kingdom), and Belshazzar's death, are recorded in Daniel 5.

Bible study on the life of Belshazzar (NTB)

King of Babylon: Daniel 5:1–30

CYRUS

Significance in summary

The founder of the Persian Empire who allowed the Jews to return to Jerusalem

Bible study on the life of Cyrus (NTB)

Issues a decree for the emancipation of the Jews and rebuilding the temple: 2 Chronicles 36:22–23; Ezra 1; 3:7; 4:3; 5:13–14; 6:3
Prophecies concerning: Isaiah 13:17–22; 21:2; 41:2; 44:28; 45:1–4, 13; 46:11; 48:14–15

DANIEL

Significance in summary

One of the Jewish exiles in Babylon who rose to great prominence in Nebuchadnezzar's court through his God-given wisdom and ability to interpret dreams

Meaning of name

God is my judge

Bible dictionary/encyclopedia entry (IBD)

One of the four great prophets, although he is not once spoken of in the Old Testament as a prophet. His life and prophecies are recorded in the book of Daniel. He was descended from one of the noble families of Judah (Dan. 1:3), and was probably born in Jerusalem, during the reign of Josiah. At the first deportation of the Jews by Nebuchadnezzar (the kingdom of Israel had come to an end nearly a century before), or immediately after his victory over the Egyptians at the second battle of Carchemish, in the fourth year of the reign of Jehoiakim, Daniel and three other noble youths were carried off to Babylon, along with part of the vessels of the temple. There he was obliged to enter into the service of the king of Babylon, and in accordance with the custom of the age received the Chaldean name of Belteshazzar, i.e., "prince of Bel," or "Bel protect the king!" His residence in Babylon was probably in the palace of Nebuchadnezzar, now identified with a mass of shapeless mounds called the Kasr, on the right bank of the river.

His training in the schools of the wise men in Babylon (Dan. 1:4) was to fit him for service to the empire. He was characterized during this period for his piety and his strict observance of the Mosaic law (1:8–16), and he gained the confidence and esteem of those who were over him.

At the close of his three years of discipline and training in the royal schools, Daniel was characterized by his proficiency in the "wisdom" of his day, and was brought out into public life. He soon became known for his skill in the interpretation of dreams (1:17; 2:14), and rose to the rank of governor of the province of Babylon; he became "chief of the governors" over all the wise men of Babylon. He made known and also interpreted Nebuchadnezzar's dream; and many years afterwards, when he was an old man, amid the alarm and consternation of the terrible night of Belshazzar's impious feast, he was called in at the instance of the queen mother (perhaps Nitocris, the daughter of Nebuchadnezzar) to interpret the mysterious handwriting on the wall. He was rewarded with a purple robe and elevation to the rank of "third ruler." The place of "second ruler" was held by Belshazzar as associated with his father, Nabonidus, on the throne (5:16). Daniel interpreted the handwriting, and that night Belshazzar the king of the Chaldeans was slain.

After the taking of Babylon, Cyrus, who was now master of all Asia from India to the Dardanelles, placed Darius, a Median prince, on the throne. During the two years of Darius's reign Daniel held the office of first of the "three presidents" of the empire, and was thus practically at the head of affairs, no doubt interesting himself in the prospects of the captive Jews (Daniel 9), whom he had the happiness of seeing restored to their own land; he did not return with them but remained in Babylon. His fidelity to God exposed him to persecution, and he was cast into a den of lions but was miraculously delivered; after this event Darius issued a decree enjoining reverence for "the God of Daniel" (6:26). Daniel "prospered in the reign of Darius, and in the reign of Cyrus the Persian," whom he probably greatly influenced in the matter of the decree which put an end to the captivity.

His series of prophetic visions opened up the prospect of a glorious future for the people of God, and must have imparted peace and gladness to his spirit in his old age. The time and circumstances of his death are not recorded. He probably died at Susa, about eighty-five years old.

Ezekiel, with whom he was contemporary, mentions him as a pattern of righteousness (Ezek. 14:14, 20) and wisdom (28:3).

Bible study on the life of Daniel (NTB)

A Jewish captive, also called Belteshazzar; educated at the king's court: Daniel 1
Interprets visions: Daniel 2; 4–5
Promotion and executive authority of: Daniel 2:48–49; 5:11, 29; 6:2
Conspiracy against, cast into the lions' den: Daniel 6
Prophecies of: Daniel 4:8–9; 7–12; Matthew 24:15
Abstinence of: Daniel 1:8–16
Wisdom of: Daniel 1:17; Ezekiel 28:3
Devoutness of: Daniel 2:18; 6; 9–10; 12; Ezekiel 14:14
Courage and fidelity of: Daniel 4:27; 5:17–23; 6:10–23

MICHAEL

Significance in summary

An archangel whom Daniel describes as the guardian of the Jewish people

Meaning of name

who is like God?

Bible study on the life of Michael (NTB)

His message to Daniel: Daniel 10:13, 21; 12:1
Contention with the devil: Jude 9
Fights with the dragon: Revelation 12:7

DARIUS I

Significance in summary

Known as Darius the Mede, who succeeded Belshazzar as ruler in Babylon

Meaning of name

he that informs himself

Bible study on the life of Darius (NTB)

The Mede, king of Persia: Daniel 5:31; 6; 9:1

DARIUS II

Significance in summary

King of Persia who encouraged the Jews to complete their rebuilding of the temple

Meaning of name

he that informs himself

Bible study on the life of Darius (NTB)

Emancipates the Jews: Ezra 5–6; Haggai 1:1, 15; Zechariah 1:1

Return from Exile

Nehemiah • Sanballat • Tobiah • Darius III • Geshem • Ezra • Zerubbabel (Sheshbazzar) • Esther • Xerxes (Ahasuerus) • Haman • Mordecai • Haggai • Zechariah • Malachi • Joshua

Introduction (CBC)

The people of God were taken into captivity because they flouted the Lord's laws and because of their consequent idolatry (1 Kings 14:21–24; 15:1–3; 16:1–20; 21:1–24; 23:31–37; 2 Chron. 36:1–21).

The people were not oppressed during their stay in Babylon although they sat down by the rivers and wept, and hung their harps on the willow trees, and declared that they could not sing the Lord's songs in a strange land (Ps. 137:1–6). It is probable that many of them followed the advice of the prophet Jeremiah and built their own houses to live in (Jer. 29:3–7). There were great prospects for the ambitious Hebrews, and some of them arose to positions of great distinction in the Babylonian empire (Dan. 2:48; Neh. 1:1–11).

Quite possibly the custom of erecting synagogues originated during the Babylonian captivity.

In the first year of his reign, Cyrus, king of Persia, in fulfillment of the prophecy of Jeremiah, proclaimed throughout his territories that the Lord had ordered him to build Him a house at Jerusalem, and he gave permission for the captives to return (2 Chron. 36:22–23; Ezra 1:1–4). He also gave back to the captives the vessels that had been taken from the house of the Lord by Nebuchadnezzar (Ezra 1:5–11). As a result of this decree, many captives returned to their native land (Ezra 2:1–70; Neh. 7:1–69).

In the second year after the return, the foundation of the temple was laid to the weeping of the old men and the shouting of the young (Ezra 3:1–13). As soon as the enemies of Judah heard that the work had begun, they asked Zerubbabel if they could join them in the work. When their request was denied, they did everything they could to hinder the work; finally they succeeded in having the work suspended (Ezra 4:1–24). In the second year of Darius, king of Persia, two new prophets (Haggai and Zechariah) encouraged the people (Ezra 5:1–17). Finally, under Darius, the building was completed, and the people showed their great joy and reverence for the Lord (Ezra 6:1–22).

NEHEMIAH

Significance in summary

Governor of Jerusalem who organized the rebuilding of the city's walls

Meaning of name

the Lord comforts

Bible dictionary/encyclopedia entry (IBD)

The son of Hachaliah (Neh. 1:1), and probably from the tribe of Judah. His family must have belonged to Jerusalem (Neh. 2:3). He was one of the "Jews of the dispersion," and in his youth was appointed to the important office of royal cupbearer at the palace of Shushan. The king, Artaxerxes Longimanus, seems to have been on friendly terms with his attendant. Through his brother Hanani, and perhaps from other sources (Neh. 1:2; 2:3), he heard of the desolate condition of the holy city, and was filled with sadness. For many days he fasted and mourned and prayed for the place of his fathers' sepulchers. At length the king observed his sadness of countenance and asked the reason of it. Nehemiah explained it all to the king, and obtained his permission to go to Jerusalem to act as governor of Judea. He went up in the spring of

446 BC (eleven years after Ezra), with a strong escort supplied by the king, and with letters to all the pashas of the provinces through which he had to pass, as also to Asaph, keeper of the royal forests, directing him to assist Nehemiah. On his arrival he surveyed the city and formed a plan for its restoration, a plan which he carried out with great skill and energy, so that it was completed in about six months. He remained in Judea for thirteen years as governor, carrying out many reforms, despite much opposition (Neh. 13:11). He built up the state on the old lines, "supplementing and completing the work of Ezra," and making all arrangements for the safety and good government of the city. At the close of this important period of his public life, he returned to Persia to the service of his royal master at Shushan or Ecbatana.

Very soon after this corruption returned, showing the worthlessness of the professions that had been made at the feast of the dedication of the walls of the city (Nehemiah 12). Malachi now appeared among the people with words of solemn warning; Nehemiah again returned from Persia (after an absence of some two years), and was grieved to see the widespread moral degeneracy that had taken place during his absence. He restored the orderly administration of public worship and the outward observance of the law of Moses. Of his subsequent history we know nothing. Probably he remained at his post as governor till his death (about 413 BC) at a good old age. The place of his death and burial is unknown.

Nehemiah was the last of the governors sent from the Persian court. Judea after this was annexed to the satrapy of Coele-Syria, and was governed by the high priest under the jurisdiction of the governor of Syria; the internal government of the country became more and more a hierarchy.

Bible study on the life of Nehemiah (NTB)

Son of Hachaliah: Nehemiah 1:1
The cupbearer of Artaxerxes, a very trusted position: Nehemiah 1:11; 2:1
Is grieved over the desolation of his country: Nehemiah 1
Is sent by the king to rebuild Jerusalem: Nehemiah 2:1–8
Register of the people whom he led from Babylon: Nehemiah 7
Register of the priests and Levites: Nehemiah 12:1–22
Rebuilds Jerusalem: Nehemiah 2–6
His administration as ruler of the people: Nehemiah 5–6; 8–11; 13

SANBALLAT

Significance in summary

The leader of the opponents of the Jews as they set about rebuilding the walls of Jerusalem

Meaning of name

the god Sin has given life

Bible dictionary/encyclopedia entry (SBD)

A Moabite of Horonaim (Neh. 2:10, 13; 13:28). He held apparently some command in Samaria at the time Nehemiah was preparing to rebuild the walls of Jerusalem (Neh. 4:2), and from the moment of Nehemiah's arrival in Judea he set himself to oppose every measure for the welfare of Jerusalem. The only other incident in his life is his alliance with the high priest's family by the marriage of his daughter with one of the grandsons of Eliashib, but the expulsion from the priesthood of the guilty son of Joiada by Nehemiah promptly followed. Here the scriptural narrative ends.

Bible study on the life of Sanballat (NTB)

An enemy of the Jews in rebuilding Jerusalem after the Babylonian captivity: Nehemiah 2:10, 19; 4; 6; 13:28

TOBIAH

Significance in summary

One of the men who attempted to stop Nehemiah from rebuilding the walls of Jerusalem

Meaning of name

the Lord is good

Bible dictionary/encyclopedia entry (IBD)

An "Ammonite" who joined with those who opposed the rebuilding of Jerusalem after the exile (Neh. 2:10). He was a man of great influence, which he exerted in opposition to the Jews; he sent letters to Nehemiah "to put him in fear" (Neh. 6:17–19). Eliashib the priest prepared for him during Nehemiah's absence "a chamber in the courts of the house of God," which on his return grieved Nehemiah, and he "cast forth all the household stuff of Tobiah out of the chamber" (13:7–8).

Bible study on the life of Tobiah (NTB)

Ancestor of a family of Babylonian captives: Ezra 2:60; Nehemiah 7:62
An enemy of the Jews in the time of Nehemiah: Nehemiah 2:10, 19; 4:3, 7–8
Conspires to injure and intimidate Nehemiah: Nehemiah 6:1–14, 19
Subverts nobles of Judah: Nehemiah 6:17–18
Allies himself with Eliashib, the priest: Nehemiah 13:4–9

DARIUS III

Significance in summary

King who ruled Persia in the time of Nehemiah

Meaning of name

he that informs himself

Bible study on the life of Darius (NTB)

The Persian: Nehemiah 12:22

GESHEM

Significance in summary

One of Nehemiah's opponents

Meaning of name

rainstorm

Bible study on the life of Geshem (NTB)

Also called Gashmu, an Arab; opposed Nehemiah in building Jerusalem: Nehemiah 2:19; 6:1–6

EZRA

Significance in summary

Leader of a group of exiles who returned to Jerusalem, where he instilled God's laws into them

Meaning of name

the Lord helps

Bible dictionary/encyclopedia entry (SBD)

A famous scribe and priest. He was residing in Babylon at the time of Artaxerxes Longimanus. The origin of his influence with the king does not appear, but in the seventh year of his reign he obtained leave to go to Jerusalem, and to take with him a company of Israelites. The journey from Babylon to Jerusalem took just four months; the company brought with them a large freewill offering of gold, silver, and silver vessels. It appears that Ezra's great purpose was to effect a religious reformation among the Palestine Jews. His first step was to enforce separation on all who had married foreign wives (Ezra 10:1). This was accomplished in little more than six months after his arrival at Jerusalem. With the detailed account of this important transaction Ezra's autobiography ends abruptly, and we hear nothing more of him until thirteen years afterwards, in the twentieth year of Artaxerxes, we find him again at Jerusalem with Nehemiah. It seems probable that after effecting the above reformations he returned to the king of Persia. The functions he executed under Nehemiah's government were purely of a priestly and ecclesiastical character. The date of his death is uncertain. There was a Jewish tradition that he was buried in Persia.

Bible study on the life of Ezra (NTB)

A famous scribe and priest: Ezra 7:1–6, 10, 21; Nehemiah 12:36
Appoints a fast: Ezra 8:21
Commissioned by Artaxerxes, returns to Jerusalem with a large group of Jews: Ezra 7:8
His charge to the priests: Ezra 8:29
Exhorts people to put away their heathen wives: Ezra 9; 10:1–17
Reads the law: Nehemiah 8
Reforms corruptions: Ezra 10; Nehemiah 13
Dedicates the wall of Jerusalem: Nehemiah 12:27–43

ZERUBBABEL (SHESHBAZZAR)

Significance in summary

As governor of Judah, helped build up the foundations of the temple in Jerusalem

Meaning of name

seed of Babylon

Bible dictionary/encyclopedia entry (IBD)

The son of Salathiel or Shealtiel (Hag. 1:1; Zorobabel, Matt. 1:12); also called the son of Pedaiah (1 Chron. 3:17–19), that is, according to a frequent usage of the word "son," the grandson or the nephew of Salathiel. He is also known by the Persian name of Sheshbazzar (Ezra 1:8, 11). In the first year of Cyrus, king of Persia, he led the first band of Jews, numbering 42,360 (Ezra 2:64), exclusive of a large number of servants, who returned from captivity at the close of the seventy years. In the second year after the return, he erected an altar and laid the foundation of the temple on the ruins of that which had been destroyed by Nebuchadnezzar (3:8–13; 4–6). All through the work he occupied a prominent place, inasmuch as he was a descendant of the royal line of David.

Bible study on the life of Zerubbabel (NTB)

Also called Sheshbazzar; directs the rebuilding of the altar and temple after his return from captivity in Babylon: Ezra 3:2–8; 4:2, 3; 5:2, 14–16; Haggai 1:12–14
Leads the emancipated Jews back from Babylon: Ezra 1:8–11; 2; Nehemiah 12
Appoints the Levites to inaugurate the rebuilding of the temple: Ezra 3:2–8
Prophecies relating to: Haggai 2:2; Zechariah 4:6–10
Called Zorobabel in the genealogy of Joseph: Matthew 1:12; Luke 3:27

ESTHER

Significance in summary

A Jewess, who replaced Queen Vashti as King Ahasuerus's wife.

Meaning of name

myrtle

Bible dictionary/encyclopedia entry (SBD)

Esther (a star), the Persian name of Hadassah (myrtle), daughter of Abihail, the son of Shimei, the son of Kish, a Benjamite. Esther was a beautiful Jewish maiden. She was an orphan, and had been brought up by her cousin Mordecai, who had an office in the household of Ahasuerus, king of Persia—supposed to be the Xerxes of history—and lived at "Shushan the palace." When Vashti was dismissed from being queen, the king chose Esther to the place on account of her beauty, not knowing her race or parentage; when Haman the Agagite suggested that the Jews should be destroyed, the king gave him full power and authority to kill them all. The means taken by Esther to avert this great calamity from her people and her family are fully related in the book of Esther. The Jews still commemorate this deliverance in the yearly festival Purim, on the fourteenth and fifteenth of Adar (February, March).

Bible study on the life of Esther (NTB)

Also called Hadassah; niece of Mordecai: Esther 2:7, 15
Chosen queen: Esther 2:17
Tells the king of the plot against his life: Esther 2:22
Fasts on account of the decree to destroy the Israelites; accuses Haman to the king; intercedes for her people: Esther 4–9

XERXES (AHASUERUS)

Significance in summary

The king of Persia who married Esther

Bible study on the life of Xerxes (NTB)

King of Persia, history of: Esther 1

HAMAN

Significance in summary

Plotted the downfall of Mordecia

Bible dictionary/encyclopedia entry (SBD)

Prime minister of the Persian king Ahasuerus. He is called an "Agagite," which seems to denote that he was descended from the royal family of the Amalekites, the bitterest enemies of the Jews, as Agag was one of the titles of the Amalekite kings. He or his parents were brought to Persia as captives taken in war. He was hanged on the gallows which he had erected for Mordecai the Jew (Esther 7:10).

Bible study on the life of Haman (NTB)

Prime minister of Ahasuerus: Esther 3:1
Plotted against Esther and the Jews; thwarted by Esther and Mordecai and hanged: Esther 3–9

MORDECAI

Significance in summary

Esther's cousin and guardian who helped save the Jews from destruction

Bible study on the life of Mordecai (NTB)

A Jewish captive in Persia: Esther 2:5–6
Foster father of Esther: Esther 2:7
Informs Ahasuerus of a conspiracy against his life and is rewarded: Esther 2:21–23; 6:1–11
Promoted in Haman's place: Esther 8:1–2, 15; 10:1–3
Intercedes with Ahasuerus for the Jews; establishes the festival of Purim in commemoration of their deliverance: Esther 8–9

HAGGAI

Significance in summary

A minor prophet who contrasted the luxurious homes the exiles built themselves with the ruined state of the temple

Meaning of name

born on a feast day

Bible dictionary/encyclopedia entry (IBD)

One of the twelve so-called minor prophets. He was the first of the three (Zechariah, his contemporary, and Malachi, who was about one hundred years later, being the other two) whose ministry belonged to the period of Jewish history which began after the return from captivity in Babylon. Scarcely anything is known of his personal history. He may have been one of the captives taken to Babylon by Nebuchadnezzar. He began his ministry about sixteen years after the return. The work of rebuilding the temple had been stopped by the Samaritans. After having been suspended for fifteen years, the work was resumed through the efforts of Haggai and Zechariah (Ezra 6:14), who by their exhortations encouraged the people to take advantage of the favorable opportunity that had arisen in a change in the policy of the Persian government.

Bible study on the life of Haggai (NTB)

One of the minor prophets; urges the Jews to rebuild the temple: Ezra 5:1; 6:14; Haggai 1

ZECHARIAH

Significance in summary

A minor prophet who encouraged the returned exiles to carry on re-building the temple.

Meaning of name

the Lord remembers

Bible dictionary/encyclopedia entry (IBD)

A prophet of Judah, the eleventh of the twelve minor prophets. Like Ezekiel, he was of priestly extraction. He describes himself (Zech. 1:1) as "the son of Berechiah." In Ezra 5:1 and 6:14 he is called "the son of Iddo," who was properly his grandfather. His prophetic career began in the second year of Darius, about sixteen years after the return of the first company from exile. He was contemporary with Haggai (Ezra 5:1).

Bible study on the life of Zechariah (NTB)

Son of Berechiah: Zechariah 2:4
Prophesied during the reign of Darius: Ezra 4:24; 5:1; 6:14; Zechariah 1:1, 7; 7:1
Probably the priest mentioned in: Nehemiah 12:16; Ezra 8:3, 11, 16

MALACHI

Significance in summary

The last of the Old Testament prophets who challenged the returned exiles to be wholly dedicated to the Lord

Meaning of name

my messenger

Bible dictionary/encyclopedia entry (IBD)

The last of the minor prophets, and the writer of the last book of the Old Testament canon (Mal. 4:4–6). Nothing is known of him beyond what is contained in his book of prophecies. Some have supposed that the name is simply a title descriptive of his character as a messenger of Jehovah, and not a proper name. There is reason, however, to conclude that Malachi was the ordinary name of the prophet.

He was contemporary with Nehemiah (compare Mal. 2:8 with Neh. 13:15; Mal. 2:10–16 with Neh. 13:23). Since no allusion is made to him by Ezra, and he does not mention the restoration of the temple, we can infer that he prophesied after Haggai and Zechariah, and when the temple services were still in existence (Mal. 1:10; 3:1, 10). It is probable that he delivered his prophecies about 420 BC, after the second return of Nehemiah from Persia (Neh. 13:6).

Bible study on the life of Malachi (NTB)

Last of the minor prophets: Malachi 1:1
Reproves God's people for their impiety: Malachi 1–2; 3:7–15
Foretells the coming of the Messiah: Malachi 3:1–6
Predicts the judgments on the wicked and consolations of the righteous: Malachi 4:1–3
Foretells the coming of the forerunner of the Messiah: Malachi 4:4–6

JOSHUA

Significance in summary

High priest in Jerusalem after the exiles returned

Meaning of name

God is salvation

Bible study on the life of Joshua (NTB)

Also called Jeshua; the high priest of the captivity: Ezra 2:2
Assists Zerubbabel in restoring the temple: Ezra 3; 4:1–6; 5; Haggai 1:1, 12–14; 2:2

Part Two

People in the New Testament

Jesus and His Contemporaries

Jesus Christ • Mary, Jesus' mother • Joseph • Elizabeth (Elisabeth) • Zechariah (Zacharias) • Quirinius (Cyrenius) • John the Baptist • Herod Antipas • Philip, son of Herod the Great • Philip, tetrarch of Ituraea and Trachonitis • Herodias • Salome • Anna • Simeon • Tiberius Claudius Caesar • Herod the Great • Augustus • Simon, Jesus' brother

The Twelve Apostles and Their Contemporaries

Simon Peter • Andrew • Bartholomew (Nathanael) • James, son of Zebedee • Herod Agrippa I • James, son of Alphaeus • John • Judas (Thaddaeus) • Judas Iscariot • Matthew (Levi) • Zebedee • Salome • Thomas (Didymus) • Simon • Philip

Jesus' Enemies

Annas • Caiaphas • Pilate • The Pharisees • Simon, the Pharisee • The Sadducees

Jesus' Friends

Nicodemus • Jairus • Zacchaeus • Mary Magdalene • Simon, the leper • Bartimaeus • Lazarus • Mary • Martha • Joseph of Arimathea • Barabbas • Simon of Cyrene • Alexander, son of Simon of Cyrene • Joanna • Mary, mother of James and Joseph • Cleopas

The Acts of the Apostles

Matthias • Joseph (Barsabbas) • Jude • Alexander, a Jewish leader • Theudas • Sapphira • Stephen • Ananias, Sapphira's husband • Simon Magus • Philip • Ethiopian eunuch • Aeneas • Dorcas (Tabitha) • Cornelius • Mary, mother of John Mark • Simeon (Niger) • Simon the tanner • Agabus • James, brother of Jesus • Rhoda • Sergius Paulus • Philippian jailer

The Apostle John and His Circle

Diotrephes • Gaius, recipient of John's third letter • Demetrius, a committed Christian

The Apostle Paul and His Circle

Gamaliel • Paul • Ananias from Damascus • Aristarchus • Jason of Thessalonica • Silas • Titus • Timothy • Eunice • Tychicus • John Mark • Barnabas • Alexander from Ephesus • Clement • Julius • Gaius from Macedonia • Luke • Theophilus • Gallio • Trophimus • Gaius from Derbe • Gaius from Corinth

Paul's Friends and Converts

Aquila • Priscilla • Apollos • Crescens • Crispus • Dionysius • Epaphras • Onesimus • Philemon • Onesiphorus • Epaphroditus • Lydia • Jason, a Jewish Christian • Phoebe • Sosthenes, a ruler of Corinthian synagogue • Sosthenes, a Corinthian believer • Stephanas • Publius • Eutychus

Paul's Enemies

Aretas • Demetrius, the silversmith • Ananias, the high priest • Demas • Elymas • Hymenaeus • Alexander, the coppersmith

Roman Rulers

Claudius • Felix • Festus • Agrippa II • Bernice • Drusilla

Jesus and His Contemporaries

Jesus Christ • Mary, Jesus' mother • Joseph • Elizabeth (Elisabeth) • Zechariah (Zacharias) • Quirinius (Cyrenius) • John the Baptist • Herod Antipas • Philip, son of Herod the Great • Philip, tetrarch of Ituraea and Trachonitis • Herodias • Salome • Anna • Simeon • Tiberius Claudius Caesar • Herod the Great • Augustus • Simon, Jesus' brother

JESUS CHRIST

Significance in summary

The Son of God who came as Messiah and Savior

Meaning of name of Jesus

the Lord is salvation

Bible dictionary/encyclopedia entry (SBD)

The name Jesus signifies savior. It is the Greek form of Jehoshua (Joshua). The name Christ signifies anointed. Jesus was both priest and king. Among the Jews priests were anointed as their inauguration to their office (1 Chron. 16:22). In the New Testament the name Christ is used as equivalent to the Hebrew Messiah (anointed), the name given to the long-promised prophet and king whom the Jews had been taught by their prophets to expect (Matt. 11:3; Acts 19:4). The use of this name, as applied to the Lord, always has a reference to the promises of the prophets. The name of Jesus is the proper name of our Lord, and that of Christ is added to identify Him with the promised Messiah. Other names are sometimes added to the names Jesus Christ, thus, "Lord," "a king," "King of Israel," "Emmanuel," "Son of David," "chosen of God."

Jesus Christ was born of the Virgin Mary, God being His father, at Bethlehem of Judea, six miles south of Jerusalem. The date of His birth was probably in December, 5 BC, four years before the era from which we count our years. That era was not used until several hundred years after Christ. The calculations were made by a learned monk, Dionysius Exiguus, in the sixth century, who made an error of four years, so to get the exact date from the birth of Christ we must add four years to our usual dates; for example, AD 1882 is really 1886 years since the birth of Christ. At the time of Christ's birth Augustus Caesar was emperor of Rome, and Herod the Great was king of Judea but subject of Rome. God's providence had prepared the world for the coming of Christ, and this was the best time in all its history.

All the world was subject to one government, so the apostles could travel everywhere; the door of every land was open for the gospel. The world was at peace, so the gospel could have free course. The Greek language was spoken everywhere with their other languages. The Jews were scattered everywhere with synagogues and Bibles.

Jesus, having a manger at Bethlehem for His cradle, received a visit of adoration from the wise men of the East. When forty days old He was taken to the temple at Jerusalem; His parents returned to Bethlehem and soon took Him to Egypt to escape Herod's massacre of the infants there. After a few months there, Herod having died in April, 4 BC, the family returned to their Nazareth home, where Jesus lived until He was about thirty years old, subject to His parents, and increasing "in wisdom and stature and in favor with God and man." The only incident recorded of His early life is His going up to Jerusalem to the Passover when He was twelve years old, and His conversation with the learned men in the temple. But we can understand the childhood and youth of Jesus better when we remember the influences He grew up with.

The natural scenery was rugged and mountainous but full of beauty. He breathed the pure air. He lived in a village, not in a city.

The Roman dominion was irksome and galling. The people of God were subject to a foreign yoke. The taxes were heavy. Roman soldiers, Roman laws, and Roman money constantly reminded them of their subjection. When Jesus was ten years old, there was a great insurrection (Acts 5:37) in Galilee. He who was to be King of the Jews heard and felt all this.

Conversations about the Jews' hopes of a Redeemer, of throwing off their bondage, of becoming the glorious nation promised in the prophets, were in the very air He breathed.

Within His view and His boyish excursions were many remarkable historic places—rivers, hills, cities, plains—that would keep in mind the history of His people and God's dealings with them.

Jesus was probably raised in a typical manner. Education for Jewish children began at first under the mother's care. At five they would learn the law, first by extracts written on scrolls of the more important passages, the Shema, or Psalms 114, 118, 136, and then by catechetical teaching in school. At twelve they accepted responsibility for obedience of the law, and on their thirteenth birthday would put on for the first time the phylacteries which were worn at the recital of daily prayers. In addition to this, Jesus no doubt learned the carpenter's trade of His reputed father Joseph, and, as Joseph probably died before Jesus began His public ministry, He may have contributed to the support of His mother.

Jesus began His ministry when He was about thirty years old. Having been baptized by John early in the winter of 26–27, He spent most of His year in Judea and around the lower Jordan; in December He went northward to Galilee through Samaria. The next year and a half, from December, AD 27, to October or November, AD 29, He spent in Galilee and northern Palestine, mainly near the Sea of Galilee. In November, 29, Jesus made His final departure from Galilee, and the rest of His ministry was in Judea and Perea, beyond Jordan, until His crucifixion, AD 30. After three days He demonstrated His divinity by rising from the dead; and after appearing on eleven different occasions to His disciples over a period of forty days, He finally ascended to heaven, where He is the living, ever-present, all-powerful Savior of His people. Jesus Christ, being both human and divine, is the true Savior of men and women. In this, as in every action and character, He is shown to be "the wisdom and power of God unto salvation." As human, He reaches down to our natures, sympathizes with us, shows us that God knows all our feelings and weaknesses and sorrows and sins, and brings God near to us humans, who otherwise could not realize the infinite and eternal as a father and friend. He is divine, in order that He may be an all-powerful, all-loving Savior, able and willing to defend us from every enemy, to subdue all temptations, to deliver from all sin, and to bring each of His people, and the whole Church, into complete and final victory. Jesus Christ is the center of the world's history, as He is the center of the Bible.

Bible study on the life of Jesus

There is a scarlet thread running from the book of Genesis to Malachi prophesying and describing the coming Messiah who would deliver

His people. The descriptions of Jesus' birth through to His ascension, as recorded in the four Gospels of Matthew, Mark, Luke, and John, place on record how Jesus fulfilled these Old Testament prophecies. From the book of Acts to Revelation, we continue to view the person of Jesus with all His wonderful attributes which are summed up in the different names given to Him.

Below is a list of the names of Jesus which can be seen in, or which sum up, each of the sixty-six books of the Bible.

Bible Book	**Name of Jesus**
Old Testament	
Genesis	Creator
Exodus	Deliverer
Leviticus	Eternal Sacrifice
Numbers	Trusted Guide
Deuteronomy	Redeeming Prophet
Joshua	Captain of Our Salvation
Judges	Steadfast Judge and Lawgiver
Ruth	Kinsman Redeemer
1 Samuel	Interceding King
2 Samuel	Anointed King
1 Kings	Wise King
2 Kings	Reigning King
1 Chronicles	Sovereign King
2 Chronicles	Glory of the Lord
Ezra	Faithful Scribe
Nehemiah	Rebuilder
Esther	Hidden Teacher
Job	Dayspring and Faithful One
Psalms	Shepherd and Song
Proverbs	Wisdom
Ecclesiastes	Only Hope
Song of Solomon	The Bridegroom
Isaiah	Prince of Peace
Jeremiah	Righteous Branch and Friend
Lamentations	Weeping Prophet
Ezekiel	Watchman and Wheel in the Sky
Daniel	Rescuer
Hosea	Faithful Husband
Joel	God's Outpouring of the Holy Spirit
Amos	Burden Bearer
Obadiah	Highest Authority
Jonah	God's Mercy
Micah	Messenger of the Gospel

Bible Book	Name of Jesus
Old Testament	
Nahum	Avenger of God's Elect
Habakkuk	Firm Foundation
Zephaniah	Prince of Peace and Glory of Israel
Haggai	Restorer of God's Lost Heritage
Zechariah	Merciful Father
Malachi	Glorious Promise
New Testament	
Matthew	King of the Jews
Mark	Son of God and Wonder Worker
Luke	Son of Man
John	Word Made Flesh
Acts	Power on High
Romans	Salvation and Justifier
1 Corinthians	Gift of the Spirit
2 Corinthians	Victory
Galatians	Liberator
Ephesians	Chief Cornerstone
Philippians	Provider and Supplier
Colossians	Fullness of God
1 Thessalonians	Soon Coming King
2 Thessalonians	Messiah
1 Timothy	Mediator
2 Timothy	Faithful Witness
Titus	Faithful Pastor and Blessed Hope
Philemon	Friend That Is Closer than a Brother
Hebrews	High Priest
James	Great Physician
1 Peter	Chief Shepherd
2 Peter	Savior
1 John	Righteousness
2 John	Everlasting Love
3 John	Truth
Jude	Majesty and Power
Revelation	King of Kings and Lord of Lords

MARY, Jesus' mother

Significance in summary

The mother of Jesus

Meaning of name

form of Miriam, meaning loved by God

Bible dictionary/encyclopedia entry (IBD)

The wife of Joseph, the mother of Jesus, called the "Virgin Mary," though never so designated in Scripture (Matt. 2:11; Acts 1:14). Little is known of her personal history. Her genealogy is given in Luke 3. She was from the tribe of Judah and the line of David (Ps. 132:11; Luke 1:32). She was connected by marriage with Elisabeth, who was of the line of Aaron (Luke 1:36).

While Mary lived in Nazareth with her parents, before she became the wife of Joseph, the angel Gabriel announced to her that she would be the mother of the promised Messiah (Luke 1:35). After this she went to visit her cousin Elisabeth, who was living with her husband Zacharias (probably at Juttah, Josh. 15:55; 21:16, in the neighborhood of Maon), at a considerable distance, about one hundred miles, from Nazareth. Immediately on entering the house she was greeted by Elisabeth as the mother of her Lord, and then offered her hymn of thanksgiving (Luke 1:46–56; compare 1 Sam. 2:1–10). After three months Mary returned to Nazareth to her own home. Joseph was supernaturally made aware (Matt. 1:18–25) of her condition, and took her to his own home.

Soon after this the decree of Augustus (Luke 2:1) required that they should proceed to Bethlehem (Micah 5:2), some eighty or ninety miles from Nazareth; while they were there they found shelter in the inn provided for strangers (Luke 2:6–7). But as the inn was crowded, Mary had to retire to a place among the cattle, and there she gave birth to her son, who was called Jesus (Matt. 1:21), because He was to save His people from their sins. This was followed by the presentation in the temple, the flight into Egypt, and their return in the following year and residence at Nazareth (Matthew 2). There for thirty years Mary, the wife of Joseph the carpenter, resides, filling her own humble sphere, and pondering the strange things that had happened to her. During these years only one event in the history of Jesus is recorded—His going up to Jerusalem when twelve years old, and His being found among the doctors in the temple (Luke 2:41–52). Probably also during this period Joseph died, for he is not again mentioned.

After the commencement of our Lord's public ministry little notice is taken of Mary. She was present at the marriage in Cana. A year and a half after this we find her at Capernaum (Matt. 12:46, 48–49), where Christ uttered the memorable words, "'Who is my mother? and who are my brethren?' And he stretched forth his hand toward his disciples, and said, 'Behold my mother and my brethren!'" (Matt. 12:48–49). The next time we find her is at the cross along with her sister Mary, and

Mary Magdalene, and Salome, and other women (John 19:26, see also Mark 15:40). From that hour John took her to his own home. She was with the little company in the upper room after the Ascension (Acts 1:14). From this time she disappears from public notice. The time and manner of her death are unknown.

Bible study on the life of Mary (NTB)

The mother of Jesus: Matthew 1:16; Luke 1:26–38; 2:5–19
Visits her cousin, Elisabeth: Luke 1:39–56
Attends the feast at Jerusalem, misses Jesus on the return, seeks and finds Him in the temple area: Luke 2:48–51
Is present with Jesus at a marriage feast in Cana of Galilee: John 2:1–10
Seeks Jesus when He is teaching in a house: Matthew 12:46–47; Mark 3:31; Luke 8:19
Present at the cross: John 19:25–27
Is committed to the care of John: John 19:27
Lives with the disciples in Jerusalem: Acts 1:14
Prophecies concerning: Isaiah 7:14; Luke 2:35

JOSEPH

Significance in summary

Jesus' earthly father

Meaning of name

may (God) add

Bible dictionary/encyclopedia entry (IBD)

The foster-father of our Lord (Matt. 1:16; Luke 3:23). He lived at Nazareth in Galilee (Luke 2:4). He is called a "just man." He was by trade a carpenter (Matt. 13:55). He is last mentioned in connection with the journey to Jerusalem, when Jesus was twelve years old. It is probable that he died before Jesus entered His public ministry. This is concluded from the fact that Mary only was present at the marriage feast in Cana of Galilee. His name does not appear in connection with the scenes of the crucifixion along with that of Mary (John 19:25).

Bible study on the life of Joseph (NTB)

Husband of Mary: Matthew 13:55; Mark 6:3; Matthew 1:18–25; Luke 1:27

His genealogy: Matthew 1:1–16; Luke 3:23–38
An angel appears and testifies to the innocence of his betrothed: Matthew 1:19–24
Lives at Nazareth: Luke 2:4
Belongs to the town of Bethlehem: Luke 2:4
Goes to Bethlehem to be enrolled: Luke 2:1–4
Jesus born to: Matthew 1:25; Luke 2:7
Presents Jesus in the temple: Luke 2:22–39
Returns to Nazareth: Luke 2:39
Warned in a dream to escape to Egypt in order to save the infant's life: Matthew 2:13–15
Warned in a dream to return to Nazareth: Matthew 2:19–23
Attends the annual feast at Jerusalem with his family: Luke 2:42–51

ELIZABETH (ELISABETH)

Significance in summary

Mother of John the Baptist

Meaning of name

God is my oath

Bible dictionary/encyclopedia entry (SBD)

The wife of Zacharias and mother of John the Baptist. She was herself of the priestly family, and related to the mother of our Lord (Luke 1:36).

Bible study on the life of Elizabeth (NTB)

The wife of Zacharias and the mother of John the Baptist: Luke 1:5–60

ZECHARIAH (ZACHARIAS)

Significance in summary

Father of John the Baptist

Meaning of name

the Lord remembers

Bible dictionary/encyclopedia entry (IBD)

A priest of the course of Abia, the eighth of the twenty-four courses into which the priests had been originally divided by David (1 Chron. 23:1–19). Only four of these courses or "families" of the priests returned from the exile (Ezra 2:36–39), but they were then redistributed under the old designations. The priests served at the temple twice each year, and only for a week each time. Zacharias's time had come for this service. During this period his home would be one of the chambers set apart for the priests on the sides of the temple ground. The offering of incense was one of the most solemn parts of the daily worship of the temple, and lots were drawn each day to determine who should have this great honor, an honor no priest could enjoy more than once during his lifetime.

While Zacharias ministered at the golden altar of incense in the holy place, it was announced to him by the angel Gabriel that his wife, Elisabeth, who was also of a priestly family, would give birth to a son who was to be called John, and that he would be the forerunner of the long-expected Messiah (Luke 1:12–17). As a punishment for his refusing to believe this message, Zacharias was struck dumb and "not able to speak, until the day that these things should be performed" (v. 20). Nine months passed, and Elisabeth's child was born, and when in reply to an inquiry Zacharias wrote on a writing tablet, "His name is John," his mouth was opened, and he praised God (vv. 60–79).

Bible study on the life of Zechariah (NTB)

The father of John the Baptist: Luke 1:5–80; 3:2

QUIRINIUS (CYRENIUS)

Significance in summary

The Roman governor of Syria when Mary and Joseph went to Bethlehem

Bible study on the life of Quirinius (NTB)

Governor of Syria when Jesus was born: Luke 2:2

JOHN THE BAPTIST

Significance in summary

The forerunner to Jesus Christ, whose mission was to prepare the way for the Messiah

Meaning of name

the Lord is gracious

Bible dictionary/encyclopedia entry (IBD)

We have only fragmentary and imperfect accounts of John the Baptist in the Gospels. He was of priestly descent. His father, Zacharias, was a priest of the course of Abia (1 Chron. 24:10), and his mother, Elisabeth, was of the daughters of Aaron (Luke 1:5). The mission of John was the subject of prophecy (Matt. 3:3; Isa. 40:3; Mal. 3:1). His birth, which took place six months before that of Jesus, was foretold by an angel. John was a Nazarite from his birth (Luke 1:15; Num. 6:1–12). He spent his early years in the mountainous tract of Judah lying between Jerusalem and the Dead Sea (Matt. 3:1–12).

At length he came into public life, and great multitudes from "every quarter" were attracted to him. The sum of his preaching was the necessity of repentance. He denounced the Sadducees and Pharisees as a "generation of vipers," and warned them of the folly of trusting external things (Matt. 3:7–8). As a preacher, John was practical and discriminating. He encouraged the common people to embrace charity and consideration for others instead of self-love. He cautioned the publicans against extortion and the soldiers against crime and plunder. His doctrine and manner of life roused the entire south of Palestine, and people from all parts flocked to the place where he was, on the banks of the Jordan. There he baptized thousands unto repentance.

The fame of John reached the ears of Jesus in Nazareth (Matt. 3:5), and He came from Galilee to be baptized of John to "fulfill all righteousness" (3:15). John's special office ceased with the baptism of Jesus, who must now "increase" as a king coming to his kingdom. He continued, however, for a while to bear testimony to the Messiahship of Jesus. He pointed Him out to his disciples, saying, "Behold the Lamb of God." His public ministry was suddenly (after about six months) brought to a close by his being cast into prison by Herod, whom he had reproved for the sin of having taken to himself the wife of his brother Philip (Luke 3:19). He was shut up in the castle of Machaerus, a fortress on the southern extremity of Peraea, nine miles east of the Dead Sea, and here he was beheaded. His disciples, having consigned the headless body to the grave, went and told Jesus all that had occurred (Matt. 14:3–12). John's death occurred apparently just before the third Passover of our Lord's ministry. Our Lord Himself testified regarding him that he was a "burning and a shining light" (John 5:35).

Bible study on the life of John the Baptist (NTB)

Prophecies concerning: Isaiah 40:3; Malachi 4:5–6; Luke 1:11–17
Miraculous birth of: Luke 1:11–20, 57–65
Lives in the desert: Matthew 3:1; Mark 1:4; Luke 1:80; 3:2–3
Mission of: Matthew 17:11; Mark 1:2–8; Luke 1:15–17, 76–79; 3:4–6; John 1:7–8, 15, 22–28, 31–34; 5:32–35; Acts 13:24–25; 19:4
Ministry of: Matthew 3:1–3; Mark 1:4; Luke 3:2–3; John 1:6–8
His influence on the public mind: Matthew 3:5–6; 14:5; 21:32; Mark 1:5; 11:32; Luke 3:7, 15; 20:6; John 1:35–40
Testifies to the messiahship of Jesus: Matthew 3:11–12; Mark 1:7–8; Luke 3:16–17; John 1:15, 26–36; 3:23–36; 5:32–33; 10:41; Acts 13:25
Teaches his disciples to pray: Luke 11:1
Teaches his disciples to fast: Luke 5:33
Baptizes Jesus: Matthew 3:13–16; Mark 1:9–11; Luke 3:21–22; John 1:32
The testimony of Jesus concerning: Matthew 17:12–13; 21:32; Mark 9:13; John 5:32–35
His ministry not attested by miracles: John 10:41
Reproves Herod Antipas on account of his incest; Herod imprisons him, and beheads him: Matthew 4:12; 14:1–12; Mark 6:16–29; 9:13; Luke 3:18–20
Sends two disciples to Jesus: Matthew 11:2–6; Luke 7:18–23
Herod Antipas falsely supposes him to be Jesus: Matthew 14:1–2; 16:14; Mark 6:14, 16; Luke 9:19
Character of: Mark 6:20; John 5:35
Jesus' discourses on: Matthew 11:7–19; Luke 7:24–33

HEROD ANTIPAS

Significance in summary

Son of Herod the Great, responsible for John the Baptist being beheaded

Meaning of name

heroic

Bible dictionary/encyclopedia entry (SBD)

Herod Antipas was the son of Herod the Great by Malthake, a Samaritan. He first married a daughter of Aretas, king of Arabia Petraea, but afterward Herodias, the wife of his half-brother, Herod Philip. Aretas, indignant at the insult offered to his daughter, found a pretext for invading the territory of Herod, and defeated him with great loss. This defeat, according to the famous passage in Josephus, was attributed by many to the murder of John the Baptist, which had been committed by Antipas shortly before, under the influence of Herodias (Matt. 14:3–12; Mark 6:17–28; Luke 3:19–20). At a later time the ambition of Herodias proved the cause of her husband's ruin. She urged him to go to Rome to gain the title of king, but he was opposed at the court of Caligula by the emissaries of Agrippa, and condemned to perpetual banishment at Lugdunum, AD 39. Herodias voluntarily shared his punishment, and he died in exile. The city of Tiberias, which Antipas founded and named in honor of the emperor, was the most conspicuous monument of his long reign.

Bible study on the life of Herod Antipas (NTB)

Tetrarch of Galilee: Luke 3:1; 23:7
Incest of: Matthew 14:3–4; Mark 6:17–19
Beheads John the Baptist: Matthew 14:3–11; Mark 6:16–28
Desires to see Jesus: Luke 9:7, 9; 23:8
Tyranny of: Luke 13:31–32
Jesus tried by: Luke 23:6–12, 15; Acts 4:27

PHILIP, son of Herod the Great

Significance in summary

Son of Herod the Great whose wife, Herodias, left him to marry Herod Antipas

Meaning of name

lover of horses

Bible dictionary/encyclopedia entry (SBD)

Herod Philip I (Mark 6:17) was the son of Herod the Great and Mariamne. He married Herodias the sister of Agrippa I by whom he had a daughter, Salome. He was excluded from all share in his father's possessions because of his mother's treachery, and lived afterward in a private station.

Bible study on the life of Herod Philip I (NTB)

The brother of Herod Antipas and the husband of Herodias: Matthew 14:3; Mark 6:17; Luke 3:19

PHILIP, tetrarch of Ituraea and Trachonitis

Significance in summary

Ruled Ituraea for thirty-seven years

Bible dictionary/encyclopedia entry (SBD)

Herod Philip II was the son of Herod the Great and Cleopatra. He received as his own government Batanea Trachonitis, Auramtis (Gaulanitis), and some parts around Jamnia, with the title of tetrarch (Luke 3:1). He built a new city on the site of Paneas, near the sources of the Jordan, which he called Caesarea Philippi (Matt. 16:13; Mark 8:27), and raised Bethsaida to the rank of a city under the title of Julias and died there AD 34. He married Salome, the daughter of Herod Philip I and Herodias.

Bible study on the life of Philip, another son of Herod (NTB)

Tetrarch of Ituraea: Luke 3:1

HERODIAS

Significance in summary

The estranged wife of Philip, son of Herod the Great, who became the wife of Herod Antipas

Bible study on the life of Herodias (NTB)

Daughter of Aristobulus: Matthew 14:3, 6; Mark 6:17, 19, 22; Luke 3:19

SALOME

Significance in summary

The daughter of Herodias, who danced before Herod Antipas

Bible dictionary/encyclopedia entry (IBD)

"The daughter of Herodias," not named in the New Testament. On the occasion of the birthday festival held by Herod Antipas, who had married her mother Herodias, in the fortress of Machaerus, she came in and danced, and pleased Herod (Mark 6:14–29). John the Baptist, at that time a prisoner in the dungeons underneath the castle, was at her request beheaded by order of Herod. His head was given to Salome; in turn she gave it to her mother, whose revengeful spirit was gratified.

ANNA

Significance in summary

A prophetess in Jerusalem who encountered the baby Jesus at the time of his presentation in the temple

Meaning of name

grace

Bible dictionary/encyclopedia entry (ISBE)

A "prophetess," daughter of Phanuel, from the tribe of Asher, and thus a Galilean, living in Jerusalem at the time of Jesus' birth (Luke 2:36–38). She must have been considerably over one hundred years old, having been a widow eighty-four years after a short married life of seven (see the Revised Version [British and American]). Exceptionally devout and gifted in spirit, she worshiped so constantly "with fastings and supplications night and day," that she is said to have "departed not from the temple." Some have mistakenly supposed that this signified permanent residence in the temple. The fact that her lineage is recorded indicates the distraction of her family. Tradition says that the tribe of Asher was noted for the beauty and talent of its women, who for these gifts, were qualified for royal and high-priestly marriage. While the tribe of Asher was not among the tribes that returned from the Babylonian exile to Palestine, many of its chief families must have done so as in the case of the prophetess. The period of war and national oppression, through which Anna's early life was passed, created in her, as in the aged Simeon, an intense longing for the "redemption" promised through the Messiah. This hope of national deliverance sustained her through more than four decades of patient waiting. In the birth of Jesus her faith was abundantly rewarded, and she became a grateful and ceaseless witness "to all them that were looking for the redemption of Jerusalem," that the day of their spiritual deliverance had come.

Bible study on the life of Anna (NTB)

A devout widow: Luke 2:36–37

SIMEON

Significance in summary

A devout Jew who met the baby Jesus in the temple and praised God in a prayer now known as the Nunc Demittis

Meaning of name

he hears

Bible dictionary/encyclopedia entry (SBD)

A devout Jew, inspired by the Holy Spirit, who met the parents of our Lord in the temple, took the baby in his arms, and gave thanks for what he saw and knew of Jesus (Luke 2:25–35).

Bible study on the life of Simeon (NTB)

Blesses Jesus (when an infant) in the temple: Luke 2:25–35

TIBERIUS CLAUDIUS CAESAR

Significance in summary

The emperor of Rome during Jesus' lifetime

Meaning of name

son of Tiber

Bible study on the life of Tiberius (NTB)

An important emperor of Rome: Luke 3:1

HEROD THE GREAT

Significance in summary

The deceitful and murderous king of Judea when Jesus was born

Meaning of name

heroic

Bible dictionary/encyclopedia entry (SBD)

This family though of Idumean origin and thus alien by race, was Jewish in faith.

Herod the Great was the second son of Antipater, an Idumean, who was appointed procurator of Judea by Julius Caesar, 47 BC. Immediately after his father's elevation when only fifteen years old, he received the government of Galilee and shortly afterward that of Coele-Syria. Though Josephus says he was 15 years old at this time, it is generally conceded that there must be some mistake, as he lived to be 69 or 70 years old, and died in 4 BC; hence he must have been 25 years old at this time. In 41 BC he was appointed by Antony Tetrarch of Judea. Forced to abandon Judea the following year, he fled to Rome, and received the appointment of King of Judea. In the course of a few years, by the help of the Romans he took Jerusalem (37 BC), and completely established his authority throughout his dominions. The terrible acts of bloodshed which Herod perpetrated in his own family were accompanied by others among his subjects equally terrible, from the number who fell victims to them. According to the well-known story he ordered the nobles whom he had called to him in his last moment to be executed immediately after his decease, that so at least his death might be attended by universal mourning. It was at the time of his fatal illness that he must have caused the slaughter of the infants at Bethlehem (Matt. 2:16–18). He adorned Jerusalem with many splendid monuments. The temple was the greatest of these works. The restoration was begun in 20 BC, and the temple itself was completed in a year and a half. But fresh additions were constantly made in succeeding years, so that it was said the temple was "built in forty and six years" (John 2:20); the work continued long after Herod's death. Herod died of a terrible disease at Jericho, in April, 4 BC, at the age of 69, after a long reign of thirty-seven years.

Bible study on the life of Herod the Great (NTB)

King of Judah (Herod the Great): Matthew 2

AUGUSTUS

Significance in summary

The imperial name of Octavian, Julius Caesar's nephew, who became emperor of Rome

Meaning of name

august

Bible study on the life of Augustus (NTB)

An important Roman emperor: Luke 2:1; Acts 25:21, 25; 27:1

SIMON, Jesus' brother

Significance in summary

One of Jesus' half-brothers

Meaning of name

hearing

Bible dictionary/encyclopedia entry (IBD)

One of the brothers of our Lord (Matt. 13:55; Mark 6:3).

Bible study on the life of Simon (NTB)

A physical half-brother of Jesus: Matthew 13:55; Mark 6:3

The Twelve Apostles and Their Contemporaries

Simon Peter • Andrew • Bartholomew (Nathanael) • James, son of Zebedee • Herod Agrippa I • James, son of Alphaeus • John • Judas (Thaddaeus) • Judas Iscariot • Matthew (Levi) • Zebedee • Salome • Thomas (Didymus) • Simon • Philip

Introduction (TT)

The selection by Jesus of twelve from the group of disciples who had gradually gathered around Him is an important landmark in the Gospel history. It divides the ministry of our Lord into two parts, nearly equal, probably, as to duration, but unequal as to the extent and importance of the work done in each respectively. In the earlier period Jesus labored single-handed; His miraculous deeds were confined for the most part to a limited area. But by the time the Twelve were chosen, the work of the kingdom had assumed such dimensions as to require organization and division of labor. The teaching of Jesus was beginning to be of a deeper and more elaborate nature, and His gracious activities were taking on ever-widening range.

These twelve were to be something more than traveling companions or menial servants of the Lord Jesus Christ. They were to be, in the meantime, students of Christian doctrine, and occasional fellow laborers in the work of the kingdom, and eventually Christ's chosen trained agents for propagating the faith after He Himself had left the earth. From the time of their being chosen, indeed, the Twelve entered on a regular apprenticeship for the great office of apostleship, in the course of which they were to learn, in the privacy of an intimate daily fellowship with their Master, what they should be, do, believe, and teach, as His witnesses and ambassadors to the world. Henceforth the training of these men was to be a constant and prominent part of Christ's personal work.

The time when this election was made, though not absolutely determined, is fixed in relation to certain leading events in the Gospel history. John speaks of the Twelve as an organized company at the period of the feeding of the five thousand, and of the discourse on the bread of life in the synagogue of Capernaum, delivered shortly after that miracle. From this fact we learn that the Twelve were chosen at least one year before the crucifixion; for the miracle of the feeding took place, according to the fourth evangelist, shortly before a Passover season. From the words spoken by Jesus to the men whom He had chosen, in justification of His seeming doubt of their fidelity after the multitude had deserted Him, "Did I not choose you the twelve, and one of you is a devil?" we conclude that the choice was then not quite a recent event. The twelve had been together long enough to give the false disciple opportunity to show his real character.

Turning now to the synoptic evangelists, we find them fixing the position of the election with reference to two other most important events. Matthew speaks for the first time of the Twelve as a distinct body in connection with their mission in Galilee. He does not, however, say that they were chosen immediately before, and with direct reference to, that mission. He speaks rather as if the apostolic fraternity had been previously in existence, his words being, "When He had called unto Him His twelve disciples." Luke, on the other hand, gives a formal record of the election, as a preface to his account of the Sermon on the Mount, so speaking as to create the impression that the one event immediately preceded the other. Finally, Mark's narrative confirms the view suggested by these observations on Matthew and Luke, that is that the Twelve were called just before the Sermon on the Mount was delivered, and some considerable time before they were sent on their preaching and healing mission.

The number of the apostolic company is significant, and was doubtless a matter of choice, not less than was the composition of the selected band. A larger number of eligible men could easily have been found in a circle of disciples which afterwards supplied not fewer than seventy auxiliaries for evangelistic work; and a smaller number might have served all the present or prospective purposes of the apostleship. The number twelve was recommended by obvious symbolic reasons. It happily expressed in figures what Jesus claimed to be, and what He had come to do, and thus furnished a support to the faith and a stimulus to the devotion of His followers. It significantly hinted that Jesus was the divine Messianic King of Israel, come to set up the kingdom whose advent was foretold by prophets in glowing language, suggested by the days of Israel's history, when all the tribes of the chosen nation were united under the royal house of David. That the number twelve was designed to bear such a mystic meaning, we know from Christ's own words to the apostles on a later occasion, when, describing to them the rewards awaiting them in the kingdom for past services and sacrifices, He said, "Verily I say unto you, that ye which have followed me, in the regeneration, when the Son of man shall sit in the throne of His glory, ye also shall sit on twelve thrones, judging the twelve tribes of Israel."

SIMON PETER

Significance in summary

One of the twelve apostles and leader in the early church

Meaning of name

rock

Bible dictionary/encyclopedia entry (SERK)

Peter originally bore the very common Jewish name of Shimeon, Simeon, or Simon (cf. Acts 15:14; 2 Peter 1:1), the first of these forms being the earliest, and the last the latest. He also had the Aramaic honorary surname of Kepha (Gk. *Kephas*), or "Rock," which was translated into its Greek equivalent *Petros*, "Peter."

Christ himself, however, called His apostle "Peter" only three times, (John 1:42; Matt. 16:18; Luke 22:34), elsewhere using either the name "Simon" (Matt. 27:5; Mark 14:37; Luke 22:31) or, in more solemn moments, "Simon son of John" (Matt. 16:17; John 1:42; 21:15–17).

The phraseology of the Evangelists varies. Mark calls the apostle Simon until he receives the surname of Peter (Mark 3:16), after which he is called Peter; and a similar, though less consistent, course is followed by the other two synoptics (cf. Matt. 4:18; 8:14; 16:16; Luke 5:8). In Acts he is invariably called Peter (Acts 10:13; 11:7). In the Fourth Gospel he is called Simon only when first mentioned, elsewhere being usually called Simon Peter, Peter alone being used only when the double name either precedes or follows. Paul almost invariably terms him Cephas (1 Cor. 1:12; 3:22; 9:5; 15:5; Gal. 1:18; 2:9, 11, 14), the use of Peter here being extremely rare (Gal. 2:7–8).

The father of the apostle Peter was named John (John 1:42; 21:15) or, in abbreviated form, Jona (Matt. 16:17). Peter was probably from Bethsaida (John 1:44), although Mark 1:21, 29 makes him a resident of Capernaum, the apparent contradiction being explicable by the fact that at marriage (cf. 1 Cor. 9:5) he had moved to Capernaum, where he became a fisherman with his younger brother Andrew, in the Sea of Galilee (Matt. 4:18; Mark 1:16; Luke 5:3). Andrew had become one of the disciples of John the Baptist (John 1:40), and it was this younger brother who brought Peter into contact with Jesus (John 1:42).

Generally speaking, the character of Peter is described with essential harmony in all the Gospels. He appears as well-meaning, freedom-loving, and courageous, yet changeable and capricious (Matt. 11:7ff.).

At first sight it seems strange that Jesus should have given the epithet of "Rock" to such a character, yet He saw beneath the surface and grasped the inherent strength and stability that underlay the changing and inconstant exterior. Nor did Peter prove unworthy of this confidence. His trust became ardent devotion; and his quick resolution was strengthened and steadied. Yet in the account of his walking on the water (Matt. 14:28–31) his natural instability of character, even after being under the influence of Jesus for a long time, is clearly seen, while his denial of Christ still more strongly marks his wavering and his weakness. Nevertheless, he had already shown himself worthy of his title, as when at Caesarea Philippi he boldly declared Jesus to be the Christ, not a mere precursor of the Messiah (Matt. 16:13ff; Mark 8:27ff.; Luke 9:18ff.; John 6:66ff.), especially as this was the same time when many, disappointed in Jesus, were abandoning Him.

Yet even the faith of Peter was contaminated with hopes of the earthly power and glory of Christ. He incurred the severe rebuke of his master by deprecating the necessity of such sufferings (Matt. 16:23–24; Mark 8:33), yet on the mount of transfiguration he again wished to make permanent the glory there apocalyptically revealed (Matt. 17:3; Mark 9:5; Luke 9:33). Equally typical was his desire to extend forgiveness as far as possible, though he still fell far short of the Christian ideal (Matt. 28:21–22); and the same statement holds true of the words in which he reminds Christ how both he and the other disciples had left all to follow Him (Matt. 19:27; Mark 10:28; Luke 18:28).

As the time of the passion approached, flaws in Peter's character are further exposed. In the scene recorded in John 13:6 and following, his impetuosity is revealed, as well as a certain lack of understanding of the love of Jesus which was to reach its culmination in the passion. Immediately afterward he vowed, despite the prophecy of the denial, to remain faithful to Jesus even if this meant death (Matt. 26:33ff.; Mark 14:29ff.; Luke 22:33–34; John 13:37–38). But he had overestimated his strength, nor could he even keep awake for his master's sake in Gethsemane (Matt. 26:40; Luke 22:45). It is true that he drew his sword when Jesus was seized (Matt. 26:51; Mark 14:47; Luke 22:50; John 18:10–11), but when he saw that this was useless, he fled with the other disciples (Matt. 26:56 and parallels).

Nevertheless, he made his way into the palace of the high priest, where he was put to the real test, only to deny Jesus with the utmost vehemence (Matt. 26:69ff.; Mark 14:66ff.; Luke 7:56ff.; John 18:15ff.). This last fall receives only a partial explanation from the vacillating character of Peter; the real reason seems to lie in the fact that inaction undermined his resolution, which activity would have kept consistent. Yet in all this he never really lost faith in Christ for an instant, and when he became aware of what he had almost unconsciously done, his remorse and shame, while finally purifying his character, kept him away from Christ until after the resurrection. Then, however, his old energy reappeared, and though at the tomb he was outstripped in running by the younger disciple John, he was still the first to find that the grave was empty (John 20:3ff.), and in the account of the appearance of the risen Christ at the Sea of Tiberias, the old character of Peter once more becomes manifest (John 21:7ff.).

The temperament of Peter, as here outlined, was inseparably connected with his position of preeminence among the apostles. Not only was he closely associated with the two sons of Zebedee, James and John, and once with his own brother, Andrew, as one of the favorite and most trusted disciples of Jesus (Mark 5:37; 9:2; 13:3ff.; 14:33ff.; Luke 8:51; 9:28), and not only were he and John commissioned to make preparations for the Last Supper (Luke 22:8ff.), but the entire content of the Gospels mark him as preeminent over the other disciples. This position seems to have been due essentially to his quick resolution and to his energy, and it was confirmed by Jesus both for the present and for the future; for the present by addressing to him questions and answers which concerned the other disciples as well (Matt. 17:25ff., 18:22; 26:40; John 13:36); and for the future by the remarkable words recorded in Matthew 16:18–19, a prerogative which even temporary wavering could not annul (cf. Luke 22:31–32).

The apostolic work of Peter in Judea and the neighboring districts after the resurrection of Jesus is recorded mainly in Acts, although the Pauline epistles contain a few valuable allusions. After the ascension, Peter, undismayed by the threats of the Sanhedrin at Jerusalem, preached and worked in Samaria and along the Syro-Phenician coast, especially in Lydda, Joppa, and Cassarea (Acts 8:14ff.; 9:32–10:48), performing many miracles (Acts 3:4ff.; 5:15; 9:34, 40). Returning to Jerusalem, he was imprisoned under Herod Agrippa after the death of James, the brother of John (Acts 12:1ff.), but after escaping, he left the city, though he seems again to have returned there after Herod's death. Paul visited him there three years after his conversion (Gal. 1:18), and he was there at the time of the council of the apostles recorded in Galatians 2:1–9. With Jerusalem as a base, he visited other churches (Gal. 2:11), accompanied by his wife (1 Cor. 9:5).

As to the position of Peter as the leader of the apostolic church, Acts and the Pauline epistles are in agreement. He took first place in the meeting which chose Matthias to succeed Judas Iscariot (Acts 1:15ff.), he was the spokesman of the whole company of apostles both in winning a large body of Jewish converts (Acts 2:14ff.) and in defending the Gospel against the Jewish hierarchy (Acts 4:8ff.; 19ff.; 5:29ff.), he reformed conditions within the mother church at Jerusalem, he watched over relations with other Christian communities (Acts 8:14ff.; 9:32ff.), and he was the first to receive a pagan into the new church (Acts 10:1ff.).

On the other hand, he enjoyed no absolute preeminence. He labored in Samaria together with John (Acts 8:14), and he was called to account for associating with gentiles (Acts 11:3ff.). At the council of the apostles, moreover, he was not only not the leader, but was even subordinate, in a sense, to James (Acts 15:6ff.). In the same way Paul at first describes Peter as the leader of the church at Jerusalem (Gal. 1:18), but by the time of the apostolic council he was, although still the virtual representative of the mission to the Jews, only one of the three pillars of the church, the other two being James and John (Gal. 2:8–9).

Except for the prophecy in John 21:18 and following and Peter's letters, the New Testament says nothing about the closing years of Peter. The sole remaining source is tradition, which seems to preserve a kernel of truth in the story that the apostle went to Rome toward the end of his life and there suffered martyrdom under Nero.

Bible study on the life of Peter (NTB)

Called Simon Bar-jona and Cephas: Matthew 16:16–19; Mark 3:16; John 1:42

A fisherman: Matthew 4:18; Luke 5:1–7; John 21:3

Call of: Matthew 4:18–20; Mark 1:16–18; Luke 5:1–11

His wife's mother healed: Matthew 8:14; Mark 1:29–30; Luke 4:38

An apostle: Matthew 10:2; 16:18–19; Mark 3:16; Luke 6:14; Acts 1:13

An evangelist: Mark 1:36–37
Confesses Jesus as Christ: Matthew 16:16–19; Mark 8:29; Luke 9:20; John 6:68–69
Walks on water: Matthew 14:28–31
Sent with John to prepare the Passover: Luke 22:8
His disloyalty foretold by Jesus, and his profession of fidelity: Matthew 26:33–35; Mark 14:29–31; Luke 22:31–34; John 13:36–38
Cuts off the ear of Malchus: Matthew 26:51; Mark 14:47; Luke 22:50
Follows Jesus to the high priest's palace: Matthew 26:58; Mark 14:54; Luke 22:54; John 18:15
His denial of Jesus, and his repentance: Matthew 26:69–75; Mark 14:66–72; Luke 22:55–62; John 18:17–18; 18:25–27
Visits the sepulcher: Luke 24:12; John 20:2–6
Jesus sends message to, after the resurrection: Mark 16:7
Jesus appears to: Luke 24:34; 1 Corinthians 15:4–5
Present at the Sea of Tiberias when Jesus appeared to His disciples: John 21:1–23
Preaches at Pentecost: Acts 2:14–40
Accused by the council; his defense: Acts 4:1–23
Imprisoned and scourged; his defense before the council: Acts 5:17–42
Receives Paul: Galatians 1:18; 2:9
Visits Lydda; heals Aeneas: Acts 9:32–34
Has a vision of a sheet containing clean and unclean animals: Acts 10:9–16
Receives the servant of the centurion; goes to Caesarea; preaches and baptizes the centurion and his household: Acts 10
Advocates, in the council of the apostles and elders, the preaching of the gospel to the Gentiles: Acts 11:1–18; 15:7–11
Imprisoned and delivered by an angel: Acts 12:3–19
Writes two epistles: 1 Peter 1:1; 2 Peter 1:1
Miracles of Peter:
Cures the sick: Acts 5:15–16
Cures Aeneas: Acts 9:34
Raises Dorcas: Acts 9:40
Causes the death of Ananias and Sapphira: Acts 5:5; 5:10
Peter and John cure a lame man: Acts 3:2–11
Peter and other apostles delivered from prison: Acts 5:19–23; 12:6–11; Acts 16:26

ANDREW

Significance in summary

One of the twelve apostles, introduced his brother Peter to Jesus

Meaning of name

manly

Bible dictionary/encyclopedia entry (IBD)

Andrew was from Bethsaida in Galilee (John 1:44), and was the brother of Simon Peter (Matt. 4:18; 10:2). On one occasion John the Baptist, whose disciple he then was, pointing to Jesus, said, "Behold the Lamb of God" (John 1:40); Andrew, hearing him, immediately became a follower of Jesus, the first of his disciples. After he had been led to recognize Jesus as the Messiah, his first care was to bring his brother Simon to Jesus. For a while after this, the two brothers seem to have pursued their usual calling as fishermen, and did not become the stated attendants of the Lord until after John's imprisonment (Matt. 4:18–19; Mark 1:16–17). Very little is related of Andrew. He was one of the confidential disciples (John 6:8; 12:22), and with Peter, James, and John inquired of our Lord privately regarding his future coming (Mark 13:3). He was present at the feeding of the five thousand (John 6:9), and he introduced the Greeks who desired to see Jesus (John 12:22), but of his subsequent history little is known. It is noteworthy that Andrew three times brings others to Christ: (1) Peter; (2) the lad with the loaves; and (3) certain Greeks. These incidents may be regarded as a key to his character.

Bible study on the life of Andrew (NTB)

An apostle; a fisherman: Matthew 4:18
Of Bethsaida: John 1:44
A disciple of John: John 1:40
Finds Peter, his brother, and brings him to Jesus: John 1:40–42
Call of: Matthew 4:19; Mark 1:16
Asks the Master privately about the destruction of the temple: Mark 13:3–4
Tells Jesus of the Greeks who sought to see Him: John 12:20–22
Reports the number of loaves at the feeding of the five thousand: John 6:8
Meets with the disciples after the Lord's ascension: Acts 1:13

BARTHOLOMEW (NATHANAEL)

Significance in summary

One of the twelve apostles

Meaning of name

son of Talmai

Bible dictionary/encyclopedia entry (IBD)

Generally supposed to have been the same as Nathanael. In the synoptic Gospels Philip and Bartholomew are always mentioned together, while Nathanael is never mentioned; in the fourth Gospel, on the other hand, Philip and Nathanael are similarly mentioned together, but nothing is said of Bartholomew. He was one of the disciples to whom our Lord appeared at the Sea of Tiberias after His resurrection (John 21:2). He was also a witness of the ascension (Acts 1:4, 12–13).

Bible study on the life of Bartholomew/Nathanael (NTB)

One of the apostles: Matthew 10:3; Mark 3:18; Luke 6:14; Acts 1:13
Becomes a disciple of Jesus: John 1:45–49; 21:2

JAMES, son of Zebedee

Significance in summary

One of the twelve apostles, a son of Zebedee

Meaning of name

form of Jacob

Bible dictionary/encyclopedia entry (IBD)

There were two apostles called James. This James was the son of Zebedee and Salome and an elder brother of John the apostle. He was by trade a fisherman, in partnership with Peter (Matt. 20:20; 27:56). With John and Peter he was present at the transfiguration (Matt. 17:1; Mark 9:2), at the raising of Jairus's daughter (Mark 5:37–43), and in the Garden with our Lord (14:33). Because, probably, of their boldness and energy, he and John were called Boanerges, that is, "sons of thunder." He was the first martyr among the apostles, having been beheaded by King Herod Agrippa (Acts 12:1–2), AD 44 (compare Matt. 4:21; 20:20–23).

Bible study on the life of James (NTB)

Son of Zebedee and Salome: Matthew 4:21; 27:56; Mark 15:40; 16:1
Brother of John and a fisherman: Luke 5:10
Called to be an apostle: Matthew 4:21–22; 10:2; Mark 1:19–20; Luke 6:14; Acts 1:13
Surnamed Boanerges by Jesus: Mark 3:17
An intimate companion of Jesus, and present with Him:
  At the great catch of fish: Luke 5:10
  At the healing of Peter's mother-in-law: Mark 1:29
  At the raising of the daughter of Jairus: Mark 5:37; Luke 8:51
  At the transfiguration of Jesus: Matthew 17:1; Mark 9:2; Luke 9:28
  In Gethsemane: Matthew 26:37; Mark 14:33
Asks Jesus concerning His second coming: Mark 13:3
Bigotry of: Luke 9:54
Civil ambitions of: Matthew 20:20–23; Mark 10:35–41
Present at Lake Tiberias when Jesus revealed Himself to the disciples after His resurrection: John 21:2; 1 Corinthians 15:7
Martyred: Acts 12:2

HEROD AGRIPPA I

Significance in summary

Grandson of Herod the Great, persecuted the early church and had James son of Zebedee killed

Meaning of name

heroic

Bible dictionary/encyclopedia entry (SBD)

Herod Agrippa I was the son of Aristobulus and Berenice, and grandson of Herod the Great. He was brought up in Rome, and was thrown into prison by Tiberius, where he remained until the accession of Caligula, who made him king, first of the tetrarchy of Philip and Lysanias; afterward the dominions of Antipas were added, and finally Judea and Samaria. Unlike his predecessors, Agrippa was a strict observer of the law, and he sought with success the favor of the Jews. It is probable that it was with this view he put to death James the son of Zebedee, and further imprisoned Peter (Acts 12:1 ff.).

Bible study on the life of Herod Agrippa I (NTB)

Son of Aristobulus: Acts 12:1–23

JAMES, son of Alphaeus

Significance in summary

James the son of Alphaeus, one of the two apostles named James

Meaning of name

form of Jacob

Bible dictionary/encyclopedia entry (IBD)

The son of Alphaeus, or Cleopas, "the brother" or near kinsman or cousin of our Lord (Gal. 1:18–19), called James "the Less," or "the Little," probably because he was of low stature. He is mentioned along with the other apostles (Matt. 10:3; Mark 3:18; Luke 6:15). He had a separate interview with our Lord after His resurrection (1 Cor. 15:7), and is mentioned as one of the apostles of the circumcision (Acts 1:13). He appears to have occupied the position of head of the church at Jerusalem, where he presided at the council held to consider the case of the Gentiles (Acts 12:17; 15:13–29; 21:18–24). This James was the author of the epistle which bears his name.

Bible study on the life of James (NTB)

Son of Alphaeus: Matthew 10:3; Mark 3:18; Luke 6:15; Acts 1:13; 12:17
Brother of Jesus: Matthew 13:55; 27:56; Mark 6:3; Luke 24:10; Galatians 1:19; 2:9, 12
The brother of Judas: Luke 6:16; Jude 1:1
The brother of Joses: Mark 15:40
Witness of Christ's resurrection: 1 Corinthians 15:7
Addresses the gathering at Jerusalem in favor of liberty for the Gentile converts: Acts 15:13–21
Disciples sent by, to Antioch: Galatians 2:12
Hears of the success attending Paul's ministry: Acts 21:18–19
Epistle of: James 1:1

JOHN

Significance in summary

Son of Zebedee, brother of James, and one of the most prominent twelve apostles

Meaning of name

the Lord is gracious

Bible dictionary/encyclopedia entry (CCEB)

The author of the fourth Gospel was the younger of the two sons of Zebedee, a fisherman on the Sea of Galilee, who lived in Bethsaida, where were born Peter and Andrew his brother, and Philip also. His mother's name was Salome, who, though not without her imperfections (Matt. 20:20–28), was among the women who accompanied the Lord on one of His preaching circuits through Galilee, ministering to His bodily wants; she also followed Him to the cross, and bought sweet spices to anoint Him after His burial. John's father, Zebedee, appears to have been wealthy, owning a vessel of his own and having hired servants (Mark 1:20).

Our evangelist, whose occupation was that of a fisherman with his father, was beyond doubt a disciple of John the Baptist, and one of the two who had the first interview with Jesus. He was called while engaged at his secular occupation (Matt. 4:21–22), and again on a memorable occasion (Luke 5:1–11), and was finally chosen as one of the twelve apostles (Matt. 10:2). He was the youngest of the Twelve, and he and James his brother were named "Boanerges," which the evangelist Mark (Mark 3:17) explains to mean "Sons of thunder," no doubt from their natural vehemence of character. They and Peter constituted that select triumvirate whom we see on the mount of transfiguration in Luke 9:28. But the highest honor bestowed on this disciple was his being admitted to the bosom place with his Lord at the table, as "the disciple whom Jesus loved" (John 13:23; 20:2; 21:7; 20:24), and to have committed to him by the dying Redeemer the care of His mother (John 19:26–27). There can be no reasonable doubt that this distinction was due to a sympathy with His own spirit and mind on the part of John; it is brought out wonderfully in his writings, which, in Christ-like spirituality, heavenliness, and love, surpass all the other inspired writings.

After Pentecost, we find John in constant but silent company with Peter, the great spokesman and actor in the infant church until the accession of Paul. While his love for the Lord Jesus drew him spontaneously to the side of Peter, and his chastened vehemence made him ready to stand courageously by him, his modest humility, as the youngest of all the apostles, made him an admiring listener and faithful supporter of his brother apostle rather than a speaker or separate actor.

Ecclesiastical history is uniform in stating that John went to Asia Minor; that he lived in Ephesus, where he superintended the churches of that region; and that he long survived the other apostles. Whether the mother of Jesus died before this, or went with John to Ephesus, where she died and was buried, is not agreed.

In the reign of Domitian (AD 81–96) John was banished to "the isle that is called Patmos" (a small, rocky, and almost uninhabited island in the Aegean Sea), "for the word of God and for the testimony of Jesus Christ" (Rev. 1:9). Irenaeus and Eusebius say that this took place near the end of Domitian's reign. John's return from exile took place during the brief but tolerant reign of Nerva; he died at Ephesus in the reign of Trajan, at an age above 90.

Bible study on the life of John (NTB)

The apostle intimately associated with Jesus: John 13:23–26; 21:20
Is present when Jesus performs the following miracles:
The healing of Peter's mother-in-law: Matthew 8:14–15; Mark 1:30–31; Luke 4:38–39
The raising of the daughter of Jairus: Mark 5:37; Luke 8:51
The two catches of fish: Luke 5:10; John 21:1–7
The transfiguration: Matthew 17:1; Mark 9:2; Luke 9:28
Is present with Jesus in the Garden of Gethsemane: Matthew 26:37; Mark 14:33; Luke 22:39
Intolerance of: Mark 9:38; Luke 9:49–50, 54–56
Civil ambitions of: Matthew 20:20–24; Mark 10:35–41
Prepares the Passover meal: Matthew 26:18–19; Mark 14:13–16; Luke 22:8–13
Present at the trial of Jesus which took place in front of the high priest: John 18:15–16
Present at the crucifixion: John 19:26–27
Present at the grave site of Jesus: John 20:2–8
Present when Jesus made Himself known at the Lake Galilee: John 21
Present with Peter in the temple courtyard: Acts 3:1–11
Lives in Jerusalem: Acts 1:13
Is entrusted with the care of Mary, mother of Jesus: John 19:26
Imprisoned by the rulers of the Jews: Acts 4:1–19
Sent by the Jerusalem congregation with the commission to Samaria: Acts 8:14–17
A pillar of the ekklesia (body of Christ): Galatians 2:9
Writes three letters to Christian congregations: 1 John; 2 John; 3 John
Writes his apocalyptic vision from Patmos Island: Revelation 1:9
Prophecy concerning: Revelation 10:11

JUDAS (THADDAEUS)

Significance in summary

Son of James, and one of the twelve apostles

Meaning of name

praise

Bible dictionary/encyclopedia entry (IBD)

Thaddaeus, the name of one of the apostles (Mark 3:18), called "Lebbaeus" in Matthew 10:3, and in Luke 6:16, "Judas the brother of James"; John (14:22), probably referring to the same person, speaks of "Judas, not Iscariot." These different names all designate the same person, that is, Jude or Judas, the author of the epistle.

Bible study on the life of Judas (NTB)

An apostle, probably identical with Lebbaeus or Thaddaeus: John 14:22

JUDAS ISCARIOT

Significance in summary

One of the twelve apostles and the betrayer of Jesus

Bible dictionary/encyclopedia entry (SBD)

Judas of Kerioth is sometimes called "the son of Simon" (John 6:71; 13:2, 26), but more commonly *Iscariotes* (Matt. 10:4; Mark 3:19; Luke 6:16, and elsewhere). The name Iscariot has received many interpretations. The most probable is from Ish Kerioth, that is, "man of Kerioth," a town in the tribe of Judah (Josh. 15:25). Of the life of Judas before the appearance of his name in the lists of the apostles we know absolutely nothing. What that appearance implies, however, is that he had previously declared himself a disciple. He was drawn, as the others were, by the preaching of John the Baptist, or his own Messianic hopes, or the "gracious words" of the new Teacher, to leave his former life, and to obey the call of the prophet of Nazareth. The choice was not made, we must remember, without a provision of its issue (John 6:64). The germs of the evil, in all likelihood, unfolded themselves gradually. The rules to which the Twelve were subject in their first journey (Matt. 10:9–10) sheltered him from the temptation that would have been most dangerous to him. The new form of life, of which we find the first traces in Luke 8:3, brought that temptation with it. As soon as the Twelve were recognized as a body, traveling hither and thither with their Master, receiving money and other offerings, and redistributing what they received to the poor, it became necessary that someone should act as the steward of the small society, and this fell to Judas (John 12:6; 13:29). He found himself entrusted with larger sums of money than before, and with this there came covetousness, unfaithfulness, embezzlement. Several times he showed his tendency to avarice and selfishness. This grew worse and worse, until he betrayed his Master for thirty pieces of silver.

What was Judas's motive in betraying Christ? (1) Anger at the public rebuke given him by Christ at the supper in the house of Simon the leper (Matt. 26:6–14); (2) avarice, covetousness, the thirty pieces of silver (John 12:6); (3) an ambition to be the treasurer, not merely of a few poor disciples, but of a great and splendid temporal kingdom of the Messiah; (4) perhaps disappointment because Christ insisted on foretelling His death instead of receiving His kingdom; (5) perhaps hoping by his treachery to gain a position of honor and influence in the Pharisaic party.

Judas, when he saw the results of his betrayal, repented (Matt. 27:3–10). He made ineffectual struggles to escape, by attempting to return the reward to the Pharisees, and when they would not receive it, he cast it down at their feet and left (Matt. 27:5). Then, Judas, in his despair, went out and hanged himself (Matt. 27:5) at Aceldama, on the southern slope of the valley of Hinnom, near Jerusalem, and in the act he fell down a precipice and was dashed into pieces (Acts 1:18). "And he went to his own place" (Acts 1:25).

Bible study on the life of Judas Iscariot (NTB)

Chosen as an apostle: Matthew 10:4; Mark 3:19; Luke 6:16; Acts 1:17
The treasurer of the disciples: John 12:6; 13:29
His protest against the breaking of the container of ointment: John 12:4–6
His bargaining to betray Jesus for a sum of money: Matthew 26:14–16; Mark 14:10–11; Luke 22:3–6; John 13:2
His apostasy: John 17:12
Betrays the Lord Jesus: Matthew 26:47–50; Mark 14:43–45; Luke 22:47–49; John 18:2–5; Acts 1:16–25
Returns the money to the rulers of the Jews: Matthew 27:3–10
Hangs himself: Matthew 27:5; Acts 1:18
Prophecies concerning: Matthew 26:21–25; Mark 14:18–21; Luke 22:21–23; John 13:18–26; 17:12; Acts 1:16, 20; Psalms 41:9; 109:8; Zechariah 11:12–13

MATTHEW (LEVI)

Significance in summary

One of the twelve apostles and author of the Gospel that bears his name

Meaning of name

gift of the Lord

Bible dictionary/encyclopedia entry (ISBE)

Matthew the apostle and evangelist is listed in Matthew 10:3; Mark 3:18; Luke 6:15; Acts 1:13, though his place is not constant in this list, varying between the seventh and the eighth places and exchanging positions with Thomas. The name occurring in the two forms Matthaios, and Maththaios, is a Greek reproduction of the Aramaic Mattathyah, that is, "gift of Yahweh," and is equivalent to Theodore. Before his call to the apostolic office, according to Matthew 9:9, his name was Levi. The identity of Matthew and Levi is practically beyond all doubt, as is evident from the predicate in Matthew 10:3 and from a comparison of Mark 2:14; Luke 5:27 with Matthew 9:9. Mark calls him "the son of Alphaeus" (Mark 2:14), although this cannot have been the Alphaeus who was the father of James the Less; for if this James and Matthew had been brothers this fact would doubtless have been mentioned, as is the case with Peter and Andrew, and also with the sons of Zebedee. Whether Jesus, as He did in the case of several others of His disciples, gave him the additional name of Matthew is a matter of which we are not informed.

As he was a customs officer (*ho telones*, Matt. 10:3) in Capernaum, in the territory of Herod Antipas, Matthew was not exactly a Roman official, but was in the service of the tetrarch of Galilee, or possibly a subordinate officer, belonging to the class called *portitores*, serving under the *publicani*, or superior officials who farmed the Roman taxes. As such he must have had some education, and doubtless in addition to the native Aramaic must have been acquainted with the Greek.

His ready acceptance of the call of Jesus shows that he must have belonged to that group of publicans and sinners who in Galilee and elsewhere looked longingly to Jesus (Matt. 11:19; Luke 7:34; 15:1). Just at what period of Christ's ministry he was called does not appear with certainty. Unlike the first six apostles, Matthew did not enter the group from among the pupils of John the Baptist.

These are practically all the data furnished by the New Testament on the person of Matthew, and what is found in post-biblical and extrabiblical sources is chiefly the product of imagination and in part based on mistaking the name of Matthew for Matthias. Tradition states that he preached for fifteen years in Palestine and that after this he went to foreign nations, the Ethiopians, Macedonians, Syrians, Persians, Parthians, and Medea being mentioned. He is said to have died a natural death either in Ethiopia or in Macedonia. The stories of the Roman Catholic church that he died the death of a martyr on September 21 and of the Greek church that this occurred on November 10 are without any historical basis. Clement of Alexandria gives the explicit denial of Heracleon that Matthew suffered martyrdom.

Bible study on the life of Matthew (NTB)

Also called Levi; a receiver of customs (taxes for the Romans): Matthew 9:9; Mark 2:14

Becomes a disciple of Jesus: Matthew 9:9–10; 10:3; Mark 2:14–15; 3:18; Luke 5:27–29; 6:15; Acts 1:13

ZEBEDEE

Significance in summary

A well-off fisherman and father of the apostles James and John

Meaning of name

gift of the Lord

Bible dictionary/encyclopedia entry (IBD)

A Galilean fisherman, the husband of Salome, and the father of James and John, two of our Lord's disciples (Matt. 4:21; 27:56; Mark 15:40). He seems to have been a man of some position in Capernaum, for he had two boats (Luke 5:4) and "hired servants" (Mark 1:20) of his own. No mention is made of him after the call of his two sons by Jesus.

Bible study on the life of Zebedee (NTB)

Father of James and John, who were nicknamed "Boanerges": Matthew 4:21; 20:20; 27:56; Mark 1:20

SALOME

Significance in summary

The wife of Zebedee and mother of the apostles James and John

Bible dictionary/encyclopedia entry (IBD)

The wife of Zebedee and mother of James and John (Matt. 27:56), and probably the sister of Mary, the mother of our Lord (John 19:25). She sought for her sons places of honor in Christ's kingdom (Matt. 20:20–21; compare 19:28). She witnessed the crucifixion (Mark 15:40), and was present with the other women at the sepulcher (Matt. 27:56).

Bible study on the life of Salome (NTB)

Mother of James and John: Matthew 27:56; Mark 15:40; 16:1
Asks Jesus to promote her sons: Matthew 20:20–21
Present at the crucifixion of Jesus of Nazareth: Mark 15:40
Present at the grave site of Jesus: Mark 16:1–2

THOMAS (DIDYMUS)

Significance in summary

One of the twelve apostles

Meaning of name

twin

Bible dictionary/encyclopedia entry (IBD, SBD)

IBD

Twin, one of the Twelve (Matt. 10:3; Mark 3:18, etc.). He was also called Didymus (John 11:16; 20:24), which is the Greek equivalent of the Hebrew name. All we know regarding him is recorded in the fourth Gospel (John 11:15–16; 14:4–5; 20:24–29). From the circumstance that in the lists of the apostles he is always mentioned along with Matthew, who was the son of Alphaeus (Mark 3:18), and that these two are always followed by James, who was also the son of Alphaeus, it has been supposed that these three, Matthew, Thomas, and James, were brothers.

SBD

Thomas is said to have been born in Antioch. In the catalogue of the apostles he is coupled with Matthew (Matt. 10:3; Mark 3:18; Luke 6:15) and with Philip (Acts 1:13). He was slow to believe and subject to despondency yet full of ardent love for his Master. The latter trait was shown in his speech when our Lord determined to face the dangers that awaited Him in Judea on His journey to Bethany. Thomas said to his fellow disciples, "Let us also go, that we may die with him" (John 11:16). His unbelief appeared in his question during the Last Supper:

"Thomas saith unto him, Lord, we know not whither thou goest; and how can we know the way?" (John 14:5).

He was absent—possibly by accident, perhaps characteristically—from the first assembly when Jesus appeared after the resurrection. The others told him what they had seen. He broke forth into an exclamation, the terms of which convey to us at once the vehemence of his doubt, and at the same time the vivid picture that his mind retained of his Master's form as he had last seen Him lifeless on the cross (John 20:25). On the eighth day he was with them at their gathering, perhaps in expectation of a recurrence of the visit of the previous week, and Jesus stood among them. Jesus uttered the same salutation, "Peace be unto you," and then turning to Thomas, as if this had been the special object of His appearance, told Thomas to touch His hands and side. The effect on him was immediate. The words in which Thomas expressed his belief contain a far higher assertion of his Master's divine nature than is contained in any other expression used by apostolic lips—"My Lord and my God." The answer of our Lord sums up the moral of the whole narrative: "Because thou hast seen me, thou hast believed: blessed are they that have not seen, and yet have believed" (John 20:29).

In the New Testament we hear of Thomas only twice again, once on the Sea of Galilee with the seven disciples, where he is ranked next after Peter (John 21:2), and again in the assemblage of the apostles after the ascension (Acts 1:13). The earlier traditions, as believed in the fourth century, represent him as preaching in Parthia or Persia, and as finally buried at Edessa. The later traditions carry him farther east. His martyrdom, whether in Persia or India, is said to have been occasioned by a lance, and is commemorated by the Latin Church on December 21, the Greek Church on October 6, and by the Indians on July 1.

Bible study on the life of Thomas (NTB)

One of the twelve apostles; called Didymus: Matthew 10:3; Mark 3:18; Luke 6:15
Present at the raising of Lazarus: John 11:16
Asks Jesus the way to the Father's house: John 14:5
Absent when Jesus first appeared to the disciples after the resurrection: John 20:24
Skepticism of: John 20:25
Sees Jesus after the resurrection: John 20:26–29; 21:1–2
Lives with the other apostles in Jerusalem: Acts 1:13–14
Loyalty of, to Jesus: John 11:16; 20:28

SIMON

Significance in summary

Known as Simon the Zealot, one of the twelve apostles

Meaning of name

hearing

Bible dictionary/encyclopedia entry (IBD)

One of the twelve apostles, called the Canaanite (Matt. 10:4; Mark 3:18). This word "Canaanite" does not mean a native of Canaan, but is derived from the Syriac word Kanean or Kaneniah, which was the name of a Jewish sect. The Revised Version has "Cananaean," marg., "or Zealot." He is also called "Zelotes" (Luke 6:15; Acts 1:13; RSV, "the Zealot"), because previous to his call to the apostleship he had been a member of the fanatical sect of the Zealots. There is no record regarding him.

Bible study on the life of Simon (NTB)

One of the twelve apostles; a revolutionary and a patriot; called "The Canaanite" (from the Hebrew root meaning "religious zeal"): Matthew 10:4; Mark 3:18

Called "Zelotes": Luke 6:15; Acts 1:13

PHILIP

Significance in summary

One of the twelve apostles; came from Bethsaida

Meaning of name

lover of horses

Bible dictionary/encyclopedia entry (SBD)

Philip was from Bethsaida, the city of Andrew and Peter (John 1:44), and apparently was among the Galilean peasants of that district who flocked to hear the preaching of John the Baptist. The manner in which John speaks of him indicates a previous friendship with the sons of Jona and Zebedee, and a consequent participation in their messianic hopes. The close union of the two in John 6 and 12 suggests that he may have owed to Andrew the first tidings that the hope had been fulfilled. The statement that Jesus found him (John 1:43) implies a previous seeking. In the lists of the twelve apostles, in the Synoptic Gospel, his name is as uniformly at the head of the second group of four as the name of Peter is at that of the first (Matt. 10:3; Mark 5:18; Luke 6:14), and the facts recorded by John give the reason of this priority. Philip apparently was among the first company of disciples who were with the Lord at the commencement of His ministry at the marriage at Cana, on His first appearance as a prophet in Jerusalem (John 2). The first three Gospels tell us nothing more of him individually. John with his characteristic fullness of personal reminiscences, records a few significant utterances (John 6:5–9; 12:20–22; 14:8). No other fact connected with the name of Philip is recorded in the Gospels. He is among the company of disciples at Jerusalem after the ascension (Acts 1:13) and on the day of Pentecost. After this all is uncertain and apocryphal. According to tradition he preached in Phrygia and died at Hierapolis.

Bible study on the life of Philip (NTB)

One of the twelve apostles: Matthew 10:3; Mark 3:18; Luke 6:14; Acts 1:13
Call of: John 1:43
Brings Nathanael to Jesus: John 1:45–50
Assists in caring for the multitude whom Jesus miraculously feeds: John 6:5–7
Brings to Jesus certain Greeks who desire to see Him: John 12:20–22
Asks Jesus to show the Father: John 14:8–13

Jesus' Enemies

ANNAS

Significance in summary

The high priest who questioned Jesus after His arrest

Meaning of name

grace

Bible dictionary/encyclopedia entry (IBD)

Was high priest AD 7–14. In AD 25 Caiaphas, who had married the daughter of Annas (John 18:13), was raised to that office, and probably Annas was now made president of the Sanhedrin, or deputy or coadjutor of the high priest, and thus was also called high priest along with Caiaphas (Luke 3:2). By the Mosaic law the high-priesthood was held for life (Num. 3:10), and although Annas had been deposed by the Roman procurator, the Jews may still have regarded him as legally the high priest. Our Lord was first brought before Annas, and after a brief questioning of Him (John 18:19–23) was sent to Caiaphas, when some members of the Sanhedrin had met, and the first trial of Jesus took place (Matt. 26:57–68). This examination of our Lord before Annas is recorded only by John. Annas was president of the Sanhedrin before which Peter and John were brought (Acts 4:6).

Bible study on the life of Annas (NTB)

Associate high priest with Caiaphas: Luke 3:2; John 18:13, 19, 24; Acts 4:6

CAIAPHAS

Significance in summary

The high priest who chaired Jesus' trial before the Sanhedrin

Meaning of name

depression

Bible dictionary/encyclopedia entry (IBD)

The Jewish high priest (AD 27–36) at the beginning of our Lord's public ministry, in the reign of Tiberius (Luke 3:2), and also at the time of His condemnation and crucifixion (Matt. 26:3, 57; John 11:49; 18:13–14). He held this office during the whole of Pilate's administration. His wife was the daughter of Annas, who had formerly been high priest, and was probably the vicar or deputy (Heb. *sagan*) of Caiaphas. He was of the sect of the Sadducees (Acts 5:17), and was a member of the council when he gave his opinion that Jesus should be put to death "for the people, and that the whole nation perish not" (John 11:50). In these words he unconsciously uttered a prophecy. Like Saul, he was a prophet in spite of himself. Caiaphas had no power to inflict the punishment of death, and therefore Jesus was sent to Pilate, the Roman governor, that he might pronounce the sentence against Him (Matt. 27:2; John 18:28). At a later period his hostility to the gospel is still manifest (Acts 4:6).

Bible study on the life of Caiaphas (NTB)

High priest: Luke 3:2
Son-in-law of Annas: John 18:13
Prophesies concerning Jesus: John 11:49–51; 18:14
Jesus tried before: Matthew 26:2–3, 57, 63–65; John 18:24, 28
Peter and other disciples accused before: Acts 4:1–22

PILATE

Significance in summary

The Roman procurator of Judea who gave orders for Jesus to be crucified

Meaning of name

javelin carrier

Bible dictionary/encyclopedia entry (IBD)

After His trial before the Sanhedrin, Jesus was brought to the Roman procurator, Pilate, who had come up to Jerusalem as usual to preserve order during the Passover, and was now residing, perhaps, in the castle of Antonia, or maybe in Herod's palace. Pilate came from his palace and met the deputation from the Sanhedrin, who, in reply to his inquiry as to the nature of the accusation against Jesus, accused Him of being a "malefactor." Pilate was not satisfied with this, and they further accused Him (1) of sedition, (2) of preventing the payment of the tribute to Caesar, and (3) of assuming the title of king (Luke 23:2). Pilate now withdrew with Jesus into the palace (John 18:33) and examined Him in private (vv. 37–38); and then going out to the deputation still standing before the gate, he declared that he could find no fault in Jesus (Luke 23:4). This only aroused them to more furious clamor, and they cried that he excited the populace "throughout all Jewry, beginning from Galilee." When Pilate heard of Galilee, he sent Jesus to Herod Antipas, who had jurisdiction over that province. Herod sent Him back again to Pilate, clad in a purple robe of mockery (23:11–12).

Pilate now proposed that as he and Herod had found no fault in Him, they should release Jesus. But his wife (Claudia Procula) sent a message to him imploring him to have nothing to do with the "just person." Pilate asked the crowd, "What shall I do with Jesus?" The fierce cry immediately followed: "Let him be crucified." Pilate yielded, and sent Jesus away to be scourged. This scourging was usually inflicted by lictors; but since Pilate was only a procurator he had no lictor, and his soldiers inflicted this terrible punishment. This done, the soldiers began to deride Jesus.

Pilate then led Jesus before the people, saying, "Behold the man!" This angered the crowd even more. Pilate took Jesus back into the Praetorium and asked Him, "Knowest thou not that I have power to crucify thee?" (John 19:10). Jesus answered, "Thou couldest have no power at all against me, except it were given thee from above" (John 19:11).

After this Pilate seemed more resolved than ever to let Jesus go. The crowd perceiving this cried out, "If thou let this man go, thou art not Caesar's friend" (John 19:12). This settled the matter. He was afraid of being accused to the emperor. He washed his hands in the sight of the people, saying, "I am innocent of the blood of this just person" (Matt. 27:24). The mob cried, "His blood be on us, and on our children" (Matt. 27:25). Pilate was stung by their insults and said, "Shall I crucify your King?" (John 19:15). The fatal moment had now come. They exclaimed they had no king but Caesar, and Jesus was led away to be crucified.

Learning that Jesus was dead, Pilate gave up the body to Joseph of Arimathea to be buried. Pilate's name now disappears from the Gospel history. References to him, however, are found in the Acts of the Apostles (3:13; 4:27; 13:28), and in 1 Timothy 6:13. In AD 36 the governor of Syria brought serious accusations against Pilate, and he was banished to Vienne in Gaul, where, according to tradition, he committed suicide.

Bible study on the life of Pilate (NTB)

Roman governor of Judaea during the time of Jesus' ministry: Matthew 27:2; Luke 3:1
Causes the slaughter of certain Galileans: Luke 13:1
Tries Jesus and orders His crucifixion: Matthew 27; Mark 15; Luke 23; John 18:28–40; 19; Acts 3:13; 4:27; 13:28; 1 Timothy 6:13
Allows Joseph of Arimathaea to take Jesus' body: Matthew 27:57–58; Mark 15:43–45; Luke 23:52; John 19:38

THE PHARISEES

Bible dictionary/encyclopedia entry (EDNTW)

Pharisee is from an Aramaic word *peras* (found in Dan. 5:28), signifying "to separate," owing to a different manner of life from that of the general public. The Pharisees and Sadducees appear as distinct parties in the latter half of the second century BC, though they represent tendencies traceable much earlier in Jewish history, tendencies which became pronounced after the return from Babylon (537 BC). The immediate progenitors of the two parties were, respectively, the Hasideans and the Hellenizers; the latter, the antecedents of the Sadducees, aimed at removing Judaism from its narrowness and sharing in the advantages of Greek life and culture. The Hasideans, a transcription of the Hebrew *chasidim*, that is, "pious ones," were a society of men zealous for religion, who acted under the guidance of the scribes, in opposition to the godless Hellenizing party. The Hellenizers were a political sect, while the Hasideans, whose fundamental principle was complete separation from non-Jewish elements, were the strictly legal party among the Jews, and were ultimately the more popular and influential party. In their zeal for the Law they almost deified it and their attitude became merely external, formal, and mechanical. They laid stress, not on the righteousness of an action, but on its formal correctness. Consequently their opposition to Christ was inevitable; His manner of life and teaching was essentially a condemnation of theirs; hence His denunciation of them (see Matt. 6:2, 5, 16; 15:7; 23).

While the Jews continued to be divided into these two parties, the spread of the testimony of the Gospel must have produced what in the public eye seemed to be a new sect, and in the extensive development which took place at Antioch, Acts 11:19–26, the name "Christians" seems to have become a popular term applied to the disciples as a sect, the primary cause, however, being their witness to Christ. The opposition of both Pharisees and Sadducees (still mutually antagonistic, Acts 23:6–10) against the new "sect" continued unabated during apostolic times.

A Bible study on the Pharisees (NTT)

A sect of the Jews: Acts 15:5
The strictest observers of the Mosaic ritual: Acts 26:5
By descent, especially esteemed: Acts 23:6
Zealous of tradition: Mark 7:3, 5–8; Galatians 1:14
Believed in the resurrection: Acts 23:8
Had disciples: Luke 5:33; Acts 22:3
Came to John for baptism: Matthew 3:7
As a body, rejected John's baptism: Luke 7:30
Imputed Christ's miracles to Satan's power: Matthew 9:34; 12:24
Sent officers to apprehend Christ: John 7:32, 45
Often sought to destroy Christ: Matthew 12:14; 21:46; John 11:47, 53, 57

SIMON, the Pharisee

Significance in summary

A Pharisee in whose house "a woman of the city which was a sinner" anointed Jesus' feet with ointment (Luke 7:36–38)

Meaning of name

hearing

Bible study on the life of Simon the Pharisee (NTB)

Jesus dines with: Luke 7:36–44

THE SADDUCEES

Bible dictionary/encyclopedia entry (TCB)

The word Sadducee is the Greek form of the Hebrew *zaddukim*, which is derived from one Zadok, said to be the founder of the sect, who was a disciple of Antigonus of Socoh (200–170 BC). They were the aristocratic and conservative party politically; and, doctrinally (generally speaking) they denied the teaching of the Pharisees, even the doctrine of the resurrection.

Bible study on the life of the Sadducees (NTB)

Rebuked by John the Baptist: Matthew 3:7–9; Luke 3:7–9
Reject the doctrine of the resurrection: Matthew 22:23–34; Mark 12:18–27; Luke 20:27–40; Acts 23:7–8
Jesus warns His disciples against: Matthew 16:6–12
Persecute the apostles: Acts 4:1–3; 5:17–33

Jesus' Friends

Nicodemus • Jairus • Zacchaeus • Mary Magdalene • Simon, the leper • Bartimaeus • Lazarus • Mary • Martha • Joseph of Arimathea • Barabbas • Simon of Cyrene • Alexander, son of Simon of Cyrene • Joanna • Mary, mother of James and Joseph • Cleopas

NICODEMUS

Significance in summary

The leading rabbi who first visited Jesus at night and was told about the necessity of new birth

Meaning of name

conqueror of the people

Bible dictionary/encyclopedia entry (ISBE)

A Pharisee and a "ruler of the Jews," mentioned only by John. He interviewed Christ at Jerusalem and was taught by Him the doctrine of the new birth (John 3:1–15); defended Him before the Sanhedrin (John 7:50–52); and assisted at His burial (John 19:39–42).

The meeting, which probably took place in the house of John (John 3:1–15), was one of the results of our Lord's ministry at Jerusalem during the first Passover (compare John 3:2 with John 2:23). Although Nicodemus had been won to believe in the divine nature of Christ's mission, his faith was yet very incomplete in that he believed Him to be inspired only after the fashion of the Old Testament prophets. To this faint-hearted faith corresponded his timidity of action, which displayed itself in his coming "by night," lest he should offend his colleagues in the Sanhedrin and the other hostile Jews (John 3:2). In reply to the veiled question which the words of Nicodemus implied, and to convince him of the inadequacy of mere intellectual belief, Christ proclaimed to him the necessity for a spiritual regeneration: "Except a man be born again, he cannot see the kingdom of God" (John 3:3). This was interpreted by Nicodemus only in its materialistic sense, and therefore confused him (John 3:4). But Christ, as on another occasion when dealing with His questioners on a similar point of doctrine (compare John 6:52–53), answered his perplexity only by repeating His previous statement (John 3:5). He then proceeded to give further explanation. The rebirth is not outward but inward; it is not of the body but of the soul (John 3:6). Only those who have experienced it as a change in themselves, wrought by the Divine Power, are qualified to judge either its reality or its effects (John 3:7–8). But Nicodemus, since such experience had not yet been his, remained unenlightened (John 3:9). Christ therefore condemned such blindness in one who professed to be a teacher of spiritual things (John 3:10), and emphasized the reality in His own life of those truths which He had been expounding (John 3:11).

The meeting, though apparently fruitless at the time, was not without its effect on Nicodemus. At the Feast of Tabernacles, when the Sanhedrin was enraged at Christ's proclamation of Himself as the "living water" (John 7:37–38), Nicodemus was emboldened to stand up in His defense. Yet here also he showed his natural timidity. He made no personal testimony of his faith in Christ, but sought rather to defend Him on a point of Jewish law (John 7:50–52; compare Exod. 23:1; Deut. 1:16–17; 17:6; 19:15).

By an open act of reverence Nicodemus at last made public profession of his being of the following of Christ. His wealth enabled him to provide the mixture of myrrh and aloes, with which the body of Jesus was embalmed (John 19:39).

The Gospel of Nicodemus and other apocryphal works narrate that Nicodemus gave evidence in favor of Christ at the trial before Pilate, that he was deprived of office and banished from Jerusalem by the hostile Jews, and that he was baptized by Peter and John. His remains were said to have been found in a common grave along with those of Gamaliel and Stephen.

Bible study on the life of Nicodemus (NTB)

A Jewish rabbi who becomes a disciple of Jesus: John 3:1–10; 7:50–53
Helps bury Jesus: John 19:39

JAIRUS

Significance in summary

A ruler of the synagogue whose daughter Jesus raised from the dead

Meaning of name

he will enlighten

Bible dictionary/encyclopedia entry (IBD)

A ruler of the synagogue at Capernaum, whose only daughter Jesus restored to life (Mark 5:22; Luke 8:41). Accompanied by Peter, James, and John, and the father and mother of the girl, Jesus went to the bed where the body lay, and said, "Talitha cumi," that is, "Maid, arise." Immediately she arose (Mark 5:42).

Bible study on the life of Jairus (NTB)

A ruler of the synagogue in Capernaum: Matthew 9:18
Daughter of, restored to life: Matthew 9:18, 23–26; Mark 5:22–43; Luke 8:41–56

ZACCHAEUS

Significance in summary

A wealthy tax collector in Jericho who became a disciple of Jesus

Meaning of name

pure

Bible dictionary/encyclopedia entry (IBD)

A superintendent of customs; a chief tax-gatherer (*publicanus*) at Jericho (Luke 19:1–10). The collection of customs at Jericho, which at this time produced and exported a considerable quantity of balsam, was undoubtedly an important post, and would account for Zacchaeus being a rich man. When Christ passed through Jericho on His way to Jerusalem, Zacchaeus, being short, climbed up a sycamore tree so he could see Him. When our Lord reached the spot He addressed Zacchaeus by name and told him to come down, because He intended that day to abide at his house. This led to the remarkable interview recorded by the evangelist, and to the striking parable of the ten pounds (Luke 19:12–27).

At Er-riha (Jericho) there is a large square tower, which goes by the traditional name of the House of Zacchaeus.

Bible study on the life of Zacchaeus (NTB)

Hosts Jesus: Luke 19:1–10

MARY MAGDALENE

Significance in summary

Healed of demon-possession by Jesus; the first person to see Jesus alive after His resurrection

Meaning of name

form of Miriam, meaning loved by God

Bible dictionary/encyclopedia entry (IBD)

Mary Magdalene, that is, Mary of Magdala, a town on the western shore of the Lake of Tiberias. She was one of the women who ministered to Christ "of their substance" (Luke 8:3). Their motive was that of gratitude for deliverances He had wrought for them. Out of Mary were cast seven demons. Gratitude to her great Deliverer prompted her to become His follower. These women accompanied Him also on His last journey to Jerusalem (Matt. 27:55; Mark 15:41; Luke 23:55). They stood near the cross. There Mary remained until the body was taken down and laid in Joseph's tomb. With Salome and Mary the mother of James (Matt. 28:1; Mark 16:2), she came to the sepulcher, bringing sweet spices to anoint the body of Jesus. They found the sepulcher empty but saw the "vision of angels" (Matt. 28:5). She hurried to tell Peter and John and immediately returned to the sepulcher. There the risen Lord appeared to her. This is the last record regarding Mary of Magdala, who now returned to Jerusalem. The idea that this Mary was "the woman who was a sinner," or that she was unchaste, is altogether groundless.

Bible study on the life of Mary Magdalene (NTB)

Possessed of devils, delivered by Jesus: Mark 16:9; Luke 8:2–3
Present at the crucifixion: Matthew 27:56; Mark 15:40; John 20:1, 11–13

Recognizes Jesus after the resurrection: Matthew 28:8–10; Mark 16:9; John 20:14–18

SIMON, the leper

Significance in summary

A leper in Bethany in whose house Jesus was anointed with perfume shortly before His crucifixion

Meaning of name

hearing

Bible dictionary/encyclopedia entry (IBD)

A leper of Bethany, in whose house Mary anointed our Lord's head with ointment "as he sat at meat" (Matt. 26:6–13; Mark 14:3–9).

Bible study on the life of Simon the leper (NTB)

Jesus dines with: Matthew 26:6; Mark 14:3

BARTIMAEUS

Significance in summary

A blind beggar in Jericho whom Jesus healed

Meaning of name

son of Timaeus

Bible dictionary/encyclopedia entry (IBD)

Son of Timaeus, one of the two blind beggars of Jericho (Mark 10:46; Matt. 20:30). His blindness was miraculously cured because of his faith.

Bible study on the life of Bartimaeus (NTB)

A blind man, healed by Jesus: Mark 10:46–52; Matthew 20:29–34; Luke 18:35–43

LAZARUS

Significance in summary

Brother of Mary and Martha

Meaning of name

God has helped

Bible dictionary/encyclopedia entry (ISBE)

The home of the Lazarus mentioned in John 11:1 was Bethany. He was the brother of Martha and Mary (John 11:1–2; see also Luke 10:38–41). All three were especially loved by Jesus (John 11:5), and more than once, He was entertained at their home (Luke 10:38–41; John 11). As intimated by the number of condoling friends from the city, and perhaps from the costly ointment used by Mary, the family was probably well-to-do. In the absence of Jesus, Lazarus was taken sick, died, and was buried, but, after having been in the grave four days, was brought back to life by the Savior (John 11:3, 14, 17, 43–44). As a result many Jews believed on Jesus, but others went and told the Pharisees, and a council was therefore called to hasten the decree of the Master's death (John 11:45–53).

Later, six days before the Passover, at a feast in a home in Bethany where Martha served, Lazarus sat at table as one of the guests, when his sister Mary anointed the feet of Jesus (John 12:1–3). Many of the common people came, not only to see Jesus but also the risen Lazarus; they believed in Jesus, were enthusiastic in witnessing for Him during the triumphal entry, and attracted others from the city to meet Him (John 12:9, 11, 17–18). For that reason the priests plotted to murder Lazarus (John 12:10). This is all that we really know about the man, for whether the Jews accomplished his death we are not informed, but it seems probable that, satiated with the death of Jesus, they left Lazarus unharmed.

The purpose of Jesus' miracle seems to have been: (1) to show Himself as Lord of life and death just before He should be Himself condemned to die; (2) to strengthen the faith of His disciples; (3) to convert many Jews; and (4) to cause the priests to hasten their movements so as to be ready when His hour had come.

Bible study on the life of Lazarus (NTB)

Sickness and death of: John 11:1–14
Resurrection of: John 11:38–44; 12:17–18
Had dinner with Jesus: John 12:1–2, 9
Plotted against by the chief priests: John 12:10–11

MARY

Significance in summary

Sister of Martha and Lazarus

Meaning of name

form of Miriam, meaning loved by God

Bible dictionary/encyclopedia entry (IBD)

Mary, the sister of Lazarus, is brought to our notice in connection with the visits of Jesus to Bethany. She is contrasted with her sister, Martha, who was "cumbered about many things" when Jesus was their guest, while Mary had chosen "the good part." Her character also appears in connection with the death of her brother (John 11:20, 31, 33). On Jesus' last visit to Bethany, Mary brought a pound of costly ointment and anointed his feet as he reclined at table in the house of Simon, who had been a leper (Matt. 26:6; Mark 14:3; John 12:2–3). This was an evidence of her overflowing love to the Lord. Nothing is known of her subsequent history. It would appear from this act of Mary's, from the fact that they possessed a family vault (11:38), and because a large number of Jews from Jerusalem came to console them after the death of Lazarus (11:19), that this family at Bethany was wealthy.

Bible study on the life of Mary (NTB)

Sits at Jesus' feet for instruction: Luke 10:38–42
Beloved of Jesus: John 11:1, 5
Anoints Jesus: Matthew 26:7–13; Mark 14:3–9; John 11:2; 12:3

MARTHA

Significance in summary

Sister of Mary and Lazarus

Meaning of name

lady

Bible dictionary/encyclopedia entry (SBD)

The facts recorded in Luke 10 and John 11 indicate a character devout after the customary Jewish type of devotion, sharing in Messianic hopes and accepting Jesus as the Christ. When we first meet Martha (Luke 10:38–42) her spirit is "cumbered about much serving," and she is "troubled about many things." Her love, though imperfect in its form, is recognized as true, and she has the distinction of being one whom Jesus loved (John 11:5). Her position as the elder sister is that of the head and manager of the household. In the supper at Bethany (John 12:2) her old character shows itself, but she is no longer "cumbered," no longer impatient.

Bible study on the life of Martha (NTB)

Sister of Mary and Lazarus: John 11:1
Ministers to Jesus: Luke 10:38–42; John 12:2
Loved by Jesus: John 11:5

JOSEPH of Arimathea

Significance in summary

A Jew who provided the tomb for the body of Jesus

Meaning of name

may (God) add

Bible dictionary/encyclopedia entry (IBD)

A native of Arimathea, probably the Ramah of the Old Testament (1 Sam. 1:19), a man of wealth, and a member of the Sanhedrin (Matt. 27:57; Luke 23:50), an "honorable counselor, who waited for the kingdom of God." As soon as he heard of Christ's death, he went boldly (lit. "having summoned courage, he went") to Pilate, and asked for the body of Jesus. Pilate having learned from the centurion that the death had really taken place, granted Joseph's request, who immediately, having purchased fine linen (Mark 15:46), proceeded to Golgotha to take the body down from the cross. There, assisted by Nicodemus, he took down the body and wrapped it in the linen, sprinkling it with the myrrh and aloes which Nicodemus had brought (John 19:39), and then conveyed the body to the new tomb hewn by Joseph himself out of a rock in his garden. There they laid it, in the presence of Mary Magdalene, Mary the mother of Joses, and other women, and rolled a great stone to the entrance, and departed (Luke 23:53, 55). This was done in haste, "for the Sabbath was drawing on" (compare Isa. 53:9).

Bible study on the life of Joseph of Arimathea (NTB)

Asks for the body of Jesus for burial in his own tomb: Matthew 27:57–60; Mark 15:42–47; Luke 23:50–56; John 19:38–42

BARABBAS

Significance in summary

The condemned criminal Pilate released to the people

Meaning of name

father's son

Bible dictionary/encyclopedia entry (IBD)

A notorious robber whom Pilate proposed to condemn to death instead of Jesus, whom he wished to release, in accordance with the Roman custom (John 18:40; Mark 15:7; Luke 23:19). The Jews were so bent on the death of Jesus that they demanded that Barabbas should be pardoned (Matt. 27:16–26; Acts 3:14). This Pilate did.

Bible study on the life of Barabbas (NTB)

A prisoner released by Pilate: Matthew 27:16–26; Mark 15:7–15; Luke 23:18–25; John 18:40; Acts 3:14

SIMON of Cyrene

Significance in summary

A Jew from Cyrene who was forced to carry Jesus' cross

Meaning of name

he hears

Bible dictionary/encyclopedia entry (IBD)

A Jew of Cyrene, in North Africa, then a province of Libya. A hundred thousand Jews from Palestine had been settled in this province by Ptolemy Soter (323–285 BC), where by this time they had greatly increased in number. They had a synagogue in Jerusalem for those of their number who went to the annual feasts. Simon was seized by the soldiers as the procession wended its way to the place of crucifixion as he was passing by, and Christ's heavy cross was laid on his shoulders. Perhaps they seized him because he showed sympathy with Jesus. He was the "father of Alexander and Rufus" (Matt. 27:32). This Simon may have been one of the "men of Cyrene" who preached the word to the Greeks (Acts 11:20).

Bible study on the life of Simon of Cyrene (NTB)

A man from the city of Cyrene who was compelled to carry Jesus' cross: Matthew 27:32; Mark 15:21; Luke 23:26

ALEXANDER, son of Simon of Cyrene

Significance in summary

A son of Simon of Cyrene

Meaning of name

defender of man

Bible study on the life of Alexander (NTB)

Son of Simon, the man who bore the cross of Jesus: Mark 15:21

JOANNA

Significance in summary

Wife of Cuza, who was on Herod Antipas's staff; supported Jesus' ministry and was one of those who discovered that Jesus' tomb was empty

Meaning of name

possibly feminine form of John

Bible study on the life of Joanna (NTB)

Wife of Cuza, the steward of Herod, and a disciple of Jesus: Luke 8:3; 24:10

MARY, mother of James and Joseph

Significance in summary

Mother of James the younger and Joseph, who was also called Joses

Meaning of name

form of Miriam, meaning loved by God

Bible study on the life of Mary (NTB)

Sister of Mary the mother of Jesus, and wife of Cleophas: John 19:25

Mother of James and Joses: Matthew 27:56; Mark 15:40; John 19:25
At the grave site of Jesus: Matthew 27:61; Mark 15:47
Assists in preparing the corpse of Jesus for burial: Matthew 28:1; Mark 16:1
A witness of the resurrection: Luke 24:10

CLEOPAS

Significance in summary

One of the two disciples who met the risen Jesus on the road to Emmaus

Meaning of name

renowned father

Bible dictionary/encyclopedia entry (IBD)

Abbreviation of Cleopatros; one of the two disciples with whom Jesus conversed on the way to Emmaus on the day of the resurrection (Luke 24:18). We know nothing definitely regarding him. It is not certain that he was the Clopas (Cleophas) of John 19:25, or the Alphaeus of Matthew 10:3, although he may have been so.

Bible study on the life of Cleopas (NTB)

A disciple to whom Jesus appeared after His resurrection: Luke 24:18

The Acts of the Apostles

Matthias • Joseph (Barsabbas) • Jude • Alexander, a Jewish leader • Theudas • Sapphira • Stephen • Ananias, Sapphira's husband • Simon Magus • Philip • Ethiopian eunuch • Aeneas • Dorcas (Tabitha) • Cornelius • Mary, mother of John Mark • Simeon (Niger) • Simon the tanner • Agabus • James, brother of Jesus • Rhoda • Sergius Paulus • Philippian jailer

MATTHIAS

Significance in summary

The man who was chosen to take the place of Judas Iscariot as one of the Twelve

Meaning of name

gift of the Lord

Bible dictionary/encyclopedia entry (SBD)

The apostle elected to fill the place of the traitor Judas (Acts 1:26). All we know of Matthias for certain is that he had been a constant attendant of the Lord Jesus during the whole course of His ministry; Peter declared this to be the necessary qualification of one who was to be a witness of the resurrection. It is said that he preached the gospel and suffered martyrdom in Ethiopia.

Bible study on the life of Matthias (NTB)

Chosen as an apostle in the place of Judas: Acts 1:15–26

JOSEPH (BARSABBAS)

Significance in summary

Nickname of Joseph, one of the two men from whom the replacement for Judas Iscariot was made. Matthias was chosen, not Joseph

Meaning of name

son of Saba

Bible study on the life of Barsabbas (NTB)

Surnamed Justus; one of the two people nominated in place of Judas: Acts 1:21, 22–23

JUDE

Significance in summary

The younger half-brother of Jesus, and author of the New Testament letter that bears his name

Meaning of name

form of Judah, meaning praise

Bible study on the life of Jude (NTB)

One of the half-brothers of Jesus: Matthew 13:55; Mark 6:3

ALEXANDER, a Jewish leader

Significance in summary

A Jewish leader in Jerusalem and a member of the high priest's family

Meaning of name

defender of man

Bible study on the life of Alexander (NTB)

A relative of the high priest, present at the defense of Peter and John: Acts 4:6

THEUDAS

Significance in summary

Leader of an abortive rebellion, referred to by Gamaliel as he counseled the Sanhedrin to be tolerant of the apostles

Meaning of name

gift of God

Bible study on the life of Theudas (NTB)

A Jewish insurrectionist: Acts 5:36

SAPPHIRA

Significance in summary

Was struck dead, with her husband, Ananias, as they tried to deceive the early church

Meaning of name

beautiful, sapphire

Bible dictionary/encyclopedia entry (IBD)

The wife of Ananias was a partner in his guilt and also in his punishment (Acts 5:1–11).

Bible study on the life of Sapphira (NTB)

Falsehood and death of: Acts 5:1–10

STEPHEN

Significance in summary

The first Christian martyr

Meaning of name

crown

Bible dictionary/encyclopedia entry (HCC)

Stephen is known best as the proto-martyr of the Christian church, introducing the heroic period of persecutions. He also deserves to be called the first great apologist for Christianity, since it was this that brought on his death as a martyr (circa 36 or 37 AD).

As his name and his relationships in the church at Jerusalem seem to imply (Acts 6:3), Stephen was a Hellenist, that is, a Greek-speaking Jew. Thus he belonged to that class of Jews usually residing outside of Palestine who, though distinguished from the orthodox Palestinian Jew by a broader outlook on life due to a more liberal education, were Jews nonetheless. Of his conversion to Christianity we know nothing, though there is a tradition that he was among the seventy. As Stephen by his life and work marks a period of transition in the development of the early Christian church, so his name is connected with an important new departure within the organization of the church itself, namely, the institution of the office of the seven (Acts 6:1), who were entrusted with the administration of the work of relief in the church at Jerusalem—the foundation of the diaconate. Of the seven men, all Hellenists, Stephen is by far the most distinguished.

Stephen more than met the requirements of the office to which he was elected (Acts 6:3); the record characterizes him as "a man full of faith and of the Holy Spirit" (Acts 6:5), that is, of an enthusiastic faith and of a deep spirituality. His preaching has given him the place he holds in history (Acts 22:20). In itself that is not surprising, for in the early Christian church every Christian was at once a witness for Christ, and lay-preaching was common. The seven from the first were occupied with essentially spiritual work, as also the later diaconate was engaged in something far different from mere charity organization. But Stephen was especially qualified for this high work, having been endued by the Holy Spirit with apostolic gifts, not only that of preaching, but also that of working miracles (Acts 6:8). In his freer views of Jewish law and customs, due to his deeper conception and better understanding of the essence of Christianity, he even excelled the apostles.

He burst the bonds of Judaism, by which the other apostles were still bound, by teaching that the temple and the Law of Moses were evanescent and that Christianity was destined to supersede Judaism (Acts 6:14). These freer views of Stephen, though possibly attributable to his Hellenic culture, were certainly not of Hellenistic origin, for these views are what brought him into controversy with the Hellenistic synagogues of Jerusalem. The true source of Stephen's freer views of the Mosaic Law and the temple was Christ's own teachings, Stephen showing a wonderfully ripened understanding of them, paralleled only by that of Paul some time later. Christ's words regarding the temple (John 4:20–24;

Mark 13:2) not only led Stephen to see that the true worship of God was not confined to the temple, but opened his eyes as to the purely formal character of this worship in that day, which, far from being true worship, had become a mere ceremonialism (Mark 7:6), and in the words of Christ (John 2:19) he saw an intimation of the new temple which was to take the place of the old. As Christ had been drawn into controversy with Pharisees and scribes on account of these freer views, and as His word about the temple was used to frame the accusation against Him in His trial, so also in the case of Stephen. He did not hesitate to preach his views, choosing the Hellenistic synagogues for this purpose, and soon became engaged in controversies there. But, as the record says, his opponents "were not able to withstand the wisdom," that is, better understanding, convincing knowledge, "and the Spirit," or the deep earnestness and spirituality, "by which he spake" so convincingly (Acts 6:10; Matt. 10:19–20). Seeing themselves beaten, they declared him a blasphemer and a heretic by using the same foul means that the enemies of Jesus had resorted to—suborning false witnesses to the plot, stirring up the people against him, appealing to their Jewish prejudices and to the scribes and elders, members of the Sanhedrin—and thus they eventually brought about his arraignment.

The accusation which they brought against him, through the introduction of false witnesses, included a twofold charge, one against his person, a charge of blasphemous words against Moses which would make him also a blasphemer of God, and one against his teaching, charging him with revolutionary and radical statements concerning the temple and the Law (compare Mark 14:58; 13:2; 15:29).

The charge against Stephen's person was a baseless accusation. There was no blasphemy on the part of Stephen, save by perversion of his words. The charge against his teaching was both false and true. It was false as an implied insinuation that he impugned the divine origin and character of the temple and the Mosaic Law, but it was true as far as he conceived both to be only of a temporary nature and serving a merely provisional purpose. It is a significant fact that Stephen was not arraigned before the Sanhedrin as being a Nazarene though at bottom it was the real cause of his arraignment. Thus also his defense before the Sanhedrin, though the name of Jesus was not mentioned until the very last, was in reality a grand apology for Christ.

While the assembly was awed by the holiness written on the countenance of Stephen (Acts 6:15), the question of the high priest "Are these things so?" broke in on the silence. It drew forth from Stephen that masterful pleading which belongs to the highest type of oratory. It is not so much a plea in self-defense as a grand apology for the cause which Stephen represents.

In appealing to their reason Stephen calls up picture after picture from Abraham to Moses; the speech exhibits vividly the continuity and the progress of the divine revelation which culminated in Jesus of Nazareth, the same thought as that expressed by Christ in Matthew 5:17 of the principal agreement between the Old Testament and the New Testament revelation.

The aim of Stephen was to point out to his hearers the true meaning of Jewish history and Jewish Law in reference to the present in such a way that they might better understand and judge the present and adjust their conduct to it accordingly. Their knowledge of Jewish history and Jewish religion as he would convey it to them would compel them to clear him of the accusation against him as blasphemer and false teacher.

In accordance with the accusation against him, his defense was a twofold one: personal defense and defense of his teaching.

The charge of blasphemy against God and contempt of the Law is implicitly repudiated by the tenor of the whole speech. The courteous and endearing terms in Stephen's address (Acts 7:2) to the council, and the terms "our fathers" and "our race" in Acts 7:2, 19 by which he closely associates himself with his hearers, his declaration of the divine majesty of Yahweh with which the speech opens (7:2), of the providential leading of the patriarchs (7:8, 10), his recognition of the Old Testament institutions as divinely decreed (7:8), his reference to the divine sanction of the Law and its condemnation of those who had not kept it (7:53), at the close of his speech, show clearly his reverence, not only for the past history of the Jewish race, but as well for its Sacred Writings and all of its religious institutions. It makes evident beyond doubt how ungrounded the accusation of blasphemy against him was.

The fundamental differences between Stephen and his opponents lay in that he judged Old Testament history from the prophetic point of view, to which Jesus had also allied Himself, while his opponents represented the legalistic point of view, so characteristic of the Jewish thought of that day. The significance of this difference is borne out by the fact on which Stephen's refutation hinges, namely, the fact, proved by the history of the past, that the development of the divine revelation and the development of the Jewish nation, so far from combining, move in divergent lines, due to a disposition of obstinate disobedience on the part of their fathers, and that therefore not he but they were disobedient to the divine revelation.

The main arguments of the speech may be summed up as follows:

1. God's self-manifestation to Israel in revealing His covenant and His will, so far from being bound to one sanctuary and conveyed to

one single person (Moses), began long before Moses and long before there was a temple.

2. The Jews to whom these revelations were granted, so far from being thankful at all stages of their history, had been slow to believe and understand them because they "would not be obedient" (Acts 7:39, 57). They resisted the purpose of God by obstinately opposing those through whom God worked. Thus their fathers had turned away from Moses at the very moment when he was receiving God's greatest revelation, and, instead of obeying the "living oracles" (7:38) he gave them, turned to idol-worship for which God punished them by the Babylonian captivity (7:39–43). They had killed the prophets who had protested against the dead ritualism of the temple-worship and raised their voice in behalf of a true spiritual worship as that of the tabernacle had been (7:44–50, 52). This disposition of disobedience reached its culmination in that awful crime of betrayal and murder committed by the present generation on the "Righteous One" whose coming the prophets had predicted.

Though the name of Jesus does not occur until in Stephen's dying prayer, his hearers could not fail to notice the hidden reference to Him throughout the entire speech and to draw parallels intended by Stephen: as Joseph and Moses, types of the Messiah, had been rejected, scorned, and ill-treated (Acts 7:9, 27, 39), before being raised to be ruler and deliverer, so Jesus had also been repulsed by them.

The climax of his speech is reached in Acts 7:51–53, when Stephen, suddenly turns on his hearers, and, the accused becoming the accuser, charges them openly with the sin of resisting the Holy Spirit, with the murder of the prophets and the Righteous One, and with continual disobedience to the Law.

Stephen's directness made the accusers mad with fury, and doubtless through their demonstrations they stopped the speech. But Stephen was given a vision of the "glory of God," which he had mentioned in the beginning of his speech (Acts 7:2), and of Jesus, whose cause he had so gallantly defended (Acts 7:55). This marks one of the most historic moments in the history of Israel, as his words constitute the most memorable testimony ever uttered in behalf of Christ: "Behold, I see the heavens opened, and the Son of man"—the only place where this title is uttered by any other person than Jesus—"standing on the right hand of God" (Acts 7:56).

Now the audience could restrain its rage no longer, and the catastrophe followed immediately. Contrary to Roman law and order they took Stephen, and without awaiting sentence against him, stoned him to death, the punishment prescribed in Mosaic Law for a blasphemer (Deut. 17:7; Lev. 24:14–16). Stephen was taken outside the city (Lev. 24:14; compare

Luke 4:29); the witnesses threw the first stone at him (compare Deut. 17:7) after taking off their upper garments and laying them at the feet of a young man named Saul (Acts 7:58)—afterward Paul, now about 30 years old—who evidently had charge of the whole proceedings.

Stephen died as he had lived, a faithful witness to his Master whom he acknowledged as such amid the rain of stones hurled at him, loudly calling on His name, "Lord Jesus, receive my spirit" (Acts 7:59; compare Luke 23:46), and whose spirit he exemplified so nobly when, with a final effort, bending his knees, he "cried with a loud voice, Lord, lay not this sin to their charge" (Acts 7:60; compare Luke 23:34). "And when he had said this, he fell asleep" (Acts 7:60; compare 1 Cor. 15).

The impression made by Stephen's death was even greater than that made by his life. Though it marks the beginning of the first great persecution of Christians, the death of the first Christian martyr resulted in the greatest acquisition Christianity has probably ever made, the conversion of Saul of Tarsus. Judged by his teaching, Stephen may be called the forerunner of Paul. He was one of the first to conceive of the fact that Christianity represented a new order of things and as such would inevitably supersede the old order. Thus his teachings forecast that greatest controversy of the first Christian century, the controversy between Judaism and Christianity, which reached its culmination in the Council of Jerusalem, resulting in the independence of the Christian church from the fetters of Judaistic legalism.

Bible study on the life of Stephen (NTB)

Appointed one of the committee of seven to oversee the daily ministration: Acts 6:3, 5–6
Faith and power of: Acts 6:5, 8–10
False charges against: Acts 6:11–15
Defense of: Acts 7
Stoned: Acts 7:54–60; 8:1; 22:20
Burial of: Acts 8:2
Gentle and forgiving spirit of: Acts 7:59–60

ANANIAS, Sapphira's husband

Significance in summary

Was struck dead, with his wife, Sapphira, as they tried to deceive the early church

Meaning of name

protected by the Lord

Bible dictionary/encyclopedia entry (IBD)

One of the members of the church at Jerusalem, who conspired with his wife, Sapphira, to deceive fellow believers, and who immediately died after he had lied (Acts 5:5). By common agreement the members of the early Christian community devoted their property to the work of furthering the gospel and of assisting the poor and needy. The proceeds of the possessions they sold were placed at the disposal of the apostles (Acts 4:36–37). Ananias might have kept his property had he so chosen; but he professed agreement with the believers in the common purpose, and had of his own accord devoted it all, as he said, to these sacred ends. Yet he retained a part of it for his own ends, and thus lied in declaring that he had given it all. His sin called for a special mark of divine indignation.

Bible study on the life of Ananias (NTB)

A covetous member of the church at Jerusalem; falsehood and death of: Acts 5:1–11

SIMON MAGUS

Significance in summary

A well-known sorcerer in Samaria who attempted to buy miraculous powers from Peter and John

Meaning of name

hearing

Bible dictionary/encyclopedia entry (IBD)

A sorcerer of great repute for his magical arts among the Samaritans (Acts 8:9–11). He afterwards became a professed convert to the faith under the preaching of Philip the deacon and evangelist (8:12–13). His profession was, however, soon found to be hollow. His conduct called forth from Peter a stern rebuke (8:18–23). From this moment he disappears from the church's history. The term "Simony," as denoting the purchase for money of spiritual offices, is derived from him.

Bible study on the life of Simon Magus (NTB)

Converted by Philip: Acts 8:9–13
Rebuked by Peter: Acts 8:18–24

PHILIP

Significance in summary

An evangelist who had four prophesying daughters; was also one of the seven deacons in the early church

Meaning of name

lover of horses

Bible dictionary/encyclopedia entry (IBD)

One of the "seven" (Acts 6:5), also called "the evangelist" (21:8–9). Philip was one of those who were "scattered abroad" by the persecution that arose after the death of Stephen. He went first to Samaria, where he labored as an evangelist with much success (8:5–13). While he was there he received a divine command to proceed toward the south, along the road leading from Jerusalem to Gaza. These towns were connected by two roads. Philip was directed to take the one that led through the desert area of Hebron. As he traveled along this road he was overtaken by a chariot in which sat a man of Ethiopia, the eunuch or chief officer of Queen Candace, who was at that moment reading, probably from the Septuagint version, a portion of the prophecies of Isaiah (53:6–7). Philip entered into conversation with him, and expounded these verses, preaching to him the glad tidings of the Savior. The eunuch received the message and believed; he was baptized, and then "went on his way rejoicing." Philip was instantly caught away by the Spirit after the baptism. He was next found at Azotus; he continued his evangelistic work until he came to Caesarea. He is not mentioned again for about twenty years, when he is still found at Caesarea (Acts 21:8) when Paul and his companions were on the way to Jerusalem. He then finally disappears from the page of history.

Bible study on the life of Philip (NTB)

One of the seven servants (Greek: diakonos): Acts 6:5
Successfully preaches in Samaria: Acts 8:4–14
Expounds the Scriptures to the Ethiopian eunuch whom he baptizes: Acts 8:27–38
Caught away by the Spirit to Azotus, preaches in the cities, and goes to Caesarea: Acts 8:39, 40
Lives at Caesarea and entertains Paul: Acts 21:8
Has four daughters (prophetesses): Acts 21:9–10

ETHIOPIAN EUNUCH

Significance in summary

Led to Christ by Philip the evangelist

Bible dictionary/encyclopedia entry (IBD)

The chief officer or prime minister of state of Candace, queen of Ethiopia. He was converted to Christianity by Philip (Act 8:27). The northern part of Ethiopia formed the kingdom of Meroe, which for a long period was ruled over by queens, and it was probably from this kingdom that the eunuch came.

Bible study on the life of the Ethiopian eunuch (NTB)

Conversion and baptism: Acts 8:26–39

AENEAS

Significance in summary

A paralytic in Lydia who was healed by Peter

Meaning of name

praise

Bible study on the life of Aeneas (NTB)

Healed: Acts 9:33–34

DORCAS (TABITHA)

Significance in summary

Also known as Tabitha; a Christian disciple in Joppa who was brought back to life by Peter

Meaning of name

gazelle

Bible dictionary/encyclopedia entry (IBD)

A pious Christian widow at Joppa whom Peter restored to life (Acts 9:36–41). She was a Hellenistic Jewess, called Tabitha by the Jews and Dorcas by the Greeks.

Bible study on the life of Dorcas (NTB)

A pious woman of Joppa: Acts 9:36–42

CORNELIUS

Significance in summary

A Roman centurion at Caesarea who, with his household, embraced Christ, as a result of Peter visiting his house

Meaning of name

of a horn

Bible dictionary/encyclopedia entry (IBD)

A centurion whose history is narrated in Acts 10. He was a "devout man," and like the centurion of Capernaum, believed in the God of Israel. His residence at Caesarea probably brought him into contact with Jews who communicated to him their expectations regarding the Messiah; and thus he was prepared to welcome the message Peter brought him. He became the first fruit of the Gentile world to Christ. He and his family were baptized and admitted into the Christian church (Acts 10:1, 44–48).

Bible study on the life of Cornelius (NTB)

A Roman centurion: Acts 10

MARY, mother of John Mark

Significance in summary

The mother of Mark

Meaning of name

form of Miriam, meaning loved by God

Bible dictionary/encyclopedia entry (IBD)

Mary, the mother of John Mark, was one of the earliest of our Lord's disciples. She was the sister of Barnabas (Col. 4:10), and joined with him in disposing of their land and giving the proceeds of the sale into the treasury of the church (Acts 4:37; 12:12). Her house in Jerusalem was the common meeting-place for the disciples there.

Bible study on the life of Mary (NTB)

Mother of Mark and sister of Barnabas: Acts 12:12; Colossians 4:10

SIMEON (NIGER)

Significance in summary

Also known by the name Niger; was a teacher and prophet at the church in Antioch

Meaning of name

he hears

Bible study on the life of Simeon (NTB)

A disciple; also called Niger: Acts 13:1

SIMON the tanner

Significance in summary

A tanner at whose house Peter stayed

Meaning of name

hearing

Bible dictionary/encyclopedia entry (IBD)

A Christian at Joppa, a tanner by trade, with whom Peter lodged on one occasion (Acts 9:43).

Bible study on the life of Simon the tanner (NTB)

Peter stays with him: Acts 9:43; 10:6, 17, 32

AGABUS

Significance in summary

A prophet from Jerusalem who predicted a famine and that Paul would be arrested if he returned to Jerusalem

Meaning of name

locust

Bible study on the life of Agabus (NTB)

A prophet: Acts 11:28; 21:10

JAMES, brother of Jesus

Significance in summary

One of Jesus' half-brothers who, after Jesus' resurrection, became a believer in Jesus and leader in the church

Meaning of name

form of Jacob

Bible dictionary/encyclopedia entry (IBD)

The son of Alphaeus, or Cleopas, "the brother" or near kinsman or cousin of our Lord (Gal. 1:18, 19), called James "the Less," or "the Little," probably because of his low stature. He is mentioned along with the other apostles (Matt. 10:3; Mark 3:18; Luke 6:15). He had a separate interview with our Lord after His resurrection (1 Cor. 15:7), and is mentioned as one of the apostles of the circumcision (Acts 1:13). He appears to have occupied the position of head of the Church at Jerusalem, where he presided at the council held to consider the case of the Gentiles (Acts 12:17; 15:13–29; 21:18–24). This James was the author of the epistle which bears his name.

Bible study on the life of James (NTB)

Brother of Jesus: Matthew 13:55; Mark 6:3; Galatians 1:19

RHODA

Significance in summary

A servant who heard Peter's voice at the door of Mary, the mother of Mark

Meaning of name

rose

Bible study on the life of Rhoda (NTB)

A Christian girl in Jerusalem: Acts 12:13

SERGIUS PAULUS

Significance in summary

A Roman deputy who became a Christian after seeing Paul make Elymas blind

Bible study on the life of Sergius Paulus (NTB)

A Roman deputy and convert of Paul: Acts 13:7–12

PHILIPPIAN JAILER

Significance in summary

A man who committed himself to Jesus after fearing that his prisoners, Paul and Silas, had escaped

Bible study on the life of the Philippian Jailer (NTB)

From Philippi, converted: Acts 16:27–34

The Apostle John and His Circle

Diotrephes • Gaius, recipient of John's third letter • Demetrius, a committed Christian

DIOTREPHES

Significance in summary

A church leader who refused to welcome the apostle John

Meaning of name

nourished by Zeus

Bible study on the life of Diotrephes (NTB)

A false teacher: 3 John 9

GAIUS, recipient of John's third letter

Significance in summary

Person to whom John wrote his third short letter

Bible study on the life of Gaius (NTB)

Man to whom John's third epistle was addressed: 3 John 14

DEMETRIUS, a committed Christian

Significance in summary

The Christian whom John mentions and praises in his third letter

Meaning of name

belonging to Demeter

Bible study on the life of Demetrius (NTB)

A Christian mentioned in: 3 John 12

The Apostle Paul and His Circle

Gamaliel • Paul • Ananias from Damascus • Aristarchus • Jason of Thessalonica • Silas • Titus • Timothy • Eunice • Tychicus • John Mark • Barnabas • Alexander from Ephesus • Clement • Julius • Gaius from Macedonia • Luke • Theophilus • Gallio • Trophimus • Gaius from Derbe • Gaius from Corinth

GAMALIEL

Significance in summary

A well-known rabbi who taught Paul

Meaning of name

God is my reward

Bible dictionary/encyclopedia entry (IBD)

The son of Rabbi Simeon, and grandson of the famous Rabbi Hillel. He was a Pharisee, and therefore the opponent of the party of the Sadducees. He was noted for his learning, and was president of the Sanhedrin during the reigns of Tiberius, Caligula, and Claudius, and died, it is said, about eighteen years before the destruction of Jerusalem.

When the apostles were brought before the council, charged with preaching the resurrection of Jesus, Gamaliel, as a zealous Pharisee, counseled moderation and calmness. By a reference to well-known events, he advised them to "refrain from these men." If their work or counsel was of man, he said, it would come to nothing; but if it was of God, they could not destroy it, and therefore ought to be on their guard lest they should be "found fighting against God" (Acts 5:34–40). Paul was one of his disciples (22:3).

Bible study on the life of Gamaliel (NTB)

Speech of, before the Sanhedrin: Acts 5:33–40
Paul's teacher: Acts 22:3

PAUL

Significance in summary

A great missionary leader in the early church who wrote thirteen of the New Testament letters

Meaning of name

small

Bible dictionary/encyclopedia entry (IBD)

Tarsus was the seat of a famous university, higher in reputation even than the universities of Athens and Alexandria, the only others that then existed. Here Saul was born, and here he spent his youth, doubtless enjoying the best education his native city could afford. His father was a Pharisee from the tribe of Benjamin, of pure and unmixed Jewish blood (Acts 23:6; Phil. 3:5). We learn nothing regarding his mother.

We read of his sister and his sister's son (Acts 23:16), and of other relatives (Rom. 16:7, 11–12). Though a Jew, his father was a Roman citizen. How he obtained this privilege we are not informed. The fact that Saul was freeborn was a valuable privilege, and one that was to prove of great use to him. It was decided that he should go to college and become a rabbi. According to Jewish custom, however, he first learned a trade—tentmaking.

His preliminary education having been completed, Saul was sent, when about thirteen years old probably, to the great Jewish school of sacred learning at Jerusalem as a student of the law. Here he became a pupil of the celebrated rabbi Gamaliel, and here he spent many years in an elaborate study of the Scriptures.

After his student years, he probably left Jerusalem for Tarsus, where he may have been engaged in connection with some synagogue for some years. But we find him back again at Jerusalem very soon after the death of our Lord.

For some two years after Pentecost, Christianity was quietly spreading its influence in Jerusalem. At length Stephen, one of the seven deacons, testified that Jesus was the Messiah, and this led to much excitement among the Jews and much disputation in their synagogues. Persecution arose against Stephen and the followers of Christ generally, in which Saul of Tarsus took a prominent part. He was at this time probably a member of the great Sanhedrin, and became the active leader in the furious persecution by which the rulers then sought to exterminate Christianity.

Hearing that fugitives had taken refuge in Damascus, he obtained letters from the chief priest authorizing him to proceed with persecuting the Christians. This was a long journey of about 130 miles, which would occupy perhaps six days. At the last stage of his journey, within sight of Damascus, as he and his companions rode on, a brilliant light shone round them. Saul was laid prostrate in terror on the ground, a voice sounding in his ears, "Saul, Saul, why persecutest thou me?" The risen Savior was there, clothed in the vesture of His glorified humanity. In reply to Saul's anxious inquiry, "Who art thou, Lord?" the Lord said, "I am Jesus whom thou persecutest" (Acts 9:5; 22:8; 26:15).

This was the moment of his conversion. Blinded by the dazzling light (Acts 9:8), his companions led him into the city, where, for three days, he neither ate nor drank (9:11). Ananias, a disciple living in Damascus, was informed in a vision of the change that had happened to Saul, and was sent to him to open his eyes and admit him by baptism into the Christian church (9:11–16). The whole purpose of Saul's life was now permanently changed.

Immediately after his conversion he went to Arabia (Gal. 1:17), perhaps of "Sinai in Arabia," for the purpose, probably, of devout study and meditation on the marvelous revelation that had been made to him. Coming back, after three years, to Damascus, he began to preach the gospel "boldly in the name of Jesus" (Acts 9:27), but was soon obliged to flee (9:25; 2 Cor. 11:33) from the Jews and go to Jerusalem. Here he tarried for three weeks, but was again forced to flee (Acts 9:28–29) from persecution. He now returned to his native Tarsus (Gal. 1:21), where, for probably about three years, we lose sight of him. The time had not yet come for his entering on his great life-work of preaching the gospel to the Gentiles.

At length the city of Antioch, the capital of Syria, became the scene of great Christian activity. There the gospel gained a firm footing, and the cause of Christ prospered. Barnabas, who had been sent from Jerusalem to superintend the work at Antioch, found it too much for him, and remembering Saul, he set out to Tarsus to seek for him. Saul responded to the call, and came to Antioch, which for a year became the scene of his labors. The disciples now, for the first time, were called "Christians" (Acts 11:26).

The church at Antioch proposed to send out missionaries to the Gentiles, and Saul and Barnabas, with John Mark as their attendant, were chosen for this work. This was a great epoch in the history of the church as the disciples began to give effect to the Master's command: "Go ye into all the world, and preach the gospel to every creature."

The three missionaries went out on the first missionary tour. They sailed from Seleucia, the seaport of Antioch, across to Cyprus, some eighty miles to the southwest. Here at Paphos, Sergius Paulus, the Roman proconsul, was converted, and now Saul took the lead, and was ever afterward called Paul. The missionaries now crossed to the mainland, and then proceeded six or seven miles up the river Cestrus to Perga (Acts 13:13), where John Mark deserted the work and returned to Jerusalem. The two then proceeded about one hundred miles inland, passing through Pamphylia, Pisidia, and Lycaonia. The towns mentioned in this tour are the Pisidian Antioch, where Paul delivered his first address of which we have any record (13:16–51; compare 10:30–43), Iconium, Lystra, and Derbe. They returned by the same route to encourage the converts they had made and to ordain elders in every city to watch over the churches which had been gathered. From Perga they sailed to Antioch.

After remaining a long time, probably until AD 50 or 51, in Antioch, a great controversy broke out in the church there regarding the relation of the Gentiles to the Mosaic law. Paul and Barnabas were sent as deputies to consult the church at Jerusalem. The council or synod which was held there (Acts 15) decided against the Judaizing party, and the deputies, accompanied by Judas and Silas, returned to Antioch, bringing with them the decree of the council.

After a short rest at Antioch, Paul said to Barnabas: "Let us go again and visit our brethren in every city where we have preached the word of the Lord, and see how they do" (Acts 15:36). Mark proposed again to accompany them; but Paul refused to allow him to go. Barnabas was resolved to take Mark, and he and Paul had a sharp contention. They separated, and never again met. Paul, however, afterward spoke honorably of Barnabas, and sent for Mark to come to him at Rome (Col. 4:10; 2 Tim. 4:11).

Paul took with him Silas, instead of Barnabas, and began his second missionary journey about AD 51. This time he went by land, revisiting the churches he had already founded in Asia. But he longed to enter into "regions beyond," and still went forward through Phrygia and Galatia

(16:6). Contrary to his intention, he stayed in Galatia, because of some physical ailment (Gal. 4:13–14). Bithynia, a populous province on the shore of the Black Sea, lay before him, and he wished to enter it, but the way was shut; the Spirit guided him to Troas, on the northwestern coast of Asia Minor (Acts 16:8). Of this long journey from Antioch to Troas we have no account except some references to it in his Epistle to the Galatians (4:13).

As he waited at Troas for indications of the will of God, he saw in a vision a man crying, "Come over into Macedonia, and help us" (Acts 16:9). Paul recognized in this vision a message from the Lord; the very next day he set sail across the Hellespont, which separated him from Europe, and carried the tidings of the gospel into the Western world. In Macedonia, churches were planted in Philippi, Thessalonica, and Berea. Leaving this province, Paul passed into Achaia, "the paradise of genius and renown." He reached Athens but left after a brief stay (17:17–31). The Athenians had received him coldly, and he never visited that city again. He passed over to Corinth, the seat of the Roman government of Achaia, and remained there a year and a half, laboring with much success. While at Corinth, he wrote his two Epistles to the church of Thessalonica, his earliest apostolic letters, and then sailed for Syria. He was accompanied by Aquila and Priscilla, whom he left at Ephesus. He landed at Caesarea, and went to Jerusalem; having "saluted the church" there, he left for Antioch, where he stayed for "some time" (Acts 18:20–23).

Paul then began his third missionary tour. He journeyed by land in the "upper coasts" (the more eastern parts) of Asia Minor, and at length made his way to Ephesus, where he stayed for about three years, engaged in ceaseless Christian labor.

Very shortly before his departure from Ephesus, the apostle wrote his first Epistle to the Corinthians. The silversmiths, whose traffic in the little images they made was in danger, organized a riot against Paul, and he left the city and proceeded to Troas (2 Cor. 2:12); from there after some time he went to meet Titus in Macedonia. Here, after hearing the report Titus brought from Corinth, he wrote his second Epistle to that church. Having spent probably most of the summer and autumn visiting the churches in Macedonia, he then came into Greece, where he stayed for three months, probably spending the greater part of this time in Corinth (Acts 20:2). During his stay in this city he wrote his Epistle to the Galatians and also the great Epistle to the Romans. Leaving Achaia, he crossed into Asia Minor; he then sailed for Tyre, finally reaching Jerusalem, probably in the spring of AD 58.

While at Jerusalem, at the feast of Pentecost, he was almost murdered by a Jewish mob in the temple. Rescued from their violence by the Roman commandant, he was conveyed as a prisoner to Caesarea, where, from various causes, he was detained a prisoner for two years in Herod's praetorium (Acts 23:35).

At the end of these two years Felix was succeeded in the governorship of Palestine by Porcius Festus, before whom the apostle was again heard. But judging it right at this crisis to claim the privilege of a Roman citizen, he appealed to the emperor (Acts 25:11). Such an appeal could not be disregarded, and Paul was at once sent on to Rome under the charge of Julius, a centurion of the "Augustan cohort." Here he was permitted to occupy his own hired house, under constant military custody. This privilege was accorded to him, no doubt, because he was a Roman citizen, and as such could not be put into prison without a trial. The soldiers who kept guard over Paul were changed at frequent intervals, and thus he had the opportunity of preaching the gospel to many of them. During this period the apostle wrote his Epistles to the Colossians, Ephesians, Philippians, and to Philemon, and probably also to the Hebrews.

At length this first imprisonment came to a close, Paul having been acquitted, probably because no witnesses appeared against him. Once more he set out on his missionary labors, probably visiting western and eastern Europe and Asia Minor. During this period of freedom he wrote his first Epistle to Timothy and his Epistle to Titus. The year of his release was marked by the burning of Rome, which Nero saw fit to attribute to the Christians. A fierce persecution now broke out against the Christians. Paul was seized, and once more conveyed to Rome a prisoner. During this imprisonment he probably wrote the second Epistle to Timothy, the last he ever wrote.

Bible study on the life of Paul (NTB)

Born in the city of Tarsus: Acts 9:11; 21:39; 22:3

Educated at Jerusalem in the school of Gamaliel: Acts 22:3; 26:4

A zealous Pharisee: Acts 22:3; 23:6; 26:5; 2 Corinthians 11:22; Galatians 1:14; Philippians 3:5

A Roman citizen: Acts 16:37; 22:25–28

Persecutes the Christians; present at and gives consent to the stoning of Stephen: Acts 7:58; 8:1, 3; 9:1; 22:4

His vision and conversion: Acts 9:3–22; 22:4–19; 26:9–15; 1 Corinthians 9:1; 15:8; Galatians 1:13; 1 Timothy 1:12–13

Called to be an apostle: Acts 22:14–21; 26:16–18; Romans 1:1; 1 Corinthians 1:1; 9:1–2; 15:9; Galatians 1:1, 15–16; Ephesians 1:1; Colossians 1:1; 1 Timothy 1:1; 2:7; 2 Timothy 1:1, 11; Titus 1:1, 3

Is persecuted by the Jews: Acts 9:23, 24

Escapes by being let down from the wall in a basket; goes to Jerusalem: Acts 9:25–26; Galatians 1:18–19
Sent to the Gentiles: Acts 13:2–3, 47–48; 22:17–21; Romans 11:13; 15:16; Galatians 1:15–24
Teaches at Antioch (in Syria) for one year: Acts 11:26
Visits much of the island of Cyprus: Acts 13:4
Visits Antioch (in Pisidia), and preaches in the synagogue: Acts 13:14–41
Persecuted and expelled: Acts 13:50–51
Visits Iconium, and preaches to the Jews and non-Jews; is persecuted; escapes to Lystra; goes to Derbe: Acts 14:1–6
Heals an immobile man: Acts 14:8–10
The people attempt to worship him: Acts 14:11–18
Is persecuted by certain Jews from Antioch and Iconium, and is stoned: Acts 14:19; 2 Corinthians 11:25; 2 Timothy 3:11
Revisits Pisidia, Pamphylia, Perga, Attalia, and Antioch, in Syria, where he lived: Acts 14:24–28
Returns to Antioch, accompanied by Barnabas, Judas, and Silas, with letters to the Gentiles: Acts 15:22, 25
Makes his second tour of the congregations: Acts 15:36
Chooses Silas as his companion, and passes through Syria and Cilicia, strengthening the congregations: Acts 15:36–41
Goes through Phrygia and Galatia; attempts to go to Bithynia, but is restrained by the Spirit: Acts 16:6–7
Goes to Macedonia: Acts 16:8–10
Persecuted, beaten, and cast into prison with Silas; after an earthquake shakes the prison, preaches to the jailer, who believes: Acts 16:19–34
Is released by the civil authorities on the grounds of his being a Roman citizen: Acts 16:35–39; 2 Corinthians 6:5; 11:25; 1 Thessalonians 2:2
Debates on Mars' hill (at the meeting of the Areopagus Council) with Greeks: Acts 17:16–34
Visits Corinth; lives with Aquila and his wife, Priscilla (Prisca), who were tentmakers; joins in their trade: Acts 18:1–3
Persecuted by Jews; sails to Syria, accompanied by Aquila and Priscilla: Acts 18:12–18
Visits Ephesus, where he leaves Aquila and Priscilla; visits Caesarea; crosses over the country of Galatia and Phrygia, strengthening the disciples: Acts 18:18–23
Returns to Ephesus; lays his hands on the disciples, who are baptized with the Holy Spirit; remains in Ephesus for two years; heals the sick: Acts 19:12

Sends Timothy and Erastus into Macedonia, but he himself remains in Asia for a period of time: Acts 19:21–22
Proceeds to Macedonia after strengthening the congregations in that region; comes into Greece and lives for three months; returns through Macedonia, accompanied by Sopater, Aristarchus, Secundus, Gaius, Timothy, Tychicus, and Trophimus: Acts 20:1–6
His defense: Acts 21:33–40; 22:1–21
Is confined in the fortress: Acts 22:24–30
Is brought before the Sanhedrin; his defense: Acts 22:30; 23:1–5
Is escorted to Caesarea by a military guard: Acts 23:23–33
Is confined in Herod's judgment hall in Caesarea: Acts 23:35
His trial before Governor Felix; remains in custody for two years: Acts 24
His trial before Governor Festus; appeals to be heard by Caesar: Acts 25:1–12
His examination before Herod Agrippa II: Acts 25:13–27; 26
Is taken to Rome in the custody of Julius, a centurion, and a detachment of soldiers: Acts 27:1–5
Transferred to a ship of Alexandria; sails by way of Cnidus, Crete, Salamis, and the Fair Havens: Acts 27:6–8
The ship encounters a storm and is wrecked; all on board take refuge on the island of Melita (Malta): Acts 27:14–44
Is delayed in Melita (Malta) for three months; proceeds on the voyage; delays at Syracuse; sails by Rhegium and Puteoli: Acts 28:11–13
Arrives at Rome; is delivered to the captain of the guard; is permitted to live by himself in custody of a soldier: Acts 28:14–16
Lives in his own rented house for two years, preaching and teaching: Acts 28:30–31
Supports himself: Acts 18:3; 20:33–35
Sickness of, in Asia: 2 Corinthians 1:8–11
Has "a thorn in the flesh": 2 Corinthians 12:7–9; Galatians 4:13–14
Persecutions endured by: Acts 9:16, 23–25, 29; 16:19–25; 20:22–24; 21:13, 27–33; 22:22–24; 23:10, 12–15; Romans 8:35–37; 1 Corinthians 4:9, 11–13; 2 Corinthians 1:8–10; 4:8–12; 6:4–5, 8–10; 11:23–27, 32–33; 12:10; Galatians 5:11; 6:17; Philippians 1:30; 2:17–18; Colossians 1:24; 1 Thessalonians 2:2, 14–5; 3:4; 2 Timothy 1:12; 2:9–10; 3:11–12; 4:16–17

ANANIAS from Damascus

Significance in summary

A Christian living in Damascus who restored Paul's sight to him after his conversion

Meaning of name

protected by the Lord

Bible dictionary/encyclopedia entry (IBD)

A Christian at Damascus (Acts 9:10). He became Paul's instructor; but when or by what means he himself became a Christian we have no information. He was "a devout man according to the law, having a good report of all the Jews which dwelt" at Damascus (22:12).

Bible study on the life of Ananias (NTB)

A Christian in Damascus: Acts 9:10–18; 22:12–16
Restores Paul's sight: Acts 9:17–18

ARISTARCHUS

Significance in summary

A Christian from Thessalonica who was a companion with Paul both on his travels and in his imprisonment

Meaning of name

best ruler

Bible study on the life of Aristarchus (NTB)

A companion of Paul: Acts 19:29; 20:4; 27:2; Colossians 4:10; Philemon 1:24

JASON of Thessalonica

Significance in summary

A Christian in Thessalonica who looked after Paul and Silas in his home

Meaning of name
healing

Bible study on the life of Jason (NTB)
A Christian at Thessalonica: Acts 17:5–7, 9

SILAS

Significance in summary
Paul's traveling companion during most of his second missionary journey

Meaning of name
wood-dweller

Bible dictionary/encyclopedia entry (IBD)
A prominent member of the church at Jerusalem; also called Silvanus. He and Judas, surnamed Barsabbas, were chosen by the church there to accompany Paul and Barnabas on their return to Antioch from the council of the apostles and elders (Acts 15:22), as bearers of the decree adopted by the council. He assisted Paul there in his evangelistic labors, and was also chosen by him to be his companion on his second missionary tour (Acts 16:19–24). He is referred to in the epistles under the name of Silvanus (2 Cor. 1:19; 1 Thess. 1:1; 2 Thess. 1:1; 1 Peter 5:12). There is no record of the time or place of his death.

Bible study on the life of Silas (NTB)
Sent to Paul, in Antioch (of Syria), from Jerusalem: Acts 15:22–34
Becomes Paul's companion: Acts 15:40–41; 2 Corinthians 1:19; 1 Thessalonians 1:1; 2 Thessalonians 1:1
Imprisoned with Paul in Philippi: Acts 16:19–40
Driven, with Paul, from Thessalonica: Acts 17:4–10
Left by Paul at Berea: Acts 17:14
Rejoins Paul at Corinth: Acts 17:15; 18:5
Carries Peter's letter to Asia Minor: 1 Peter 5:12

TITUS

Significance in summary

Assisted the apostle Paul in Corinth and was appointed to pastor the church in Crete

Meaning of name

honored

Bible dictionary/encyclopedia entry (CCEB)

It is strange that Titus is never mentioned by name in Acts, and there seems none of those mentioned in that book who exactly answers to him. He was a Greek, and therefore a Gentile (Gal. 2:1, 3), and was converted by Paul (Titus 1:4). He accompanied the apostle from Antioch to Jerusalem to consult the apostles respecting the circumcision of Gentile converts (Acts 15:2); and, agreeably to the decree of the council there, was not circumcised. He was in company with Paul at Ephesus, from where he was sent to Corinth to commence the collection for the Jerusalem saints, and to determine the effect of the first Epistle on the Corinthians (2 Cor. 7:6–9; 8:6; 12:18). He next proceeded to Macedon, where he joined Paul, who had been already eagerly expecting him at Troas (2 Cor. 2:12–13, "Titus my brother"; 2 Cor. 7:6). He was then employed by the apostle in preparing the collection for the poor saints in Judea, and became the bearer of the second Epistle to the Corinthians (2 Cor. 8:16–17). Paul calls him "my partner and fellow-helper concerning you" (2 Cor. 8:23). His being located in Crete (Titus 1:5) was after Paul's first imprisonment, and shortly before the second, about AD 67, ten years subsequent to the last notice of him in 2 Corinthians (12:18), AD 57. Tradition represents him to have died peaceably in Crete, as archbishop of Gortyna, at an advanced age.

Bible study on the life of Titus (NTB)

Paul's love for: 2 Corinthians 2:13; 7:6–7, 13–14; 8:23; Titus 1:4
With Paul in Macedonia: 2 Corinthians 7:5–6
Affection of, for the Corinthians: 2 Corinthians 7:15
Sent to Corinth: 2 Corinthians 8:6, 16–22; 12:17–18
Character of: 2 Corinthians 12:18
Accompanies Paul to Jerusalem: Galatians 2:1–3
Left by Paul in Crete: Titus 1:5
To rejoin him in Nicopolis: Titus 3:12
Paul writes to: Titus 1:1–4
With Paul in Rome: 2 Timothy 4:10
Goes to Dalmatia: 2 Timothy 4:10

TIMOTHY

Significance in summary

A young traveling companion and assistant of the apostle Paul

Meaning of name

honoring God

Bible dictionary/encyclopedia entry (ISBE)

Timothy was one of the best known of Paul's companions and fellow-laborers. He was evidently one of Paul's own converts, as the apostle describes him as his beloved and faithful son in the Lord (1 Cor. 4:17); in 1 Timothy 1:2 he writes to "Timothy, my true child in the faith"; and in 2 Timothy 1:2 he addresses him as "Timothy, my beloved child."

In 2 Timothy 3:10 and 11 Paul mentions that Timothy had fully known the persecutions and afflictions which came to him at Antioch, Iconium, and Lystra. These persecutions occurred during the apostle's first visit to these towns. Timothy seems to have been one of those who were converted at that time, as we find that on Paul's next visit to Lystra and Derbe, Timothy was already one of the Christians there: "He came to Derbe and Lystra. And behold, a certain disciple was there, named Timothy" (Acts 16:1).

Timothy was now chosen by Paul to be one of his companions. This was at an early period in Paul's apostolic career, and it is pleasing to find that to the end of the apostle's life Timothy was faithful to him.

Timothy's father was a heathen Greek; this fact is twice mentioned (Acts 16:1, 3). His mother was a Jewess, but Timothy had not been circumcised in infancy, probably owing to objections made by his father. Timothy's mother was Eunice, and his grandmother Lois. Paul mentions them by name in 2 Timothy 1:5. It is evident that Eunice was converted to Christ on Paul's first missionary journey to Derbe and Lystra, because, when he next visited these cities, she is spoken of as a Jewess who believed (Acts 16:1).

Before Timothy could begin his work as a Christian missionary, both to Jew and Gentile, two things needed to be done. In order to conciliate the Jewish Christians, who would otherwise have caused trouble, which would have weakened Timothy's position and his work as a preacher of the gospel, Paul took Timothy and circumcised him. Paul was willing to agree to this because Timothy's mother was a Jewess. It was therefore quite a different case from that of Titus, where Paul refused to allow circumcision to be performed (Acts 15:2)—Titus being, unlike Timothy, a Gentile by birth. The other act performed for

Timothy's benefit before he set out with Paul was that he was ordained by the local council of presbyters in Derbe and Lystra.

Showing the importance which Paul assigned to this act of ordination, he refers to it in a letter to Timothy written many years afterward: "Neglect not the gift that is in thee, which was given thee by prophecy, with the laying on of the hands of the presbytery" (1 Tim. 4:14). In this ordination Paul himself took part, for he writes, "I put thee in remembrance that thou stir up the gift of God, which is in thee by the putting on of my hands" (2 Tim. 1:6).

Prepared for the work, Timothy went with Paul on his second missionary journey. We find Timothy at Berea (Acts 17:14), having evidently accompanied Paul to all the places visited by him up to that point, namely, Phrygia, the region of Galatia, Mysia, Troas, Neapolis, Philippi, Amphipolis, Apollonia, Thessalonica, and Berea. Paul next went—and went alone, on account of the persecution at Berea—to Athens (Acts 17:15).

Paul left Athens before Silas and Timothy were able to rejoin him; he had proceeded to Corinth. Timothy evidently remained with Paul during the year and six months of his residence in Corinth, and also throughout this missionary journey to its end. From Corinth Paul wrote the Epistle to the Romans and sent them a salutation from Timothy, "Timothy, my fellow worker, greets you" (Rom. 16:21). It was Paul's custom to associate with his own name that of one or more of his companions in the opening salutations in the Epistles. Timothy's name occurs in 2 Corinthians 1:1; Philippians 1:1; Colossians 1:1; Philemon 1:1. It is also found, along with that of Silvanus, in 1 Thessalonians 1:1 and 2 Thessalonians 1:1.

On Paul's third missionary journey, Timothy again accompanied him, though he is not mentioned until they reached Ephesus. After two years there, Paul made plans to go to Jerusalem. He sent on before him "into Macedonia two of them that ministered unto him, [Timothy] and Erastus" (Acts 19:22).

From Ephesus Paul wrote the first Epistle to the Corinthians (1 Cor. 16:8), and in it he mentioned (1 Cor. 16:10) that Timothy was then traveling to Corinth, apparently an extension of the journey into Macedonia. After commending him to the Corinthians, Paul stated that Timothy was to return to him from Corinth, and report on the state of the Corinthian church.

Soon thereafter the riot in Ephesus occurred; when it was over, Paul left Ephesus and went to Macedonia and Greece. In Macedonia he was rejoined by Timothy, whose name is associated with his own, in the opening salutation of the second Epistle, which he now wrote to Corinth. Timothy accompanied him into Greece, where they stayed for three months.

From Greece the apostle once more set out toward Jerusalem, with Timothy and others accompanying him (Acts 20:4). "We that were of Paul's company" (Acts 21:8), as Luke terms the friends who now traveled with Paul—and Timothy was one of them—touched at Troas and a number of other places, and eventually reached Jerusalem, where Paul was apprehended. This terminated his apostolic journeys for the time.

The details of how Timothy was now employed are not recorded until he is found once more with Paul—during his first imprisonment in Rome. But, from that point onward, there are many notices of how he was occupied in the apostle's service. He is mentioned in three of the Epistles written by Paul at this time—in Colossians 1:1 and Philemon 1:1, he calls Timothy "our brother," and in Philippians 1:1 he says, "Paul and Timothy, servants of Christ Jesus."

Paul's hope was realized: he was set free, and once again Timothy was his companion in travel. Perhaps it was in Philippi that they rejoined each other, for not only had Paul expressed his intention of sending Timothy there, but he had also said that he hoped himself to visit the Philippian church (Phil. 1:26; 2:24). From this point onward it is difficult, perhaps impossible, to trace the course of Paul's journeys, but he tells us that he had left Timothy as his representative in Ephesus (1 Tim. 1:3); soon after, he wrote the first Epistle to Timothy, in which he gave full instructions regarding the affairs of the Ephesian church, until Paul himself again revisited Ephesus: "These things write I unto thee, hoping to come unto thee shortly" (1 Tim. 3:14).

From the second Epistle we learn that Paul was imprisoned a second time, and feeling that on this occasion his trial would be followed by an adverse judgment and by death, he wrote from Rome to Timothy at Ephesus, affectionately requesting him to come to him. The fact that at that time, when no Christian friend was with Paul except Luke (2 Tim. 4:11), it was to Timothy he turned for sympathy and aid, closing with the request that his own son in the faith should come, to be with him in his last hours, shows how true and tender was the affection which bound them together. Whether Timothy was able to reach Rome, to be with Paul before his execution is unknown.

Nothing further is known of Timothy. Of all Paul's friends, with the exception, perhaps, of Luke, Paul's beloved friend, Timothy was regarded by him with the tenderest affection; he was his dearly loved son, faithful and true.

Bible study on the life of Timothy (NTB)

Parentage of: Acts 16:1

Reputation and Christian faith of: Acts 16:2; 1 Corinthians 4:17; 16:10; 2 Timothy 1:5; 3:15

Circumcised; becomes Paul's companion: Acts 16:3; 1 Thessalonians 3:2
Left by Paul at Berea: Acts 17:14
Rejoined Paul at Corinth: Acts 17:15; 18:5
Sent into Macedonia: Acts 19:22
Rejoined by Paul; accompanies Paul to Asia: Acts 20:1–4
Sent salutation to the Romans: Romans 16:21
Sent to the Corinthians: 1 Corinthians 4:17; 16:10–11
Preached to the Corinthians: 2 Corinthians 1:19
Sent to the Philippians: Philippians 2:19, 23
Sent to the Thessalonians: 1 Thessalonians 3:2, 6
Left by Paul in Ephesus: 1 Timothy 1:3
Confined with Paul in Rome: Philippians 2:19–23; Philemon 1:1; Hebrews 13:23
Zeal of: Philippians 2:19–22; 1 Timothy 6:12
Power of: 1 Timothy 4:14; 2 Timothy 1:6
Paul's love for: 1 Corinthians 4:17; Philippians 2:22; 1 Timothy 1:2, 18; 2 Timothy 1:2–4
Paul writes to: 1 Timothy 1:1–2; 2 Timothy 1:1–2

EUNICE

Significance in summary

Timothy's godly mother

Meaning of name

good victory

Bible study on the life of Eunice (NTB)

A Jewess, mother of Timothy: 2 Timothy 1:5

TYCHICUS

Significance in summary

One of Paul's trusted friends whom Paul sent to the Christians at Ephesus, while Paul himself was in his last imprisonment

Meaning of name

fortuitous

Bible study on the life of Tychicus (NTB)

An Asian companion of Paul; accompanies Paul from Greece to Asia: Acts 20:4
With Paul in Nicopolis: Titus 3:12
With Paul in Rome: Ephesians 6:21–22; Colossians 4:7–8
Paul's amanuensis (copyist) in writing to the Ephesians and Colossians: see postscripts to Ephesians and Colossians
Sent to Ephesus: Ephesians 6:21, 22; 2 Timothy 4:12
Sent to Colosse: Colossians 4:7–8

JOHN MARK

Significance in summary

Writer of the second Gospel who accompanied Paul on his first missionary journey

Bible dictionary/encyclopedia entry (SERK)

In Acts 12:12 and 25, a John Mark is named as one of the Christians of Jerusalem, at whose mother's house the meetings of the community were held. He was also a companion of Barnabas and Paul on their missionary journey to Antioch and Cyprus (Acts 13:5) but left them when they reached Asia Minor. Because of this defection, Paul refused to take him along on the second missionary journey, and this caused a separation between Barnabas and Paul, Barnabas and Mark going together and Paul and Silas becoming companions.

Mark is mentioned by Paul several times in his epistles (Col. 4:10, "Mark, the cousin of Barnabas"; 2 Tim. 4:11; Philemon 24), always in favorable terms. He was a Jew (Col. 4:11), and, like the Jesus Justus of that passage and other Jews of the period, took a Roman name in addition to his Jewish name. Acts 12:12 suggests that his father was already dead in the early years of Christianity. Mark appears to have been younger than Paul and Peter, but still old enough to have been an adult at the time of the crucifixion. Tradition identifies him with the man described in Mark 14:13 as "bearing a pitcher of water" and with the young man of verses 51 and 52, and also makes him one of the seventy disciples. His missionary activity is recognized by Paul, and the last historical datum is that of his presence in Rome about AD 63. Legend makes him the founder of the church in Egypt and bishop of Alexandria.

Bible study on the life of John Mark (NTB)

A cousin of Barnabas: Colossians 4:10
A disciple of Jesus: Acts 12:12, 25; 13:5, 13
Paul and Barnabas contend concerning: Acts 15:36–39
A convert of Peter: 1 Peter 5:13
Fellow worker with Paul at Rome: Colossians 4:10–11; 2 Timothy 4:11; Philemon 1:24

BARNABAS

Significance in summary

A Jewish Christian who accompanied Paul on his missionary journeys

Meaning of name

son of encouragement

Bible dictionary/encyclopedia entry (IBD)

Barnabas's name stands first on the list of prophets and teachers of the church at Antioch (Acts 13:1). Luke speaks of him as a "good man" (11:24). He was born of Jewish parents from the tribe of Levi. He was a native of Cyprus, where he had a possession of land (Acts 4:36–37), which he sold. His personal appearance is supposed to have been dignified and commanding (Acts 14:11–12). When Paul returned to Jerusalem after his conversion, Barnabas took him and introduced him to the apostles (9:27). They had probably been companions as students in the school of Gamaliel.

The prosperity of the church at Antioch led the apostles and the believers in Jerusalem to send Barnabas there to oversee the movement. He found the work so difficult that he went to Tarsus in search of Paul to assist him. Paul returned with him to Antioch and labored with him for a year (Acts 11:25–26). At the end of this period the two were sent to Jerusalem with the contributions the church at Antioch had made for the poorer brethren there (11:28–30). Shortly after they returned, bringing John Mark with them, they were appointed as missionaries to the heathen world, and in this capacity visited Cyprus and some of the principal cities of Asia Minor (Acts 13:14). Returning from this first missionary journey to Antioch, they were again sent to Jerusalem to consult with the church there regarding the relation of Gentiles to the church (Acts 15:2: Gal. 2:1). This matter having been settled, they returned again to Antioch, bringing the decree of the council as the rule by which Gentiles were to be admitted into the church.

When about to set forth on a second missionary journey, a dispute arose between Paul and Barnabas as to the propriety of taking John Mark with them again. The dispute ended by Paul and Barnabas taking separate routes. Paul took Silas as his companion and journeyed through Syria and Cilicia while Barnabas took John Mark, and visited Cyprus (Acts 15:36–41). Barnabas is not again mentioned by Luke in the Acts.

Bible study on the life of Barnabas (NTB)

Also called Joses; a Levite who gave his possessions to be owned in common with other disciples: Acts 4:36–37
Brings Paul to the apostles: Acts 9:25–27
Accompanies Paul to Jerusalem: Acts 11:30
Returns with Paul to Antioch: Acts 12:25
Goes with Paul to Seleucia: Acts 13
A prophet: Acts 13:1
An apostle: Acts 14:14
Goes with Paul to Iconium: Acts 14:1–7
Called Jupiter (Zeus): Acts 14:12–18
Goes to Derbe: Acts 14:20
Is sent as an emissary to Jerusalem: Acts 15; Galatians 2:1–9
Disaffected toward Paul: Acts 15:36–39
Is reconciled to Paul: 1 Corinthians 9:6
Piety of: Acts 11:24
Devotion of, to Jesus: Acts 15:26

ALEXANDER from Ephesus

Significance in summary

A spokesman for the Jews during the riot in Ephesus

Bible study on the life of Alexander (NTB)

A Jew from Ephesus: Acts 19:33

CLEMENT

Significance in summary

A Philippian Christian whom Paul called his fellow worker

Meaning of name

merciful

Bible study on the life of Clement (NTB)

A disciple at Philippi: Philippians 4:3

JULIUS

Significance in summary

The centurion who was in charge of Paul during his journey to stand trial in Rome

Bible study on the life of Julius (NTB)

A centurion: Acts 27:1, 3, 43

GAIUS from Macedonia

Significance in summary

One of Paul's traveling companions who was seized by a crowd during a riot in Ephesus

Bible study on the life of Gaius (NTB)

A Macedonian, and a companion of Paul; seized at Ephesus: Acts 19:29

LUKE

Significance in summary

A doctor who accompanied Paul on his travels and the author of the third Gospel and Acts

Meaning of name

light-giving

Bible dictionary/encyclopedia entry (ISBE)

The name Luke (*Loukas*) is apparently an abbreviation for Loukanos. Old Latin manuscripts frequently have the words *cata Lucanum* as the title of the third Gospel.

Paul alone names Luke (Col. 4:14; 2 Tim. 4:11; Phil. 1:24). Luke does not mention his own name in the Gospel or in the Acts. Compare the silence of the fourth Gospel concerning the name of the apostle John. There was no particular occasion to mention Luke's name in the Gospel, except as the author, if he had so wished. The late legend that Luke was one of the seventy sent out by Jesus is pure conjecture, as is the story that Luke was one of the Greeks who came to Philip for an introduction to Jesus (John 12:20), or the companion of Cleopas in the walk to Emmaus (Luke 24:13). The clear implication of Luke 1:2 is that Luke himself was not an eyewitness of the ministry of Jesus.

In Colossians 4:14 Luke is distinguished by Paul from those "of the circumcision" (Aristarchus, Mark, Jesus Justus). Epaphras, Luke, and Demas form the Gentile group. He was believed by the early Christian writers to have come directly from heathendom to Christianity. He may or may not have been a Jewish proselyte. His first appearance with Paul at Troas (compare the "we" sections, Acts 16:10–12) is in harmony with this idea. The classic introduction to the Gospel (Luke 1:1–4) shows that he was a man of culture (compare Apollos and Paul). He was a man of the schools, and his Greek has a literary flavor only approached in the New Testament by Paul's writings and by the Epistle to the Hebrews.

We know that Luke lived in Philippi for a considerable period. He first meets Paul at Troas just before the vision of the man from Macedonia (Acts 16:10–12), and a conversation with Paul about the work in Macedonia may well have been the human occasion of that vision and call. Luke remains in Philippi when Paul and Silas leave (Acts 16:40, "They . . . departed"). He is here when Paul comes back on his third journey bound for Jerusalem (Acts 20:3–5). He also shows a natural pride in the claims of Philippi to the primacy in the province as against Amphipolis and Thessalonica (Acts 16:12, "the first of the district"). On the whole, we may consider Philippi as the home of Luke, though he was probably a man who had traveled a great deal, and may have been with Paul in Galatia before coming to Troas. He may have ministered to Paul in his sickness there (Gal. 4:14). His later years were spent chiefly with Paul away from Philippi (compare Acts 20:3–28, 31, on the way to Jerusalem, at Caesarea, the voyage to Rome, and in Rome).

Paul (Col. 4:14) expressly calls Luke "the beloved physician." He was Paul's medical adviser, and doubtless prolonged his life and rescued him from many a serious illness. He was a medical missionary, and probably kept up his general practice of medicine in connection with his work in Rome. He probably practiced medicine in Malta (Acts 28:9). He shows his fondness for medical terms in his books.

Luke was the more or less constant companion of Paul from Philippi on the return to Jerusalem on the third journey until the two years in Rome at the close of the Acts. He was apparently not with Paul when Philippians 2:20 was written, though, as we have seen, he was with Paul in Rome when he wrote Colossians and Philemon. He was Paul's sole companion for a while during the second Roman imprisonment (2 Tim. 4:11). His devotion to Paul in this time of peril is beautiful.

One legend regarding Luke is that he was a painter. It is true that he has drawn vivid scenes with his pen. The early artists were especially fond of painting scenes from the Gospel of Luke. The allegorical figure of the ox or calf in Ezekiel 1 and Revelation 4 has been applied to Luke's Gospel.

Bible study on the life of Luke (NTB)

A physician: Colossians 4:14
Wrote to Theophilus: Luke 1:1–4; Acts 1:1–2
Accompanies Paul on his tour of Asia and Macedonia: Acts 16:10–13; 20:5–6
To Jerusalem: Acts 21:1–18
To Rome: Acts 27; 28; 2 Timothy 4:11; Philemon 24

THEOPHILUS

Significance in summary

Man to whom Luke addressed his Gospel and the Acts

Bible dictionary/encyclopedia entry (IBD)

From the fact that Luke applies to him the title "most excellent," the same title Paul uses in addressing Felix (Acts 23:26; 24:3) and Festus (26:25), it has been concluded that Theophilus was a person of rank, perhaps a Roman officer.

Bible study on the life of Theophilus (NTB)

A Christian to whom Luke addressed the books of Luke and Acts: Luke 1:3; Acts 1:1

GALLIO

Significance in summary

The Proconsul of Achaia who refused to condemn Paul in Corinth

Bible study on the life of Gallio (NTB)

Proconsul (governor) of Achaia; dismisses complaint of Jews against Paul: Acts 18:12–17

TROPHIMUS

Significance in summary

A Christian from Ephesus who became one of Paul's traveling companions

Bible study on the life of Trophimus (NTB)

Accompanies Paul from Greece to Asia: Acts 20:4
With Paul in Jerusalem; made the occasion of an attack on Paul: Acts 21:27–30
Left ill at Miletus: 2 Timothy 4:20

GAIUS from Derbe

Significance in summary

A Christian from Derbe who traveled with Paul to Jerusalem

Bible study on the life of Gaius (NTB)

A man of Derbe; accompanied Paul from Macedonia: Acts 20:4

GAIUS from Corinth

Significance in summary

A Corinthian Christian baptized by Paul

Bible study on the life of Gaius (NTB)

A Corinthian, whom Paul baptized: Romans 16:23; 1 Corinthians 1:14

Paul's Friends and Convert s

Aquila • Priscilla • Apollos • Crescens • Crispus • Dionysius • Epaphras • Onesimus • Philemon • Onesiphorus • Epaphroditus • Lydia • Jason, a Jewish Christian • Phoebe • Sosthenes, a ruler of Corinthian synagogue • Sosthenes, a Corinthian believer • Stephanas • Publius • Eutychus

AQUILA

Significance in summary

A Jewish Christian who, with his wife, Priscilla, befriended and supported Paul

Bible dictionary/encyclopedia entry (SBD)

A Jew whom Paul found at Corinth (AD 52) on his arrival from Athens (Acts 18:2). He was a native of Pontus, but had fled with his wife, Priscilla, from Rome, following an order of Claudius commanding all Jews to leave the city. He and Priscilla became acquainted with Paul, who stayed and worked with them making tents. On the departure of the apostle from Corinth, a year and eight months after, Priscilla and Aquila accompanied him to Ephesus. There they remained and there they taught Apollos. At what time they became Christians is uncertain.

Bible study on the life of Aquila (NTB)

Christian at Corinth: Acts 18:1–3, 18–19, 26
Friendship of, for Paul: Romans 16:3–4
Paul sends salutations to: 2 Timothy 4:19

PRISCILLA

Significance in summary

A Christian woman who, with her husband, Aquila, supported Paul

Bible dictionary/encyclopedia entry (IBD)

The wife of Aquila (Acts 18:2), who is never mentioned without her. Her name sometimes takes the precedence of his (Rom. 16:3; 2 Tim. 4:19). She took part with Aquila in instructing Apollos (Acts 18:26).

Bible study on the life of Priscilla (NTB)

A disciple at Corinth: Acts 18:1–3, 18–19, 26; Romans 16:3–4; 1 Corinthians 16:19; 2 Timothy 4:19

APOLLOS

Significance in summary

A Jew from Alexandria who became an influential teacher in the early church

Bible dictionary/encyclopedia entry (IBD)

A Jew "born at Alexandria," a man well versed in the Scriptures and eloquent (Acts 18:24; RSV, "learned"). He came to Ephesus (about AD 49), where he spoke "boldly" in the synagogue (18:26), although he did not know as yet that Jesus of Nazareth was the Messiah. Aquila and Priscilla instructed him more perfectly in "the way of God," that is, in the knowledge of Christ. He then proceeded to Corinth, where he met Paul (Acts 18:27; 19:1). He was very useful there in watering the good seed Paul had sown (1 Cor. 1:12) and in gaining many to Christ. His disciples were much attached to him (1 Cor. 3:4–7, 22). He was with Paul at Ephesus when he wrote the first Epistle to the Corinthians; Paul makes kindly reference to him in his letter to Titus (3:13). Some have supposed, although without sufficient ground, that he was the author of the Epistle to the Hebrews.

Bible study on the life of Apollos (NTB)

An eloquent, Christian convert at Corinth: Acts 18:24–28; 19:1; 1 Corinthians 1:12; 3:4–7
Refuses to return to Rome: 1 Corinthians 16:12
Paul writes Titus about: Titus 3:13

CRESCENS

Significance in summary

One of Paul's friends when Paul was a prisoner in Rome

Bible study on the life of Crescens (NTB)

A disciple with Paul at Rome: 2 Timothy 4:10

CRISPUS

Significance in summary

The chief official of the synagogue in Corinth whom Paul baptized after his conversion

Bible study on the life of Crispus (NTB)

A leader of a synagogue at Corinth: Acts 18:8; 1 Corinthians 1:14

DIONYSIUS

Significance in summary

A member of the supreme court in Athens who became a Christian

Bible study on the life of Dionysius (NTB)

A convert of Paul: Acts 17:34

EPAPHRAS

Significance in summary

A leader of the church at Colosse and prisoner with Paul in Rome

Bible study on the life of Epaphras (NTB)

A co-laborer with Paul: Colossians 1:7; 4:12; Philemon 1:23

ONESIMUS

Significance in summary

A runaway slave who became a Christian

Bible dictionary/encyclopedia entry (IBD)

After robbing his master Philemon at Colosse, Onesimus fled to Rome, where he was converted by the apostle Paul, who sent him back to his master with the Epistle which bears his name. In it he beseeches Philemon to receive his slave as a "faithful and beloved brother." Paul offers to pay to Philemon anything his slave had taken, and to bear the wrong he had done him. He was accompanied on his return by Tychicus, the bearer of the Epistle to the Colossians (Phil. 1:16, 18).

Bible study on the life of Onesimus (NTB)

A fugitive slave and subsequent convert of Paul: Colossians 4:9; Philemon 1:10

PHILEMON

Significance in summary

A Christian to whom Paul addressed his Epistle on behalf of Onesimus

Meaning of name

friendship

Bible dictionary/encyclopedia entry (SBD)

Philemon was a native probably of Colosse, or at all events lived in that city when the apostle wrote to him: first, because Onesimus was a Colossian (Col. 4:9), and secondly because Archippus was a Colossian (Col. 4:17), whom Paul associates with Philemon at the beginning of his letter (Philem. 1–2). Some sources say that Philemon became bishop of Colosse, and died as a martyr under Nero. He was indebted to the apostle Paul as the medium of his personal participation in the gospel. It is not certain under what circumstances they became known to each other. It is evident that on becoming a disciple he gave no common proof of the sincerity and power of his faith. His character as shown in the Epistle to him, is one of the noblest which the sacred record makes known to us.

Bible study on the life of Philemon (NTB)

Paul's letter to: Philemon 1:25

ONESIPHORUS

Significance in summary

A Christian who helped Paul during his imprisonment in Rome

Meaning of name

who brings profit

Bible study on the life of Onesiphorus (NTB)

A Christian of Ephesus: 2 Timothy 1:16–17; 4:19

EPAPHRODITUS

Significance in summary

A Philippian Christian who took a gift from the church at Philippi to Paul during his imprisonment in Rome

Meaning of name

handsome, agreeable

Bible study on the life of Epaphroditus (NTB)

A messenger of Paul: Philippians 2:25; 4:18
Sick at Rome: Philippians 2:26–27, 30

LYDIA

Significance in summary

A businesswoman from Thyatira who became a Christian through Paul's ministry

Bible dictionary/encyclopedia entry (SBD)

The first European convert of Paul, and afterward his hostess during his first stay at Philippi (Acts 16:14–15, 40). Lydia was a Jewish proselyte at the time of the apostle's coming; it was at the Jewish Sabbath-worship by the side of a stream (Acts 16:13), that the preaching of the gospel reached her heart. Her native place was Thyatira, in the province of Asia. Thyatira was famous for its dyeing works; Lydia was connected with this trade, as a seller either of dye or of dyed goods. We infer that she was a person of considerable wealth.

Bible study on the life of Lydia (NTB)

A woman of Thyatira, who with her household was converted through the preaching of Paul: Acts 16:14–15
Entertains Paul and Silas: Acts 16:15, 40

JASON, a Jewish Christian

Significance in summary

A Jewish Christian mentioned by Paul at the end of his letter to the Romans

Meaning of name

healing

Bible study on the life of Jason (NTB)

Probably Paul's relative: Romans 16:21

PHOEBE

Significance in summary

A deaconess in Cenchrea, a neighboring church to Corinth

Meaning of name

radiant

Bible study on the life of Phoebe (NTB)

A servant of the congregation at Cenchrea: Romans 16:1

SOSTHENES, a ruler of Corinthian synagogue

Significance in summary

The ruler of the synagogue at Corinth when Paul was taken to court by the Jews

Bible study on the life of Sosthenes (NTB)

Chief ruler of the synagogue in Corinth: Acts 18:17

SOSTHENES, a Corinthian believer

Significance in summary

A Christian known to the believers at Corinth

Bible study on the life of Sosthenes (NTB)

A Christian with whom Paul wrote the first letter to the Corinthians: 1 Corinthians 1:1

STEPHANAS

Significance in summary

Man who, with his family, was among the first people to become Christians in Achaia

Meaning of name

crown

Bible study on the life of Stephanas (NTB)

A Christian in Corinth, whose household Paul baptized: 1 Corinthians 1:16; 16:15, 17

PUBLIUS

Significance in summary

Malta's chief official who helped Paul and whose father Paul healed

Bible study on the life of Publius (NTB)

Father of, healed by Paul: Acts 28:7–8

EUTYCHUS

Significance in summary

A young man from Troas who fell asleep while listening to Paul preach

Meaning of name

fortunate

Bible study on the life of Eutychus (NTB)

Restored to life by Paul: Acts 20:9–11

Paul's Enemies

Aretas • Demetrius, the silversmith • Ananias, the high priest • Demas • Elymas • Hymenaeus • Alexander, the coppersmith

ARETAS

Significance in summary

The governor of Damascus who tried, unsuccessfully, to arrest Paul

Meaning of name

goodness, virtuous

Bible study on the life of Aretas (NTB)

A ruler of Syria: 2 Corinthians 11:32

DEMETRIUS, the silversmith

Significance in summary

The silversmith in Ephesus who orchestrated a riot against Paul

Meaning of name

belonging to Demeter

Bible study on the life of Demetrius (NTB)

A silversmith, noted for raising a riot: Acts 19:24–38

ANANIAS, the high priest

Significance in summary

The high priest at Paul's trial before the Sanhedrin in Jerusalem

Meaning of name

protected by the Lord

Bible dictionary/encyclopedia entry (IBD)

The high priest before whom Paul was brought in the procuratorship of Felix (Acts 23:2–5). Ananias was so enraged at Paul's noble declaration, "I have lived in all good conscience before God until this day," (Acts 23:1) that he commanded one of his attendants to strike him on the mouth. Smarting under this unprovoked insult, Paul quickly replied, "God shall smite thee, thou whited wall" (v. 3). Being reminded that Ananias was the high priest, to whose office all respect was to be paid, he answered, "I wist not, brethren, that he was the high priest" (v. 5). The expression may mean that Paul had at the moment overlooked the honor due to the high priest, or that Paul spoke ironically, as if he had said, "The high priest breaking the law! God's high priest a tyrant and a lawbreaker! I see a man in white robes, and have heard his voice, but surely it cannot, it ought not to be, the voice of the high priest." Others think that from defect of sight Paul could not observe that the speaker was the high priest. In all this, however, Paul, with all his excellency, comes short of the example of his divine Master, who, when He was reviled, reviled not again.

Bible study on the life of Ananias (NTB)

High priest, before whom Paul was tried: Acts 23:2–5; 24:1; 25:2

DEMAS

Significance in summary

One of Paul's friends and helpers who later deserted him

Bible study on the life of Demas (NTB)

A companion of Paul: Colossians 4:14; Philemon 1:24
Deserts Paul: 2 Timothy 4:10

ELYMAS

Significance in summary

A Jewish false prophet at Paphos whom Paul struck blind

Meaning of name

sorcerer

Bible study on the life of Elymas (NTB)

A false prophet, punished with blindness: Acts 13:8, 10

HYMENAEUS

Significance in summary

A heretical teacher condemned by Paul in both of his letters to Timothy

Bible study on the life of Hymenaeus (NTB)

A false teacher: 1 Timothy 1:20; 2 Timothy 2:17

ALEXANDER, the coppersmith

Significance in summary

A coppersmith who opposed Paul

Meaning of name

defender of man

Bible dictionary/encyclopedia entry (BC)

We first come on Alexander, a coppersmith of Ephesus, when called on as a clever speaker before a mob of metalsmiths (Acts 19:33). Next he finds it apparently in his interest to be baptized and seen openly with Paul. But Paul's side does not turn out to be as serviceable to him as he expected, so we eventually find him in complete shipwreck of his faith (1 Tim. 1:20). In the end, Alexander is portrayed as a bitter man who so hates Paul that he hunts him down and does him much evil (2 Tim. 4:14).

Bible study on the life of Alexander (NTB)

A coppersmith: 1 Timothy 1:20; 2 Timothy 4:14

Roman Rulers

Claudius • Felix • Festus •
Agrippa II • Bernice • Drusilla

CLAUDIUS

Significance in summary

The Roman Caesar who expelled Christians from Rome

Meaning of name

lame

Bible study on the life of Claudius (NTB)

Emperor of Rome: Acts 11:28; 18:2

FELIX

Significance in summary

The Roman governor of Judea who tried Paul in Caesarea and imprisoned him for two years

Meaning of name

happy

Bible study on the life of Felix (NTB)

Tries Paul: Acts 23:24–35; 24
Trembles under Paul's preaching: Acts 24:25
Leaves Paul in prison: Acts 24:26–27; 25:14

FESTUS

Significance in summary

Succeeded Felix as Roman governor of Judea and sent Paul to trial in Rome after Paul had appealed to Caesar

Meaning of name

swine-like

Bible study on the life of Festus (NTB)

Also called Porcius Festus, the Roman governor of Judaea, and successor to Governor Felix: Acts 24:27
Tries Paul: Acts 25:26

AGRIPPA II

Significance in summary

The ruler of Galilee from whom Festus sought advice about the imprisoned Paul

Bible dictionary/encyclopedia entry (SBD)

Herod Agrippa II was the son of Herod Agrippa I. In AD 62 the emperor gave him the tetrarchs formerly held by Philip and Lysanias, with the title of king. The relation in which he stood to his sister Bernice (Acts 25:13) was the cause of grave suspicion. It was before him that Paul was tried (Acts 26).

Bible study on the life of Agrippa II (NTB)

King: Acts 25:26

BERNICE

Significance in summary

Daughter of Agrippa I

Meaning of name

victorious

Bible study on the life of Bernice (NTB)

Daughter of Agrippa: Acts 25:13, 23; 26:30

DRUSILLA

Significance in summary

Wife of Felix, Roman governor of Judea who tried Paul

Bible study on the life of Drusilla (NTB)

A Jewess, wife of Felix: Acts 24:24

Part Three

All the People of the Bible

This list identifies all the proper names of people mentioned in the Bible. They are in alphabetical order, using names as found in the King James Version of the Bible. Variant spellings are included in parentheses after the name of the person.

I've also included meanings of Bible names from Roswell D. Hitchcock's dictionary, *Hitchcock's New and Complete Analysis of the Holy Bible*, which was first published in 1874. Hitchcock was the Washburn Professor of Church History in the Union Theological Seminary, New York City.

Alphabetical List of Bible Names

Aaron *[a teacher; lofty; mountain of strength]*
The older brother of Moses and Miriam (Exod. 4:14; Num. 12; 17).

Abagtha *[father of the winepress]*
One of the seven eunuchs in the Persian court of Ahasuerus (Esther 1:10).

Abda *[a servant; servitude]*
1. Father of Adoniram (1 Kings 4:6).
2. Son of Shammua (Neh. 11:17), called Obadiah (1 Chron. 9:16).

Abdeel *[a vapor; a cloud of God]*
Father of Shelemiah (Jer. 36:26).

Abdi *[my servant]*
1. One of David's song leaders (1 Chron. 6:44).
2. One who married a foreign wife in the exile (Ezra 10:26).

Abdiel *[servant of God]*
Ancestor of a clan of Gad (1 Chron. 5:15).

Abdon *[servant; cloud of judgment]*
1. A judge who ruled Israel for eight years (Judg. 12:13, 15).
2. A descendant of Benjamin (1 Chron. 8:23).
3. Firstborn son of Jehiel, son of Gideon (1 Chron. 8:30; 9:36).
4. Son of Micah, a contemporary of Josiah (2 Chron. 34:20).

Abednego *[servant of light; shining]*
Name given to Azariah, one of Daniel's three friends (Dan. 1:7).

Abel *[vanity; breath; vapor]*
The second son of Adam, murdered by his brother, Cain (Gen. 4:1–10).

Abi *[my father]*
Mother of King Hezekiah (2 Kings 18:2). Abi is a contraction of Abijah, as in 2 Chronicles 29:1. See Abi-albon; Abiezer.

Abia (Abiah, Abijah) *[the Lord is my father]*
1. Son of Becher, the son of Benjamin (1 Chron. 7:8).
2. Wife of Hezron (1 Chron. 2:24).
3. Son of Rehoboam and successor to Judah's throne, and ancestor of Jesus Christ (1 Chron. 3:10; Matt. 1:7). Also known as Abijam.

Abi-albon (Abiel) *[most intelligent father]*
One of David's valiant men (2 Sam. 23:31). Also called Abiel (1 Chron. 11:32).

Abiasaph *[consuming father; gathering]*
One of the descendants of Korah, and head of the Korhites (Exod. 6:24). Also written as Ebiasaph (1 Chron. 6:23, 37; 9:19).

Abiathar *[excellent father; father of the remnant]*
High priest and the only one of the sons of Ahimelech the high priest who escaped Saul's slaughter (1 Sam. 22:1).

Abida (Abidah) *[father of knowledge]*
A son of Midian (Gen. 25:4; 1 Chron. 1:33).

Abidan *[father of judgment]*
Chief of the tribe of Benjamin at the time of the exodus (Num. 1:11; 2:22; 7:60, 65; 10:24).

Abiel *[God my father]*
See Abi-albon; Ner.

Abiezer *[father of help]*
1. Eldest son of Gilead, and descendant of Manasseh (Josh. 17:2; 1 Chron. 7:18).
2. One of David's mighty men (2 Sam. 23:27; 1 Chron. 11:28).

Abigail *[the father's joy]*
1. The beautiful wife of Nabal, a wealthy owner of goats and sheep in Carmel (1 Sam. 25:14).
2. A sister of David, married to Jether the Ishmaelite, and mother, by him, of Amasa (1 Chron. 2:17).

Abihail *[the father of strength]*
1. Father of Zuriel, chief of the Levitical father of Merari, a contemporary of Moses (Num. 3:35).
2. Wife of Abishur (1 Chron. 2:29).
3. Son of Huri, of the tribe of Gad (1 Chron. 5:14).
4. Wife of Rehoboam (2 Chron. 11:18).
5. Father of Esther (Esther 2:15; 9:29).

Abihu *[he is my father]*
Son of Aaron (Exod. 6:23).

Abihud *[father of praise; confession]*
Son of Bela (1 Chron. 8:3).

Abijah *[the Lord is my father]*
1. A son of Jeroboam of Israel who died as a youth (1 Kings 14:1–18).
2. A priest who sealed the covenant between God and Israel after the exile (Neh. 10:7).
3. See Abia.

Abijam *[father of the sea]*
See Abia 3.

Abimael *[a father sent from God]*
A son of Joktan (Gen. 10:26–28).

Abimelech *[father of the king]*
1. The name of several Philistine kings, was probably a common title of these kings, like that of Pharaoh among the Egyptians and that of Caesar and Augustus among the Romans. Hence in the title of Psalm 34:1 the name of Abimelech is given to the king, who is called Achish in 1 Samuel 21:11.
2. Son of the judge Gideon (Judg. 8:30–10:1).
3. See Ahimelech.

Abinadab *[father of a vow, or of willingness]*
1. A Levite in whose home the ark of the covenant was housed for twenty years (1 Sam. 7:1; 1 Chron. 13:7).
2. Second son of Jesse, David's brother (1 Sam. 16:8; 17:13).
3. A son of Saul, who was killed with his brothers at the battle on Mount Gilboa (1 Sam. 31:2).
4. Father of one of the twelve chief officers of Solomon (1 Kings 4:11).

Abiner
See Abner.

Abinoam *[father of beauty]*
Father of Barak (Judg. 4:6, 12; 5:1, 12).

Abiram *[high father; father of deceit]*
1. A Reubenite, son of Eliab, who with Korah organized a conspiracy against Moses and Aaron (Num. 16:27).
2. Eldest son of Hiel who died when his father began to rebuild Jericho (1 Kings 16:34).

Abishag *[ignorance of the father]*
A beautiful Shunammite taken into David's harem to comfort him in his old age (1 Kings 1:1–4).

Abishai *[the present of my father]*
A son of David's sister, one of David's mighty men (2 Sam. 26:6–9).

Abishalom (Absalom) *[father of peace]*
Father of Maachah, the wife of Rehoboam (1 Kings 15:2, 10); called Absalom in 2 Chronicles 11:20–21.

Abishua *[father of salvation]*
1. A descendant of Benjamin (1 Chron. 8:4).
2. Son of Phinehas, descendant of Aaron (1 Chron. 6:4–5, 50).

Abishur *[father of the wall; father of uprightness]*
Son of Shammai (1 Chron. 2:28–29).

Abital *[the father of the dew or of the shadow]*
One of David's wives (2 Sam. 3:4; 1 Chron. 3:3).

Abitub *[father of goodness]*
A descendant of Benjamin (1 Chron. 8:11).

Abiud *[father of praise]*
Son of Zerubbabel and ancestor of Jesus Christ (Matt. 1:13).

Abner (Abiner) *[father of light]*
Captain under Saul and Ishbosheth (1 Sam. 14:50–51).

Abraham (Abram) *[father of a great multitude]*
The son of Terah, and founder of the great Hebrew nation (Genesis 11–25).

Abram *[high father]*
The earlier name of Abraham (Gen. 11:26).

Absalom *[father of peace]*
Third son of David by Maachah who tried to usurp the throne from his father (2 Sam. 13–19).

Achaicus *[a native of Achaia; sorrowing; sad]*
A Corinthian Christian who visited Paul at Philippi (1 Cor. 16:17).

Achan (Achar) *[he that troubleth]*
An Israelite who, when Jericho was taken, hid some of the spoil in his tent (Josh. 7:1–24).

Achar
See Achan.

Achaz *[one that takes or possesses]*
Greek form of Ahaz. See Ahaz.

Achbor *[a rat; bruising]*
1. Father of Baalhanan, king of Edom (Gen. 36:38–39; 1 Chron. 1:49).
2. A person sent to bring Urijah from Egypt (Jer. 26:22; 36:12).

Achim *[preparing; revenging; confirming]*
Ancestor of Jesus Christ (Matt. 1:14).

Achish *[thus it is; how is this]*
1. A Philistine king of Gath to whom David fled for safety (1 Sam. 21:27–29).
2. Another king of Gath who reigned in Solomon's time (1 Kings 2:39–40).

Acsah (Achsah) *[adorned; bursting the veil]*
A daughter of Caleb (1 Chron. 2:49).

Adah *[an assembly]*
1. One of Lamech's wives (Gen. 4:19–20).
2. One of Esau's wives (Gen. 36:2, 4, 10, 12, 16).

Adaiah *[the witness of the Lord]*
1. Father of Jedidah, King Josiah's mother (2 Kings 22:1).
2. A Levite ancestor of Asaph (1 Chron. 6:41).
3. A son of Shimhi (1 Chron. 8:12–21).
4. A Levite descended from Aaron (1 Chron. 9:12; Neh. 11:12).
5. Father of a commander who supported Jehoiada (2 Chron. 23:1).
6. A person who married a foreign wife during the exile (Ezra 10:29).
7. Another person who married a foreign wife during the exile (Ezra 10:39).
8. A person whose descendants lived in Jerusalem (Neh. 11:5).

Adalia *[one that draws water; poverty; cloud; death]*
The fifth son of Haman (Esther 9:8).

Adam *[earthy; red]*
The first man (Genesis 2–3).

Adbeel *[vapor or cloud of God]*
A son of Ishmael (Gen. 25:13; 1 Chron. 1:29).

Addan
See Addon.

Addar
A son of Bela (1 Chron. 8:3).

Addi *[my witness; adorned; prey]*
An ancestor of Jesus Christ (Luke 3:28).

Addon (Addan) *[basis; foundation; the Lord]*
A man who could not prove his Jewish ancestry after he returned from exile (Neh. 7:61).

Ader (Eder)
A son of Beriah (1 Chron. 8:15).

Adiel *[the witness of the Lord]*
1. A descendant of Simeon (1 Chron. 4:36).
2. A descendant of Aaron (1 Chron. 9:12).
3. Father of Azmaveth, David's treasurer (1 Chron. 27:25).

Adin *[adorned; voluptuous; dainty]*
1. Ancestor of a family who returned from Babylon with Zerubbabel (Ezra 2:15; Neh. 7:20).
2. A descendant who returned with Ezra (Ezra 8:6).
3. A family who sealed the covenant with God in Jerusalem after the exile (Neh. 10:14–16).

Adina *[same as Adin]*
One of David's commanders (1 Chron. 11:42).

Adino
A chief of David's mighty men (2 Sam. 23:8); sometimes identified with Jashobeam 1.

Adlai *[my witness; my ornament]*
Father of an overseer of David's herds (1 Chron. 27:29).

Admatha *[a cloud of death; a mortal vapor]*
One of the seven princes of Persia (Esther 1:14).

Adna *[pleasure; delight]*
1. A person who returned with Ezra and had married a foreign wife (Ezra 10:30).
2. A priest, descendant of Harim in the days of Joiakim (Neh. 12:15).

See also Adnah.

Adnah *[eternal rest]*
1. A Manassite who joined David at Ziklag (1 Chron. 12:20).
2. The chief commander over 300,000 men of Judah who were in Jehoshaphat's army (2 Chron. 17:14).

See also Adna.

Adoni-bezek *[the lightning of the Lord; the Lord of lightning]*
A king of Bezek who was captured by Israel (Judg. 1:5–7).

Adonijah *[the Lord is my master]*
1. A son of David executed by Solomon for trying to usurp the throne (2 Sam. 3:4).
2. A Levite who taught the Law during Jehoshaphat's reign (2 Chron. 17:8).
3. A person who sealed the covenant with God after the exile (Neh. 10:16).
4. See Tob-adonijah.

Adonikam *[the Lord is raised]*
Ancestor of returned captives (Ezra 2:13).

Adoniram *[my Lord is most high; Lord of might and elevation]*
See Hadoram 3.

Adoni-zedek *[justice of the Lord; lord of justice]*
The Amorite king of Jerusalem defeated by Joshua (Josh. 10:1–27).

Adoram *[their beauty; their power]*
See Hadoram 3.

Adrammelech *[the cloak, glory, grandeur or power of the king]*
Son of the Assyrian king Sennacherib, who, with his brother Sharezer, murdered their father (2 Kings 19:37; Isa. 37:38).

Adriel *[the flock of God]*
Son of Barzillai, to whom Saul gave his daughter Merab, although he had previously promised her to David (1 Sam. 18:19).

Aeneas *[praised; praiseworthy]*
A paralytic at Lydda healed by Peter (Acts 9:33–34).

Agabus *[a locust; the father's joy or feast]*
A Christian prophet in the apostolic age (Acts 11:28; 21:10).

Agag *[roof; upper floor]*
Possibly the title of the kings of Amalek.
1. A king mentioned by Balaam (Num. 24:7).
2. A king whose life Saul spared (1 Samuel 15).

Agar *[a stranger; one that fears]*
The Greek form of Hagar. See Hagar.

Agee *[a valley; deepness]*
Father of one of David's three mightiest men (2 Sam. 23:11).

Agrippa *[one who causes great pain at his birth]*
See Herod.

Agur *[stranger; gathered together]*
An unknown Hebrew sage who wrote Proverbs 30.

Ahab *[uncle or father's brother]*
1. Israel's seventh king who married Jezebel (1 Kings 16:28–22:40).
2. A false prophet killed by Nebuchadnezzar (Jer. 29:21–22).

Aharah *[a smiling brother; a meadow of a sweet savor]*
See Ahiram.

Aharhel *[another host; the last sorrow; a brother's sheep]*
A descendant of Judah (1 Chron. 4:8).

Ahasai
A priest of the family of Immer (Neh. 11:13).

Ahasbai *[trusting in me; a grown-up brother]*
Father of Eliphelet, one of David's thirty-seven commanders (2 Sam. 23:34).

Ahasuerus *[prince; head; chief]*
The name of one Median and two Persian kings mentioned in the Old Testament.
1. Father of Darius the Mede (Dan. 9:1).
2. Another name for Cambyses, king of Persia (Ezra 4:6).
3. King of Persia whom Esther married (Esther 1:1).

Ahaz *[one that takes or possesses]*
1. The eleventh king of Judah (1 Kings 15:38–16:20).
2. A descendant of Benjamin (1 Chron. 8:35–36; 9:41–42).

Ahaziah *[seizure; vision of the Lord]*
1. Son of Ahab and Jezebel, the eighth king of Israel (1 Kings 22:51–52).
2. Sixth king of Judah, son of Jehoram and Athaliah (2 Kings 8:24–29).
3. See Jehoahaz.

Ahban
Son of Abishur of Judah (1 Chron. 2:29).

Aher
A descendant of Benjamin (1 Chron. 7:12). See also Ahiram.

Ahi *[my brother; my brethren]*
1. Head of a family of Gad (1 Chron. 5:15).
2. A descendant of Shamer, of the tribe of Asher (1 Chron. 7:34).

Ahiah (Ahijah) *[brother of the Lord]*
1. A grandson of Phinehas and great-grandson of Eli (1 Sam. 14:3, 18).
2. One of Solomon's scribes (1 Kings 4:3).
3. Son of Bela, descendant of Benjamin (1 Chron. 8:7).

Ahiam *[mother's brother; brother of a nation]*
One of David's mighty men (1 Chron. 11:35).

Ahian *[brother of wine]*
A descendant of Manasseh (1 Chron. 7:19).

Ahiezer *[brother of assistance]*
1. A prince of Dan who helped Moses take a census (Num. 1:12; 2:25; 7:66).
2. The Benjamite head of a group of archers in David's day (1 Chron. 12:3).

Ahihud *[brother of vanity, or of darkness, or of joy, or of praise; witty brother]*
1. The son of Shelomi and prince of the tribe of Asher (Num. 34:27).

2. Chieftain of the tribe of Benjamin (1 Chron. 8:7).

Ahijah *[brother of the Lord]*

1. A prophet from Shiloh who prophesied the splitting up of the ten tribes (1 Kings 11:29–30).
2. Father of Baasha, king of Israel, who conspired against Nadab (1 Kings 15:29–30).
3. Son of Jerahmeel (1 Chron. 2:25).
4. One of David's mighty men (1 Chron. 11:36).
5. A person who sealed the new covenant with God after the exile (Neh. 10:26).
6. A Levite in David's reign who looked after the temple treasures (1 Chron. 26:20).

See also Ahiah; Ahimelech

Ahikam *[a brother who raises up or avenges]*

One of the delegates sent to consult Huldah the prophetess (2 Kings 22:12, 14).

Ahilud *[a brother born, or begotten]*

Father of Jehoshaphat, the recorder in the reigns of David and Solomon (2 Sam. 8:16; 20:24).

Ahimaaz *[a brother of the council]*

1. Son of Zadok who stayed loyal to David (2 Sam. 15:27; 17:15–22).
2. Saul's wife's father (1 Sam. 14:50).
3. One of Solomon's commanders (1 Kings 4:15).

Ahiman *[brother of the right hand]*

1. One of the three giant Anakim who lived in Mount Hebron (Num. 13:22–23).
2. A Levite temple porter (1 Chron. 9:17).

Ahimelech *[my brother is a king; my king's brother]*

1. One of the priests of Nob, killed for helping David (1 Sam. 21:1–8; 22:9–20).
2. A priest, son of Abiathar (2 Sam. 8:17).
3. A Hittite friend of David (1 Sam. 26:6).

Ahimoth *[brother of death]*

A descendant of Kohath (1 Chron. 6:25).

Ahinadab *[a willing brother; brother of a vow]*

Son of Iddo, one of Solomon's twelve royal merchants (1 Kings 4:14).

Ahinoam *[beauty of the brother; brother of motion]*

1. The daughter of Ahimaaz and wife of Saul (1 Sam. 14:50).
2. Born in Jezreel; married to David during his itinerant life (1 Sam. 25:43).

Ahio *[his brother; his brethren]*

1. Son of Abinadab, in whose house the ark of the covenant stayed for twenty years (2 Sam. 6:3–4; 1 Chron. 13:7).
2. A Benjamite, one of the sons of Beriah (1 Chron. 8:14).
3. A descendant of Saul (1 Chron. 8:31; 9:37).

Ahira *[brother of iniquity; brother of the shepherd]*

Chief of the tribe of Naphtali (Num. 1:15; 2:29).

Ahiram (Aharah; Aher; Ehi) *[brother of craft or of protection]*

A descendant of Benjamin (Num. 26:38); called Ehi in Genesis 46:21 and Aharah in 1 Chronicles 8:1.

Ahisamach *[brother of strength]*

One of the architects of the tabernacle (Exod. 31:6; 35:34; 38:23).

Ahishahar *[brother of the morning or dew; brother of blackness]*

One of the sons of Bilhan, the grandson of Benjamin (1 Chron. 7:10).

Ahishar *[brother of a prince; brother of a song]*

The controller of Solomon's household (1 Kings 4:6).

Ahithophel *[brother of ruin or folly]*
Leader of Absalom's conspiracy against David (2 Samuel 15–17).

Ahitub *[brother of goodness]*
1. The son of Phinehas and grandson of Eli (1 Sam. 14:3; 22:9, 11–12).
2. Father of Zadok the high priest (1 Chron. 6:7–8).
3. A high priest who served in Nehemiah's day (1 Chron. 6:11).

Ahlai *[beseeching; sorrowing; expecting]*
1. Daughter of Sheshan, whom he gave in marriage to his Egyptian slave Jarha (1 Chron. 2:31, 35).
2. Father of one of David's mighty men (1 Chron. 11:41).

Ahoah *[a live brother; my thorn or thistle]*
A son of Bela (1 Chron. 8:4).

Aholiab *[the tent of the father]*
A skilled weaver and embroiderer, whom Moses appointed with Bezaleel to erect the tabernacle (Exod. 35:30–35).

Aholibamah (Oholibamah) *[my tabernacle is exalted]*
One of Esau's wives (Gen. 36:2, 5, 14, 18).

Ahumai *[a meadow of waters; a brother of waters]*
A descendant of Judah (1 Chron. 4:2).

Ahuzam *[their taking or possessing vision]*
A son of Ashur, a descendant of Judah through Caleb (1 Chron. 4:6).

Ahuzzath *[possession; seizing; collecting]*
One of the friends of the Philistine king Abimelech (Gen. 26:26).

Aiah (Ajah) *[vulture, raven; an isle; alas, where is it?]*
1. Son of Zibeon, a descendant of Seir and ancestor of one of the wives of Esau (1 Chron. 1:40).
2. Father of Saul's concubine, Rizpah (2 Sam. 3:7).

Akan
See Jaakan.

Akkub *[footprint; supplanting; crookedness; lewdness]*
1. A descendant of Zerubbabel and son of Elioenai (1 Chron. 3:24).
2. One of the doorkeepers at the east gate of the temple (Neh. 11:19).
3. Ancestor of a family of porters (Neh. 7:45).
4. Ancestor of Nethinim, who returned from the exile with Zerubbabel (Ezra 2:45).
5. A Levite who assisted Ezra in expounding the Law to the people (Neh. 8:7).

Alameth
A son of Becher (1 Chron. 7:8).

Alemeth *[hiding; youth; worlds; on the dead]*
A descendant of Jonathan (1 Chron. 8:36; 9:42).

Alexander *[one who assists men]*
1. Son of Simon the Cyrenian, who was compelled to carry Jesus' cross (Mark 15:21).
2. One of the relatives of Annas the high priest (Acts 4:6).
3. A Christian with Paul in Ephesus when Demetrius the silversmith led a mob in a riot (Acts 19:33).
4. An Ephesian Christian who deserted his Christian faith (1 Tim. 1:20).
5. A coppersmith who harmed Paul greatly (2 Tim. 4:14).

Aliah (Alvah)
A leader of Edom (1 Chron. 1:51), called Alvah in Genesis 36:40.

Alian (Alvan) *[high]*
A descendant of Seir (1 Chron. 1:40), called Alvan in Genesis 36:23.

Allon *[an oak; strong]*
A Simeonite, ancestor of Ziza (1 Chron. 4:37).

Almodad *[measure of God]*
The first of the descendants of Joktan (Gen. 10:26; 1 Chron. 1:20).

Alphaeus *[a thousand; learned; chief]*
1. The father of Levi (Matthew) (Mark 2:14).
2. The father of the apostle James (Matt. 10:3; Mark 3:18; Acts 1:13).

Alvah *[his rising up; his highness]*
See Aliah.

Alvan
See Alian.

Amal *[labor; iniquity]*
A descendant of Asher, son of Helem (1 Chron. 7:35).

Amalek *[a people that licks up]*
A son of Eliphaz by his concubine Timnah, grandson of Esau and chief of Edom (Gen. 36:12, 16; 1 Chron. 1:36).

Amariah *[the Lord says; the integrity of the Lord]*
1. Grandfather of Zadok the high priest (1 Chron. 6:7, 52).
2. Son of Azariah, high priest in Solomon's reign (1 Chron. 6:11).
3. The high priest in Jehoshaphat's reign (2 Chron. 19:11).
4. A descendant of Kohath (1 Chron. 24:23).
5. A person appointed to distribute tithes (2 Chron. 31:15).
6. A person who married a foreign wife during the exile (Ezra 10:42).
7. A priest who sealed the new covenant with God after the exile (Neh. 10:3; 12:2, 13).
8. A person whose descendants lived in Jerusalem after the exile (Neh. 11:4).
9. An ancestor of Zephaniah the prophet (Zeph. 1:1).

Amasa *[sparing the people]*
1. David's nephew who joined in Absalom's rebellion (2 Samuel 18–21).
2. A prince of Ephraim, son of Hadlai, in Ahaz's reign (2 Chron. 28:12).

Amasai *[strong]*
1. A Kohathite, father of Mahath and ancestor of Samuel (1 Chron. 6:25, 35).
2. Chief of the captains of Judah and Benjamin, who deserted to David while an outlaw at Ziklag (1 Chron. 12:18).
3. One of the priests who blew a trumpet before the ark of the covenant (1 Chron. 15:24).
4. Another Kohathite, in Hezekiah's reign (2 Chron. 29:12).

Amashai *[the people's gift]*
Son of Azareel, a priest in the time of Nehemiah (Neh. 11:13).

Amasiah
One of Jehoshaphat's chief commanders (2 Chron. 17:16).

Amaziah *[the strength of the Lord]*
1. Son of Joash, and eighth king of Judah (2 Kings 12:21–14:20).
2. A descendant of Simeon (1 Chron. 4:34).
3. A Levite descendant from Merari (1 Chron. 6:45).
4. Idolatrous priest of the golden calf at Bethel (Amos 7:10, 12, 14).

Ami (Amon) *[mother; fear; people]*
One of Solomon's servants (Ezra 2:57), called Amon in Nehemiah 7:59.

Aminadab *[same as Amminadab]*
Greek form of Amminadab. See Amminadab.

Amittai *[true; fearing]*
Father of the prophet Jonah (2 Kings 14:25; Jonah 1:1).

Ammiel *[the people of God]*
1. The spy from the tribe of Dan who spied out the land of Canaan (Num. 13:12).
2. Father of Machir of Lodebar, David's friend (2 Sam. 9:4–5; 17:27).
3. The sixth son of Obed-edom (1 Chron. 26:5) and one of the doorkeepers of the temple.
4. See Eliam.

Ammihud *[people of praise]*
1. Father of Elishama, the chief of Ephraim (Num. 1:10; 2:18).
2. A Simeonite, father of Shemuel (Num. 34:20).

3. The father of Pedahel, prince of the tribe of Naphtali (Num. 34:28).
4. The father of Talmai, king of Geshur (2 Sam. 13:37).
5. A descendant of Pharez, son of Judah (1 Chron. 9:4).

Amminadab (Aminadab) *[my people is liberal]*
1. Aaron's father-in-law (Exod. 6:23).
2. A prince of Judah and ancestor of Christ (Num. 1:7; 2:3; Ruth 4:19–20; Matt. 1:4).
3. A son of Kohath (1 Chron. 6:22).
4. A person who helped bring the ark of the covenant from the house of Obed-edom (1 Chron. 15:10–11).

Ammishaddai *[the people of the Almighty; the Almighty is with me]*
Father of Ahaizer, a leader of Dan during the desert journey (Num. 1:12; 2:25).

Ammizabad *[dowry of the people]*
The son of Benaiah, who commanded part of David's army (1 Chron. 27:6).

Amnon *[faithful and true; tutor]*
1. David's eldest son who dishonored his half-sister Tamar, and so was murdered by her brother (2 Sam. 13:1–29).
2. Son of Shimon, from Caleb's family (1 Chron. 4:20).

Amok *[a valley; a depth]*
A priest who returned to Jerusalem with Zerubbabel (Neh. 12:7, 20).

Amon *[faithful; true]*
1. One of Ahab's governors (1 Kings 22:26; 2 Chron. 18:25).
2. King of Judah, son and successor of Manasseh, who reigned for two years (2 Kings 21:19–25).
3. See Ami.

Amos *[loading; weighty]*
A prophet during the reigns of Uzziah and Jeroboam (Amos 1:1).

Amoz *[strong; robust]*
Father of the prophet Isaiah (Isa. 1:1).

Amplias *[large; extensive]*
A Christian at Rome to whom Paul sent greetings (Rom. 16:8).

Amram *[an exalted people; their sheaves; handfuls of corn]*
1. A Levite of the family of the Kohathites, and father of Moses (Exod. 6:18, 20).
2. A son of Dishon and descendant of Seir (1 Chron. 1:41).
3. One of the sons of Bani in the time of Ezra, who had married a foreign wife during the exile (Ezra 10:34).
4. See Hemdan.

Amraphel *[one that speaks of secrets]*
A Hamite king of Shinar who fought against Sodom and Gomorrah (Gen. 14:1, 9).

Amzi *[strong, mighty]*
1. A Levite of the family of Merari (1 Chron. 6:46).
2. An ancestor of returned exiles (Neh. 11:12).

Anah *[one who answers; afflicted]*
1. The mother of one of Esau's wives (Gen. 36:2, 14, 25).
2. A leader of Edom (Gen. 36:20).
3. A son of Zibeon (Gen. 36:24).

Anaiah
1. Stood with Ezra during the reading of the Law (Neh. 8:4).
2. A person who signed the covenant with Nehemiah after the exile (Neh. 10:22).

Anak *[a collar; ornament]*
Ancestor of the giant Anakim (Num. 13:22).

Anan
A person who signed the covenant with Nehemiah after the exile (Neh. 10:26).

Anani *[a cloud; prophecy; divination]*
The seventh son of Elioenai, descended from the royal line of Judah (1 Chron. 3:24).

Ananiah *[the cloud of the Lord]*
Ancestor of Azariah, who helped to rebuild the wall of Jerusalem (Neh. 3:23).

Ananias *[the cloud of the Lord]*
1. A high priest in Jerusalem who opposed Paul (Acts 23:2; 24:1).
2. A disciple in Jerusalem who was struck dead for trying to deceive the apostles (Acts 5:1–11).
3. A disciple in Damascus (Acts 9:10–17) who helped Saul after his vision.

Anath *[answer; song; poverty]*
Father of the judge Shamgar (Judg. 3:31; 5:6).

Anathoth *[answer; song; poverty]*
1. Son of Becher (1 Chron. 7:8).
2. A person who signed the new covenant after the Exile (Neh. 10:19).

Andrew *[a strong man]*
One of Jesus' twelve apostles (John 1:40; Matt. 4:18).

Andronicus *[a man excelling others]*
A Christian in Rome to whom Paul sent greetings (Rom. 16:7).

Aner *[answer; song; affliction]*
One of the three Amorite chiefs of Hebron who helped Abraham to fight off the four invading kings (Gen. 14:13, 24).

Aniam *[a people; the strength or sorrow of people]*
A descendant of Manasseh (1 Chron. 7:19).

Anna *[gracious; one who gives]*
A prophetess in Jerusalem at the time of Jesus' presentation in the temple (Luke 2:36).

Annas *[one who answers; humble]*
The high priest who tried Jesus (Luke 3:2; John 18:13).

Antipas *[for all, or against all]*
Christian martyr in Pergamos (Rev. 2:13).

Antothijah *[answers or songs of the Lord; afflictions]*
A son of Shashak (1 Chron. 8:24).

Anub *[same as Anab]*
A descendant of Judah, through Caleb (1 Chron. 4:8).

Apelles *[exclusion; separation]*
A Roman Christian greeted by Paul (Rom. 16:10).

Aphiah *[speaking; blowing]*
An ancestor of King Saul (1 Sam. 9:1).

Aphses
Chief of the eighteenth temple chorus (1 Chron. 24:15).

Apollos *[one who destroys; destroyer]*
A Jew from Alexandria who was mighty in the Scriptures (Acts 18:24; 19:1).

Appaim *[face; nostrils]*
A son of Nadab (1 Chron. 2:30).

Apphia *[productive; fruitful]*
A Christian woman mentioned with Philemon and Archippus (Philem. 2).

Aquila *[an eagle]*
A Jew whom Paul found at Corinth on his arrival from Athens (Acts 18:2).

Ara *[cursing; seeing]*
A son of Jether (1 Chron. 7:88).

Arad *[a wild ass; a dragon]*
1. A king defeated by Israel near Mount Hor (Num. 21:1).
2. One of the chief men of Aijalon (1 Chron. 8:15).

Arah *[the way; a traveler]*
1. An Asherite, of the sons of Ulla (1 Chron. 7:39).
2. Ancestor of a family returned from the exile (Ezra 2:5).
3. Grandfather of the wife of Tobiah, who opposed Nehemiah's rebuilding of the temple (Neh. 6:18).

Aram *[highness; magnificence; one that deceives; curse]*
1. A son of Shem (Gen. 10:22–23).
2. A son of Abraham's nephew, Kemuel (Gen. 22:21).
3. A descendant from Asher (1 Chron. 7:34).
4. The Greek form of Ram. See Ram.

Aran *[an ark; their curse]*
A son of Seir (Gen. 36:28).

Araunah *[ark; song; joyful cry]*
A Jebusite who sold his threshing floor on Mount Moriah to David as a site for an altar to Jehovah (2 Sam. 24:16–24). See also Ornan.

Arba *[four]*
An ancestor of the Anakim (Josh. 14:15; 15:13; 21:11).

Archelaus *[the prince of the people]*
Son and successor of Herod the Great who ruled over Idumea, Judea, and Samaria (Matt. 2:22).

Archippus *[a master of horses]*
A Christian teacher in Colosse (Col. 4:17).

Ard *[one that commands; he that descends]*
1. A son of Benjamin (Gen. 46:21).
2. A son of Bela (Num. 26:40).

Ardon *[ruling; a judgment of malediction]*
A son of Caleb (1 Chron. 2:18).

Areli *[the light or vision of God]*
A son of Gad (Gen. 46:16; Num. 26:17).

Aretas *[agreeable, virtuous]*
Aretas IV's deputy who attempted to arrest Paul (2 Cor. 11:32).

Aridai
The ninth son of Haman, killed by the Jews (Esther 9:9).

Aridatha
The sixth son of Haman, hanged with his father (Esther 9:8).

Arieh
An Israelite killed by Pekah (2 Kings 15:25).

Ariel *[altar; light or lion of God]*
Sent by Ezra to find attendants for the temple (Ezra 8:16).

Arioch *[long; great; tall]*
1. The king of Ellasar, who fought against Sodom and Gomorrah (Gen. 14:1, 9).
2. The captain of Nebuchadnezzar's bodyguard (Dan. 2:14–15).

Arisai
Haman's eighth son, killed by the Jews (Esther 9:9).

Aristarchus *[the best prince]*
One of Paul's traveling companions who accompanied him on his third missionary journey (Acts 19:29).

Aristobulus *[a good counselor]*
A resident at Rome, some of whose household are greeted in Romans 16:10.

Armoni
Son of Saul by Rizpah (2 Sam. 21:8).

Arnan *[rejoicing; sunlight]*
A descendant of David and founder of a family (1 Chron. 3:21).

Arod
A son of Gad (Num. 26:17).

Arphaxad *[a healer; a releaser]*
The son of Shem and ancestor of Jesus Christ (Gen. 10:22, 24; Luke 3:36).

Artaxerxes *[the silence of light; fervent to spoil]*
1. King of Persia who had Ezra and Nehemiah in his court (Ezra 4:7; Neh. 2:1).
2. Another king of Persia (Ezra 6:14).

Artemas *[whole, sound]*
One of Paul's companions (Titus 3:12).

Arza
Steward to Elah, king of Israel (1 Kings 16:9).

Asa *[physician; cure]*
1. Third king of Judah, and ancestor of Jesus Christ (1 Kings 15:8–16; Matt. 1:7–8).
2. Head of a Levite family (1 Chron. 9:16).

Asahel *[creature of God]*
1. David's nephew who was killed by Abner (2 Sam. 2:18).
2. One of the Levites who taught the Law (2 Chron. 17:8).
3. A Levite in Hezekiah's reign who was in charge of the tithes and dedicated things in the temple (2 Chron. 31:13).

4. A priest, father of Jonathan, in Ezra's time, who took a census of foreign wives (Ezra 10:15).

Asahiah (Asaiah)

King Josiah's servant who was sent to find out about the book of the law, which Hilkiah found in the temple (2 Kings 22:12, 14).

Asaiah *[the Lord hath wrought]*

1. A prince of Simeon in Hezekiah's reign (1 Chron. 4:36).
2. A Levite who helped to bring the ark of the covenant from the house of Obed-edom to the city of David (1 Chron. 15:6, 11).
3. A resident in Jerusalem (1 Chron. 9:5).
4. See also Asahiah.

Asaph *[who gathers together]*

1. A Levite, son of Berechiah, one of the leaders of David's choir (1 Chron. 6:39).
2. The father or ancestor of Joah, and recorder to Hezekiah (2 Kings 18:18, 37).
3. The keeper of the royal forest (Neh. 2:8).
4. A Levite whose descendants lived in Jerusalem (1 Chron. 9:15).

Asareel *[the beatitude of God]*

A descendant of Judah through Caleb (1 Chron. 4:16).

Asarelah (Azarael)

One of the sons of Asaph, a musician (1 Chron. 25:2).

Asenath *[peril; misfortune]*

Joseph's Egyptian wife (Gen. 41:45) and mother of Manasseh and Ephraim.

Aser

Greek form of Asher. See Asher.

Ashbea

A family of linen workers (1 Chron. 4:21).

Ashbel *[an old fire]*

Second son of Benjamin and ancestor of the Ashbelites (Gen. 46:21; Num. 26:38; 1 Chron. 8:1).

Ashchenaz (Ashkenaz)

A son of Gomer (1 Chron. 1:6).

Asher *[happiness]*

The eighth son of Jacob, by Zilpah, Leah's handmaid (Gen. 30:13).

Ashkenaz *[a fire that spreads]*

See Ashchenaz.

Ashpenaz

Nebuchadnezzar's chief court official (Dan. 1:3).

Ashriel

See Asriel.

Ashur *[who is happy; or walks; or looks]*

Son of Hezron by his wife Abiah (1 Chron. 2:24; 4:5) who became founder of the town of Tekoa.

Ashvath

One of the sons of Japhlet, of the tribe of Asher (1 Chron. 7:33).

Asiel *[the work of God]*

A descendant of Simeon and grandfather of Jehu (1 Chron. 4:35).

Asnah

One whose descendants returned from the exile to Jerusalem with Zerubbabel (Ezra 2:50).

Asnapper *[unhappiness; increase of danger]*

A person who brought men from Susa and Elam to Samaria (Ezra 4:10).

Aspatha

Third son of Haman, killed by the Jews (Esther 9:7).

Asriel (Ashriel) *[help of God]*

1. A son of Gilead (Num. 26:31; Josh. 17:2).
2. A son of Manasseh (1 Chron. 7:14).

Asshur (Assur)

1. A son of Shem and ancestor of Assyria (Gen. 10:22).
2. A descendant of Ham who built Nineveh (Gen. 10:11).

Assir *[prisoner; fettered]*

1. A son of Korah (Exod. 6:24; 1 Chron. 6:22).

2. A son of Ebiasaph and a forefather of Samuel (1 Chron. 6:23, 37).
3. A son of Jeconiah, king of Judah (1 Chron. 3:17).

Assur
See Asshur.

Asyncritus *[incomparable]*
A Christian in Rome, greeted by Paul (Rom. 16:14).

Atarah *[a crown]*
A wife of Jerahmeel, and mother of Onam (1 Chron. 2:26).

Ater *[left hand; shut]*
1. Ancestor of a family of gatekeepers of the temple who returned with Zerubbabel (Ezra 2:42; Neh. 7:45).
2. A person who sealed the covenant with Nehemiah (Neh. 10:17).
3. Ancestor of a family who returned to Jerusalem after the exile (Ezra 2:16; Neh. 7:21).

Athaiah *[the Lord's time]*
A descendant of Judah who lived in Jerusalem after the return from Babylon (Neh. 11:4).

Athaliah *[the time of the Lord]*
1. Daughter of Ahab and Jezebel (2 Kings 11:1–20).
2. A son of Jeroham (1 Chron. 8:26–27).
3. Father of a returned exile (Ezra 8:7).

Athlai *[my hour or time]*
One of the sons of Bebai who turned away from his foreign wife because of Ezra's exhortation (Ezra 10:28).

Attai *[same as Athlai]*
1. A descendant of Pharez (1 Chron. 2:35–36).
2. A person who joined David at Ziklag (1 Chron. 12:11).
3. A son of King Rehoboam (2 Chron. 11:20).

Augustus Caesar *[increased, augmented]*
The imperial name of Octavian who became Roman emperor and during whose reign Jesus was born (Luke 2:1).

Azaliah *[near the Lord]*
The father of Shaphan the scribe in Josiah's reign (2 Kings 22:3; 2 Chron. 34:8).

Azaniah *[hearing the Lord; the Lord's weapons]*
The father of a person who sealed the new covenant with God after the exile (Neh. 10:9).

Azarael (Azareel)
1. A Levite musician (Neh. 12:36).

Azareel *[help of God]*
1. A Korhite who joined David in his retreat at Ziklag (1 Chron. 12:6).
2. A Levite musician of the family of Heman in the time of David (1 Chron. 25:18).
3. Son of Jeroham, and prince of the tribe of Dan when David numbered the people (1 Chron. 27:22).
4. One of the sons of Bani who turned away from his foreign wife because of Ezra's teaching (Ezra 10:41).
5. A priest who lived in Jerusalem after the return from Babylon (Neh. 11:13).
6. A trumpeter at the dedication of the rebuilt temple (Neh. 12:36).

Azariah *[he that hears the Lord]*
A common name in Hebrew, and especially in the families of the priests of the line of Eleazar, whose name has precisely the same meaning as Azariah.
1. Son of Ahimaaz (1 Chron. 6:9).
2. A ruler of Solomon's officers (1 Kings 4:5).
3. A descendant of David's high priest (1 Kings 4:2).
4. Tenth king of Judah, more often called Uzziah (2 Kings 14:21; 15:1, 6, 8, 17, 23, 27; 1 Chron. 8:12).
5. Son of Ethan (1 Chron. 2:8).
6. Son of Jehu of the family of the Jerahmeelites (1 Chron. 2:38–39).
7. A son of Ahimaaz (1 Chron. 6:9).
8. A high priest and grandson of seven (1 Chron. 6:10).
9. A son of Hilkiah the high priest under Josiah (1 Chron. 6:13–14).

10. Son of Zephaniah, a Kohathite, and ancestor of Samuel the prophet (1 Chron. 6:36).
11. A prophet who went to Asa (2 Chron. 15:1).
12. 13. Two sons of King Jehoshaphat (2 Chron. 21:2).
14. Son of Jeroham, one of the captains of Judah in the time of Athaliah who helped Joash gain the throne (2 Chron. 23:1).
15. Another man who helped Joash (2 Chron. 23:1).
16. A high priest who opposed Uzziah (2 Chron. 26:17–20).
17. Son of Johanan, one of the captains of Ephraim in Ahaz's reign (2 Chron. 28:12).
18. A Kohathite, father of Joel, in Hezekiah's reign (2 Chron. 29:12).
19. A Merarite, son of Jehalelel, in Hezekiah's reign, who helped cleanse the temple (2 Chron. 29:12).
20. The high priest in Hezekiah's reign (2 Chron. 31:10, 13).
21. Ancestor of Zadok and Ezra (Ezra 7:3).
22. A person who repaired part of the wall of Jerusalem (Neh. 3:23–24).
23. One of the leaders who went up from Babylon with Zerubbabel (Neh. 7:7).
24. One of the Levites who helped Ezra in instructing the people about the Law (Neh. 8:7).
25. A prince of Judah (Neh. 12:33).
26. One of the priests who sealed the covenant with Nehemiah (Neh. 10:2).
27. One who accused Jeremiah of being a false prophet (Jer. 43:2).
28. The original name of Abednego (Dan. 1:6–7, 11, 19). See Abednego.

Azaz *[strong one]*

A descendant of Reuben (1 Chron. 5:8).

Azaziah *[strength of the Lord]*

1. A Levite musician in David's reign appointed to play the harp as the ark of the covenant was brought up from the house of Obed-edom (1 Chron. 15:21).
2. The father of Hoshea, prince of the tribe of Ephraim when David numbered the people (1 Chron. 27:20).
3. One of the Levites in Hezekiah's reign who was in charge of the tithes (2 Chron. 31:13).

Azbuk

Father of a man named Nehemiah (Neh. 3:16).

Azel

A descendant of Saul (1 Chron. 8:37–38).

Azgad *[a strong army; a gang of robbers]*

1. A person whose descendants returned from the exile with Zerubbabel (Ezra 2:12).
2. A person who came back to Jerusalem with Ezra (Ezra 8:12).
3. A person who sealed the new covenant with God after the exile (Neh. 10:15).

Aziel

See Jaaziel.

Aziza

A person who married a foreign wife during the exile (Ezra 10:27).

Azmaveth *[strong death; a he-goat]*

1. One of David's mighty men (2 Sam. 23:31; 1 Chron. 11:33).
2. A descendant of Saul (1 Chron. 8:36; 9:42).
3. The father of Jeziel and Pelet, two of the skilled Benjamite slingers and archers who joined David at Ziklag (1 Chron. 10:3).
4. Overseer of the royal treasures during David's reign (1 Chron. 27:25).

Azor *[a helper; a court]*

An ancestor of Jesus Christ (Matt. 1:13–14).

Azriel *[help of God]*

1. A chief of the tribe of Manasseh (1 Chron. 5:24).
2. Father of a ruler of Naphtali in David's reign (1 Chron. 27:19).

3. The father of Seraiah, one of Jehoiakim's officers (Jer. 36:26).

Azrikam *[help, revenging]*
1. A descendant of Zerubbabel and son of Neariah of the royal line of Judah (1 Chron. 3:23).
2. Eldest son of Azel and descendant of Saul (1 Chron. 8:38; 9:44).
3. A Levite, ancestor of Shemaiah, who lived in the time of Nehemiah (1 Chron. 9:14; Neh. 11:15).
4. Governor of Ahaz's house (2 Chron. 28:7).

Azubah *[forsaken]*
1. Wife of Caleb, son of Hezron (1 Chron. 2:18–19).
2. Mother of King Jehoshaphat (1 Kings 22:42; 2 Chron. 20:31).

Azur *[he that assists or is assisted]*
1. Father of the false prophet Hananiah (Jer. 28:1). See also Azzur.
2. Father of a prince whom Ezekiel saw in a vision (Ezek. 11:1).

Azzan *[their strength]*
Father of a chief of Issachar (Num. 34:26).

Azzur *[same as Azur]*
A person who sealed the covenant with Nehemiah (Neh. 10:17).
See also Azur.

Baal *[master; lord]*
1. A descendant of Reuben (1 Chron. 5:5).
2. The fourth son of Jehiel, and grandfather of Saul (1 Chron. 8:30; 9:36).

Baal-hanan
1. The seventh of the kings of Edom (Gen. 36:38–39).
2. One who looked after olive and sycamore trees in David's time (1 Chron. 40:14).

Baalis *[a rejoicing; a proud lord]*
King of the Ammonites at the time of Nebuchadnezzar's destruction of Jerusalem (Jer. 40:14).

Baana (Baanah) *[in the answer; in affliction]*
1. One of Solomon's royal merchants (1 Kings 4:12).
2. Another of Solomon's merchants, responsible for Asher (1 Kings 4:16).
3. Father of Zadok, who assisted in rebuilding the wall of Jerusalem under Nehemiah (Neh. 3:4).
4. Father of one of David's mighty men (2 Sam. 23:29).
5. A captain in Ish-bosheth's army (2 Sam. 4:2).
6. One who returned from the exile with Zerubbabel (Ezra 2:2).

Baara *[a flame; purging]*
One of the wives of Shaharaim, a descendant of Benjamin (1 Chron. 8:8).

Baaseiah *[in making; in pressing together]*
An ancestor of Asaph the singer (1 Chron. 6:40).

Baasha *[he that seeks or lays waste]*
Israel's third king (1 Kings 15:16–16:13).

Bakbakkar
A Levite who returned from the Babylonian captivity (1 Chron. 9:15).

Bakbuk
A person whose descendants returned from captivity (Ezra 2:51; Neh. 7:53).

Bakbukiah
A Levite in the time of Nehemiah (Neh. 11:17; 12:9).

Balaam *[the ancient of the people; the destruction of the people]*
A prophet who was asked to curse Israel but instead blessed Israel (Num. 22:5).

Balac
Greek form of Balak. See Balak.

Baladan *[one without judgment]*
Father of the king of Babylon in Hezekiah's reign (2 Kings 20:12).

Balak (Balac) *[who lays waste or destroys]*
The king of Moab who asked Balaam to curse the Israelites (Num. 22:24).

Bani

1. A Gadite, one of David's mighty men (2 Sam. 23:36).
2. A Levite and descendant of Merari (1 Chron. 6:46).
3. A descendant of Pharez (1 Chron. 9:4).
4. Father of a family who returned from captivity with Zerubbabel (Ezra 2:10).
5. One whose descendants had taken foreign wives during the exile (Ezra 10:34).
6. One who had taken a foreign wife during the exile (Ezra 10:38).
7. A Levite who helped to repair Jerusalem's wall (Neh. 3:17).
8. A Levite who helped in the devotions of the people (Neh. 9:4; 10:13).
9. A person who sealed the new covenant with God after the exile (Neh. 10:14).
10. A Levite whose son was an overseer of the Levites after the exile (Neh. 11:22).

Barabbas *[son of shame, confusion]*

A criminal in Jerusalem who was in prison during Jesus' trial and was released by Pilate (Mark 15:7; Luke 28:18; John 18:40).

Barachel *[that bows before God]*

Father of Elihu (Job 32:2, 6).

Barachiah (Berechiah)

Father of Zechariah the prophet (Zech. 1:1).

Barachias (Berechiah) *[same as Barachel]*

Father of the prophet whom the Jews killed (Matt. 23:35).

Barak *[thunder or in vain]*

Judge Deborah's general (Judg. 4:6–5:15).

Bariah

A descendant of David (1 Chron. 3:22).

Bar-jesus *[son of Jesus or Joshua]*

See Elymas.

Bar-jona *[son of Jona; of a dove]*

See Jona 1.

Barkos

An ancestor of captives returning from the exile (Ezra 2:53; Neh. 7:55).

Barnabas *[son of the prophet or of consolation]*

A Jewish Christian who traveled with Paul (Acts 4:36; 11:22–30), originally called Joses, but called Barnabas by the apostles.

Barsabas *[son of return; son of rest]*

See Joseph 11.

Bartholomew *[a son that suspends the waters]*

One of the twelve apostles of Christ (Matt. 10:3; Mark 3:18; Luke 6:14; Acts 1:13).

Bartimaeus *[son of the honorable]*

A blind beggar from Jericho whom Jesus healed on his last journey to Jerusalem (Mark 10:46).

Baruch *[who is blessed]*

1. Jeremiah's friend and scribe (Jer. 32:12–13).
2. The son of Zabbai, who assisted Nehemiah in rebuilding the wall of Jerusalem (Neh. 3:20).
3. A descendant of Perez who returned from the exile (Neh. 11:5).

Barzillai *[son of contempt; made of iron]*

1. A wealthy Gileadite who showed hospitality to David when he fled from Absalom (2 Sam. 17:27).
2. A Meholathite whose son Adriel married Michal, Saul's daughter (2 Sam. 21:8).
3. Son-in-law of Barzillai the Gileadite (Ezra 2:61; Neh. 7:63–64).

Bashemath (Basmath) *[perfumed; confusion of death; in desolation]*

1. A daughter of Solomon (1 Kings 4:15).
2. One of Esau's wives (Gen. 26:34).
3. Another wife of Esau whom he married to appease his father (Gen. 36:3–4, 13).

Bathsheba (Bathshua) *[the seventh daughter; the daughter of satiety]*
Wife of Uriah the Hittite who married King David and became Solomon's mother, and ancestor of Jesus Christ (2 Sam. 11:3; 12:24; 1 Kings 1:11–2:19; Matt. 1:6); called Bathshua in 1 Chronicles 3:5.

Bathshua *[same as Bathsheba]*
1. Another name for Bathsheba. See Bathsheba.
2. The wife of Judah (Gen. 38:2).

Bavai
Son of Henadad, ruler of the district of Keilah in the time of Nehemiah (Neh. 3:18).

Bazlith (Bazluth)
A person whose descendants returned from the exile with Zerubbabel (Neh. 7:54).

Bealiah *[the god of an idol; in an assembly]*
A Benjamite who went to David at Ziklag (1 Chron. 12:5).

Bebai *[void, empty]*
1. An ancestor of captives who returned from Babylon with Zerubbabel (Ezra 2:11; Neh. 7:16).
2. An ancestor of some returning from the exile with Ezra (Ezra 8:11).
3. One who sealed a new covenant with God after the exile (Neh. 10:15).

Becher *[first begotten; firstfruits]*
A son of Ben-hadad I, the king of Syria (Num. 26:35); maybe the same as Bered in 1 Chron. 7:20.

Bechorath *[firstfruits]*
Ancestor of Saul (1 Sam. 9:1).

Bedad *[alone; solitary]*
The father of Hadad, fourth king of Edom (Gen. 36:35; 1 Chron. 1:46).

Bedan *[according to judgment]*
1. Mentioned in 1 Samuel 12:11 as a judge of Israel between Jerubbaal (Gideon) and Jephthah.
2. The son of Gilead, and descendant of Manasseh (1 Chron. 7:17).

Bedeiah (Bedaiah) *[the only Lord]*
One of the sons of Bani, in the time of Ezra, who had taken a foreign wife (Ezra 10:35).

Beeliada (Eliada) *[an open idol]*
One of David's sons, born in Jerusalem (1 Chron. 14:7); called Eliada in 2 Sam. 5:16.

Beera (Beerah) *[a well; declaring]*
1. Son of Zophah, of the tribe of Asher (1 Chron. 7:37).
2. A prince of Reuben who was taken captive to Assyria (1 Chron. 5:7).

Beeri *[my well]*
1. The father of Judith, one of the wives of Esau (Gen. 26:34).
2. Father of the prophet Hosea (Hos. 1:1).

Bela (Belah) *[destroying]*
1. A king of Edom (Gen. 36:31–33; 1 Chron. 1:43–44).
2. Eldest son of Benjamin (Gen. 46:21).
3. Son of Ahaz, a Reubenite (1 Chron. 5:8).

Belshazzar *[master of the treasure]*
The last king of Babylon who saw the miraculous appearance of the handwriting on the wall, just before his death (Daniel 5).

Belteshazzar *[who lays up treasures in secret]*
Name given to Daniel in Babylon (Dan. 1:7).

Ben *[a son]*
A Levite, one of the porters appointed by David for the ark of the covenant (1 Chron. 15:18).

Benaiah *[son of the Lord]*
1. The son of Jehoiada the chief priest whom David made the third leader of his army (1 Kings 1:8–2:46).
2. One of David's thirty mighty men (2 Sam. 23:30).
3. Head of a family of the tribe of Simeon (1 Chron. 4:36).
4. A Levite in the time of David (1 Chron. 15:18, 20; 16:5).

5. Father of one of David's counselors (1 Chron. 27:34).
6. The grandfather of Jahaziel (2 Chron. 20:14).
7. An overseer of the temple during Hezekiah's reign (2 Chron. 31:13).
8. 9. 10. 11. Four men who married foreign wives during the exile (Ezra 10:25, 30, 35, 43).
12. The father of Pelatiah, a prince of Judah (Ezek. 11:1, 13).

Ben-ammi *[son of my people]*
The son of the younger daughter of Lot, and ancestor of the Ammonites (Gen. 19:38).

Ben-hadad *[son of Hadad, or noise]*
The name of three kings of Damascus.
1. Ben-hadad I, supreme in Syria; made an alliance with Asa and conquered a large part of the north of Israel (1 Kings 15:18).
2. Ben-hadad II, son of Ben-hadad I, also king of Damascus; laid siege to Samaria (1 Kings 20; 2 Kings 6:24; 8:7, 9).
3. Ben-hadad III, son of Hazael, who presided over the disintegration of the Syrian empire (2 Kings 13:3, 24–25).

Ben-hail *[son of strength]*
One of the princes whom King Jehoshaphat sent to teach the Law in the cities of Judah (2 Chron. 17:7).

Ben-hanan *[son of grace]*
A prince of Judah under Jehoshaphat (1 Chron. 4:20).

Beninu
A Levite who sealed the covenant with Nehemiah (Neh. 10:13–14).

Benjamin *[son of the right hand]*
1. The youngest of the children of Jacob (Gen. 35:18, 24).
2. A descendant of Benjamin (1 Chron. 7:10).
3. A descendant of Harim (Ezra 10:32).
4. Someone who helped rebuild the wall of Jerusalem (Neh. 3:23).
5. Someone who helped to dedicate the wall of Jerusalem (Neh. 12:34).

Beno *[his son]*
A descendant of Merari (1 Chron. 24:26–27).

Benoni *[son of my sorrow, or pain]*
Name given to Rachel's child as she died giving birth to him (Gen. 35:18).

Ben-zoheth *[son of separation]*
A descendant of Judah (1 Chron. 4:20).

Beor (Bosor) *[burning; foolish; mad]*
1. The father of Bela, one of the early Edomite kings (Gen. 36:32; 1 Chron. 1:43).
2. Father of Balaam (Num. 22:5; 24:3, 15; 31:8).

Bera *[a well; declaring]*
A king of Sodom (Gen. 14:2).

Berachah *[blessing; bending the knee]*
A Benjamite who linked up with David at Ziklag (1 Chron. 12:3).

Berachiah *[speaking well of the Lord]*
See Berechiah 2.

Beraiah *[the choosing of the Lord]*
1. A son of Asher (Gen. 46:17).
2. A son of Ephraim (1 Chron. 7:23).
3. A descendant of Benjamin (1 Chron. 8:13).
4. A descendant of Levi (1 Chron. 23:10–11).

Berechiah
1. A descendant of Jehoiakim (1 Chron. 3:20).
2. Father of Asaph, the leading singer (1 Chron. 6:39).
3. Father of Meshullam, who assisted in rebuilding the wall of Jerusalem (Neh. 3:4, 30; 6:18).
4. A Levite who lived close to Jerusalem (1 Chron. 9:16).
5. A doorkeeper for the ark of the covenant (1 Chron. 15:23).
6. One of the tribe of Ephraim in the time of Ahaz (2 Chron. 28:12).
7. Father of Zechariah (Zech. 1:1, 7).

Bered *[hail]*
A descendant of Ephraim (1 Chron. 7:20).

Beri *[my son; my corn]*
Son of Zophah, of the tribe of Asher (1 Chron. 7:36).

Beriah *[in fellowship; in envy]*
1. A son of Asher (Gen. 46:17; Num. 26:44–45).
2. A son of Ephraim (1 Chron. 7:20–23).
3. A Benjamite (1 Chron. 8:13, 16).
4. A Levite (1 Chron. 23:10–11).

Bernice *[one that brings victory]*
The eldest daughter of Herod Agrippa I (Acts 12:1).

Berodach-baladan *[the son of death]*
Possibly another form of Merodach-baladan (2 Kings 20:12). See Merodach-baladan.

Besai *[a despising; dirty]*
A person who went to Jerusalem with Zerubbabel (Ezra 2:49; Neh. 7:52).

Besodeiah *[counsel of the Lord]*
Father of one of the repairers of the wall of Jerusalem (Neh. 3:6).

Beth-rapha *[house of health]*
A descendant of Judah through Caleb (1 Chron. 4:12).

Bethuel *[filiation of God]*
The son of Nahor by Milcah; nephew of Abraham, and father of Rebekah (Gen. 22:22–23; 24:15, 24, 47; 28:2).

Bezai *[eggs]*
1. An ancestor of captives returning from the exile (Ezra 2:17; Neh. 7:23).
2. A person who sealed the new covenant with God after the Exile (Neh. 10:18).

Bezaleel *[in the shadow of God]*
1. The son of Uri, the son of Hur, of the tribe of Judah and one of the architects of the tabernacle (Exod. 31:1–6).
2. One of the sons of Pahath-moab who had taken a foreign wife (Ezra 10:30).

Bezer *[vine branches]*
Son of Zophah, one of the heads of the houses of Asher (1 Chron. 7:37).

Bichri *[first-born; firstfruits]*
An ancestor of Sheba (2 Sam. 20:1).

Bidkar *[in compunction, or sharp pain]*
Jehu's captain who executed Jehoram, son of Ahab (2 Kings 9:25).

Bigtha
One of the seven eunuchs of King Ahasuerus's harem (Esther 1:10).

Bigthan (Bigthana) *[in the press; giving meat]*
A eunuch who conspired with Teresh against King Ahasuerus (Esther 2:21).

Bigvai *[in my body]*
1. A leader who returned to Jerusalem with Zerubbabel (Ezra 2:2).
2. An ancestor of some of the people who returned to Jerusalem after the exile (Ezra 2:14; Neh. 7:19).
3. A descendant of a captive who returned to Jerusalem with Ezra (Ezra 8:14).
4. A family who sealed the new covenant with God after the exile (Neh. 10:16).

Bildad *[old friendship]*
The second of Job's three friends (Job 2:11).

Bilgah *[ancient countenance]*
1. A priest in the time of David, in the temple service (1 Chron. 24:14).
2. A priest who returned from Babylon with Zerubbabel (Neh. 12:5, 18).

Bilgai
One who sealed the new covenant with God after the exile (Neh. 10:16); possibly the same person as Bilgah 2.

Bilhah *[who is old or confused]*
The maidservant of Rachel (Gen. 29:29) and concubine of Jacob, to whom she

bore Dan and Naphtali (Gen. 30:3–8; 35:25; 46:25; 1 Chron. 7:13).

Bilhan *[who is old or confused]*
1. A Horite chief living in Mount Seir (Gen. 36:27; 1 Chron. 1:42).
2. A Benjamite, son of Jediael (1 Chron. 7:10).

Bilshan *[in the tongue]*
One of Zerubbabel's companions on his expedition from Babylon (Ezra 2:2; Neh. 7:7)

Bimhal
One of the sons of Japhlet in the line of Asher (1 Chron. 7:33).

Binea *[son of the Lord]*
One of the descendants of Saul (1 Chron. 8:37; 7:43).

Binnui *[building]*
1. A Levite, father of Noadiah (Ezra 8:33).
2. One who had taken a foreign wife during the exile (Ezra 10:30).
3. Another Israelite who had also taken a foreign wife (Ezra 10:38).
4. A Levite, son of Henadad, who helped to repair the wall of Jerusalem under Nehemiah (Neh. 3:24; 10:9).
5. A Levite who returned to Jerusalem with Zerubbabel (Neh. 12:8).

Birsha *[an evil; a son who beholds]*
A king of Gomorrah (Gen. 14:2).

Birzavith
A descendant of Asher (1 Chron. 7:31).

Bithiah *[daughter of the Lord]*
Daughter of a Pharaoh, and wife of Mered (1 Chron. 4:18).

Biztha
The second of the seven eunuchs in King Ahasuerus's harem (Esther 1:10).

Blastus *[that buds or brings forth]*
Herod Agrippa I's personal servant (Acts 12:20).

Boanerges *[son of thunder]*
A name meaning sons of thunder, given by Jesus to the two sons of Zebedee, James and John (Mark 3:17).

Boaz *[in strength]*
A wealthy Bethlehemite relative of Elimelech, the husband of Naomi, who married Ruth and redeemed the estates of her deceased husband Mahlon (Ruth 4:1).

Bocheru *[the firstborn]*
A descendant of King Saul (1 Chron. 8:38).

Bohan *[in them]*
A Reubenite (Josh. 15:6; 18:17).

Booz *[in strength]*
Greek form of Boaz. See Boaz.

Bosor
Greek form of Beor. See Beor.

Bukki *[void]*
1. Son of Abishua and father of Uzzi; an ancestor of Ezra and descendant of Aaron (Ezra 7:4; 1 Chron. 6:5, 51).
2. Son of Jogli, prince of the tribe of Dan (Num. 34:22).

Bukkiah *[the dissipation of the Lord]*
A Kohathite Levite, of the sons of Heman, one of the temple musicians (1 Chron. 25:4, 13).

Bunah *[building; understanding]*
A son of Jerahmeel, of the family of Pharez in Judah (1 Chron. 2:25).

Bunni *[building me]*
1. An ancestor of Shemaiah the Levite (Neh. 11:15).
2. A Levite who helped Ezra teach the Law (Neh. 9:4).
3. One who sealed the new covenant with God after the exile (Neh. 10:15).

Buz *[despised; plundered]*
1. The second son of Milcah and Nahor, and brother of Abraham (Gen. 22:21).
2. A descendant of Gad (1 Chron. 5:14).

Buzi *[my contempt]*
Father of Ezekiel the prophet (Ezek. 1:3).

Caesar
In the New Testament Caesar always refers to the Roman emperor, the sovereign of Judea (John 19:12, 15; Acts 17:7).

Caiaphas *[he that seeks with diligence; one that vomits]*
The Jewish high priest who took a leading role in the trial of Jesus (Matt. 26.3, 57; John 11:49; 18:13–14, 24, 28; Acts 4:6).

Cain *[possession, or possessed]*
The eldest son of Adam and Eve who killed his brother, Abel (Gen. 4:1–25).

Cainan (Kenan) *[possessor; purchaser]*
1. Son of Enos and ancestor of Jesus (Gen. 5:9; Luke 3:37).
2. Son of Arphaxad and ancestor of Jesus (Luke 3:36). His name does not occur in the Hebrew text of Genesis 10:24; 11:12, only in the Septuagint text. This adds weight to the argument that the early lists in Genesis were not always meant to be complete lists.

Calcol *[nourishing]*
A descendant of Judah (1 Chron. 2:6).

Caleb (Chelubai) *[a dog; a crow; a basket]*
1. Son of Jephunneh, one of the twelve spies sent by Moses to Canaan (Num. 13:6).
2. A son of Hezron and grandfather of Caleb 1 (1 Chron. 2:18–19, 42).
3. A son of Hur (1 Chron. 2:50).

Canaan *[merchant; trader; one that humbles and subdues]*
The fourth son of Ham and grandson of Noah (Gen. 10:6; 1 Chron. 1:8).

Candace *[who possesses contrition]*
A dynastic title of the queen of Ethiopia (Acts 8:27).

Caphtorim
The personification of Crete, a son of Mizrain (Gen. 10:14; 1 Chron. 1:12).

Carcas *[the covering of a lamb]*
The seventh of the seven eunuchs in King Ahasuerus's harem (Esther 1:10).

Careah *[bald; ice]*
See Kareah.

Carmi *[my vineyard; lamb of the waters]*
1. The fourth son of Reuben (Gen. 46:9; Exod. 6:14; 1 Chron. 5:3).
2. A man of the tribe of Judah, father of Achan (Josh. 7:1, 18; 1 Chron. 2:7).
3. Another son of Judah (1 Chron. 4:1), sometimes identified as Carmi 2.

Carpus *[fruit; fruitful]*
A Christian at Troas (2 Tim. 4:13).

Carshena *[a lamb; sleeping]*
One of the seven princes of Persia and Media, during Ahasuerus's reign (Esther 1:14).

Casluhim *[hopes of life]*
Son of Mizraim (Gen. 10:14; 1 Chron. 1:12).

Cephas *[a rock or stone]*
See Peter.

Chalcol *[who nourishes, consumes, and sustains the whole]*
A wise man with whom Solomon was compared (1 Kings 4:31).

Chedorlaomer *[roundness of a sheaf]*
A king of Elam, in the time of Abraham, who fought against the kings of Sodom, Gomorrah, Admah, Zeboim, and Zoar (Gen. 14:17).

Chelal *[as night]*
A man who took a foreign wife during the exile (Ezra 10:30).

Chelluh *[all]*
A man who took a foreign wife during the exile (Ezra 10:35).

Chelub *[a basket]*
1. A descendant of Judah (1 Chron. 4:11).

2. Father of Ezri (1 Chron. 27:26).

Chenaanah *[broken in pieces]*
1. Son of Bilhan (1 Chron. 7:10).
2. Father of the false prophet Zedekiah (1 Kings 22:11, 24; 2 Chron. 18:10, 23).

Chenani *[my pillar]*
A Levite in Ezra's time (Neh. 9:4).

Chenaniah *[preparation, or disposition, or strength, of the Lord]*
1. Leader of the Levites when David carried the ark of the covenant to Jerusalem (1 Chron. 15:22).
2. One of David's commanders (1 Chron. 26:29).

See also Conaniah.

Cheran *[anger]*
One of the sons of Dishon the Horite (Gen. 36:26; 1 Chron. 1:41).

Chesed *[as a devil, or a destroyer]*
Fourth son of Nahor (Gen. 22:22).

Chileab *[totality; the perfection of the father]*
A son of David by Abigail (2 Sam. 3:3), possibly also called Daniel in 1 Chron. 3:1.

Chilion *[finished; complete; perfect]*
The son of Naomi and husband of Orpah (Ruth 1:2–5; 4:9).

Chimham *[as they; like to them]*
A friend and supporter of David (2 Sam. 19:37–38, 40).

Chislon *[hope, trust]*
Father of Elidad, the prince of the tribe of Benjamin (Num. 34:21).

Chloe *[green herb]*
A woman who knew about the problems at Corinth (1 Cor. 1:11).

Christ *[anointed]*
See Jesus Christ.

Chushan-rishathaim *[blackness of iniquities]*
The king of Mesopotamia who oppressed Israel for eight years (Judg. 3:8, 10).

Chuza *[the seer or prophet]*
Manager of the household of Herod Antipas who helped Jesus and the apostles (Luke 8:3).

Cis
Greek form of Kish. See Kish.

Claudia *[lame]*
A Christian woman who sent greetings to Timothy (2 Tim. 4:21).

Claudius Caesar
The fourth Roman emperor, who banished Jews from Rome (Acts 18:2).

Claudius Lysias
A Roman officer in Jerusalem (Acts 23:26).

Clement *[mild; good; merciful]*
A fellow worker with Paul at Philippi (Phil. 4:3).

Cleopas
One of the two disciples going to Emmaus on the day of the resurrection (Luke 24:18).

Cleophas *[the whole glory]*
The husband of Mary, the sister of Mary the mother of Jesus (John 19:25).

Col-hozeh *[every prophet]*
1. Father of Shallum, who helped rebuild the wall of Jerusalem (Neh. 3:15).
2. A man from the tribe of Judah in the time of Nehemiah (Neh. 3:15; 11:5).

Conaniah (Cononiah)
1. A Levite appointed as overseer of the tithes in the temple (2 Chron. 31:12–13).
2. One of the chiefs of the Levites in the time of Josiah (2 Chron. 35:9).

See also Chenaniah.

Coniah *[strength of the Lord]*
See Jehoiachin.

Cononiah
See Conaniah.

Core
Greek form of Korah. See Korah.

Cornelius *[of a horn]*
A Roman centurion in the Italian cohort stationed in Caesarea who was converted to Christ (Acts 10:1).

Cosam *[divining]*
Ancestor of Jesus Christ (Luke 3:28).

Coz *[a thorn]*
A descendant of Judah (1 Chron. 4:8).

Cozbi *[a liar; sliding away]*
Daughter of Zur, a chief of the Midianites (Num. 25:6–18).

Crescens *[growing; increasing]*
An assistant with Paul at Rome (2 Tim. 4:10).

Crispus *[curled]*
Ruler of the Jewish synagogue at Corinth (Acts 18:8) who was converted to Christ and baptized with his family by Paul (1 Cor. 1:14).

Cush *[Ethiopians; blackness]*
1. Eldest son of Ham (Gen. 10:6–8).
2. A descendant of Benjamin who opposed David (Psalm 7, title).

Cushi *[Ethiopians; blackness]*
1. Father of Zephaniah (Zeph. 1:1).
2. Great-grandfather of Jehudi (Jer. 36:14).
3. The messenger who told David about the defeat of Absalom (2 Sam. 18:21–25, 31–32).

Cyrenius (Quirinius) *[who governs]*
The Greek form of the Roman name of Quirinius. His full name was Publius Sulpicius Quirinius. He was governor of Syria when Jesus was born (Luke 2:2).

Cyrus *[as miserable; as heir]*
The founder of the Persian empire who allowed the Jews to return to Jerusalem after their exile (2 Chron. 36:22–23; Ezra 1:1–4; 3:7; 4:3; 5:13, 17; 6:3).

Dalaiah *[the poor of the Lord]*
A descendant of the royal family of Judah (1 Chron. 3:24).

Dalphon *[the house of caves]*
The second of the ten sons of Hamam (Esther 9:7).

Damaris *[a little woman]*
An Athenian woman converted to Christ through Paul's preaching (Acts 17:34).

Dan *[judgment; he that judges]*
The fifth son of Jacob and ancestor of one of the tribes of Israel (Gen. 30:6).

Daniel *[judgment of God; God my judge]*
1. The second son of David, by Abigail the Carmelitess (1 Chron. 3:1). See Chileab.
2. A prophet during the reigns of Nebuchadnezzar and Cyrus, noted for his faith and courage (Dan. 2; 6:1–2).
3. A descendant of Ithamar, who returned with Ezra (Ezra 8:2).

Dara
A son of Zerah (1 Chron. 2:6). Possibly the same as Darda. See Darda.

Darda *[home of knowledge]*
Wise man to whom Solomon was compared (1 Kings 4:31). See also Dara.

Darius *[he that informs himself]*
1. A king in Cyrus's control; also known as Darius the Mede (Dan. 5:30–6:28).
2. The fourth king of Persia (Ezra 4:5).
3. Darius II who ruled Persia and Babylon (Neh. 12:22).

Darkon *[of generation; of possession]*
A servant of Solomon whose descendants returned from Babylon with Zerubbabel (Ezra 2:56; Neh. 7:58).

Dathan *[laws or rites]*
A Reubenite chieftain, son of Eliab, who joined the conspiracy of Korah the Levite (Num. 16:1; 26:9; 11:6; Ps. 106:17).

David *[well-beloved, dear]*
Israel's greatest king, and ancestor of Jesus Christ (1 Sam. 16–1 Kings 2:11; Matt. 1:6).

Deborah *[word; thing; a bee]*
1. Rebekah's nurse (Gen. 35:8).
2. A prophetess who judged Israel (Judges 4–5).

Dedan *[their breasts; friendship; a judge]*
1. The name of a son of Raamah, son of Cush (Gen. 10:7; 1 Chron. 1:9).
2. A son of Jokshan, son of Keturah (Gen. 25:3; 1 Chron. 1:32).

Dekar *[force]*
One of Solomon's chief officials (1 Kings 4:9).

Delaiah *[the poor of the Lord]*
1. A priest during David's reign (1 Chron. 24:18).
2. A priest who urged Jehoiakim not to destroy Jeremiah's scroll (Jer. 36:12, 25).
3. Ancestor of a post-exilic family who lost its genealogy (Ezra 2:60; Neh. 7:62).
4. Father of Shemaiah (Neh. 6:10).

Delilah *[poor; small; head of hair]*
The Philistine woman who was used to find out the source of Samson's strength (Judges 16).

Demas *[popular]*
A companion of Paul during his first imprisonment at Rome who later deserted the apostle (Phil. 1:24; Col. 4:14).

Demetrius *[belonging to corn, or to Ceres]*
1. A silversmith who made models of Artemis at Ephesus and who led the opposition against Paul (Acts 19:24–41).
2. A Christian disciple praised by John (3 John 12).

Deuel *[the knowledge of God]*
Father of Eliasaph, the "captain" of the tribe of Gad at the time of the numbering of the people at Sinai (Num. 1:14; 7:42, 47; 10:20). The same man is mentioned again in Numbers 2:14 but here the name appears as Ruel.

Diblaim *[cluster of figs]*
Mother of Gomer, Hosea's wife (Hosea 1:3).

Dibri *[an orator]*
A Danite, father of Shelomith (Lev. 24:11).

Didymus *[a twin; double]*
A surname of the apostle Thomas (John 11:16; 20:24; 21:2).

Diklah *[his diminishing]*
A son of Joktan (Gen. 10:27; 1 Chron. 1:21).

Dinah *[judgment; who judges]*
The daughter of Jacob by Leah (Gen. 30:21).

Dionysius *[divinely touched]*
An eminent Athenian converted to Christ by the preaching of Paul (Acts 17:34).

Diotrephes *[nourished by Jupiter]*
A person who opposed John's authority (3 John 9).

Diphath
See Riphath.

Dishan *[a threshing]*
The youngest son of Seir the Horite (Gen. 36:21, 28, 30; 1 Chron. 1:38, 42).

Dishon *[fatness; ashes]*
1. The fifth son of Seir (Gen. 36:21, 30; 1 Chron. 1:38).
2. A grandson of Seir (Gen. 36:25).

See also Dishan.

Dodai *[beloved]*
See Dodo.

Dodanim (Rodanim)
The son of Javan (Gen. 10:4; 1 Chron. 1:7).

Dodavah *[love]*
Father of Eliezer who denounced Jehoshaphat's alliance with Ahaziah (2 Chron. 20:37).

Dodo (Dodai) *[his uncle]*
1. The grandfather of Tola (Judg. 10:1).
2. One of David's thirty commanders and father of Eleazar (2 Sam. 23:9; 1 Chron. 11:12).
3. Father of Elhanan (2 Sam. 23:24).

Doeg *[careful, who acts with uneasiness]*
King Saul's servant who killed the priests of Nob (1 Sam. 21:7; 22:9–19).

Dorcas *[a doe]*
See Tabitha.

Drusilla *[watered by the dew]*
A Jewess, daughter of Herod Agrippa I who heard Paul preach (Acts 24:24–25).

Ebal *[ancient heaps]*
1. One of the sons of Shobal the son of Seir (Gen. 36:23; 1 Chron. 1:40).
2. Obal, the son of Joktan (1 Chron. 1:22).

Ebed *[a servant; laborer]*
1. A companion of Ezra as he returned to Jerusalem (Ezra 8:6).
2. Father of Gaal who rebelled against Abimelech (Judg. 9:26–35).

Ebed-melech *[the king's servant]*
An Ethiopian eunuch who rescued Jeremiah (Jer. 38:7–12).

Eber (Heber) *[one that passes; anger]*
1. Son of Salah and great-grandson of Shem (Gen. 10:24; 1 Chron. 1:19).
2. Head of a family of Gad (1 Chron. 5:13).
3. 4. Two descendants of Benjamin (1 Chron. 8:12, 22).
5. A priest in the time of Joiakim the son of Jeshua (Neh. 12:20).

Ebiasaph *[a father that gathers or adds]*
See Abiasaph.

Eden *[pleasure; delight]*
1. A descendant of Gershom (2 Chron. 29:12).
2. A Levite in the time of Hezekiah (2 Chron. 31:15).

Eder *[a flock]*
A Levite of the family of Merari in the time of David (1 Chron. 23:23; 24:30).

Edom *[red, earthy; of blood]*
The name given to Esau, the firstborn son of Isaac and twin brother of Jacob, when he sold his birthright (Gen. 25:30).

Eglah *[heifer; chariot; round]*
One of David's wives during his reign in Hebron (2 Sam. 3:5; 1 Chron. 3:3).

Eglon *[same as Eglah]*
A king of Moab who opposed Israel in the time of the judges (Judg. 3:12–17).

Ehi
See Ahiram.

Ehud *[he that praises]*
1. Son of Gera, of the tribe of Benjamin, the second judge of the Israelites (Judg. 3:15).
2. Great-grandson of Benjamin (1 Chron. 7:10; 8:6).

Eker *[barren, feeble]*
A descendant of Judah (1 Chron. 2:27).

Eladah *[the eternity of God]*
A descendant of Ephraim through Shuthelah (1 Chron. 7:20).

Elah *[an oak; a curse; perjury]*
1. One of the rulers of Edom (Gen. 36:41; 1 Chron. 1:52).
2. One of Solomon's chief officials (1 Kings 4:18).
3. The son and successor of Baasha (1 Kings 16:6–14).
4. The father of Hoshea (2 Kings 15:30).
5. A son of Caleb, the son of Jephuneh (1 Chron. 4:15).
6. A descendant of Benjamin (1 Chron. 9:8).

Elam *[a young man; a virgin; a secret]*
1. A son of Shem (Gen. 10:22; 1 Chron. 1:17).
2. A descendant of Benjamin (1 Chron. 8:24).
3. A descendant of Korah (1 Chron. 26:3).
4. A leader of the people who sealed the new covenant with God after the exile (Neh. 10:14).
5. A priest in Nehemiah's time who helped to cleanse Jerusalem (Neh. 12:42).
6. One whose descendants returned from exile (Ezra 2:7).

7. Another whose descendants returned from exile (Ezra 2:31).
8. Another whose descendants returned from exile (Ezra 8:7).
9. One of the priests who accompanied Nehemiah at the dedication of the new wall of Jerusalem (Neh. 12:42).

Elasah *[the doings of God]*
1. A priest in the time of Ezra who had married a Gentile wife (Ezra 10:22).
2. Son of Shaphan, one of the two men sent on a mission by King Zedekiah to Nebuchadnezzar at Babylon (Jer. 29:3).
3. See Eleasah.

Eldaah *[knowledge of God]*
A son of Midian (Gen. 25:4).

Eldad *[favored of God; love of God]*
One of two elders who, despite remaining in the camp, received the prophetic power of Moses (Num. 11:16, 26).

Elead *[witness of God]*
A descendant of Ephraim (1 Chron. 7:21).

Eleasah
1. Son of Helez, one of the descendants of Judah, of the family of Hezron (1 Chron. 2:39).
2. Son of Rapha or Rephaiah; a descendant of Saul through Jonathan and Merib-baal or Mephibosheth (1 Chron. 8:37; 9:43).

Eleazar *[help of God, court of God]*
1. Third son of Aaron, and successor to the high priest's office (Exod. 6:23; Num. 3:32).
2. The son of Abinadab who kept the ark of the covenant (1 Sam. 7:1).
3. One of the three principal mighty men of David's army (2 Sam. 23:9; 1 Chron. 11:12).
4. A Merarite Levite, son of Mahli and grandson of Merari (1 Chron. 23:21–22; 24:28).
5. A priest who accompanied Ezra when he returned to Jerusalem (Ezra 8:33).
6. A priest who took part in the feast of dedication under Nehemiah (Neh. 12:42).
7. One of the sons of Parosh, who had married a foreign wife (Ezra 10:25).
8. The son of Eliud, and ancestor of Jesus Christ (Matt. 1:15).

Elhanan *[grace, or gift, or mercy of God]*
1. A distinguished warrior in the time of King David who killed Lahmi, Goliath's brother (2 Sam. 21:19; 1 Chron. 20:5).
2. One of David's mighty men (2 Sam. 23:24; 1 Chron. 11:26).

Eli *[the offering or lifting up]*
High priest at Shiloh and judge of Israel (Samuel 1–4).
See also Heli.

Eliab *[God is my father; God is the father]*
1. Son of Helon and leader of the tribe of Zebulun at the time of the census in the wilderness of Sinai (Num. 1:9; 2:7; 7:24, 29; 10:16).
2. A Reubenite, father of Dathan and Abiram (Num. 16:1, 12; 26:8–9; 11:6).
3. One of David's brothers (1 Sam. 16:6; 17:13, 28; 1 Chron. 2:13).
4. An ancestor of Samuel the prophet; a Kohathite Levite, son of Nahath (1 Chron. 6:27).
5. One of David's warriors (1 Chron. 12:9).
6. A Levite musician in the time of David (1 Chron. 15:18, 20; 16:5).
7. See Eliel.

Eliada (Eliadah) *[knowledge of God]*
1. One of David's sons (2 Sam. 5:16).
2. A mighty man of war, a Benjamite, who led 200,000 men (2 Chron. 17:17).
3. Father of Rezon, who opposed Solomon (1 Kings 11:23).
4. See Beeliada.

Eliah *[God the Lord]*
See Elijah.

Eliahba *[my God the Father]*
One of the thirty of David's guard (2 Sam. 23:32; 1 Chron. 11:33).

Eliakim *[resurrection of God]*
1. Son of Hilkiah, master of Hezekiah's household (2 Kings 18:18, 26, 37).
2. The original name of Jehoiakim king of Judah (2 Kings 23:34; 2 Chron. 36:4).
3. A priest in the time of Nehemiah, who assisted at the dedication of the new wall of Jerusalem (Neh. 12:41).
4. Ancestor of Jesus Christ (Matt. 1:13).

Eliam *[the people of God]*
1. Father of Bath-sheba, the wife of David (2 Sam. 11:3).
2. One of David's thirty warriors (2 Sam. 23:34).

Elias *[God the Lord, the strong Lord]*
The Greek form of Elijah. See Elijah.

Eliasaph *[the Lord increases]*
1. Head of the tribe of Dan at the time of the census in the wilderness of Sinai (Num. 1:14; 2:14; 7:42, 47; 10:20).
2. A prince of Gershon (Num. 3:24).

Eliashib *[the God of conversion]*
1. A priest in the time of King David (1 Chron. 24:12).
2. A descendant of David (1 Chron. 3:24).
3. High priest at Jerusalem at the time of the rebuilding of the walls under Nehemiah (Neh. 3:1, 20–21).
4. A singer in the time of Ezra who had married a foreign wife (Ezra 10:24).
5. A son of Zattu who in the time of Ezra had married a foreign wife (Ezra 10:27).
6. A son of Bani who in the time of Ezra had married a foreign wife (Ezra 10:36).
7. Someone who helped Ezra resolve the problem with foreign wives (Ezra 10:6), possibly the same person as 3.

Eliathah *[thou art my God]*
A musician in the temple in the time of King David (1 Chron. 25:4, 27).

Elidad *[beloved of God]*
The man chosen to represent the tribe of Benjamin in the division of the land of Canaan (Num. 34:21).

Eliel *[God, my God]*
1. One of the heads of the tribe of Manasseh on the east of Jordan (1 Chron. 5:24).
2. A forefather of Samuel the prophet (1 Chron. 6:34).
3. A descendant of Benjamin (1 Chron. 8:20).
4. Another descendant of Benjamin (1 Chron. 8:22).
5. A captain of David's guard (1 Chron. 11:46).
6. Another of the same guard (1 Chron. 11:47).
7. One of the Gadite heroes who came to David when he was in the wilderness of Judah hiding from Saul (1 Chron. 12:11).
8. A chief of Judah (1 Chron. 15:9).
9. A Kohathite Levite who helped to move the ark of the covenant from the house of Obed-edom to Jerusalem (1 Chron. 15:11).
10. A Levite in the time of Hezekiah; one of the overseers of the offerings made in the temple (2 Chron. 31:13).
11. See Eliab.

Elienai *[the God of my eyes]*
A descendant of Benjamin (1 Chron. 8:20).

Eliezer *[help, or court, of my God]*
1. Abraham's chief servant (Gen. 15:2).
2. Second son of Moses and Zipporah.
3. A descendant of Benjamin (1 Chron. 7:8).
4. A priest in the reign of David (1 Chron. 15:24).
5. Son of Zichri, ruler of the Reubenites in David's reign (1 Chron. 27:16).
6. Son of Dodavah, of Mareshah in Judah; a prophet who rebuked Je-

hoshaphat for joining Ahaziah king of Israel (2 Chron. 20:37).
7. A leading Israelite who persuaded others to return to Jerusalem (Ezra 8:16).
8. 9. 10. Three men who married foreign wives during the exile (Ezra 10:18, 23, 31).
11. Son of Jorim, and an ancestor of Jesus Christ (Luke 3:29).

Elihoenai
Son of Zerahiah who with two hundred men returned from the captivity with Ezra (Ezra 8:4). See also Elioenai.

Elihoreph *[god of winter, or of youth]*
One of Solomon's scribes (1 Kings 4:3).

Elihu *[he is my God himself]*
1. The youngest of Job's so-called comforters (Job 32:2, 4–6).
2. A person who joined David at Ziklag (1 Chron. 12:20).
3. A Korhite Levite in the time of David (1 Chron. 26:7).
4. See Eliab 3.
5. See Eliab 4.

Elijah (Eliah; Elias) *[God the Lord, the strong Lord]*
1. God's prophet who opposed idolatry and was taken up to heaven in a chariot of fire (1 Kings 17:1–2 Kings 2:11).
2. A chief of the tribe of Benjamin (1 Chron. 8:27).
3. A person who married a foreign wife during the exile (Ezra 10:26).
4. Another person who married a foreign wife during the exile (Ezra 10:21).

Elika *[pelican of God]*
A Harodite, and one of David's guards (2 Sam. 23:25).

Elimelech *[my God is king]*
Naomi's husband and father-in-law of Ruth (Ruth 1:2–3).

Elioenai *[toward him are mine eyes; or to him are my fountains]*
1. Eldest son of Neariah, the son of Shemaiah, and descendant of David (1 Chron. 3:23–24).
2. Head of a family of the Simonites (1 Chron. 4:36).
3. A chief of Benjamin (1 Chron. 7:8).
4. A priest in the days of Nehemiah (Neh. 12:41).
5. A priest in the days of Ezra who married foreign wives (Ezra 10:22).
6. An Israelite of the sons of Zattu who married a foreign wife (Ezra 10:27).
7. A doorkeeper of the temple (1 Chron. 26:3).
8. See Elihoenai.

Eliphal *[a miracle of God]*
One of David's guard (1 Chron. 11:35).

Eliphalet (Eliphelet) *[the God of deliverance]*
1. The last of David's thirteen sons (2 Sam. 5:16; 1 Chron. 14:7).
2. Another of David's sons (1 Chron. 6:3).
3. One of David's mighty men (2 Sam. 23:34).
4. A descendant of Benjamin and Saul (1 Chron. 8:39).
5. A person who returned from the exile with Ezra (Ezra 8:13).
6. A person who took a foreign wife during the exile (Ezra 10:33).

Eliphaz *[the endeavor of God]*
1. A son of Esau and Adah, and the father of Teman (Gen. 36:4; 1 Chron. 1:35–36).
2. The leader of Job's three friends (Job 2:11; 4:1; 15:1).

Elipheleh
A Levite who supervised the choral service of the temple when the ark of the covenant was returned (1 Chron. 15:18, 21).

Eliphelet
See Eliphalet.

Elisabeth (Elizabeth) *[the oath, or fullness, of God]*
The wife of Zacharias and mother of John the Baptist (Luke 1:5–57).

Eliseus
The Greek form of Elisha. See Elisha.

Elisha (Elishah; Eliseus) *[salvation of God]*
1. The disciple and successor of Elijah (1 Kings 19:16–17).
2. Eldest son of Javan and grandson of Noah (Gen. 10:4).

Elishama *[God hearing]*
1. Grandfather of Joshua (1 Chron. 7:26).
2. A son of King David (1 Sam. 5:16; 1 Chron. 3:8; 14:7).
3. Another son of David (1 Chron. 3:6), also called Elishua.
4. A descendant of Judah (1 Chron. 2:41).
5. The father of Nethaniah and grandfather of Ishmael (2 Kings 25:25; Jer. 41:1).
6. Secretary to King Jehoiakim (Jer. 36:12, 20–21).
7. A priest in the time of Jehoshaphat (2 Chron. 17:8).

Elishaphat *[my God judgeth]*
Son of Zichri; one of the captains of hundreds in the time of Jehoiada (2 Chron. 23:1).

Elisheba *[the oath, or fullness, of God]*
Aaron's wife (Exod. 6:23).

Elishua *[God is my salvation]*
See Elishama 3.

Eliud *[God is my praise]*
An ancestor of Jesus Christ (Matt. 1:15).

Elizaphan (Elzaphan)
1. A chief of the family of Kohath (Num. 3:30).
2. Prince of the tribe of Zebulun (Num. 34:25).
3. An ancestor of some of the Levites who cleansed the temple in Hezekiah's reign (Num. 1:5).

Elizur *[God is my strength; my rock; rock of God]*
A chief of the tribe of Reuben (Num. 1:5; 2:10; 7:30, 35; 10:18).

Elkanah (Elkonah) *[God the zealous; the zeal of God]*
1. Grandson of Korah (Exod. 6:24).
2. Father of Samuel (1 Sam. 1–23).
3. A descendant of Levi (1 Chron. 6:25).
4. A descendant of Levi (1 Chron. 6:26).
5. A Levite ancestor of Berechiah (1 Chron. 9:16).
6. A Korhite who joined David at Ziklag (1 Chron. 12:6).
7. A doorkeeper for the ark of the covenant (1 Chron. 15:23).
8. An officer in the household of Ahaz king of Judah (2 Chron. 28:7).

Elmodam *[the God of measure, or of the garment]*
An ancestor of Jesus Christ (Luke 3:28).

Elnaam *[God's fairness]*
The father of Jeribai and Joshaviah, two of David's guards (1 Chron. 11:46).

Elnathan *[God hath given; the gift of God]*
1. Father of Nehushta, Jehoiakim's queen (2 Kings 24:8).
2. 3. 4. Three Levites in the time of Ezra (Ezra 8:16).

Elon *[oak; grove; strong]*
1. The father of the wife of Esau (Gen. 26:34; 36:2).
2. A son of Zebulun (Gen. 46:14; Num. 26:26).
3. A judge who ruled Israel for ten years (Judg. 12:11–12).

Elpaal *[God's work]*
A descendant of Benjamin (1 Chron. 8:11).

Eluzai *[God is my strength]*
One of the warriors of Benjamin who joined David at Ziklag (1 Chron. 12:5).

Elymas *[a magician, a corrupter]*
The Arabic name for the Jewish sorcerer Bar-jesus (Acts 13:6).

Elzabad *[the dowry of God]*
1. One of the Gadite heroes who came across the Jordan to David (1 Chron. 12:12).
2. A Korhite Levite (1 Chron. 26:7).

Elzaphan *[God of the northeast wind]*
See Elizaphan.

Emmor *[an ass]*
The father of Sychem (Acts 7:16).

Enan *[cloud]*
Father of a prince of Naphtali (Num. 1:15).

Enoch *[dedicated; disciplined]*
1. The eldest son of Cain (Gen. 4:17).
2. The son of Jared, father of Methuselah, and ancestor of Jesus Christ (Gen. 5:21; Luke 3:37).

Enos (Enosh) *[mortal man; sick; despaired of; forgetful]*
The son of Seth and ancestor of Jesus Christ (Gen. 4:26; 5:6–7, 9–11; Luke 3:38).

Epaenetus (Epenetus)
A Christian at Rome to whom Paul sent his greetings (Rom. 16:5).

Epaphras *[covered with foam]*
A fellow worker with the apostle Paul who was sent to work in Colosse (Col. 1:7–8; 4:12).

Epaphroditus *[agreeable; handsome]*
A Philippian Christian who worked so hard that he became ill (Phil. 2:25; 4:18).

Ephah *[weary; tired]*
1. Concubine of Caleb (1 Chron. 2:46).
2. A descendant of Judah (1 Chron. 2:47).
3. A grandson of Abraham (Gen. 25:4).

Ephai
One whose children were left in Judah after the exile to Babylon (Jer. 40:8; 41:3).

Epher *[dust; lead]*
1. A grandson of Abraham (Gen. 25:4).
2. One of the descendants of Judah (1 Chron. 4:17).
3. One of the heads of the families of Manasseh on the east of Jordan (1 Chron. 5:24).

Ephlal *[judging; praying]*
A descendant of Pharez through Jerahmeel (1 Chron. 2:37).

Ephod
Father of Hanniel of the tribe of Manesseh (Num. 34:23).

Ephraim *[fruitful; increasing]*
The second son of Joseph by his wife Asenath, and ancestor of one of the twelve tribes of Israel (Gen. 41:52; 48:1).

Ephratah (Ephrath) *[abundance; bearing fruit]*
Second wife of Caleb the son of Hezron, mother of Hur and grandmother of Caleb the spy (1 Chron. 2:19, 50).

Ephron *[dust]*
The son of Zochar, a Hittite, from whom Abraham bought the field and cave of Machpelah (Gen. 23:8–17; 25:9; 49:29–30; 50:13).

Er *[watchman]*
1. Eldest son of Judah (Gen. 38:3–7).
2. A son of Judah (1 Chron. 4:21).
3. An ancestor of Jesus Christ (Luke 3:28).

Eran *[follower]*
The son of Ephraim's eldest son (Num. 26:36).

Erastus *[lovely, amiable]*
1. A Christian who worked with Paul and Timothy (Acts 19:22).
2. A Christian in Corinth who sent his greetings to Rome (Rom. 16:23).
3. The Christian who remained at Corinth (2 Tim. 4:20).

Some or all of the above may be the same person.

Eri *[my city]*
Son of Gad (Gen. 46:16).

Esaias
The Greek form of Isaiah. See Isaiah.

Esarhaddon (Esar-haddon) *[that closes the point; joy; cheerfulness]*
The son of Sennacherib and one of the greatest of the kings of Assyria (2 Kings 19:37).

Esau *[he that acts or finishes]*
The eldest son of Isaac and twin brother of Jacob (Gen. 25:25–34; 27; 36).

Esh-baal
See Ish-bosheth.

Eshban *[fire of the sun]*
One of the four sons of Dishon (Gen. 36:26; 1 Chron. 1:41).

Eshcol *[bunch of grapes]*
Brother of Mamre the Amorite and Aner, and one of Abraham's companions who tracked down the four kings who had carried off Lot (Gen. 14:13–24).

Eshek *[violence, force]*
A descendant of King Saul (1 Chron. 8:39).

Eshton
A descendant of Judah through Caleb (1 Chron. 4:11–12).

Esli *[near me; he who separates]*
A descendant of Jesus Christ (Luke 3:25).

Esrom *[dart of joy; division of a song]*
Greek form of Hezron. See Hezron.

Esther *[secret; hidden]*
The Persian name of Hadassah (myrtle), whom Ahasuerus, king of Persia, chose to be his queen, as recorded in the book of Esther.

Etam *[their bird, their covering]*
A name mentioned in Judah's genealogy (1 Chron. 4:3).

Ethan *[strong; the gift of the island]*
A wise man who lived during Solomon's reign (1 Kings 4:31; 1 Chron. 2:6).

Ethbaal *[toward the idol, or with Baal]*
King of Sidon and father of Jezebel (1 Kings 16:31).

Ethnan *[gift]*
One of the sons of Helah the wife of Ashur (1 Chron. 4:7).

Ethni *[strong]*
Leader of the ministry of song in the temple (1 Chron. 6:41).

Eubulus *[prudent; good counselor]*
A Christian at Rome who stayed faithful to Paul (2 Tim. 4:21).

Eunice *[good victory]*
Mother of Timothy (2 Tim. 1:5).

Euodia
See Euodias.

Euodias *[sweet scent]*
A Christian woman at Philippi (Phil. 4:2). According to the KJV translation this person is "Euodias" and thus a woman, but this is inaccurate, as the name should read "Euodia" referring to a man. The Revised Version and the New International Version use the word "Euodia" here.

Eutychus *[happy; fortunate]*
A young man in Troas (Acts 20:9) whom Paul restored to life.

Eve *[living; enlivening]*
Adam's wife, the first woman (Gen. 2:21–22; 3:20).

Evi *[unjust]*
One of the five kings of Midian killed by the Israelites (Num. 31:8; Josh. 13:21).

Evil-merodach *[the fool of Merodach; the fool grinds bitterly]*
The king of Babylon who released Jehoiachin from prison (2 Kings 25:27–30; Jer. 52:31).

Ezar
See Ezer.

Ezbai
Father of Naarai who was one of David's thirty mighty men (1 Chron. 11:37).

Ezbon *[hastening to understand]*

1. Son of Gad and founder of one of the Gadite families (Gen. 46:16; Num. 26:16).
2. A descendant of Benjamin (1 Chron. 7:7).

Ezekias

Greek form of Hezekiah. See Hezekiah.

Ezekiel *[the strength of God]*

One of the four major prophets, the son of a priest named Buzi, who was deported from Jerusalem to Babylon. The author of the Bible book bearing his name.

Ezer *[a help]*

1. A son of Seir (Gen. 36:21, 27, 30), who is also called Ezar (1 Chron. 1:38). See Abiezer; Romamti-ezer.
2. A son of Ephraim, killed by the inhabitants of Gath (1 Chron. 7:21).
3. A Levite who helped to repair the wall of Jerusalem (Neh. 3:19).
4. A priest who assisted in the dedication of the wall of Jerusalem under Nehemiah (Neh. 12:42).
5. A descendant of Judah through Caleb (1 Chron. 4:4).
6. One of the Gadite chiefs who fought with David (1 Chron. 12:8–9).

Ezra *[help; court]*

1. Leader of one of the groups of priests who returned to Jerusalem (Neh. 12:1).
2. A descendant of Judah through Caleb (1 Chron. 4:17).
3. A scribe and priest descended from Hilkiah (Ezra 7:1–12).

Ezri *[my help]*

Son of Chelub, superintendent of King David's farm laborers (1 Chron. 27:26).

Felix *[happy, prosperous]*

A Roman governor of Judea appointed by the emperor Claudius who presided over Paul's trial (Acts 23:23–27).

Festus, Porcius *[festive, joyful]*

Succeeded Felix as governor of Judea (Acts 24:27).

Fortunatus *[lucky, fortunate]*

A Corinthian Christian who supported the apostle Paul (1 Cor. 16:17).

Gaal *[contempt; abomination]*

Son of Ebed who helped the Shechemites in their rebellion against Abimelech (Judg. 9:1).

Gabbai *[the back]*

Leader of the family of Benjamin after the return from the exile (Neh. 11:8).

Gabriel *[God is my strength]*

An angel sent by God to announce to Zachariah the birth of John the Baptist, and to Mary the birth of Jesus Christ. He was also sent to Daniel to explain his visions (Dan. 8:16; 9:21).

Gad *[a band; a troop]*

Jacob's seventh son, and first son of Zilpah, Leah's maid (Gen. 30:11–13; 46:16, 18).

Gaddi *[my troop; a kid]*

The Manassite spy sent by Moses to explore Canaan (Num. 13:11).

Gaddiel *[goat of God; the Lord my happiness]*

A Zebulunite spy sent by Moses to explore Canaan (Num. 13:10).

Gadi

A Gadite, father of Menahem, a king of Israel (2 Kings 15:14, 17).

Gaham

Son of Nahor, Abraham's brother, by his concubine Reumah (Gen. 22:24).

Gahar

A family who returned from the captivity with Zerubbabel (Ezra 2:47; Neh. 7:49).

Gaius *[lord; an earthly man]*

1. A Macedonian who accompanied Paul on his travels, and whose life was in danger from the mob at Ephesus (Acts 19:29).
2. A man from Derbe who went with Paul from Corinth on his last journey to Jerusalem (Acts 20:4).

3. The Christian Paul stayed with when he wrote his letter to the Romans (Rom. 16:23).
4. A man baptized by Paul; is identified by some as being identical with 3. (1 Cor. 1:14; Rom. 16:23).
5. Christian to whom John's third letter is addressed (3 John 1).

Galal *[a roll, a wheel]*
1. A returned exile (1 Chron. 9:15).
2. A Levite who returned from exile (1 Chron. 9:16).

Gallio *[who sucks, or lives on milk]*
Roman proconsul of Achaia when Paul was on trial in Corinth (Acts 18:12).

Gamaliel *[recompense of God; camel of God]*
1. Son of Pedahzur, leader of the tribe of Manasseh at the census at Sinai (Num. 1:10; 20:20; 7:54, 59).
2. A Pharisee who persuaded the Sanhedrin to free the apostles (Acts 5:33–40).

Gamul *[a recompense]*
A chief priest (1 Chron. 24:17).

Gareb *[a scab]*
One of the heroes of David's army (2 Sam. 23:38).

Gashmu
See Geshem.

Gatam *[their lowing; their touch]*
Grandson of Esau, and an Edomite chief (Gen. 36:11; 1 Chron. 1:36).

Gazez *[a passing over]*
1. A son of Caleb (1 Chron. 2:46).
2. A grandson of Caleb (1 Chron. 2:46).

Gazzam *[the fleece of them]*
Man whose descendants returned to Jerusalem from exile with Zerubbabel (Ezra 2:48; Neh. 7:51).

Geber *[manly, strong]*
1. The father of one of Solomon's officers (1 Kings 4:13).
2. One of Solomon's governors (1 Kings 4:19).

Gedaliah *[God is my greatness]*
1. A leader in Jerusalem who imprisoned Jeremiah (Jer. 20:1–6).
2. Governor of Jerusalem after most of the people had been deported (Jer. 40:5–6).
3. A Levite musician (1 Chron. 25:3, 9).
4. A priest who married foreign wives during the exile (Ezra 10:18).
5. Grandfather of the prophet Zephaniah (Zeph. 1:1).

Gedeon
The Greek form of Gideon. See Gideon.

Gedor
1. A descendant of Judah (1 Chron. 4:4).
2. A descendant of Judah (1 Chron. 4:18).
3. An ancestor of Saul (1 Chron. 8:31).

Gehazi *[valley of sight]*
Elisha's dishonest servant (2 Kings 4:12–37).

Gemalli *[wares; a camel]*
Father of Ammiel, the Danite spy (Num. 13:12).

Gemariah *[accomplishment or perfection of the Lord]*
1. Son of Shaphan the scribe who tried to stop Jehoiakim from burning Jeremiah's prophecies (Jer. 36:10–11).
2. One of Zedekiah's ambassadors to Babylon (Jer. 29:3).

Genubath *[theft; robbery]*
Son of Hadad, and a member of the Edomite of the royal family (1 Kings 11:20).

Gera (Gerar) *[pilgrimage, combat; dispute]*
1. A son of Benjamin (Gen. 46:21).
2. A son of Bela (1 Chron. 8:3).
3. Father of the judge Ehud (Judg. 3:15).
4. Ancestor or father of Shimei (2 Sam. 16:5).

All of these may be identical.

Gershom *[a stranger here]*
1. The firstborn son of Moses and Zipporah (Exod. 2:22; 18:3).

2. See Gershon.
3. Descendant of Phinehas (Ezra 8:2).
4. Father of Jonathan, and a Levite in the time of the judges (Judg. 18:30).

Gershon (Gershom) *[his banishment; the change of pilgrimage]*
The eldest of the three sons of Levi (Gen. 46:11; Exod. 6:16); also called Gershom (1 Chron. 6:16–17).

Gesham
A descendant of Caleb (1 Chron. 2:47).

Geshem (Gashmu)
One of Nehemiah's opponents (Neh. 2:19).

Gether *[the vale of trial or searching]*
1. A descendant of Shem (1 Chron. 1:17).
2. Aram's third son (Gen. 10:23).

Geuel *[God's redemption]*
Son of Machi, the Gadite spy, sent into Canaan (Num. 13:15).

Gibbar *[strong, manly]*
One who returned to Jerusalem with Zerubbabel from Babylon (Ezra 2:20).

Gibea
A descendant of Caleb (1 Chron. 2:49).

Giddalti
One of the sons of Heman, put in charge of some of the temple's services (1 Chron. 25:4).

Giddel *[great]*
1. One whose descendants returned from the captivity with Zerubbabel (Ezra 2:47; Neh. 7:49).
2. Head of a family of Solomon's servants (Ezra 2:56; Neh. 7:58).

Gideon (Gedeon) *[he that bruises or breaks; a destroyer]*
Israel's fifth judge, who delivered the Israelites from the Midianites (Judges 6–8).

Gideoni *[same as Gideon]*
A Benjamite, father of Abidan (Num. 1:11; 2:22).

Gilalai *[a wheel]*
One of the priests at the consecration of the wall of Jerusalem (Neh. 12:36).

Gilead *[the heap or mass of testimony]*
1. Son of Machir, grandson of Manasseh (Num. 26:29–30).
2. The father of Jephthah the judge (Judg. 11:1–2).
3. A descendant of Gad (1 Chron. 5:14).

Ginath (Ginnetho) *[a garden]*
Father of Tibni (1 Kings 16:21–22).

Ginnetho (Ginnethon)
One of the priests who returned to Judea with Zerubbabel (Neh. 12:4).

Gispa *[coming hither]*
One of the overseers of the Nethinim (Neh. 11:21).

Gog *[roof; covering]*
1. A Reubenite (1 Chron. 5:4).
2. A leader (most probably to be interpreted symbolically) of Rosh, Meshech, and Tubal (Ezek. 38:2; 39:1, 11).

See also Magog.

Goliath *[passage; revolution; heap]*
1. A famous giant from Gath killed by the young David (1 Sam. 17:4–54).
2. Another giant, who may have been the son of 1 (2 Sam. 21:19).

Gomer *[to finish; complete]*
1. The eldest son of Japheth (Gen. 10:2–3).
2. The immoral wife of Hosea (Hos. 1:3).

Guni *[a garden; a covering]*
1. A son of Naphtali (Gen. 46:24; 1 Chron. 7:13), the founder of the family of the Gunites (Num. 26:48).
2. Father of Abdiel (1 Chron. 5:15).

Haahashtari *[a runner]*
Son of Ashur (1 Chron. 4:6).

Habaiah *[the hiding of the Lord]*
Ancestor of a priestly family (Ezra 2:61; Neh. 7:63).

Habakkuk *[he that embraces; a wrestler]*
One of the minor prophets who prophesied during the reigns of Jehoiakim and Josiah (Hab. 1:1; 3:1).

Habaziniah *[a hiding of the shield of the Lord]*
The grandfather of Jaazaniah (Jer. 35:3).

Hachaliah *[who waits for the Lord]*
The father of Nehemiah (Neh. 1:1).

Hachmoni (Hacmoni) *[a wise man]*
The father of Jehiel, and caregiver of some of David's sons (1 Chron. 27:32).

Hadad (Hadar) *[joy; noise; clamor]*
1. Son of Ishmael and grandson of Abraham (Gen. 25:15; 1 Chron. 1:30).
2. A king of Edom who defeated the Midianites (Gen. 36:35; 1 Chron. 1:46).
3. Another king of Edom (1 Chron. 1:50–51).
4. A member of the royal family of Edom (1 Kings 11:14–22).

Hadadezer (Hadarezer) *[beauty of assistance]*
King of Zobah in Syria (2 Sam. 8:3–12).

Hadar *[power; greatness]*
See Hadad 1, 3.

Hadarezer
See Hadadezer.

Hadassah *[a myrtle; joy]*
The Hebrew name of Esther. See Esther.

Hadlai *[loitering; hindering]*
The father of Amasa (2 Chron. 28:12).

Hadoram *[their beauty; their power]*
1. The fifth son of Joktan (Gen. 10:27; 1 Chron. 1:21).
2. Son of the king of Hamath (1 Chron. 18:10).
3. The organizer of forced labor under David, Solomon, and Rehoboam (2 Chron. 10:18).

Hagab *[a grasshopper]*
An ancestor of captives returning from Babylon with Zerubbabel (Ezra 2:46). See Hagaba.

Hagaba *[a grasshopper]*
An ancestor of some of the captives who came back from captivity with Zerubbabel (Neh. 7:48).

Hagar (Agar) *[a stranger; one that fears]*
An Egyptian woman, the servant of Sarah (Gen. 16:1–16).

Haggai *[feast; solemnity]*
The first of the minor prophets who prophesied after the captivity (Haggai 1:1, 3, 12).

Haggeri *[a stranger]*
The father of one of David's mighty men (1 Chron. 11:38).

Haggi *[a stranger]*
The second son of Gad (Gen. 46:16; Num. 26:15).

Haggiah *[the Lord's feast]*
A descendant of Levi (1 Chron. 6:30).

Haggith *[rejoicing]*
David's fifth wife and mother of Adonijah (2 Sam. 3:4; 1 Kings 1:6).

Hakkatan *[little]*
The father of Johanan who returned from Babylon with Ezra (Ezra 8:12).

Hakkoz *[a thorn; summer; an end]*
A priest who was in charge of a group who served in the temple (1 Chron. 24:10).

Hakupha *[a commandment of the mouth]*
An ancestor of a family who returned from Babylon with Zerubbabel (Ezra 2:61; Neh. 7:63).

Hallohesh (Halohesh) *[saying nothing; an enchanter]*
1. The father of one who repaired the wall of Jerusalem (Neh. 3:12).
2. One of the leaders of the people who sealed the covenant with Nehemiah (Neh. 10:24).

Ham *[hot; heat; brown]*
Noah's youngest son (Gen. 5:32).

Haman *[noise; tumult]*
King Ahasuerus's chief minister (Esther 3:1).

Hammedatha *[he that troubles the law]*
The father of Haman (Esther 3:1, 10; 8:5; 9:24).

Hammelech *[a king; a counselor]*
Not a proper name but a general title meaning "the king" (Jer. 36:26; 38:6).

Hammoleketh
An ancestor of Gilead (1 Chron. 7:18).

Hamor (Emmor) *[an ass; clay; dirt]*
The prince of the land and city of Shechem (Gen. 33:19; 34:2–26).

Hamran
See Hemdan.

Hamuel (Hammuel)
A descendant of Simeon (1 Chron. 4:26).

Hamul *[godly; merciful]*
The younger son of Pharez (Gen. 46:12; 1 Chron. 2:5).

Hamutal *[the shadow of his heat]*
One of King Josiah's wives (2 Kings 23:31; 24:18; Jer. 52:1).

Hanameel *[the grace that comes from God; gift of God]*
Jeremiah's cousin who sold him a field (Jer. 32:6–9).

Hanan *[full of grace]*
1. A descendant of Benjamin (1 Chron. 8:23).
2. A descendant of Benjamin through Saul (1 Chron. 8:38; 9:44).
3. One of David's heroes (1 Chron. 11:43).
4. A returned captive (Ezra 2:46; Neh. 7:49).
5. A Levite who assisted Ezra in his public exposition of the Law (Neh. 8:7).
6. A Levite who sealed the covenant with Nehemiah (Neh. 10:10).
7. Another leader who sealed the covenant with Nehemiah (Neh. 10:22).
8. Another leader who sealed the covenant with Nehemiah (Neh. 10:26).
9. A temple officer whose sons had a room in the temple (Jer. 35:4).

Hananeel *[grace, or gift, of God]*
The builder of the tower near the Sheep Gate (Neh. 3:1; Jer. 31:38).

Hanani *[my grace; my mercy]*
1. A leader in the temple services (1 Chron. 25:4, 25).
2. A prophet who was imprisoned by Asa king of Judah (2 Chron. 16:1, 7).
3. The father of the prophet Jehu (2 Kings 1:7).
4. A priest who married a foreign wife (Ezra 10:20).
5. A brother of Nehemiah (Neh. 1:2) who was made governor of Jerusalem under Nehemiah (Neh. 7:2).
6. A priest who helped purify the wall of Jerusalem (Neh. 12:36).

Hananiah *[grace; mercy; gift of the Lord]*
1. A descendant of Benjamin (1 Chron. 8:24).
2. A leader of some of David's musicians (1 Chron. 25:4, 23).
3. A general in the army of King Uzziah (2 Chron. 26:11).
4. Father of Zedekiah, one of Jehoiakim's officials (Jer. 36:12).
5. A false prophet in the reign of Zedekiah king of Judah who opposed Jeremiah (Jeremiah 28).
6. Grandfather of Irijah (Jer. 37:13).
7. The Hebrew name of Shadrach, one of Daniel's friends (Dan. 1:3, 6–7). See also Shadrach.
8. Son of Zerubbabel (1 Chron. 3:19).
9. A Levite who married a foreign wife during the exile (Ezra 10:28).
10. A priest who helped rebuild the wall of Jerusalem (Neh. 3:8).
11. A priest present at the dedication of the wall of Jerusalem (Neh. 12:12).
12. A person who helped rebuild the gate of Jerusalem (Neh. 3:30).
13. Ruler of the palace at Jerusalem under Nehemiah (Neh. 7:2).

14. An Israelite who sealed the new covenant with God after the exile (Neh. 10:23).

Haniel (Hanniel) *[the gift of God]*
1. A prince of the tribe of Manasseh (Num. 34:23).
2. A prince of the tribe of Asher (1 Chron. 7:39).

Hannah *[gracious; merciful; he that gives]*
A prophetess and mother of Samuel (1 Samuel 1).

Hanniel *[grace or mercy of God]*
See Haniel.

Hanoch *[dedicated]*
1. A grandson of Abraham (Gen. 25:4).
2. Eldest son of Reuben (Gen. 46:9).
3. Enoch, the son of Jared (1 Chron. 1:3).

Hanun *[gracious; merciful]*
1. A king of Ammon (2 Sam. 10:1–6).
2. One who repaired the valley gate of Jerusalem (Neh. 3:13).
3. A man who repaired the wall of Jerusalem (Neh. 3:30).

Haran *[mountainous country]*
1. The third son of Terah, and Abram's youngest brother (Gen. 11:26–31).
2. A descendant of Levi (1 Chron. 23:9).
3. A son of Caleb (1 Chron. 2:46).

Harbona *[his destruction; his sword]*
The third of King Ahasuerus's seven eunuchs (Esther 1:10).

Hareph *[winter; reproach]*
A son of Caleb (1 Chron. 2:51).

Harhaiah *[heat, or anger, of the Lord]*
Father of Uzziel, a builder of Jerusalem's walls (Neh. 3:8).

Harhas (Hasrah) *[anger; heat of confidence]*
Husband of the prophetess Huldah (2 Kings 22:14).

Harhur *[made warm]*
Ancestor of returned captives (Ezra 2:51; Neh. 7:53).

Harim *[destroyed; dedicated to God]*
1. A priest in charge of a section of the officials in the sanctuary of the temple (1 Chron. 24:8).
2. An ancestor of some of the returning captives (Ezra 2:32).
3. Man whose descendants married foreign wives during the exile (Ezra 10:31).
4. A person who sealed the new covenant with God after the exile (Neh. 10:5).
5. A family who sealed the new covenant with God after the exile (Neh. 10:27).
6. An ancestor of a family who sealed the new covenant with God after the exile (Neh. 12:15).

A number of people named Harim may be identical with each other.

Hariph (Jorah)
1. An ancestor of returning captives (Neh. 7:24).
2. Head of a family who sealed the new covenant with God after the exile (Neh. 10:19).

Harnepher *[the anger of a bull; increasing heat]*
A descendant of Asher (1 Chron. 7:36).

Haroeh
A descendant of Judah (1 Chron. 2:52).

Harsha *[workmanship; a wood]*
An ancestor of returning captives (Ezra 2:52; Neh. 7:54).

Harum *[high; throwing down]*
A descendant of Judah (1 Chron. 4:8).

Harumaph *[destruction]*
Father of Jedaiah the wall-builder (Neh. 3:10).

Haruz *[careful]*
Mother of King Amon (2 Kings 21:9).

Hasadiah *[the mercy of the Lord]*
A descendant of Jehoiakim (1 Chron. 3:20).

Hasenuah
A descendant of Benjamin (1 Chron. 9:7).

Hashabiah *[the estimation of the Lord]*

1. A descendant of Levi (1 Chron. 6:45).
2. Another descendant of Levi (1 Chron. 9:14).
3. The fourth of the six sons of Jeduthun (1 Chron. 25:3).
4. A descendant of Kohath (1 Chron. 26:30).
5. The son of Kemuel who was prince of the tribe of Levi in the time of David (1 Chron. 27:17).
6. A chief of the Levite clan (2 Chron. 35:9).
7. A Levite who returned with Ezra from Babylon (Ezra 8:19).
8. A chief of the family of Kohath (Ezra 8:24).
9. A person who repaired the wall of Jerusalem (Neh. 3:17).
10. A person who sealed the new covenant with God after the exile with Nehemiah (Neh. 10:11; 12:24).
11. A Levite, son of Bunni (Neh. 11:15).
12. A Levite, son of Mattaniah, one of the singers in the temple (Neh. 11:22).
13. A priest in the time of Jeshua (Neh. 12:21).
14. A chief Levite (Neh. 12:24).

Some of the above may refer to the same person, especially see 10, 12, and 14.

Hashabnah *[the silence of the Lord]*

A person who sealed the new covenant with God after the exile (Neh. 10:25).

Hashabniah *[the silence of the Lord]*

1. Father of Hattush, who helped to rebuild the wall of Jerusalem (Neh. 3:10).
2. A Levite who officiated at the fast under Ezra and Nehemiah when the covenant was sealed (Neh. 9:5).

Hashbadana

A man who assisted Ezra at the reading of the Law (Neh. 8:4).

Hashem *[named; a putting to]*

Father of several of David's guard (1 Chron. 11:34).

Hashub *[esteemed; numbered]*

1. A person who repaired the wall of Jerusalem (Neh. 3:11).
2. Another person who repaired the wall of Jerusalem (Neh. 3:23).
3. One of the heads of the people who sealed the covenant with Nehemiah (Neh. 10:23).
4. A Levite chief (1 Chron. 9:14). The KJV misspells his name as "Hashub" in Nehemiah 11:15, when it should read "Hashabia."

Hashubah *[estimation; thought]*

A descendant of Jehoiakim (1 Chron. 3:20).

Hashum *[silence; their hasting]*

1. A person whose descendants returned from the Babylonian captivity (Ezra 2:19; 10:33; Neh. 7:22).
2. A priest who assisted Ezra (Neh. 8:4).
3. Head of a family who sealed the new covenant with God after the exile (Neh. 10:18).

Hashupha (Hasupha) *[spent; made base]*

An ancestor of returning captives (Neh. 7:46).

Hasrah *[wanting]*

See Harhas.

Hassenaah

An ancestor of those who rebuilt the fish gate in Jerusalem (Neh. 3:3). He is probably identical with Senaah of Ezra 2:35.

Hasshub

See Hashub.

Hasupha

See Hashupha.

Hatach *[he that strikes]*

One of Ahasuerus's eunuchs (Esther 4:5–10).

Hathath *[fear]*

Son of Othniel (1 Chron. 4:13).

Hatipha *[robbery]*

An ancestor of returning captives (Ezra 2:54; Neh. 7:56).

Hatita *[a bending of sin]*

A temple doorkeeper whose descendants returned from the Babylonian captivity (Ezra 2:42; Neh. 7:45).

Hattil *[howling for sin]*

An ancestor of returning captives (Ezra 2:57).

Hattush *[forsaking sin]*

1. A descendant of the kings of Judah (1 Chron. 3:22).
2. A descendant of David who returned from the exile with Ezra (Neh. 3:10).
3. A priest who returned from the exile with Zerubbabel (Neh. 12:2).
4. A person who repaired the wall of Jerusalem (Neh. 3:10).

Havilah *[that suffers pain; that brings forth]*

1. Son of Cush (Gen. 10:7).
2. A descendant of Shem (Gen. 10:29).

Hazael *[that sees God]*

The murderer of Benhadad II (2 Kings 8:8–29).

Hazaiah *[seeing the Lord]*

A descendant of Judah (Neh. 11:5).

Hazarmaveth *[dwelling of death]*

The third son of Joktan (Gen. 10:26).

Hazelelponi *[sorrow of countenance]*

A daughter of Etam in the genealogy of Judah (1 Chron. 4:3).

Haziel

A descendant of Levi (1 Chron. 23:9).

Hazo *[seeing; prophesying]*

A son of Nahor, and nephew of Abraham (Gen. 22:22).

Heber *[one that passes; anger]*

1. A descendant of Asher (Gen. 46:17; Num. 26:45; 1 Chron. 7:31).
2. Used in Luke 3:35 to refer to Eber.
3. Head of the clan of Judah (1 Chron. 4:18).
4. A descendant of Benjamin (1 Chron. 8:17).
5. The husband of Jael, who killed Sisera (Judg. 4:11, 17, 21).

Hebron *[society; friendship]*

1. The third son of Kohath (Exod. 6:18; Num. 3:19; 1 Chron. 6:2, 18; 23:12).
2. A descendant of Caleb (1 Chron. 2:42–43).

Hegai (Hege) *[meditation; word; groaning; separation]*

One of Ahasuerus's eunuchs (Esther 2:8, 15).

Helah

A wife of Ashur (1 Chron. 4:5, 7).

Heldai *[the world; rustiness]*

1. A captain in the temple service (1 Chron. 27:15).
2. An Israelite who returned from the Babylonian captivity (Zech. 6:10).

Heleb *[the world; rustiness]*

One of David's mighty men (2 Sam. 23:29; 1 Chron. 11:30).

Heled *[the world; rustiness]*

See Heleb.

Helek *[part; portion]*

A descendant of Manasseh (Num. 26:30).

Helem *[dreaming; healing]*

1. A descendant of Asher (1 Chron. 7:35).
2. Another name for Heldai.

Helez *[armed; set free]*

1. One of David's guards (2 Sam. 23:26; 1 Chron. 11:27).
2. A descendant of Judah (1 Chron. 2:39).

Heli (Eli) *[ascending; climbing up]*

The father of Joseph in Luke's genealogy (Luke 3:23). His name in Hebrew is Eli.

Helkai *[same as Helek]*

The head of a priestly family (Neh. 12:15).

Helon *[window; grief]*

The father of Eliab, the prince of the tribe of Zebulun (Num. 1:9; 2:7; 7:24).

Heman *[their trouble; tumult; much; in great number]*

1. A wise man with whom Solomon is compared (1 Chron. 2:6; 1 Kings 4:31).
2. A musician appointed by David to lead singing and instrumental playing in the temple (1 Chron. 15:16–22). Psalm 88 is ascribed to him.

Hemath (Hamath)

Father of the house of Rechab (1 Chron. 2:55). Called Hamath in Amos 6:14.

Hemdan

A descendant of Seir (Gen. 36:26).

Hen *[grace; quiet; rest]*

A son of Zephaniah (Zech. 6:14).

Henadad *[grace of the beloved]*

A head of a family of the Levites who played a prominent part in rebuilding the temple (Ezra 3:9).

Henoch *[dedicated; disciplined]*

See Hanoch.

Hepher *[a digger]*

1. The youngest son of Gilead and founder of the Hepherites (Num. 26:32).
2. A man of Judah (1 Chron. 4:6).
3. One of David's guard (1 Chron. 11:36).

Hephzibah *[my delight is in her]*

The wife of King Hezekiah and the mother of Manasseh (2 Kings 21:1).

Heresh *[a carpenter]*

Head of a Levite family (1 Chron. 9:15).

Hermas *[gain; refuge]*

A Christian to whom Paul sent greetings (Rom. 16:14).

Hermes *[gain; refuge]*

A Christian to whom Paul sent greetings (Rom. 16:14).

Hermogenes *[begotten of Mercury]*

A Christian who deserted Paul (2 Tim. 1:15).

Herod *[son of a hero]*

1. Herod the Great, king of Judah when Jesus was born (Matt. 2:1–22).
2. Herod Antipas, son of Herod the Great, tetrarch of Galilee and Perea (Matt. 14:1–10).
3. Herod Philip, son of Herod the Great, tetrarch of Iturea and Trachonitis (Luke 3:1).
4. Herod Philip, another son of Herod the Great. His wife left him for Herod Antipas (Matt. 14:3).
5. Herod Agrippa I, tetrarch of Galilee; persecuted Christians (Acts 12:1–23).
6. Herod Agrippa II, son of Agrippa I; witnessed Paul's preaching (Acts 25:13–26).

Herodias

Granddaughter of Herod the Great, wife of Herod Philip; she left him to marry Herod Antipas (Matt. 14:8–11; Mark 6:24–28).

Herodion *[the song of Juno]*

A Jewish Christian to whom Paul sent greetings (Rom. 16:11).

Hesed

Father of one of Solomon's officers (1 Kings 4:10).

Heth *[trembling; fear]*

Ancestor of the Hittites (Gen. 10:15; 1 Chron. 1:13).

Hezeki

A descendant of Shaaraim (1 Chron. 8:17).

Hezekiah (Ezekias) *[strength of the Lord]*

1. Twelfth king of Judah and ancestor of Jesus Christ (2 Kings 18:5).
2. Son of Neariah, one of the descendants of the royal family of Judah (1 Chron. 3:23).
3. A person who returned from the Babylonian captivity (Ezra 2:16).

Hezion

Grandfather of Ben-hadad, king of Syria (1 Kings 15:18).
Probably to be identified with Rezon. See Rezon.

Hezir *[a bog; converted]*
1. A Levite in the time of David (1 Chron. 24:15).
2. A leader of the people who sealed the new covenant with God after the exile (Neh. 10:20).

Hezrai (Hezro) *[an entry or vestibule]*
One of David's guards (2 Sam. 23:35).

Hezron (Esrom) *[the dart of joy; the division of the song]*
1. A son of Reuben (Gen. 46:9).
2. A son of Pharez and an ancestor of Jesus Christ (Gen. 46:12; Matt. 1:3).

Hiddai (Hurai) *[a praise; a cry]*
One of David's guards (2 Sam. 23:30).

Hiel *[God lives; the life of God]*
A person who rebuilt Jericho in the reign of Ahab (1 Kings 16:34) and in whom was fulfilled the curse pronounced by Joshua five hundred years before (Josh. 6:26).

Hilkiah *[God is my portion]*
1. Palace administrator in Hezekiah's reign (2 Kings 18:18; Isa. 22:20; 36:22).
2. High priest in Josiah's reign who discovered the book of the law (2 Kings 22:4).
3. A Levite who looked after the children of the temple officials (1 Chron. 6:45).
4. A gatekeeper of the tabernacle (1 Chron. 26:11).
5. One who stood with Ezra when he read the Law to the people (Neh. 8:4).
6. A priest of Anathoth, and father of the prophet Jeremiah (Jer. 1:1).

Hillel *[he that praises]*
Father of Abdon, one of the judges of Israel (Judg. 12:13, 15).

Hinnom *[there they are; their riches]*
An unknown person after whose son a valley near Jerusalem was named (Josh. 15:8; 18:16).

Hirah *[liberty; anger]*
A friend of Judah (Gen. 38:1, 12).

Hiram (Huram) *[exaltation of life; a destroyer]*
1. A king of Tyre who sent workmen and materials to Jerusalem to build a palace for David (2 Sam. 5:11; 1 Chron. 14:1).
2. A craftsman in bronze sent by King Hiram to Solomon (1 Kings 7:13).
3. A descendant of Benjamin (1 Chron. 8:5).

Hizkiah (Hizkijah) *[the strength of the Lord]*
1. An ancestor of the prophet Zephaniah (Zeph. 1:1).
2. A person who sealed the new covenant with God after the exile (Neh. 10:17).

Hobab *[favored; beloved]*
The father-in-law or brother-in-law of Moses (Num. 10:29).

Hod *[praise; confession]*
One of the sons of Zophah (1 Chron. 7:37).

Hodaiah *[the praise of the Lord]*
A descendant of the royal line of Judah (1 Chron. 3:24).

Hodaviah *[same as Hodaiah]*
1. A chief of the tribe of Manasseh (1 Chron. 5:24).
2. A descendant of Benjamin (1 Chron. 9:7).
3. An ancestor of the returning captives (Ezra 2:40).

See also Hodaiah.

Hodesh *[a table; news]*
A wife of Shaharaim (1 Chron. 8:9).

Hodevah
See Hodaviah.

Hodiah (Hodijah)
1. The brother-in-law of Naham (1 Chron. 4:19).
2. One of the Levites who explained the Law (Neh. 8:7).
3. A person who sealed the new covenant with God after the exile (Neh. 10:18).

Hoglah *[his festival or dance]*
A daughter of Zelophehad (Num. 26:33; 27:1).

Hoham *[woe to them]*
An Amorite king killed by Joshua (Josh. 10:1–27).

Homam (Hemam) *[making an uproar]*
A Horite descendant of Esau (1 Chron. 1:39).

Hophni *[he that covers; my fist]*
A son of Eli killed at the battle of Aphek (1 Sam. 1:3; 2:22–24).

Horam *[their hill]*
A king of Gezer defeated by Joshua (Josh. 10:33).

Hori *[a prince; freeborn]*
1. A descendant of Esau (Gen. 36:22; 1 Chron. 1:39).
2. A father of one of the spies of the land of Canaan (Num. 13:5).

Hosah *[trusting]*
One of the first doorkeepers of the ark of the covenant (1 Chron. 16:38).

Hosea (Osee) *[savior; safety]*
One of Israel's prophets (Hosea 1:1–2).

Hoshaiah *[the salvation of the Lord]*
1. The father of Jezaniah or Azariah (Jer. 42:1; 43:2).
2. A man who led a procession at the dedication of the wall of Jerusalem (Neh. 12:32).

Hoshama *[heard; he obeys]*
A son or descendant of Jeconiah or Jehoiakim (1 Chron. 3:18).

Hoshea (Hosea) *[savior; safety]*
1. The nineteenth, last and best king of Israel (2 Kings 15:30).
2. The original name of Joshua. See Joshua.
3. The chief of the tribe of Ephraim in David's reign (1 Chron. 27:20).
4. A person who sealed the covenant with Nehemiah (Neh. 10:23).

Hotham (Hothan) *[a seal]*
1. A descendant of Asher (1 Chron. 7:32).
2. Father of two of David's mighty men (1 Chron. 11:44).

Hothir *[excelling; remaining]*
Organizer of some of the tabernacle services (1 Chron. 25:4, 28).

Hul *[pain; infirmity]*
Grandson of Shem (Gen. 10:23).

Huldah *[the world]*
A prophetess in King Josiah's reign (2 Kings 22:14; 2 Chron. 34:22).

Hupham *[their chamber; their bank]*
The head of a family descended from Benjamin (Num. 26:39).

Huppah
A priest in David's reign who organized some of the tabernacle services (1 Chron. 24:13).

Huppim *[a chamber covered; the sea shore]*
See Hupham.

Hur *[liberty; whiteness; hole]*
1. One of the people who held up Moses's arms during the battle with Amalek (Exod. 17:10).
2. A son of Caleb (Exod. 31:2; 35:30; 38:22).
3. A Midianite king killed by Israel (Num. 31:8).
4. One of Solomon's chief officials (1 Kings 4:8).
5. Father of a man called Caleb (1 Chron. 2:50).
6. A descendant of Judah (1 Chron. 4:1).
7. The ruler of half of Jerusalem under Nehemiah (Neh. 3:9).

Hurai
See Hiddai.

Huram *[their liberty; their whiteness; their hole]*
See Hiram.

Huri *[being angry; or same as Huram]*
A descendant of Gad (1 Chron. 5:14).

Hushah *[hasting; holding peace]*
A descendant of Judah (1 Chron. 4:4).

Hushai *[their haste; their sensuality; their silence]*
One of David's friends and advisors (2 Sam. 15:32; 16:16).

Husham
A descendant of Esau who became king of Edom (Gen. 36:34–35).

Hushim *[man of haste, or of silence]*
1. A son of Dan (Gen. 46:23).
2. A descendant of Benjamin (1 Chron. 7:12).
3. One of the two wives of Shaharaim (1 Chron. 8:8).

Huz *[counsel; woods; fastened]*
The eldest son of Nahor and Milcah (Gen. 22:21).

Hymenaeus *[nuptial; the god of marriage]*
A Christian who Paul says fell into error (1 Tim. 1:20).

Ibhar *[election; he that is chosen]*
One of David's sons born in Jerusalem (2 Sam. 5:15; 1 Chron. 3:6; 14:6).

Ibneiah (Ibnijah) *[the building of the Lord; the understanding of the Lord; son by adoption]*
1. A descendant of Benjamin (1 Chron. 9:8).
2. A Benjamite whose descendants lived in Jerusalem (1 Chron. 9:8).

Ibri *[passing over; being angry; being with young]*
A descendant of Merari in David's reign (1 Chron. 24:27).

Ibzan *[father of a target; father of coldness]*
A judge who ruled Israel for seven years (Judg. 12:8, 10).

Ichabod *[where is the glory? or, no glory]*
The son of Phinehas and grandson of Eli (1 Sam. 4:21).

Idbash *[flowing with honey; the land of destruction]*
One of the sons of Abi-etam (1 Chron. 4:3).

Iddo *[his band; power; praise]*
1. Father of Abinadab (1 Kings 4:14).
2. A descendant of Gershom (1 Chron. 6:21).
3. Commander of the tribe of Manasseh (1 Chron. 27:21).
4. A prophet who wrote about the kings of Israel (2 Chron. 9:29).
5. Grandfather of the prophet Zechariah (Zech. 1:7).
6. Leader in Casiphia when Ezra had returned to Jerusalem (Ezra 8:17).
7. A priest who returned to Jerusalem with Zerubbabel (Neh. 12:4).

Igal (Igeal) *[redeemed; defiled]*
1. One of the twelve spies sent into Canaan (Num. 13:7).
2. One of David's mighty men (2 Sam. 23:36).
3. A descendant of the house of Judah (1 Chron. 3:22).

Igdaliah *[the greatness of the Lord]*
Ancestor of a person who lived in the temple (Jer. 35:4).

Igeal *[a redeemer; redeemed; defiled]*
See Igal.

Ikkesh *[forward; wicked]*
Father of Ira, one of David's mighty men (2 Sam. 23:26; 1 Chron. 11:28; 27:9).

Ilai
See Zalmon.

Imla (Imlah) *[plentitude; circumcision]*
Father of Micaiah the prophet (2 Chron. 18:7–8).

Immer *[saying; speaking; a lamb]*
1. A priest in David's reign (1 Chron. 24:14).
2. A priest in Jeremiah's time (Jer. 20:1).
3. The father of Zadok (Neh. 3:29).
4. A person who returned from Babylon with no genealogy (Ezra 2:59).
5. A family of priests who gave their name to the sixteenth division of the temple service (1 Chron. 9:12).

Imnah (Jimna; Jimnah) *[right hand; numbering; preparing]*
1. A descendant of Asher (Gen. 46:17; 1 Chron. 7:35).
2. A son of Asher (Num. 26:44).
3. Father of Kore in Hezekiah's reign (2 Chron. 31:14).

Imrah *[a rebel; waxing bitter; changing]*
A descendant of Asher (1 Chron. 7:36).

Imri *[speaking; exalting; bitter; a lamb]*
1. A descendant of Judah (1 Chron. 9:4).
2. Father of Zaccur, one of Nehemiah's assistants (Neh. 3:2).

Iphedeiah *[redemption of the Lord]*
A descendant of Benjamin (1 Chron. 8:25).

Ir *[watchman; city; vision]*
A descendant of Benjamin (1 Chron. 7:12).

Ira *[watchman; making bare; pouring out]*
1. One of David's priests (2 Sam. 20:26).
2. One of David's mighty men (2 Sam. 23:38; 1 Chron. 11:38).
3. One of David's guards (2 Sam. 23:26).

Irad *[wild ass; heap of empire; dragon]*
A descendant of Enoch (Gen. 4:18).

Iram *[the effusion of them; a high heap]*
A leader of the Edomites (Gen. 36:43).

Iri *[fire; light]*
A descendant of Benjamin (1 Chron. 7:7).

Irijah *[the fear of the Lord]*
A captain of the gate who arrested Jeremiah in Jerusalem (Jer. 37:13–14).

Ir-nahash
A descendant of Judah (1 Chron. 4:12).

Iru
A son of Caleb (1 Chron. 4:15).

Isaac *[laughter]*
The son of Abraham and Sarah, born to them in their old age (Genesis 21–25).

Isaiah (Esaias) *[the salvation of the Lord]*
One of the major Old Testament prophets (Isaiah 1–66).

Iscah *[he that anoints]*
Abraham's niece (Gen. 11:29).

Iscariot *[a man of murder; a hireling]*
See Juda 8.

Ishbah
A descendant of Judah (1 Chron. 4:17).

Ishbak *[who is empty or exhausted]*
A son of Rapha the Philistine who was killed by Abishai (2 Sam. 21:15–22).

Ishbi-benob *[respiration; conversion; taking captive]*
One of the sons of Rapha the Philistine (2 Sam. 21:15–22).

Ish-bosheth (Esh-baal) *[a man of shame]*
The youngest of Saul's four sons, and his legitimate successor (2 Samuel 2–4).

Ishi *[salvation]*
1. A descendant of Pharez, son of Judah (1 Chron. 2:31).
2. A descendant of Judah (1 Chron. 4:20).
3. A descendant of Simeon (1 Chron. 4:42).
4. One of the heads of the tribe of Manasseh (1 Chron. 5:24).

Ishiah *[it is the Lord]*
See Isshiah.

Ishijah
See Isshiah.

Ishma *[named; marveling; desolation]*
A brother of Jezreel (1 Chron. 4:3).

Ishmael *[God that hears]*
1. Son of Abraham and Hagar (Gen. 16:15–16).
2. A descendant of Benjamin (1 Chron. 8:38).
3. Father of Zebadiah (2 Chron. 19:11).
4. A commander in the time of Jehoiada and Joash (2 Chron. 23:1).
5. A Levite who married a foreign wife during the exile (Ezra 10:22).

6. Son of Nethaniah who was known for his treachery toward Israel (Jer. 40:8–41).

Ishmaiah (Ismaiah) *[hearing or obeying the Lord]*

1. A chief of the tribe of Zebulun during David's reign (1 Chron. 27:19).
2. A chief of Gibeon who joined David at Ziklag (1 Chron. 12:4).

Ishmerai *[keeper, or keeping]*
A descendant of Benjamin (1 Chron. 8:18).

Ishod *[a comely man]*
A man of the tribe of Manasseh (1 Chron. 7:18).

Ish-pan *[hid; broken in two]*
A leader of the clan of Benjamin (1 Chron. 8:22).

Ishuah (Isuah) *[plainness; equal]*
Second son of Asher (Gen. 46:17).

Ishuai (Ishvi; Ishui; Jesui)

1. Third son of Asher (1 Chron. 7:30).
2. Second son of Saul by his wife Ahinoam (1 Sam. 14:49).

Ismachiah (Ismakiah) *[cleaving to the Lord]*
Chief officer under King Hezekiah (2 Chron. 31:13).

Ismaiah
See Ishmaiah.

Ispah *[a jasper stone]*
A descendant of Benjamin (1 Chron. 8:16).

Israel *[who prevails with God]*
See Jacob.

Issachar *[reward; recompense]*

1. Ninth son of Jacob and ancestor of one of the twelve tribes of Israel (Gen. 30:17–18).
2. A tabernacle porter (1 Chron. 26:5).

Isshiah (Ishiah; Ishijah)

1. One of David's fighting men (1 Chron. 7:3).
2. See Jesiah.
3. A man who married a foreign wife during the exile (Ezra 10:31).
4. A descendant of Moses (1 Chron. 24:21).

Isuah
See Ishuah.

Isui
See Ishui.

Ithai *[strong; my sign; a plowshare]*
One of David's guards (1 Chron. 11:31).

Ithamar *[island of the palm tree]*
Aaron's youngest son (Exod. 6:23).

Ithiel *[sign, or coming of God]*
A member of Benjamin's clan (Neh. 11:7).

Ithmah *[an orphan]*
One of David's guards (1 Chron. 11:46).

Ithra
Father of Amasa, Absalom's commander (2 Sam. 17:25).

Ithran *[remaining; searching out diligently]*

1. A descendant of Seir (Gen. 36:26).
2. A son of Zophah of Asher (1 Chron. 7:37).

Ithream *[excellence of the people]*
A son of David (2 Sam. 3:5).

Ittai

1. One of David's commanders (2 Sam. 15:11–22).
2. See Ithai.

Izehar (Izhar) *[clearness; oil]*
A Levite, the father of Korah (Num. 3:19).

Izrahiah *[the Lord ariseth; the clearness of the Lord]*
A descendant of Issachar (1 Chron. 7:3).

Izri *[fasting; tribulation]*
Leader of some temple musicians (1 Chron. 25:11).

Jaakan (Jakan) *[tribulation; labor]*
A son of Ezer, son of Seir (Deut. 10:6).

Jaakobah *[supplanter; deceiver; the heel]*
A descendant of Simeon (1 Chron. 4:36).

Jaalah (Jaala) *[ascending; a little doe or goat]*
One of Solomon's servants whose descendants returned from exile (Neh. 7:58).

Jaalam *[hidden; young man; heir]*
Head of a tribe of Edom (Gen. 36:5).

Jaanai *[answering; afflicting; making poor]*
A descendant of Gad (1 Chron. 5:12).

Jaare-oregim
Father of Elhanan, who killed Goliath the Gittite (2 Sam. 21:19).

Jaasau *[doing; my doing]*
One who married a foreign wife during the exile (Ezra 10:37).

Jaasiel (Jasiel) *[God's work]*
1. One of Saul's cousins (1 Chron. 27:21).
2. One of David's mighty men (1 Chron. 11:47).

Jaazaniah *[whom the Lord will hear]*
1. A commander of men who joined Gedaliah at Mizpah (2 Kings 25:23).
2. A leader of Reuben's clan (Jer. 35:3).
3. Son of Shaphan, who enticed people to idolatry (Ezek. 8:11).
4. Son of Azur, whom Ezekiel prophesied against (Ezek. 11:1).

Jaaziah *[the strength of the Lord]*
A descendant of Merari who lived in Solomon's reign (1 Chron. 24:26–27).

Jaaziel *[the strength of the Lord]*
A temple musician in David's reign (1 Chron. 15:18).

Jabal *[which glides away]*
Son of Lamech and Adah, a nomad (Gen. 4:20).

Jabesh *[dryness; confusion; shame]*
Father of Shallum, the fifteenth king of Israel (2 Kings 15:10–14).

Jabez *[sorrow; trouble]*
Leader of a family of Judah (1 Chron. 4:9–10).

Jabin *[he that understands; building]*
1. King of Hazor, who was defeated by Joshua (Josh. 11:1–3).
2. Another king of Hazor, who was defeated by Barak and Deborah (Judg. 4:2, 13).

Jachan *[wearing out; oppressing]*
A descendant of Gad (1 Chron. 5:13).

Jachin *[he that strengthens and makes steadfast]*
1. Fourth son of Simeon (Gen. 46:10; Exod. 6:15).
2. Head of a family of Aaron (1 Chron. 24:17).
3. A priest in Jerusalem after the Babylonian captivity (1 Chron. 9:10). See Jarib.

Jacob *[that supplants, undermines; the heel]*
1. Second son of Isaac and Rebekah (Genesis 25–50).
2. The father of Joseph, the husband of Mary (Matt. 1:15–16).

See also Heli.

Jada *[knowing]*
A descendant of Judah (1 Chron. 2:28, 32).

Jadau *[his hand; his confession]*
A person who married a foreign wife during the exile (Ezra 10:43).

Jaddua *[known]*
1. The last high priest mentioned in the Old Testament (Neh. 12:11, 22).
2. A person who sealed the new covenant with God after the exile (Neh. 10:21).

Jadon
A person who helped repair the wall of Jerusalem (Neh. 3:7).

Jael *[he that ascends; a kid]*
Wife of Heber who killed Sisera (Judg. 5:6, 24).

Jahath *[broken in pieces; descending]*

1. A descendant of Judah (1 Chron. 4:2).
2. 3. 4. 5. Four descendants of Levi (1 Chron. 23:10–11).

Jahaziah *[the vision of the Lord]*

Helped make a record of those who had foreign wives (Ezra 10:15).

Jahaziel *[seeing God]*

1. One of the heroes of Benjamin who joined David at Ziklag (1 Chron. 12:4).
2. A priest who helped bring the ark of the covenant into the temple (1 Chron. 16:6).
3. A son of Hebron (1 Chron. 23:19; 24:23).
4. A Levite who encouraged Jehoshaphat's army against the Moabites (2 Chron. 20:14).
5. A leader who returned from Babylon with Ezra (Ezra 8:5).

Jahdai

A member of Caleb's family (1 Chron. 2:47).

Jahdiel *[the unity, or sharpness, or revenge, of God]*

Head of a family of Manasseh (1 Chron. 5:24).

Jahdo *[I alone; his joy; his sharpness of wit; his newness]*

A descendant of Gad (1 Chron. 5:14).

Jahleel *[waiting for, or beseeching, or hope in, God]*

A son of Naphtali (Gen. 46:14).

Jahmai *[warm; making warm]*

Head of a clan of Issachar (1 Chron. 7:2).

Jahzeel (Jahziel) *[God hasteth, or divideth]*

The first of the four sons of Naphtali, mentioned three times (Gen. 46:24; Num. 26:48; 1 Chron. 7:13).

Jahzerah

A priest of the family of Immer whose descendants lived in Jerusalem (1 Chron. 9:12).

Jahziel

See Jahzeel.

Jair *[my light; who diffuses light]*

1. A man who on his father's side was descended from Judah, and on his mother's from Manasseh (Num. 32:41; 1 Chron. 2:22).
2. A judge who ruled Israel for twenty-two years (Judg. 10:3–5).
3. Father of Mordecai, Esther's cousin (Esther 2:5).
4. See Jaare-oregim.

Jairus *[my light; who diffuses light]*

A ruler of a synagogue near Capernaum whose daughter Jesus brought back to life (Luke 8:41).

Jakan

See Jaakan.

Jakeh

The father of Agur (Prov. 30:1).

Jakim *[rising; confirming; establishing]*

1. Head of a family descended from Aaron (1 Chron. 24:12).
2. A descendant of Benjamin (1 Chron. 8:19).

Jalon *[tarrying; murmuring]*

A descendant of Caleb the spy (1 Chron. 4:17).

Jambres *[poverty; bitter; a rebel]*

One of the Egyptian magicians who opposed Moses (Exod. 7:9–13).

James *[same as Jacob]*

1. The son of Zebedee, one of the twelve apostles killed by Herod Agrippa I (Mark 1:20; Acts 12:2).
2. The son of Alpheus, one of the twelve apostles (Matt. 10:3).
3. The brother of Jesus (Matt. 13:55), author of the New Testament letter that bears his name (James 1:1).
4. Unknown person called the "brother of Judas." Most probably this should be "Judas, the son of James" (Luke 6:16; Acts 1:13).

Jamin *[right hand; south wind]*

1. Second son of Simeon (Gen. 46:10).

2. A descendant of Ram the Jerahmeelite (1 Chron. 2:27).
3. A priest who expounded the law to the people (Neh. 8:7).

Jamlech *[reigning; asking counsel]*
A prince of the clan of Simeon (1 Chron. 4:34).

Janna *[who speaks or answers; afflicted; poor]*
An ancestor of Jesus Christ (Luke 3:24).

Jannes *[who speaks or answers; afflicted; poor]*
One of the Egyptian magicians who opposed Moses (Exod. 7:9–13).

Japheth *[enlarged; fair; persuading]*
One of Noah's three sons (Gen. 5:32).

Japhia *[enlightening; appearing]*
1. Amorite king of Lachish whom Joshua defeated (Josh. 10:3).
2. One of the sons of David born to him in Jerusalem (2 Sam. 5:15; 1 Chron. 3:7; 14:6).

Japhlet *[delivered; banished]*
A descendant of Asher through Beriah (1 Chron. 7:32–33).

Jarah (Jehoadah) *[a wood; honeycomb; watching closely]*
A son of Ahaz of the family of Saul (1 Chron. 9:42).

Jareb *[a revenger]*
Most probably a nickname for a king of Assyria (Hosea 5:13; 10:6).

Jared (Jered) *[a ruling; commanding; coming down]*
A descendant of Seth and ancestor of Jesus Christ (Gen. 5:15–20; Luke 3:37).

Jaresiah *[the bed of the Lord; the Lord hath taken away; poverty]*
A descendant of Benjamin (1 Chron. 8:17).

Jarha
An Egyptian servant who married his master's daughter (1 Chron. 2:34–35).

Jarib *[fighting; chiding; multiplying; avenging]*
1. One of the leaders under Ezra (Ezra 8:16).
2. A priest who married a foreign wife during the exile (Ezra 10:18).
3. See Jachin.

Jaroah
A descendant of Gad (1 Chron. 5:14).

Jashen *[ancient; sleeping]*
The father of one, or some, of David's guards (2 Sam. 23:32).

Jasher *[righteous; upright]*
Author of a book which is now lost (Josh. 10:13; 2 Sam. 1:18).

Jashobeam *[the people sitting; captivity of the people]*
1. One of David's mighty men (1 Chron. 11:11).
2. One who joined David at Ziklag (1 Chron. 12:6).

See also Adino.

Jashub *[a returning; a controversy; a dwelling place]*
1. A person who married a foreign wife during the exile (Ezra 10:29).
2. See Job 2.

Jashubi-lehem
A descendant of Judah by Bath-shua the Canaanitess (1 Chron. 4:22).

Jasiel *[the strength of God]*
See Jaasiel.

Jason *[he that cures]*
1. Paul's host when he stayed at Thessalonica (Acts 17:5–9).
2. One of Paul's relatives who sent greetings to Rome (Rom. 16:21).

Jathniel *[gift of God]*
A gatekeeper of the tabernacle (1 Chron. 26:2).

Javan *[deceiver; one who makes sad]*
Fourth son of Japheth (Gen. 10:2, 4).

Jaziz *[brightness; departing]*
David's chief shepherd (1 Chron. 27:31).

Jeaterai *[searching out]*
A descendant of Gershon (1 Chron. 6:21).

Jeberechiah *[speaking well of, or kneeling to, the Lord]*
Father of Zechariah, during Ahaz's reign, whom Isaiah took as a witness (Isa. 8:2).

Jecamiah (Jekamiah) *[resurrection, or confirmation, or revenge, of the Lord]*
1. A descendant of Judah (1 Chron. 2:41).
2. A son of King Jeconiah (Jehoiachim) (1 Chron. 3:18).

Jecholiah (Jecoliah) *[perfection, or power, of the Lord]*
Wife of Amaziah king of Judah, and mother of Azariah or Uzziah his successor (2 Kings 15:2).

Jeconiah (Jechonias)
Greek form of Jehoiachin. See Jehoiachin.

Jedaiah *[the hand of the Lord; confessing the Lord]*
1. A descendant of Simeon (1 Chron. 4:37).
2. A person who helped repair the wall of Jerusalem (Neh. 3:10).
3. A priest living in Jerusalem (Ezra 2:36).
4. A priest who returned from the Babylonian captivity with Zerubbabel (Neh. 11:10).
5. Another priest who returned from the Babylonian captivity with Zerubbabel (Neh. 12:7, 21).

Jediael *[the science, or knowledge, of God]*
1. A descendant of Benjamin (1 Chron. 7:6, 10–11).
2. A descendant of Korah, son of Meshelemiah (1 Chron. 26:2).
3. One of David's guards (1 Chron. 11:45).
4. One who joined David on his march to Ziklag (1 Chron. 12:20).

Jedidah *[well beloved; amiable]*
Queen of Amon and mother of King Josiah (2 Kings 22:1).

Jedidiah *[beloved of the Lord]*
The name God gave Solomon through Nathan the prophet (2 Sam. 12:25).

Jeduthun *[his law; giving praise]*
One of the three chief temple musicians (1 Chron. 9:16; 16:38–42).

Jeezer *[island of help]*
A descendant of Manasseh (Num. 26:30).

Jehaleleel (Jehalelel) *[praising God; clearness of God]*
1. A descendant of Judah through Caleb the spy (1 Chron. 4:16).
2. A descendant of Merari in Hezekiah's reign (2 Chron. 29:12).

Jehdeiah *[joy together, one Lord]*
1. A descendant of Levi in David's reign (1 Chron. 24:20).
2. One of David's chief officers (1 Chron. 27:30).

Jehezekel *[strength of God]*
A priest to whom David gave work in the sanctuary (1 Chron. 24:16).

Jehiah *[the Lord liveth]*
A Levite gatekeeper of the ark of the covenant (1 Chron. 15:24).

Jehiel
1. A singer in the tabernacle in David's reign (1 Chron. 15:18; 16:5).
2. One of the sons of Jehoshaphat king of Judah, put to death by his brother Jehoram (2 Chron. 21:2, 4).
3. A chief priest at the time of Josiah's reforms (2 Chron. 35:8).
4. A descendant of Gershon (1 Chron. 23:8).
5. A companion of the sons of David (1 Chron. 27:32).
6. A son of Heman the singer (2 Chron. 29:14).
7. A Levite in charge of the dedicated things in the temple (2 Chron. 31:13).
8. Father of a person who returned from the Babylonian captivity (Ezra 8:9).

9. Father of a person who married a foreign wife during the exile (Ezra 10:2).
10. Father of the first person to admit to taking a foreign wife during the exile (Ezra 10:2).
11. Two people who had taken foreign wives (Ezra 10:21, 26).
12. Another name for Jehiah. See Jehiah.

Jehieli

A Levite who was in charge of the treasures of the temple in David's reign (1 Chron. 26:21–22). See Jehiel.

Jehizkiah *[the strength, or taking, of the Lord]*

One who objected to those who wanted to make fellow Jews slaves (2 Chron. 28:12). See Hezekiah.

Jehoadah *[passing over; testimony of the Lord]*

See Jarah.

Jehoaddan *[pleasure, or time, of the Lord]*

Wife of King Josiah, and mother of Amaziah of Judah (2 Kings 14:2; 2 Chron. 25:1).

Jehoahaz *[possession of the Lord]*

1. The son and successor of Jehu (2 Kings 13:2–25).
2. Jehoahaz, also called Shallum, son of Josiah, whom he succeeded as king of Judah (2 Kings 23:3–34).
3. See Azariah 2.

Jehoash (Joash) *[fire of the Lord]*

1. The ninth king of Judah (2 Kings 11:21–12:21).
2. The twelfth king of Israel; son of Jehoahaz (2 Kings 13:9–14:16).

Jehohanan *[grace, or mercy, or gift, of the Lord]*

1. A Korhite Levite, one of the gatekeepers of the tabernacle (1 Chron. 26:3).
2. A chief commander of Judah under King Jehoshaphat (2 Chron. 17:15).
3. Father of Ishmael, who helped Jehoiada the priest (2 Chron. 23:1).
4. A person who married a foreign wife during the exile (Ezra 10:28).
5. A priest who returned to Jerusalem with Zerubbabel (Neh. 12:13).
6. A singer who took part in the dedication of the wall of Jerusalem (Neh. 12:42).

Jehoiachin *[preparation, or strength, of the Lord]*

King of Judah for three months and ten days, before Judah was captured by Nebuchadnezzar (2 Kings 24:8–16).

Jehoiada *[knowledge of the Lord]*

1. Father of Benaiah, one of David's chief officials (2 Sam. 8:18).
2. Leader of the Aaronites who joined David at Ziklag (1 Chron. 12:27).
3. One of David's advisors (1 Chron. 27:34).
4. High priest when Athaliah was deposed from the throne of Judah (2 Kings 11–12:9).
5. A priest replaced by Zephaniah (Jer. 29:26).
6. Son of Paseach, who helped repair the old gate of Jerusalem (Neh. 3:6).
7. See Joiada.

Jehoiakim *[avenging, or establishing, or resurrection, of the Lord]*

The name given to Eliakim by Pharaoh Necho when he made him king of Judah (2 Kings 23:34–24:6).

Jehoiarib *[fighting, or multiplying, of the Lord]*

1. A priest in Jerusalem (1 Chron. 9:10).
2. Head of a family of Aaron (1 Chron. 24:7).

Jehonadab (Jonadab) *[free giver; liberality]*

1. Descendant of Rechab who did not allow his followers to drink wine or live in houses (2 Kings 10:15, 23).
2. The son of David's brother Shimeah (2 Sam. 13:3).

Jehonathan *[gift of the Lord; gift of a dove]*

1. Son of Uzziah, a chief official in King David's storehouses (1 Chron. 27:25).
2. One of the Levites sent by Jehoshaphat to teach the Law (2 Chron. 17:8).
3. A priest (Neh. 12:18), called Jonathan in Neh. 12:35.

Jehoram (Joram) *[exaltation of the Lord]*

1. Son of Ahab king of Israel, who succeeded his brother Ahaziah, and ancestor of Jesus Christ (2 Kings 8:16–24; Matt. 1:8).
2. Israel's ninth king, killed by Jehu (2 Kings 1:17; 3:1–6).
3. A priest commissioned to teach the Law to the people (2 Chron. 17:8).

Jehoshabeath (Jehosheba)

Daughter of Jehoram, king of Judah (2 Chron. 22:11); called Jehosheba in 2 Kings 1:2.

Jehoshaphat (Josaphat) *[the Lord is judge]*

1. King of Judah, and ancestor of Jesus Christ (2 Kings 22:41–50; Matt. 1:8).
2. Recorder in David's reign (2 Sam. 8:16).
3. A priest in David's reign (1 Chron. 15:24).
4. One of Solomon's chief officials (1 Kings 4:17).
5. Son of Nimshi and father of King Jehu (2 Kings 9:2, 14).

Jehosheba *[fullness, or oath, of the Lord]*

See Jehoshabeath.

Jehozabad *[the Lord's dowry; having a dowry]*

1. A Korhite Levite who was gatekeeper of the temple and the storehouse in David's reign (1 Chron. 26:4, 15).
2. A Benjamite, captain of 180,000 armed men, in King Jehoshaphat's reign (2 Chron. 17:18).
3. A servant who killed King Joash (2 Kings 12:21).

Jehozadak *[justice of the Lord]*

See Josedech.

Jehu *[himself who exists]*

1. The founder of the fifth dynasty of the kingdom of Israel, and their tenth king (1 Kings 19:16–17; 2 Kings 9–10).
2. The prophet who brought disastrous news to Baasha of Israel (1 Kings 16:1–12).
3. A descendant of Hezron (1 Chron. 2:38).
4. A descendant of Simeon (1 Chron. 4:35).
5. One who joined David at Ziklag (1 Chron. 12:3).

Jehubbah *[hiding, binding]*

A descendant of Asher (1 Chron. 7:34).

Jehucal (Jucal) *[mighty; perfect; wasted]*

A messenger of Zedekiah (Jer. 37:3).

Jehudi *[praising; conferring]*

The person who brought Baruch to the princes and read to the king Jeremiah's prophecies (Jer. 36:21–23).

Jehudijah *[the praise of the Lord]*

Ezra's wife (1 Chron. 4:18).

Jehush *[keeping counsel; fastened]*

A member of Saul's family (1 Chron. 8:39).

Jeiel (Jehiel)

1. A leader of the tribe of Reuben (1 Chron. 5:7).
2. An ancestor of Saul (1 Chron. 9:35).
3. One of David's mighty men (1 Chron. 11:44).
4. A singer and gatekeeper in the tabernacle (1 Chron. 15:18).
5. A descendant of Asaph (2 Chron. 20:14).
6. Uzziah's recorder (2 Chron. 26:11).
7. A Levite in Hezekiah's reign (2 Chron. 29:13).
8. A chief Levite in Josiah's reign (2 Chron. 35:9).
9. One who returned to Jerusalem with Ezra (Ezra 8:13).
10. A person who married a foreign wife during the exile (Ezra 10:43).

Jekamean *[the people shall arise]*
A descendant of Levi (1 Chron. 23:19).

Jekamiah *[establishing, or revenging, of the Lord]*
See Jecamiah.

Jekuthiel *[hope, or congregation, of the Lord]*
A descendant of the spy Caleb (1 Chron. 4:18).

Jemima *[handsome as the day]*
Job's first daughter after his restoration (Job 42:14).

Jemuel *[God's day; son of God]*
See Nemuel.

Jephthae
Greek form of Jephthah. See Jephthah.

Jephthah (Jephthae)
One of Israel's judges (Judg. 11–12:7).

Jephunneh *[he that beholds]*
1. Father of Caleb the spy (Num. 13:6).
2. A descendant of Asher, eldest of the three sons of Jether (1 Chron. 7:38).

Jerah *[the moon; month; smelling sweet]*
A son of Joktan (Gen. 10:26; 1 Chron. 1:20).

Jerahmeel *[the mercy, or the beloved, of God]*
1. A son of Hezron, and grandson of Judah (1 Chron. 2:9, 25–27, 33, 42).
2. A son of Kish (1 Chron. 24:29).
3. Jehoiakim's chief official (Jer. 36:26).

Jered *[ruling; coming down]*
A son of Ezra (1 Chron. 4:18).

Jeremai *[my height; throwing forth waters]*
A person who married a foreign wife during the exile (Ezra 10:33).

Jeremiah (Jeremias) *[exaltation of the Lord]*
1. A woman whose daughter married King Josiah (2 Kings 23:31).
2. Head of a family of the clan of Manasseh (1 Chron. 5:24).
3. One who joined David at Ziklag (1 Chron. 12:10).
4. A man of Gad who joined David at Ziklag (1 Chron. 12:4).
5. Another who joined David at Ziklag (1 Chron. 12:13).
6. A priest who sealed the new covenant with God after the exile (Neh. 10:2).
7. A descendant of Jonadab (Jer. 35:3).
8. A prophet during the reigns of the last five kings of Judah (Jeremiah 1–52).

Jeremias
The Greek form of Jeremiah. See Jeremiah.

Jeremoth *[eminences; one that fears death]*
1. A son of Beriah (1 Chron. 8:14).
2. 3. Two people who married foreign wives (Ezra 10:26–27).
4. A son of Mushi (1 Chron. 23:23); called Jerimoth in 1 Chron. 24:30.
5. A person anointed by David to sing in the temple (1 Chron. 25:22); called Jerimoth in 1 Chronicles 25:4.

Jeriah (Jerijah) *[fear, or throwing down, of the Lord]*
A descendant of Hebron (1 Chron. 23:19; 24:23).

Jeribai *[fighting; chiding; multiplying]*
One of David's guards (1 Chron. 11:46).

Jeriel *[fear, or vision of God]*
A descendant of Issachar (1 Chron. 7:2).

Jerijah
See Jeriah.

Jerimoth *[he that fears or rejects death]*
1. A son of Bela (1 Chron. 7:7).
2. A person who joined David at Ziklag (1 Chron. 12:5).
3. A son of Beecher (1 Chron. 7:8).
4. A ruler of the tribe of Naphtali (1 Chron. 27:19).
5. A son of King David (2 Chron. 11:18).
6. See Jeremoth 4, 5.

Jerioth *[kettles; breaking asunder]*
Caleb's wife or concubine (1 Chron. 2:18).

Jeroboam *[he that opposes the people]*
1. The first king of the divided kingdom of Israel (1 Kings 11:24–40).
2. The thirteenth king of Israel (2 Kings 14:23–29).

Jeroham *[high; merciful; beloved]*
1. Grandfather of Samuel (1 Sam. 1:1).
2. A descendant of Benjamin (1 Chron. 9:8).
3. Head of a family of Benjamin (1 Chron. 8:27).
4. A priest whose son lived in Jerusalem after the exile (1 Chron. 9:12).
5. Father of two people who joined David at Ziglag (1 Chron. 12:7).
6. Father of Azareel, prince of Dan (1 Chron. 27:22).
7. Father of a person who helped Joash to gain Judah's throne (2 Chron. 23:1).

Jerubbaal *[he that defends Baal; let Baal defend his cause]*
The name given to Gideon by his father (Judg. 6:32).

Jerubbesheth *[let the idol of confusion defend itself]*
The name given to Gideon by those who wanted to avoid pronouncing Baal (2 Sam. 11:21).

Jerusha (Jerushah) *[banished; possession; inheritance]*
The wife of King Uzziah (2 Kings 15:33).

Jesaiah (Jeshaiah) *[health, or salvation, of the Lord]*
1. A grandson of Zerubbabel (1 Chron. 3:21).
2. A person appointed to sing in the temple (1 Chron. 25:3, 15).
3. A grandson of Moses (1 Chron. 26:25).
4. A person who returned from the Babylonian captivity (Ezra 8:7).
5. A descendant of Merari who returned from the exile (Ezra 8:19).
6. One whose descendants lived in Jerusalem (Neh. 11:17).

Jesharelah
See Asarelah.

Jeshebeab *[sitting, or captivity, of the father]*
Head of the fourteenth division of priests (1 Chron. 24:13).

Jesher *[right; singing]*
Son of Caleb (1 Chron. 2:18).

Jeshishai *[ancient; rejoicing exceedingly]*
A descendant of Gad (1 Chron. 5:14).

Jeshohaiah *[the Lord pressing; the meditation of God]*
A descendant of Simeon (1 Chron. 4:36).

Jeshua (Jeshuah) *[a savior; a deliverer]*
1. A priest in David's reign (1 Chron. 24:11).
2. One of the Levites in Hezekiah's reign (2 Chron. 31:15).
3. A priest who returned from the Babylonian captivity (Ezra 2:40).
4. Father of Jozabad the Levite (Ezra 8:33).
5. An ancestor of the returning captives (Ezra 2:6).
6. Father of one who repaired the wall of Jerusalem (Neh. 3:19).
7. A Levite who explained the Law to the people (Neh. 8:7).
8. A person who sealed the new covenant with God after the exile (Neh. 10:9).
9. See Joshua.

6, 7, 8, and 9 may refer to the same person.

Jesiah *[sprinkling of the Lord]*
1. A person who joined David at Ziklag (1 Chron. 12:6).
2. A descendant of Uzziel (1 Chron. 23:20); called Isshiah in 1 Chronicles 24:25.

Jesimiel *[naming, or astonishment, of God]*
A descendant of Simeon (1 Chron. 4:36).

Jesse *[gift; oblation; one who is]*
Father of King David and ancestor of Jesus Christ (Ruth 4:17, 22; Matt. 1:5–6).

Jesui *[even-tempered; flat country]*
See Ishuai.

Jesus *[savior; deliverer]*
A Christian who was with Paul at Rome (Col. 4:11); also called Justus.

Jesus Christ
The son of Mary who came to save people from their sins. His ministry is recorded in the four Gospels.

Jether *[he that excels]*
1. Gideon's first son (Judg. 8:20).
2. A son of Jerahmeel (1 Chron. 2:32).
3. A descendant of Caleb the spy (1 Chron. 4:17).
4. A descendant of Asher (1 Chron. 7:38).
5. See Ithra.

Jetheth *[giving]*
A chief of Edom (Gen. 36:40; 1 Chron. 1:51).

Jethro *[his excellence; his posterity]*
Moses's father-in-law (Exod. 3:1).

Jetur *[order; succession; mountainous]*
A son of Ishmael (Gen. 25:15; 1 Chron. 1:31; 5:19).

Jeuel *[God hath taken away; God heaping up]*
A descendant of Judah (1 Chron. 9:6).

Jeush *[he that is devoured]*
1. A son of Esau (Gen. 36:5, 14, 18; 1 Chron. 1:35).
2. A descendant of Benjamin (1 Chron. 7:10).
3. A descendant of Gershon (1 Chron. 23:10–11).
4. A son of Rehoboam king of Judah (2 Chron. 11:19).

Jeuz *[he that is devoured]*
A descendant of Benjamin (1 Chron. 8:10).

Jezaniah *[nourishment, or weapons, of the Lord]*
See Jaazaniah.

Jezebel *[chaste]*
1. The wife of Ahab, king of Israel (1 Kings 16:31).
2. A false prophetess at Thyatira (Rev. 2:20).

Jezer *[island of help]*
The third son of Naphtali (Gen. 46:24; Num. 26:49; 1 Chron. 7:13).

Jeziah *[sprinkling of the Lord]*
A person who married a foreign wife during the exile (Ezra 10:25).

Jeziel *[sprinkling of the Lord]*
A person who joined David at Ziklag (1 Chron. 12:3).

Jezliah
A descendant of Benjamin (1 Chron. 8:18).

Jezoar *[clear; white]*
A descendant of Caleb (1 Chron. 4:7).

Jezrahiah *[the Lord arises; brightness of the Lord]*
The leader of the singers at the solemn dedication of the wall of Jerusalem (Neh. 12:42).

Jezreel *[seed of God]*
1. A descendant of Etam (1 Chron. 4:3).
2. The eldest son of the prophet Hosea (Hosea 1:4).

Jibsam *[their drought, their confusion]*
A son of Tola, the son of Issachar (1 Chron. 7:2).

Jidlaph *[he that distills water]*
Abraham's nephew (Gen. 22:22).

Jimna
See Imnah.

Joab *[paternity; voluntary]*
1. Son of Zeruiah, David's sister (2 Sam. 2:13–32; 3:23–31).
2. A descendant of Caleb (1 Chron. 2:54).

3. A member of the tribe of Judah (1 Chron. 4:14).
4. An ancestor of the returning captives (Ezra 2:6; Neh. 7:11).
5. An ancestor of the returning captives (Ezra 8:9).

Joah *[fraternity; brother of the Lord]*

1. The son of Asaph, the recorder in Hezekiah's reign (Isa. 36:3, 11, 22).
2. A descendant of Gershon (1 Chron. 6:21).
3. A porter in the tabernacle (1 Chron. 26:4).
4. A Levite commissioned to repair the temple (2 Chron. 34:8).

Joahaz *[apprehending; possessing; seeing]*

Father of Joah, King Josiah's recorder (2 Chron. 34:8).

Joanna *[grace or gift of the Lord]*

1. An ancestor of Jesus Christ (Luke 3:27).
2. The wife of Chuza, Herod's steward, who helped Jesus and his apostles (Luke 8:3; 24:10).

Joash *[who despairs or burns]*

1. A descendant of Benjamin (1 Chron. 7:8).
2. Father of Gideon (Judg. 6:11).
3. A son of Ahab (1 Kings 22:26; 2 Chron. 18:25).
4. A descendant of Judah (1 Chron. 4:22).
5. A person who joined David at Ziklag (1 Chron. 12:3).
6. A keeper of David's stores of oil (1 Chron. 27:28).
7. See Jehoash 1, 2.

Joatham *[same as Jotham]*

Greek form of Jotham. See Jotham.

Job *[he that weeps or cries]*

1. A godly man whose severe testing resulted in great blessing (book of Job).
2. The third son of Issachar (Gen. 46:13).

Jobab *[sorrowful, hated]*

1. A son of Joktan (Gen. 10:29; 1 Chron. 1:23).
2. A king of Edom (Gen. 36:33–34; 1 Chron. 1:44–45).
3. A king of Canaan conquered by Joshua (Josh. 11:1).
4. A descendant of Benjamin (1 Chron. 8:9).
5. Another descendant of Benjamin (1 Chron. 8:18).

Jochebed *[glorious; honorable]*

Moses's mother (Exod. 6:20; Num. 26:59).

Joed *[witnessing; robbing; passing over]*

A son of Pedaiah (Neh. 11:7).

Joel *[that wills or commands]*

1. Eldest son of Samuel the prophet (1 Sam. 8:2; 1 Chron. 6:33; 15:17).
2. A descendant of Simeon (1 Chron. 4:35).
3. A descendant of Reuben (1 Chron. 5:4, 8).
4. Chief of the Gadites (1 Chron. 5:12).
5. An ancestor of the prophet Samuel (1 Chron. 6:36).
6. A descendant of Tola (1 Chron. 7:3).
7. One of David's mighty men (1 Chron. 11:38).
8. A Levite in David's reign (1 Chron. 15:7, 11).
9. A keeper of the temple treasures (1 Chron. 26:22).
10. A prince of Manasseh in David's reign (1 Chron. 27:20).
11. A Levite in Hezekiah's reign (2 Chron. 29:12).
12. A person who married a foreign wife during the exile (Ezra 10:43).
13. The son of Zichri, a Benjamite (Neh. 11:9).
14. The second of the twelve minor prophets (the book of Joel).

Joelah *[lifting up; profiting; taking away slander]*

A person who joined David at Ziklag (1 Chron. 12:7).

Joezer *[he that aids]*

A person who joined David at Ziklag (1 Chron. 12:6).

Jogli *[passing over; turning back; rejoicing]*
A prince of Dan (Num. 34:22).

Joha *[who enlivens or gives life]*
1. A descendant of Benjamin (1 Chron. 8:16).
2. One of David's guards (1 Chron. 11:45).

Johanan *[who is liberal or merciful]*
1. An officer who helped Gedaliah after the fall of Jerusalem (2 Kings 25:23).
2. Father of a priest in Solomon's reign (1 Chron. 6:9–10).
3. Son of Elioenai (1 Chron. 3:24).
4. Eldest son of Josiah, king of Judah (1 Chron. 3:15).
5. 6. Two men who joined David at Ziklag (1 Chron. 12:4, 12).
7. A person who was against enslaving Judean captives in Ahaz's reign (2 Chron. 28:12).
8. A returned exile (Ezra 8:12).
9. The son of Eliashib, one of the chief Levites (Ezra 10:6).
10. The son of Tobiah the Ammonite (Neh. 6:18).
11. A priest in Joiakim's reign (Neh. 12:22–23).

John *[the grace or mercy of the Lord]*
1. The son of Zacharias and Elisabeth, known as John the Baptist, who was beheaded by Herod (Matt. 3; 11:7–18; 14:1–10; Luke 1:13–17).
2. A son of Zebedee, one of the twelve apostles (Matt. 4:21; 10:2).
3. A relative of the high priest Annas (Acts 4:6).
4. A missionary better known by his surname Mark (Acts 12:12, 25; 13:5, 13; 15:37).

Joiada
An ancestor of the priest Jeshua (Neh. 12:10–11, 22). See Jehoiada.

Joiakim
The son of Jeshua who returned from the Babylonian captivity (Neh. 12:10).

Joiarib *[chiding, or multiplying, of the Lord]*
1. A layman who returned from Babylon with Ezra (Ezra 8:16).
2. An ancestor of a family living in Jerusalem (Neh. 11:5).
3. A priest who returned from captivity (Neh. 11:10).

Jokim *[that made the sun stand still]*
A descendant of Judah (1 Chron. 4:22).

Jokshan *[an offense; hardness; a knocking]*
A son of Abraham and Keturah (Gen. 25:2–3; 1 Chron. 1:32).

Joktan *[small dispute; contention; disgust]*
A son of Eber (Gen. 10:25; 1 Chron. 1:19).

Jona (Jonah; Jonas)
1. The father of the apostle Peter (John 1:42) who was spoken of as Simon Bar-jona (i.e., son of Jona) in Matthew 16:17.
2. A Hebrew prophet sent to preach to Nineveh (Jonah 1:1).

Jonadab *[who gives liberally]*
See Jehonadab.

Jonah (Jonas) *[a dove; he that oppresses; destroyer]*
See Jona.

Jonan *[a dove; multiplying of the people]*
An ancestor of Jesus Christ (Luke 3:30).

Jonathan *[given of God]*
1. David's nephew (2 Sam. 21:21; 1 Chron. 20:7).
2. The son of Abiathar, the high priest (2 Sam. 15:36; 17:15–21; 1 Kings 1:42–43).
3. One of David's mighty men (2 Sam. 23:32; 1 Chron. 11:34).
4. A priest of an idol shrine in Ephraim (Judg. 18:30).
5. A grandson of Onam (1 Chron. 2:32–33).
6. One of David's uncles (1 Chron. 27:32).
7. Father of one who returned with Ezra (Ezra 8:6).

8. A priest involved in the foreign wife problem (Ezra 10:15).
9. A descendant of Jeshua the high priest (Neh. 12:11).
10. A priest (Neh. 12:14).
11. A scribe in whose house Jeremiah was kept a prisoner (Jer. 37:15).
12. One who joined Gedaliah after the fall of Jerusalem (Jer. 40:8).
13. Saul's son and David's close friend (1 Sam. 14; 18:1–4; 31:2).
14. See Jehonathan 3.

Jorah *[showing; casting forth; a cauldron]*
See Hariph.

Jorai *[showing; casting forth; a cauldron]*
A chief of the tribe of Gad (1 Chron. 5:13).

Joram (Jehoram) *[to cast; elevated]*
1. A descendant of Moses (1 Chron. 26:25).
2. See Hadoram 2.
3. See Jehoram 1, 2.

Jorim *[he that exalts the Lord]*
An ancestor of Jesus Christ (Luke 3:29).

Jorkoam
A son of Raham, or the city he founded (1 Chron. 2:44).

Josabad *[having a dowry]*
See Jozabad.

Josaphat
Greek form of Jehoshaphat. See Jehoshaphat.

Jose *[raised; who pardons]*
An ancestor of Jesus Christ (Luke 3:29).

Josedech (Jehozadak; Jozadak)
Father of Jeshua the high priest (Hag. 1:1, 12, 14; Zech. 6:11).

Joseph *[increase; addition]*
1. The elder of the two sons of Jacob and Rachel who was sold into Egypt, where he rose to become prime minister (Genesis 37; 39–50).
2. Father of one of the spies sent into Canaan (Num. 13:7).
3. A son of Asaph (1 Chron. 25:2, 9).
4. A person who married a foreign wife during the exile (Ezra 10:42).
5. A priest of the family of Shebaniah (Neh. 12:14).
6. Husband of Mary, mother of Jesus (Matt. 1:16–24).
7. A converted Jew from Arimathea in whose tomb Jesus was laid (Matt. 27:57, 59).
8. One of the ancestors of Christ (Luke 3:24).
9. Another ancestor of Christ (Luke 3:26).
10. Another ancestor of Christ (Luke 3:30).
11. Joseph, called Barsabas, and surnamed Justus; one of the two people considered as a replacement for Judas (Acts 1:23).

Joses *[same as Jose]*
1. One of Jesus' half-brothers (Matt. 13:55; Mark 6:3).
2. The son of Mary, the wife of Cleophas (Matt. 27:56).

Joshah *[being; forgetting; owing]*
A descendant of Simeon (1 Chron. 4:34, 38–41).

Joshaphat
One of David's guards (1 Chron. 11:43).

Joshaviah *[the seat, alteration, or captivity of the Lord]*
One of David's guards (1 Chron. 11:46).

Joshbekashah *[it is requiring or beseeching]*
A son of Heman, David's song leader (1 Chron. 25:4, 24).

Joshua *[a savior; a deliverer]*
1. Moses' successor (Exod. 17:9–14).
2. An inhabitant of Beth-shem in the time of Eli (1 Sam. 6:14, 18).
3. A governor of Jerusalem under Josiah (2 Kings 23:8).
4. High priest when the temple was rebuilt (Hag. 1:14; 2:12; Zech. 3:1).

Josiah (Josias) *[the Lord burns; the fire of the Lord]*
1. King of Judah when the book of the law was discovered (2 Kings 22:1–

23:30); also an ancestor of Jesus Christ (Matt. 1:10–11).
2. A son of Zephaniah living in Jerusalem (Zech. 6:10).

Josias
Greek form of Josiah. See Josiah.

Josibiah *[the seat, or captivity of the Lord]*
A descendant of Simeon (1 Chron. 4:35).

Josiphiah *[increase of the Lord; the Lord's finishing]*
Father of a returned exile (Ezra 8:10).

Jotham (Joatham) *[the perfection of the Lord]*
1. The youngest son of Gideon who escaped from the massacre of his family (Judg. 9:5, 7, 21, 57).
2. The son of King Uzziah and twelfth king of Judah; also an ancestor of Jesus Christ (2 Kings 15:5–38; Matt. 1:9).
3. A son of Jahdai (1 Chron. 2:47).

Jozabad (Josabad) *[having a dowry]*
1. A person who joined David at Ziklag (1 Chron. 12:4).
2. 3. Two descendants of Manasseh who joined David at Ziklag (1 Chron. 12:20).
4. A chief officer of the dedicated things of the temple in Hezekiah's reign (2 Chron. 31:13).
5. A chief Levite in Josiah's reign (2 Chron. 35:9).
6. A Levite, son of Jeshua, in the days of Ezra (Ezra 8:33).
7. 8. Two people who had married foreign wives (Ezra 10:22–23).
9. A person who interpreted the Law (Neh. 8:7).
10. A chief Levite after the exile (Neh. 11:16).

Jozachar *[remembering; of the male sex]*
One of the murderers of Joash king of Judah (2 Kings 12:21); called Zabad in 2 Chronicles 24:26.

Jozadak
See Josedech.

Jubal *[he that runs; a trumpet]*
A son of Lamech and skilled musician (Gen. 4:21).

Jucal *[mighty; perfect]*
See Jehucal.

Juda (Judah; Judas; Jude) *[the praise of the Lord; confession]*
1. Son of Jacob by Leah and an ancestor of Jesus Christ (Gen. 29:35; Luke 3:30).
2. An ancestor of a person who helped to rebuild the temple (Ezra 3:9).
3. A person who married a foreign wife during the exile (Ezra 10:23).
4. Second in command in Jerusalem after the exile (Neh. 11:9).
5. A person who returned to Jerusalem with Zerubbabel (Neh. 12:8).
6. A prince of Judah (Neh. 12:34).
7. A priest and musician (Neh. 12:36).
8. Judas Iscariot, one of the twelve apostles; betrayed Jesus (Matt. 10:4; 26:14, 25, 47; 27:3).
9. One of Jesus' half-brothers (Matt. 13:55).
10. A Galilean who incited a rebellion against Rome (Acts 5:37).
11. A person Paul stayed with in Damascus (Acts 9:11).
12. A prophet sent to Antioch with Silas (Acts 15:22, 27).
13. See Thaddeus.

Judith *[same as Juda]*
The daughter of Beeri the Hittite, and wife of Esau (Gen. 26:34).

Julia *[downy; soft and tender hair]*
A Christian to whom Paul sent greetings (Rom. 16:7).

Julius *[same as Julia]*
The centurion who took Paul to Rome as a prisoner (Acts 27:1, 3).

Junia *[youth]*
A Christian to whom Paul sent greetings (Rom. 16:7).

Jushab-hesed *[dwelling place; change of mercy]*
A son of Zerubbabel (1 Chron. 3:20).

Justus *[just or upright]*
1. A Christian at Corinth, with whom Paul stayed (Acts 18:7).
2. See Jesus 2. 3. See Joseph 11.

Kadmiel *[God of antiquity; God of rising]*
1. An ancestor of the returning captives (Ezra 2:40; Neh. 7:43).
2. A person who helped repair the temple (Ezra 3:9).
3. A Levite who led the devotions of the people (Neh. 9:4–5; 10:9).

Kallai *[light; resting by fire; my voice]*
A priest who returned to Jerusalem with Zerubbabel (Neh. 12:20).

Kareah (Careah) *[bald; ice]*
The father of Johanan and Jonathan (Jer. 40:8).

Kedar *[blackness; sorrow]*
Ishmael's second son (Gen. 25:13; 1 Chron. 1:29).

Kedemah *[oriental; ancient; first]*
The youngest of Ishmael's sons (Gen. 25:15; 1 Chron. 1:31).

Keilah
A descendant of Caleb (1 Chron. 4:19).

Kelaiah *[voice of the Lord; gathering together]*
One of the priests who married a foreign wife during the exile (Ezra 10:23).

Kelita *[same as Kelaiah]*
1. A priest who explained the Law when it was read by Ezra (Neh. 8:7).
2. A person who sealed the new covenant with God after the exile (Neh. 10:10).

Kemuel *[God hath raised up, or established him]*
1. The son of Nahor by Milcah, and father of Aram (Gen. 22:21).
2. The son of Shiptan, and prince of the tribe of Ephraim; one of the twelve men appointed by Moses to divide the land of Canaan (Num. 34:24).
3. A Levite, father of Hashabiah, prince of the tribe in David's reign (1 Chron. 27:17).

Kenan *[buyer; owner]*
See Cainan.

Kenaz (Kenez) *[this purchase; this lamentation]*
1. A chief of Edom (Gen. 36: 42).
2. The fourth son of Eliphaz (Gen. 36:11).
3. Father of the judge Othniel (Judg. 1:13).
4. A grandson of Caleb (1 Chron. 4:15).

Keren-happuch *[the horn or child of beauty]*
Job's third daughter after his restoration (Job 42:14).

Keros *[crooked; crookedness]*
Ancestor of a clan who returned from the exile with Zerubbabel (Ezra 2:44; Neh. 7:47).

Keturah *[that makes the incense to fume]*
The wife of Abraham after the death of Sarah (Gen. 25:1; 1 Chron. 1:32).

Kezia *[superficies; the angle; cassia]*
Job's second daughter after his restoration (Job 42:14).

Kish *[hard; difficult; straw; for age]*
1. A son of Gibeon (1 Chron. 8:30).
2. The father of Saul (1 Sam. 9:1).
3. A descendant of Levi who helped cleanse the temple in Hezekiah's reign (2 Chron. 29:12).
4. Great-grandfather of Mordecai (Esther 2:5).
5. A Levite in David's reign (1 Chron. 23:21; 24:28–29).

Kishi *[hardness; his gravity; his offense]*
Father of Ethan the minstrel (1 Chron. 6:44).

Kittim *[breaking; bruising small; gold; coloring]*
Son of Javan (Gen. 10:4; 1 Chron. 1:7).

Koa *[hope; a congregation; a line; a rule]*
A prince or people living between Egypt and Syria (Ezek. 23:23).

Kohath *[congregation; wrinkle; bluntness]*
Levi's second son and start of the priestly tribe (Gen. 46:11; Exod. 6:16).

Kolaiah
1. A descendant of Benjamin (Neh. 11:7).
2. The father of the false prophet Ahab (Jer. 29:21).

Korah *[baldness; ice; frost]*
1. A son of Esau by Aholibamah (Gen. 36:5, 14, 18; 1 Chron. 1:35).
2. A son of Eliphaz (Gen. 36:16).
3. A son of Hebron (1 Chron. 2:43).
4. One of the leaders of the rebellion against Moses and Aaron who was swallowed up by the earth (Num. 16; 26:9–11).
5. Grandson of Kohath and ancestor of some sacred musicians (1 Chron. 6:22).

Kore
1. A son of Asaph whose descendants were gatekeepers in the tabernacle (1 Chron. 9:19; 26:1).
2. A Levite in Hezekiah's reign in charge of the freewill offerings (2 Chron. 31:14).

Koz
1. Ancestor of a priestly family returning from captivity (Ezra 2:61).
2. An ancestor of a person who helped repair the wall of Jerusalem (Neh. 3:4).

Kushaiah *[hardness; his gravity; his offense]*
See Kishi.

Laadah *[to assemble together; to testify; passing over]*
A descendant of Judah (1 Chron. 4:21).

Laadan *[for pleasure; devouring; judgment]*
1. A descendant of Ephraim (1 Chron. 7:26).
2. A Levite from the family of Gershom (1 Chron. 23:7–9; 26:21).

Laban *[white; shining; gentle; brittle]*
Brother of Rebekah and father of Leah and Rachel (Genesis 24–31).

Lael *[to God; to the mighty]*
A descendant of Gershon (Num. 3:24).

Lahad *[praising; to confess]*
A descendant of Judah (1 Chron. 4:2).

Lahmi *[my bread; my war]*
Brother of the giant Goliath (1 Chron. 20:5).

Laish *[a lion]*
Father of Phaltiel, to whom Saul had given Michal, David's wife (1 Sam. 25:44; 2 Sam. 3:15).

Lamech *[poor; made low]*
1. Father of Noah and ancestor of Jesus Christ (Gen. 5:25–31; Luke 3:36).
2. The father of Jabal and Jubal. He is the first recorded polygamist (Gen. 4:18–26).

Lapidoth *[enlightened; lamps]*
The husband of the prophetess Deborah (Judg. 4:4).

Lazarus *[assistance of God]*
1. The brother of Martha and Mary whom Jesus raised from the dead (John 11:1).
2. The name of a beggar in one of Jesus' parables (Luke 16:19–31).

Leah *[weary; tired]*
The daughter of Laban who became Jacob's wife (Genesis 29–31).

Lebana (Lebanah)
Leader of a family of returning exiles (Neh. 7:48).

Lebanah
See Lebana.

Lebbaeus *[a man of heart; praising; confessing]*
See Thaddeus.

Lecah
A descendant of Judah (1 Chron. 4:21).

Lehabim *[flames; inflamed; swords]*
A descendant of Mizraim (Gen. 10:13).

Lemuel *[God with them, or him]*
An unknown king often supposed to be Solomon or Hezekiah, whose words are recorded in Proverbs 31:1–9.

Letushim *[hammermen; filemen]*
A son of Dedan (Gen. 25:3).

Leummim *[countries; without water]*
A son of Dedan (Gen. 25:3).

Levi *[associated with him]*
1. The third son of Jacob by his wife Leah who went to Egypt with his father (Gen. 39:34).
2, 3. Two ancestors of Jesus Christ (Luke 3:24, 29).
4. Another name for Matthew. See Matthew.

Libni *[white; whiteness]*
1. A son of Merari (1 Chron. 6:29).
2. See Laadan.

Likhi
A descendant of Benjamin (1 Chron. 7:19).

Linus *[net]*
A Christian in Rome, known to Paul and to Timothy (2 Tim. 4:21).

Lo-ammi *[not my people]*
Symbolic name of Hosea's son (Hosea 1:9).

Lois *[better]*
Timothy's godly grandmother (2 Tim. 1:5).

Lo-ruhamah *[not having obtained mercy; not pitied]*
Symbolic name of Hosea's daughter (Hosea 1:6).

Lot *[wrapt up; hidden; covered; myrrh; rosin]*
Abraham's nephew who escaped from Sodom (Gen. 13:1–14).

Lotan *[wrapt up; hidden; covered; myrrh; rosin]*
An Edomite chief (Gen. 36:20–29; 1 Chron. 1:38–39).

Lucas *[luminous; white]*
See Luke.

Lucius *[luminous; white]*
1. A Jewish Christian who sent his greetings to the Christians at Rome (Rom. 16:21).
2. A prophet or teacher from Cyrene who ministered in Antioch (Acts 13:1).

Lud *[nativity; generation]*
A son of Shem (Gen. 10:22).

Ludim *[nativity; generation]*
A son of Mizraim (Gen. 10:13; 1 Chron. 1:11).

Luke (Lucas) *[luminous; white]*
Gospel writer, doctor, and Paul's traveling companion (Col. 4:14; 2 Tim. 4:11; Philem. 24).

Lydia *[a standing pool]*
The first European convert of Paul (Acts 18:14–15).

Lysanias *[that drives away sorrow]*
The tetrarch of Abilene (Luke 3:1).

Lysias *[dissolving]*
See Claudius Lysias.

Maacah (Maachah) *[pressed down; worn; fastened]*
1. One of David's wives and the mother of Absalom (2 Sam. 3:3).
2. A king of Maacah (2 Sam. 10:6, 8; 1 Chron. 19:7).
3. The son of Nahor, Abraham's brother (Gen. 22:24).
4. The father of Achish; king of Gath at the beginning of Solomon's reign (1 Kings 2:39).
5. The mother of Asa, king of Judah (1 Kings 15:13; 2 Chron. 15:16).
6. Caleb's concubine (1 Chron. 2:48).
7. The wife of Machir, son of Manasseh (1 Chron. 7:15–16).
8. The wife of Jehiel (1 Chron. 8:20; 9:35).
9. The father of one of David's guards (2 Chron. 11:43).
10. Father of Sephatiah, ruler of Simeon (1 Chron. 27:16).
11. See Michaiah 2.

Maadai *[pleasant; testifying]*
A person who married a foreign wife during the exile (Ezra 10:34).

Maadiah *[pleasantness; the testimony of the Lord]*
One of the priests who returned with Zerubbabel (Neh. 12:5); called Moadiah in Nehemiah 12:17.

Maai *[belly; heaping up]*
A priest who helped purify the people who returned from the exile (Neh. 12:36).

Maaseiah *[the work of the Lord]*
1. One of the Levites appointed by David to sing (1 Chron. 15:18, 20).
2. A commander who helped make Josiah king of Judah (2 Chron. 23:1).
3. A high-ranking officer in Uzziah's reign (2 Chron. 26:11).
4. A son of Ahaz, king of Judah (2 Chron. 28:7).
5. The governor of Jerusalem in Josiah's reign (2 Chron. 34:8).
6. 7. 8. 9. Four men who took foreign wives during the exile (Ezra 10:18, 21–22, 30).
10. The father of Azariah, who helped repair the wall of Jerusalem (Neh. 3:23).
11. A priest who stood with Ezra when he read the Law to the people (Neh. 8:4).
12. A Levite who explained the Law (Neh. 8:7).
13. A person who sealed the new covenant with God after the exile (Neh. 10:25).
14. A descendant of Pharez who lived in Jerusalem (Neh. 11:5).
15. A Benjamite whose descendants lived in Jerusalem (Neh. 11:7).
16. 17. Two priests who took part in the purification of the wall of Jerusalem (Neh. 12:41–42).
18. A priest whose son was sent by King Zedekiah to find out the Lord's will (Jer. 21:1; 29:25; 37:3).
19. Father of Zedekiah the false prophet (Jer. 29:21).
20. A temple officer (Jer. 35:4).
21. Grandfather of Baruch, Jeremiah's scribe (Jer. 32:12).

Maasiai *[the defense, or strength, or trust of the Lord]*
A descendant of Aaron (1 Chron. 9:12).

Maath *[wiping away; breaking; fearing; smiting]*
An ancestor of Jesus Christ (Luke 3:26).

Maaz *[wood; wooden]*
A son of Ram (1 Chron. 2:27).

Maaziah
1. A priest who sealed the new covenant with God after the exile (Neh. 10:8).
2. A priest during the reign of David who served in the sanctuary (1 Chron. 24:18).

Machbanai *[poverty; the smiting of his son]*
A person who joined David at Ziklag (1 Chron. 12:13).

Machbenah *[same as Machbanai]*
A descendant of Caleb (1 Chron. 2:49).

Machi *[poor; a smiter]*
Father of one of the spies who went with Caleb to spy out the land of Canaan (Num. 13:15).

Machir *[selling; knowing]*
1. The eldest son of Manasseh (Gen. 50:23).
2. A descendant of Manasseh living near Mahanaim (2 Sam. 9:4–5; 17:27).

Machnadebai *[smiter]*
A person who married a foreign wife during the exile (Ezra 10:40).

Madai *[a measure; judging; a garment]*
Son of Japheth (Gen. 10:2).

Magdiel *[declaring God; chosen fruit of God]*
A chief of Edom, descended from Esau (Gen. 36:43; 1 Chron. 1:54).

Magog *[covering; roof; dissolving]*
The second son of Japheth (Gen. 10:2).

Magor-missabib *[fear on every side]*
Symbolic name given to Pashur by Jeremiah (Jer. 20:1–3).

Magpiash *[a body thrust hard together]*
A person who sealed the new covenant with God after the exile (Neh. 10:20).

Mahalah *[sickness; a company of dancers; a harp]*
A descendant of Manasseh (1 Chron. 7:18). See Mahlah.

Mahalaleel (Maleleel) *[praising God]*
1. Son of Cainan and ancestor of Jesus Christ (Gen. 5:12–13, 15–17; 1 Chron. 1:2; Luke 3:37).
2. One whose descendants lived in Jerusalem (Neh. 11:4).

Mahalath *[sickness; a company of dancers; a harp]*
1. One of Esau's wives (Gen. 28:9).
2. Rehoboam's wife (2 Chron. 11:18).

Mahali *[infirmity; a harp; pardon]*
See Mahli.

Maharai *[hasting; a hill; from a hill]*
One of David's soldiers (2 Sam. 23:28; 1 Chron. 11:30; 27:13).

Mahath *[same as Maath]*
1. A descendant of Kohath who helped purify the sanctuary (1 Chron. 6:35).
2. A Levite chief officer in charge of dedicated things in Hezekiah's reign (2 Chron. 31:13).

Mahazioth *[seeing a sign; seeing a letter]*
An organizer of the temple singing (1 Chron. 25:4, 30).

Maher-shalal-hash-baz *[making speed to the spoil; he hastens to the prey]*
Symbolic name of Isaiah's son (Isa. 8:1–4).

Mahlah *[same as Mahali]*
Zelophehad's eldest daughter (Num. 27:1–11). See Mahalah.

Mahli (Mahali) *[same as Mahali]*
1. A son of Merari (Num. 3:20; 1 Chron. 6:19, 29).
2. A descendant of Levi (1 Chron. 6:47; 23:23; 24:30).

Mahlon
Ruth's first husband (Ruth 1:2–5; 4:10).

Mahol
Father of the four men of wisdom (1 Kings 4:31).

Malachi *[my messenger; my angel]*
Prophet and author of the last book of the Old Testament.

Malcham, Malchom *[their king; their counselor]*
A descendant of Benjamin (1 Chron. 8:9).

Malchiah (Malchijah; Melchiah) *[the Lord my king, or my counselor]*
1. A song leader in David's reign (1 Chron. 6:40).
2. An Aaronite whose descendants lived in Jerusalem after its captivity (1 Chron. 9:12).
3. Head of a priestly family (1 Chron. 24:9).
4. 5. 6. Three men who married foreign wives during the exile (Ezra 10:25, 31).
7. 8. 9. Three men who helped rebuild the wall of Jerusalem (Neh. 3:11, 14, 31).
10. A person who stood next to Ezra as he read the Law (Neh. 8:4).
11. A priest who helped purify the wall of Jerusalem (Neh. 10:3).
12. Father of Pashur (Jer. 21:1).

Malchiel *[God is my king, or counselor]*
A descendant of Asher (Gen. 46:17).

Malchijah
See Malchiah.

Malchiram
A descendant of King Jehoiakim (1 Chron. 3:18).

Malchi-shua
See Melchi-shua.

Malchus *[my king, kingdom, or counselor]*
The servant of the high priest whose right ear Peter cut off (Matt. 26:51; Mark 14:17; Luke 22:49, 51; John 18:10).

Maleleel *[same as Mahaleleel]*
Greek form of Mahalaleel. See Mahalaleel.

Mallothi *[fullness; circumcision]*
A person who organized singing in the temple (1 Chron. 25:4, 26).

Malluch *[reigning; counseling]*
1. A descendant of Levi (1 Chron. 6:44).
2. 3. Two people who married foreign wives during the exile (Ezra 10:29).
4. A priest who sealed the new covenant with God after the exile (Neh. 10:4); called Melicu in Nehemiah 12:14.
5. A leader who sealed the new covenant with God after the exile (Neh. 10:27).

Mamre *[rebellious; bitter; set with trees]*
An Amorite chief who sided with Abram (Gen. 14:13, 24).

Manaen *[a comforter; a leader]*
A teacher or prophet at Antioch (Acts 13:1).

Manahath
A descendant of Seir the Horite (Gen. 36:23; 1 Chron. 1:40).

Manasseh (Manasses) *[forgetfulness; he that is forgotten]*
1. The thirteenth king of Judah, son of Hezekiah, and ancestor of Jesus Christ (2 Kings 21:1–18; Matt. 1:10).
2. One whose descendants set up idolatrous images at Laish (Judg. 18:30).
3. Joseph's eldest son (Gen. 41:51; 46:20).
4. 5. Two people who married foreign wives during the exile (Ezra 10:30, 33).

Manasses
Greek form of Manasseh. See Manasseh.

Manoah *[rest; a present]*
The father of Samson (Judg. 13:2).

Maoch
The father of Achish king of Gath, who protected David (1 Sam. 27:2).

Mara (Marah) *[bitter; bitterness]*
The name Naomi adopted after her husband's death (Ruth 1:20).

Marcus *[polite; shining]*
See Mark.

Mareshah *[from the beginning; an inheritance]*
1. Father of Hebron (1 Chron. 2:42).
2. Son of Laadah (1 Chron. 4:21).

Mark (Marcus) *[same as Marcus]*
A Christian convert and missionary companion of Paul, and author of the second Gospel (Acts 12:12, 25; 15:37; Col. 4:10).

Marsena *[bitterness of a bramble]*
A prince of Persia (Esther 1:14).

Martha *[who becomes bitter; provoking]*
Sister of Mary and Lazarus (Luke 10:38, 40–41; John 11:1–39).

Mary *[rebellion]*
1. The mother of Jesus Christ (Luke 1:46–55).
2. The sister of Lazarus and Martha (Luke 10:39, 42; John 11:1–45).
3. A woman from Magdala in Galilee who followed Jesus after having seven devils expelled from her (Matt. 27:56, 61; 28:1; Luke 8:2).
4. A Roman Christian to whom Paul sent greetings (Rom. 16:6).
5. The mother of John Mark (Acts 12:12).
6. Mary, the mother of Joses (Mark 15:47) and James (Luke 24:10), the "other Mary" (Matt. 28:1), and the Mary, wife of Cleophas (John 19:25), may be the same person (Mark 15:40).

Mash *[who is drawn by force]*
Son or grandson of Shem (Gen. 10:23).

Massa *[a burden; prophecy]*
A son of Ishmael (Gen. 26:14; 1 Chron. 1:30).

Mathusala
Greek form of Methuselah. See Methuselah.

Matred *[wand of government]*
Daughter of Mezahab and mother of Mehetabel (Gen. 36:39; 1 Chron. 1:50).

Matri *[rain; prison]*
Ancestor of a tribe of Benjamin, to which Saul the king of Israel belonged (1 Sam. 10:21).

Mattan (Mattana, Mattenai) *[gifts; rains]*
1. The priest of Baal killed in front of his altars in the idol temple at Jerusalem (2 Kings 11:18; 2 Chron. 23:17).
2. The father of Shephatiah (Jer. 38:1).

Mattaniah *[gift, or hope, of the Lord]*
1. The original name of Zedekiah king of Judah (2 Kings 24:17).
2. A Levite singer and descendant of Asaph (1 Chron. 9:15).
3. A son of Heman the singer (1 Chron. 25:4).
4. A person who helped cleanse the temple (2 Chron. 29:13).
5. 6. 7. 8. Four people who married foreign wives during the exile (Ezra 10:26–27, 30, 37).
9. A descendant of Levi (Neh. 13:13).

Mattatha *[his gift]*
An ancestor of Jesus Christ (Luke 3:31).

Mattathah *[his gift]*
A person who married a foreign wife during the exile (Ezra 10:33).

Mattathias *[the gift of the Lord]*
1. An ancestor of Jesus Christ (Luke 3:25).
2. Another ancestor of Jesus Christ (Luke 3:26).

Mattenai
1. 2. Two people who married foreign wives during the exile (Ezra 10:33, 37).
3. A priest who returned from the exile (Neh. 12:19).

Matthan *[same as Mattan]*
An ancestor of Jesus Christ (Matt. 1:15).

Matthat
1. Grandfather of Joseph and ancestor of Jesus Christ (Luke 3:24).
2. Another ancestor of Jesus Christ (Luke 3:29).

Matthew *[given; a reward]*
One of the twelve apostles and author of the Gospel bearing his name (Matt. 9:9).

Matthias *[same as Mattathias]*
A Christian chosen to take Judas's place as an apostle (Acts 1:26).

Mattithiah *[same as Mattathias]*
1. A Levite responsible for baking the offering bread (1 Chron. 9:31).
2. A Levite singer and gatekeeper (1 Chron. 16:5).
3. A son of Jeduthun (1 Chron. 25:3, 21).
4. A person who married a foreign wife during the exile (Ezra 10:43).
5. One who stood with Ezra when he read the Law (Neh. 8:4).

Mebunnai *[son; building; understanding]*
See Sibbechai.

Medad *[he that measures; water of love]*
One of the elders of the Jews on whom the Spirit came (Num. 11:26–27).

Medan *[judgment; process]*
A son of Abraham and Keturah (Gen. 23:5; 1 Chron. 1:42).

Mehetabel (Mehetabeel) *[how good is God]*
1. Wife of King Hadad of Edom (Gen. 36:39).
2. Father of Delaiah who opposed Nehemiah (Neh. 6:10).

Mehida *[a riddle; sharpness of wit]*
An ancestor of the returned captives (Ezra 2:52; Neh. 7:54).

Mehir *[a reward]*
A descendant of Caleb of Hur (1 Chron. 4:11).

Mehujael *[who proclaims God]*
A descendant of Cain (Gen. 4:18).

Mehuman *[making an uproar; a multitude]*
One of Ahasuerus's eunuchs (Esther 1:10).

Mehunim
An ancestor of the returning captives (Ezra 2:50).

Melatiah *[deliverance of the Lord]*
A Gibeonite who assisted in rebuilding the wall of Jerusalem (Neh. 3:7).

Melchi *[my king; my counsel]*
1. An ancestor of Jesus Christ (Luke 3:24).
2. Another ancestor of Jesus Christ (Luke 3:28).

Melchiah *[God is my king]*
See Malchiah.

Melchisedec
Greek form of Melchizedek. See Melchizedek.

Melchi-shua (Malchi-shua) *[king of health; magnificent king]*
Third son of Saul (1 Sam. 14:49; 31:2).

Melchizedek (Melchisedec) *[king of justice]*
King and priest of Salem (Gen. 14:18–20; Ps. 110:4; Hebrews 5–7).

Melea *[supplying; supplied]*
An ancestor of Jesus Christ (Luke 3:31).

Melech *[king; counselor]*
Great-grandson of Saul (1 Chron. 8:35; 9:41).

Melicu *[his kingdom; his counselor]*
See Malluch 4.

Melzar *[circumcision of a narrow place, or of a bond]*
A person who was in charge of Daniel and his companions (Dan. 1:11, 16); may be a title rather than a proper name.

Memucan *[impoverished; to prepare; certain; true]*
A Persian prince (Esther 1:14–21).

Menahem *[comforter; who conducts them; preparation of heat]*
A usurper of Israel's throne who killed Shallum (2 Kings 15:14–23).

Menan *[numbered; rewarded; prepared]*
An ancestor of Jesus Christ (Luke 3:31).

Meonothai
A descendant of Judah (1 Chron. 4:14).

Mephibosheth *[out of my mouth proceeds reproach]*
1. Saul's son by Rizpah the daughter of Aiah, his concubine (2 Sam. 21:8).
2. Saul's grandson (2 Sam. 4:4); also called Merib-baal (1 Chron. 8:34).

Merab *[he that fights or disputes]*
Saul's daughter, promised to David, but given to Adriel (1 Sam. 14:49).

Meraiah
A priest during Joiakim's reign (Neh. 12:13).

Meraioth *[bitterness; rebellious; changing]*
1. A descendant of Aaron (1 Chron. 6:61; 7:62).
2. Another priest of the same line (1 Chron. 9:11; Neh. 11:11).
3. Another priest at the end of the exile (Neh. 12:15).

Merari *[bitter; to provoke]*
The third son of Levi and founder of a priestly clan (Gen. 46:8, 11).

Mered *[rebellious, ruling]*
A descendant of Judah (1 Chron. 4:17–18).

Meremoth *[bitterness; myrrh of death]*
1. A priest who weighed the gold and silver sacred articles of the temple (Ezra 8:33).
2. A person who married a foreign wife during the exile (Ezra 10:36).
3. A person who sealed the new covenant with God after the exile (Neh. 10:5).

Meres *[defluxion; imposthume]*
One of the seven princes of Persia (Esther 1:14).

Merib-baal *[he that resists Baal; rebellion]*
See Mephibosheth.

Merodach-baladan *[bitter contrition, without judgment]*
A Babylonian king in Hezekiah's reign (Jer. 50:2).

Mesech (Meshech) *[who is drawn by force]*
1. A son of Japheth (Gen. 10:2; 1 Chron. 1:5).
2. See Mash.

Mesha *[burden; salvation]*
1. A king of Moab who rebelled against Ahaziah (2 Kings 3:4).
2. The eldest son of Caleb (1 Chron. 2:42).
3. A descendant of Benjamin (1 Chron. 8:9).

Meshach *[that draws with force]*
The name given to Mishael after he was taken captive to Babylon (Dan. 1:7; 3:12–30).

Meshelemiah *[peace, or perfection, of the Lord]*
A descendant of Levi (1 Chron. 9:21; 26:1–2, 9).

Meshezabeel *[God taking away; the salvation of God]*
1. One whose descendants helped repair the wall of Jerusalem (Neh. 3:4).
2. A person who sealed the new covenant with God after the exile (Neh. 10:21; 11:24).

Meshillemith *[peaceable; perfect; giving again]*
A priest whose descendants lived in Jerusalem (Neh. 11:13; 1 Chron. 9:12).

Meshillemoth *[same as Meshillemith]*
1. A descendant of Ephraim (2 Chron. 28:12).
2. A priest from the family of Immer whose descendants lived in Jerusalem (Neh. 11:13).

Meshullam *[peaceable; perfect; their parables]*
1. Grandfather of Shaphan the scribe (2 Kings 22:3).
2. A descendant of King Jehoiakim (1 Chron. 3:19).
3. Head of a family of Gad (1 Chron. 5:13).
4. A descendant of Benjamin (1 Chron. 8:17).
5. One whose son lived in Jerusalem (1 Chron. 9:7).
6. One who lived in Jerusalem after the captivity (1 Chron. 9:8).
7. A descendant of Aaron and an ancestor of Ezra (1 Chron. 9:11; Neh. 11:11).
8. A priest (1 Chron. 9:12).
9. A chief officer of the temple work in Josiah's reign (2 Chron. 34:12).
10. A leader who returned to Jerusalem with Ezra (Ezra 8:16).
11. A person who helped take account of those who had foreign wives after the exile (Ezra 10:15).
12. A person who married a foreign wife during the exile (Ezra 10:29).
13. 14. Two people who rebuilt part of the wall of Jerusalem (Neh. 3:30; 6:18).
15. A prince or priest who stood with Ezra as he read the Law (Neh. 8:4).
16. A priest who sealed the new covenant with God after the exile (Neh. 10:7).
17. A person who sealed the new covenant with God after the exile (Neh. 10:20).
18. A person whose descendants lived in Jerusalem (Neh. 11:17).
19. A priest who helped dedicate the wall of Jerusalem (Neh. 12:13, 33).
20. A descendant of Ginnethon (Neh. 12:16).
21. A Levite and gatekeeper after the exile (Neh. 12:25).

Meshullemeth
Wife of Manasseh and mother of Amon (2 Kings 21:19).

Methusael *[who demands his death]*
The father of Lamech (Gen. 4:18).

Methuselah (Mathusala) *[he has sent his death]*
The longest living person recorded in the Bible and grandfather of Noah (Gen. 5:21–27).

Meunim *[dwelling places; afflicted]*
See Mehunim.

Mezahab *[gilded]*
Grandfather of Mehetabel, wife of Hadar, the eighth king of Edom (Gen. 36:39; 1 Chron. 1:50).

Miamin *[the right hand]*
1. A person who married a foreign wife during the exile (Ezra 10:25).
2. A priest who returned from the exile with Zerubbabel (Neh. 12:5).

Mibhar *[chosen; youth]*
One of David's mighty men (1 Chron. 11:38).

Mibsam *[smelling sweet]*
1. Son of Ishmael (Gen. 25:13; 1 Chron. 1:29).
2. A son of Simeon (1 Chron. 4:25).

Mibzar *[defending; forbidding; taking away]*
Chief of Edom (Gen. 36:42; 1 Chron. 1:53).

Micah (Michah) *[poor; humble]*
1. A man from Ephraim who began a pagan shrine (Judg. 17:1–18).
2. Head of a family of Reuben (1 Chron. 5:5).
3. The son of Meribbaal, the grandson of Saul (1 Chron. 8:34–35; 9:40–41).
4. A Levite whose descendants lived in Jerusalem (1 Chron. 9:15).
5. A descendant of Kohath (1 Chron. 23:20).
6. Father of Abdon who sought the Lord's guidance when the book of the Law was found (2 Chron. 34:20); called Michaiah in 2 Kings 22:12.
7. A prophet from Judah, contemporary with Isaiah and Hosea, who wrote one of the minor prophets (Jer. 26:18; Micah 1:1).

Micaiah *[who is like to God?]*
A prophet who predicted Ahab's defeat and death (1 Kings 22:8–28).

Micha (Michah) *[same as Micaiah]*
1. A son of Mephibosheth (2 Sam. 9:12).
2. A person who sealed the new covenant with God after the exile (Neh. 10:11).
3. The father of Mattaniah, a Gershonite Levite and descendant of Ashaph (Neh. 11:17, 22).

Michael *[same as Micah]*
1. One of the twelve spies who spied out the land of Canaan (Num. 13:13).
2. A descendant of Gad (1 Chron. 5:13).
3. Another descendant of Gad (1 Chron. 5:14).
4. An ancestor of Asaph (1 Chron. 6:40).
5. A chief of the tribe of Issachar (1 Chron. 7:3).
6. A Benjamite who was living in Jerusalem (1 Chron. 8:16).
7. A person who joined David at Ziklag (1 Chron. 12:20).
8. Father of Omri, a prince of Issachar (1 Chron. 27:18).
9. A son of Jehoshaphat (2 Chron. 21:2).
10. An ancestor of the returning captives (Ezra 8:8).
11. God's messenger who came to Daniel (Dan. 10:21).

Michah
See Micha.

Michaiah *[same as Micah]*
1. Ancestor of a person at the purification of Jerusalem's wall (Neh. 12:35).
2. Wife of Rehoboam (2 Chron. 13:2).
3. A prince commissioned by Jehoshaphat (2 Chron. 17:7).
4. A prince of Judah (Jer. 36:11, 13).
5. See Micah 6.

Michal *[who is perfect?]*
One of Saul's daughters who married David (1 Sam. 14:49).

Michri *[selling]*
An ancestor of a clan of Benjamin in Jerusalem (1 Chron. 9:8).

Midian *[judgment; covering; habit]*
A son of Abraham and Keturah and founder of the Midianites (Gen. 25:2; 1 Chron. 1:32).

Mijamin *[right hand]*
1. A priest in David's reign (1 Chron. 24:9).
2. A person who sealed the new covenant with God after the exile (Neh. 10:7).

Mikloth *[little wants; little voices; looking downward]*
1. A descendant of Benjamin living in Jerusalem (1 Chron. 8:32; 9:37–38).
2. One of David's chief military officers (1 Chron. 27:4).

Mikneiah
A Levite musician (1 Chron. 15:18, 21).

Milalai *[circumcision; my talk]*
A priest who helped in the purification of the wall of Jerusalem (Neh. 12:36).

Milcah *[queen]*
1. A daughter of Haran, wife of Nahor, and Abraham's brother (Gen. 11:29; 22:20, 23).
2. The fourth daughter of Zelophehad (Num. 26:33; 27:1).

Miniamin *[right hand]*
1. A Levite in Hezekiah's reign (2 Chron. 31:15).
2. A priest in Joiakim's reign (Neh. 12:17).
3. One of the priests at the dedication of the wall of Jerusalem (Neh. 12:41).

Miriam *[rebellion]*
1. The sister of Moses and Aaron (Exod. 2:4–10).
2. A woman descendant of Judah (1 Chron. 4:17).

Mirma
A descendant of Benjamin (1 Chron. 8:10).

Mishael *[who is asked for or lent]*
1. The person who removed the bodies of Nadab and Abihu (Lev. 10:4).
2. A person who stood with Ezra when he read the law to the people (Neh. 8:4).
3. One Daniel's companions in Babylon (Dan. 1:6–7).

Misham *[their savior; taking away]*
A descendant of Benjamin (1 Chron. 8:12).

Mishma *[hearing; obeying]*
1. A son of Ishmael and brother of Mibsam (Gen. 25:14; 1 Chron. 1:30).
2. A son of Simeon (1 Chron. 4:25).

Mishmannah *[fatness; taking away provision]*
A person who joined David at Ziklag (1 Chron. 12:10).

Mispereth (Mispar) *[numbering; showing; increase of tribute]*
A person who returned from the Babylonian captivity with Zerubbabel and Jeshua (Neh. 7:7); called Mispar in Ezra 2:2.

Mithredath *[breaking the law]*
1. The treasurer of Cyrus, king of Persia, through whom he restored the temple vessels (Ezra 1:8).
2. A Persian officer who protested the restoration of Jerusalem (Ezra 4:7).

Mizraim *[tribulations]*
A son of Ham and progenitor of the Egyptian nation (Gen. 10:6, 13).

Mizzah *[defluxion from the head]*
A duke of Edom (Gen. 36:13, 17; 1 Chron. 1:37).

Mnason *[a diligent seeker; an exhorter]*
A Cyprian convert who went with Paul from Caesarea to Jerusalem (Acts 21:16).

Moab *[of his father]*
Lot's son and an ancestor of the Moabites (Gen. 19:34).

Moadiah
See Maadiah.

Molid *[nativity; generation]*
A descendant of Judah (1 Chron. 2:29).

Mordecai *[contrition; bitter; bruising]*
1. A Jewish exile who helped save the Jews from extermination (Esther 2–10).
2. A leader who returned from the Babylonian captivity (Ezra 2:2).

Moses *[taken out; drawn forth]*
Israel's prophet, lawgiver, and deliverer from Egypt whose life is recorded in the book of Exodus.

Moza *[unleavened]*
1. A son of Caleb (1 Chron. 2:46).
2. A descendant of Saul (1 Chron. 8:36–37; 9:42–43).

Muppim (Shuppim, Shupham, Shephuphan) *[out of the mouth; covering]*
A descendant of Benjamin (Gen. 46:21); also called Shuppim (1 Chron. 7:12), Shupham (Num. 26:39), and Shephuphan (1 Chron. 8:5).

Mushi *[he that touches, that withdraws or takes away]*
A son of Merari, son of Levi (Exod. 6:19; Num. 3:20; 1 Chron. 6:19, 47).

Naam *[fair; pleasant]*
A son of Caleb (1 Chron. 4:15).

Naamah *[beautiful; agreeable]*
1. One of the four women whose names are preserved in the records of the world before the flood (all except Eve being Cainites); daughter of Lamech and Zillah (Gen. 4:22).
2. A wife of Solomon and mother of Rehoboam (1 Kings 14:21; 2 Chron. 12:13).

Naaman *[beautiful; agreeable]*
1. A Syrian general who was healed of his leprosy by bathing in the river Jordan (2 Kings 5; Luke 4:27).
2. Grandson of Benjamin (Gen. 26:38, 40).
3. A son of Benjamin and founder of a tribal family (Gen. 46:21).

Naarah *[young person]*
A wife of Ashur (1 Chron. 4:5–6).

Naarai *[young person]*
One of David's valiant men (1 Chron. 11:37). Probably the same person as Paarai in 2 Samuel 23:35.

Naashon *[that foretells; that conjectures]*
See Nahshon.

Naasson
The Greek form of Nahshon. See Nahshon.

Nabal *[fool; senseless]*
A wealthy Carmelite who refused to give food to David and his men (1 Samuel 25).

Naboth *[words; prophecies]*
Killed by Jezebel in order to secure his vineyard (1 Kings 21:1–18).

Nachor *[same as Nahor]*
Greek form of Nahor. See Nahor.

Nadab *[free and voluntary gift; prince]*
1. The eldest son of Aaron and Elisheba (Exod. 6:23; Lev. 10:1–3).
2. King Jeroboam I's son, who ruled Israel for two years (1 Kings 15:25–31).
3. A descendant of Jerahmeel (1 Chron. 2:28).
4. Gibeon's brother (1 Chron. 8:30).

Nagge *[clearness; brightness; light]*
One of the ancestors of Jesus Christ (Luke 3:25).

Naham *[comforter; leader]*
A descendant of Judah (1 Chron. 4:19).

Nahamaai *[comforter; leader]*
A person who returned from the Babylonian captivity with Zerubbabel and Jeshua (Neh. 7:7).

Naharai (Nahari) *[my nostrils; hot; anger]*
Joab's armor-bearer (2 Sam. 23:37).

Nahari
See Naharai.

Nahash *[snake; serpent]*
1. An Ammonite king who was defeated by Saul (1 Sam. 11:1–2).
2. Another king of Ammon (2 Sam. 10:2; 17:27).
3. The father of Abigail and Zeruiah (2 Sam. 17:25).

Nahath *[rest; a leader]*
1. A descendant of Esau (Gen. 36:13; 1 Chron. 1:37).
2. A chief officer of the temple offerings (2 Chron. 31:13).
3. See Toah.

Nahbi *[very secret]*
One of the twelve spies sent to explore Canaan (Num. 13:14).

Nahor (Nachor) *[hoarse; dry; hot]*
1. Abraham's grandfather and ancestor of Jesus Christ (Gen. 11:22–25; Luke 3:34).
2. Abraham's brother (Gen. 11:26–27).

Nahshon (Naashon) *[that foretells; that conjectures]*
A descendant of Judah and ancestor of Jesus Christ (Exod. 6:23; Num. 1:7; Matt. 1:4).

Nahum *[comforter; penitent]*
One of the twelve minor prophets who has a prophetic book named after him.

Naomi *[beautiful; agreeable]*
Ruth's mother-in-law (Ruth 1:2–4:17).

Naphish *[the soul; he that rests, refreshes himself, or respires]*
Son of Ishmael (Gen. 25:15; 1 Chron. 1:31).

Naphtali *[that struggles or fights]*
Jacob's sixth son (Gen. 30:7–8) whose descendants became one of the twelve tribes.

Narcissus *[astonishment; stupidity]*
A Roman Christian (Rom. 16:11).

Nathan *[given; giving; rewarded]*
1. Prophet and David's advisor (2 Sam. 7:2–3, 17; 2 Sam. 12:1–12).
2. King David's son and ancestor of Jesus Christ (2 Sam. 5:14; Luke 3:31).
3. Father of Igal (2 Sam. 23:36).
4. A descendant of Jerahmeel (1 Chron. 2:36).
5. One of Ezra's companions (Ezra 8:16).
6. A person who married a foreign wife during the exile (Ezra 10:39).
7. Brother of Joel, one of David's valiant men (1 Chron. 11:38).
8. Father of Solomon's chief officer (1 Kings 4:5).
9. A leader in Israel (Zech. 10:10).

Nathanael *[the gift of God]*
A Galilean who became a disciple of Jesus Christ (John 21:2). See also Bartholomew.

Nathan-melech *[the gift of the king, or of counsel]*
One of Josiah's officials (2 Kings 23:11).

Naum *[same as Nahum]*
An ancestor of Jesus Christ (Luke 3:25).

Neariah *[child of the Lord]*
1. A descendant of David (1 Chron. 3:22).
2. A descendant of Simeon (1 Chron. 4:42).

Nebai *[budding; speaking; prophesying]*
A person who sealed the new covenant with God after the exile with Nehemiah (Neh. 10:19).

Nebaioth (Nebajoth) *[words; prophecies; buds]*
Ishmael's oldest son (Gen. 25:13; 1 Chron. 1:29).

Nebat *[that beholds]*
Father of Jeroboam I (1 Kings 11:26).

Nebo *[that speaks or prophesies]*
An ancestor of the Jews who had married foreign wives during the exile (Ezra 10:43).

Nebuchadnezzar (Nebuchadrezzar) *[tears and groans of judgment]*
King of the Babylonian Empire (2 Kings 24:1, 10–11; 25:1, 8).

Nebushasban
A Babylonian prince (Jer. 39:13).

Nebuzar-adan *[fruits or prophecies of judgment]*
A Babylonian captain at the siege of Jerusalem (2 Kings 25:8, 11, 20).

Necho *[lame; beaten]*
Pharaoh of Egypt who fought Josiah at Megiddo (2 Chron. 35:20).

Nedabiah *[prince or vow of the Lord]*
A descendant of Jehoiakim, king of Judah (1 Chron. 3:18).

Nehemiah *[consolation; repentance of the Lord]*
1. Governor of Jerusalem who helped rebuild its wall (Neh. 1:1; 8:9; 12:47).
2. One of the leaders of the first return from Babylon to Jerusalem under Zerubbabel (Ezra 2:2; Neh. 7:7).
3. Son of Azbuk who helped to repair the wall of Jerusalem (Neh. 3:18).

Nehum *[comforter; penitent]*
See Rehum.

Nehushta *[made of brass]*
Daughter of Elnathan of Jerusalem, wife of Jehoiakim (2 Kings 24:8).

Nekoda *[painted; inconstant]*
1. Head of the family of the Nethinim (Ezra 2:48; Neh. 7:50).
2. The head of a family who had no genealogy after the exile (Ezra 2:60; Neh. 7:62).

Nemuel *[the sleeping of God]*
1. A descendant of Reuben (Num. 26:9).
2. A son of Simeon (Num. 26:12; 1 Chron. 4:24).

Nepheg *[weak; slacked]*
1. Korah's brother (Esther 6:21).
2. One of David's sons born in Jerusalem (2 Sam. 5:15; 1 Chron. 3:7; 14:6).

Nephishesim (Nephusim) *[diminished; torn in pieces]*
An ancestor of the returning captives (Neh. 7:62).

Nephusim *[same as Nephishesim]*
See Nephishesim.

Ner *[a lamp; new-tilled land]*
1. Saul's uncle and father of Abner (1 Sam. 14:50).
2. Saul's grandfather (1 Chron. 8:33).

Nereus *[same as Ner]*
A Roman Christian (Rom. 16:15).

Nergal-sharezer *[treasurer of Nergal]*
A Babylonian officer who released Jeremiah (Jer. 39:3, 13–14).

Neri *[my light]*
An ancestor of Jesus Christ (Luke 3:27).

Neriah *[light; lamp of the Lord]*
Baruch's father (Jer. 32:12, 16).

Nethaneel *[same as Nathanael]*
1. One of the people Moses sent to spy out the land of Canaan (Num. 1:8; 2:5; 7:18).
2. Fourth son of Jesse and David's brother (1 Chron. 2:14).
3. A priest during David's reign who blew the trumpet before the ark of the covenant when it was brought from the house of Obed-edom (1 Chron. 15:24).
4. A Levite, father of Shemaiah the scribe, in David's reign (1 Chron. 24:6).
5. Son of Obed-edom and gatekeeper of the tabernacle (1 Chron. 26:4).
6. One of the princes of Judah whom Jehoshaphat sent to teach the people (2 Chron. 17:7).
7. A chief of the Levites in Josiah's reign (2 Chron. 35:9).
8. A priest who married a foreign wife during the exile (Ezra 10:22).
9. A priest in Joiakim's reign (Neh. 12:21).
10. Levite musician at the purification ceremony of the wall of Jerusalem under Ezra and Nehemiah (Neh. 12:36).

Nethaniah *[the gift of the Lord]*
1. A musician in David's worship services (2 Kings 25:2, 12).
2. A Levite in Jehoshaphat's reign (2 Chron. 17:8).
3. The father of Jehudi (Jer. 36:14).
4. Father of Ishmael, and murderer of Gedaliah (Jer. 40:8, 14–15; 41:11).

Neziah *[conqueror; strong]*
Head of a Nethinim family who returned to Jerusalem with Zerubbabel (Ezra 2:54; Neh. 7:56).

Nicanor *[a conqueror; victorious]*
One of the seven chosen to care for the poor (Acts 6:5).

Nicodemus *[victory of the people]*
A Pharisee and ruler of the Jews who helped Joseph of Arimathaea take down and embalm the body of Jesus (John 3:1–15; 7:50–52; 19:39–42).

Nicolas *[same as Nicodemus]*
One of the seven chosen to care for the poor (Acts 6:5).

Nimrod *[rebellion, but probably an unknown Assyrian word]*
A son of Cush (Gen. 10:8–9).

Nimshi *[rescued from danger]*
An ancestor of Jehu (1 Kings 19:16; 2 Kings 9:2).

Noadiah *[witness, or ornament, of the Lord]*
1. A Levite, son of Binnui, to whom Ezra entrusted the temple's sacred vessels (Ezra 8:33).
2. The prophetess who opposed Nehemiah (Neh. 6:14).

Noah (Noe) *[repose; consolation]*
1. The patriarch who built the ark (Gen. 5:28–32; 6:8–22; 7–10).
2. One of the five daughters of Zelophehad (Num. 26:33).

Nobah *[that barks or yelps]*
A descendant of Manasseh who conquered Kenath (Num. 32:42).

Noe *[same as Noah]*
Greek form of Noah. See Noah.

Nogah *[brightness; clearness]*
A son of David (1 Chron. 3:7; 14:6).

Nohah *[rest; a guide]*
A son of Benjamin (1 Chron. 8:2).

Non *[posterity; a fish; eternal]*
See Nun.

Nun (Non) *[same as Non]*
1. A descendant of Ephraim (1 Chron. 7:27).
2. The father of Joshua (Exod. 33:11).

Nymphas *[spouse; bridegroom]*
A Christian in Laodicea to whom Paul sent greetings (Col. 4:15).

Obadiah *[servant of the Lord]*
1. Ahab's governor who tried to protect the prophets from Jezebel (1 Kings 18:3–16).
2. A descendant of David (1 Chron. 3:21).
3. A chief of the tribe of Issachar (1 Chron. 7:3).
4. A descendant of Saul (1 Chron. 8:33; 9:44).
5. A member of the tribe of Zebulun (1 Chron. 27:19).
6. A chief of the Gadites who joined David at Ziklag (1 Chron. 12:9).
7. One of the princes whom Jehoshaphat commissioned to teach the Law (2 Chron. 17:7–9).
8. A Levite chief officer of the temple work (2 Chron. 17:7–9).
9. Chief of a family who returned to Jerusalem with Ezra (Ezra 8:9).
10. A person who sealed the new covenant with God after the exile (Neh. 10:5).
11. A gatekeeper for the sanctuary of the temple (Neh. 12:25).
12. The fourth of the twelve minor prophets.
13. See Abda.

Obal *[inconvenience of old age]*
See Ebal.

Obed *[a servant; workman]*
1. Son of Boaz and Ruth, father of Jesse, and ancestor of Jesus Christ (Ruth 4:17; Matt. 1:5).
2. A descendant of Judah (1 Chron. 2:37–38).
3. One of David's mighty men (1 Chron. 11:47).
4. A Levite gatekeeper in David's reign (1 Chron. 26:7).
5. Father of Azariah, who helped Joash to become king of Judah (2 Chron. 23:1).

Obed-edom *[servant of Edom]*
1. A man who housed the ark of the covenant of the Lord for three months (2 Sam. 6:10–12).
2. One of the leading Levitical singers and doorkeepers (1 Chron. 15:18, 24).
3. A temple treasurer or official (2 Chron. 25:24).

Obil *[that weeps; who deserves to be bewailed]*
A descendant of Ishmael who looked after David's camels (1 Chron. 27:30).

Ocran *[a disturber; that disorders]*
A descendant of Asher (Num. 1:13; 2:27).

Oded *[to sustain, hold, lift up]*
1. Father of Azariah the prophet in Asa's reign (2 Chron. 15:1).
2. A Samarian prophet who persuaded the northern army to free their Judean slaves (2 Chron. 28:9–15).

Og *[a cake; bread baked in ashes]*
A giant from Bashan (Num. 21:33–35).

Ohad *[praising; confessing]*
A son of Simeon (Gen. 46:10).

Ohel *[tent; tabernacle; brightness]*
A son of Zerubbabel (1 Chron. 3:20).

Olympas *[heavenly]*
A Christian from Rome (Rom. 16:15).

Omar *[he that speaks; bitter]*
A grandson of Esau (Gen. 36:15).

Omri *[sheaf of corn]*
1. The sixth king of Israel and founder of the third dynasty (1 Kings 16:15–28).
2. A descendant of Benjamin (1 Chron. 7:8).
3. A descendant of Pharez (1 Chron. 9:4).
4. A prince of the tribe of Issachar in David's reign (1 Chron. 27:18).

On *[pain; force; iniquity]*
A Reubenite who rebelled against Moses and Aaron (Num. 16:1).

Onam *[same as On]*
1. A grandson of Seir (Gen. 36:23; 1 Chron. 1:40).
2. A son of Jerahmeel of Judah (1 Chron. 2:26, 28).

Onan *[same as On]*
Judah's second son, killed for disobeying God (Gen. 38:4–10).

Onesimus *[profitable; useful]*
A runaway slave who Paul helped by writing to his master Philemon (Philem. 10, 15).

Onesiphorus *[who brings profit]*
One of Paul's faithful friends (2 Tim. 1:16–18).

Ophir *[fruitful region]*
A son of Joktan (Gen. 10:29; 1 Chron. 1:23).

Ophrah *[dust; lead; a fawn]*
A descendant of Judah (1 Chron. 4:14).

Oreb *[a raven]*
A Midianite chief defeated by Gideon (Judg. 7:25).

Oren
A son of Jerahmeel of Judah (1 Chron. 2:25).

Ornan (Araunah) *[that rejoices]*
A Jebusite from whom David bought a piece of land, on which Solomon's temple was built (1 Chron. 21:15–25); called Araunah in 2 Samuel 24:16.

Orpah *[the neck or skull]*
Naomi's daughter-in-law (Ruth 1:4–14).

Osee
Greek form of Hosea. See Hosea.

Oshea
See Joshua.

Othni *[my time; my hour]*
A Levite who was a gatekeeper of the tabernacle in David's reign (1 Chron. 26:7).

Othniel *[the hour of God]*
Caleb's younger brother (Judg. 1:13; 3:8–11).

Ozem *[that fasts; their eagerness]*
1. The sixth son of Jesse; David's brother (1 Chron. 2:15).
2. A son of Jerahmeel (1 Chron. 2:25).

Ozias *[strength from the Lord]*
Greek form of Uzziah. See Uzziah.

Ozni *[an ear; my hearkening]*
See Ezbon 1.

Paarai *[opening]*
One of David's mighty men (2 Sam. 23:35).

Padon *[his redemption; ox yoke]*
A person who returned from the Babylonian captivity (Ezra 2:44; Neh. 7:47).

Pagiel *[prevention, or prayer, of God]*
A chief of the tribe of Asher (Num. 1:13; 2:27).

Pahath-moab *[ruler of Moab]*
1. An ancestor of the returning captives (Ezra 2:6).
2. Another who returned from the exile (Ezra 8:4).
3. The name of a family who sealed the new covenant with God after the exile (Neh. 10:14).

Palal *[thinking]*
A person who helped rebuild the wall of Jerusalem (Neh. 3:25).

Pallu (Phallu) *[marvelous; hidden]*
One of Reuben's sons (Exod. 6:14; 1 Chron. 5:3).

Palti *[deliverance; flight]*
A person selected to spy out Canaan (Num. 13:9).

Paltiel (Phaltiel) *[deliverance; or banishment, of God]*
1. A prince from the tribe of Issachar (Num. 34:26).
2. The man who married David's wife (2 Sam. 3:15).

Parmashta *[a yearling bull]*
A son of Haman (Esther 9:9).

Parmenas *[that abides, or is permanent]*
One of seven people chosen to care for the poor (Acts 6:5).

Parnach *[a bull striking, or struck]*
A descendant of Zebulun (Num. 34:25).

Parosh (Pharosh) *[a flea; the fruit of a moth]*
1. An ancestor of the returning captives (Ezra 2:3).
2. Another whose family returned from the exile (Ezra 8:3).
3. A person who married a foreign wife during the exile (Ezra 10:25).
4. A person who sealed the new covenant with God after the exile (Neh. 10:14).
5. The father of a person who helped repair the wall of Jerusalem (Neh. 3:25).

All of the above may be the same person.

Parshandatha *[given by prayer]*
A son of Haman killed by the Jews (Esther 9:7).

Paruah *[flourishing; that flies away]*
Father of Jehoshaphat (1 Kings 4:17).

Pasach *[thy broken piece]*
A descendant of Asher (1 Chron. 7:33).

Paseah *[passing over; halting]*
1. A descendant of Judah (1 Chron. 4:12).
2. A family who returned from the exile to Jerusalem with Zerubbabel (Ezra 2:49).

3. Father of Jehoiada, who helped repair the wall of Jerusalem (Neh. 3:6).

Pashur *[that extends or multiplies the hole; whiteness]*

1. Head of a priestly family (1 Chron. 9:12; Neh. 7:41).
2. A priest who sealed the new covenant with God after the exile (Neh. 10:3).
3. A priest who persecuted Jeremiah (Jer. 20:1–6).
4. Son of Melchiah, a prince of Judah (Jer. 21:1; 38:1).

Pathrusim *[mouthful of dough; persuasion of ruin]*

A descendant of Mizraim (Gen. 10:14).

Patrobas *[paternal; that pursues the steps of his father]*

A Christian in Rome to whom Paul sent his greetings (Rom. 16:14).

Paul *[small; little]*

A converted Pharisee who became the apostle to the Gentiles. The book of Acts recounts his missionary work.

Pedahel

A prince of Naphtali (Num. 34:28).

Pedahzur *[strong or powerful savior; stone of redemption]*

Father of Gamaliel (Num. 1:10).

Pedaiah *[redemption of the Lord]*

1. Father of Joel (1 Chron. 27:20).
2. Grandfather of King Josiah (2 Kings 23:36).
3. Son or grandson of Jeconiah (1 Chron. 3:18–19).
4. A person who helped repair the wall of Jerusalem (Neh. 3:25).
5. A person who stood with Ezra when he read the Law to the people (Neh. 8:4).
6. A descendant of Benjamin (Neh. 11:7).

Pekah *[he that opens; that is at liberty]*

A ruler of Israel for twenty years (2 Kings 15:25–31).

Pekahiah *[it is the Lord that opens]*

Son and successor of Menahem to Israel's throne (2 Kings 15:22–26).

Pelaiah *[the Lord's secret or miracle]*

1. A son of Elioenai (1 Chron. 3:24).
2. A Levite who helped Ezra to explain the Law (Neh. 8:7).
3. A Levite who sealed the new covenant with God after the exile (Neh. 10:10); may be the same as 2.

Pelaliah *[entreating the Lord]*

A priest whose grandson lived in Jerusalem after the exile (Neh. 11:12).

Pelatiah *[let the Lord deliver; deliverance of the Lord]*

1. A person who sealed the new covenant with God after the exile (Neh. 10:22).
2. A descendant of David (1 Chron. 3:21).
3. A captain of Simeon (1 Chron. 4:42–43).
4. An evil prince seen in Ezekiel's vision (Ezek. 11:1, 13).

Peleg (Phalec) *[division]*

Son of Eber and ancestor of Jesus Christ (Gen. 10:25; 11:16; Luke 3:35).

Pelet

1. A son of Jahdai (1 Chron. 2:47).
2. A person who joined David at Ziklag (1 Chron. 12:3).

Peleth

1. Father of On (Num. 16:1).
2. A son of Jonathan and a descendant of Pharez (1 Chron. 2:33).

Peninnah *[pearl; precious stone; the face]*

Elkanah's second wife and father of Samuel (1 Sam. 1:2).

Penuel *[face or vision of God; that sees God]*

1. A descendant of Benjamin (1 Chron. 8:25).
2. A chief or father of Gedar (1 Chron. 4:4).

Peresh *[horseman]*

Son of Machir (1 Chron. 7:16).

Perez (Phares; Pharez) *[divided]*
Eldest son of Judah and ancestor of Jesus Christ (1 Chron. 27:3; Neh. 11:4); called Pharez in Luke 3:33.

Perida (Peruda) *[separation; division]*
An ancestor of the returning captives (Neh. 7:57).

Persis *[that cuts or divides; a nail; a gryphon; a horseman]*
A Christian woman at Rome (Rom. 16:12).

Peruda *[same as Perida]*
See Perida.

Peter *[a rock or stone]*
Apostle of Jesus and leader of the early church (Matt. 4:18–20; 16:15–19; Acts 2).

Pethahiah *[the Lord opening; gate of the Lord]*
1. A leading Levite in David's reign (1 Chron. 24:16).
2. A Levite who had married a foreign wife (Ezra 10:23).
3. A descendant of Judah (Neh. 11:24).
4. A Levite who organized the devotional life of the people after Ezra had read the Law to them (Neh. 9:5).

Pethuel *[mouth of God; persuasion of God]*
Father of Joel the prophet (Joel 1:1).

Peulthai *[my works]*
A son of Obed-edom and gatekeeper in David's reign (1 Chron. 26:5).

Phalec
A Greek form of Peleg. See Peleg.

Phallu *[admirable; hidden]*
See Pallu.

Phaltiel
See Paltiel.

Phanuel *[face or vision of God]*
Father of Anna the prophetess (Luke 2:36).

Pharaoh *[that disperses; that spoils]*
1. Royal title of Egyptian kings (Gen. 12:15).
2. Father of Bithia (1 Chron. 4:18).

Phares
Greek form of Perez. See Perez.

Pharez
See Perez.

Pharosh
See Parosh.

Phebe *[shining; pure]*
A servant of the Christian church who helped Paul (Rom. 16:1).

Phichol *[the mouth of all, or every tongue]*
A commander of Abimelech's army (Gen. 21:22).

Philemon *[who kisses]*
A Christian at Colosse to whom Paul wrote a letter asking him to take back his runaway slave Onesimus (Philem. 1, 5–7).

Philetus *[amiable; beloved]*
A person condemned by Paul because of his false teaching (2 Tim. 2:17).

Philip *[warlike; a lover of horses]*
1. One of Jesus' twelve apostles (John 1:44).
2. An evangelist mentioned in Acts (Acts 6:5; 8:5–13).

Philologus *[a lover of letters, or of the word]*
A Christian in Rome to whom Paul sent greetings (Rom. 16:15).

Phinehas *[bold aspect; face of trust or protection]*
1. Aaron's grandson (Exod. 6:25).
2. Younger son of Eli (1 Sam. 1:3; 2:22–24, 34).
3. Father of Eleazer (Ezra 8:33).

Phlegon *[zealous; burning]*
A Christian to whom Paul sent greetings (Rom. 16:14).

Phurah *[that bears fruit, or grows]*
Gideon's servant (1 Sam. 14:1).

Phut (Put)
A son of Ham (Gen. 10:6; 1 Chron. 1:8).

Phuvah (Pua; Puah)
1. Issachar's second son (Gen. 46:13).
2. Father of Tola the judge (Judg. 10:1).

Phygellus *[fugitive]*
A Christian who deserted Paul (2 Tim. 1:15).

Pilate *[armed with a dart]*
See Pontius Pilate.

Pildash
Son of Nahor, brother of Abraham (Gen. 22:22).

Pileha
A person who sealed the new covenant with God after the exile (Neh. 10:24).

Piltai
A priest in Jerusalem in Joiakim's reign (Neh. 12:17).

Pinon *[pearl; gem; that beholds]*
A chief of Edom (Gen. 38:41; 1 Chron. 1:52).

Piram *[a wild ass of them]*
An Amorite king of Jarmuth killed by Joshua (Josh. 10:3).

Pispah
A descendant of Asher (1 Chron. 7:38).

Pithon *[mouthful; persuasion]*
A son of Micah and Saul's great-grandson (1 Chron. 8:35).

Pochereth *[cutting of the mouth of warfare]*
An ancestor of the returning captives (Ezra 2:57; Neh. 7:59).

Pontius Pilate *[marine; belonging to the sea]*
A Roman procurator of Judea who condemned Jesus to be crucified (Matt. 27:2–24).

Poratha *[fruitful]*
A son of Haman killed by the Jews (Esther 9:8).

Porcius Festus
See Festus.

Potiphar *[bull of Africa; a fat bull]*
Egyptian captain of the guard who became Joseph's master (Gen. 37:36; 39).

Poti-pherah *[that scatters abroad, or demolishes, the fat]*
A priest of On; Joseph's father-in-law (Gen. 41:45, 50).

Prisca
Shortened form of Priscilla. See Priscilla.

Priscilla *[ancient]*
Wife of the Jewish Christian Aquila (Acts 18:2, 18, 26; Rom. 16:3).

Prochorus *[he that presides over the choirs]*
One of the seven people chosen to care for the poor (Acts 6:5).

Pua (Puah) *[mouth; corner; bush of hair]*
See Phuvah.

Publius *[common]*
Governor of Malta who welcomed Paul (Acts 28:1–10).

Pudens *[shamefaced]*
A Christian friend of Timothy at Rome (2 Tim. 4:21).

Pul *[bean; destruction]*
See Tiglath-pileser.

Put
See Phut.

Putiel *[God is my fatness]*
Eleazer's father-in-law (Exod. 6:25).

Quartus *[fourth]*
A Christian of Corinth who sent greetings to the church in Rome (Rom. 16:23).

Quirinius
See Cyrenius.

Raamah *[greatness; thunder; some sort of evil]*
A son of Cush (Gen. 10:7).

Raamiah *[thunder, or evil, from the Lord]*
A leader who returned from the Babylonian captivity (Neh. 7:7).

Rabmag *[who overthrows or destroys a multitude]*
A title used by Nergal-sharezer of Babylonia (Jer. 39:3, 13).

Rabsaris *[chief of the eunuchs]*
This is not a proper name, but a title used by an official in the Babylonian and Assyrian government (Jer. 39:3, 13).

Rab-shakeh *[cup-bearer of the prince]*
The title of an office in the Assyrian government (2 Kings 18:17–28; 9:4, 8).

Rachab
Greek form of Rahab. See Rahab.

Rachel (Rahel) *[sheep]*
Laban's daughter and Jacob's wife (Gen. 29–35).

Raddai *[ruling; coming down]*
One of David's brothers (1 Chron. 2:14).

Ragau *[friend; shepherd]*
Greek form of Reu. See Reu.

Raguel *[shepherd, or friend of God]*
See Jethro.

Rahab (Rachab) *[large; extended]*
A prostitute in Jericho who helped Jewish spies and who became an ancestor of Jesus Christ (Josh. 2:1–21; Matt. 1:5).

Raham *[compassion; a friend]*
A descendant of Caleb (1 Chron. 2:44).

Rahel
See Rachel.

Rakem
A descendant of Manasseh (1 Chron. 7:16).

Ram (Aram) *[elevated; sublime]*
1. An ancestor of David and of Jesus Christ (Ruth 4:19; Matt. 1:3–4).
2. Son of Jerahmeel of Judah (1 Chron. 3:27).
3. Head of the family of Elihu (Job 32:2).

Ramiah *[exaltation of the Lord]*
A person who married a foreign wife during the exile (Ezra 10:25).

Ramoth *[eminences; high places]*
A person who married a foreign wife during the exile (Ezra 10:29).

Rapha (Rephaiah) *[relaxation; physic; comfort]*
1. Benjamin's fifth son (1 Chron. 8:2); called Rephaiah in 1 Chronicles 9:43.
2. A descendant of King Saul (1 Chron. 8:37).

Raphu *[relaxation; physic; comfort]*
The father of Palti, the Benjamite spy (Num. 13:9).

Reaia (Reaiah) *[vision of the Lord]*
1. A descendant of Reuben (1 Chron. 5:5).
2. An ancestor of the returning captives (Ezra 2:47).
3. A descendant of Judah (1 Chron. 4:2).

Reba *[the fourth; a square; that lies or stoops down]*
One of the five Midianite kings killed by the Israelites under Moses' leadership (Num. 31:8; Josh. 13:21).

Rebecca
Greek form of Rebekah. See Rebekah.

Rebekah (Rebecca) *[fat; fattened; a quarrel appeased]*
Isaac's wife and mother of Jacob and Esau (Gen. 22:23; 24–28).

Rechab *[square; chariot with team of four horses]*
1. A descendant of Benjamin who murdered Ish-bosheth (2 Sam. 4:2).
2. Founder of a tribe called Rechabites (2 Kings 10:15; Jeremiah 35).
3. A descendant of Hemath (1 Chron. 2:55).
4. A person who helped repair the wall of Jerusalem (Neh. 3:14).

Reelaiah *[shepherd or companion to the Lord]*
See Raamiah.

Regem *[that stones or is stoned; purple]*
A descendant of Caleb (1 Chron. 2:47).

Regem-melech *[he that stones the king; purple of the king]*
A messenger sent out by some Jews (Zech. 7:2).

Rehabiah *[breadth, or extent, of the Lord]*
Son of Eliezer, son of Moses (1 Chron. 23:17; 24:21).

Rehob *[breadth; space; extent]*
1. Father of Hadadezer king of Zobah (2 Sam. 8:3, 12).
2. A Levite who sealed the covenant with Nehemiah (Neh. 10:11).

Rehoboam (Roboam) *[who sets the people at liberty]*
Son of Solomon and ancestor of Jesus Christ (1 Kings 14:43; 12; 14; Matt. 1:7).

Rehum *[merciful; compassionate]*
1. A leader who returned from the exile in Babylon with Zerubbabel (Ezra 2:2); called Nehum in Nehemiah 7:7.
2. Artaxerxes's chancellor (Ezra 4:8, 17).
3. A Levite who helped repair the wall of Jerusalem (Neh. 3:17).
4. A person who sealed the new covenant with God after the exile (Neh. 10:25).

Rei *[my shepherd; my companion; my friend]*
One of David's friends (1 Kings 1:8).

Rekem *[vain pictures; divers picture]*
1. A Midianite king killed by the Israelites (Num. 31:8; Josh. 13:21).
2. A son of Hebron, and father of Shammai (1 Chron. 2:43–44).

Remaliah *[the exaltation of the Lord]*
Father of Pekah (2 Kings 15:25–37).

Rephael *[the physic or medicine of God]*
Son of Obed-edom (1 Chron. 26:7).

Rephah
An ancestor of Ephraim (1 Chron. 7:25).

Rephaiah *[medicine or refreshment of the Lord]*
1. Head of a family of the house of David (1 Chron. 3:21).
2. Simeonite leader in Hezekiah's reign (1 Chron. 4:42).
3. A son of Tola (1 Chron. 7:2).
4. A person who helped repair the wall of Jerusalem (Neh. 3:9).
5. See Rapha.

Resheph
A descendant of Ephraim (1 Chron. 7:25).

Reu (Ragau) *[his friend; his shepherd]*
Son of Peleg and ancestor of Jesus Christ (Gen. 11:18–21; Luke 3:35).

Reuben *[who sees the son; the vision of the son]*
Jacob and Leah's eldest son (Gen. 29:32; 35:22; 37:29) whose descendants became one of the twelve tribes of Israel.

Reuel *[the shepherd or friend of God]*
1. One of Esau's sons (Gen. 36:4).
2. A descendant of Benjamin (1 Chron. 1:35).
3. See Jethro.
4. See Deuel.

Reumah *[lofty; sublime]*
Nahor's concubine (Gen. 22:4).

Rezia
A descendant of Asher (1 Chron. 7:39).

Rezin *[goodwill; messenger]*
1. The last king of Syria (2 Kings 15:37).
2. An ancestor of the returning captives (Ezra 2:48; Neh. 7:50).

Rezon *[lean; small; secret; prince]*
A Syrian rebel who established his own government in Damascus (1 Kings 11:23).

Rhesa *[will; course]*
An ancestor of Jesus Christ (Luke 3:27).

Rhoda *[a rose]*
A servant in Mary's house (Acts 12:13).

Ribai *[strife]*
Father of Ittai, one of David's valiant men (2 Sam. 23:29); called Ithai in 1 Chronicles 11:31.

Rimmon *[exalted; pomegranate]*
Father of Ish-bosheth's murderers (2 Sam. 4:2–9).

Rinnah *[song; rejoicing]*
A descendant of Judah (1 Chron. 4:20).

Riphath *[remedy; medicine; release; pardon]*
A son of Gomer (Gen. 10:3).

Rizpah *[bed; extension; a coal]*
One of Saul's concubines (2 Sam. 3:7; 21:8–11).

Roboam
Greek form of Rehoboam.
See Rehoboam.

Rodanim
See Dodanim.

Rohgah *[filled or drunk with talk]*
A leading Asherite (1 Chron. 7:34).

Romamti-ezer *[exaltation of help]*
One of Heman's fourteen sons (1 Chron. 25:4, 31).

Rosh *[the head; top, or beginning]*
A descendant of Benjamin (Gen. 46:21).

Rufus *[red]*
1. Son of Simon of Cyrene (Mark 15:21).
2. A Christian in Rome (Rom. 16:13).

Ruth *[drunk; satisfied]*
David's grandmother and ancestor of Jesus Christ (Ruth 1:4–5; Matt. 1:5).

Sabta (Sabtah) *[a going about or circuiting; old age]*
Third son of Cush (Gen. 10:7; 1 Chron. 1:9).

Sabtecha (Sabtechah) *[that surrounds; that causes wounding]*
Fifth son of Cush (Gen. 10:7; 1 Chron. 1:9).

Sacar *[wares; a price]*
1. The father of one of David's mighty men (1 Chron. 11:35).
2. A Levite tabernacle gatekeeper in David's reign (1 Chron. 26:4).

Sadoc (Zadok) *[just; righteous]*
An ancestor of Jesus Christ (Matt. 1:14).

Sala (Salah) *[mission; sending]*
Son of Arphaxad and ancestor of Jesus Christ (Gen. 10:24; Luke 3:35).

Salathiel *[asked or lent of God]*
Greek form of Shealtiel. See Shealtiel.

Sallai *[an exaltation; a basket]*
1. A leader in the tribe of Benjamin (Neh. 11:8).
2. A priest who returned from the Babylonian captivity (Neh. 12:20); called Sallu in Nehemiah 12:7.

Sallu *[an exaltation; a basket]*
1. A descendant of Benjamin living in Jerusalem (1 Chron. 9:7).
2. See Sallai 2.

Salma (Salmon) *[peace; perfection]*
1. A son of Caleb (1 Chron. 2:51).
2. Boaz's father and ancestor of Jesus Christ (Ruth 4:20–21; Matt. 1:4–5).

Salome *[same as Salma]*
1. One of the women who witnessed Jesus' death (Mark 15:40; 16:1).
2. Herodias's daughter (Matt. 14:6).

Salu
Father of Zimri (Num. 25:14).

Samgar-nebo
One of the king of Babylon's commanders (Jer. 39:3).

Samlah *[his raiment; his left hand; his astonishment]*
A king of Edom (Gen. 36:36; 1 Chron. 1:47–48).

Samson *[his sun; his service; there the second time]*
A judge of Israel, famed for his strength (Judg. 13:24; 14–16).

Samuel (Shemuel) *[heard of God; asked of God]*
Israel's famous prophet, kingmaker, and last judge (1 Sam. 1:20; 3–13; 15–16).

Sanballat *[bramble bush; enemy in secret]*
A leading opponent of the Jews as they rebuilt the wall of Jerusalem (Neh. 2:10; 6:1–14).

Saph *[rushes; sea moss]*
A descendant of Rapha the giant (2 Sam. 21:18); called Sippai in 1 Chronicles 20:4.

Sapphira *[that relates or tells]*
Ananias's dishonest wife whom God struck dead (Acts 5:1–10).

Sara
Greek form of Sarah. See Sarah.

Sarah (Sara; Sarai) *[lady; princess; princess of the multitude]*
Abraham's wife and mother of Isaac (Gen. 17–18; 20–21) whose name was changed from Sarai to Sarah.

Sarai
See Sarah.

Saraph
A descendant of Judah (1 Chron. 4:22).

Sargon *[who takes away protection]*
The king of Assyria who completed the siege of Samaria and deported the Israelites (Isa. 20:1).

Sarsechim *[master of the wardrobe]*
A Babylonian prince (Jer. 39:3).

Saruch *[branch; layer; lining]*
Greek form of Serug. See Serug.

Saul (Shaul) *[demanded; lent; ditch; death]*
1. Israel's first king (1 Samuel 9–31).
2. Paul's original name (Acts 13:9).
3. See Shaul 1.

Sceva *[disposed; prepared]*
A Jew living in Ephesus during Paul's second visit to that town (Acts 19:14–16).

Seba *[a drunkard; that turns]*
Cush's eldest son (Gen. 10:7; 1 Chron. 1:9).

Secundus *[second]*
A Thessalonian Christian (Acts 20:4).

Segub *[fortified; raised]*
1. The youngest son of Hiel who rebuilt Jericho (1 Kings 18:34).
2. A grandson of Judah (1 Chron. 2:21–22).

Seir (Seirath) *[hairy; goat; demon; tempest]*
A leading Horite (Gen. 36:20–21).

Seled *[affliction; warning]*
A descendant of Judah (1 Chron. 2:30).

Sem
Greek form of Shem. See Shem.

Semachiah *[joined to the Lord]*
A tabernacle gatekeeper in David's reign (1 Chron. 26:7).

Semei *[hearing; obeying]*
An ancestor of Jesus Christ (Luke 3:26).

Sennacherib *[bramble of destruction]*
An Assyrian king who unsuccessfully invaded Judah (2 Kings 19; Isa. 37:17, 21, 37).

Senuah
A descendant of Benjamin (Neh. 11:9).

Seorim *[gates; hairs; tempests]*
A priest in David's reign (1 Chron. 24:8).

Serah *[lady of scent; song; the morning star]*
A daughter of Asher (Gen. 46:17; 1 Chron. 7:30).

Seraiah *[prince of the Lord]*
1. One of David's scribes (2 Sam. 8:17); called Sheva in 2 Samuel 20:25, and Shavsha in 1 Chronicles 18:16.
2. The high priest in Zedekiah's reign (2 Kings 25:18; 1 Chron. 6:14).
3. The person Gedaliah advised to give in to Babylon (2 Kings 25:23; Jer. 40:8).
4. Othniel's brother (1 Chron. 4:13–14).
5. A descendant of Simeon (1 Chron. 4:35).
6. A priest who returned to Jerusalem with Zerubbabel (Ezra 2:2).
7. A leader sent to capture Jeremiah (Jer. 36:26).
8. A prince of Judah who went to Babylon (Jer. 51:59, 61).
9. A son of Hilkiah living in Jerusalem after the exile (Neh. 11:11).

Sered *[dyer's vat]*
Zebulun's eldest son (Gen. 46:14; Num. 26:26).

Sergius Paulus *[net]*
A Roman proconsul in Cyprus when the apostle Paul visited the island with Barnabas (Acts 13:7).

Serug (Saruch) *[branch; layer; twining]*
Nahor's father and ancestor of Jesus Christ (Gen. 11:20; Luke 3:35).

Seth (Sheth) *[put; who puts; fixed]*
Adam and Eve's son and ancestor of Jesus Christ (Gen. 4:25–26; Luke 3:38).

Sethur *[hid; destroying]*
The Asherite spy, sent out to spy out the land of Canaan (Num. 13:13).

Shaaph *[fleeing; thinking]*
1. A descendant of Jahdai (1 Chron. 2:47).
2. Caleb's son (1 Chron. 2:49).

Shaashgaz *[he that presses the fleece; that shears the sheep]*
One of Ahasuerus's eunuchs (Esther 2:14).

Shabbethai *[my rest]*
1. One of Ezra's assistants (Ezra 10:15).
2. A person who explained the Law to the people (Neh. 8:7).
3. A leading Levite in Jerusalem (Neh. 11:16).

These three may be identical with each other.

Shachia *[protection of the Lord]*
A descendant of Benjamin (1 Chron. 8:10).

Shadrach *[tender, nipple]*
The name given to Hananiah in Babylon (Daniel 1–3).

Shage *[touching softly; multiplying much]*
Father of Jonathan the Hararite, one of David's guards (1 Chron. 11:34).

Shallum *[perfect; agreeable]*
1. The youngest son of Naphtali (1 Chron. 7:13); also called Shillem in Genesis 46:24 and Numbers 26:49.
2. A descendant of Simeon (1 Chron. 4:25).
3. A descendant of Shesham (1 Chron. 2:40–41).
4. A usurper of Israel's throne who reigned for one month (2 Kings 15:10–14).
5. The husband of Huldah the prophetess (2 Kings 22:14; 2 Chron. 34:23).
6. See Jehoahaz.
7. See Meshullam.
8. A tabernacle gatekeeper (1 Chron. 9:17).
9. Father of Jehizkiah, an Ephraimite (2 Chron. 28:12).
10. 11. Two people who married foreign wives during the exile (Ezra 10:24, 42).
12. A person who helped repair the wall of Jerusalem (Neh. 3:12).
13. A person who helped repair the gate of Jerusalem (Neh. 3:15).
14. One of Jeremiah's uncles (Jer. 32:7).
15. Father of one of the temple officers in Jehoiakim's reign (Jer. 35:4).

Shalmai *[my garment]*
An ancestor of the returning captives (Ezra 2:46; Neh. 7:48).

Shalman *[peaceable; perfect; that rewards]*
The king of defeated Beth-arbel (Hosea 10:14).

Shalmaneser *[peace; tied; chained; perfection; retribution]*
King to whom Hoshea became subject (2 Kings 17:3).

Shama
One of David's guards (1 Chron. 11:44).

Shamariah *[throne or keeping of the Lord]*
See Shemariah.

Shamed *[destroying; wearing out]*
A son of Elpaal the Benjamite (1 Chron. 8:12).

Shamer *[keeper; thorn; dregs]*
1. A descendant of Merari (1 Chron. 6:46).
2. A descendant of Asher (1 Chron. 7:34); called Shomer in 1 Chronicles 7:32.

Shamgar *[named a stranger; he is here a stranger]*
One of Israel's judges (Judg. 3:31).

Shamhuth *[desolation; destruction]*
A commander of David's army (1 Chron. 27:8).

Shamir (Shamer) *[prison; bush; lees; thorn]*
A son of Micah, a Levite (1 Chron. 24:24).

Shamma
A descendant of Asher (1 Chron. 7:37). See Shammah.

Shammah *[loss; desolation; astonishment]*
1. Esau's grandson (Gen. 36:13, 17; 1 Chron. 1:37).
2. Jesse's son, and David's brother (1 Sam. 16:9; 17:13); called Shimeah in 2 Samuel 13:3; 21:21 and Shimma in 1 Chronicles 2:13.
3. One of David's three greatest mighty men (2 Sam. 23:11).
4. Another of David's mighty men (2 Sam. 23:23); called Shammoth in 1 Chronicles 11:27.
5. Another of David's mighty men (2 Sam. 23:25).

Shammai *[my name; my desolations]*
1. A descendant of Judah (1 Chron. 2:28, 32).
2. A descendant of Caleb (1 Chron. 2:44–45).
3. Ezra's son or grandson (1 Chron. 4:17).

Shammoth *[names; desolations]*
See Shammah.

Shammua (Shammuah) *[he that is heard; he that is obeyed]*
1. A Reubenite sent out to spy the land of Canaan (Num. 13:4).
2. One of David and Bathsheba's sons (1 Chron. 14:4); called Shimea in 1 Chronicles 3:5.
3. A Levite who led the temple worship after the exile (Neh. 11:17); called Shemaiah in 1 Chronicles 9:16.
4. The head of a priestly family in Nehemiah's time (Neh. 12:18).

Shamsherai *[there a singer or conqueror]*
A descendant of Benjamin (1 Chron. 8:26).

Shapham *[rabbit; wild rat; their lip; their brink]*
A chief of Gad (1 Chron. 5:12).

Shaphan *[rabbit; wild rat; their lip; their brink]*
1. Josiah's scribe who read him the Law (2 Kings 22:3; 2 Chron. 34:8–21).
2. Father of a chief officer in Josiah's reign (2 Kings 22:12; 2 Chron. 34:20).
3. Father of Elasah (Jer. 29:3).
4. Father of Jaazaniah whom Ezekiel saw in a vision (Ezekiel 8:11).

Shaphat *[judge]*
1. One of the men sent to spy out the land of Canaan (Num. 13:5).
2. Elisha the prophet's father (1 Kings 19:16, 19).
3. One of the six sons of Shemaiah (1 Chron. 3:22).
4. One of the chiefs of the Gadites in Bashan (1 Chron. 5:12).
5. One of David's herdsmen (1 Chron. 27:29).

Sharai *[my lord; my prince; my song]*
A person who married a foreign wife during the exile (Ezra 10:40).

Sharezer *[overseer of the treasury, or of the storehouse]*
1. A son of the Assyrian king Sennacherib, who, with his brother, murdered their father (2 Kings 19:37).
2. A person sent to consult the priests and prophets (Zech. 7:2).

Shashai *[rejoicing; mercy; linen]*
A person who married a foreign wife during the exile (Ezra 10:40).

Shashak *[a bag of linen; the sixth bag]*
A descendant of Benjamin (1 Chron. 8:14, 25).

Shaul (Saul) *[asked; lent; a grave]*
1. A descendant of Levi (1 Chron. 6:24).
2. A son of Simeon (Gen. 46:10; Exod. 6:15; 1 Chron. 4:24).
3. Edom's sixth king (1 Chron. 1:48–49); called Saul in Genesis 36:37 (AV).

Shavsha
See Seraiah.

Sheal
A person who married a foreign wife during the exile (Ezra 10:29).

Shealtiel *[asked or lent of God]*
Father of Zerubbabel and ancestor of Jesus Christ (Ezra 3:2, 8; 5:2; Hag. 1:1, 12, 14; 2:2, 23; Matt. 1:12).

Sheariah *[gate of the Lord; tempest of the Lord]*
One of Saul's descendants (1 Chron. 8:38; 9:44).

Shear-jashub *[the remnant shall return]*
Symbolic name given to one of Isaiah's sons (Isa. 7:3).

Sheba *[captivity; old man; repose; oath]*
1. A chief of Gad (1 Chron. 5:13).
2. Someone who was beheaded for rebelling against David (2 Samuel 20).
3. One of Abraham's grandsons (Gen. 25:3).
4. A descendant of Shem (Gen. 10:28).
5. A descendant of Ham (Gen. 10:7).

Shebaniah *[the Lord that converts, or recalls from captivity]*
1. A Levite who guided the devotions of the people (Neh. 9:4–5).
2. 3. Two priests who sealed the new covenant with God after the exile with Nehemiah (Neh. 10:4, 12, 14).
4. One of the priests appointed by David to blow the trumpet before the ark of the covenant (1 Chron. 15:24).

Sheber *[breaking; hope]*
A descendant of Jephunneh (1 Chron. 2:48).

Shebna *[who rests himself; who is now captive]*
1. Hezekiah's scribe (Isa. 36:3–22; 2 Kings 18:18).
2. The treasurer who was replaced by Eliakim (Isa. 22:15).

Shebuel *[turning, or captivity, or seat, of God]*
1. A son of Gershom (1 Chron. 23:16; 26:24).
2. A son of Haman, leading singer in the sanctuary (1 Chron. 25:4); called Shubael in 1 Chronicles 25:20.

Shecaniah *[habitation of the Lord]*
1. A priest in David's reign (1 Chron. 24:11).
2. A priest in Hezekiah's reign (2 Chron. 31:15).

Shechaniah *[habitation of the Lord]*
1. Head of a family in David's house (1 Chron. 3:21–22).
2. 3. Two people whose descendants returned from the Babylonian captivity (Ezra 8:3, 5).
4. A person who married a foreign wife during the exile (Ezra 10:2).
5. Father of a person who repaired the wall of Jerusalem (Neh. 3:29).
6. The father-in-law of one of Nehemiah's opponents (Neh. 6:18).
7. A priest who returned from the Babylonian captivity (Neh. 12:3).

Shechem (Sychem) *[part; portion; back early in the morning]*
1. The son of Hamor who defiled Dinah (Gen. 33:19; 34).
2. A descendant of Manasseh (Num. 26:31).
3. Another descendant of Manasseh (1 Chron. 7:19).

Shedeur *[field of light; light of the Almighty]*
A person who helped different people (Num. 1:5; 2:10; 7:30, 35).

Shehariah *[mourning or blackness of the Lord]*
A descendant of Benjamin (1 Chron. 8:26).

Shelah *[that breaks; that unties; that undresses]*
Judah's youngest son (Gen. 38:5–26).

Shelemiah *[God is my perfection; my happiness; my peace]*
1. See Meshelemiah.

2. 3. Two people who married foreign wives during the exile (Ezra 10:39, 41).
4. Father of Hananiah (Neh. 3:30).
5. A priest in charge of the treasury (Neh. 13:13).
6. An ancestor of the person who was sent by the princes to bring Baruch (Jer. 36:14).
7. The person ordered to catch Baruch and Jeremiah (Jer. 36:26).
8. Father of the person sent to Jeremiah to ask for prayers (Jer. 37:3; 38:1).
9. Father of the person sent to arrest Jeremiah (Jer. 37:13).

Sheleph *[who draws out]*
A son of Joktan (Gen. 10:26; 1 Chron. 1:20).

Shelesh *[captain; prince]*
A descendant of Asher (1 Chron. 7:35).

Shelomi *[my peace; my happiness; my recompense]*
Father of a prince of Asher (Num. 34:27).

Shelomith *[my peace; my happiness; my recompense]*
1. Mother of a person stoned for blasphemy in the desert (Lev. 24:11).
2. Daughter of Zerubbabel (1 Chron. 3:19).
3. A descendant of Levi and Kohath (1 Chron. 23:18).
4. A person in charge of the treasury in David's reign (1 Chron. 26:25–28).
5. A descendant of Gershon (1 Chron. 23:9).
6. One of Rehoboam's children (2 Chron. 11:20).
7. An ancestor of the returning captives (Ezra 8:10).

Shelomoth *[my peace; my happiness; my recompense]*
A descendant of Izhar (1 Chron. 24:22).

Shelumiel *[same as Shelemiah]*
A chief of Simeon who assisted Moses at the time of the exodus (Num. 1:6; 2:12; 7:36).

Shem (Sem) *[name; renown]*
Noah's eldest son and ancestor of Jesus Christ (Gen. 5:32; Luke 3:36).

Shema *[hearing; obeying]*
1. A son of Hebron (1 Chron. 2:43–44).
2. A descendant of Reuben (1 Chron. 5:8).
3. A chief of the tribe of Benjamin (1 Chron. 8:13).
4. A person who stood with Ezra when he read the Law to the people (Neh. 8:4).

Shemaah
Father of two valiant men who joined David (1 Chron. 12:3).

Shemaiah *[that hears or obeys the Lord]*
1. A prophet who warned Rehoboam against war (1 Kings 12:22; 2 Chron. 11:2).
2. A descendant of David (1 Chron. 3:22).
3. A prince of the tribe of Simeon (1 Chron. 4:27).
4. Son of Joel (1 Chron. 5:4).
5. A descendant of Merari (1 Chron. 9:14; Neh. 11:15).
6. A person who helped bring the ark of the covenant to the temple (1 Chron. 15:8, 11).
7. A scribe in David's reign (1 Chron. 24:6).
8. A tabernacle gatekeeper (1 Chron. 26:4, 6–7).
9. A Levite Jehoshaphat sent to teach the people (2 Chron. 17:8).
10. A person who helped cleanse the temple (2 Chron. 29:14).
11. A Levite in Hezekiah's reign (2 Chron. 31:15).
12. A chief Levite in Josiah's reign (2 Chron. 35:9).
13. One of the sons of Adonikam who returned with Ezra (Ezra 5:13).
14. One of Ezra's messengers (Ezra 8:16).
15. 16. Two people who married foreign wives during the exile (Ezra 10:21, 31).
17. A person who helped repair the wall of Jerusalem (Neh. 3:29).

18. A person who attempted to intimidate Nehemiah (Neh. 6:10).
19. A person who sealed the new covenant with God after the exile (Neh. 10:8; 12:6, 18).
20. A person who helped purify the wall of Jerusalem (Neh. 12:36).
21. A member of the choir when the wall of Jerusalem was dedicated (Neh. 12:42).
22. A person who wanted the priests to reprimand Jeremiah (Jer. 29:24, 31).
23. Urijah the prophet's father (Jer. 26:20).
24. The father of Delaiah (Jer. 36:12).
25. See Shammua.

Shemariah (Shamariah) *[God is my guard]*

1. A Benjamite warrior who joined David at Ziklag (1 Chron. 12:5).
2. A son of King Rehoboam (2 Chron. 11:19).
3. 4. Two people who married foreign wives during the exile (Ezra 10:32, 41).

Shemeber *[name of force; name of the strong]*

The king of Zeboim in the time of Abraham (Gen. 14:2).

Shemer *[guardian; thorn]*

The owner of the hill on which the city of Samaria was built (1 Kings 16:24).

Shemida (Shemidah) *[name of knowledge; that puts knowledge]*

Manasseh's grandson (Num. 26:32; Josh. 17:2).

Shemiramoth *[the height of the heavens]*

1. A Levite singer (1 Chron. 15:18).
2. A person sent by Jehoshaphat to teach the Law (2 Chron. 17:8).

Shemuel *[appointed by God]*

1. A commissioner appointed from the tribe of Simeon to divide the land of Canaan (Num. 34:20).
2. Son of Tola, and one of the chiefs of the tribe of Issachar (1 Chron. 7:2).
3. See Samuel.

Shenazar *[treasurer of a tooth]*

Jeconiah's son or grandson (1 Chron. 3:18).

Shephathiah (Shephatiah) *[the Lord that judges]*

1. David's fifth son (2 Sam. 3:4; 1 Chron. 3:3).
2. Father of Meshullam who lived in Jerusalem (1 Chron. 9:8).
3. A person who joined David at Ziklag (1 Chron. 12:5).
4. A prince of Simeon in David's reign (1 Chron. 27:16).
5. A son of Jehoshaphat (2 Chron. 21:2).
6. An ancestor of the returning captives (Ezra 2:4; Neh. 7:9).
7. One of Solomon's servants whose descendants returned from Babylon (Ezra 2:57).
8. An ancestor of the returning captives (Ezra 8:8).
9. A descendant of Pharez (Neh. 11:4).
10. One of the princes of Judah who advised Zedekiah to put Jeremiah in a cistern (Jer. 38:1).

Shephi (Shepho) *[beholder; honeycomb; garment]*

A descendant of Seir the Horite (1 Chron. 1:40); called Shepho in Genesis 36:23.

Shephuphan *[serpent]*

See Muppim.

Sherah *[flesh; relationship]*

A woman descendant of Ephraim (1 Chron. 7:24).

Sherebiah *[singing with the Lord]*

1. A priest who returned from the Babylonian captivity (Ezra 8:18, 24).
2. A Levite who sealed the new covenant with God after the exile (Neh. 10:12).

Sheresh

A descendant of Manasseh (1 Chron. 7:16).

Sherezer

See Sharezer.

Sheshai *[six; mercy; flax]*
One of Anak's sons killed by Caleb (Num. 13:22).

Sheshan *[lily; rose; joy; flax]*
A descendant of Judah through Jerahmeel (1 Chron. 2:31, 34).

Sheshbazzar *[joy in tribulation; joy of the vintage]*
The prince of Judah Cyrus entrusted with the temple vessels (Ezra 1:8, 11; 5:14–16).

Sheth
A chief of the Moabites (Num. 24:17).

Shethar *[putrefied; searching]*
One of the seven princes of Persia and Media (Esther 1:14).

Shethar-boznai *[that makes to rot; that seeks those who despise me]*
One of the officials of the king of Persia (Ezra 5:3, 6; 6:6, 13).

Sheva *[vanity; elevation; fame; tumult]*
1. A son of Caleb (1 Chron. 2:49).
2. See Seraiah 1.

Shilhi (Shilhim) *[bough; weapon; armor]*
King Jehoshaphat's grandfather (1 Kings 22:42; 2 Chron. 20:31).

Shillem *[peace; perfection; retribution]*
See Shallum.

Shiloni
Zechariah's father (Neh. 11:5).

Shilshah *[three; chief; captain]*
Zophah's son (1 Chron. 7:37).

Shimea *[that hears, or obeys; perdition]*
1. A descendant of Merari (1 Chron. 6:30).
2. Father of Berachiah (1 Chron. 6:39).
3. See Shammua 2.

Shimeah (Shimeam) *[that hears, or obeys; perdition]*
A member of King Saul's family who lived in Jerusalem (1 Chron. 8:32), called Shimeam in 1 Chron. 9:38.

Shimeath *[that hears, or obeys; perdition]*
The mother of a person who helped murder King Jehoash (2 Kings 12:21; 2 Chron. 24:26).

Shimei (Shimhi; Shimi) *[that hears or obeys; my reputation; my fame]*
1. A descendant of Gershon (1 Chron. 6:17, 42).
2. A descendant of Benjamin who cursed David when he was running away from Absalom (2 Sam. 16:5–13).
3. One of David's loyal officers (1 Kings 1:8).
4. One of Solomon's officers (1 Kings 4:18).
5. King Jeconiah's grandson (1 Chron. 3:19).
6. A man who had sixteen sons and six daughters (1 Chron. 4:26–27).
7. A descendant of Reuben (1 Chron. 5:4).
8. A son of Libni (1 Chron. 6:29).
9. Father of a chief of Judah (1 Chron. 8:21).
10. A Levite (1 Chron. 23:9).
11. A Levite singer in David's reign (1 Chron. 25:17).
12. The Ramathite who was in charge of David's vineyards (1 Chron. 27:27).
13. A Levite who helped cleanse the temple under Zedekiah (2 Chron. 29:14).
14. A Levite in charge of the temple offerings in Hezekiah's reign (2 Chron. 31:12–13).
15. 16. 17. Three men who married foreign wives during the exile (Ezra 10:23, 33, 38).
18. Mordecai's grandfather (Esther 2:5).
19. A probable descendant of Shimei (Zech. 12:13).

Shimeon *[that hears or obeys; that is heard]*
A person who married a foreign wife during the exile (Ezra 10:31).

Shimhi
See Shimei.

Shimi
See Shimei.

Shimma *[same as Shimeah]*
See Shammah 2.

Shimon *[providing well; fatness; oil]*
A descendant of Caleb (1 Chron. 4:20).

Shimrath *[hearing; obedient]*
A descendant of Benjamin (1 Chron. 8:21).

Shimri *[thorn; dregs]*
1. Head of a family of Simeon (1 Chron. 4:37).
2. The father of Jediael, one of David's guards (1 Chron. 11:45).
3. A tabernacle gatekeeper in David's reign (1 Chron. 26:10).
4. A Kohathite Levite who helped cleanse the temple (2 Chron. 29:13).

Shimrith (Shomer) *[same as Shimri]*
A Moabitess, mother of Jehozabad, one of King Joash's assassins (2 Chron. 24:26); called Shomen in 2 Kings 12:21.

Shimrom (Shimron) *[same as Shimri]*
Issachar's fourth son (1 Chron. 7:1).

Shimshai *[my son]*
A scribe who wrote to the king of Persia objecting to the rebuilding of the wall of Jerusalem (Ezra 4:8–9, 17, 23).

Shinab *[father of changing]*
The king of Admah in the time of Abraham (Gen. 14:2).

Shiphi *[multitude]*
Father of a chief of Simeon (1 Chron. 4:37).

Shiphrah *[handsome; trumpet; that does good]*
One of the Hebrew midwives when Moses was born (Exod. 1:15–21).

Shiphtan
Father of Kemuel, a prince of the tribe of Ephraim (Num. 34:24).

Shisha *[of marble; pleasant]*
Father of Elihoreph and Ahiah, two of Solomon's scribes (1 Kings 4:3).

Shishak *[present of the bag; of the pot; of the thigh]*
Another name for Sesconchis I, king of Egypt (1 Kings 11:40).

Shitrai *[gatherer of money]*
One of David's herdsmen (1 Chron. 27:29).

Shiza *[this gift]*
Father of Adina, one of David's valiant men (1 Chron. 11:42).

Shobab *[returned; turned back; a spark]*
1. Son of David by Bath-sheba (2 Sam. 5:14; 1 Chron. 3:5; 14:4).
2. A son of Caleb (1 Chron. 2:18).

Shobach *[your bonds; your chains]*
King Hadarezer of Syria's commander (2 Sam. 10:15–18); called Shophach in 1 Chronicles 19:16.

Shobai *[turning captivity]*
A tabernacle gatekeeper who returned with Zerubbabel (Ezra 2:42; Neh. 7:45).

Shobal *[path; ear of corn]*
1. A son of Seir the Horite (Gen. 36:20; 1 Chron. 1:38).
2. A son of Caleb, the son of Hur (1 Chron. 2:50, 52).
3. A son of Judah (1 Chron. 4:1–2).

Shobek *[made void; forsaken]*
A person who sealed the new covenant with God after the exile (Neh. 10:24).

Shobi
A person who helped David when he fled from Absalom (2 Sam. 17:27).

Shoham *[keeping back]*
A descendant of Merari (1 Chron. 24:27).

Shomer *[keeper; dregs]*
1. See Shamer 2.
2. See Shimrith.

Shophach *[pouring out]*
See Shobach.

Shua *[crying; saving]*
Daughter of Heber (1 Chron. 7:32).

Shuah (Shua) *[ditch; swimming; humiliation]*

1. A Canaanite whose daughter Judah married (Gen. 38:2, 12; 1 Chron. 2:3).
2. Abraham and Keturah's son (Gen. 25:2; 1 Chron. 1:32).
3. Chelub's brother (1 Chron. 4:11).

Shual *[fox; path; first]*

Zophah's third son (1 Chron. 7:36).

Shubael *[returning captivity; seat of God]*

1. A son or descendant of Amram (1 Chron. 24:20).
2. See Shebuel 2.

Shuni *[changed; sleeping]*

Son of Gad, and founder of the family of the Shunites (Gen. 46:16; Num. 26:15).

Shupham

See Muppim.

Shuppim *[wearing them out; their shore]*

1. A gatekeeper in David's reign (1 Chron. 26:16).
2. See Muppim.

Shuthelah *[plant; verdure; moist; pot]*

1. A son of Ephraim (Num. 26:35–36).
2. Another descendant of Ephraim (1 Chron. 7:21).

Siaha (Sia) *[moving; help]*

An ancestor of the returning captives (Neh. 7:47).

Sibbechai (Mebunnai) *[bough; cottage; of springs]*

A strong man who killed a Philistine giant (2 Sam. 21:18; 1 Chron. 20:4); called Mebunnai in 2 Samuel 23:27.

Sidon (Zidon) *[hunting; fishing; venison]*

The eldest son of Canaan, son of Ham (Gen. 10:15); called Zidon in 1 Chronicles 1:13.

Sihon *[rooting out; conclusion]*

An Amorite king defeated by Israel (Num. 21:21–31).

Silas (Silvanus) *[three, or the third]*

A member of the early Christian Church who accompanied Paul on some of his missionary journeys (Acts 15:22, 32–34; 2 Cor. 1:19; 1 Thess. 1:1; 2 Thess. 1:1).

Silvanus *[who loves the forest]*

See Silas.

Simeon (Simon) *[that hears or obeys; that is heard]*

1. Jacob's second son by Leah (Gen. 29:33).
2. A devout Jew, inspired by the Holy Spirit, who met Mary and Joseph in the temple when Jesus was a baby (Luke 2:25–35).
3. An ancestor of Jesus Christ (Luke 3:30).
4. A disciple and prophet at Antioch (Acts 13:1).

Simon *[that hears; that obeys]*

1. Original name of the apostle Peter (Matt. 4:18).
2. Another of the twelve apostles, called Simon the Canaanite or Simon the Zealot (Matt. 10:4).
3. One of Jesus Christ's half-brothers (Matt. 13:55; Mark 6:3).
4. A leper in Bethany (Matt. 26:6).
5. A Cyrenian who was forced to carry Jesus' cross.
6. A Pharisee in whose house Jesus was anointed (Luke 7:40, 43–44).
7. Judas Iscariot's father (John 6:71).
8. A magician who tried to buy gifts of the Holy Spirit (Acts 8:9, 13, 18, 24).
9. A Christian convert living at Joppa in whose home Peter stayed (Acts 9:43).

Sippai *[threshold; silver cup]*

See Saph.

Sisamai *[house; blindness]*

A descendant of Sheshan (1 Chron. 2:40).

Sisera *[that sees a horse or a swallow]*

1. Captain of Jabin's army who was murdered by Jael (Judg. 4:1–22).
2. An ancestor of the returning captives (Ezra 2:53; Neh. 7:55).

So *[a measure for grain; vail]*

A king of Egypt (2 Kings 17:3–7).

Socho *[tents; tabernacles]*
Hebor's son (1 Chron. 4:18).

Sodi *[my secret]*
Father of Geddiel, the man sent to spy out the land of Canaan (Num. 13:10).

Solomon *[peaceable; perfect; one who recompenses]*
David and Bathsheba's son, Israel's second king, and ancestor of Jesus Christ (1 Kings 1:11; 2:11; Matt. 1:6–7).

Sopater (Sosipater) *[who defends the father]*
A man from Berea who accompanied Paul to Asia (Acts 20:4).

Sophereth *[scribe, numbering]*
One of Solomon's servants whose descendants returned from Babylon with Zerubbabel (Ezra 2:55; Neh. 7:57).

Sosipater *[same as Sopater]*
A man who sent greetings to the Roman Christians (Rom. 16:21).

Sosthenes *[savior; strong; powerful]*
1. Chief ruler of the synagogue at Corinth (Acts 18:12–17).
2. A Christian who joined Paul in addressing the Corinthian church (1 Cor. 1:1).

Stachys *[spike or ear of corn]*
A Christian in Rome to whom Paul sent his greetings (Rom. 16:9).

Stephanas *[crown; crowned]*
One of the first believers in Achaia (1 Cor. 1:16; 16:15).

Stephen *[same as Stephanas]*
The first Christian martyr (Acts 6:5–9; 7:59; 8:2).

Suah *[speaking; entreating; ditch]*
A son of Zophah and descendant of Asher (1 Chron. 7:36).

Susanna *[lily; rose; joy]*
A woman who ministered to Jesus Christ (Luke 8:3).

Susi *[horse; swallow; moth]*
Father of one of the men sent to spy out the land of Canaan (Num. 13:11).

Syntyche *[that speaks or discourses]*
A woman who belonged to the church of Philippi (Phil. 4:2).

Tabbaoth *[good; goodness]*
An ancestor of the returning captives (Ezra 2:43; Neh. 7:46).

Tabeal (Tabeel) *[good God]*
1. Father of the person the kings of Israel and Damascus planned to make king of Judah (Isa. 7:6).
2. A Persian official who tried to prevent the rebuilding of the wall of Jerusalem.

Tabitha *[clear-sighted; a roe deer]*
A woman from Joppa whom Peter raised from the dead (Acts 9:36–42).

Tabrimon *[good pomegranate; the navel; the middle]*
Ben-hadad I's father (1 Kings 15:18).

Tahan *[beseeching; merciful]*
1. A descendant of Ephraim (Num. 26:35).
2. Another descendant of Ephraim (1 Chron. 7:25).

Tahath *[fear; going down]*
1. A Kohathite Levite, ancestor of Samuel and Heman (1 Chron. 6:24, 37).
2. A descendant of Ephraim (1 Chron. 7:20).
3. A grandson of the above (1 Chron. 7:20).

Tahpenes *[standard; flight; temptation]*
An Egyptian queen who protected Hadad, Solomon's enemy (1 Kings 11:18–20).

Tahrea *[anger; wicked contention]*
Son of Micah, descendant of Mephibosheth (1 Chron. 9:41).

Talmai *[my furrow; that suspends the waters; heap of waters]*
1. A man or clan defeated by Caleb (Num. 13:22; Josh. 15:14; Judg. 1:10).
2. King of Geshur and David's father-in-law (2 Sam. 3:3; 13:37).

Talmon
A Levite in Ezra's day (1 Chron. 9:17).

Tamar (Thamar) *[palm; palm tree]*
1. The wife of Er, Perez's mother, and ancestor of Jesus Christ (Gen. 38:6, 11, 13; Ruth 4:12; Matt. 1:3).
2. David's daughter, violated by Amnon (2 Sam. 13:1–32).
3. Absalom's daughter (2 Sam. 14:7).

Tanhumeth *[consolation; repentance]*
Father of one of Gedaliah's captains (2 Kings 25:23; Jer. 40:8).

Taphath *[distillation; drop]*
A daughter of Solomon (1 Kings 4:11).

Tappuah *[apple; swelling]*
A descendant of Judah (1 Chron. 2:43).

Tarshish *[contemplation; examination]*
1. A son of Javan and grandson of Noah (Gen. 10:4; 1 Chron. 1:7).
2. One of the seven princes of Persia (Esther 1:14).

Tartan *[a general—official title]*
The title of a high-ranking Assyrian officer (2 Kings 18:17).

Tatnai *[that gives; the overseer of the gifts and tributes]*
A Persian governor of Samaria in Zerubbabel's time (Ezra 5:3, 6; 6:6, 13).

Tebah *[murder; butchery; guarding of the body; a cook]*
A son of Nahor, Abraham's brother (Gen. 22:24).

Tebaliah *[baptism, or goodness, of the Lord]*
A Levite gatekeeper in David's reign (1 Chron. 26:11).

Tehinnah *[entreaty; a favor]*
A descendant of Judah (1 Chron. 4:12).

Telah *[moistening; greenness]*
A descendant of Ephraim (1 Chron. 7:25).

Telem *[their dew; their shadow]*
A person who married a foreign wife during the exile (Ezra 10:24).

Tema *[admiration; perfection; consummation]*
The ninth son of Ishmael (Gen. 25:15; 1 Chron. 1:30).

Temah (Thamah)
An ancestor of the returning captives (Ezra 2:53).

Teman (Temani) *[the south; Africa; perfect]*
1. Esau's grandson (Gen. 36:11; 1 Chron. 1:36).
2. One of Edom's chiefs (Gen. 36:42).

Terah (Thara) *[to breathe; scent; blow]*
Abram's father and ancestor of Jesus Christ (Gen. 11:24–32; Luke 3:34).

Teresh
A eunuch who plotted to assassinate Ahasuerus (Esther 2:21; 6:2).

Tertius *[third]*
A person who acted as a scribe for Paul (Rom. 16:22).

Tertullus *[third]*
An orator who spoke against Paul before Felix (Acts 24:1–8).

Thaddeus *[that praises or confesses]*
One of the twelve apostles (Matt. 10:3; Mark 3:18).

Thahash *[that makes haste; that keeps silence]*
Nahor's son (Gen. 22:24).

Thamah *[that blots out; that suppresses]*
See Temah.

Thamar
Greek form of Tamar. See Tamar.

Thara
Greek form of Terah. See Terah.

Tharshish
A descendant of Benjamin (1 Chron. 7:10).

Theophilus *[friend of God]*
An unknown person to whom Luke addressed his Gospel and the Acts of the Apostles (Luke 1:3; Acts 1:1).

Theudas *[flowing with water]*
Leader of a rebellion against the Romans (Acts 5:36).

Thomas *[a twin]*
One of Jesus' twelve apostles (Matt. 10:3).

Tiberius *[good vision]*
Third emperor of the Roman Empire (Luke 3:1).

Tibni *[straw; hay]*
A rival of Omri's for Israel's throne (1 Kings 16:21–22).

Tidal *[that breaks the yoke; knowledge of elevation]*
King of Goyim who invaded the cities of the plain (Gen. 14:1, 9).

Tiglath-pileser (Pul; Tilgath-pilneser) *[that binds or takes away captivity]*
King of Assyria (2 Kings 15:29); also known as Pul (2 Kings 15:19).

Tilon *[murmuring]*
A descendant of Judah (1 Chron. 4:20).

Timaeus *[perfect; admirable; honorable]*
Father of the blind man, Bartimaeus (Mark 10:46).

Timna (Timnah) *[forbidding]*
1. One of Esau's concubines (Gen. 36:12).
2. A daughter of Seir the Horite (1 Chron. 1:39).
3. One of Edom's chiefs (Gen. 36:40).
4. A son of Eliphaz (1 Chron. 1:36).

Timon *[honorable; worthy]*
One of the seven deacons (Acts 6:1–6).

Timotheus (Timothy) *[honor of God; valued of God]*
One of Paul's converts and friends to whom he wrote 1 Timothy and 2 Timothy (Acts 16:1).

Tiras
Japheth's youngest son (Gen. 10:2).

Tirhakah *[inquirer; examiner; dull observer]*
A king of Ethiopia and Egypt who helped Hezekiah against Sennacherib (2 Kings 19:9; Isa. 37:9).

Tirhanah
A descendant of Hezron (1 Chron. 2:48).

Tiria *[searching out]*
A descendant of Judah (1 Chron. 4:16).

Tirshatha *[a governor]*
A title of the governor of Judea under the Persians (Neh. 8:9; 10:1).

Tirzah *[benevolent; complaisant; pleasing]*
Zelophehad's youngest daughter (Num. 26:33; 27:1; Josh. 17:3).

Titus *[pleasing]*
A converted Grecian whom Paul appointed to be pastor on Crete (Gal. 2.1, 3; 2 Cor. 2:13; Titus 1:4).

Toah *[weapon; dart]*
An ancestor of Samuel (1 Chron. 6:34); called Nahath in 1 Chronicles 6:26 and Tohu in 1 Samuel 1:1.

Tob-adonijah *[my good God; the goodness of the foundation of the Lord]*
A Levite sent by Jehoshaphat to teach the Law (2 Chron. 17:8).

Tobiah (Tobijah) *[the Lord is good]*
1. A Levite sent by Jehoshaphat to teach the Law (2 Chron. 17:8).
2. An ancestor of the returning captives who lost their genealogy (Ezra 2:60).
3. One of Sanballat's servants who opposed Nehemiah (Neh. 2:10–20).
4. A leader who returned from the Babylonian captivity (Zech. 6:10, 14).

Togarmah *[which is all bone]*
A son of Gomer (Gen. 10:3).

Tohu *[that lives; that declares]*
See Toah.

Toi (Tou) *[who wanders]*
A king of Hamath (2 Sam. 8:9–10).

Tola *[worm; grub; scarlet]*
1. A son of Issachar (Gen. 46:13).
2. A judge of Israel (Judg. 10:1).

Tou
See Toi.

Trophimus *[well educated; well brought up]*
A Christian convert who became one of Paul's traveling companions (Acts 21:27–29).

Tryphena *[delicious; delicate]*
A Christian woman at Rome to whom Paul sent greetings (Rom. 16:12).

Tryphosa *[thrice shining]*
A Christian woman at Rome to whom Paul sent greetings (Rom. 16:12).

Tubal *[the earth; the world; confusion]*
A son of Japheth (Gen. 10:2; 1 Chron. 1:5).

Tubal-cain *[worldly possession; possessed of confusion]*
A son of Lamech and expert metal-worker (Gen. 4:22).

Tychicus *[casual; by chance]*
A disciple and messenger of Paul (Acts 20:4; 2 Tim. 4:20).

Tyrannus *[a prince; one that reigns]*
A Greek teacher in whose school Paul taught at Ephesus (Acts 19:9).

Uel *[desiring God]*
A son of Bani, who during the captivity had married a foreign wife (Ezra 10:34).

Ulam *[the porch; the court; their strength; their folly]*
1. A descendant of Manasseh (1 Chron. 7:17).
2. A descendant of Benjamin (1 Chron. 8:39–40).

Ulla *[elevation; leaf; young child]*
A descendant of Asher (1 Chron. 7:30).

Unni *[poor; afflicted; that answers]*
1. One of the Levite singers (1 Chron. 15:18, 20).
2. A Levite who returned to Jerusalem with Zerubbabel (Neh. 12:9).

Ur *[fire, light, a valley]*
Father of one of David's mighty men (1 Chron. 11:35).

Urbane (Urbanus) *[courteous]*
A Christian in Rome to whom Paul sent greetings (Rom. 16:9).

Uri *[my light, my fire]*
1. The father of Bezaleel, one of the architects of the tabernacle (Exod. 31:1–2).
2. The father of Geber, one of Solomon's officers in Gilead (1 Kings 4:19).
3. One of the gatekeepers of the temple in Ezra's time (Ezra 10:24).

Uriah (Urias; Urijah) *[the Lord is my light or fire]*
1. A Hittite soldier in David's army (2 Sam. 11:11).
2. High priest in Ahaz's reign (2 Kings 16:10–16).
3. A prophet murdered by Jehoiakim (Jer. 26:20–23).
4. The father of Meremoth (Ezra 8:33; Neh. 3:4, 21).
5. A person who stood at Ezra's side as he read the Law (Neh. 8:4).
6. A person Isaiah called on as a witness (Isa. 8:2).

Uriel *[same as Uriah]*
1. A chief of the sons of Kohath (1 Chron. 6:24; 15:5).
2. Father of Michaiah, one of Rehoboam's sons (2 Chron. 13:2).

Uthai *[my iniquity]*
1. A son of Bigvai who returned to Jerusalem with Ezra (Ezra 8:14).
2. A descendant of Judah (1 Chron. 9:4).

Uz *[counsel; words]*
1. Eldest son of Aram (Gen. 10:23).
2. A son of Dishon (Gen. 36:28).

Uzai *[he]*
The father of Palal who helped Nehemiah to rebuild the wall of Jerusalem (Neh. 3:25).

Uzal *[wandering]*
A son of Joktan (Gen. 10:27; 1 Chron. 1:21).

Uzza (Uzzah) *[strength; goat]*
1. A man struck dead by God when he touched the ark of the covenant (2 Sam. 6:2–7).
2. A descendant of Ehud (1 Chron. 8:7).
3. An ancestor of the returning captives (Ezra 2:49; Neh. 7:51).
4. A descendant of Merari (1 Chron. 6:29).
5. A Levite, son of Jeduthun, who helped cleanse the temple (2 Chron. 29:14).
6. Son of Harhaiah, who helped repair the wall of Jerusalem (Neh. 3:8).

Uzzi *[my strength; my kid]*
1. Son of Bukki and father of Zerahiah (1 Chron. 6:5–6; Ezra 7:4).
2. A descendant of Issachar (1 Chron. 7:1–3).
3. A descendant of Benjamin (1 Chron. 7:7).
4. The father of Elah, a descendant of Benjamin (1 Chron. 9:8).
5. An overseer of the Levites at Jerusalem (Neh. 11:22).
6. Chief of a priestly family of Jedaiah (Neh. 12:19).

Uzzia *[the strength, or kid, of the Lord]*
One of David's guards (1 Chron. 11:44).

Uzziah (Ozias) *[the strength, or kid, of the Lord]*
1. The tenth king of Judah and ancestor of Jesus Christ (2 Chron. 26; Matt. 1:8–9); called Azariah in 2 Kings 15:1–8.
2. A Levite descended from Kohath and ancestor of Samuel (1 Chron. 6:24).
3. A descendant of Judah (Neh. 11:4).
4. Father of Jehonathan, one of David's overseers (1 Chron. 27:25).
5. A priest who married a foreign wife during the exile (Ezra 10:21).

Uzziel *[the strength, or kid, of the Lord]*
1. The ancestor of the Uzzielites (Exod. 6:18).
2. Captain of the sons of Simeon (1 Chron. 4:42).
3. A son of Bela and grandson of Benjamin (1 Chron. 7:7).
4. A temple musician in David's reign (1 Chron. 25:4).

Vajezatha *[sprinkling the chamber]*
One of the sons of Haman killed by the Jews (Esther 9:9).

Vaniah *[nourishment, or weapons, of the Lord]*
A son of Bani who married a foreign wife (Ezra 10:36).

Vashni *[the second; changed; a tooth]*
A son of Samuel (1 Chron. 6:28).

Vashti *[that drinks; thread]*
Queen of Ahasuerus who was divorced when she refused to attend Ahasuerus's great feast (Esther 1:1).

Vophsi *[fragrant; diminution]*
A descendant of Naphtali (Num. 13:14).

Zaavan (Zavan) *[trembling]*
A descendant of Seir (Gen. 36:27). Called Zavan in 1 Chronicles 1:42.

Zabad *[dowry; endowed]*
1. A descendant of Jeruhmeer of Judah (1 Chron. 2:36–37).
2. An Ephraimite and son of Tahath (1 Chron. 7:21).
3. Son of Alai and one of David's guards (1 Chron. 7:21).
4. 5. 6. People who married foreign wives during the exile (Ezra 10:27, 33, 43).
7. See Jozachar.

Zabbai *[flowing]*
1. One of the descendants of Bebai who had married a foreign wife in the days of Ezra (Ezra 10:28).
2. Father of Baruch who assisted Nehemiah in rebuilding the city wall (Neh. 3:20).

Zabbud
One of the sons of Bigvai, who returned to Jerusalem with Ezra (Ezra 8:14).

Zabdi (Zimri) *[same as Zabad]*
1. Father of Carmi (Josh. 7:1, 17–18); called Zimri in 1 Chronicles 2:6.
2. A descendant of Benjamin (1 Chron. 8:19).
3. One of David's storekeepers (1 Chron. 21:27).
4. A descendant of Mattaniah (Neh. 11:17); called Zichri in 1 Chronicles 9:15.

Zabdiel
1. Father of Jashobeam, a chief of David's guards (1 Chron. 27:2).
2. An overseer of the priests (Neh. 11:14).

Zabud
Solomon's officer and friend (1 Kings 4:5).

Zaccai *[pure meat; just]*
An ancestor of the returning captives (Ezra 2:9; Neh. 7:14).

Zacchaeus *[pure; clean; just]*
A tax collector in Jericho who became a follower of Jesus (Luke 19:1–10).

Zaccur (Zacchur) *[of the male kind; mindful]*
1. A descendant of Simeon (1 Chron. 4:26).
2. Father of Shammua, one of the men who spied out the land of Canaan (Num. 13:4).
3. A descendant of Merari (1 Chron. 24:27).
4. Son of Asaph the singer (1 Chron. 25:2, 10; Neh. 12:35).
5. The son of Imri who helped Nehemiah rebuild the city wall (Neh. 3:2).
6. A Levite who sealed the covenant with Nehemiah (Neh. 10:18).
7. Father of Hanan (Neh. 13:13).

Zachariah (Zechariah) *[memory of the Lord]*
1. Son and successor of Jeroboam II (2 Kings 14:29; 15:8–11).
2. Father of Abi, mother of Hezekiah (2 Kings 18:2); called Zechariah in 2 Chronicles 29:1.

Zacharias *[memory of the Lord]*
Greek form of Zechariah.
1. Father of John the Baptist (Luke 1:5).
2. The prophet whom the Jews stoned between the altar and the temple (Matt. 23:35).

Zacher (Zechariah)
Son of Jehiel (1 Chron. 8:31); called Zechariah in 1 Chronicles 9:37).

Zadok *[just; justified]*
1. A high priest in David's reign (2 Sam. 8:17; 15:24–36).
2. Father of Jerushah, wife of King Uzziah and mother of King Jotham (2 Kings 15:33; 2 Chron. 27:1).
3. Son of Ahitub (1 Chron. 6:12).
4. A young man of mighty valor (1 Chron. 12:28).
5. 6. Two people who repaired the wall of Jerusalem (Neh. 3:4, 29).
7. A person who sealed the covenant with Nehemiah (1 Chron. 10:21).
8. A scribe under Nehemiah (Neh. 13:13).

Zaham *[crime; filthiness; impurity]*
Rehoboam's son (2 Chron. 11:19).

Zalaph *[shadow; ringing; shaking]*
The father of a person who helped rebuild Jerusalem's wall (Neh. 3:30).

Zalmon (Ilai) *[his shade; his image]*
An Ahohite, one of David's guards (2 Sam. 23:28).

Zalmunna *[shadow; image; idol forbidden]*
A Midianite king killed by Gideon (Judg. 8:5–21).

Zanoah *[forgetfulness; desertion]*
A member of Caleb's family (1 Chron. 4:18).

Zaphnath-paaneah *[one who discovers hidden things]*
A name given by Pharaoh to Joseph (Gen. 41:45).

Zara *[east; brightness]*
Greek form of Zara or Zerah. See Zerah.

Zarah
See Zerah.

Zattu (Zatthu) *[olive tree]*
1. An ancestor of the returning captives (Ezra 2:8; Neh. 7:13).
2. A person who sealed the covenant (Neh. 10:14).

Zavan
See Zaavan.

Zaza *[belonging to all]*
A son of Jonathan (1 Chron. 2:33).

Zealotes
See Simon 2.

Zebadiah *[portion of the Lord; the Lord is my portion]*
1. A descendant of Benjamin (1 Chron. 8:15).
2. A son of Elpaal (1 Chron. 8:17).
3. One of the sons of Jeroham of Gedor who joined David (1 Chron. 12:7).
4. A descendant of Levi through Kohath (1 Chron. 26:2).
5. A son of Asahel (1 Chron. 27:7).
6. Head of a family who returned from the exile (Ezra 8:8).
7. A priest who had married a foreign wife during the exile (Ezra 10:20).
8. A Levite sent by Jehoshaphat to teach the Law (2 Chron. 17:8).
9. A son of Ishmael (2 Chron. 19:11).

Zebah *[victim; sacrifice]*
Midianite king killed by Gideon (Judg. 8:5–21).

Zebedee *[abundant; portion]*
Father of the apostles James and John (Matt. 4:21).

Zebina *[flowing now; selling; buying]*
A person who married a foreign wife during the exile (Ezra 10:43).

Zebudah *[endowed; endowing]*
Wife of Josiah and mother of King Jehoiakim (2 Kings 23:36).

Zebul *[a habitation]*
Ruler of Shechem (Judg. 9:28–41).

Zebulun (Zebulon) *[dwelling; habitation]*
Jacob's tenth son and ancestor of one of the twelve tribes (Gen. 30:20; 1 Chron. 2:1).

Zechariah *[same as Zachariah]*
1. A chief of the tribe of Reuben (1 Chron. 5:7).
2. A Levite gatekeeper in David's reign (1 Chron. 9:21).
3. A Levite who helped organize temple singing (1 Chron. 15:18, 20).
4. One of the priests who accompanied the ark of the covenant from the house of Obed odom (1 Chron 15:24).
5. A descendant of Levi through Kohath (1 Chron. 24:25).
6. A descendant of Levi through Merari (1 Chron. 26:11).
7. Father of Iddo (1 Chron. 27:21).
8. A prince of Judah sent to teach the people the Law (2 Chron. 17:7).
9. A Levite who encouraged Jehoshaphat against Moab (2 Chron. 20:14).
10. A son of Jehoshaphat (2 Chron. 21:2).
11. A son of the high priest Jehoiada (2 Chron. 24:20).
12. A prophet in the reign of Uzziah (2 Chron. 26:5).
13. A Levite who helped cleanse the temple (2 Chron. 29:13).
14. A descendant of Levi in Josiah's reign (2 Chron. 34:12).
15. A prince of Judah in Josiah's reign (2 Chron. 35:8).
16. One of the twelve minor prophets (Zech. 1:1).
17. The leader of the sons of Pharosh who returned with Ezra (Ezra 8:3).
18. A person who returned from the exile (Ezra 8:11).
19. A person who married a foreign wife during the exile (Ezra 10:26).
20. One of the chiefs of the people who stood next to Ezra as he expounded the Law (Neh. 8:4).
21. A descendant of Perez (Neh. 11:4).
22. A person whose descendants lived in Jerusalem (Neh. 11:5).

23. A priest, son of Pashur (Neh. 11:12).
24. A priest in Joiakim's reign (Neh. 12:16).
25. One of the priests who blew the trumpets at the dedication of the city wall (Neh. 12:35, 41).
26. One of the people Isaiah took as a witness (Isa. 8:2).
27. See Zachariah.
28. See Zacher.

Zedekiah *[the Lord is my justice; the justice of the Lord]*

1. The last king of Judah (2 Kings 24:18–25:7).
2. A false prophet who encouraged Ahab to attack the Syrians (1 Kings 22:11).
3. A false prophet (Jer. 21–23).
4. A prince of Judah in Jehoiakim's reign (Jer. 36:12).

Zeeb *[wolf]*

A prince of Midian killed by Gideon (Judg. 7:25; 8:3).

Zelek *[the shadow or noise of him that licks or laps]*

An Ammonite, one of David's guards (2 Sam. 23:37; 1 Chron. 11:39).

Zelophehad *[the shade or tingling of fear]*

Gilead's grandson (Josh. 17:3).

Zemira *[song; vine; palm]*

One of the sons of Becher, a descendant of Benjamin (1 Chron. 7:8).

Zenas *[living]*

A Christian who had been a teacher of the Law (Titus 3:13).

Zephaniah *[the Lord is my secret]*

1. One of the twelve minor prophets (Zeph. 1:1).
2. One of Samuel's ancestors (1 Chron. 6:36).
3. A priest who opposed the Babylonian rule (Jer. 21:1; 2 Kings 25:18).
4. Son of Josiah the priest (Zech. 6:10).

Zephi (Zepho) *[that sees and observes; that expects or covers]*

A son of Eliphaz (1 Chron. 1:36).

Zephon (Ziphion) *[that sees and observes; that expects or covers]*

A son of Gad (Num. 26:15), called Ziphion in Genesis 46:16.

Zerah *[east; brightness]*

1. A son of Reuel, son of Esau (Gen. 36:13; 1 Chron. 1:37).
2. Father of Jobab (Gen. 36:33).
3. A son of Judah and Tamar (Gen. 38:30; 1 Chron. 2:4).
4. A son of Gershon (1 Chron. 6:21).
5. A Levite (1 Chron. 6:41).
6. A king of Ethiopia who fought against Asa (2 Chron. 14:9).
7. See Zohar.

Zerahiah *[the Lord rising; brightness of the Lord]*

1. A priest in the line of Eleazar (1 Chron. 6:6, 51; Ezra 7:4).
2. Head of a family who returned from the captivity with Ezra (Ezra 8:4).

Zeresh *[misery; strange; dispersed inheritance]*

Wife of Haman the Agagite (Esther 5:10, 14; 6:13).

Zereth *[perplexity]*

A descendant of Judah (1 Chron. 4:7).

Zeri

A musician in David's reign (1 Chron. 25:3).

Zeror *[root; that straitens or binds; that keeps tight]*

An ancestor of Kish, the father of Saul (1 Sam. 9:1).

Zeruah *[leprous; wasp; hornet]*

The mother of Jeroboam I (1 Kings 11:26).

Zerubbabel (Zorobabel) *[a stranger at Babylon; dispersion of confusion]*

1. The leader of a group who returned from the exile, and an ancestor of Jesus Christ (Ezra 3–5; Matt. 1:12–13).
2. An ancestor of Jesus Christ (Luke 3:27), perhaps the same as 1.

Zeruiah *[pain or tribulation of the Lord]*
The mother of Joab, Abishai, and Asahel; David's sister (1 Sam. 26:6; 1 Chron. 2:16).

Zetham
Son or grandson of Laadan (1 Chron. 23:8).

Zethan
A descendant of Benjamin (1 Chron. 7:10).

Zethar *[he that examines or beholds]*
One of Ahasuerus's seven eunuchs (Esther 1:10).

Zia *[sweat; swelling]*
A descendant of Gad (1 Chron. 5:13).

Ziba *[army; fight; strength]*
One of Saul's stewards (2 Sam. 9:2–13).

Zibeon *[iniquity that dwells]*
1. A Hivite (Gen. 36:2).
2. A son of Seir (1 Chron. 1:38, 40).

Zibia *[the Lord dwells; deer; goat]*
A descendant of Benjamin (1 Chron. 8:9).

Zibiah *[the Lord dwells; deer; goat]*
Mother of King Joash (2 Kings 12:1; 2 Chron. 24:1).

Zichri *[that remembers; that is a man]*
1. A son of Ishar (Exod. 6:21).
2. A descendant of Benjamin (1 Chron. 8:19).
3. A descendant of Benjamin of Shashak (1 Chron. 8:23).
4. A descendant of Benjamin of Jeroham (1 Chron. 8:27).
5. Son of Asaph (1 Chron. 9:15).
6. A descendant of Eliezer in the time of Moses (1 Chron. 26:25).
7. Father of Eliezer, a descendant of Reuben (1 Chron. 27:16).
8. Father of Amasiah (2 Chron. 11:16).
9. Father of Elishaphat (2 Chron. 23:1).
10. A courageous man who killed the son of King Ahaz (2 Chron. 28:7).
11. Father of Joel (Neh. 11:9).
12. A priest of the family of Abijah (Neh. 12:17).

Zidkijah *[justice of the Lord]*
A priest who signed the covenant with Nehemiah (Neh. 10:1).

Ziha *[brightness; whiteness; drought]*
1. Man whose children returned with Zerubbabel (Ezra 2:43; Neh. 7:46).
2. Leader of the Nethinim in Ophel (Neh. 11:21).

Zilpah *[distillation from the mouth]*
A Syrian given by Laban to his daughter Leah as a servant (Gen. 29:24) and by Leah to Jacob as a concubine; the mother of Gad and Asher (Gen. 30:9–13; 35:26; 37:2; 46:18).

Zilthai *[my shadow; my talk]*
1. A Benjamite (1 Chron. 8:20).
2. One of the commanders of Manasseh who deserted to David at Ziklag (1 Chron. 12:20).

Zimmah *[thought; wickedness]*
1. A Gershonite Levite, son of Jahath (1 Chron. 6:20).
2. Another Gershonite, son of Shimei (1 Chron. 6:42), possibly the same as the preceding.
3. Father of ancestor of Joab, a Gershonite in Hezekiah's reign (2 Chron. 29:12).

Zimran *[song; singer; vine]*
The eldest son of Keturah (Gen. 25:2; 1 Chron. 1:32).

Zimri *[my field; my vine]*
1. The son of Salu, a Simeonite chief, killed by Phinehas (Num. 25:14).
2. Fifth sovereign of the separate kingdom of Israel (1 Kings 16:9–20).
3. One of the five sons of Zerah, the son of Judah (1 Chron. 2:6).
4. Son of Jehoadah and descendant of Saul (1 Chron. 8:36; 9:42).
5. An obscure name, mentioned in Jeremiah 25:25 in probable connection with Dedan, Tema, Buz, Arabia.

Zina *[shining; going back]*
The second son of Shimei the Gershonite (1 Chron. 23:10).

Ziph *[this mouth or mouthful; falsehood]*
Son of Jehaleleel (1 Chron. 4:16).

Ziphah
A son of Jehaleleel (1 Chron. 4:16).

Ziphion
Son of Gad (Gen. 46:18); elsewhere called Zephon.

Zippor *[bird; sparrow; crown; desert]*
Father of Balak king of Moab (Num. 22:2, 4, 10, 16).

Zipporah *[beauty; trumpet; mourning]*
Daughter of Reuel, the priest of Midian, wife of Moses and mother of his two sons Gershom and Eliezer (Exod. 2:21; 4:25; 18:2).

Zithri *[to hide; demolished]*
One of the sons of Uzziel the son of Kohath (Exod. 6:22).

Ziza *[same as Zina]*
1. Son of Shiphi, a chief of the Simeonites in Hezekiah's reign (1 Chron. 4:37).
2. Son of Rehoboam, granddaughter of Absalom (2 Chron. 11:20).

Zizah *[same as Zina]*
A Gershonite Levite, second son of Shimei (1 Chron. 23:11); called Zina in 1 Chronicles 23:10.

Zobebah *[an army; warring]*
Son of Coz, of the tribe of Judah (1 Chron. 4:8).

Zohar *[white; bright; dryness]*
1. Father of Ephron the Hittite (Gen. 23:8; 25:9).
2. One of the sons of Simeon (Gen. 46:10; Exod. 6:15).

Zoheth *[separation; amazing]*
Son of Ishi of the tribe of Judah (1 Chron. 4:20).

Zophah *[viol; honeycomb]*
Son of Helem or Hotham the son of Heber, an Asherite (1 Chron. 7:35–36).

Zophai
A Kohathite Levite, son of Elkanah and ancestor of Samuel (2 Chron. 6:26).

Zophar *[rising early; crown]*
One of Job's three friends (Job 2:11; 11:1; 20:1; 42:9).

Zorobabel (Zerubbabel) *[same as Zerubbabel]*
An ancestor of Jesus Christ (Matt. 1:12–13; Luke 3:27).

Zuar *[little; small]*
Father of Nethaneel the chief of the tribe of Issachar at the time of the Exodus (Num. 1:8; 2:5; 7:18, 23; 10:15).

Zuph *[that beholds, observes, watches; roof; covering]*
A Kohathite Levite, ancestor of Elkanah and Samuel (1 Sam. 1:1; 1 Chron. 6:35); called Zopha in 1 Chronicles 6:26.

Zur *[stone; rock; that besieges]*
1. Father of Cozbi and one of the five princes of Midian killed by the Israelites when Balaam was taken (Num. 25:15; 31:8).
2. Son of Jehiel, the founder of Gideon (1 Chron. 8:30; 9:36).

Zuriel *[rock or strength of God]*
Son of Abihail, and chief of the Merarite Levites at the time of the exodus (Num. 3:35).

Zurishaddai *[the Almighty is my rock and strength]*
Father of Shelumiel, the chief of the tribe of Simeon at the time of the exodus (Num. 1:6; 2:12; 7:36, 41; 10:19).

Index of Names in Parts 1 and 2

For additional names, see the alphabetical listing of names in Part 3 beginning on page 385.